APR 30'89   REL

MEN AND GODS ON THE ROMAN NILE

JACK LINDSAY

Men and Gods
on the Roman Nile

BARNES & NOBLE, Inc.
NEW YORK
PUBLISHERS & BOOKSELLERS SINCE 1873

First published in the United States
in 1968
by Barnes & Noble, Inc.
New York, N.Y.

To Hugh MacDiarmid

Your name on this page I write
because of your ranging mind
which stands on the heaving centre
yet is eager to know and enter
all things in this universe
so strangely, simply designed:

aware of mysterious dusk
with its flight of flurrying wings
and the naked noonbodies of light
that the Greeks hacked out of stone:
all men, and brooding alone,
in the variety of things.

Live through the ritual mime
of the deep Egyptian night
and the bright engrossing play
of the busy Nile of day:

Man's the image we seek and find
in the shifting labyrinth,
in the transformations of time.

Jack Lindsay

Printed in Great Britain

Contents

Illustrations

Author's Note

THIS is my third book on Roman Egypt. The wealth of surviving papyri from the Graeco-Roman period gives us a unique opportunity of getting inside the lives of people in a section of the ancient world. Each of the books is complete in itself, though naturally they supplement one another and I trust enrich the picture. *Daily Life in Roman Egypt* sought to set out everyday details and provide a broad basis. *Leisure and Pleasure in Roman Egypt* dealt with games, festivals, gardens, and so on, and out of the material emerged an account of the Dionysiac cult in its final phases, with the poet Nonnos as its subtle prophet. Here the theme is the Nile, the activities on its waters and banks, and the ideas and emotions which it aroused. Though the main point of focus is the busy world of Roman Egypt, which the papyri reveal, in order to get deep inside the minds of the people we have to keep looking back into the Pharaonic past. Only thus the full richness of Romano-Egyptian culture can be appreciated. Despite all the convulsions there was a deep element of continuity in Egyptian life and thought.

Many points thus come up: the extent to which the Greeks and Romans knew about Africa below the First Cataract of the Nile, and the reasons why they did not know more and did not bring about a more effective penetration; the image of the universe which the early Egyptians built up and which survived in varying degrees till the end, and the part this image played in determining the ideas of the Greeks; the way in which the Nile pervaded Egyptian life and religion; the early creation-myths and their later effects. On this side of our inquiry we come at the end to a detailed investigation of the legend of the hero Perseus and the maiden Andromeda whom he rescued from a sea-monster; we examine his connections with Egypt and ask how he and the others in this legend found their way into the sky as the only connected set of constellations. As a result we find that we have not only explored many aspects of Egyptian and Graeco-Roman Egyptian culture, but have gained an idea of how the two cultures fruitfully interacted.

J. L.

I

The Nile

THE great river-valleys played an essential part in the rise of civilisation: in Mesopotamia, India, China, as well as Egypt. But no other river had quite the character of the Nile with its regular summer-flood and its narrow strip of fertile land between two desert expanses. That the Nile should dominate Egyptian life and thought in many ways was natural; and in this book we explore some of those ways. Few aspects of Egyptian life were unrelated to the great river, its rise and fall, its fertilising powers, its use as a highway or as source of valuable commodities like fish and papyrus-reed. In turn, efforts to understand the universe and man's place in it were linked with a continual brooding on the mysterious waters. Only the Sun had as important a part in Egyptian life and thought.

The chant, *Adoration of the Nile*, sought to express the deep gratitude of the Egyptian, his unfailing sense of awe and his dependence on the waters:

Praise to you, Nile, who issue from the Earth and come to nourish Egypt. Of hidden nature, a darkness in the daytime . . .
That waters the meadows, he that Re [the sungod] has created to nourish all cattle. That gives drink to the desert places which are far from water. It is his dew that falls from heaven.
Beloved of Geb [the earthgod], director of the corngod. That makes every workshop of Ptah flourish.
Lord of the fish, that makes the waterfowl go upstream . . . that makes barley and creates wheat so as to cause temples to keep festivals. If he is sluggish, nostrils are stopped up and all men impoverished; the victuals of the gods are diminished and millions of men perish . . .[1]

This chant is unlike the old hymns to deities: it is rather a cry of thanks for the blessings brought by the river. No doubt it was used at the Flood Festival. That it was widely known is shown by the copies made, with varying degrees of correctness, by schoolboys on sherds from Der el-Medineh.[2]

The enigma of the yearly flood and the immense length of the river, lost in the remote depths of Africa, were important ingredients in the reverence and wonder that were aroused. Lucan declared:

> Your desire, Roman, to explore the Nile
> was felt by the Kings of Egypt, Persia, Macedon.
> Every age has wished to find and hand on the truth;
> but the Nile's secret nature has always won.
> Alexander, the great king, envied the Nile
> which Memphis worships; he sent explorers out
> through farthest Aethiopia; the parched sky
> with its fierce zone halted them; they saw
> the Nile steaming. Sesostris westwards reached
> the world's limits, yoked kings to his chariot,
> but drank your waters, Rhone and Po, before
> the Nile's sources. Madman Cambyses drove
> westward to where the Longlived People dwelt,
> but starving he fed on his own men and gained
> no knowledge, Nile, of you. Even lying legend
> has never ventured to announce your springs.[3]

He has packed enough "lying legend" into his own lines, with the references to the Pharaoh Sesostris conquering Europe and to the Persian Cambyses reaching the Makrobioi, a tribe of Aithiopians said to live 120 years. (The Twelfth Dynasty in Egypt had produced the image of the ideal ruler, and gradually the picture of Sesostris, great conqueror and builder, was formed, probably based at the outset on the three pharaohs with the name Senusret.) It is also more than doubtful if Alexander ever sent out an expedition to find the sources—though the ancients did in fact know much more about the Nile than Lucan suggests. His lines, however, suggest well enough the Nile's reputation.

The first known explorer to reach the source of the Blue Nile was the Portuguese priest Pedro Paez in 1615; Jeronimo Lobo was there in 1662; and Bruce arrived in 1772. Lake Tana in Aithiopia was the place, about 2,750 miles from the Mediterranean and

6,000 ft. above sea-level—though sometimes the Little Abbai, feeding the lake, is regarded the true source. The grey-green waters slip out on to a shore broken by low islands, edged with black lava boulders and thick with greenery. Hardly half an hour across the lake are Coptic monasteries where priests walk at morning and evening round their thatched circular churches with cross and censer. Soon after leaving the lake, the river runs wildly over rocks and shallows, amid acacia and lotus, banyan, palms, and waterferns. Then after some twenty miles comes the roar of the Tiasasat Falls, some 150 ft. high, and a long wet cloud hangs over the valley. The river begins to make its great cut through the plateau, a curve of 400 miles, first south, then west and north, until it pours out of the mountains into the hot plains of the Sudan. Tributaries in scores come in at every stage; but except for a few hamlets where the valley widens, there are no inhabitants. The animals are mainly crocodiles and hippopotami. Some 470 miles from Lake Tana, and 4,500 ft. lower, villages reappear, of Amharic and Galla peoples with ancient roots in the region. Gold is still washed out in the foothills. As the river comes down to the Sudanese border, settlements of pagan Negro tribes with conical grass-huts show up through the heavy heat. The waters have lost their vehemence.

1. The Two Niles

The desert is yet lacking and the river runs over black granite rocks with occasional cataracts. On the banks is scrub forest, bleached white except in the rainy season, fever-trees with ochre trunks and sage-coloured leaves, or bulging baobabs.

We reach the ancient kingdom of Sennar, the heart of the Moslem Sudan. (At Sennar there is now a dam with a railway across it; mechanical pumps replace the old water-wheels.) The Blue Nile widens and warms as it slows down. The area still has a wet season, but north of Sennar the shrubs end and sand begins to take over a few yards from the banks. Two tributaries come in from the east and the reinforced river rushes on to meet the White Nile at Khartum. After the meeting, for several miles the grey or palegreen waters of the White Nile can be distinguished from the darker hue of the Blue—blue in a certain light, but more usually brown. The Nile still has some 1,900 miles to the sea.

The White Nile rises, already a considerable stream, close to Jinja in Uganda: the main outlet of Lake Victoria, the largest lake in Africa. (The outlet has been controlled by a dam since 1954, covering the original Ripon Falls.) H. J. Speke and James Grant reached it in July 1862 and named it. Some fifty miles on, it passes through a small lake, Kioga, then leaves the high plateau by the Murchison Falls and soon enters the northern tip of Lake Albert, one of a group forming part of the Great Rift Valley. Now it flows through parkland country with elephants, lions, leopards, giraffes. Navigable save for a stretch of rapids between Nimuele and Juba, it goes on through south and central Sudan. At one point it passes through 350 miles of the swampy Sudd, which for long barred the exploration of the Upper Nile. In modern times the way through was not achieved till 1839–42. Equally swampy is the basin of the Bahr el-Ghazal, River of Gazelles, a left-bank tributary. Small groups of Nilotic tribesmen, Nuer, Shilluk, and Dinka, live in the region. Darkskinned, tall (well over six feet), they herd cattle and carry on a rough form of agriculture as well as hunting hippopotami. The small Lake No marks the end of the swamps. An important right-bank tributary, the Sobal, comes in, and the Nile flows on to Khartum along a broad flat plain, now inhabited by folk of mixed Arab and Negro stocks.

The White Nile has come a longer distance than the Blue and is quieter. It may be called the parent stream, but the main strength of the combined rivers proceeds from the Blue, which brings in six-sevenths of the volume of water and hurls itself down as a torrent for six months. By June its force is so great that the White is pushed back at the meeting-point and the Blue hurtles past with hundreds of tons of grit and soil for Egypt. In January the rush subsides and the White reasserts itself.

There is one more tributary from the highlands before the Nile, now a warm brown softflowing river, enters the rainless regions. About 180 miles down from Khartum, at Meroe, some 200 ruined pyramids show up in the desert, then the Nile goes down over a series of long cataracts. More temples and fortresses appear. We are in Nubia, often invaded for slaves, gold, ivory. Caravan routes strike off into the desert where all is stark rock and barren yellow sands.[4]

In the Graeco-Roman period the Cataracts were often taken as the point above which the Nile was lost in obscurity. Thus Diodoros of Sicily describes them:

. . . The Nile is the only river that makes its way along without violence or onrush of waves, except at the so-called Cataracts. This is a place only about ten stades in length, but with a steep descent. It is shut in by cliffs to form a narrow cleft, rugged all the way and ravine-like, full as well with huge boulders that stand out of the water like peaks. And since the river is spilt about these boulders with tremendous force and often turned back, so that it hurtles in the opposite direction as a result of the obstructions, remarkable whirlpools are formed. The middle space, too, for the whole length is filled with foam produced by the back-rush of the water, and strikes those who approach it with great terror. Indeed the descent of the river is so swift and furious that it appears to the eye like the very rush of an arrow.

At floodtime of the Nile, when the peaked rocks are covered and the entire rapids hidden by the large volume of water, some men sail down the cataract when they find the winds against them [and thus checking their speed]; but no man can make his way up it, since the force of the river defeats every human device. And there are still other cararacts of this kind, though the biggest is the one on the border between Aithiopia and Egypt.[5]

On entering Egypt the Nile slows down in a narrow trench bordered by the desert, all the way to Cairo. The valley is less than six miles wide in places south of Aswan and varies from five to twelve downstream. Mudhut villages and clusters of palmtrees by the banks, feluccas on the river with long thin pennants to show the wind—though the wind has lost its force. Primitive water-machines are to be seen as well as modern control-works and barrages. Near Aswan are the quarries, which, with those of Silsileh, provided much building-stone. Aswan was a great caravan centre in its day as well as the southernmost post of the Roman Empire. As we go down over the last cataract at Philai, past the island temples and the plantations (now wheat and sugarcane), we see camels and donkeys along the banks with palms and tamarisks on the banks. The birds have a tame look, white egrets in the swamps, pigeons on all the roofs, herons and storks in the shallows. The buffalo, released from the waterwheel, comes to lie down in the mud. Crocodile and hippopotamus have now gone.

One after another we pass the great temple-sites: Kom Ombo dominating a riverbend, Karnak and Luxor, Dendera and Abydos. The Nile begins to lose its mud at Cairo, a hundred miles from the sea. It spreads into canals and waterways, into the green fan of the Delta. Its falling silt has gradually pushed out the limits of the land. Of its seven ancient mouths, only two remain, at Rosetta and Damietta; but at flood-height it still stains the sea for miles out.[6]

Egypt has greatly changed over the millennia. In the Pleistocene epoch it had a series of rainy periods, followed by various undrastic changes. There are three main areas in historical Egypt: the alluvial lands of valley and delta, the low desert bordering the river on both sides, and the desert uplands beyond. But in the earlier rainy periods these divisions did not apply. The three areas were then fairly uniform, even if sparsely inhabited. The Nile, which may not be more than some 14,000 years old, and its tributaries, swept down masses of gravels and sands from the higher parts, where there seems to have been enough moisture to grow a fair amount of vegetation.[7] Much less water came down from the African interior; but in winter there was a good flow from what were later the desert wadis, which were eroded and sent down their gravels. Deposits of ten to fifteen feet deep in Upper Egypt date from the last main pluvial phase. Then, about this time or soon after, came the largescale downflow of water from Aithiopia with silts in the summer and early autumn.

The distribution of Upper-Palaeolithic artefacts suggests that men lived in the floodplain area, where they could hunt game of the water and the woodland as well as steppe creatures coming down to drink. Fishing became important in early Neolithic times. In the subpluvial period (about 5000 to 350 B.C.) farmers began a settled life, while much of the uplands, with a rich fauna, were occupied by hunting folk. Stone implements found in the desert show that in the past a much larger population, carrying on a pastoral way of life, could exist there than the scattered Arab tribesmen of our own day. Only five miles from the Red Sea coast a grave of the late predynastic or early dynastic period has been discovered.[8]

The river dropped the coarser sands near its banks, but took the finer silts and clays farther out in its flooding. As it receded, the raised section along the banks cut the floodplain from the normal Nile channel, and the plain held the water for months. Only in a few places, however, did sporadic swamps come about: patches of papyrus marsh or stagnant pools filled with the Egyptian and the blue lotus, reeds and sedge, waterbirds, crocodiles and hippopotami. The situation in the Delta was complicated by the many small branches; the raised banks were also slighter and the pools often ended in marsh or lake, or in brackish lagoons near the sea with sand-ridges or turtlebacks. The coastline seems to have altered little in the last 8,000 years. The trees were acacia, tamarisk, sycamore, or Egyptian willow in the higher parts of the valley.[9]

Men could settle there or on the low desert edges. After the flood they threw seeds of their crops on the damp earth or grazed their herds on the lush grasses. On the return of the flood they retired to the banks or the desert edge. The Delta's turtlebacks similarly enabled settlers to use and to evade the flood. Amid the small streams and marshes there were large sheltered spaces where they could live without waiting for the alluvial deposits to dry out. Hence Athribis, Tanis, Mendes and other townships were early founded there. But even outside the floodplain there was sufficient water for long to feed considerable vegetation. Tree roots have been found in the desert, well beyond the floodwaters,

B

and datable from the Neolithic Badarean period to the Fourth Dynasty.

Definite confirmation is found in the Fifth and the Sixth Dynasty reliefs (in the tombs of Ptahhotep and Mereruka at Saqqara and of Djau at Deir el-Gabrawi, and in the temples of Sahure and Nyuserre at Abusir) which show characteristic, irregular low desert-terrain with acacia and sycamore, acacia and tamarisk in an open parkland association with grass tufts and desert shrubs, which made up an "acacia desert-grass savanna" vegetation due to infrequent but ecologically important rains. Just as with the acacia shrubs of the eastern desert today, such copses could have been concentrated near or within the wadis, where accessory ground moisture would have been available.[10]

At the beginning there were small Neolithic communities, scattered about and rather cut off from one another. The organisation into districts or nomes came later. Gradually the groups must have learned to co-operate in draining swamps and controlling the yearly flood. Out of these contacts would come the building up of larger units embracing several villages, with a growth of uniformity in culture; the ancient phrase that speaks of the Portions of the Gods possibly refers to a system of holding land in common and of apportioning it to families by the elders of tribe or clan. If we may judge by analogy, in due course the economic co-operation would bring about the first stages of political controls, an increase in inequalities, and the rise of war-chieftains. Finally something like a centralised organisation of the irrigation systems and primitive forms of the State would emerge. The dependence of the farmers on a steady and effective control of irrigation would facilitate the growth of stable and ever-wider forms of political domination. A strong absolutist state had appeared with the first dynastic union: the earliest nation-state in history, since in Mesopotamia at the time there were still numbers of separate autonomous cities.[11]

Between the First and the Fourth Dynasty a worsening of climatic conditions, which had begun earlier, became more decisive. The rhinoceros, elephant, giraffe, and gerenuk gazelle went, and by the Sixth Dynasty aridity such as is now found had asserted its grip. Dunes crept along the western line. Low Niles in the First Intermediate Period led to famines, and Old Kingdom records show a lowering of flood-levels. From about 2350 to 500 B.C. the situation was unfavourable, then conditions much like the present came in.

Rain has never been entirely absent. A papyrus of the 2nd century A.D. from Oxyrhynchos mentions the sort of storm that is still not uncommon in the area during January:

Moros to my Lord Epimachos, greeting. I write to let you know we have winnowed the barley of the man from the Oasis on the 8th and we never had so much trouble in winnowing it. God rained and the wind was irresistible. Panares knows how we toiled to manage the transference of all the rest with the gods' help. The total was 38 artabai 4 choinikes. I disposed beforehand of 12½ art. 8 choin. of what we got. [Artaba = about 40 litres, but varies.]

I inquired about the price of annual grass. It was sold in the village at 7 drachmai the load, as Panares too knows. After many inquiries I found some that was dry, and not needing ready money—four months' credit. You'll explore the problem of how you're to transport it, and if you please, write to me about it and say what proportion I'm to dispose of beforehand from the large holding—and whether you want me to mix with the rest the barley of the man from the Oasis. I've stored my share in the room belonging to your father. I supplicate on behalf of you and all your children and all your brothers and . . . I pray for your health, My Lord.[12]

Problems of the Nile were with the people at all periods, whether connected with the dreaded failure of the water to rise high enough or with difficulties brought about by an all-too-good flood and weakenings of the embankments. The Pyramid Texts, seeking for an image of the dead king's powers of destruction against his enemies, declare: "Their hearts fall into his fingers, their entrails to the inhabitants of heaven [birds], their blood to the inhabitants of earth [beasts], their inheritance to the poor, their farms to a high Nile."[13] And in the Prophecy of Neferty, known from a papyrus of the period of Thotmose III as well as from two writing-boards and three ostraka of the New Kingdom, though composed under the Twelfth Dynasty, we read as a picture of the worst that could happen to Egypt:

How fares the land? The sun is veiled and will not shine that men may see. None will live when the storm veils it. All men are dulled [?] through the lack of it.

Drought has come and the sun is obscured—perhaps by storms of dust and sand, or perhaps by the withdrawal of the sungod from the lives of men as a dire omen.

I will speak of what is before me, and foretell nothing that is not also [already] come.

The River of Egypt is empty, men cross over the water on foot. Men will search for water in which the ships may sail. Its road is become a bank and the bank is become water. [The Delta streams shrink and stray from their beds.] . . . The southwind [of heat] will drive away the northwind [of coolness], and the sky has still only the one wind. The birds no longer hatch their eggs in the swamps of the Delta, but the strange bird has made herself a nest near to men and lets them approach her in her necessity. Moreover those good things are ruined, the fishponds where were the slittings [of fish], which shone with fish and wildfowl. All good things are passed away and the land is laid low with misery. . . .[14]

2. Animals of the Nile

On the other hand, when the Nile is controlled and functions well, men are happy and the land prosperous. A poet, seeking images for Sesostris III, declares:

How great is the Lord for his City: he is like a Dyke that keeps back the river in its waterfloods . . .

How great is the Lord for his City: he is like the shade of the Season of Overflowing for coolness in summer.

How great is the Lord for his City: he is like a corner warm and dry in time of winter.

How great is the Lord for his City: he is like a mountain that keeps back the storm-blast at the time when the sky is in riot.

How great is the Lord for his City: he is like Sekmet to foes that cross his boundaries.[15]

And joy at the accession of Ramses IV is similarly expressed:
"High Niles have come from their sources, that they may refresh
the hearts of others." And in the quietist prayers of the humble,
which we shall later consider in relation to the Theban nekropolis,
the secret sources of renewal and consolation are felt to be the
springs of water amid barren sand: "You who bring water to a
place afar, come, deliver me, the silent one, Thoth, you sweet
well for one who thirsts in the wilderness. It is closed to him who
finds words to say, it is open to him who keeps silent. The silent
one comes and finds the well."[16]

On the other hand, "to go down to the riverbank" (perhaps to
drown oneself) was an expression for disaster. Kamose boasts,
after defeating the Hyksos, "I destroyed his wall, I slew his folk,
I caused his wife to go down to the riverbank".[17] For the peasant
the Nile was an inescapable part of both happiness and misery.
Details changed, but the broad facts were not so unlike in
Pharaonic or in Graeco-Roman Egypt. Some phrases in the
following account are obscure, but the general bearing is poignantly
plain. The Porters here are minor officials, and the Negroes are
police:

The water is in flood and he is soaked. He stands preparing himself.
He spends the day cutting instruments for cultivating the corn; he
spends the night twisting rope. He spends the noon-hour doing a
craft-job so that he may equip himself to go out into the fields like
any warrior. The tillage is clear of water and lies before him. He goes
out to draw his yoke, and many days pass by while he follows after
the herdsman. When he has drawn his span, he comes back with it
so that he may make a place for it in the fields. At dawn of day, going
out to make an early start, he doesn't find it in its place. He spends
three days looking for it and finds it in the mud, but even the hides
are gone—the wolves have chewed them. He goes out with his
cloak in his hand to beg a span for himself. When he reaches the field,
he finds . . . He spends time cultivating barley, but the worm is behind
him. It finishes off the seed that is cast to the ground, and he never
sees a green blade. He does it [at last] with three sowings of borrowed
corn. His . . . has fallen to the traders, but has brought nothing in
exchange.

And now the Scribe lands on the bank registering the harvest. The
Porters are in attendance, and the Negroes with staffs. "Give us corn,"

they say. There is none. He is stretched out and beaten; he is bound and thrown into the canal; he sinks as one drowned. His wife is bound in his presence; his children are in fetters. His neighbours leave them and take to flight. All is over. The corn is not there.[18]

A Fayum document of A.D. 42, of twenty-two columns, gives a daily account of the movement of cereals. Apparently all wheat and barley had been taken out of the granaries before 23 Epeiph; and we may have here a confirmation of Dion's statement that Rome was stricken with famine in this year. However, no doubt shipments were made from the southern Fayum as quickly as possible while the flood was at its height. In the 2nd century we meet a complaint about lack of water.[19]

3. Benefits of the Nile: showing the Nile,
Isis, Horos, Nymphs, and Etesian Winds (Tassa Farnese onyx).

Demarios and Eirene to their dearest Syros, very many greetings. We know that you are distressed about the deficiency of water. This has happened not only to us but to many, and we know that nothing has occurred through any fault of yours. We know now your zeal and attentiveness to the work of the holding, and we hope that with god's help the field will be sown. Put down to our account all you spend on cultivating the holding. Get from Ninnaros for Eirene's account the share that belongs to her, and similarly from Hatres for Demarios' account the share that belongs to him. We pray for your health.[20]

This was probably a local matter, but it may possibly have

referred to the insufficient floods which we know occurred in the years A.D. 129–130. Juvenal was probably writing his Satire XV at this time, when, describing village-brawls that involved cannibalism, he comments:

> What extreme hunger, what beleaguering army
> drove them to dare so monstrous a crime? I cry.
> Should the Memphian land run dry, could they not try
> anything else to shame the unrising Nile?[21]

He seems alluding to the tradition that in the distant past human sacrifices were made to the Nile in time of famine and failing flood.

A letter of about 255 B.C. to Kleon the chief engineer of the Fayum, from his son at Alexandreia, suggests that if he cannot resign his post he may at least ask for a holiday in the low-water months. "If possible, make every effort to gain your release for good, or, if you see no chance of that, at least for the time of low Nile, at which season there is no danger [of burst dykes] and Theodoros can be left to take your place so that you may spend this season at least with us."[22] In the late 2nd century B.C. a farmer of Kerkesephis wrote to a man (probably of Kerkeosiris): "You must hear about our plain having been flooded, we have not so much as food for our cattle. So please firstly give thanks to the gods and secondly save many lives by seeking out in the neighbourhood of your village 5 arourai for our maintenance in order that we may get food from it. If you do so, I'll be eternally obliged."[23] The gods are to be thanked, just as another person, describing devastation by the flood, still called the Nile the Most Sacred.[24] A notice of the 1st century, sent round as a peremptory order to a number of village elders, shows how a sudden emergency could arise:

To the Elders of the undermentioned Villages. Send out irrigation-guards to the banks of the Upper Patemite District: from Skar, 100 . . . from Thatis, 100; from Temnkoris of the Shepherds, 100 . . . from Sinageris, 100; from Telbouthis, 100. Sebastos 9th.[25]

The terse tone and the large numbers of men called out suggest that some serious breach of the systems of embankments had happened.

In the late 5th or early 6th century, Phoibammon, a subordinate or agent at Gessias, a Herakleopolite village, wrote to a notary "my master the all-virtuous Aphhous":

Today I came to Oxyrhynchos with Alis on account of the tow-ropes. Let your Nobility deign to come at once by night, so that you may reach Gessias. For the grapes have been destroyed through the flood and our master is absent every day. Be sure too to send builders at once with the men of Gessias to the vineyard to finish the tank and prevent the water from flooding the land. Do not neglect this, master.

I have given the Lord Eulogios a copy of Proximos' letter requesting that the officialis Philoxenos should desist from annoying the riparii— sending it through the men from Palosis, master.[26]

A Nilometer at Elephantine noted the river levels and provided the basis on which the Prefect could work out the amount of tribute he would demand.[27] In the later years of the 2nd century A.D. a record of the floods under the Romans was engraved on the walls of the staircase.[28] Plinius says the highest level known up to his days came under Claudius, and the first entry on the first column of the inscription seems to record this event: ". . . year of Claudius Caesar 25 cubits. . . . year of Tiberius Caesar 25 cubits 3 palms. . . ." Plinius says that 16 cubits were the norm of a good flood; Strabon says 14. But variations in standards of measurement may derive from the selection of different sites along the Nile.

A rise of 16 cubits is good. If less, the irrigation is incomplete. If more, the slow subsidence of the flood obstructs cultivation: the land is soaked and the proper moment for seeding is lost. If the flood is low, the parched land does not yield a crop. In either case the Province is deeply concerned. With 12 cubits famine is the result; with 13 the country goes hungry; 14 cubits bring cheer; 15 security; and 16 the joys of prosperity. (Plinius)

I have heard that the Nile rises to 28 cubits at Syene and Elephantine; around Koptos, the mart for Indian and Arabic trade, to 21 cubits; at Memphis and the peoples now regarded as Greeks, the rise is 7 cubits less, or 14 cubits; lower down at the Delta the flood is reduced to 7 cubits and finally to 2. (Aristeides)[29]

Sixteen cubits was officially taken as the level of a good flood. Coins show the Nile with the figure 16, but whether they com- memorate a good year or merely state what was the desired

height of the waters is not clear. Other coins with Euthenia and
the Cornucopia seem to belong to the same category.[30] The
number 16 appears in a Nile-rite at Oxyrhynchos: because there
had been a good year, because this was the conventional number
associated with the Nile, or because it was hoped magically to
make the Nile reach that level:

To the Strategos, articles for the Sacrifice of the Most Sacred Nile on
30 Pauni: 1 calf, 2 jars of sweet wine, 16 wafers, 16 garlands, 16 cones,
16 cakes, 16 green palm branches, 16 reeds likewise, oil, honey, milk,
every spice but frankincense.[31]

The participation of the strategos shows the state-importance of
the event.

Excessive floods are recorded under Claudius and for A.D. 131;
the Nilometer inscriptions show that a large proportion of good
floods came under Tiberius and Nero; and Philon mentions good
harvests under the prefect Flaccus (c. A.D. 32–8).[32] Things went
well also under Vespasian, Hadrian, Commodus, Caracalla,
Gordian.[33] Strabon says that Augustus' improvements of the
irrigation system were so thorough that even a rise of 12 cubits
brought in a big revenue, and when the river fell to 8 cubits,
when Petronius was prefect, there was no famine.[34] Things seem
to have gone badly in the 40s if we may take the high proportion
of grass and pasturage at Tebtynis in 42 and 45–6 to show a low
level of the Nile; and the fact that there was a famine at Rome
in 42 supports this interpretation.[35] The low average rental on
crownland at Krodilopolis in 46–7 is additional evidence. The
flood in 77 must have been low, for next year the harvest at
Hermopolis was abnormally early and the price of wheat went
up.[36] The younger Plinius mentions a famine in Egypt about
A.D. 100, when Rome sent wheat to Alexandreia. A run of low
floods preceded Hadrian's Edict of 136; and another such run is
suggested by the surrender of a lease in 221 at Philadelpheia.[37]

We can guess at low flood-levels from other pieces of evidence.
A famine at Rome may result from a bad Egyptian harvest or
from conditions in Africa, which supplied an even larger part of
the annona than Egypt did. Sudden increases in wheat prices in
Egypt may reflect local dearths or a general failure in the

Mediterranean world. Distributions of seed-corn, if they were general, imply a bad harvest in the previous year.[38] From the 2nd century on, declarations of unflooded land appear, but we do not know if they indicate a flood failure or some need to register land outside the basins.[39]

We have some Ptolemaic documents in demotic in which the question of the level of the flood is taken into consideration. In one, a son engages to give his mother two artabai of wheat, $\frac{1}{2}$ art. of oil, and $\frac{1}{4}$ art. of salt yearly, plus a garment every two years; but if the Nile fails to reach the level of 18 cubits, she is to do his housekeeping.[40] At first it seems odd that such an important matter does not intrude more into legal documents, especially those concerned with farming and land-rents. But the situation seems to have been covered partly by law; at least under the Ptolemies we find the Kanopos Decree dealing with measures to be taken by the king in the event of a famine caused by the inadequate rising of the Nile.[41] And there were doubtless also various customary procedures for meeting such difficult years when a large number of persons would be hard hit. Hazards of various kinds could be covered in leases; in 132–1 B.C. we find a clause dealing with the possible effects of war; and we also find guarantees against hazard "apart from drought and flooding". Failure of crop was not, however, ranked as a danger against which one could thus seek legal protection.[42]

2

The Southern Barriers

BEFORE, however, we turn to the people on and by the Nile, it would be as well to consider further just how much the ancients did know of the sources of the river, and what held them up from an effective penetration into Africa.[1] Two barriers played the main role in cutting Central Africa from the Mediterranean world, apart from the obstructions of the desert: the cataracts on the Nile and the swamps of the Sudd. To defeat the cataracts a well-organised and permanent system of transhipments at the difficult points was needed; but even if that had been done, there was the yet worse problem of the marshes of the Bahr el-Ghazal.[2]

Still, the Egyptians of the Middle and New Kingdoms had moved into the Sudan and made settlements there, at Kerma, Soleb, Sesebi; the temple of Barkal showed the strength of their penetration. Further, there are the pictures of Nubian tributes on the walls of Theban tombs, such as that of Rekhmare; and finally there came the Nubian conquest of Egypt. In 730 B.C. Piankhi of Napata occupied Upper Egypt and gained the nominal submission of Lower Egypt; Shabaka conquered the Delta by 715. A single kingdom stretched from the Sea to Abyssinia. This twenty-fifth Kushite or Aithiopian dynasty ruled for half a century, with Thebes under the control of a Divine Wife. Then the northern princes revolted and opened the way to the invading Assyrians, who sacked Thebes. Psammetichos in the Delta crushed other local rulers, threw off the Assyrian protectorate and drove the Aithiopians from Upper Egypt about 660.

There were thus periods when the Egyptians must have learned a great deal about the Sudan and Aithiopia. The contact was by the desert-route that drives southwards, cutting across the bends of the Nile and thus reaching fresh water-supplies, and using transhipment at the cataracts. Hence the import into Egypt of products from Kerma, Napata, Meroe—the last two points commanding roads to the mines of the eastern desert and to the Red Sea. A New Kingdom text—in the tomb of Rekhmire, vizier of Thotmose III—informs us that certain officials "report on the rains of heaven" as well as on the rising of Sothis and the state of the Nile. Exactly how far their observations on rainfall went, we however have no clue. We are on more solid ground with a text of the time of Tanarka (684 B.C.): "A downpour of the sky in Nubia has made the mountains flourish." This seems the only example in Egyptian literature of a scientific explanation of the yearly flood; and it is significant that it occurs under the Aithiopian dynasty. A Saite text, mentioning the falling of rain on the Mountain of Punt (Aithiopia) attributes it to the benevolence of the goddess Neit towards king Psammetichos I; she "has brought [the King] the Nile to preserve his army".[3]

4. Negro Head
(balsam-container from Lamaurelle)

5. Egyptian Head
(Louvre balsam-container)

There are no representations of Negroes in the art of the Old and the Middle Kingdoms. Excavations in Lower Nubia show that at the time of the Old Kingdom the population there was Hamitic, though there may have been some slight negroid mixture. What is called the A-group seem to have been folk of predynastic Egypt retreating south from the pressure of the forerunners of the Pharaonic Egyptians. Population expanded and at least in Lower Nubia there was an increase in prosperity. At the end of the Second Dynasty the Egyptians invaded Nubia, and we meet the B-group, whose culture shows some links with that of the A-group, but also many differences—perhaps through a general breakdown, perhaps through the influx of new groups from the south. Tribal movements indeed may have been going on fairly strongly from the First Intermediate Period of Egypt, pressing in on the Nubians, who were however still substantially Hamitic. When in the Intermediate Period the Egyptians withdrew, the Nubians (probably swollen by folk coming in from the south-west) developed an independent culture known as that of the C-group. The newcomers seem, like the earlier inhabitants of Lower Nubia, of the Brown or Mediterranean race; but certain negroid characteristics have been noticed in the skeletons from the graves. The culture of the A- and B-groups was still the basis on which Nubia developed.

With the New Kingdom the situation was much changed through contacts with Punt along the Red Sea and through the southward extension of the Egyptian frontier. The Middle Kingdom had pushed only slightly into the region of the Second Cataract; but Thotmose I reached up to Napata, 600 km. beyond the previous line. The representations of his conquest in the Temple of Amun, however, do not show Negroes; the Egyptians had not penetrated as far as the Fourth Cataract. But expeditions and skirmishes no doubt soon took them more south, into Negro territory. Negro chieftains acknowledged the Pharaoh's supremacy by a yearly tribute. In some cases we may assume that their lands had not been subjugated; but such gifts would be worth while, ensuring their safety from raids. Also, Negro tribesmen from deeper Africa may have come to the new trade-sites for barter; some may have even have gone into Egyptian territory along the Napata route. Contacts were going on under Thotmose II and III, as we can see from the tombs. Meanwhile, in Lower Nubia the Egyptian element was increasing through colonisation, and many local women married Egyptians. In Upper Nubia (Kush) at Kerma we find graves with a more negroid culture, and it was probably from such an area that the black troops of the Egyptian army were recruited. A start seems to have been made as early as the Twelfth Dynasty.[4]

The first Greeks in Egypt in the historical period were not unaware of some of the southern links. Some of them, probably mercenaries in the army of Psammetichos II in 591 B.C., cut inscriptions on the leg of one of the colossi of the great temple of Abu Simnel. The longest text runs:

When King Psammetichos came to Elephantine, this was written by those who sailed with Psammetichos son of Theokles and they came beyond Kerkis as far as the river permits. Those who spoke foreign tongues were led by Potasimto, the Egyptians by Amasis.

A Karnak inscription also mentions the expedition and states that it reached Pnubs (Tumbus) and that after finally beating the Nubians it occupied the Land of Shas (perhaps the Dongola reach, which includes Napata). No doubt the limit that "the river permits" was the 2nd Cataract; for no attempt to occupy the region beyond seems to have been made. The expedition retired to the 2nd Cataract; and the Carian mercenaries who put their names on the pilasters of the Temple of Buhen and on the rocks of the hill of Sheikh Suliman at Kor were doubtless members of the garrison. Napata remained the religious capital of the Nubians, but the political capital moved farther south to Meroe between the 5th and 6th Cataracts.[5]

Between Napata and the 2nd Cataract the desert-crossing was a hard one. It could be used only when the region was pacified and there was an organised system. So, from time to time when things went wrong, communications broke down along the line between the 2nd and 4th Cataracts. On the other hand, at Meroe there was enough summer rain to encourage a spiny vegetation that served as cattle-fodder; and the trees supplied fuel for crafts that needed fire.[6] The area could carry on even if relations with Egypt were severed. A track supplied with wells gave access to the Red Sea. The period between the expedition of Psammetichos II and the advent of the Ptolemies seems to have been one when communications lapsed. Herodotos has a tale of the garrison left by Psammetichos for three years without relief; the soldiers discussed their grievances and went off in a body to Aithiopia. The king gave chase and caught them up. He begged them not to abandon their wives, children, and gods; but one of them "in reply pointed to his private parts and said that wherever those were, there'd be no lack of wives and children." The Aithiopian king allowed them to drive out some of his subjects with whom he was on bad terms, and take their land. "As a result the Aithiopians learned Egyptian manners and became more civilised."[7]

Herodotos knew of the east-west direction of the Nile from Bahr Jebet or Bahr el-Ghazal. In stating that the deserters were installed at Four Months' Navigation or March from Elephantine, he remarks, "and the Nile flows from the region of the Night and Sunset". And adds, "as to what lies beyond, no one can speak of it with certainty; for this land is desert on account of the heat". It follows that the Egyptian tradition in his time did not know of a marshy region, though it told of the way in which at one place the Nile flowed east-west. The desert was imagined to continue indefinitely.[8]

The Persian Kambyses was said to have attempted a southern expedition, which perished in the desert.[9] All that seems to have survived in men's minds was a memory of the perils of the 2nd Cataract. Herodotos says: "The most I could learn was that past Elephantine the country rises steeply; and in that part of the river boats have to be hauled along by ropes (one rope on each side) rather as a man drags an ox. If the rope snaps, the boat is gone in an instant, carried away by the force of the stream."[10]

However, about this time "a group of wild young fellows, sons of chieftains" of the Nasamonians of Syrtis, to the east of Kyrene, "on coming to manhood, planned all sorts of extravagant adventures among themselves, one of which was to draw lots for five of their number to explore the Libyan desert and try to penetrate farther than had ever been done before". They crossed the desert, reached a region of fruit-trees, and were there attacked by "some little men, of less than middle height, who seized them and carried them off". These small men "took their captives through a vast tract of marshy country, and beyond it came to a town, all the inhabitants of which were of the same small stature, and all black. A great river with crocodiles in it flowed past the town from west to east,"[11]

Herodotos seems to have got the direction of this expedition wrong; he speaks of it crossing the desert on a westerly course. And what is the great river flowing east–west? If the young men had indeed gone southwest, they came on the Niger; but if Herodotos has confused his orientations—note how he compares the Nile and the Danube—then the river was the Nile, as we are told at the outset of the story: "Some folk of Kyrene informed me that during a visit to the Oracle of Ammon they chanced in the course of conversation with Etearchos the Ammonian King to strike the theme of the Nile and the riddle of its sources." Etearchos then narrated the tale of the young Nasamonians.[12]

Now let us turn back to Herodotos' account of the upper reaches of the Nile. He halts at Elephantine, but clearly other writers had a factual knowledge that reached to the 4th Cataract. This knowledge may have derived from a period when the Egyptians commanded the communications with the 4th Cataract, or it may merely prove that (despite the alleged check to Kambyses) traders kept on going all the while to Napata for Sudanese products. Herodotos somewhat confusedly attributes the landscape of the Cataract to the whole Dodekaschoinos: the Greek translation of the Egyptian name, the Land of the Twelve Furlongs, for the reach between Hiera Sykaminos and Philai. But the time he allots, four days, is verified by voyages in the Roman period. As twelve *schoinoi* represent some 120 kilometres, about 30 km. were covered in a day. The end of this stretch is marked by an island Tachampso (apparently Derar) at Hiera Sykaminos.[13] Then the reckoning is not given in days till the traveller is forced to leave his boat, no doubt at the 2nd Cataract. At 30 km. a day, the passage from Derar to Wadi Halfa would take seven or eight days. After that came a forty-day trudge to

Kerma along rocky roads with sandy pockets, at about 10 km. a day—slow-going, but understandable for foot-travellers with only donkeys, oxen or porters to carry the wares or baggage. Camels in caravans had not yet come in. At Kerma the traveller returned to a boat and went on to Meroe (Kareima, with Merowe opposite on the left bank), a site known to the Hellenistic Greeks. In Herodotos' time, however, the place was no metropolis, and he therefore probably refers to Napata, nearby, just below the 4th Cataract.[14] What he calls the Temple of Zeus would be the temple of Barkal dedicated to Amun-Re and partly cut into the rock.

Here for long lay the limits of Greek knowledge of Africa. According to Herodotos' calculation the land of the Deserters would have been on the White Nile in the section where, pressed by the Bahr el-Ghazal, it flows from west to east, up to the confluent of the Sobat, with the uninhabitable marshes behind. A recent traveller thus describes the swampy area:

. . . at the point where the Sobat comes in from the Abyssinian mountains, a short distance above the present town of Malakal, the river turns west, the air grows more humid, the banks more green, and this is the first warning of the great obstacle of the Sudd that lies ahead. There is no more formidable swamp in the world than the Sudd. The Nile loses itself in a vast sea of papyrus ferns and rotting vegetation, and in that foetid heat there is a spawning tropical life that can hardly have altered since the beginning of the world . . . The region is neither land nor water. Year by year the current keeps bringing down more floating vegetation, and packs it into solid chunks perhaps twenty feet thick and strong enough for an elephant to walk on. But then this debris breaks away in islands and forms again in another place, and this is repeated in a thousand indistinguishable patterns and goes on for ever.

The pharaonic Egyptians were not ignorant of the marshlands; at least under Ramses II at Luxor we find the extent of his power described as including "the Great Circle, the Sea, the Southern Countries of the Land of the Negro as far as the Marshlands, as far as the Limits of Darkness, even to the Four Pillars of Heaven".

If we turn back to Homer, however, we find that the much earlier

C

Greeks seem to have known rather more about Africa. Homer knew the Pygmies of Central Africa, though Strabo, some seven hundred years later, doubted their existence.[15] Homer's picture of the pygmies fighting the cranes provides the location—though, as the pygmies have doubtless moved much more south than his day, that location was certainly not where they now dwell. Under the Sixth Dynasty Herkhuf, on his fourth exploration of the south, wrote to the young Pepi II that he was bringing back a dancing dwarf from the Land of Yam. Pepi was delighted:

Come northward to the court at once and bring with you the pygmy that you have brought living, in good condition, and healthy, from the Land of the Horizon-folk, for the amusement of the king, to rejoice and gladden his heart. When the pygmy is in the boat, appoint trustworthy persons to be on either side of him. Take care that he doesn't fall into the water. When he sleeps at night, appoint trust-worthy persons to sleep beside him in the cabin and make an inspection ten times a night. My Majesty desires to see this pygmy more than the gifts of Sinai and of Punt.

It is uncertain whether this pygmy was a real one or a pathological dwarf, as the ancient Egyptian word is obscure. If he were the former, then the expedition would seem to have gone far into southern Sudan or the dancer must have been brought up and sold in barter in the Land of Yam. Egyptian kings or dignitaries were eager to obtain dwarf dancers and entertainers, who were felt to be vessels of sacred power.[16]

Nubian pressure—the result perhaps of Negro pressure from farther south—led the pharaohs of the New Kingdom to respond with attacks that brought Egyptian controls up as far as the 4th Cataract. Negroes were imported as messengers, mercenaries, house-slaves.[17] Now the statuettes of dwarfs certainly show a negroid aspect and represent Pygmies.[18] The temples in the region of the 4th Cataract, fortified, served as the bases for the economic exploitation of the more southern parts which had not been reached by the Egyptian armies. About the same time there were close trading and artistic relations with the Minoan and the Mykenean worlds. Ostrich eggs have been found in the Aegean; and the so-called Captain of the Black Guard painted on the wall at Knossos may well reveal the use of Negro soldiery—unless the dark hues derive from some art-convention. There is no reason why Egyptian tales of the Pygmies should not have reached the Aegean at this time and provided Homer with his imagery. Hekataios describes disguised Pygmies making castanet-noises as they fight with cranes.[19]

6. Pygmies fighting Cranes

Another interesting point is Homer's knowledge of the Aithiopians. They live on the edge of the world somewhere, close to the sun in its ascent or descent, in the extreme east or west; they are visited by the gods, but we hear nothing of human visitors. They thus have the mythical or semi-mythical quality of people who live remotely on the horizon-edge, both in this world and in the spirit-world—the sort of thing that comes up strongly in the Egyptian concept of the Akhit. They are Horizon-folk like the denizens of the mysterious land from which Herkhuf's dwarf came. But though Homer has no clear idea where or what the Aithiopians are, he is probably echoing some account brought into the Aegean from Egypt. Since they seem to exist in a Bronze-Age context, we may carry the tale back into the Mykenean world. Menelaos' story of his voyage to Egypt in the *Odyssey* suggests, not the southern route natural for a Cretan, but a more northerly roundabout course likely to be followed by Achaians who had outposts in Rhodes, Cypros, and Syria, and who traded with Phoinikian ports.[20]

The reference in the *Iliad* to Egyptian Thebai seems to represent a general impression of splendour, probably derived from the reign of Amenophis III.[21] Articles of his period are those most widely found in Greece and the Aegean.[22] After that came the loss of Syria, which drove Egypt back on herself and led to the rise of the Phoinikian traders. The picture of Thebes with its hundred gates through which could pass two hundred men with war-chariots may be an hyperbole to express the city's magnificence, though Diodoros says that some persons thought the reference was to "the great propylai in front of the temples". He adds: "Twenty thousand chariots did in fact, we are told, pass out of it in war; for there were once scattered along the River from Memphis on to the Thebes over against Libya a hundred post-stations, each with accommodation for two hundred horses, the foundations of which are pointed out to this day."[23] But by the 9th century B.C. Thebes had fallen from its high estate and the mummies of its kings had been taken from their tombs and hidden away. The Homeric reference then must derive from Mykenean days; and the *Odyssey*'s reuse of the picture is a mere quotation.[24]

In narrating Menelaos' adventures in the Delta, the poet thinks that the isle of Pharos is a full day's journey from the mainland, to which it is in fact attached.[25] Proteus, the shaman of trans-formations met on the isle, is thought to have a name which reflects the Egyptian title *Prouti*.[26] (The term Pharaoh appears to have come via Hebrew from the title *Per-aa*.) But the objects mentioned as taken by Helen from Thebes—gold distaff, wheeled basket, silver basket with gilded rims—are plainly Phoinikian in character.[27] The only Odyssean passage that seems to have genuine contemporary roots is the tale told by Odysseus when he pretends to be a Cretan adventurer captured while carrying on piracy along the Egyptian coast; and this is just the sort of thing we should imagine the Phoinikians telling.[28]

It seems plausible then that a certain amount of stories about Egypt entered the Aegean in the Mykenean period. After that communications were interrupted by the Dark Ages in Greece and a difficult period in Egypt. They were resumed when Greek trade expanded afresh in the wake of the Phoinikians. Naukratis was founded in the Delta by Milesians in the 7th century B.C. as a trade-emporion, with the income from customs dues going to the temple of Neith at Sais and several Greek cities joining in the development of the site. But the knowledge of the farther south had now weakened in Egypt and reached the sort of stage which we find set out in Herodotos. Things grew even worse in the next century or so, as we can see by considering the representations of Negroes on Greek vases. There are many such in the 6th century and the first half of the 5th—interest being aroused first through Naukratis and then through the presence of Aithiopians in Xerxes' armies. After that the theme loses its grip.[29]

The Ptolemies resumed the efforts to penetrate into the south. Ptolemy II sent an expedition to open up Aithiopia, but with the aim, it seems, rather of gaining knowledge of the routes and of developing trade connections than of making any considerable conquests. Didoros says that till his reign "not only did no Greek ever cross over into Aithiopia, but none ascended even as far as the boundaries of Egypt, to such an extent were all these regions inhospitable to foreigners and totally dangerous. But after this king had made an expedition into Aithiopia with an army of Greeks, being the first to do so, the facts about that country have thenceforth been more accurately ascertained."[30] A coin of the king has been found at Buhen; and the names of Kyreneans engraved on a pilaster of the temple there may well be those of some of his mercenaries.[31] A scrap of papyrus found at Elephantine may be a report of the Greek garrison there about this time. "To King Ptolemaios Pertaios son of Arnuphis, greeting . . . the Aithiopians came down and besieged . . . constructing a stockade, I and my two brothers . . . as reinforcements, and we took up . . ." If the conjecture is correct, it seems that the Greeks did not by any means have things all their own way.[32] Under Ptolemy IV the Nubians extended their rule over the whole Dodekaschoinos as far as Philai, where there are the remains of a temple bearing the name of king Arkamon. At Dakkeh he built the inner shrine of the temple, but the outer hall was added by Ptolemy IV and the pronaos by Ptolemy IX. It appears then that the Nubian hold was brief and that the Ptolemies reasserted their control. In any event relations between Egypt and Nubia continued peaceable, and the Nubian kingdom of Meroe went on with its settlement of Lower Nubia undisturbed.[33]

In these conditions individual Greeks travelled south, even beyond Meroe. There were several authors of *Aithiopika* cited by

Plinius: Dalios, Aristokreon, Bion, Basilis, and Simonides the Younger, who lived five years in Meroe. The life of the nomadic as well as the settled areas was known; and Agatharkides described the atrocious Nubian goldmines.[34] Eratosthenes knew that at the level of Meroe and to the west of the Nile's double bend there were Nubian tribes independent of Aithiopia. (Perhaps anarchic conditions round here were one of the barriers to southward movements and played their part in provoking the expedition of Ptolemy II.[35]) Meroe's latitude was known from the time of Ptolemy I in a remarkably correct way; the observations went back to Philon who made a reconnaissance of the Red Sea at that time.[36]

But in general the Ptolemies decided that the penetration into Africa by land was too difficult. They wanted the southern products, especially elephants for fighting purposes, but now they turned to the Red Sea as an alternative route and put their energies into developing sea-trade. Plinius gives conflicting lengths of time for the journey from Elephantine to Meroe; and he sets monsters there: Blemyes, whose heads lack ears and whose eyes are fixed in their chests. Also he mentions a series of towns below Meroe which in his time had faded out.[37] Clearly, under the Ptolemies and the early Empire, the routes across the desert and up the Nile were not being used, although we find some graffiti in the temples of Lower Nubia.[38] Military and religious establishments stretched south of the 1st Cataract as far as Kasr Ibrim, becoming important under the Romans, but as a defensive system, not as a launching ground for expeditions farther south.

At first, indeed, the Romans were much interested in Lower Nubia. Under Augustus the great temple of Kalabsha, dedicated to the Nubian god Mandoulis, was built, and additions were made to shrines at Debod, Dendur and Dakkeh. An earlier building on the Kalabsha site seems the work of Amenhotep II, refounded by one of the Ptolemies. Clearly the intention was to push the frontier southwards. In 29 B.C. the prefect Cornelius Gallus managed to make the envoys of the Merotic king sign a treaty turning all Lower Nubia into a protectorate. The Nubians bided their time and a chance soon came to strike. When in 23 the third prefect failed in an Arabian expedition, they "attacked the Thebaid", says

Strabo, "and the garrison of three cohorts at Syene, and by surprise captured Syene, Elephantine, and Philai, enslaved the inhabitants, and pulled down Caesar's statues". The new prefect G. Petronius, set out with less than 10,000 infantry and 800

7. Pygmies and Crocodile

horsemen. He drove the Nubians back to Pselkis, an Aithiopian city, and sent ambassadors to demand what they had taken, and to ask the reasons for their making war. They declared they had been wronged by the Nomarchs; he replied that these were not the country's rulers, but Caesar was. When they asked for three days to consider, but did nothing as they should, he attacked and forced them into battle.

He quickly put them to rout, as they were badly marshalled and badly armed. They carried big oblong shields, made of raw oxhide, and for weapons had only axes, pikes, or swords. Some were driven into the city, others fled into the desert, yet others took refuge in an island nearby after wading across the channel—for, on account of the current, crocodiles were not numerous there. Among the fugitives were the generals of Queen Kandake, who was ruler of the Aithiopians in my time, a masculine sort of woman, blind in one eye.

Kandake is Meroitic for queen. The queen in question seems to have been Amanirenas. Strabon goes on:

He captured every one of these, sailing after them in rafts and ships, and sent them without delay down to Alexandreia. He also assaulted Pselkis and took it. If the multitude of those killed in battle is added to the number of captives, those who escaped must have been few indeed. From Pselkis, Petronius went on to Premnis, a fortified city, after passing through the sand-dunes where Kambyses' army had been overwhelmed by a wind-storm. He gained the fortress at the first onset. Then he set out for Napata, the royal residence. Kandake's son was there and she herself was staying at a place nearby. She sent envoys to treat for friendship and offered to hand back the captives and the statues from Syene, but Petronius attacked and captured Napata as well, after the son had fled. He razed the place to the ground, enslaved its people, and then, deciding that the regions beyond would be hard to traverse, he turned back with his booty.

But he improved the fortifications of Premnis, threw in a garrison and two years' food for 400 men, then set off for Alexandreia. He sold some of the captives as plunder and sent a thousand to Caesar [Augustus] who had recently returned from Cantabria; the others died of diseases. Meanwhile Kandake marched with many thousands against the garrison; but Petronius set out to relieve them and arrived first at the fortress. After he had made the place secure by various devices, ambassadors arrived. He bade them go to Caesar. They asserted that they did not know who Caesar was, or where to find him. So he gave them escorts and they went on to Samos, where, after despatching Tiberius to Armenia, Caesar had paused, intending to move on to Syria. Then, when they had gained all they pleaded for, he even remitted the tributes he had imposed.[39]

So runs the Roman version; but what the Nubians say on a stele at Meroe suggests that their defeat was not so complete. A head of Augustus was found at Meroe, apparently under the threshold of a small temple; it was probably buried ritually as an important trophy. No doubt it was the head of a statue carried away from Syene as a token of Meroitic victory.[40] Also, it is significant that the Roman frontier was withdrawn to the former point, Hiera Sykaminos, in the Dodekaschoinos. Still, the Meroitic realm now steadily declined. Intrusive warring powers, the Blemyes and the Nobatai, worsened the situation. Towns and villages were destroyed or left to sink down; many parts of the country were depopulated. The Blemyes gradually occupied all Nubia and by the mid-3rd century were strong enough to attack the Roman frontier.

The southern desert was unknown. Nero sent two centurions to seek for the springs of the Nile and to investigate the possibilities of offensive action against the Aithiopians. They seem to have reached the Sudd. Seneca informs us:

I have heard the narration of two centurions whom Nero, that great lover of all good things, but above all of truth, had sent to discover the Nile's sources. After a long journey, directed by the help of the King of Aethiopia and with his recommendation to neighbouring princes, they penetrated into the beyond. There, they declared, they came on vast marshland. Its inhabitants had no idea of its extent and despaired of ever finding out. Plants and water were so entangled that any passage through on foot or by boat was impossible. Scarcely could a very small boat, made to carry one person, make its way there. And there, they said, they saw two rocks from which burst out a huge force of water. Whether this was the source of the Nile or a tributary, whether it was born there or came up after a long subterranean course —can you doubt that a great lake under the earth feeds it, whatever it is? Waters, scattered about in various places, must come together, forced into the depths, in order to jet out with such violence.[41]

We see that the Romans had not got beyond Dodek and that though the relations with Aithiopia were amicable, they were slight and sporadic.[42] A certain amount of trade in slaves, skins, ivory, ebony, ostrich eggs, feathers, must have gone on at frontier-posts by barter—there was no Aithiopian coinage till the kings of Axum took over, though even the caravan-folk of Arabia struck Hellenised pieces.[43] The Aithiopians were no sea-folk and clearly their rulers made no consistent effort to organise trade.[44]

8. Pygmies in the countryside

In the Memnonia one of the sightseers at an uncertain date under the Romans was "Kladon the envoy to Aithiopia and his companions". We also find a man from Pselkis (Dakkeh).[45] There is further extant a letter, written under Trajan, from a soldier stationed at Pselkis, who was about to go off on some expedition; unfortunately he does not specify in what direction. He is so worried about the problem of getting downriver to visit his mother (no doubt at Karanis) that he has no time in a long letter for much else. He was probably serving in an auxiliary cohort.

Satornilos to his mother, very many greetings. Before all else I pray for your health and prosperity. I want you to know I've sent you three letters this month. I've received in full the monthly allowance you sent me by Ioulios and a basket of olives by the lad of Ioulios. I want you to know another male child has been born to me—his name, the gods willing, is Agathos Daimon.

If I get a chance of carrying out my plan, I'm coming to you with letters. I want you to know it's now three months since I came to Pselkis, and I've not yet found a chance to come to you. I was scared of coming just now because they're saying: The Prefect is on route. Scared of him taking the letters from me and sending me back to the troops, so that I'm put to the expense all for nothing.

Still, I want you to know that if another two months pass and I don't come to you before the month Hathyr, I have eighteen more months of sitting in garrison till I enter Pselkis again and come to you.

All those who come will bear witness to you how I daily try to come. If you want to see me a little, I greatly desire it and daily pray the gods to give me quickly a good chance for coming.

Everything is ready for the expedition, awaiting a chance. If I get the chance, I'm coming to you. Take care of my children's pigs for me, so that if my children come they may find them. At the next chance, please send to Ioulas, the son of Ioulios, whatever allowance you can, and let him be as a son of mine, just as you love me and I love my children. If his brother as well is at leisure, send him to me at once so that I may send my children and their mother to you by him.

Send me an extra jar of olives for a friend of mine. Don't fail to do it. You know that whatever you give to Ioulios, he brings me: which he indeed promised me to do. Write to me whatever he does. Salute Sokmenios and his children and . . . and Sabeinos and Thaisas and her children and brothers and my sister Tabenka and her children and her relations-in-law. And write to me if she has had a child.

Salute Tasokmenis and my lady sister Sambas and Soueris and her children and Sambous and all the relations and friends, each by name. Gemella salutes you all as do Didymarion and the newly-born Agathos Daimon and Epiktetos. Salute Gemellus and . . . the wife of . . . lianos. And it was no great matter . . . I pray for the health of you all.[46]

Why he should fall foul of the Prefect if he were carrying letters, it is hard to say. The context suggests that he hopes to be sent with letters downstream and thus get a chance to call on his mother; but his worry about the Prefect makes the mission seem unofficial and without proper authorisation.

The longing to get downstream in this letter reminds us of a letter, probably a piece of fiction, which occurs among those set out as models for schoolboys in the New Kingdom. There, however, the writing is highly lyrical and competent:

Behold, my heart has gone forth secretly. It hastens away to a place that it knows. It voyages downstream, so that it may see Memphis. . . . But I sit and wait for [a messenger] so that he may tell how Memphis is faring. I get no message and my heart leaps in my breast.

Come to me, Ptah, take me to Memphis, and let me look on you unhindered.

I spend the day with my heart dreaming. My heart is not in my body, all my limbs . . . my eye is weary with looking, my ear is not . . . my voice is . . . , so that it speaks all manner of things in a topsy-turvy way. Be gracious to me. . . .[47]

It is a pity that the text is not complete; for in its way it stands out as a prose draft of the derangement of desire that cries passionately in Sappho's ode on the nearness of the beloved.

At Pselkis excavations have shown great burial grounds of the same sort as those found farther north; but on the west bank, north of the temple, a vast amount of Roman pottery was dug up, including many bowls of fine blue glaze, near to a small brick building. Most of the jars were doubtless used for wine, and the building seems to have been a canteen for the soldiers in the garrison. If so, our Satornilos may have drunk his griefs away there. The place, however, may have been a custom-house at which cargoes were brought ashore. Protecting the temple on its south and west sides lay a fortified encampment, where the garrison was housed. This fort was occupied between A.D. 100 and 250 as part of the defence system against the Meroites and Blemyes. (In 297 the frontier retreated to the 1st Cataract.) Signs of fire on the brickwork and copper sheathing of the wooden door of the west gate suggest that the fort was finally stormed. But that was long after Satornilos and his woes.[48]

There is another angle from which we may approach the question of how much the Greeks knew of the Nile. We find a persistent tradition that the yearly flood was caused by equatorial rains and the melting of snow in Aithiopia. Strabon attempts to make Homer the first to propound this thesis because he calls the great river of Egypt *diipetes*: "come from Zeus, come from the rains of heaven". But this may be no more than a conventional epithet.

9. Pygmies in the countryside

Homer uses it also of the river Spercheios, and in the sense of *divine* it is applied to bronze, ether, even fire. We cannot then attach any special significance to Homer's epithet except to note that he knew of the Egyptian River and its deeply sacred character. For him it rose out of the spiritworld (which could be either sky, ocean, underworld); but that does not necessarily mean any link with the equatorial rains and the snows of Aithiopia.[49]

The first Greek to set clearly out the snow-thesis seems Anaxagoras of Klazomenai, born about 500 B.C. He "declared that the cause of the rising", says Diodoros, "is the melting snow in Aithiopia", and the poet Euripides, a pupil of his, is in agreement. At least he writes: "He quit Nile's waters, the fairest that come out of earth, that out of the Blackman's-home, Aithiopia, flow with the fullness of flood when the snows are melting."[50] The idea may have reached the Greek world through mercenaries returned from Egypt or through the Persians. Later, it was through the Troglodytes of the Red Sea coast that Agatharkides claimed to have learned that the Nile in the south collected water from many confluents.[51] It is possible that Aischylos had anticipated Anaxagoras; for in his *Suppliants* he speaks of "the sacred land of Zeus where grow all fruits, the snowfertilised meadow that Typhon's fury assails, and the Nile with its waters inviolably healthful", and in *Prometheus Bound* he shows his interest in Nilotic geography: "You'll reach a distant land, a darkened tribe, who dwell close by the Fountains of the Sun, where runs the river Aithops. Along its banks wander until you reach the Cataract where from the Bybline Mountains the Nile pours out its hallowed kindly waters. This will guide you to Egypt's Delta."[52]

Other Greeks, such as Promachos of Samos, repeated this thesis of the Nile's birth from mountain snows.[53] Poseidonios thought that rain caused the floods, and cited Homer, Thrasyalkes, Aristotle, and Kallisthenes. Thrasyalkes, a physical philosopher of the mid-5th century, is the first thinker whom we can definitely say set out the rain-thesis. John of Lydia summarised his views. "Thrasyalkes of Thasos argued that the Etesian winds bring on the Nile; Aithiopia is surrounded by mountains higher than those of the part of the world we inhabit, and when it receives the clouds driven up by the Etesian winds, the Nile-flood is produced."[54] Demokritos in the second half of the 5th century went further. He tried to describe the origin of rains in a torrid zone, and was said to have visited Egypt and Aithiopia about 410. "Demokritos upholds that at the winter solstice, the northern regions are covered with snow; at the summer solstice, once the sun has changed his course's orientation, the snow begins to melt and the humidity that results from this melting gives birth to clouds that the Etesian winds seize and carry southwards. When these clouds mass in Aithiopia and Lybia, abundant precipitations are caused, which stream down and make the Nile rise."[55]

We see then again that the writers of the 5th century had some definite points of knowledge whether or not they built up correct theories upon them. The following century was much more vague. Ephoros tried to explain the flood as the result of water being sucked up by the summer sun out of the spongy soil. He had seen or been told of the way the water sank down into cracks in the mud, and thought the process could be reversed. He thus excluded from his consideration the rocky areas and the whole Aithiopian background.[56]

Nothing substantial was added to the knowledge of Africa in the following Graeco-Roman centuries; but efforts to rationalise and generalise the previous findings were made. Here the astronomers played the main role. According to Agatharkides (as handed down by Diodoros) the Egyptians began the reasoning.

Certain of the philosophers in Memphis have undertaken to provide an explanation of the flooding, which is incapable of disproof rather than credible, yet is accepted by many. They divide the earth into three parts and say that one part is that forming our inhabited world, the second is exactly opposite to these regions in its seasons, and the third lies between the two and is uninhabited on account of its heat. If the Nile rose in winter, it would obviously be getting its additional waters from our zone, since it is at that season in particular that we experience our heavy rains. But as the flood on the contrary occurs in the summer, it is probably in the regions opposite to us that winter storms are occurring, and the surplus waters of those far-off regions flow into the world we inhabit.

For this reason no man can journey to the sources of the Nile, as the river flows from the opposite zone through that which is uninhabited. A further witness to this fact is the excessive sweetness of the Nile waters. In the course of the river through the torrid zone it is tempered by the heat and as a result is the sweetest of all rivers; for it is the law of nature that what is fiery always sweetens what is wet.[57]

Against this thesis it was argued that in a spherical earth water could not flow uphill over the equator, that in any event the matter was not capable of proof or disproof, and that the fish in a river flowing through the torrid zone would be all killed.

Some idea of the earth as a sphere was needed for such arguments to be at all effective; but ancient ideas of symmetry may have sketched out a plan of three zones on a flat earth. The Egyptians thought of the year as three-seasoned. A Pyramid Text, calling on the deadman to "stand up as Anubis", adds: "The Three Beginnings will be celebrated for you; you purify yourself on the day of the New Moon, you dawn on the First of the Month." The Three Beginnings are the three year-divisions: New Year's Day, 1 Tybi, and 1 Pachon, or Winter, Spring, and Summer, each of four months. Considering a temperate and a torrid zone, Egyptian priests might have been drawn to add a third zone, temperate and set beyond the desert area, both for symmetry and to explain the Nile sources. If so, it was left to the

Greeks to rationalise and finally to provide astronomic precisions.[58]

The idea of zones of sky and earth was widely accepted. Pythagoras had recognised the obliquity of the ecliptic, and the zones traced in heaven by the sun were considered to have their reflections on earth: the lines of the solstices, the equinoxes, the equator, the arctic and antarctic zones. Parmenides seems to have first made the correlations and stated that habitable regions stopped at the tropics, though Strabon attributes the zonal division to Poseidonios. The latter seems to have made the torrid zone double what it is in fact. So we see that the memory of the southern marshes had been lost and a hopeless desert was thought to stretch across vast spaces.[59]

From the period of Alexander the Great, however, more correct information about Africa became available, no doubt mainly through the connections along the Red Sea. We find again references to the marshland and to the high mountains of Aithiopia that gave birth to rivers with opposed orientations—among which the Nile came down from a Mountain of Silver.[60] The astronomers intruded again, using the new materials to estimate the volume and measure the meridian of the earth. Aristotle had a figure for the latter measurement, though it was too big. For such calculations it was necessary to take two places on the same meridian, at different latitudes, and compare the angles of the point at which the sun or a star reached its highest altitude. For the Greeks the meridian they could explore at its greatest length passed through Egypt. Aristotle did not know the latitude of Syene, but perhaps his pupil Dikaiarchos, about 300 B.C., used that latitude for a measurement of the earth's meridian based on the arc separating Syene and Lysimacheia. Thus, the advances being made by astronomers, often at Alexandreia, were linked with the growth of precise knowledge about Africa. Philon, exploring for Ptolemy II, determined the latitude of Meroe; and his observation allowed Eratosthenes to determine the distance of Meroe from the equator. Meroe's parallel provided him with one of the four sides of his map, and the new Aithiopian capital remained the essential landmark of Ptolemaios' geography, in which we find knowledge of the mountains running up to 15 degrees of south latitude.[61]

The key-role played by the trade in the Black Sea in this expansion of horizons is shown by the way in which the accounts of Strabon and Diodoros follow the coast and then later move inland.

Eratosthenes, mapmaker, has collected measurement and (what seems new) directions that allow him to mark out, between Meroe and the 2nd Cataract, the great loop of the Nile line a reversed N. However, apart from the distance between Atbara and Meroe, which is correct, the lengths he gives of different sections of the Nile are somewhat too long. This exaggeration might derive from the difficulty of the journey. Only, the sections in question are not settled by their navigability; what matters is now not the cataracts or transhipments that interested Herodotos' informant, who was anxious to facilitate travelling. Eratosthenes' account (preserved by Strabon) responds solely to the mapmaker's interests. He knew the Atbara and the Blue Nile (Astapous), which he makes come from lakes to the east of the Nile, and which enclose the island of Meroe, to the south of which has been marked another island, evidently between the White and the Blue Niles, where he sets the Deserters of Psammetichos.

After him, without doubt, we distinguish in a toponymic note of Strabon a new progress towards the south. For, in mentioning the *Astapous*, which is clearly the Blue Nile according to the etymology given by Diodoros, the Water come out of Darkness—allusion to the dark colour of the affluent—Strabon adds: "Others call it *Astasobas* and think the Astapous is another watercourse coming from certain lakes of the South and constituting the right branch of the Nile." This Astasobas perhaps preserves for us the name of the Sobat, which Strabon and his sources had trouble in locating and confused with the Blue Nile, while at the same time knowing something about the southern lakes.[62]

3

The Sacred River

Now let us look at the name Neilos for the river. It is of un-known origin. Homer did not know it and it appeared first in Hesiod. One interesting point is that the numerical value of the Greek letters (50, 5, 10, 30, 70, 200) makes up 365, the number of days in a year. The ancients were not likely to miss such a detail, which would at once seem to hold a strange magical significance. Heliodoros in his romance says of the folk of Meroe in Aithiopia:

They glorified the Festivals of the Nile and extolled the River, which they called Horos and Lifegiver of the whole of Egypt, Saviour of Upper Egypt and Father and Creator of Lower Egypt, through his yearly bringing-down a fresh silt [nea ilys] whence his Greek name of Neilos. He it is they say that announces the Seasons of the Year, the Summer by his Flood, the Autumn by his Ebb, the Spring by the Flowers growing along his banks and the crocodiles laying their eggs. The Nile indeed, they hold, is nothing other than the Year itself, as is proved by his name, in which the letters, translated into figures, add up to 365, the number of days in the year.[1]

The epithet zeidoros there used has some interest; it is a word other-wise found only in verse and is applied to the earth as the giver of grain (zeia, one-eared wheat) by Homer and Hesiod. But it was also explained as connected with zao, meaning Lifegiver. Nonnos applied it to Helios; and as at this late period Horos was taken to be a sungod, Life-giving must be the meaning. Its use thus exem-plifies the way in which Greek and Egyptian modes of thought are often learnedly entangled in such writers as Heliodoros. Similarly it is noteworthy that Diodoros' interpretation of Astapous as a Nile-name, "come out of darkness", reminds us of the ancient chant in honour of the Nile, "a darkness in the day-time", and "You Light that come from the Darkness".[2]

D

The magical force of the name Neilos is brought out by the fact that *Abraxas*, much used in late formulas of magic, has the same numerical value. It occurs in texts ranging from the 2nd century A.D. to the Christian epoch; and as we never find the name Neilos in such charms, it has been conjectured that Abraxas here takes the place of Neilos as the Year and in some way represents it.[3]

The Egyptians themselves used various words to express the nature of the river and its waters, with special reference to the flood.[4] *Hapi*, however, is the main term, and alone it has something like a geographical sense.[5] Yet to translate it simply as the Nile is somewhat rash, as we shall see. Hapi is above all the sacred virtue of the Nile, and as such he is called the Great Lord of Provisions, Lord of Fishes, Father of all the Gods, Vivifier, Creator of Things that exist. The Greeks and Romans never transliterated the name, though they must have known it well. It was still being used in hieroglyphic texts of the Roman period, for example on the walls of the temple at Esneh; and it occurs in Demotic and Coptic names.[6]

Hapi was one of the fifteen great gods.[7] Representations of him are found all along the valley from Tanis in the northern Delta to Amara in Nubia.[8] We cannot satisfactorily analyse his name for its meaning; it probably goes back to predynastic times.[9] On the temple walls it refers not so much to the river itself as a geographical fact as to its waters which were needed to complete the rites, to make them effectively work—just as Nepri refers to wheat, but not to any particular field of it. Hapi is shown at times pouring out water from libation-vases; and we are told of Osiris being revived by water jetting from the breasts of male-female Hapi and from a vase in his left hand.[10] When the Egyptians wanted to render homage to the actual Nile and its flood, they turned to the flowing river itself, as at Gebel Silsileh and elsewhere.[11]

Representations of Hapi are to be found from the Old Kingdom on to Roman times. The traits are consistent. He appears as an hermaphrodite, with female breasts and male genitals, naked save for a narrow belt that comes down under the navel so as to hold up his big pendulous belly. From the belt hang three strips of leather or cloth, two red and one white, or one white and two green. These strips stay together when he is in repose, but part when he walks. He also wears a wig and at times a beard-case. He bears on his head a cluster of lotus-flowers or waterplants (with slight differences according as to whether he represents Upper or Lower Egypt). If an emblem, for instance of a nome, has to be set on his head, he holds the cluster in his hands. Hapis nearly always bear offerings. Thus, they hold in their left hand a footless portable table on which is set bread, flowers, perfumes, fish and so on— things due to the fertilising flood. They wear the ankh-sign of life twisted on the arm as a bracelet.[12] The women shown at times alternating with Hapis are not consorts; they are priestesses, super-numeraries, or agricultural deities.

Hapis then are numerous. We see processions of them on the temple walls, on intercolumnations, on the walls of stairs or the base of walls. They move to the centre of the motive set above them; they converge to the depths of the temple or some other significant point. At Medamud we meet as many as 145. Some-times each Hapi may stand for a particular nome; we meet forty-two provincial Hapis. But in the unity and the multiplicity there is no contradiction for the Egyptians, who could think at one and the same time of a unifying force or principle and of an indefinite number of local manifestations.[13]

This multiplication of forms cannot be exemplified in the case

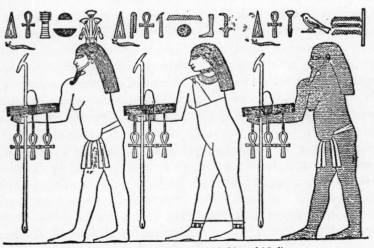

10. Hapis and Companions: Nekhebit and Nadj-ur

of any other great gods, and shows that the stress was on the sacred and fertilising water, not on a rivergod as such. The Hapi-processions go back to about 2550 B.C. at Sahure and continue into the Greek period, for instance on the Isis Temple at Behbet under Ptolemy II.[14] Further, though Hapis appear in pictures of ritual and Hapi had temples at Neilopolis, Heliopolis, Memphis, he had no statues in wood or stone as far as we know. The chant in his honour states, "He cannot be figured in stone, he is invisible, he has neither servants nor ministers, he cannot be brought forth from his secret places, it is unknown where he is, he is not to be found in ornamented sanctuaries, there is no habitation which will contain him, he cannot be imagined in your heart." He thus has the odd position of expressing a sacred and fertilising force without which neither gods nor men can function, yet is not in any precise way a separate god. He is necessary to all cult, but has no liturgical cult of his own. What he does have are festivals of thanksgivings and joy.[15]

He is often shown in double form, standing or kneeling, and bringing together with a symmetrical gesture the papyrus of the north and the south, thus symbolising the Union of the Two Lands. At Lisht we find the gods Hu and Sia depicted as Nile-gods in such a rite of Union. The dialogue runs: "*Hu:* I unite for you the portions of Horos and Seth. *Sia:* I unite for you the thrones of Geb." We see Hapi's indeterminate position as a god; the others can mask in his image. The Two Niles, though used to express the separation-and-union of the Two Lands (Upper and Lower Egypt), are not mere reflections of this division; they certainly have their roots in what we may call the concept of the unity-of-opposites in a primitive system of dialectics. Such dualities represent much more than a mere form of intensified statement; and the relation to the Two Lands is secondary. Indeed, the persistence of the notion of the Two Lands, despite various historical aspects, itself shows the strength of the concept in question.[16] Sometimes one Hapi is red, the other blue: the pair perhaps representing the Nile in flood and at low levels.[17] But Aristeides of Smyrna, who travelled much in Egypt in the 2nd century A.D., says the colours stand for earth and heaven.[18] They might then be emblems for different theologies of the Nile: one deriving the river from the earth

(Hermopolis Magna), the other from the sky by means of rain (Thebes and Memphis).[19] But we also find a single Hapi. He then appears in a ritual scene where he plays a minor part; he accompanies the pharaoh who is bringing offerings to the gods.[20] When we meet a statue with Hapi's attributes, it represents the pharaoh himself and has no special meaning. The gods were often represented in the traits of the dedicating king, for instance Amun as Tutankhamen.[21]

Hapi's peculiar role is brought out by the ancient Pyramid Texts. In one sense the Nile pervades these inscriptions, for they are much concerned with the safe passage of the dead king over the waters between the two worlds. The Nile, though unnamed, here appears both as the dividing line between the world of the living and the spiritworld, and as an aspect of the spiritworld itself —what Okeanos was for the Greeks. Because of the way in which underworld images are translated into the heavens, the Nile becomes ritually a sky-stream. The importance of the Nile waters appears in the Utterances which deal with *kbh.w*. The verb (*kbh*) means to be cool or to cool; the noun (plural in form though used as a singular) designates the particles or elements of which water is composed. "This is your cool water, Osiris; this is your cool water, N [the deadman], which went forth from your son, which went forth from Horus."[22] It is used to express the cool morning sky of a dawn ascent: "To say, N, [free] course is given to you by Horos; you are adorned as the only star in the sky. Your two wings are grown as [those of] a falcon; great of breast like the *gnhsw*-falcon, whose descent was seen, after he had traversed the sky. You voyage the *kbh.w* by the watercourse of Re-Harakhte," the Sun.[23] Again, in an ascension-text:

To say: Gods of the West, gods of the East, gods of the South, gods of the North—these four pure reed-floats, which you placed for Osiris, for his ascension to heaven, that he might ferry over to *kbh.w*, while his son Horos was at hand, [whom] he reared and whom he caused to dawn as a great god in *kbh.w*, place them for N.

Are you Horos, son of Osiris? Are you, N, the god, the eldest, son of Hathor? are you the seed of Geb? Osiris has ordained that N dawn as a second Horos. Those four souls, who are in Heliopolis, have written it in the register of the two Great Gods who are in *kbh.w*.[24]

A noun of the same root, *Kbh.t*, was used to personify the goddess of fresh libation-water. A spell tells of the deadman's safe arrival in the spiritworld:

To say: The mouth of the earth opens for Osiris N, Geb said to him, "N is great like a king, mighty like Re."
"Come in peace," say the Two Enneads to N.
The eastern door of heaven is open for him, to the abode of *kas*. The great Nut gives her arms to him, she of the long horn, she of the protruding breast. She will nurse N. She will not wean him. She takes him herself to heaven, she does not cast him down to the earth. She makes this N remain as chief of the two *'itr.t* palaces. He descends into the boat like Re, on the shores of the Winding Watercourse.
N rows in the *hnbw*-boat, where he takes the helm, towards the field of the Two Lower Heavens, to the beginning of the Land of the Marsh of Reeds. His arm is taken by Re. His head is raised up by Atum. His forward cable is taken by Isis. His stern cable is seized by Nephthys.
Kbh.w.t places him at her side and puts him among the *hnti.w-š*, as the herdsmen of [his] calves.[25]

This text seems an Osirian adaptation of a plainer one. In it Geb the earthgod hails the deadman and the gods welcome him to the abode of the *kas* (the spirits or other-selves).[26] The sky-goddess Nut nurses and suckles him in the new-birth, and takes him up to heaven. He travels in the sun-boat, aided by the gods. The Lower Heaven is the Underworld (*nn.t* or *niw* usually transliterated as Nun); here a dual form seems used and the reference is to the Two Anti-Skies (in a symmetrical image of upper and lower worlds), the kingdom of the ordinary dead.[27] The Marsh of Reeds seems here to be set in heaven at the point where the underworld is divided from the beginning of the upperworld.

Kbh.w.t is the goddess personifying fresh libation water, the sacred Nile-water. She completes the successful advent in heaven by putting the deadman among the Guardians of the Lake, whose duty is to provide him with nourishment. They are a sort of foremen of farmers on the royal domain in the spiritworld, the heavenly equivalents of the *hnti.w-š* of earth; they are to serve the deadman as if they were the herders of his calves. In another text *Kbh.w.t* is called the Daughter of the mortuary god Anubis with his head of jackal or dog, who is a spirit-guide, a pathfinder, like Hermes in Greece, and thus the personification of the shamanist priest whose ritual performances guide the spirits of the dead through various dangers and barriers into a safe place in the other-world.[28] *Kbh.w.t* was in fact the cult-name of Wadit, goddess of Buto in the 10th Nome of Lower Egypt, where she was wor-shipped in the form of an uraeus or cobra (a symbol of royalty). With her cool water she quickened the heart of the deadman.[29] The heart-quickening refers to the ritual washing; for a text states: "She approaches him [the deadman] with these her four *nmis.t* jars, with which she refreshes the heart of the Great God, on the day of awakening." These jars were used in purification ceremonies.[30]

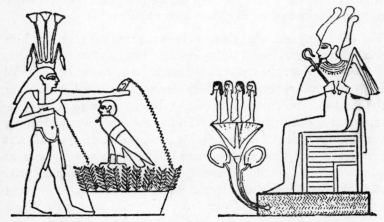

11. The Nile revives the soul of Osiris; Osiris in the water, Lotus with the four Sons of Horos

She had originally represented the serpent in the inner sanc-tuary, the *abaton*, and was also associated with the Nile-source (imagined at the 1st Cataract), the waters in which the viscera of murdered Osiris were found and which were supposed to come from the sky in the form of star-dew. "You purify yourself in the dew of the stars."[31] She herself was a star. "The stars follow your beloved *Kbh.w.t*, who is chief of your attendants."[32] The *kbh.w* had its home in Egypt. "Osiris N take to yourself this your libation, which is offered to you by Horos, in your name of He-who-is-

to-come-from-the-Cataract.''[33] The deadman gained his release
from earth by the purifying libation; but his goal was the same
purification in the spiritworld, which would continue to give him
life:

You ascend as the morning star and voyage as the *hnti* [master of the
heavenly Ocean]. Those who are in Nun fear you, you command the
spirits. Isis laments for you, Nephthys moans for you, the great
mni.t smites evil for you, as for Osiris in his suffering.

Nunite, Nunite, guard yourself against the Great Sea.

Be seated on this your firm throne so that you may command those
of the secret places.

The double doors of heaven are open for you, the double doors of
the *kbh.w* are open for you, so that you may ferry over to the Marsh of
Reeds and till the barley and reap the spelt—so that your livelihood
may be thereby secured, like Horos, son of Atum.[34]

The dead king ascended from Nun, the primeval Ocean, where
were the ordinary dead, who respected him, and he voyaged as
the *hnti*-star over the heavens, where he was master of the dead
kings who had gone ahead of him. He apparently ruled also over
the dead in Nun from his heavenly throne—though he may be
imagined as daily returning to Nun like the other stars and ruling
the dead there directly. The *mni.t* is a stake or landpeg which was
personified as a mourning woman.[35] The form *nun* in the next
sentence seems a gentilic, meaning something like Nunite or Nun-
man; we find Osiris called by this name on his arrival in heaven;
and the Nunite, or Man from Nun, is warned against the Great
Sea. Elsewhere we find the dead man told to "beware of the
Ocean: to say four times". And to "sail, arrive, protect yourself
against the Great Sea".[36]

We may further note of *Kbhwt*, who is called the sister of the
dead king, that as serpent-goddess of the Tenth Nome in Upper
Egypt she welcomes the newcomer at heaven's door. "Greetings,
Daughter of Anubis, who are at the windows of heaven, you
friend of Thoth who is at the double rail [end] of the ladder. Open
the way for N, so that he may pass." Anubis guides as far as
heaven; Thoth the moongod guides through the regions there.
The deadman climbs a ladder with a single rail at the bottom
which is stuck into the ground.[37] In heaven he works the fields

like a farmer. Atum, who seems originally a creator-god, is a sun-god in these texts, especially of the evening.

12. Nile with Offerings; Mer, god of the Whole Flood

The location of the Cool Water is both on the horizon of heaven and the 1st Cataract. "Stand at the doorway of the Horizon. Open the double doors of the *kbhw*."[38] The phrase "the *kbhw* of Horos and Seth", used of North or South, seems to refer to the whole of Egypt, the full length of the (known) Nile, from the Sea, the Nile-mouths, to the Cataract.[39] *Kbhw* is also the mythical birthplace of the sungod Re as well as the full extent of the heaven, or one part of it—especially the east whence the sun ascends. Like heaven it has double doors.

Though then the direct references to the Nile are few in the Pyramid Texts, the Nile as the source of libations and purifications and as the earthly double of the oceanic waters of life-death passage plays a pervasive part.[40] Every morning the Sun was thought to purify and renew himself by passing through the oceanic waters; the deadman had to do likewise in rising from his tomb. During his lifetime the king performed a daily purification at sunrise in the House of Morning before entering the temple to officiate as priest. Similar purifications were made at the birth of a royal heir or before the coronation. The Nile-water restored vital fluids to the body as well as representing the oceanic water of sun-resurrection.[41] "N is purified with these four *nmst* jars filled at the divine lake in Ntrw." The word *nmst* has been compared with the Babylonian *namsa*, a jar for pouring water. In a papyrus we see a mummified deity, *Mw-ntri*, who seems the personification of the waters needed by the dead for purification; out of his mouth pours a stream. The City of Ntrw was in Lower Egypt, sacred to Isis; but though the water from temple lakes and other sacred spots had their peculiar virtues, the ultimate source of all such magical potences was the Nile itself. In myth Horos washes the dead king's body, as he and Thoth washed the sungod. Or the deadman may bathe with the sungod in the pool of the Marsh of Reeds and be dried by Horos and Thoth.[42]

The moment of successful flooding is imagined as the moment of rebirth, when the deadman can best hope to make his passage across the death-waters. "The *mn*'-canal is open; the Winding Watercourse is inundated; the Marshes of Reeds are filled. N. will certainly ferry over to yonder eastern side of heaven, to the place where the gods will give him birth, where he will certainly be born, new and young . . ."[43]

These aspects might be much extended; but what has been said is enough to bring out the importance of Nile-water in Egyptian religion and thought. Hapi is ubiquitous and yet "he cannot be figured in stone".

In the Graeco-Roman period there developed something of a tendency to treat the Nile as a rivergod in the normal Greek way. No colossal statue of him is known; and the statuettes we hear about in the texts seem always to be offerings to other gods. Even in the Roman period he remains a god paying homage or making his offerings to other gods: the source of fertility, but not singled out as a fertility-god, as for example Min was. On the island of Bigeh in a modest position in the lefthand corner of a relief of the Antonine period, we see him with his lotus-head-gear, kneeling and holding two vases that pour out waters. But he is also surrounded by a serpent and set amid a mass of rocks on which stand two birds. He represents the Nile at its mysterious source, an oceanic power and at the same time localised at the

13. Nile-gods and Cavern with awaiting Death-monster; Nile-god at Bigeh

1st Cataract.[44] The picturesque aspect of the image is Graeco-Roman, though it has its roots in ancient ideas. A Pyramid Text declares:

This your Cavern there is the Broad-Hall of Osiris N, which brings the wind. The Northwind refreshes. It raises you as Osiris N. *Šsmw* [god of the wine and oil press] comes to you, bearing water and wine. *Hnti-mnwtf* [Horos] comes, bearing the vases which are before the two *'itrt* palaces. You stand, you sit like Anubis, Chief of the Nekropolis. Aker [earth-god] stands up for you. Shu [god of air] dries for you.

They tremble who see the Inundation when it tosses. [But] the marshes laugh. The shores are become green. The Divine Offerings descend. The Face of Men brightens. The Heart of the Gods rejoices.

"Deliver N from his bandages, which restrain the living, O gods,"
is in the mouth of those who run to them on the good day of running
[while running is good].

"Seth is guilty. Osiris is justified," is in the mouth of the gods, on
the good day of the going upon the mountains.

When Inundations are upon the land, he who hastens with his
soul goes to his Cave. [But] you march behind your spirit towards
Knm-'iwnw like the successor of *Hrti*, chief of Nsat.[45]

This is a chant to Osiris in his character as the Nile. The Egyptians
called this sort of symbolism an address to someone or something
"over the head of another"—that is, the speaker seems to be
addressing a certain person but is in fact looking beyond him to
another, who is mysteriously identified with him to the extent of
the words and imagery used. Thus in another text the dismembered wild-bull is addressed, but the real theme is the rebel Seth.
In the spell cited above, Osiris and Nile are first identified; then
the Osirian King, as Osiris, is contrasted with Seth; next the
Osiris-Nile rises in flood, which expresses the defeat of Seth,
the Enemy, and the triumphal resurrection of the deadman as
Osiris. The Nile Cavern is equated with the Broad Hall of the
Osirian Underworld, and we learn that the Winds as well as the
Waters come out of the Cavern, the holes or fissures that lead
down to the Osirian realm. The northwind raises the Nile in
the same way as the Osirian Deadman is raised from the tomb.
(We thus find Isis represented as a Falcon waving her wings to
bring air to raise the dead.) The god *Šsmw* brings water and wine.
Anubis sits or stands as the waters rise or fall: an image that
brings out further their relation to the underworld. Aker represents the Two Doors of the Earth, East and West, through which
the sun passes; he is usually, as here, coupled with Shu. As the flood
ebbs, the earth stands up and the air dries it. (Aker is depicted as
a double sphinx with human heads, a lion, or two lions seated
back to back.) An appeal is made to the gods to deliver the deadman from the mummy-bandages of death—as the Nile, delivered
at flood-time, expands over its banks. Their verdict of salvation
is given on the day of going-on-the-mountain: the day of burial
in the desert-cliffs often called mountains or hills. To hurry at
flood-time is perilous and liable to lead back into the cave from

which the waters came (as if they receded into it): the cave which connects with the underworld. *Knm-'iwnw* is obscure, apparently meaning him-whom-the-winds-enfold; it may stand for a region in heaven. *Hrti* was an early clan-god in ram-form, at Letopolis; in one Pyramid Text he appears as playing the same role as Osiris. His second cult-place Nsat is perhaps set near Buto in one text, near Memphis in another.

One more text is worth citing in full for its revelation of this kind of ancient imagery.

The waters of life which are in the sky, the waters of life which are in the earth come. The sky burns for you, the earth trembles for you, before the birth of the god.

The two mountains divide, a god comes into being, the god has power over his body. The two mountains divide, N comes into being, N has power over his body.

Behold N, his feet shall be kissed by the pure waters which come into being through Atum, which the penis of Shu makes, which the vulva of Tefnut brings into being. They have come to you, they have brought you the pure waters which issue from their Father. They purify you, they fumigate you, N, with incense.

You lift up the sky with your hand. You tread down the earth with your foot.

A libation is poured out at the gate of N. The face of every god is washed. You wash your arms, Osiris. You wash your arms, N. Your rejuvenescence is a god. Your third is a *wd*-offering. The perfume of an 'Ihtwtt serpent is on N. A *bnbn* bread is in the house of Seker. A leg of meat is in the house of Anubis.

N is intact. The '*itr.t* palace is standing. The month [the moon] is born. The nome lives, which measurements have traced. You till the barley, you till the spelt, with which N will be presented for ever.[46]

Here is a chant in praise of the flood and its blessing. The image of the flood is used to depict the dead king reborn in heaven, the dead king rejuvenated as Osiris, the dead king securely prospering as the newborn Osiris. The living waters come out of the sky, out of a cow's body, out of the vagina of a sky-woman, out of the earth. Thunder and lightning announce the god's birth, the dead-man's rebirth as a god. The Two Mountains refer both to the ridges of the vulva between which the waters or the child come forth, and to the mountains or rocks of the Cataract. The flood is one with *kbhw*, the cool and fresh water-libation. *Wd* is some kind of offering, but why it is the third is not clear; the *'Ihtwtt* is the white crown with the uraeus, which was deified and described as giving birth to the king as well as bringing incense; the cone-like *bnbn* may have been a form of bread used as offerings in the Heliopolitan cult under the Old Kingdom. In any event we are told that the king-reborn-as-Osiris is going to have some special perfume, bread, and meat. The Moon is born at the same time. In another text we find the dead king called the Scribe of the Divine Book: that is, Thoth the moongod.

This spell is then a powerful poem in which the image of the flood is used to express the renewal of nature and man, and is then directed specifically to express the resurrection of the dead king in a world which reflects the earth in a static abstracted way. The Eyptian method of symbolism is in fact given a triple force; for the Flood is identified with Osiris who is identified with the deadman.

The image of the dual crags or sides of a fissure (expressing also the vaginal passage of birth) continued to be used to define the sources of the Nile. About 2000–1700 B.C. we read, "If the Nile come out from the holes of his sources . . ."[47] About 1000 we meet all the good things "that the Nile brings from his cavern".[48] In the Ptolemaic period the Nile still "comes out of his gulfs of abysses".[49] The Herodotean statement that the Nile-sources flowed both north and south from between the two mountains Krophi and Mophi, which lay between Syene and Elephantine, had a factual basis, it has been suggested, in the strong back-current felt for about 100 km. on the left bank above the Cataract. But though such a phenomenon may have strengthened the idea, the keypoint lies in the image of the twin-rocks, which are the gateway of life and death, and which thus reveal a double current. (The notion that the Nile springs lay at this point was long held. An address by the Divan of Cairo to General Menou spoke of Shellal, the Cataract or the village above it, "where the Nile has its source".[50])

We may note further that the image of the cavernous gateway of life and death had its link with that of the underworld as a

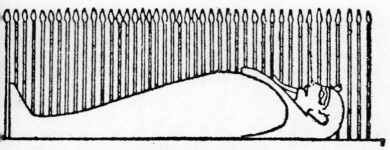

14. Osiris rising in the grain-crop

great cavern of winding waters and that of the cliff-tomb as a
cave. On a stele of the early Eighteenth Dynasty at Thebes, the
"Chief of the Weavers of the God's Wife Ahmose, (also) called
Pesiur", is shown seated with his wife before a table of offerings
on which water is being poured by a lector-priest "making
libation and incense of all good things and pure"; the main text
refers to Osiris providing for the kas of the pair "all things good
and pure given by Heaven, created by Earth, and brought by
Nile from his Cavern".[51] Texts such as those on the Cenotaph of
Seti I at Abydos bring out profusely the image of the death-cave.
Osiris is shown lying on his back with erect penis, the sundisk
above him and a serpent surrounding him—as a serpent surrounded Hapi at Bigeh. The nightsun addresses the corpse: "I cause my
disk to rest in your cavern. I protect your soul and your shadow.
The darkness goes from you(?). The Nehaher serpent who is in the
cave joins your corpse. I truly pass by your cavern, giving orders
to your followers."[52] Other typical texts from the Cenotaph are:

This great god, he passes the time in charge of his cavern. His words of
his guidance (?) he calls to the Chief of the Underworld. He it is who
lights those who are in the paw of the Aker [here shown as a sphinx];
he unites his body. The god sees the rays of the god after he has
passed by him. . . .
    Re says to this cavern: O Osiris, ichneumon-like one, upon his
Wer-serpent, taking hold of the unique one which came forth from
his body, namely the hair of his lower jaw, the secret of his beard, and
it is not known what comes forth from it. Damuty praises him and
greets the corpses that are with him: You are the gods who place the

souls in the Place of Slaughtering, while they struggle for him from whom they came forth, the great gods of the West: O behold I pass by you to take care of you, ichneumon-like one, to light the darkness of your corpses, to strengthen your soul. O Osiris, you are the unique one who became two, you are the two who became Osiris, the great one of the West. . . .

The entering of this great god in the darkness. This great god passed by the cavern of Him who is great in his belly, whose head is in the dark and whose hinderpart is in the dark, to whose cave neither gods nor spirits nor dead approach, and by whom they do not pass, except this great god who is in heaven. The gods who are in their caverns and those who are in their caves, and those who are in their abodes, and those who are at peace upon their corpses—the gods, the spirits, and the dead, they say when they see Re, they rejoice when he has entered: O Come to us, Lord of the Disk. . . .[53]

The second of these passages provides a good example of the primitive dialectics already mentioned. Osiris, the one in two, and the two in one, we must remember, is also in one aspect the Nile, the river that issues from his loins; he is the Nile in its cave, also one in two and two in one, and he is the deadman in his cave of death and resurrection.

But because of the oddly impersonal nature of Hapi in a polytheistic world, the question arises: What great god controls or commands the issuing-forth of the waters? what great god is master of the flood? The hieroglyphic texts imply that a great god allows Hapi to emerge from his cave or pair of caves. This god opens the bolts so that "the flood comes from the cave under his [two] sandals".[54] In a syncretising hymn to Amun ("Re belongs to him as his Face and his Body is Ptah"), that god is depicted as releasing the waters. "He enters, the two caverns are under his feet. The Nile appears from the hollow beneath his sandals."[55]

I have shown in my book *The Clashing Rocks* that there is a world-wide series of images in ritual-myth dealing with twin-rocks that open and close. This myth has its origin in ritual-experience and the rocks own a central role in the shamanist passage into the spiritworld. Krophi and Mophi, or the two caverns of the Nile, belong to this series; for it is stated that the Nile source is closed and opened, bolted and unbolted. Often, in primitive thinking, ritual-fantasies and actual geography merge in the schemes of the passage-myth, and the journey involves an essential movement over or through water. Okeanos in early Greek thought, and Nun in Egyptian, are typical images of the water that has to be crossed—water that lies round the rim of the world (and also underlies the world), yet also merges with the spirit-sphere. At such primitive levels of conception, that sphere is both identical with the actual world (deep inside it as the source of life, energy, and transformation) and yet also somewhere beyond, an ancestral and ideal dreamtime.

15. Sun-boat

The oceanic passage into the spiritworld appears in a richly developed form in the Sumerian epic of Gilgamesh. It is common in Greek myth, in the journeys of Herakles, Perseus, Iason, Odysseus and others. We have no corresponding Egyptian myth, though it may have existed. There is an abundance of Egyptian sacred texts, which often imply all sorts of myths, but not many direct myth-narratives have come down. What is certain is that no culture had a more complex and sustained development of the shamanist type of spirit-journey in terms of ritual, solar and mortuary. The movement of the sungod Re by day over the sky-ocean and by night through the underearth-ocean is the most ritually elaborated of all direct offshoots from that journey. In the Pyramid Texts, aimed at guiding the dead king across the waters and into the heavens, we meet a shamanist system in a

E

clear form, though political and religious developments have made the right to the magical directions the monopoly of the kingship. In one sense the history of Egyptian religion is the history of the way in which the cult of Osiris, originally connected with the underworld, invaded the solar world and brought back to everyone the right which the kings had usurped.[56] During this process the right became moralised; and though the magicks were still essential, it was felt that the deadman had to prove in a death-judgment that he deserved eternal life. One very old Pyramid Text preserves the ideas of a period, perhaps the Second Dynasty, when Osiris was felt as the enemy of the solar religion and a spell was needed to prevent him and his kind from entering the solar tomb, the pyramid enclosure. In the exorcising spell he was bidden go back to the banks of the Nile. "Let him be gone. Let him go to Nedit. Let him be gone to the Transgressor." Nedit was at Abydos; and there Osiris was found dead. The spell thus seeks to deny and prevent his resurrection from the waters.[57] The Transgressor seems a crocodile, as there was a crocodile-god with this name at Horbeit in the Delta under the Old Kingdom. The spell attempts to return Osiris to his death, so that he will be swallowed by the crocodile without hope of revival or re-emergence.[58]

4

Dogstar, Ganymedes, Ptah, Khnum

Sothis the Dogstar, the Seirios of the Greeks, heralded the Flood and so was taken as its cause. Her heliacal rising occurred close in time to the rising of the waters. (When a star is seen coming up at the beginning of dawn, but disappears from sight in a short while through the rapid approach of daylight, this momentary advent is a heliacal rising.) Egyptian astronomer-priests therefore set the turn into a new year at her heliacal appearance, which thus played a key-part in the regulation of agriculture. Already on an ivory tablet of the First Dynasty we read, "Sothis, Opening of the Year, the Flood". And in the Pyramid Texts she is the Year (star). "It is Sothis your daughter who loves you, who secures your livelihood in this her name of Year, who conducts N when N comes to you."[1] She is called in these texts the Sister of the deadman and seems his Wife. "Your sister comes to you, rejoicing for love of you. You have placed her on your penis, so that your seed may go into her, [while] it is pointed like Sothis." (Sothis, Horos, and N's seed are all called *pointed*, as well as Re and the heavenly Osiris. It seems to mean pre-eminent and to be used for celestial royalty.) Horos is thus born of Sothis through the deadman (Osiris). N himself appears also as the son and father of Sothis. She, like the Morning Star, guides him; they lead him to the Marsh of Offerings north of the Marsh of Reeds. She bears as title, "she of (or in) pure or clean places" and she washes N's hands at his birth as star or god.

In coffin-texts Sothis appears as She who makes Re ascend into the Boat of Day: a reference to her role as Year-marker, Year-regulator. She seems the unnamed Third who "has opened the doors of Re" (in a parallelism with the phrase: "Open the door that Hathor has made"); that is, she controls or aids the yearly course of the sun. Elsewhere the Third is "the Lady of Threats on the Road of the Storm", reminding us of the Pyramid Texts where Sothis aids the deadman across the storms. Again, "I am the Lady of Powers that guide those who are in their Caverns" seems a reference to her control of the flood; for the term used (*tpht*) was the name of the mythical cavern of the 1st Cararact.[2] But as we have seen in the last chapter those-in-their-caverns are also the dead. The cavern of life-death is also the Nile source.

We see then that Sothis is considered as more than herald or cause of the Flood; she is also its goddess and in one sense is the flood itself. "The birth of Sothis will be prevented if you [Re] prevent N from coming to the place where you are." That is, time will cease; the flood will not come about; life will end.[3]

As the cause or force of the flood she had special relations with the 1st Cataract. The New Year was celebrated there with much pomp, and the New Year was her Rising.[4] (She herself had no temple; like Hapi she had no organised cult of her own, yet was

16. Sothis with Horos

worshipped.) At Dendera in Graeco-Roman times we read "Sothis who gives the flood each year" and "Sothis who gives the Nile from its cavern".[5] She thus became in late times confounded with Satis who had usurped the place of the Frog-goddess in the triad of Elephantine; her original home was in the island of Sahel and she may have been of Sudani origin.[6] In the Pyramid Texts

Satis appears as washing the deadman with her four pitchers from Elephantine.[7] And the deadman says in the *Book of the Dead*, "I was in Ab (Elephantine) in the Temple of Satitt".[8]

Sothis was also identified, much earlier, with Isis. When the deadman copulated with Sothis, he was also Osiris copulating with Isis. We read that Isis is "Mistress of the Year's beginning" at Syene; and on the ceiling of the Theban Ramasseum the heliacal rising of Sothis is shown under the form and with the name of Isis.[9] Under the Ptolemies the tradition was strongly entrenched. "Isis of Behdet gives the king a high Nile."[10] Plutarch tells us that "among the stars Sothis is the one consecrated by the Egyptians to Isis because it brings the water". And he thinks a Pythagorean influence underlies the Egyptian calling of Isis's soul Sothis.[11]

In the expanded Isis-cult of the Roman period Isis is said to bring, not only the Nile-flood, but the flood of the Eleutheros in Tripoli and that of the Ganges in India. "Mistress of the earth, you bring the flooding of rivers."[12] And a charm, perhaps used at floodtime in the Delta (Boubastis, Bouto, Pelousion), runs:

I invoke you, Lady Isis, by whom comes the Good Daimon . . . Isis–Sothis, in your morning, Boubastos, find the water, the current of water, Boutos, in your morning . . . protect me thanks to the god's great and marvellous names . . . for I am he who is established at Pelousion . . . I spread my sweat.[13]

The speaker identifies himself with Osiris-Nile, and speaks, during a sacrifice "after taking some of the divine seed of Nile-reed" by moonlight.

As a result of these identifications of Isis with Dogstar, we find her represented under the Romans with a dog.[14] A terracotta lamp shows the head of Sothis coming out of a dog's spine. Such lamps were probably used during vigils on the eve of the Sothis Advent as promise of the flood.[15] On another lamp Isis holds a horn-of-plenty, seated on a dog with a star over its head.[16] Coins carried the image. Trajan sought to honour Egyptian gods who cared for imperial prosperity; under him were struck coins that show Isis-Sothis seated on a dog that runs to the right with its head turned back. The goddess holds an object which may be a sceptre but is more likely a torch.[17] Under Hadrian the theme was

17. An Hour; Sothis; Nile as Aquarius

revived (134-8) on a coin issued by the Roman Senate, and again on a bronze put out under Antoninus in 157-8. Certainly the return of the Sothic year in A.D. 139, which happened only every 1,460 years (when Sothis rose on the first of the month Thoth), contributed to the attention paid to the Star in these years.[18] But in any event the growing interest in astrology and star-worship would attract attention to Isis-Sothis.

The Iseum in the Campus Martius at Rome, repaired about A.D. 38, had a statue of Isis on a dog. The Isiac Table of silver-incrusted bronze has the dog under the throne on which Isis sits.[19]

The dog had now insinuated itself into the myths. Ailian said, "legend reports that this dog was that of Orion".[20] Diodoros declared at more length:

The dog is useful both for hunting and for protecting man. That is why they represent the god they call Anubis with a dog's head, show-ing thus that he was the bodyguard of Osiris and Isis. There are some, however, who explain that dogs guided Isis in her search for Osiris and protected her from wildbeasts and wayfarers, and that they helped her in her search through the affection they felt for her, by barking. And this is the reason why at the Festival of Isis the procession is led by dogs. In this way those who introduced the rite showed the kindly service rendered by this animal in ancient times.[21]

In the mosaic at Praeneste Anubis appears beside the procession of the sacred vase containing the water of new life.[22] Apuleius, describing the Isiac procession seen by his hero Lucius, says that after the initiates came the gods, "here was he, terrible, the messenger of the gods above and below, lofty, with face sometimes black, sometimes golden, lifting up on high his dog's head and bearing in his left hand his caduceus, in his right a green palm-branch".[23]

Though the turning of Sothis into an actual dog is a rationalisation of the Graeco-Roman period, and though there is no ancient connection of Isis with dogs, the dog-aspect of Anubis gave some substance to these fantasies. And there is an ancient Egyptian folktale in which the dog has a life-death role. This tale has been variously called *The Predestined Prince, The Doomed or Foredoomed Prince, The Bewitched Prince;* it stands at the head of a very wide-spread series of stories with similar motives and formulas. It begins, "Once upon a time, we are told, there was a King of Egypt to whom was born a male child. He had asked the gods of his time to give him a son, and they ordered that one should be born. He lay that night with his wife and she became with child. And when she had completed the months of birth, she bore a boy. Then came the Hathors to decide his destiny. They said, 'He will die through crocodile or snake, or again through a dog'. The people around the baby heard these words and reported them to his Majesty. Then his Majesty's heart became extremely sad, and he had a house of stone built on a desert plateau. He furnished it with servants and all sorts of good things from his palace; for the child was not to venture outside it. When the child was grown up, he went up on its terrace and saw a dog following a man who was walking along the road. Then he said to the servitor at his side, 'What is that that goes behind the man who walks on the road?' And the man replied, 'It's a dog'. And the child said, 'Bring me one like it'. So the servitor went to repeat this conversation to his Majesty. And his Majesty said, 'Let him have a frisky young dog so that his heart may not grow sad'. And they brought him a dog."

The Hathors are the birth-fates or fairies. In another tale, *The Two Brothers,* they are said to number seven. They have countless analogies in later folktales; but we may note here the birth-fairies who attend the young princess in the tale of the Sleeping Beauty, where the doom pronounced is explained by the spite of the excluded wicked fairy.

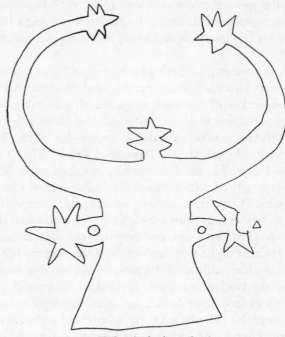

18. Hathor (early slate palette)

When the secluded prince had grown up yet more, he told his father, "What use is it for me to stay inactive here? See, I am promised to Fate. Let me then be left free to do as I wish till the day when God will carry out his will." He was given a chariot with weapons of all sorts and a squire, and he drove off along the riverbank with his dog—northwards on to the desert uplands. There he lived on the game he killed, till he came to the chief of Naharin (the Land of the Two Rivers: properly the area between the Upper Euphrates and the Orontes, but used loosely for northern Syria). The chief's only child was a daughter, for whom he had built a house with a window 66 cubits high. All the princes of Syria were brought here and told, "He who reaches my daughter's window will have her for wife". Now, when the Egyptian prince arrived, he was well received and declared that he was the son of an official, who had fled from a persecuting stepmother. Brought before the princess's window, he jumped up to it. The girl embraced him and fell in love. Her father objected to marriage with a fugitive from Egypt; but when she insisted, he gave in. They were married, and later the prince told her of the prophecy. She replied, "Have the dog who follows you killed".

He objected, "No, I won't allow my dog to be killed. I have brought it up since it was a puppy."

After that she watched over him and wouldn't let him go out alone. But the crocodile of his fate had followed him, and one day they met. However, a water-spirit would not allow the crocodile to attack, while the crocodile on his side prevented the spirit from leaving the water. Daily they fought from dawn for three months. Then one day, as the evening breeze came, the prince slept on his couch and his wife filled a bowl of wine and another of beer. A snake crept from its hole to sting the prince, but the bowls attracted it. It drank, became drunk, and lay on its back. The wife cut it to pieces with her axe. Finally the prince went strolling in his domain, without his wife but with his dog. The dog, gaining the power to speak, said something [gap in manuscript] Whatever it was, the prince ran, with the dog after him. He leaped into the water, where the crocodile seized him and dragged him to where the water-spirit usually was. But for some reason the spirit was absent. The crocodile said, "I am your fate, which pursues you. Now for three months I have fought with the water-spirit. Well, I am disposed to set you free. If my enemy comes here to fight and you wish to take my part, kill the water-spirit. . . ." The water-spirit returns next day.

There the manuscript breaks off. Whether the conclusion was happy or not is uncertain. But certainly the dog must have finally and unwittingly caused the prince's death. Thus the prophecy would be accomplished. No doubt the youth was then resurrected by a magician, perhaps undergoing some metamorphosis, as happens with the hero of The Two Brothers. The winning of the girl by a great leap occurs in a series of folktales, Russian, Polish, Finnish, Indian: the hero there has to jump up to a castle's third story, jump over a tower (in a tale of the Avars of the Caucasus),

19. Sothis-Sirius

or catch a flower held by a girl on top of a column. (These later heroes ride a horse; the Egyptian prince is superior to his rivals in magical power.) The originating elements of the tale-type clearly lie in initiation-ritual: seclusion, test, ordeal, death-and-revival. But our tale has moved far away from its primary bases and has been sophisticated into a romance. The role of the dog, however, is what interests us here. It shows, in a very simplified way, the elements which made Anubis the guide into the deathworld and at the same time the guardian of the dead.[24]

But Sothis, even when merged with Isis, could not effectively provide a force generally accepted as causing and liberating the Nile-flood. Two Greek texts show an awareness that some divine figure or energy was needed to give a mythologically satisfactory explanation of the great release of waters at the Cataracts. The first is a (lost) passage in a poem by Pindar. Philostratos in his *Life of Apollonios* tells us of the 3rd Cataract:

Peaks overhang the Nile, at most eight stades in height; but the eminence faces the mountains, a lofty brow of rock like a mysterious quarry, and the springs of the Nile cling to the mountain-edge till they topple over and fall on the rocky height, from which they pour into the Nile in whitening billows. The effect on the senses made by this cataract, which is many times larger than the previous ones, and the echo surging against the mountains, makes it very hard to hear what you are told about the river. The farther road leading up to the river's

first springs was impracticable, they tell us, and impossible to consider. . . . They have many stories of the daimons that haunt it, tales like
those that Pindar in his wisdom hymns about the daimon he sets over
these springs to preserve the due proportions of the Nile.[25]

It would be interesting to know just what tales Pindar told of
this daimon. However, a scholiast on Aratos informs us, "The
Pourer (Aquarius in the sky) seems to take his name from the
gesture he makes; in effect he holds a vase from which he pours
quantities of water which is compared with the Nectar of Ganymedes. It is Ganymedes, say the commentators on Pindar, represented by a statue of a hundred fathoms (about 180 metres),
the stirrings of whose feet provoke the Nile-flood."[26] It would
seem then that Pindar equated the Nile-daimon with Ganymedes,
who served the Olympian Gods with nectar. In the Zodiac of
Dendera (painted under Caligula), the Pourer (Hydrochoos,
Aquarius) is again identified with the Nile-god.[27] And Aquarius
was often identified with Ganymedes, who was also called the
Star in the Cloak (chlamys). In one codex the Cloak reaches from
Ganymedes' right shoulder to his left hand, which is stretched out
towards Capricorn.[28]

The strong beliefs held about the magical and sweet qualities of
Nile-water must have helped the identification of its Pourer with
Ganymedes. But we are still far from finding the Nile-Master.
Ganymedes was ravished to heaven by the Eagle of Zeus and
carried out the will of the highgod in his pourings.

As for the Colossos which was supposed to represent him, the
height is impossible; and the idea that the statue agitated its feet
belongs to an idea of magical movement which, especially in the
Roman period, coalesced around the Magnet. It has been suggested, however, that the movement of the rising and nearing
waters has been transferred to the feet. A papyrus speaks of the
"dyke that is above the footgear of Ptah, and that which is below"
(to the south of the statue, and to its north). And no doubt the
trickling and the rushing of water towards the feet of a statue,
especially a colossal one, could have the effect of an attraction, in
which the water obeyed the feet or the sandals of the stone god.[29]

The second Greek text comes from the *Imagines* of another

Philostratos, a member of the same family as the author of the *Life*. He describes a picture in which the pygmies, as heralds of the flood, are sporting over the rivergod, bringing him flowers, weaving him garlands, playing sistra—while the crocodiles stay in the depths. At the flood

the Nile lays Egypt open to boats and when the water has been drunk by the fields, he gives the folk a fertile land to till. In Aithiopia, where he rises, a daimon is set over him as his steward, and this daimon it is that sends forth the water in accordance with the seasons. He has been painted so as to seem heaven-high, and he plants his foot on the springs, with his head bent forward like Poseidon. Towards him the River looks and prays that his babes may be many.[30]

Here again the daimon is colossal and has as his function the regulation of the flow. But there is nothing in Egyptian iconography that corresponds to the description, unless a sky-upholding figure like Shu has been mistaken for a Nile-controller.

There seems then no definite god who is Lord of the Nile. Any god, however, who had risen to sufficient importance through political circumstances might have this position claimed for him by his priests. Thus, about 2500 B.C. Ihy, son of Hathor, was god of Gebelein, then the most southern point of the Egyptian kingdom and one of the places where at that time the flood-advent was observed.[31] He claimed, "I am a strong and glorious lord, I am he who makes the flood rise".[32] Again, "I am the weary one, who is in Nun" (the primeval ocean).[33] He was assimilated to the two gods of the Ogdoad who represented water, whether Nun from which the flood ultimately came, or the flood itself in its work.[34] Again,

I have sought the place where I shall be, in my name of the Flood, and I have found it in Punt. I have built a house which will be the house of coming into the world while my mother is under a sycamore.[35]

It seems that he, as the Nile-flood, is claiming to have been born in Punt, Aithiopia as the paradisiac land of scents. "My perfume is the oliban, which is given to my mother for her head, my odour is the incense that is given to my mother for her fumigation," and so on.[36]

Ihy's power over the flood no doubt derived from his father
Osiris. Because of his death-by-water at the hands of his brother
Seth, Osiris came to symbolise water; because of his resurrection
out of the water, he came to represent the rebirth of vegetation
out of the inundated earth. Yet, despite this important relation to
the Nile-waters, he did not emerge as the god controlling the
springs.[37]

Creator-gods obviously had a strong position as claimants for
that control. Ptah of Memphis was a potter-god and patron of
craftsmen, identified by the Greeks with Hephaistos and by the
Romans with Vulcan; he was a creator and thus connected with
the flood. "The canals are full of water afresh and the earth is
flooded with the love" of Ptah; Ptah, the Nile, Father of the Gods,
who gives Life to the Two Lands; Ptah "who makes the Nile
come out of his cavern and the nutritious plants grow green."[38]
He creates Hapi.[39]

20. Ptah-Nunu; Ptah-Tenen; Ptah of Memphis

As creator he had links with Nun and with Earth. He became
Ptah-Nun and also Ptah-Tenen, merging with Ta-tenen, the
Uplifted Earth, who seems to represent the primeval mound or
hill rising up out of Nun. Ptah was at his apogee under the Nine-

teenth Dynasty, and about that time an important hymn was composed in his honour:

Your feet are on the earth and your head is in the heights above in
your form of Dweller-in-the-Tuat [Underworld]. You bear up the
work you have made, you support yourself by your own divine
strength, and you hold yourself up by the vigour of your own hands. . . .

The words come forth from your nostrils and the heavenly waters
from your mouth, and the staff of life [grain] comes forth on your
back. You make the earth fruitful, gods and men have abundance,
and they see the cow-goddess Mehurit in your field. . . .

You are the Great God who has stretched out the heavens, who
makes the disk revolve in the body of Nut and enter into the body of
Nut in your name of Re. You are the moulder of gods and men and
everything which is produced, you are the creator of all lands and
countries and the Great Green Sea in your name of Kheper-Ta. You
are the Bringer of Hapi from his Source, making the staff of life
flourish. . . .

You make fertile the watery mass of heaven and make water appear
on the mountains to give life to men and women in your name of
Ari-Ankh [Life-Maker]. You are the Babe born daily, the Aged One on
the limits of eternity. . . .[40]

Ptah was the patron of those who made vases in which
fresh Nile-water was sent to Asia Minor under the Ptolemies, and
all round the Mediterranean under the Romans. A Ptolemaic
funerary inscription declares, "Let Hapi give you fresh water in a
jar that Ptah has fashioned".[41] And a chant to the Nile says that
Hapi "makes all the workshops of Ptah prosper".[42] Under the
Romans an important Nilometer was placed at Memphis.[43] Ptah,
says Cicero, was Son of Neilos and Guardian (custos) of Egypt;
Lucan says that Memphis itself "measures the Nile when it rises
to flood the fields".[44]

Another god who put in a strong claim to be the Nile-master was
Khnum, largely because of his site on the Island of Elephantine by
the 1st Cataract. "Khnum is there," says a Ptolemaic text, "his
sandals set on the flood."[45] Herodotos tells us that he gave Egypt
the Nile "coming out of two caves".[46] In the Roman as in the
Ptolemaic period he ordered the coming of the waters.

For you I make the Nile fall in waves when its day comes. (Edfu)

The wave of the flood comes out and the northwind descends on the south at the command of this venerable god. (Esneh)[47]

 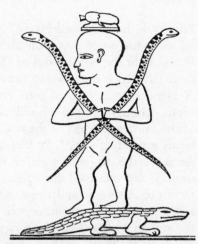

21. Ptah as Guardian; Ptah as Lord of the Magicians

He was represented with outstretched hands over which flowed water; also with a jug above his head—the hieroglyph of his name.[48] A late legend told how he withheld the waters till his sanctuary and priesthood were properly provided for.[49]

Another reason for his strong claim was that like Ptah he was a craft-patron and a creator-god. At Philai he was said to have made men out of clay on a potter's wheel; in the Ptolemaic period he was depicted there as the Potter, a ram-headed man, seated at the wheel, which he worked with his foot. He fashioned a man, accompanied by Thoth who held a palmbranch notched to mark the years of the man's life. The frog-goddess Heket also accompanied him. At Antinoe she was patroness of women in childbirth.[50]

In texts of the New Kingdom he is called:

Builder of men, maker of the gods, the Father who was from the beginning.

Maker of the things that are, creator of the things that will be, source of things that are, father of fathers, mother of mothers.

Father of the fathers of the gods and goddesses, lord of the things created by himself, maker of heaven, earth, Tuat, waters [and] mountains. Supporter of the sky on its four pillars, raising it up to all eternity.[51]

Like Ptah, he fashioned Hapi.[52] And like Ptah, as a world-pillar, he had a huge size that reminds us of Philostratos' Nile-daimon. He brought the Nile up out of Ocean at two caverns, we saw, and there divided it into two sections, sending one north, one south. A Dendera text tells of four rivers, flowing east, west, north, south—though only two goddesses of the flood are known: Mert of the south and Mert of the north. Sometimes he had four rams' heads instead of one.[53] At Elephantine he made up a triad with Anukis and Satis (who replaced Heket as his consort). Anukis restrained and mastered the waters, and was thought to make them return to Aithiopia and the southern wind; she was lady of the ebb.[54] Satis (whom we have seen as identified with Sothis) drove the waters over the rocks to Egypt and the northern wind; she was lady of the rise. "They give the fresh water that comes from Elephantine," says a prayer.[55] Under the Romans Khnum became the god of the Third Nome at Esneh (Latopolis). "He it is, master of the watery world [Nun] who breaks the bolt that closes it in and opens the two rocks to cover you with his flood."[56] He is now the "ram guide of the water", and his face is sometimes coloured

22. The two Merts

green or dark blue. Eusebios says of his statue at Elephantine that it is dark in colour "because the moon in its revolution brings the water".[57]

An inscription made with blunted chisel or hammer on one side of a large rounded granite-block on the island of Sahel tells of Khnum and a Seven Years' Famine. It purports to record a royal decree sent to Matar, the Governor of the South, who was Commander of all who dwelt in Abu or Elephant City.[58]

This royal decree has been brought to you to inform you that Misery has laid hold of me as I sit in the Great Hall of the Palace, and my heart is grievously afflicted because Hapi has not come forth during the time of my reign to his proper height for seven years. Grain is very scarce, herbs and vegetables are altogether lacking, and everything that men eat for food is of the poorest. A man now robs his neighbour, they go away in order not to return. The child wails, the young man sinks down exhausted, and the hearts of the old are crushed with despair; their legs give way under them and they sink to the ground, and their arms are [folded] inside them. The Shennu Nobles are destitute, and the storehouses are closed, and nothing comes out of them but wind. Everything is in a state of ruin.

My mind has remembered going back to a time past, that I had asked for information from the Ibis [of Thoth], from the Kheri-Heb I-em-Heteb, the Son of Ptah south of the Wall.

This last-named person was Imouthes, highpriest and magician of Memphis, who flourished under King Djeser of the Third Dynasty, and who was later deified and made one of the chief gods of Memphis. The House of Life mentioned in the next paragraph was the Hermopolitan Temple Library with the Books of Thoth, and the Souls-of-Re were the papyrus-rolls there.

"Where is the birthplace of Hapi? which is the town of the [Flood]? Who is the god to whom sacrifices should be offered up there?"

He answered that it was "necessary for me to go to the Governor of Hermopolis, whose beneficence strengthened the hearts of all men in their duty." Then I would go into the House of Life and I would unroll the Souls-of-Re and I would lay my hands on them.

Then Matar went on his journey and returned with imformation about the Flood.

F

He told me everything which men had written about it, and he revealed to me secret wonders which the men of old had experienced on their way thither, the like of which no king had known since the time of Re. And he announced the following to me:

There is a city in the middle of the stream from which Hapi makes his appearance; its name is Abu. It is the chief city, the first city of the nome, on the way to Wawat [Nubia], the beginning of that land; it is the Stairway of Gebb [the earth-god]. It is the Support of Re where he makes his calculation to prolong the life of everyone. Its name is Medjemdjem Ankh [something like the Pleasure-place of Life]. The Two Qerti [the underground caverns through which the Nile rises out of Nun] is the name of the water, and these are the Two Breasts from which all good things come.

It is the Bed of Hapi, in which he renews his youth . . . by which he causes the flooding of the land. He comes and has union as he journeys, as a man has union with a woman and produces offspring. He rises to the height of 28 cubits [at Abu], and in the town of Sma-Bhtet [in the Delta] his height may be reckoned as 7 cubits.

The god Khnum is the god of the place. [It is the place of] the soles of his feet. . . . The bolt of the door is in his hand; the double doors [of the Qerti] fall open when he wishes. There he is called Shu who dwells on the Riverbanks of the District. There he keeps an account of all the products of the Land of the South and of the Land of the North, so as to give each god his proper share.

The region is described:

Huge mountains of stone [granite] are round about its domain on the east side, and they contain stone, and the quarrymen come there, and people of all kinds who seek to build any god-house in the South and North, or [byres] for sacred animals, or royal pyramids, or statues of every kind. They place them in the god-house and in the sanctuary chamber. And their sweetsmelling offerings are presented before the face of Khnum during his circuit, and so with garden-herbs and flowers of every kind.

After learning these things about Abu, Matar went into the temple of Khnum.

I was sprinkled with water. I went into the secret places and a great offering was made of cakes and wine and geese and oxen and all good things to the deities of Abu. I lay on a couch with life and strength in my heart.

Matar thus seems to have carried out the practice of incubation in Khnum's temple. Sleeping there, he would hope for the god to visit him in a dream. According to the inscription, the god appeared:

I found the god standing in front of me. I made him be at peace with me. I prayed to him and made adoration before him and his heart was at peace with me. He made himself visible and said:

"I am Khnum who fashioned you. My two arms [or hands] are behind you to make your body strong and give health to your limbs. I now give you commands. The stones in the quarries have been there from time immemorial and yet there is no work going on in them for building the god-houses or for repairing what has fallen into decay or for hewing out shrines for the gods of the South and the North or for doing what a king ought to do for his lord. For I am the Lord of Building. I am he who built [fashioned] himself and Nun the great [Ocean] which existed in primeval time, at whose will Hapi spills [over his banks]. I ordain the work which men do, and I direct all the people in their hours. [I am] Tennu [Tanen, the primeval mound] the Father of the gods, [and of] the great god Shu, the Lord of the Earth. The two openings are in a chamber under me and I have the power to let the Inundation flow. Hapi is my kinsman. When he has embraced the fieldland, his embrace provides life for every nose—according to the extent of his embrace. [With] old age [comes weakness].

"But I shall make the Nile rise [again] for you and in no year shall it fail to do so and to produce fatness in the whole land. Herbs and trees will flourish and bow their heads beneath [the weight] of their produce. The goddess Renutt [of harvest] will be at the head of everything and every product will increase by hundreds of thousands according to the cubit of the year [on the Nilometer]. The people will be filled according to the desire of their hearts and all want will cease. And the emptiness of their granaries will come to an end. The land of Tamer-t [Egypt] will be [again] a region of cultivated land and the fields will be yellow with crops of grain. And there will be wealth and prosperity in the land among the people as there was in days of old."

Matar awoke in happiness and promulgated a decree in which various concessions are made to the god, that is to his temple and its priests, in return for the benefits conferred. We now see the importance of the document to the priesthood of Abu in confirming and extending a large number of privileges. The god's terri-

23. Khnum creating Man on the potter's wheel, aided by Thoth (marking the years of life)

tory was defined. He was to get an increased payment from all farmers including those who brought new ground into cultivation; he was to get a tenth from all fishermen, fowlers, "those who traffic in the waters", hunters of wild game or of lions in the hills, for the catches they brought into the city; a tenth of all calves in his region for the temple-byres "as animals sealed for the burnt offerings which are offered up daily"; a tenth of all gold, ivory, ebony, spices, precious stones, woods and other products brought in by Nubians.[59]

And I shall give to you the land containing minerals and good land for cultivation, and nothing of it is to be diminished or withheld . . . And the scribes and revenue-officers will inspect the same and be satisfied that the rendering is correct.

Further, I shall make the masons and ore-hewers (?) and metalworkers and gold-smelters and sculptors and ore-crushers and furnacemen and handicraftsmen of all kinds, who work in hewing, cutting,

and polishing stones and in gold, silver, copper, lead, and every woods-
man and carpenter working in wood, to pay tithe on all work done.

And tithe will be paid on all natural products and on all the precious
stones and minerals which are brought down from the uplands, and on
all quarried stones; and there will be an inspector over the weighing of
the gold, silver, copper, and precious stones.

And everything the metalworkers need for the house of gold, for
making images of the gods and the repairs of statues, and the workmen
also, will be exempted from the tithe. And everything which [in the
past] has been given to the Storehouse is to be given again to [their]
children. And everything which is delivered to your god-house will
be [in abundance] as in times of old.

5

Craft-gods and Creation

THERE is, we see, an important relation to craft-process in both Ptah and Khnum. They are also demiurges, who make men, who support the universe they have created, and who control the oceanic waters of the underworld. Is this complex of characteristics a matter of chance or does it develop organically out of their position of craft-gods? (Craft-process in these early days always combines magical lore with technical knowledge.) Let us see if Greek mythology helps us to answer the question. The main figures there who embody craft-process are Athene, Hephaistos, and Prometheus. At first glance they seem wholly unlike Ptah and Khnum, but if we look more closely many parallels emerge, at least with the two male figures; for Athene, despite her connection with weaving and other crafts, remains essentially a city-goddess.

Hephaistos is at root a craft-magician, concerned with fire-transformations.[1] In the myth of his exile we find a link with water and the spirit-journey. Hera throws him into the sea where he is received by Thetis and Eurynome, and where he learns the craft of forging *daidala*. Eurynome was a daughter of Okeanos; she was honoured at a sanctuary in Phigalia, Arkadia, where she had the form of a fish-goddess bound by a thread of gold. In the *Argonautika* of Apollonios, Orpheus chants a theogony in which the first masters of snowy Olympos are Ophion and the Okeanid Eurynome; they give way to Kronos and Rhea, being swallowed up in Okeanos (or Tartaros). Ophion, by his name, shows himself a snake-god, and Okeanos curls like a snake round the world.[2] Whether Eurynome had the tail of fish or snake, she was a creature of the underworld; her name was one of the names of death and she was perhaps consort of Eurynomos, also a chthonic spirit.[3]

Hephaistos then has his links with Okeanos and goes down into the waters as part of an ordeal or initiation-passage that provides him with the technical and magical lores of his craft. He was also connected with world-mountains or sky-pillars, especially of a volcanic kind, where the fire and smoke make a suitable underworld-lair for a smith-god. Zeus threw him out of Olympos and he landed on Lemnos where the volcanic mount Moschylos was connected with both his forge and the fire that Prometheus stole from heaven.[4] Aitna, where he also had his smithy, was an important world-mount.[5] At Tyre we meet the Ambrosial Stones, a pair of world-pillars, associated with Okeanos, Hephaistos, and Athene.[6] In short, we find a complex of world-pillars, Okeanos, and water-passage, loosely but definitely linked with Hephaistos. He also had the power of making living creatures. Hesiod says he made Pandora, while Athena clothed her. In the *Iliad* he is the only person able to make objects endowed with movement.[7]

Prometheus shows the same complex, but in a much more powerful form. He is the patron of potters and metallurgists, all craftsmen who work with fire for purposes of transformation. He is a culture-hero who brings things useful for men from the spirit-world; and he is associated like his brother Atlas with world-pillars. Indeed his pillar-aspect seems primary in certain respects.[8] Like Khnum, he is a creator of men, whom he moulds in clay; in a late myth he appears after the Flood with a torch of heavenly fire and gives life to the stones thrown by Deukalion and Pyrrha.[9] Deukalion, the Greek Noah, was his son. We do not find Prometheus making the water-passage, but he was connected with Okeanos. In Aischylos' play the chorus, who are the friends of Prometheus, are the Okeanids, and Okeanos himself appears on a winged steed. No doubt Aischylos cast round for some Titan who could be made to sympathise with his hero; but the role of Okeanos is none the less significant. Note the phrases with which Prometheus welcomes him:

> How have you dared, leaving
> the stream that bears your name, the rockroofed caves
> selfborn, to try this ironteeming land?

Further, the Telchines, one of the mythical groups that reflect metal-working fraternities, were amphibious; Rhea was said to have confided Poseidon to their care so that they might rear him together with the Okeanid Kapheira. They were connected with floods, and were either drowned or dispersed by water.[11]

The complex of ideas and images under consideration then appears unmistakably in the Greek craft-figures, though it is not allowed to concentrate and develop as it did with Ptah and Khnum. However, we see that the culture-hero of a craft fraternity can easily become a creator-god who makes all things with his hands and who has a special relation to Okean, Nun, the primeval waters that have to be traversed in the journey into the spirit-world. We realise how in a land like Egypt, dominated by the Nile, the demiurge expanded his Okean-association into a claim to control the river-sources, where earthly water and Nun were magically one.

The Egyptian image of the primeval waters was very ancient. We found it pervading the Pyramid Texts; and it carried on into such late writings as the *Hermetica*: "who has ordered fresh water to come out of the Ocean to spread over habited and uninhabited earth for the subsistence and creation of all men."[12]

The world-picture is an elaboration of that which we find

24. Doubling of the Cosmic Image

emerging in tribal society at the totemic and subtotemic level: a ritual mound as world-centre, and both the sacred sites and the camp of the group oriented to the four points of the horizon (as determined by the east-west movement of the sun). The central point may be vertically expressed by poles as well as mounds. Such systems of orientation were highly developed among the North American Indians. The Australians too made the tribal camp a diagram of their society: a circle divided into semicircles and quarters according to the divisions of the tribe. Thus, with each totemic clan assigned to its proper place, the camp reproduces the world of nature as seen by the tribe—or we might say, in reverse terms, that nature is seen as organised in the same way as the tribe. The Ponkas of the Missouri, a tribe with two moieties, four phratries and eight clans, had a circular camp with the entry normally in the west. In the first quarter, left of the entry, was the phratry of fire; in the second quarter, behind it, was the phratry of wind; in the third quarter, right of the entry, was the phratry of water; and behind it, in the fourth quarter, was the phratry of earth. The Zunis of New Mexico had four divisions of north, south, east, west, one of the centre, and two concerned with verticality (nadir and zenith); each division had its own totemic creature or plant, and each of the four earth-divisions had also a colour and a set of correlatives (yellow, red, white, white; wind, winter and war, fire, summer and tillage, frost, autumn and magic, water, spring and peace). The original basis seems to have been four.[13]

Why the encircling waters should be added to the earth-round is not so clear. No doubt the reason lay in the notion of birth as an emergence from the womb-waters and death as a passage back over the waters to the spiritworld. The earth-mound was thus imagined as rising out of enclosing waters—with Flood-myths to express the dangers of the crucial lifedeath passage. It is perhaps significant that the nearest Egyptian parallels to a flood-legend are the tales of Osiris or Horos floating in a chest at birth or death. Such myths in turn link with the widespread tales of heroes set afloat at birth, which we shall later discuss in connection with Moses.

In the Jesuit *Relation* of 1637 we learn of the North American

Indians: "They believe that the earth is entirely flat, and that its ends are cut off perpendicularly; that souls go away to the end which is at the setting Sun and that they build their cabins upon the edge of the great precipice which the earth forms, at the base of which is nothing but water." A Flood-myth illustrates the image. The Great Hare and other animals were on a raft in mid-waters, with only waterfowl in sight. The Hare said that even a grain of soil could form the earth. The Beaver vainly dived, then the Musk-rat, who came up at last almost dead but with one grain of soil in a clenched foot. From this the earth was made in the form of a mountain (still growing even today). Around it goes for ever circling the Great Hare.

But the ultimate reason for the idea of world-waters we need not explore here. Enough to point out generally how the Egyptian world-scheme, like that of other ancient peoples, had its root in

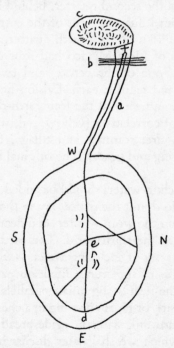

25. Cosmic Map by a Thompson River Indian: (a) western trail to underworld; b) river; (c) land of dead; (d) surise point; (e) central point. (*Mem. Am. Mus. NH* ii 343)

early tribal systems of ritual and social organisation. The Maori said of sunset, "The sun has returned to Hades", just as the Egyptian thought it had gone down into the Tuat.[14]

We must note further that the surrounding river or ocean can become in the geography of the spirit-journey a long river like the Nile. In Siberian shamanist cultures:

The early concepts about the upper and lower worlds turn out to be exact copies of concepts about surrounding nature. This explains the identical terms for all worlds: buga or dunne, the origin of which goes back to the remote past. The shaman's concept of the three worlds was different and the names for them were different. If the first worlds, upper and lower, were in a vertical arrangement (above and below the earth), in the second arrangement the upper world has been moved to the east and the lower world to the north, and they are connected by the long river, Engdekit, with its source in the upper and its mouth in the lower world. The river flows first to the west and then to the north. The headwaters of its tributaries are connected to our world and their basins are considered the property of individual shamans (the helper-spirits live along them). Seven or nine 'heavens' are situated between the upper world and the source of Engdekit; along the lower course of the river are the tribal worlds of the dead. . . .[15]

Such schemes are essentially the same as those we find in the Egyptian *Book of the Dead*, where the passage along the water-course is attended with a series of dangers. The difference is that the shamans help directly in the Siberian systems, while the more sophisticated Egyptian methods for procuring a safe passage involve a complicated set of spells and ritual acts connected with a settled priesthood. Shamanist improvisation is gone and the spells are written down, fixed.

There was then nothing original about the general scheme of earth and surrounding water, underworld and overworld, with water-passages derived from underworld-imagery and sky-passages in which the movement along a cavernous darkness or a water-space, with various danger-points to be encountered, has become an ascent into a world of light. We meet all these elements also in the Sumerian world-picture, where the world-mount, represented in ritual, appears as the ziqqarat instead of the pyramid— a communal centre instead of one monopolised (at the outset) by a kingship. And generally similar systems can be met all over the world in tribal societies at various stages of development. What is unique in Egypt is the extreme degree of theological refinement and ritual elaboration.

As we have seen, the Egyptians built up a creation-myth out of the ritual-mound or world-centre. The primeval hill rose up out of the waters of Nun and provided the basis of the earth on which men, animals, and plants might grow. This creation-event had happened in some ancient myth-time, and was happening every day. The acts of ritual repeated the moment of creation and stabilised the universe. The earth floated in Nun as well as being surrounded by it. Life had arisen out of Nun and was perpetually reborn from it. The sun rose out of the waters every morning and died into them at eve. The Nile spurted up out of Nun through the deep caverns, the Qerti.

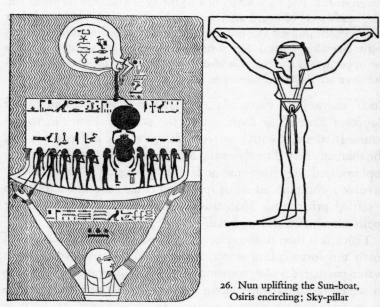

26. Nun uplifting the Sun-boat, Osiris encircling; Sky-pillar

An important expression of these cosmic ideas is to be found in the picture on the sarcophagus of Seti I, in which the solar boat is thrust up on the arms of Nun, while, opposite, Osiris allows the sun to be reborn in the form of a scarab from the sky-goddess Nut. Seti was the first great king after Akhnaten's heresy who felt deeply about religious matters. In his cenotaph at Abydos he embodied the image of the earth-island or hill surrounded by water.

The entrance [of the Central Hall] leads on to a ledge, with the water deep below, where one stands closed in by two projecting piers. Neither the ledge in front of the cells on the sides nor the island can be reached. On the other hand we have a double flight of steps which lead down from the island into the water. They were considered very important indeed. This is not only shown by the fact that in the construction of the island the space which they were to occupy was left open and is as well finished as the other parts of its outer sides, while the steps were actually worked into the great blocks. It is also evident from the indications of steps which are apparent on the western side, where they evidently were not yet finished (like so much in the building) when the work had to be stopped. Obviously the steps were considered an essential feature of the building, though they lead nowhere. And there remains only one possibility: as the Central Hall with its island in water can never have been used, it must have been merely the expression in stone of an idea.[16]

The same image is embodied in the Steps of Osiris at Abydos, near which every dead man prayed to be interred. The king, identified with Osiris, could build his own steps. When, with the Fifth Dynasty, the Re-religion became that of the state, the primeval hill rising out of Nun as the place of creation and renewal had a central part in the cult-imagery. When later the cults of Re and Osiris fused, the hill was the site of Osiris' tomb and resurrection, as well as of the birth and death, ascent and descent, of the sun. The primeval hill at Hermopolis and elsewhere was represented by a double flight of stairs, and on such a flight we find representations of Osiris entombed and Osiris ruler of the dead. "The Pillars of the god Shu were not as yet created, when he [Re] was upon the steps of him that dwells in Khemenu [Hermopolis]." Shu lifted the sky upon these steps when the universe was created. The papyrus of Ani goes on, "I am the great god who created himself, even Nun, who made his names become the Company of the Gods as gods."[17]

The rise and fall of the water round the island of Seti's Cenotaph would be connected with Osiris, drowned yearly in the flood and then rising afresh out of the waters. The Tomb of Osiris on Bigeh near Philai was covered yearly by the flood; and in late texts of the Hour-Watches, the place where the drowned Osiris was found is located "on that north shore of Abydos".[18] We may note further that the ritual island was more than the primeval hill; it was also the island of the blessed in which the Sungod lived or arose. This island, originally set in Heliopolis, was during the New Kingdom located in Abydos. "The island of the Justified is Abydos," says the Book of the Dead.[19] Herodotos remarked that the rooms built for the Burial of Cheops in his Pyramid were situated on an island, created by canals filled with water from the Nile. This was an erroneous belief, though the pyramids were grandiose versions of the primeval hill; but the holding of it was none the less significant. (All the temples which rise in steps from the front up to the holy-of-holies at the back repeat the image of the primeval hill.)

It is interesting to note also that the picture of Nun lifting up the sunboat, and Osiris encircling the Underworld, mentioned above, occurs only three times. On the sarcophagus, in one of the Books of the Dead, and in Seti's Cenotaph, at the end of the entrance-passage before we turn to the Central Hall with its island and its water. In the papyrus the picture precedes the depiction of a similar sort of hall (drawn, in the Egyptian way, partly in plan, partly in section). We see the pillars in plan, a blue colour indicates the encircling waters, and below is shown the double flight of steps (the primeval hill with the Osirian dead upon it.)[20]

The way in which such a sanctuary as the Cenotaph was felt to be actually as well as symbolically a world-image, an other-world-site, can be seen in a graffito here: "Adoration of Re-Harakhti, Lord of the Two Lands . . . the Great God, King of the Gods, Lord of Horos, with pointed Atef-crown . . . King . . . may he save the scribe . . . from the demons that are in this place. May he save the scribe Pedamun from the demons that are in this place." Pedamun feels that the spirits of the dead, the underworld-gods, who are continually described in the texts as lurking in their caverns, are dangerously all round him.[21]

Above the earth was the cover of the sky, coming down to rest on the horizons. Not that there was any single notion about the way it hung above. One picture shows it apparently floating aloft. But such a state of suspension would be perilous. So we get the four posts at the four cardinal points. "I have set . . . the terror of you as far as the four pillars of heaven." A not uncommon simile was: firm "as heaven resting upon its four posts". Every door or gate was "built like heaven upon its four pillars". When the sun was seen as the boat of Re, it was given four rudders.[22]

The heaven-support was also represented as a single figure, the air-god Shu. A Pyramid Text declares:

I am the great spoken Word. I am a delivered one. I am worthy of deliverance. I am delivered from all evil things. Further, to say: Men and gods, your arms under me, while you rise me and lift me up to heaven, as the arms of Shu under the sky as he lifted her up—to heaven, to heaven, to the great seat, among the gods.[23]

Nut, the sky-goddess, is depicted as crouching or stretched over the earth, with her fingers or toes touching it, while sun, moon, and stars adorn her body. Shu may take some of her weight on his raised hands as she stands upright. He is also shown kneeling with his arms holding up the sky with its sun. He wears one or more feathers on his head, and the four pillars are his emblem.

27. Shu bearing up Solar Disk; Shu god of light and atmosphere

He and his consort Tefnut are said to weep copiously; their tears
(? dew) falling on the ground are changed to incense-bearing
plants. (From these the Christians later pressed out the oil which
formed the chrism used by the Copts in rites of consecration.[24])

A dedication of the time of Ptolemy VIII on the second Pylon
at Karnak shows how these ideas worked out in the later phases.
Thebes is defined as the mound or hill of creation.

It happened while His Majesty [Amun] was hiding his head over against
his frontiers and the Earth was in the depth of the Flood, that he
[Amun] put his foot on her. He threw off his torpor altogether when he
set himself on her surface. This was the terrain that became the mound
which emerged at the beginning.[25]

Amun, hiding his head, was immersed in Nun; he floated inert
till at a certain moment he found himself on the ground which
was perhaps already pushing itself up out of the waters and which
was later to become Thebes. The term here for Flood is *wrm*,
one of the many flood-names; we find it given to one of the
bearers of offerings, the Hapis, on the lower walls of temples.[26]
The *hmws-wt*, the female spirits of places, things, elements,
depicted in similar positions on shrines of the late period, were all
created together at the beginning when the earth existed only as
the emergent Mound of Thebes. As the other towns did not yet
exist, the spirits owned parts of the Mound; then, as the rest of
the world came into existence, what we may call these seminal
town-patterns were transferred from the primeval mound to sites
in the widened earth-surface.[27]

Such Theban claims go far back. They were already current
under the Ramessides, though not in so theologically schematic a
form. Hymns declared, "Thebes is the Prototype for all Towns ...
since she begot men in herself to found all towns in her true name;
for they were given the name of towns in subordination to
Thebes, the Eye of Re."[28] This argument in part was based on the
doctrine that words by their sounds express or embody the
essential properties of things; since *The Town* was the outstanding
name for Thebes, and other places took over the sound of this
name in calling themselves towns, so they must have been derived
from Thebes, subordinate to her as copies.

A Ptolemaic text found a more plainly material explanation. Thebes was "the Mothertown where the gods have been born and all beings produced. Her soil has been distributed to found the Two Lands and the towns are named after her." Again, Thebes was "called the Orb of the whole Earth. Its angle-stones are set at the Four Pillars. They are then with the winds and they uphold the Firmament of Him-who-is-Hidden [Amun]." So the Theban dominion extends all over the earth. "With the winds" means: to the earth's limits.[29]

Amun then as the lord of Thebes, with its special relation to Nun, could claim to be master of the Nile. The Ptolemaic pylon-inscriptions tell us:

The water mounts up at the command of its divine image [Amun], him under whose authority are the harvests. The place that Nun [-Amun] reaches: it is His Majesty Harakhti who brings the Flood there promptly. When the soil of the Town-of-Life is dried out, the Nile [Ptah] is produced . . . goods to her deities, so that those who sleep in her bosom are without care. . . . her harvests.

Dishes are made according to his desire, truly. How great, how noble is he who is in his company and sees [realised] what his heart can imagine. His Majesty [Amun] is content . . . in their temple. Egypt flourishes with life. Sekhmet does not launch her pest. The Flood bears off the bull and surfeits the Two Lands. There is no lack of joy or gaiety in the people. The harvests of   field are not retarded. The Prince is assured on his throne; all foreign lands are under his sandals for eternity.[30]

The references to the harvests suggest Min, who at Thebes had become fused with Amun. As Kamenphis there he was lord of all the manifestations of natural fecundity; and generative power was thought to be incarnated in his statue. A description of the Festivals of Bouto tells us that in years of dearth an appeal was launched to him, asking that the crops grow and the plants burst open at their moment of flowering.[31] The sleepers in Thebes' bosom are the dead, who shared a special beatitude through lying in her soil.[32] Sekmet represents the yearly fever, which was thought to be brought on by a bad wind. "O Year, who bring to birth the wind, grant that Hathor, Lady of Dendera, may be pure from all malign contagion."[33] The fever was called the Carnage

G

of the Year, and in wintertime it regularly played havoc with the Egyptians. Bearing-off-the-bull (with a determinative showing that the term refers to the action of water) can only relate to the rite of breaking the dykes, which officially inaugurated the Flood. As a propitiatory offering, a throat-slit bull was doubtless set on the chosen spot; a breach was made; the water rushed in and carried off the life—as if it were gleefully accepting the sacrifice.[34]

A Ptolemaic text of an ancient myth, inscribed on a black granite shrine, describes the god Shu as having once reigned as a king on earth.[35] He carried out many building operations. "He irrigated the towns and the settlements and the nomes, and he erected the walls of Egypt and built temples in the Land of the South and the Land of the North." The shrine was dedicated to Sept, wargod and warden of eastern frontier and marshlands of Lower Egypt, and was set up at Qes (Qesem), sanctuary of the 20th Nome there, which was called by the priests Aat-Nebes. The text seeks to glorify Aat-Nebes, using the myth as the basis. Shu visits the place.

Then every door of Het-Nebes [was] built like heaven upon its four pillars. And the temple of Sept was built anew for the Majesty of Shu, for it was the temple which he loved. The doors were fixed with all the fittings as regards direction to the south and the north and the west and the east. The temples were built on the sites on which they had originally stood, everyone of them, everywhere. Eight halls were constructed on the west, eight on the east, and eight on the large forecourt of the eastern horizon.[36]

But the enemy, "the dwellers in the red lands", the deserts, attacked. "Wherever they came they destroyed everything." So Shu fortified all the sacred buildings in the region of Aat-Nebes, where the gods were the watchdogs of the land, their sanctuaries "the four pillars of heaven, which watch over the . . . of the Eternal Horizon, that is the sanctuary of Shu in the Temple of Nebes". They "raise up Re into the heavens from the Tuat", and are "the lords of the eastern hills who deliver Re from Apepi" (the serpent seeking to swallow the Sun).

Shu continued to reign till he grew old and sick. Then "his court became unruly and calamity invaded the land. Great strife

28. Nut and the Earthgod (snake-headed)

broke out in the palace and a revolt among Shu's associates. Then Geb looked on his mother [Tefnut] and loved her greatly. His heart yearned for her, and for this reason he wandered about the land, suffering greatly. The Majesty of Shu had gone up into heaven together with his followers." Tefnut came from Memphis "to Shu's palace at the time of noon, while Great Company of the Gods were on their eternal course, on the road of their father Re-Harmakhis". Geb met her at Pkharti and "laid hands on her with great violence". For nine days there was blackness and winds. Then Geb "as seen on the place [throne] of his father and all those who were in the palace smelt the earth before him".

Geb had thus raped his mother and exiled his father—"Shu having fled from the earth to heaven before him". He assumed power but had one ordeal before all was well. He took out the serpent Aart from the temple by the east gate of Aat-Nebes and wanted to put it on his head as Shu had done. But the serpent stung him. Geb went into the Field of Henna-plants north of the city, but could not drive out the venom. The gods in his following told him, "Let the Aart of Re be carried there and let your Majesty go and look upon its Mysteries and your Majesty will receive healing". Geb did so. He had "the Aart of Aart's Temple set on his head and caused a great coffer of real stone to be made for it. The coffer was hidden in a place in Aart's Temple near the Divine Aart of the Majesty of Re. And the burning head flowed forth from the body of the Majesty of Geb." Geb resolved to carry on Shu's work of building, rebuilding, and irrigation.[37]

Apparently Geb seeks to take over the Aart-serpent of the Sun-god Re without the correct ceremonies and secrecies. Shu appears as the perfect ruler, producing stable buildings and irrigation-systems; yet even he grows old and infirm. Geb, who usurps his place, ends by accepting him as the pattern of good kingship. The foursquare world is being continually threatened, by enemy attack from outside and by decay and revolt from within, but reasserts itself. The revolt of the young god against his father reminds us of the conflicts in Greek mythology, Kronos against Ouranos, and Zeus against Kronos. Indeed, in another myth, we have the motive of the old god swallowing the younger ones, though here it is the Mother who is cannibalistic:

These stars sail to the end of the sky on her outside at night whilst they show themselves and are seen. They sail in her inside in the daytime while they do not show themselves and are not seen. They enter after this god [the sungod] and they come forth after him. Then they sail after him on the supports of Shu while they rest on their places after his Majesty has set in the Western horizon.

They enter her mouth in the place of her head in the West. Then she ate them. Then Geb quarreled with Nut, because he was angry with her because of the eating of her young ones. Her name was called: She who eats pig[let]s—because she ate them.

Then her father Shu lifted her and raised her to his head. He said: "Beware of Geb. Let him not quarrel with her because she eats their children. She shall give birth to them and they shall live [again] and they shall come forth in the place at her behind in the East every day, even as she gave birth.[38]

The imagery derives from the intensely-felt anthropomorphic conception of the whole universe. The dead are swallowed up by the Mother and achieve a second birth through her anus as she evacuates them. (This idea of an anal second-birth as the achievement of immortality derives from the myth and ritual of initiation-rebirth.) The above-cited text is from the Cenotaph of Seti I at Abydos, in which we also find these texts connected with the king's ritual of immortality:

Twilight, heaven of the gods, the place from which the birds come: This is from its north-western side up to its north-eastern side, [viz.]the opening of the Underworld which is on her northern side. Her hinder part is in the east, her head in the west. . . .

Her head is in the western horizon, so that she may eat in the West [*i.e.* eat up the dead]. . . .

The Majesty of this god enters into her mouth in the Underworld. The Underworld is opened when he sails into it. The stars enter after him and they come forth after him, and they hasten to their places. . . .

He bursts forth (?) afterwards [or outside]. Then he opens the thighs of his Mother Nut and then he departs towards the sky. . . .

The Majesty of this god comes forth from her hinder part. . . .He opens with his splitting, he swims on. . . . Then he goes slowly towards the earth.[39]

We see the sundisk lying on Nut's foot as if she had dropped him there and he was about to start his upward journey along her leg (as the beetle is shown doing). We also find the progress of the night-sun through Nut calculated in terms of the twelve hours. The sun enters her at dusk, and at each hour moves through one part of her body: "the hand, the lip, the tooth, the throat, the breast, the . . . , the . . . , the intestine, the bowels, the vulva, the spine, the thigh".[40]

The notion of Nun the primeval ocean as circular seems inherent in the image of the mound or hill arising from the waters; and we do find some further evidence for the circle—for instance, the picture of Osiris bent in a ring round the underworld.[41] Under the Thirtieth Dynasty there occurs a sarcophagus relief of the goddess Nut curved over in an arch with the sun passing through her body, which encloses a circular world-map. On the edge of the circle are written the names of foreign lands; next, the names of the nomes are given inside another circle; in the central area appear the regions of the underworld-gods.[42] This map, however, may well show ideas borrowed from Babylonia, where the world-Ocean was certainly circular and flowed under the earth as did the Egyptian Nun.[43] Each Egyptian temple, we saw, repeated the ritual-myth of the world-mound; it stood on a "hill", even if one mounted only a few steps or came up a ramp at each entrance from court or hall to the holy of holies, which was thus set at a definitely higher level than the entrance.[44] The Sumerian temple was a Bond of Heaven and Earth or Great Binding-post (*dimgal*); we meet two ritual foundations, that above or of heaven, and that of the *abzu*, the waters of the underworld. Babylon was founded on the *bab apsi*, the Gate of the Apsu.[45]

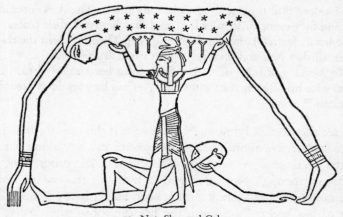

29. Nut, Shu, and Geb

But the primitive mind could think of the world as both square and rounded. The ancient Chinese said: "Heaven is round, Earth square." And John Donne could write, "At the round earths imagin'd corners, blow your trumpets, Angells . . . ." The Egyptian may well have thought of the arched woman-sky (or cow-sky) resting on rounded waters while the earth itself was most easily graspable as a square or oblong. The quadrangular or cubic concept of form in Egyptian art has often been noted, as compared with the rotundity of Sumerian forms with their basis in the cylinder. On plainlands the horizon appeared rounded; in Egypt, with the long line of the Nile, bounded on each side by desert cliffs or hills, the world might more plausibly seem an oblong.

30. Archaic statement: "6,000 Asiatic Prisoners"

And indeed an ancient determinative used in words expressing various lands is such a shape. It can be seen in the archaic period in a design that may be interpreted, "The Falcon N has brought back 6000 enemy prisoners". The oblong represents the foreign land, defined by an Asiatic head. The Egyptians had two categories of land, the alluvial valley with its name the Dark Brown, "the country black as a heap of charcoal", and the Clear Rose or the Flamingo-coloured Country of barren warm-hued sand on either side. A similar determinate to the plain oblong was a thin oblong laid sideways with three points or crests rising up from it. This stood for mountainous country, the desert-cliffs seen in elevation, with the three crests standing for any plural number. It came to designate any foreign land, whether Libya, Nubia or Babylonia; and by the principle of extension the plain oblong was applied even to the names of seas.[46]

Before leaving this section we may note that the Blessed Isles, in terms of what we have called shamanist geography, can be located in the sunset-west as the otherworld (and in late times raised to the skies); but they reflect at the same time the scheme of the primal hill-island and oceanic waters. In the *Contendings of Horos and Seth*, one episode is set in the Island of the Middle, where the Ennead gather:

The gods of the Ennead then went in a boat to the Isle of the Middle and sat down, eating bread. And lo, Isis came and she approached Anti the ferryman [who has been told not to admit her and] who was seated not far from his boat. She had changed herself into an old woman and walked all bent, a little golden ring on her hand. And she said to him, "I've come so that you can carry me over to the Isle of the Middle. I've brought this pot of meal for the lad. He's been watching cattle for five days in the Isle of the Middle and he's hungry."

He replied, "I've been told not to let any woman go over."

But she objected. "What's that you say? Haven't you been told that on account of Isis?"

He said, "What will you give me for carrying you to the Isle of the Middle?"

She replied, "I'll give you this small loaf of bread."

He said, "What do I care for your small loaf? Am I to ferry you to the Isle of the Middle after I've been told: Don't take any woman—ferry you for your small loaf?"

So she replied, "I'll give you the golden ring on my hand."

He said, "Give me the golden ring."

She gave it and he ferried her over to the Isle of the Middle. And while she walked on under the trees, she saw the gods of the Ennead sitting down and eating bread before the Universal Master in his Pavilion.[47]

Seth sees her. She changes herself into a young girl and he desires her. She tells him that she is a herdsman's widow and that a stranger is threatening to disinherit her son. She asks Seth to be the latter's champion. Seth takes her side. Then she changes into a kite, flies to the top of a tree, and tells Seth that with his own mouth he has condemned himself and vindicated Horos.

This Isle of the Middle, where the gods assemble before the Pavilion of the lord of all things, can only be a form of the cosmic isle-hill, though this aspect no longer has any particular significance in the myth. After the gods have punished Anti by cutting off his toes (so that he becomes the Clawed One), "they went by boat on to the western bank and sat on the mountain", staying there till evening. This site is only a somewhat rationalised version of the Isle.[48]

A nekropolis, which was likely to be on higher ground, was also in some sense the cosmic hill-island, since it was the place of assembly of the dead, the spirits. It was itself the underworld with its caverns. Thus, the nekropolis of Thoth's city Hermopolis was *Hmnw*, and this was also the Island of Flame.[49] At Dendera the king presenting a figure of Maat is called Son of the Lord of *Hmnw*, Child of Sia in the Island of Flame.[50] In an Edfu text the sacred Tree of the Hermopolite Nome is said to grow in the Island of Flame.[51] Sacred trees were associated with the burial centres; they were themselves reflections of the world-tree or world-pillar, and thus equivalents in their way of the world-hill.[52] In a Hymn to Thoth he is said to have made shrines for the gods and goddesses in the Isle of Flame. The gods here are no doubt the dead buried at Hermopolis and become Osirises. In late texts the dead dwell on the Isle.[53] In another hymn, of the time of Rameses IV, the Island of Flame is Thoth's Birthplace.[54] Also, later, the Island was where the Ogdoad of Hermopolis made the sungod come forth from the abyss and where he was suckled by a Cow.[55]

We see that here we touch essentially on a doctrine unrelated to that of Re or Osiris, the Island of Fire is the Hermopolitan version of the cosmic hill-island and has its own myth of creation.[56]

In the Pyramid Texts it is an island in the sea that the dead have to cross or a place of judgment or ordeal where the dead have to prove their power before being admitted to blessedness in the sky or the Happy Fields.

N comes out of the Isle of Flame [after] he, N, has set truth there in place of error.

N is the Bull of Heaven who suffered want and decided to live on the being of every god, who ate their entrails (?) when it came [to pass] that their belly was full of magic from the Isle of Flame.[57]

Like the cosmic hill, the Isle of Flame is a source of power or magic.[58]

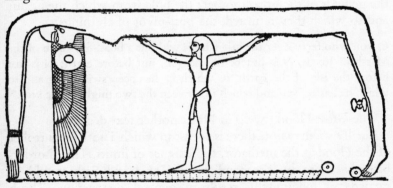

31. Shu upholding Nut

The Books of the Dead give us further details. There were seven words that caused a slaughter on the Island; a great god lives there, the golden youth who comes forth from the lotus-flower.[59]

Hail, you [Herfhaf] who bring the Ferryboat of Re, you hold your course firmly and directly in the northwind as you sail up the River towards the Island of Fire which is Khert-Neter.

This comes from the chapter which was to enable the deadman to gather words of power and magic in Khert-Neter, the Other-world; these words would gain him the help of the Ferryman and enable him to pass through the danger-points of the spirit-journey.[60] We also find Hmnw identified with the world-pillar. "Re was on the highplace of *Hmnw*, before that which Shu raised aloft came into being."[61] The tale occurs often in Coffin Texts, especially those from Bersheh.

In texts of the Greek period the Ogdoad, the eight primal deities, were formed in Thebes; they descended to their home, the Isle of Flame; there they created Light and took their place in Hermopolis beside their Father. Here we see syncretism at work. Thebes claims to be the primal site; but the cosmic hill, in its form as the Isle of Flame, moves to Hermopolis; and at the same time Re of Hermopolis asserts himself and comes forth on the Isle.[62]

Finally, if we look back at the Pyramid Texts, we find that the world-centre, the primal hill-island, was also identified with the genitals of the great mother: the hole from which men came and to which they returned, the post-pivot of all things:

O you who ferry over the just who is without a boat, ferryman of the Marsh of Reeds, N is just before heaven, just before earth; N is just before the Isle of the Earth, to which he has been swimming and to which he has arrived and which is between the two thighs of the Nut.[63]

The Great Flood dwells in Nut, another text declares.

Finally we may note there is a sense in which Thoth is controller of the Flood as the mediator, the assigner of limits. The disorders brought about by the conflicts of Horos and Seth would, if carried on indefinitely, result in general destruction. Thoth declared, "I am he who limits the flood, who separates the two men". The separating of Horos and Seth was linked with the setting of a boundary between cosmos and the flood-chaos. Other equations were with the keeping apart of heaven and earth, earth and underworld, right and left, black and red, birth and conception, life and dominion, rulership and strength. The concept of limits meant that the world was symmetrically divided. The horizontal division was traversed by a vertical one, that of above and below; and Horos and Seth were again involved. The primeval flood was also divided into two: the *kbhw* of the north and that of the south. And other gods besides Thoth could take over the separating function, Amun or Geb.[64]

6

Oceanic Nile

THE Greek image of Okeanos was essentially the same as that of Nun or Abzu; and it is impossible to estimate how far either of the latter contributed to it. No doubt both Egypt and the Near East played their part in influencing Greece, from far back in the 2nd millennium B.C. Neither Babylonia, Syria, nor Greece worked out the detailed schemes of the Night-Sun that developed in Egypt, though all these regions had the same general world-system. Egypt seems, as we noted, to have infiltrated ideas into Crete and the Aegean in the later Minoan and the Mykenean periods. It is of interest that in the rather dim notions of the Greeks about a judgment in the underworld the two Cretan brothers Minos and Rhadamanthys, together with Aiakos, are those in charge. In the *Odyssey* Minos is a judge in Hades, but merely it seems as a king carrying on his functions as on earth. In both Homer and Pindar, Rhadamanthys is lord of the Elysian fields. We have an impression of ideas carried on from earlier phases which have been very imperfectly incorporated in the Olympian religion.

Homer knows a remote land called Aigyptos with a great river of the same name. The reference to the splendours of Thebes in Egypt occurs in both *Iliad* and *Odyssey*; but there is much more about Aigyptos in the *Odyssey* as one would expect from its theme of sea-wanderings. The knowledge or memory of this river-land presumably goes back to Mykenean days, but is now smudged with a haze of romanticised tradition. No direct knowledge of recent times appears. The adjective Aigyptios, *Ai–ku–pi–ti–jo*, has been found on a table from Knossos, which has been dated of the 15th century B.C. and which seems in any event to bring the word well back into the 2nd millennium.[1] The origin of the name is obscure. There is no clear relation to any Egyptian word, though etymologies such as that meaning the Castle-of-the-Ka-of-Ptah have been suggested. Possibly it is an old Aegean or Cretan word related to *aiges* (waves), *aigaion* (Aegean), and *Aigeus* (an epithet of Poseidon), and derived from some such form as **Aiga*, prehellenic for Sea. If something of the sort is correct, we may take Aigyptos to be a vague term, partly geographical, partly mythical, used by the Mykeneans for the whole area lying south of Crete. It would thus in meaning be akin to Okeanos, indeed expressing the oceanic image in its southern bearings. In Homer's epics a certain amount of factual knowledge has been mixed with the more mythical aspects. Egypt is a fabulous and wealthy place with a heavenfed river; and the two aspects, the rich land and the Okeanid stream, are not clearly differentiated. (According to Aulus Gellius the name Aeria was once given to both Crete and Egypt.) By Hesiod's time the land and the river are distinguished, and the river is called Neilos. Contacts seem to have been re-established, directly or indirectly.[2]

The *Iliad* suggests that the Okeanos-complex comes from an earlier substratum of religion than the Olympians. Okeanos is an alien and opposed power. Zeus calls the gods to his council on Olympos, and Thetis ranges about to bring them in. She fetches the Rivers, who put on their human shapes. "There was no River that failed to come, save Okeanos." Even Poseidon came, but not the world-ocean. Again, Homer goes out of his way to pose against Zeus the chthonic river Acheloos and Okeanos.

> With Zeus not even King Acheloios may vie
> nor the great might of deeply-flowing Okean
> from whom all rivers flow and every sea
> and all the springs and the deep wells of the earth:
> even he is afraid of the lightning of great Zeus,
> and his dread thunder when it crashes from heaven.[3]

The *Etymologicum Magnum* says that Ouranos, Heaven, is a title of Okeanos. We see how right Aischylos was to link Okeanos and Prometheus.

Hesiod, we noted, is the first writer known to use the name Neilos. The *Theogony* states, "And Tethys bore to Okeanos eddying rivers, Neilos, Alpheios", and so on. Neilos is the first-mentioned river in the catalogue.[4] Pindar calls Okean "the father of springs", and so, like Homer, shows a belief in a great underlying ocean or a network of underground streams reaching out to the ocean-circle. Thales of Miletos, who probably visited Egypt in the 7th century, heard there of Okean-Nun as the source of the Nile, but with his busy mind questing for rational causation he was more interested in the thesis that the flood came about through the force of the Etesian winds, which blew as the river started to rise.[5] Hekataios, soon after 494 B.C., conjectured that the Nile was connected in the south to the Ocean and attributed the flood to this connection; he had talked with Egyptian priests.[6] Herodotos cites his opinion without naming him, but rejects the Ocean as a mere fable.[7]

Diodoros says, "The Egyptians consider Okeanos to be their river Nile, on which also their gods were born . . .", alluding to Homer's statement that all the gods were born from Okeanos. He also says, "The Egyptians speak of the Nile as Okeanos". Elsewhere he says the Nile was first called Okeane, then Aetos (Eagle) on account of its speed, then Aigyptos after one of the kings, and finally Neilos after another king.[8] Various rationalisations were attempted. Dikaiarchos, a disciple of Aristotle, thought the Nile joined up with the Atlantic Ocean; King Juba of Carthage, who died A.D. 23, held the Nile rose in the Atlas Mountains; and so on.[9] Nonnos simplifies the matter by describing the Nile as *autogonos*,

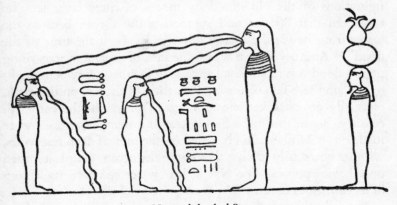

32. Nun and the dual Stream

self-created. The epithet recalls the ancient chant which sees the Nile as unique, self-created, of unknown essence, also Aischylos' epithet for the caves of Ocean. But in fact the epithet is typical of Nonnos's efforts to define a universe of spontaneous Dionysiac energy.[10]

The linking of Nile and Ocean occurs on Egyptian coinage of the Roman period. The Nile is naturally common as a cointype (in the form of a Graeco-Roman rivergod); but on an Alexandrian coin of the Antonines we find a woman clad in a stola, who holds up in her right hand two corn-ears, in her left a horn-of-plenty, and stands between two ship-prows. The prow on the right has its sail spread and a rivergod on either side. The righthand god is bearded and holds a rudder; the lefthand is beardless, with a reed in one hand, a horn-of-plenty in the other—underneath is inscribed what seems to read *Okeanos*. The woman is Euthenia (Abundance); the rivers, Nile and Ocean. The Nile is uniformly shown on Alexandrian coins with reed and horn, while the rudder is Ocean's property.[11]

A young Greek in Egypt says in his epitaph: "No more the fresh water of Okean I'll drink. . . . If you bring me here some water drawn from the Nile, sprinkle on me some drops of it awhile."

Horapollon in the late 4th century A.D. stated that the Nile-flood was called Nun by the Egyptians and tried to link Nun with the Greek *neon* (new). Explaining one of the hieroglyphic figurations of the Nile-flood by means of three large jars, he remarked that "the second symbolises the Ocean because the water from beside the Ocean flows in Egypt at the time of the flood".[12] Another way in which the idea of oceanic waters rising up in a flood was rationalised appears in the theories which sought to explain the Nile's phases by the action of the sun on the earth, especially on its subterranean waters. Timaios, in the early 5th century, began this line of argument and many variations were made on it.[13] Others simply relied on the idea of deep reservoirs, without necessarily linking them with the ocean. Statius summed up this viewpoint: "The Nile at low water contracts itself deep in its enormous caverns."[14]

The only texts that interest us here are those which show how the Greeks held to the idea of a link of all rivers with Okeanos. Plato seems to have drawn directly or indirectly on Egyptian sources for his picture of an underground system of rivers which starts and ends in the central reservoir of Tartaros. He elaborates this picture at length in the *Phaidon* and fuses it with an account of afterdeath rewards and penalties which no doubt owes much to Orphic doctrine. He describes a network of cavities and chasms into the earth, and a system of oscillations that control rivers of water, fire, liquid mire, lava, and make them move up or down.

One of the chasms in the earth is extremely large and pierced right through the whole earth: it is that which Homer speaks of as very far off, where is the deepest abyss beneath the earth, and which elsewhere he and many other poets have called Tartaros. For into this cavern all rivers flow together and from it flow out again. . . .

He uses the analogy of the pump to explain the way in which the rivers rise up out of Tartaros, and propounds a very complex pattern of risings, fallings, circlings, which end by producing the seas, lakes, rivers and springs of the earth. There are four great streams: Okeanos flows all round the earth; Acheron flows in a contrary direction, through desert places, and passes under the earth, to fall into the Acherousian lake (where the souls of most men who die arrive to pass a certain time before being rein-

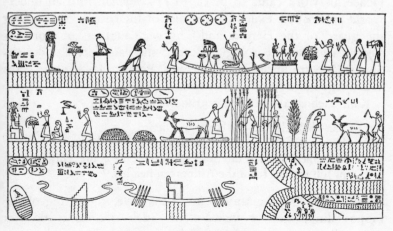

33. The Tuat or Underworld and its Rivers

carnated as animals); Pyriphlegethon runs between the first two and quickly falls into a vast region of boiling water and mud, then circles round till it reaches the Acherousian lake without mingling with it, and finally discharges into the lower parts of Tartaros; Styx is opposite to this third river, and also sinks and circles in a contrary direction to the current of fire, meeting the Acherousian lake without mingling with it, and discharging into the Stygian lake on the opposite side to Pyriphlegethon.[15]

We cannot here go into the question of Orphism and the origin of such eschatological beliefs as these of Plato in the *Phaidon* and other dialogues. Probably the belief of an afterdeath judgment which there plays an important part derived from certain indigenous elements given a new expansive force by the general development of Greek society and exploding within the Olympian system; but there certainly seem also Egyptian elements, some absorbed far back in Mykenean days, others brought into the Greek world through the renewed contacts which the foundation of Naukratis in the Delta expressed. It is impossible that Plato's picture of Tartaros could have come about without all the theorisings on the question of the Nile.[16] The same may be said of Pherekydes' earlier account of the cosmos as involving five Caves or Recesses, *antra* or *mychoi*, also called Ditches or Gates, *bothroi* or *pylai*, and assigned to Fire, Vapour, Water, and so on. Hence his work came to be called *Pentemychos*. Into an underworld precinct are exiled the enemies of the cosmic order under the guard of the Harpies and Thyella, daughters of Boreas— clearly seen as meteorological forces; the dark forces under the Snaky One are hurled into Okeanos. Pherekydes sees the earth as a winged tree suspended in space.

Kallimachos says of Leto on the island of Delos:

> She gladly halted her bitter wandering, sat
> by the stream of Inopos which the earth sends out
> in deepest flood at the time when the Nile comes crashing
> in full torrent from the Aithiopian heights.[17]

Plinius adds, "At the same time as the Nile, the spring of the Inopos diminishes or increases."[18] Such statements do not necessarily assume an underground connection; they might mean there was some magical sympathy or that the same natural causes were operating at places far apart. But on Delos there certainly was a ritual acceptance of the virtual identity of Inopos and Nile. The reservoirs for water to be used in the rites of Serapeia A and B were joined by a canal to the Inopos, and thus the local river supplied what was ritually considered Nile-water. Kallimachos, in his Hymn to Artemis, writes:

> But when the Nymphs encircle you in a dance
> near to the springs of Egyptian Inopos.[19]

Pausanias says that the Delians told him that "the Inopos comes from the Nile".[20] A rationalisation or a confusion resulting from the notion of intercommunicating waters led to the idea that the great rivers were all part of one another. The Persians thought the Nile and the Indus were sections of one river.[21] Pausanias said:

The water near Atlas, which provides a beginning to three streams, does not turn any of these streams into a river, as the sand swallows it up at once. So the Aithiopians dwell near no River Okeanos. The water from Atlas is muddy and near the source were crocodiles of not less than two cubits, which, when the men came near, dashed down into the spring. Many have had the idea that it is the reappearance of this water out of the sand that gives the Nile to Egypt. Mount Atlas is so high that its peaks are said to touch heaven. . . .[22]

Of the Asopos, he said that among the Phliasians and the Sikyonians tales are told that:

its water is foreign and not native, in that the Maiandros, descending from Kelainai through Phrygia and Karia, and emptying itself into the sea at Miletos, goes to the Peloponnesos and forms the Asopos. I remember hearing a similar story from the Delians that the Inopos comes to them from the Nile. Further there is a story that the Nile itself is the Euphrates, which disappears into a marsh, rises again beyond Aithiopia, and becomes the Nile.[23]

Lucan put these ideas into verse:

> Some think there yawn in the Earth
> air-vents, huge fissures in its hollow frame.
> There, water unseen, deep down, moves to and fro
> and is called from the frosty North to the Equator,

H

> when the Sun, straight above Meroe, parches the Earth
> that thus attracts water. Po and Ganges are drawn
> through a secret world, and many-mouthed Nile discharges
> from a single source all rivers, down to the Sea.[24]

The Greeks further had tales that the Alpheos, flowing in the Peloponnesos to Olympia, went underground and passed through the seas to mix with the spring Arethousa in Sicily.[25] Pomponius Mela, geographer of the mid-1st century A.D., declared, "If there does exist another world [orbis] and there are antipodean people opposite to us to the south, we can hold without too far outraging truth that the Nile finds its origin there and penetrates below the seas in an underearth cavern, then comes up again in our part of the world, where it rises at the time of the solstice because the land of its origin is then in midwinter."[26]

The persistence of the idea of the Nile as an Oceanic River is revealed by the acclamations of the Roman period. Dion of the Golden Mouth, describing a festival at Antioch, mentions the acclamations greeting the donor on his arrival at the theatre. Some of the people hailed him as Generous Nile, others as Ocean.[27] Again in the 2nd century A.D., at Hermopolis, the councillors shouted in praise of a gymnasiarch, "O Oceanic Heraklammon!"[28] A report of a public meeting held in the late 3rd or early 4th century at Oxyrhynchos in honour of a prytanis is worth citing in full; it shows in extended form the complicated acclamations in which people were drilled in the later Roman period, and it demonstrates effectively the way in which the Oceanic epithet was used to build up a feeling of someone's boundless generosity. The display was made during a visit of the Prefect.

When the Assembly had met, [the people cried out] "The Roman Power for ever! Lords Augusti! Prosperous Prefect! Prosperity to our Ruler! Hail, Oceanic President, Oceanic Glory of our City, Oceanic Disokoros Chief Citizen, under you our Blessings increase evermore, Source of our blessings. . . . Prosperity to the Patriot, Prosperity to the Lover of Right! Source of our Blessings, Founder of the City . . . Oceanic . . . . Let the President receive the vote on this great day. You deserve many votes, for many are the Blessings, President, that we enjoy through you. This Petition we make to our Ruler about the President, with Good Wishes to our Ruler [katholikos], asking for the City's President, Beneficent Ruler, for the City's Founder, Lords Augusti for ever!

"This Petition to our Ruler about the President for the Honest Man's Governor, the Equitable Governor, the City's Governor, the City's Patron, the City's Benefactor, the City's Founder, Prosperous Prefect, Prosperous Ruler, Beneficent Ruler, Beneficent Prefect!

"We beseech you, Ruler, about the President, let the President receive the vote! Let the President receive the vote of this great day. This is the first necessity!"

The Prefect replied, "I acknowledge with great pleasure the honour you do me, but I ask you to reserve these demonstrations for a legitimate occasion, when you may make them in safety and I be justified in accepting them."

The People cried out, "Many votes do you deserve. . . . The Roman Power for ever! Prosperous Prefect, Protector of Honest Men, our Ruler! We ask, Ruler, for the City's President, the City's Benefactor, the City's Founder! We beg you, Ruler, to preserve the City for Our Lords! Beneficent Ruler, we beg you for the City's Wellwisher, the City's Patriot!"

Aristion the Advocate [syndikos] said, "We shall refer the matter to the Most High Council."

The People: "We ask, Ruler, for the City's Patron, the Faithful General, Peace of the City, Oceanic Disokorides, Chief Citizen, Oceanic Seuthes, Chief Citizen, Equitable Governor, Equitable Citizen. True and Upright Advocates, True and Upright Assessors! Hurrah for all who love the City! Long Live the Lords Augusti!"[29]

The more that local freedoms faded out, the more fulsome became the compliments addressed to the men in power.

The same image of Oceanic Bounty appears in the tale told by Philostratos of the meeting between his hero Apollonios and Vespasian at Alexandreia. Vespasian, about to become emperor, turned round to the Egyptians there and said, "You shall draw on me as you do on the Nile."[30] The Nile, as the bestower of a universal bounty which draws all men together, at least in Egypt, in a common humanity, appears in another anecdote about Apollonios, who rebukes the Alexandrians for their partisan violence at horseraces. "I see you rushing at one another with drawn swords and ready to hurl stones, all over a horse-race.

I'd like to call down fire on such as city." He asks, "Cannot you respect the Nile, the common mixing-bowl (*krater*) of Egypt? But why mention the Nile to men whose gauges measure a rising tide of blood rather than of water."[31]

Philostratos is thinking of the banquet that Alexander the Great gave at Opis after the mutinous Macedonians had been reconciled to his imperial purposes. Both Macedonians and Persians attended, and Alexander prayed for *homonoia*, unity of outlook, between the two peoples. Eratosthenes says that by this act he broke with Aristotle's teaching—to treat Greeks as friends, barbarians as animals—and preferred to divide men into good or bad without concern for race; for he believed he had a mission to harmonise mankind, reconcile the world, and mix men's lives and customs as in a loving-cup. We may read too much into the *krater* of communion at Opis. Alexander had no vision of human unity

34. Osiris in Judgment at the top of his Stairs

and equality; but in expressing his imperial needs he was indeed giving voice to the widened horizons opening in his age.[32] The krater itself continued to be an important image of the act of communion and baptism whereby men entered into a new life, a new fellowship.

An Hermetic treatise, entitled *The Krater*, sets out the myth, in the form of a dialogue between Hermes (Thoth) and his disciple Tat. (Hermetic doctrines developed during the 2nd and 3rd centuries A.D.)

Tat: Tell me then, Father, why did not God impart Intellect to all men?

Hermes: It was his will, my son, that Intellect should be placed in the midst as a prize that human souls may win.

Tat: And where did he place it?

Hermes: He filled a great Krater with Intellect and sent it down to earth, and he appointed a herald and bade him make proclamation to the hearts of men: Dip yourself in this Krater, you who are able; you who believe you will ascend to Him who sent this Krater down; you who know for what purpose you have been born.

Now those who paid heed to the proclamation and were baptised in Intellect, they got a share of Gnosis [knowledge of God] and they became Perfect Men because they received Intellect.[33]

The *Pistis Sophia*, a Gnostic treatise of the 3rd century A.D., written in Coptic, tells of two vessels, one of oblivion and one of wisdom, presented to the soul by astral powers.

In the Hermetic *Krater* two rites are fused: the bath of purification and initiation, and the absorption of a sacred drink. The mystic doctrines of the Holy Grail seem to be in a direct descent from the Gnostic idea of the Krater; and indeed the very word Graal or Grail may derive from Krater.[34]

The correlation of the Nile-flood with imagery of love and union, however, goes far back into the Egyptian past:

You are beautiful in your body, happy of demeanour; the love of you is in all mankind like a great Nile.

You are a great protector of your peasants; your great repasts are plentiful like a high Nile.

The Nile in flood came by love for him.[35]

The last sentence occurs three times on an hieratic ostrakon, once in black and twice in red; it must be part of a writing exercise.[36]

Here is a prayer written on parchment about the 6th century, which shows the idea of the oceanic Nile carrying on into Christian times. It opens with an invocation to the Nile, then adds the Constantinopolitan Creed and a Psalm.

Sign of most holy Nile. Sign for the rites of abundance. The water has been let loose. The canals are made oceanic through the flood, by flowing currents. Rule the canal many-watered great-named Nile. Since Meroe you rejoice, cheerfully, sweetly flood the earth that will bear fruit by your many currents of water, consider the whole earth of Egypt wetted by the rains appearing in their time, they turn into gold for each man. Form choruses in honour of the waters, all together pray three times: Come, Nile, rise to the joyous sixteen cubits' height.[37]

Sign is *semasia*, the name which the Nile-festival gained, at least under the Romans. The Rite of Abundance seems mentioned in an account of the Public Games at Oxyrhynchos in the 2nd century A.D. where we find *hierodouloi* or temple-slaves *plou* . . . (*ta plousia* is the term that the invocation uses for the Nile's gifts). "Rains" are no doubt here used to express the inundation which does for Egypt what rains do for other lands.[38]

In the *Hymn to the Aten* of Tell el Amarna, with its effort to build a world-picture that embraces both Egypt and the other lands, we read:

You make the Nile in the Underworld; you bring it at your will to cause the people of Egypt to live, for you have made them for yourself, O lord of them all, who grow tired through them, O lord of every land who shine for them, you Disk of the Day, great of dignity. All the distant lands, you make their life. You set a Nile in heaven that it may descend for them and make floods on the mountains like the sea, so as to water their fields in their towns. How excellent are your plans you Lord of Eternity. The Nile in heaven is your [gift] to the foreign peoples and all herds that go on their feet, but the [true] Nile comes from the Underworld for Egypt.[39]

The same ideas were current in the Roman period. Philon wrote: "Their not being watered like others by rain, but regularly flooded each year by the overflowing of the river, makes the Egyptians deify the Nile by divine reason (*logos*) because it is the antithesis of the sky and they find there grounds for being proud of their land."[40] He also defends the miracle of manna in the wilderness by bringing in the Nile: "It has seemed good to him for the air to produce food instead of water since the earth has often brought forth rain: for when the River in Egypt yearly overbrims in floods and irrigates the fields, what is that but a rain showered up from below?"[41] Euripides had said, "The Nile waters the fields of Egypt instead of the rains of Zeus." Parmenides exclaimed in words that became famous, "Egyptian Zeus, O Nile!" And this sort of phrase carried on into the Latin poets, Tibullus and Lucan.[42] Hence the way in which "rain" is used for the Nile's overflow.[43]

Before we end this section it would be worthwhile to cite another text of the 6th century announcing the extent of the Nile's rise at Takona on three successive days in Mesore. The text is of interest in showing how carefully the levels were still noted and how Christ has now taken the position of Khnum and the others as Lord of the Nile.

To the most honourable Kalos, Secretary of the Illustrious House [probably that of Apion]. I again bring Good Tidings to your Honour that the Blessed Fertilising River of Egypt has risen by the power of 20 finger-breadths of new water.

From 5th Mesore till 7th it rose twelve finger-breadths, so that there are 2 cubits, 20 finger-breadths of new water. There were added also to this $\frac{1}{2}$ cubit from the water in the reservoir 16 finger-breadths, total 5 cubits, leaving 3 cubits, 12 finger-breadths in the reservoir. Altogether, including the water in the reservoir, 8 cubits, 12 finger-breadths.

Last year on the same dates the water rose 36 finger-breadths, making 5 cubits, 7 finger-breadths of new water, there being 5 cubits, 10 finger-breadths in the reservoir; altogether, including the water in the reservoir, 10 cubits, 17 finger-breadths.

I inform your Honour of all this for your information. Farewell in the Lord. The daily figures are: On the 5th it rose 4 finger-breadths, on the 6th 4, on the 7th 4: total, 12 finger-breadths. . . .[44]

7

People on the Nile

So far we have been dealing with some of the historical problems of the Nile, the reasons for the failure in antiquity to reach its sources, the ideas that men had about it, and the great structure of religious emotion and thought which they raised upon it. Now let us look more closely at the people who pondered these problems, absorbed in some degree or other the religious attitudes, and whose lives were bound up with the Nile, its rising and its ebbing, and its use as a broad highway. In one sense we could cite almost any of the papyri, since hardly any event or difficulty could come up in Egypt without some bearing, direct or indirect, on the waters of the Nile; but here we shall concern ourselves with the documents which deal with travelling and bring out, one way or another, the motives of the people moving up and down the river. As usual, we find that the documents from the Egyptian sands provide us with a picture of social and personal life which is quite unparalleled in the ancient world. In a thousand ways these people come close to us and we feel their physical presence, their emotional strains and stresses. We gain all sorts of insights into their daily lives, their hopes and fears, their greeds and irritations, their amiable impulses and affections. The papyri and ostraka can be grouped under various heads: personal, commercial, legal, military, administrative—though there is inevitably a continual tangle of purposes and motivations. We shall attempt to make some convenient classifications, but these must not be taken in any rigid sense. Little family-emotions slide over into larger questions, and the other way round. What emerges out of the total picture is the vivid and unique kaleidoscope that Egypt alone can give us of personal life in the Graeco-Roman world.

First, as an introduction, is a small group of letters of the Ptole-

maic period, letters written to or by Adamas in the 2nd century
B.C. The man was a sitologos, an official dealing with the collection and carriage of corn; and though the letters are personal ones,
his problems of transport by land and water intrude:

(1) Adamas to Dionysios, greeting. Ptolemaios has not dealt mode-
rately with me, as to the collector; he has sworn to Psenemmous,
Dionysios and Aristandros who've engaged to provide 100 transport-
beasts. . . . If they still find the gods propitious, let them provide them
and take away the corn in the store, for they'll hardly appease the
fellow [apparentlyPtolemaios].

But if they suppose that Petosiris and his brother, who are under
Hippalos' protection, will provide the animals, then they think
foolishly. Let them know that Ptolemaios son of Hermokrates is waiting
till he gets the animals after paying their price. Goodbye, 18th year,
Epeiph. . . .

I have sent a written order to give to . . . 20 artabai of wheat and
one of wheat to his servants: total 21.

(2) Adamas to his Father, greeting . . . and that we are in the greatest
danger as to the mixed wheat and barley at Poan, amounting to 200
art. of wheat, until we see what line the dioiketes takes—in case he
makes an unfavourable decision. . . .

(3) His Father to Adamas. Don't omit sending home news of how
things go with you, what they are like, and showing prudence so that I
won't have to come up about this same affair. For Aniketos the agent
of Eubios the archiphylakites. . . .

35. Nilotic scene, with Pygmies

(4) Herodoros to Adamas, greeting. After I had set out with Ammonios, having taken the animals from Oxyrhyncha, when we had carried down the wheat from Ibion and . . . [finding] the bridge fallen down, we returned to Oxyrhyncha with nothing to do.

I couldn't get away from Herakleides so as to go up, because he said we'd proceed to Kameionoi . . . and send even now a man to be there so that I myself may sail to the folk at Theognis and the other villages and see to my holding. Goodbye, 9th year, 12 Thoth.

(5) Heliodoros to Adamas his brother, greeting and goodhealth. As our brother was detained from the 28th on the business at the metropolis which I communicated to you, and as Argeios made an inquiry about it on the 29th and found nothing, I decided to report to you, knowing that . . .

Another note may be from the same man as the last.

Heliodoros to Epidoros, greeting. If you're in health and all else goes as you wish, I'm glad. I too am getting on pretty well. I have written to you before so as to have a chat with you before I sail down, and now, if you agree, I'll be obliged if you'll meet me, preferably on the 20th. . . .[1]

Turning now to the Roman period, we can group the letters in various ways, even though the themes overlap. Many letters deal with purchases or presents that are being sent along to relatives or friends, and are of interest in showing the sort of goods that people wanted and often went to much trouble to buy and transport. Here is a letter of the 1st century A.D. in which a father writes to his son, who is staying in Alexandreia. Nikanor is perhaps another son. "Apollonios to his son Apollonios, greeting. I've received through Heraklas the boxes with the books, as you write, and the half-chous jar of oil which Nikanor writes he has sent. Tell Nikanor that Heraklas the boatman [has] to pay us the 600 dr. for his freights; he was here today. I found the boat sailing down and thought I ought to let you know what I said. You'll receive through Origas two variegated wristbands, one scarlet, one purple, which your brother Pausanias went to the expense of having made some time ago and presented to you. Write and acknowledge their receipt. If I can privately buy a cloak for you, I'll send it at once. If I can't I'll have it made for you at home. The blankets have been cut out. The account, as you write, will be sent by Diogas to Nikanor through Heraklas. A pattern of the colour of the dress being made is enclosed here. Give it to Nikanor to consider, so that if he likes it he may write to us—it hasn't yet been given out. We are going to use local purple. Goodbye. 6 Mechair".[2]

The boxes of books are an unusual consignment, but clothes are often mentioned. Here is a letter of the 2nd century:

"Kornelios to his sweetest son Hierax, greeting. Everyone in the household salutes you and all those with you. As for the man you write to me so often about, claim nothing till I come to you —happily I trust—with Vesteinos and the donkeys. For if the gods will, I'll arrive soon after Mecheir is over—at the moment I have urgent business on hand. Take care not to cause offence to any of the persons at home, and give your attention wholly to your books. Devote yourself to learning and then they will bring you profit. Receive by Onnophris the white robes which are to be worn with the purple cloaks, the others you should wear with the myrtle-coloured ones. I'll send you by Anoubas both the cash and the monthly supplies and the other pair of scarlet cloaks. You won me over by the dainties and I'll send you the price of these too by Anoubas. Till Anoubas arrives you must pay for your own and your household's provisions out of your own money, till I send you some. For the month of Tybi there is for yourself what you like, for Phronimos 16 dr., for Abaskantos and his companions and Myron 9 dr., for Sekoundos 12 dr., Send Phronimos to Asklepiades in my name and let him get from him an answer to the letter I wrote, and send it. Let me know what you want. Goodbye, my son."[3]

Another 2nd century letter deals with a land-journey. The friend addressed was at Bacchias, only some 11 km. or 7 miles from Karanis where the letter was written: a short distance for a walk or a donkey-jog. He seems, however, to have been previously travelling about more widely. The complaint at receiving no letters is common. "Apol[lonios?] to Apollinarios, his brother, greeting. Having learned that you're at Bacchias I salute you, brother, and urge you to write at once about your health. I've already used up a papyrus-roll in writing to you, and I've had barely one letter back, in which you informed me that I should have received the cloaks and the pig. The pig I didn't receive, but the cloaks I got. Farewell, 4 Parmouthi." Perhaps the writer thought he had been over-curt, for a postscript followed, in a different hand, "I pray for your good health and pleasure, brother. Please receive 4 good lettuces, a bundle of beets, 21 bulbs, 16 (?) greens, and 3 good semi-salted fish. Theon, my brother, salutes you and urges you to come to us from Bacchias. For observe that those coming from there arrive within the second hour. To Apollinarios, his friend."[4]

The last words show that *brother* is here no more than a term of affection or respect, and illustrate the difficulty of being sure what relationship is meant by family-terms. Sister can mean sister or wife—and indeed both sister and wife. And so on. In the next letter, of the late 2nd or early 3rd century, written on a cleaned piece of used papyrus, a sailor seems used as the bearer of articles. "Nikanor to Ninnaros his brother, greeting. Knowing your goodness to all, I now ask you to do me this one service. Please demand from Tithois the sailor a garment consisting of a brown tunic, inside which was a linen cloth, a worn towel, and some wool. All these things were inside the brown tunic, and it was sealed with white clay. And with it send back to me all the other garments, making the total six, to the Oxyrhynchite nome from which I obtained all the aforesaid articles. I therefore write to you, brother, to see if they are in someone else's possession. Please tell me at once about this. I pray for you health." It is not clear if Nikanor suspects the sailor of dishonesty or if he is merely instructing Ninnaros to look out for him.[5] Now to the 3rd century:

(1) Pausanias to his father Ioulios Alexandros, greeting. Before all else I pray for your health and do adoration on your behalf before the gods of the country. Receive from Syros a basket of 80 eggs and a jug with 3 chinikes of mustard and ½ chous of radish oil and a jug with ½ chous of honey and the dagger.

From Agatheneros receive a honeycomb and a pot of 10 cakes and 3 honeysweet garlands; give these to my sister and warmly salute her.

Receive from the letter's bearer a basket holding 40 eggs and a Kanopic basket with 4 pairs of loaves and 6 pairs of dung-celery.

The cobbler says he won't give up either the cloak or the money without Ioustos, for he says: The cloak hasn't yet been redeemed and I've altogether failed to find Philoxenos.

I went to Ammonios' mother and she says: I have no food now and the petitions haven't yet been got ready.

Bring me 2 hides, a wrap, and a small crate . . . five years old, and some shoes. Send me now an open-work covering with a . . .[6]

(2) Demarchos to his sister Taor, very many greetings. I want you to know that you wrote to me about what Agathinos did to me. Well, if I live and come to my homeland I'll have my revenge. And for the moment I ask you strongly, my lady sister, to go to the Street of the Theatre and find out about the stone bowl in the boat and warn them all there, Philkyros and Zosimos, to keep a watch on it in case Agathinos should make up his mind to take the bowl.

Write me a reply through the man from Antinoopolis, about whom I sent to you, and write the list there—that you've received this and that. If the man from Antinoopolis wants anything, provide him with it and come with him to meet Tasoitas. Send your cloak and the jar of pickled fish and two kotylai of good oil. I pray for your health. You'll receive three bags from the man from Antinoopolis who is taking this letter.[7]

(3) Nemesianos to his brother Sarapammon, many greetings. You did well in sending me the file, but you sent one that's too fine. So I send it back to you by Apollon with the pattern so that you may go by it. You write in your letter: I send you a boy's linen-cloth. And I've received nothing. Apollon told me: He gave me nothing. O send you the tripod by Apollon, and if you want anything else reply to me by the same Apollon so that I may send it to you. And do your best to get me the file and send it by Apollon, and look out for a file that files not only wood but iron tools . . . and indicate . . . I pray for your lasting health.[8]

(4) To my brother Diodoros, many greetings from Loukis and Sarapion. Before all else we pray for your prosperity and that of your whole house. Many times in the day we expect you to come to us. It would be kind for you to go to Aretion the baker and obtain from him 4 talants which he had from us when he was at Alexandria. See that you don't neglect this. If you get the 4 talants from him, when you come to us, buy us some provisions for our use and obtain stores and send them to us. You must know that I have written to Aretion to give you the 4 talants.

As you said you'd like . . . , I'll send it to you when it's brought. I got the Knidian jar of vinegar from Ammonas, and I have sent you by him a basket of dainties and a . . . We greet our sister and her daughter Helenous and her daughter. Greet Aphynchis and Techosis and Ptolemaios from us. If you hear that Aretion's going to accuse you about the copper, write to me and I'll send him an addition. I pray for your lasting health.[9]

The writer was not the brother of Diodoros; in the address he merely calls himself a friend. Next we meet a woebegone soldier:

(5) . . . to my dearest mother, many greetings. Above all I pray that you and everyone else are in good health. You'll do well if on getting this letter you send me 200 dr. When my brother Geminos came, I'd only 20 staters left. Now I haven't got one; for I bought a mule-waggon and spent every copper on it. I've written this to you as I want you to know of it. Please send me a woollen cloak, a leather . . . , a pair of girdles and leather coats, olive oil, a basin as you said, . . . , a couple of pillows, and . . . In future, mother, send my monthly allowance more promptly.

When I visited you, you said, "Before you go to your camp, I'm sending one of your brothers," and you sent me nothing but let me go off without a thing . . . not even a thing besides. You didn't say [I'd go] without even a copper. But you sent me like a dog. And father came here and didn't even give me a leather penny.

Everyone laughs at me. "His dad is a soldier. He's given him nothing."

He told me, "If I go home, I'll send you everything." He never sent a thing. Why? Valerius' mother sent him a suit of underwear, a jar of oil, a basket of meats, a garment, and 200 dr. . . . So I beg you, mother, send to me. Don't leave me like this.

36. Nilotic landscape, with Crocodile

I went off on a visit. I borrowed a copper from a comrade and from the adjutant. My brother Gemellos sent me a letter and trousers. I'd like you to know I'm grieved because I didn't go near my brother and he's grieved too for the same reason. He sent me a letter rebuking me for going off somewhere else. I write this so that you may know about it, mother. You'll do well on getting my letter if you send things quickly. Know that my brother Gemellos has gone to . . . Greetings to you all at home. Greeting to Apollinarion, Valerios, and Geminos. Greetings to all who love me.[10]

For the 4th century we may take another letter in which message and family troubles are intermixed. "Ploutarchos to my Lord Brother Theoninos, greeting. I prostrate myself daily on your behalf before the Lord God so that I may find you whole in health. I want to see you. My Lord Brother, whatever commission you laid on me . . . to take to Alexandreia, I haven't hesitated nor again neglected. My father has done many bad things to me and I'm waiting for you to come. Do everything then, My Lord Brother, to get the money when you are coming down, and buy me the prescription and get the variegated tunic from Megale. But only don't delay. I pray for your enduring health." The Lord God might here be the Christian God, but could also be Sarapis.[11] Though this book is not much concerned with the Byzantine period we may end this section with two letters from it, which show the same concern about the transmission of articles. A Christian letter of the late 4th or early 5th century mentions parchment:

To my most Beloved Brother Seras from Amyntas, greeting. As I have just been given a favourable opportunity by a man who is going to you, I thought I must send you a greeting, while praying at the same time to the Divine Providence of God that He will ever preserve you to us.

Receive through the bearer of this letter of mine the skin of parchments in 25 quaternions to the value of 14 talants of silver, and if there is any need for me, besides these, to take from those others, answer me and I'll do it. You must know, if you wish, that their value is 6 talants, and that after the law-court I was encouraged to send those few small commissions.

Receive through Api the tunic and the cloak, and let him clean

them at once. Aphyngios the fuller has the other cloak. Greet Ammonios
and his sisters. Aurelios sends you many salutations, also to my Lord
and Brother Herminos and Leon and to all our friends in peace.
[I pray for your preservation] in health and happiness in the Lord
God.[12]

And this, from the 7th century, deals mainly with food-supplies.
It is written by Rheme, perhaps a trainer, certainly connected with
a stable; and we feel behind it the large estates, more or less self-
sufficient, of the new system.

Before all things I salute you and greet your Godguarded Lordship.
Victor, who has gone off, also brought 220 art. barley and 72 art.
wheat and 297 kouri of wine and 12 sheep—poor ones: a man can't
eat them—and 6 sucking-pigs and 12 cambric garments and 39 fowls
and 6 solidi and 2 flagons of radish-oil and 5 sectarii of Spanish oil
and 200 eggs and $2\frac{1}{2}$ kouri of honey and a little pepper.

And Victor said, "I can't stay here," and because of his saying,
"I can't stay," see, I've sent him to you with your horses that are here.
One of them, look you, died 4 months ago, and another, has been
quite unable to work for just a month today. And look now, I have
sent the said Victor so that he may give it to the . . . and bring it here
with 30 more art. barley: these you ought to send, and if I need more
chopt hay I'll write to you about that too.

The 6 solidi you sent for the pay of the grooms and cost of camel-
freight and other things and on account of the cabbage for the
countryhouse, will, I know, not be enough. If then I don't write to
you and your lads come, don't listen to them or send anything whatever there till, as aforesaid, I write to you. For barley and wine and
poultry and all the expenses I know that the money will suffice for
the 2 months, except for hay and chaff and the grooms' pay I don't
know if it will suffice or not.

And I have sworn Victor to come up and come to me; and as for
the purgative I got it and thank you for it. The sum for expenses
which you sent here, I took half of it for the posting-station, and the
other half I paid in at the harbour till the rising of the water, and I'll
take it up to the monastery by boat.

If you've sent anything for the posting-station, set out in a single
account details of what you sent, and send it to me, as the store-
keeper at Herakleopolis brought with him the expenses for 4 months
and stole them and left only the expenses of 2 months. Unless I write

to you and seal my letter, send nothing more, if you will trust me in this matter. And write to me how you are.[13]

These letters then give us some idea of the sort of objects which in small parcels, boxes, or pots went up and down the Nile. The preponderance of food, clothing, and textile materials is fairly typical. The mixture of food and family problems is pleasantly illustrated by a short letter of Apia in the 2nd century to her "brother Zoilos". She writes: "Don't let Sarapion idle and roam about, but throw him into some trade. I have baked bread. I'll send you some loaves by Ptolemaios when he may take them."[14] In two lists of the 5th or early 6th century (each headed: List of Articles placed in the Boat) the things are almost all food but hardly the sort of thing to be taken along for meals on the voyage:

3 wallets, 1 cupboard-door, 1 double bag, 1 mat of bread, 4 jars of wine, 2 jars of fish sealed, 2 jars of meat sealed, 1 pot of preserves sealed, 1 flask of . . . sealed. I flash of annise sealed, 1 pot from the kiln, 1 pot of garlic sauce, 1 . . . , 1 oilflask, 3 saucepans, a basket with 2 pots of cheese, 1 can of oil sealed, 5 wooden locks with the keys, 2 young wild geese, 2 fowls, 1 silver chest, 1 calf wineskin, 1 pot of cummin.

3 Askalon jars of wine, 1 jar of soap, 2 jars of cedar oil, 1 flagon of sauce, 1 vessel of Spanish oil, 7 Gazz jars of pickled fish, 5 empty vessels, 1 empty Askalon jar, 1 empty Gaza jar, 1 empty flagon, 1 basket of papyrus, 1 rug.[15]

We have already encountered various details about comings and goings. Other documents give us further pictures of the arrangements being made, the problems of travelling, the uncertainties. In a Ramessid papyrus of magico-medical recipes we find medicine against travel-weariness in a group also dealing with difficulties in urinating or in weaning a child, trouble over mother's milk, a child's thirst or a blow in the eyes.[16] A charm "to ensure the safety of anyone travelling by water" had to be recited over an egg-shaped lump of clay which was then thrown into the Nile.

A water spell . . . a veritable Mystery of the House of Life. "Egg of the water which is poured out upon the earth. Existing One of the Eight

I

Gods of Khmenu [Hermopolis], Chief of the Heavens, Chief in the Tuat, Dweller in the Nest, President of Merdjesdjes. I have come forth with you from the water. I have risen up with you from out of the divine Nest. I am the god Min of Koptos."

This spell shall be recited over an egg of dung, which shall be placed in the hand of a man in the bows of a boat. If anything appear on the water, cast the egg on the water.

The "anything" is probably a crocodile, but the spell is conveniently vague, so as to cover all water-terrors. Another runs

"I am the Chosen One of millions of years, he who comes forth from the Tuat, whose name is not known. If his divine name be cut on the riverbank, it will slice it away; and if on the earth, it will cause a fire to break out. I am the god Shu in the form of Re. I have my seat in the Eye of the Father. If that which is on the water opens its mouth or works violence with its arms, I will cause the earth to fall into the water. The south shall become the north, and the earth likewise."

Recite the above four times and [put] in the hand of the man a drawing of the Udjat [Re's Eye] with the figure of the god An-her on it.

To stop the attack of a water-monster the man stood before the cabin with a hard egg in his hand and declared, "O Egg of the Water that has been spread over the earth, essence of the divine apes, the great one in the heaven above and in the earth below, who dwell in the nests that are in the waters, I have come forth with you from the water, I have been with you in your nest, I am Amsu of Koptos, I am Amsu, Lord of Kebu". He would then appear in the water in the form of the god Amsu, and the monster would flee. Another spell against water-monsters runs:

Hail, Lord of the Gods! Drive away from me the lions of the land of Meru [?Meroe] and the crocodiles that come forth from the river and the bite of all poisonous reptiles that crawl forth from their holes. Get you back, O crocodile Mak, you son of Seth! Don't move by means of your tail! Don't work your legs and feet! Don't open your mouth! Let the water before you turn into a consuming fire, O you whom the Thirty-seven Gods made, and the serpent of Re put in chains, O you who were fettered with links of iron before the boat of Re! Get back, crocodile Mak, you son of Seth!

These words were to be recited over a figure of Amun painted on clay; the god was to have four ram-heads on one neck, under his feet was to be a figure of the crocodile Mak, and left and right of him were to be dogheaded apes (the dawn-spirits who sang hymns of praise as Re daily rose). In the Theban Recension of the Book of the Dead the deadman had to repulse a crocodile that came to take from him his magical words (vignette: the deadman spearing four crocodiles) but he also sought in his transformations to become a crocodile as well as a bennu-bird (phoenix), heron, ram, swallow, serpent. The scribe Ani had his chapter on becoming a crocodile (the god of Sekhem), as well as the Great Fish of Kamur, so that he might traverse waters unafraid. However, apart from crocodiles, the Nile-journeys could be tiring and anxious. In the early 2nd century we find a man complaining. "The voyage past the Antaiopolite nome is most troublesome; daily I am burdened on account of it and I am extremely worn out with the business."[17]

In A.D. 30 a woman Zois wrote to her brother Ischyrion, "No one has brought me a letter about the bread but if you send a letter by Kollouthos, an artaba will come to you at once. If you want to go off to Alexandreia, Apollos son of Theon is leaving tomorrow. Goodbye."[18] About the same time Hermogenes wrote to his brother Ischyras, "Please put on board for me 200 empty jars, as I asked you before. You have the 16 dr. of silver by Saras, and I have given Hermas 12 dr. to give you. If you specially require 2 pieces of wood to bring down to me the wheel of the machine, they will be brought to you by . . . For the rest, goodbye."[19]

In the 2nd century we find a man held up by the delay of the ship with the corn-supply going down to Alexandreia for the government. Perhaps steps were taken to keep the river clear for such important flotillas. "Sopatros to his sister, very many greetings. Not yet up to today has the ship of the annona sailed and enabled us to sail too, and what's more, there's nothing for me to do here. They say that on the 15th we hope to get away with god's help. I pray you and the children are well." The sister here was perhaps his wife.[20]

In the 3rd century Eutycheis wrote to her mother: "I want

you to know that from the 30th Tybi I arrived at Tyrannis and can't find the means of reaching you. The camel drivers refuse to go to Oxyrhyncheite. Not only that. I went to Antinoopolis to find a boat and couldn't." Now she was held up till she found the boat and could sail. Meanwhile she had run out of moneys and borrowed, and she asked her mother to pay the sum to the bearers of the letter.[21]

37. Nilotic landscape, Crocodile seizing victim

Letters made arrangements for meetings. "Damas, assistant, to Artemidora my sister, greeting. Before all else I make daily supplication for you. Please come up to the metropolis at the New Year, as I am also coming up to the city. Salute your mother and your father. I pray your health is good" (late 2nd century).[22] In the 3rd century we find the river-boat a bad place for a young girl. Probably she was scared of going overboard or sinking rather than of the rough company; the boat was the small kind, *pakton*. "To the Most Honourable Apollon from Didymos, greeting. The total yield of Dionysos' vineyards from the 6 presses is 5,132-chor measures, 121 doubles, 37 two-chor measures, and foreign vessels to the number of 8: into which were bottled a total of 211 measures, and for the distribution a total of 123 measures: making for the whole vineyard 5,464. I have sent the animals with the carpenter and Sotas and the builder, who has quitted today the burning of the baked bricks—having given him his pay as the lady wrote to me. Think about the way we're to come, if you don't want us to come on the animals here. If we find a boat on which the little girl can embark, we'll come that way. But if you want to send the animals for us to Lagas' places, so that we may arrive after travelling by night, send them. At any rate don't leave us the small boat I sent with Isidoros, for the little one didn't dare to embark on that. I pray for your health."[23]

We meet letters of introduction or recommendation. In A.D. 6 a note introduces Apollonios to Sarapion, who is described as strategos and gymnasiarch: an odd association of ranks, for it was Roman policy to see that the strategoi did not hold office in a nome where they owned property. The explanation, however, may be that Sarapion was gymnasiarch in another nome than that where he held office, that the title was merely honorific, or that at this early date in the Roman epoch the rule had not yet been established.[24] In A.D. 16 Theon wrote to his brother Herakleides, royal-clerk of the Oxyrhynchite and Kynopolite nomes: "Hermophilos the bearer of this letter is [friend or relative] of . . . erios, and asked me to write to you. Hermopholis says he has business at Kerkemounis. If you please then, help him along as is right. For the rest take care of your health."[25] The writer of a 2nd-century letter observes, "Very many thanks, brother, for your care of me. Your recommendation was extremely useful."[26] In the next century:

Aristandros to his son Apion, greeting. Theon our son is coming to you on his way to the city of Nikias through an urgent unfinished negotiation of which you have perhaps been long aware from his father. I think that while he was still alive he wrote to you about it. Indeed you love him both for his own sake and for his father's memory. But I know this letter of mine will also be a great help to him if he wants anything with Apion, royal scribe of the Prosopite nome, or anyone else, if you will ask them and not delay in writing to them. I pray for your lasting health and happiness, my son.[27]

Apion is basiliko-grammateus of the Letopolite nome. He is the son of the writer, but Theon, called "our son" is only a friend since we learn that his father is dead. Another example of the use of family terms to convey friendship.

How useful such a letter could be, at least in later times, is brought out by a note of the 6th–7th century. "See, I have sent the son of Abraham, of Kl . . . , with his memoranda. Will your True Brotherliness make up his account and discharge him speedily without molestation, and not permit the secretaries or anyone else to wrong him."

A Christian letter of the 4th century shows a rhetorical form of introduction:

To my Lord Brother S[arapion] Paulos [wishes] welldoing. A man who has acquired a mirror or holds in his hand something of that kind in which faces are shown, does not need anyone to inform him or to testify as to the character that lies upon him, and his complexion, and his looks, how they are. He himself has become a witness by himself and can speak about his own likeness. And when someone speaks to him or explains about his beauty and the comeliness about him, he does not then believe. For he is not like the rest who are in ignorance and who stand far from the mirror that sets out the likenesses of all.

And it is the same with you, my good friend. As through a mirror you have beheld my implanted affection and love for you eternally renewed.

Now, as to the acquaintances of ours who are bringing down the letter to you, I [need to] write, [in view of] your friendship and affection for all, especially for our Brethren. So welcome them in love as friends: they are not catechumens but belong to the group of Ision and Nikolaos—and if you do anything for them, you have done it for me. All the Brethren here salute you. Greet also the Brethren with you, elect and catechumens alike. I pray you may be strong. And if you can write to the others about [them], don't hesitate, so that they may receive them in each place.[28]

Catechumens (converts not yet baptised) were not allowed to remain in the Mass of the Faithful. The special group of Ision and Nikolaos may be monks, but the term used, *idioi*, means simply "one's own" and can have a family, partisan, or sectarian sense. It might merely mean the *pistoi*, the faithful who have been baptised.[29]

Paulos was well schooled in the rhetoric of the day. The proem of an artistically conceived letter aimed at winning the recipient's interest and goodwill by compliment and by an adroit turning of some commonplace so that it was made applicable to the circumstances and the person addressed. Theorists mainly advised the use of colloquial speech, but practitioners usually preferred display of some sort. By the 4th century some literary groups considered the letter a form of art. Gregory Naziansen in his thirty commendatory letters keeps to a set pattern: preamble (compliment or effort to gain goodwill), introduction of person bearing the letter (with various praises), and something likely to win the recipient into doing as asked. The first section was given the most variation or elaboration, especially in accordance with the recipient's social position; it might almost fade out in addressing someone of low rank. The only one of Gregory's letters close to that of Paulos is addressed to the Prefect of Constantinople in A.D. 369. When we add that the cultural level of the Christian clergy in 4th-century Egypt was very low, it seems that Paulos and Sarapion (if that is the name) were men of considerable importance and education in the Christian community. The stress on welcoming the bearers "as friends" suggests that enemies were about and that there was trouble in the Church. The letter thus no doubt belongs to one of the moments when the Meletian and Arian controversies were rending the groups of the faithful. Paulos is letting S. know that the letter-bearers are on the same side of the conflict as they both are.[30]

Mirror-imagery in Greek literature goes back to Alkaios and Pindar. It is common in Hellenistic times and is used mostly in one of three ways: the mirror's clean pure surface symbolises the soul's purity; the reflection expresses the Sokratic injunction "know yourself"; it represents the mere image of reality, not the inner or ultimate truth of things. The second usage was common among Cynic and Stoic preachers and was given a more mystical turn in the neoplatonic tradition; it is found several times in Philon. The third usage also appears in Cynico-Stoic diatribe as well as in Philon, Seneca, Plutarch, Hermetic writings.[21] In *On the Migration of Abraham* Philon provides an example of the mirror rather surprisingly used to express essential truth:

[in deep slumber] the mind, roaming abroad and straying past the confines of the outward senses and of all the other bodily affections, begins to associate with itself, looking on truth as at a mirror and discarding all the imaginations contracted from the outward sense, becomes inspired with the truest divination of the future by means of dreams.[32]

We may perhaps recall too the Jewish tradition of the heavens "strong as a molten mirror", with open windows through which the rain might pour—later Rabbinic speculations said holes were made by the extraction of two stars.[33]

Here is a letter of the late 3rd century making arrangements for a meeting. The woman addressed seems the man's wife, perhaps also his sister:

. . . that I may not trouble him about provisions, as I wrote to him that I was coming by the 30th. Otherwise arrange with him for his coming by the 13th Phamenoth. As for the deposit of corn, don't neglect worrying Thonios. As for my tools, tell the men I am sending the expenses for them, and leave the tools with them till I send the expenses.

When you come, bring the old cushion that's up in the dining-room. Salute my children—avert the evil-eye from them!—and our mother and your sister and all our friends.[34]

Alexandreia was often the place to which trips were made, some-times for personal reasons, often in connection with legal or administrative matters. The writer of the following letter, dated 2 B.C., was in a not-unusual net of worries:

I want you and the [oikonomos?] of Caesar to read this, for though I (?) have had trouble with others, you must help him for our friend-ship's sake. I am thoroughly upset over Helenos' loss of the money.

When Damas arrived in Alexandreia we went to Epaphroditos and found that he hadn't received or paid out anything. So I want you to know that I've given him instructions to go to Takona for the rents, and now I've sent him off to collect them all have put the management of the whole thing in his hands. Whatever service he may need from you, stand by him and he'll be as amenable on everything for you as much as for me.

Owing to my worries I was unable to meet Apollonios the Libyan to tell him about this. Write to me yourself about anything you want, and I'll see to it without delay. Damas has agreed with me in all matters. It's good for him to go quickly; for he'll instruct you. Take care to keep healthy. Look after all your household. Goodbye.[35]

In A.D. 104 Theonas wrote to Apion, a pastophoros of the temple of Isis at Oxyrhynchos. "I want you to know that as soon as I arrived in Alexandreia I at once attended to the matter about which you asked me. I found the man prospering on the whole.

Greet all my friends. I send you the actual proclamation of the Prefect so that you may hurry and do what concerns you. Goodbye."[36]

In the 3rd century a man wrote to his children that he had arrived at Schedia, the point on the Nile where boats turned westward for Kanopos and Alexandreia. (Strabon tells us: "Schedia is four schoinoi distant from Alexandreia; it is a settlement of the city and contains the station for the cabin-boats on which the prefects sail to Upper Egypt. And at Schedia is also the station for paying duty on goods brought down from above or below it; and for this purpose a *schedia* (raft or pontoon-bridge) has been laid across the river, from which the place gets

38. Rhinoceros and Palm

its name.") "Herakleios to Theon and Sarapias his darling sons, greeting. I write this letter first, second and third to you as I come into Schedia at midnight so that you may be cheerful at nothing going wrong with us. The winds with a wild bluster . . . Apion, Longeinos, Agathos, Philargyros send you good wishes. I pray you're all in good health and doing well."[37]

The western branch of the Nile flowing from Schedia to Alexandreia was called the channel of the Good Spirit. It was not used for commercial purposes in the Roman period, but in A.D. 80–1 we find it being cleared. "When G. Tettius Africanus Cassianus Priscus was Prefect", an inscription tells us, "the river called the Good Spirit was dug and restored to its ancient form in length, breadth and depth to the rock, and fourteen engraved stones were set up on each bank." The purpose was perhaps to supply Alexandreia with water or to help in irrigation.[38]

In the same century, probably the later decades, a woman from Philadelpheia in the Fayum, visited Alexandreia; two of the persons she mentions have Semitic names. "Isis to Thermouthion her mother, very many greetings. I make daily supplication for you before the Lord Sarapis and his Fellow-gods. I want you to know I've arrived safe and sound in Alexandreia in four days. I send my best wishes to my sister and the children and Elouath and his wife and Dioskorous and her husband and children and Tamalis and her husband and son and Heron and Ammonarion and her children and husband and Sanpat and her children. And if Apion wants to join the army, let him come. Everyone's becoming a soldier. I pray for the health of all your household."[39]

Finally here are two letters of the Byzantine period about journeys to and from Alexandreia. In 580 a banker paid a sum of money to a man, who wrote, "This sum I am prepared to take to Alexandreia, apart from accidents sent by Heaven and dangers and mischance by River, and pay it to Ioannes and Symeonios the most illustrious money-changers and bring a written receipt from the illustrious agent Theodoros." The document has been crossed out so that we know the receipt was duly brought. And in 612 Makarios, banker, paid 3 solidi less 12 carats, to some boatmen who were to go to Alexandreia and convey an advocate back to Oxyrhynchos.[40]

8

More People on the Nile

WE have seen how anxieties keep intruding into the messages.
Here are some more letters which give us insight into the emotions
that stirred the men and women moving up and down the Nile
in these years. Theon, in the first century, wrote to his "sister
Sarapous". "Above all else as I bade you do when I was with you,
look after yourself so that you'll keep in good health for me, and
don't worry about me because I'm away from home, for I'm
well acquainted with these parts and am not a stranger here."
The letter here breaks off but he seems to go on with some remark
about the possibility of his soldiering.[1]

An interesting group of letters in Latin and Greek of the early
2nd century reveals the preoccupations of a family. The main
writer is Claudius Terentianus; but we also have a letter from his
father and two by the latter's sister, and there are glimpses of
other members of the family. They seem all to live near or in
Alexandreia, though only one letter is definitely from that city.
Business-matters come up, but the main connections seem to be
military. The father, Claudius Tiberianus, has the military title of
speculator, which, under the empire, could designate special
adjutants, messengers, and the like. Terentianus himself is much
involved with army-activities and gives us a glimpse of some
popular outburst which he was concerned in putting down.[2]

Claudius Tiberianus to Longinus Priscus, his Lord and Patron, very
many greetings. You know quite well in what way I left you . . .
to come to you soon . . . . When I brought to Alexandreia with me . . .
I found that the boats had already gone off and I didn't sell it.

Know, my Lord, that I am in Alexandreia. If I find an opportunity,
I hope to come to you soon. I beg you, my Lord, deign to write to

me where you are stationed, so that I may be able to find you there quickly and bring the . . . by boat.

As I was about to send you the letter that Sempronius Claudius the frumentarius [commisariat officer] will deliver to you, I found at his place, by dint of thought and good luck, also the two letters that you want, and I send them to you under seal. I beg you, my Lord . . . I prepared . . . wooden staves . . . Claudius my son sends his salutations to you.

In the next letter a family-tragedy is confusedly set down by Tabitheus. "Before all else I pray for your health and make obeisance for you in the presence of Our Lord Souchos. I was happy that you sent my son so that I might greet him. But you have not. . . . For Satorneilos has not found out what I did for him. I bought 3 mnai of linen and sent them. Don't blame me if you didn't deliver them to Metellus the soldier. I want you to write about a friend; deliver them to him at once. I was annoyed a lot. This year I was able to send you the robe; I didn't send it last year but I sent and sold them to Kabin the attendant. When I went down from our home at Tonis and came to Satorneilos' lodging and saw our things—may the evil-eye not touch them—I didn't approve that he, my son, should trust Menas; and after he had killed him he told me not to be distressed. I told Satorneilos that I was sleepless from worry. As you caused me damage to the extent of 1,200 dr., let them go as my son's ransom."

Thus, after a grumbling account of business-matters, she slides into the disaster which one would expect to be the first thing to be described. She had disapproved of Menas as steward during her last visit to her son Satorneilos. Since then, Menas had exposed his unreliability by appropriating for himself and his family the rations meant for the son. The latter heard and in a fit of fury killed Menas. Tabitheus continues:

"And I went down to Alexandreia with my son. For this reason a madness took hold of him, as he didn't approve that he [Menas] and his family should consume the rations. If god wills and you receive the rations that I put up for you, do not you also . . . then. As to last year's rations, I didn't prepare them . . . prepared them last year. I sent them from Alexandreia as late as the second shipment upstream. And he became ill. I was tortured

39. Landscape, with Fisher

with the grief that he caused me, but I was utterly happy that he remained alive. I have consistently urged him: Take a taste of Alexandreia. And he says to me: I don't want to. I thank the gods that he is like you; no one can mock him. Salute all your people, each by name. How much damage have I incurred this last year, on account of Satorneilos. He wasn't liable for it, nor was I, but I have incurred damage on every side. Goodbye."

The way she jumps from one subject to another may derive from her distraction; but she seems more concerned about her losses than about the troubles of her son. For the murdered man she has no thought at all, and there is no indication of any process against Satorneilos for the killing. The law in the Roman and Byzantine periods, as well as the Ptolemaic, distinguished between premeditated and unpremeditated killing, violence in the act, and poisoning. Robbery with murder was not rated as a special kind of homicide. We find considerations of motive intruding more and more; and by the 4th–5th centuries *eros*, which deranged the murderer to the point of mania, was taken as an extenuating circumstance in the practice of the governor's court. Perhaps already in the 2nd century the question of mania was coming up; for we find it stressed in our letter. The right of prosecution, also a duty, rested in principle with the victim's family. Members of the family acted as accusers—though in certain cases, such as the murder of officials, the state intervened. In the 2nd century homicide was punished by voluntary exile; but in the 4th century, after the triumph of Christianity, common homicide was punished by crucifixion and killing in a rage by *damnatio in metallum*, condemnation to the mines. In the 2nd century we find the murderer's property confiscated, apart from a tenth that was reserved for his children.[3]

From the silence of Tabitheus about any legal action and her remark about her son's ransom, it seems that the family of Menas were bought off and that they kept silent. Perhaps, it has been suggested, the failure of the Gnomon, which deals with various situations involving confiscation of property, to recognise a customary procedure of compensating a murdered man's family, may account for the dearth of murder-cases in the papyri. Generally a private settlement was more advantageous for both parties than a public prosecution.

The reference to rations shows the military status of Tiberianus and Satorneilos. Both seem to get their monthly rations from Tabitheus. Other texts show soldiers dependent on their families for these rations and for supplies of clothing. Tabitheus sent linen to her son (though Tiberianus neglected to deliver it), and a robe or gown to her brother.[4]

Next comes another letter, apparently from Tabitheus to her brother. There are grumblings in it, but not the distractions of the previous letter. She seems writing in late June or in July:

[When I heard] you had come to Alexandreia, I was happy together with my whole family. [Please write in answer] that you are at once coming to us, since your son (?) . . . waited for you during your absence till today. And to the present moment we wait for you [daily] together with the children. I therefore ask you to come to us immediately: we will make obeisance together with the children if you come up. . . .

Your daughter Segathis is now serving me. She is prudent and . . . capable. She sent your son (?) Isidoros to you so that [he might take you] your belts [in the company] of soldiers, because she remains in attendance on me for fear [the flood] may come with great [violence]—

as I cannot leave my house on account of . . . Isidoros and Segathis
salute you, and we salute . . . the children.

I received a letter from Claudius your son [in which I learned] that
as soon as you come to me [you will take] me to Alexandreia along
with Segathis. . . . Up to the present moment you have not been
willing to come.[5]

Next comes a letter from Terentianus, his son, who is also in the
army and takes part in putting down some riot or revolt of the
Alexandrians.

Claudius Terentianus to Claudius Tiberianus his Father and Lord,
very many greetings. Before all else I pray for your health and success,
which are my wish, and I make obeisance for you . . . daily in the
presence of Our Lord Sarapis and the Gods sharing his Temple.

I got your letter, from which I learned you also sailed up in the boat
you found going to the Arsinoite nome. I want you to know that I
went at your request to register the document and was at a loss since
I needed the person in whose name it was drawn so that he might
record it. For without him I'm unable to register it.

I also looked up Papirius Apollinarius and told him what I had heard
from the notaries, and he said to me: Let it go until he is able to come
down. Inasmuch as you are neglecting your affairs by staying in the
country, come to Alexandreia since I have been waiting in Alexandreia.

As his exasperation grows, Terentianus forgets the tone of
extreme respect with which he began, and in this is not unlike
many others of these letter-writers. He goes on:

Having gone up into the country, you are neglecting them totally;
but even when you were here, you neglected to settle them. . . . If
you sail down, they can be despatched. You write to me that you have
sent . . . through Anoubion; but he doesn't know that you wrote to
me here and has given me nothing. From the day that you went
upcountry, until today, for the first time, I have received the letter
and the basket through Aurelios; and please take the trouble to write
to Anoubion so that he won't disregard me . . . and I ask you if you
are able to send me some sandals without delay, as I now derive much
benefit from them.

For you know we are working hard now, in view of the fact we're
suppressing the uproar and anarchy of the city.

You'll do well to send down to me . . . and to Gemellus three . . . I
want you to know that after the above had been written to you, the

basket was brought to me . . . by Anoubion's father, and now at last I have it.

Since I've found no one to send because I'm ill, you will then do well to conclude your business quickly and sail down to me. For the illness at the moment is no laughing matter, and it's even necessary for me to be fed by someone else, as you will hear when you come to the city.

Isidoros and Sempronius and all who love you truly and completely send many salutations to you as well as to Zotike, whom you will bring down with you when you come because you know that we are going to need her here.

Salute all your friends, each by name. I pray for your health through many years.

He writes again to Tiberianus, who has in the meantime come to Alexandreia and gone off again. The themes of tumult and illness recur. The letter opens with the formulas wishing the recipient good health and adds: "I myself am in good health and make obeisance," etc., but at once goes on, "I want you to know that although I was ordered to go out on duty in your absence I was quite unable to go down to Neopolis.[6] For it was at that time that . . . so violent an attack of illness and for five days couldn't write you anything, not to mention going up to you. Nor was anyone of us able to pass the camp-gate. I give thanks to the god that after the five days . . . so great a disturbance, in which I was

40. Nilotic views

wounded . . . he found the transgressors of the laws. . . . I have recovered from my illness, and I am the more grateful to you for coming down. . . ."

Again we find him writing, "I marvel that after you sailed upcountry you did not write to me about your wellbeing, but till today I have been anxious because you were indisposed when you left me. You will deliver to Tabitheus the letter of the dioiketes for the strategos, and let her make every effort to deliver it to the strategos at once, so that he may reply quickly to what has been written to him. I also was intending to sail up, but till today I haven't yet disposed of my affairs, which remain unsettled. And if you know about Nemesianos, where he is staying, write to me, as we are anxious about him too."

What the legal matter is that worries him is not clarified, but it seems connected with the document he earlier mentioned. For the next letter returns to a similar difficulty. "I want you to know, my Lord Father, that from the day you left me till today, I have kept close to Aemilius, demanding an explanation about those matters, and he protested that that man's chirographs are different and can't be registered without the consent of the archidikastes. . . . I therefore gave him . . . another 32 dr. At that he said: If you blame me—either you or your father—take back from me . . . which you gave me. For I submitted another petition to the archidikastes through the same channel that he had used for submitting his petition. So I hope soon to get them from him duly completed and to forward. . . ."

Finally Terentianus writes to his sister, Tasoucharion: "Receive a basket from the man who delivers this letter to you, and write back to me what you find in it. And I have sent another basket by Valerius the goldsmith. Please write to me when you get it, about both your health and anything you need. For I hope soon to go upcountry to you. Do everything possible to provide for me two kerania, of the largest size, of olyra and an art. of radish oil. I sent you the marjoram that gives out the oil. And if you received from Ptolemaios what I wrote . . . write to me. . . . Our children salute you. . . . Salute . . . with all his house, and Ptolemaios the son of Arios together with their wives and children. Salute Ptolemaios and Tiberinus and . . . to send a fresh

K

bundle of asparagus by Melas, since we ask it of you, further
send one bundle (?). All the persons in the house salute you, each
by name. I sent you papyrus so that you might be able to write
to me about your health. I pray you may always be well."

Illness was one of the themes in the last batch of letters. In the
2nd century Apollinarios spent some days with Theon; then, on
leaving, he fell ill. Theon wrote, "If we hadn't learned that with
the help of the gods you're now well after what you write you
went through, we'd have left everything and rushed to you. For
nothing is more precious than you are to us. But even though
we're here, we are praying for your health. You deserve it.
Alexandros the builder came straightway after your departure;
and when he was told you had stayed several days with us on
his account—so you might spend some time with him—he was
miserable at missing you. He kept on mentioning you all the
while in our presence. . . . Let me then know the price, so I may
pay it over to your brother Apollonios. All the men of our household and the women salute you. I pray for your health, most
esteemed. . . ."[7]

Strained family-relations at a distance were liable to cause much
anxiety. A correspondent, probably a woman, wrote to Kopres in
the 2nd century: "I know your hot temper and your wife
inflames you, declaring hourly that I give you nothing. But when
I came up, I gave you some small change, as I'd got my allowances that very month and I'd had nothing to give you before.
I'm keeping nothing back from you. I give you credit in everything. Yet your wife says: She credits you in nothing. . . ." On
the margin is added: "Nobody can love you, for she moulds you
to her own disposition."[8] Valerius Gemellus, a soldier stationed
at Koptos, wrote to his brother, "Before all else I pray for your
health and make obeisance for you unceasingly in the presence of
the Hair at Koptos. I ask you to write to me and the gods ask
the same thing of you. Even if I do not know . . . , you ought to
grant me this one favour. In response to my appeal, brother, be
reconciled with me so that I may enjoy your confidence while I
am in the service. Besides, you have not even regarded me as is
right with a brother, have you now? from the time I left home.

But I regarded you in the manner of a pious brother, as I do Sarapis. Above all, there is no other hope like the candid intercourse of brothers and our own people. Do not fail to inform me about your wellbeing, and do persuade mother. (2nd hand) Please write to me as I asked you. I pray for your health. Before all else I give thanks to my Lady Sister Thermoutharion in the presence of the gods and . . . your wellbeing. Salute. . . ."[9]

From such letters as this last we gain a feeling of the strength of family feeling among the people, even if at the same time there is continual conflict and arguments about property. This Gemellus seems piously inclined, unless he keeps drawing in the gods only to give force to his entreaties. Isis was Isis Trichomatos at Koptos. Here she learned of the death of Osiris and cut off her hair in mourning. At this late period her Hair was exhibited as a holy relic.[10] In passages such as the following, from the funerary papyrus of Ani, the Hair has a protective role and at the same time is something that is to be shorn—perhaps a part sacrificed for the sake of the whole:

Let the Osiris Ani be safely guarded. He is Isis and he is found with her hair spread over him; it is shaken out over his brow. He was conceived by Isis and engendered by Nephthys, and they have cut away from him the thing that should be cut from him.

Fear follows after you, terror is about your arms. You have been embraced for millions of years by arms; mortals go round about you. You smite down the mediators of your foes and you seize the arms of the powers of darkness. Your two sisters are given to you for your delight [Isis and Nephthys]. You have created what is in Kher-aha and what is in Anu [Heliopolis]. Every god fears you, for you are exceedingly great and terrible, you avenge every god on the man who curses him, and you shoot arrows at him. You live as you will. You are Uatchet, the Lady of Flame, evil befalls those who set themselves up against you.

What is this? "Hidden in form, given of Menhu" is the name of the tomb. "He who sees what is on his hand" is the name of Qerau, or, as others saw, it is the name of the Block.

Now, he whose mouth shines and whose head moves is the penis of Osiris, but others say it is the penis of Re. "You spread your hair and I shake it out over his brow," is said of Isis, who hides in her hair and draws it round about her.[11]

But by the time of our papyrus-letter the Hair of Koptos has doubt-less only a vague though strong aura of holiness. Loukian, the sceptic, remarks that the Tegeans display "the Skin of the Kalydonian Boar, the Thebans the Bones of Geryon, and the Memphites the Tresses of Isis".

Another letter of the same century, in clumsy script, fails to make clear what the trouble is. "Tarem . . . to Chairemon her father." After the usual preface she says, "Gonas is truly sorry for what he did. He is not the only one to whom such a thing has happened. I give thanks to the gods that his mental and bodily health have come back to him. Don't bother to come up to us for the botheration is not slight. If I get the chance, I'll take Persion and go down the river with him. I salute my sisters and their children and their husbands and my brother and Panisneus salutes you all one by one and Ancharenis my son salutes you." Panisneus seems the writer's husband, but who Gonas was is not clear—perhaps another brother of hers.[12]

Anxiety was naturally exacerbated if an absent one had gone into an area where some epidemic was raging. In the late 2nd or early 3rd century Taeis wrote to her son: ". . . since then there have been many deaths in Alexandreia. Just as you were my guide while you were with us, now again may you guide me although you are absent. I want you to know that we are carrying out fertilisation of the dates that are in Apate. If Taseus follows my instructions, she should receive from me a basket of . . . I have paid all the public dues, thanks to you. The little papyrus that you told me not to give to anyone, I didn't give away. You yourself, I said, will give it." Apparently plague had been active at Alexandreia.[13]

Family worries which include anxiety over a plague outburst make up a letter of the 3rd century from Pausanias to his brother Herakleides. "I think my brother Sarapammon has told you the cause of my going down to Alexandreia, and I've previously written to you about the little Pausanias becoming a legionary soldier. As, however, he no longer wanted to join a legion but a cavalry-squadron, on learning this I was obliged to go down to him, though I didn't want to. So, after many entreaties from his mother and sister to transfer him to Koptos, I went down to

Alexandreia and tried out many methods till at last he was transferred to the squadron at Koptos. I desired then to pay you a visit on the upward voyage, but we were limited by the furlough granted to the boy by the most illustrious Prefect, and for this reason I couldn't visit you. If the gods will, I'll then try to get to you for the festival of Amesysia. Please then, brother, see to the mortgage-deed, so that it can be prepared in the usual way. I urge you, brother, to write to me about your safety, as I heard at Antinoopolis that there has been plague in your [Oxyrhynchite] neighbourhood. Then don't neglect this, so I may rest assured about you. Many salutations to my Lady Mother and my sister and our children, from whom avert the evil eye. Pausanias salutes you. I pray for the health of you and all your household."[14]

The Koptos squadron was no doubt that to which Gemellus with the cult of Isis' Hair belonged. Before the 3rd century a transfer from legion to cavalry-unit would have involved a question of status; for a legionary gained Roman citizenship on enlistment, unlike the recruit in an auxiliary corps. But Pausanias was no doubt enlisting after the Constitutio Antoniniana had given citizenship to all free persons in the empire, and so any problems of status would have been wiped out.

Sudden deaths could create problems. In the late 6th century we meet a harried tax-collector in the Herakleopolite nome. "On reaching Gessias I found that only four gold pieces had been collected and I may be forced on my way back from Herakleopolis to spend three days here until the money has been raised. For, as I learned, Philoxenos, who has come from Herakleopolis, has been only two days collecting, and, as your Excellence knows, the number of solidi required is considerable and it is necessary for everyone to make up his accounts. It is truly a labour to

41. Country scene

grapple with the accounts as the man who was from the beginning in control of the business has died and God knows I have been at a total loss, for I haven't got the money nor have I been able to stay and master the accounts, as I'm in a hurry to reach my master Artemios. So as not to let the ship go full of ballast, I've sent off the soldiers' wine. May God's Own Son be my witness that I have not a thorough grasp of the accounts, because those who were in control here till recently have confused the accounts of wine for the 8th and 9th Indictions."[15]

Husbands parted from their pregnant wives waited eagerly for news. In I B.C., Hilarion, who seems to have come to Alexandreia from Oxyrhynchos for work—perhaps at the docks—wrote to his wife, "I beg and beseech you to take care of the child, and as soon as we get paid our wages, I'll send them to you. If, as may well happen, you have a baby, let it live if it's a boy; but if it's a girl, expose it. You told Aphrodisias to hand on the message: Don't forget me. How can I ever forget you? I beg you not to be anxious."[16] The loving tone of the letter makes even more callous the remark about a baby girl. In the 3rd century Sarapasto wrote to his "sister Diogenis", his wife or else the wife of Horion: "I pray always to all the gods for you and you know from experience my devotion even if I don't write to you. But you have never thought it worthwhile to send your good wishes in a letter. A year today I've been absent from you and all that time you haven't thought it worthwhile to let me know about yourself and your brother Horion, how he's doing. I love him dearly. Have you produced a male child? I pray that you'll agree about all this, as you wholly deserve. Let me know now about anything you want here, for with the god's help I'm hastening to set off to you. I greet you all and pray for your health."[17]

Here are four notes of the 3rd century:

(1) Chairemon to Serapion . . . greetings. Before all else I pray you are well and I make my obeisance daily before the Lord Sarapis. I want you to know that . . . you have sent me no word from the day that I came to Alexandreia. If then you love me, do not neglect to write to me. I salute . . . Sarapias and her children. Pasoxis (?) the carpenter salutes you and your children and . . . his wife.[18]

(2) To my Lord Brother Pamates, Isidoros, very many greetings.

As soon as you receive my letter, hasten to sail down to me in the city before I go away, as I have need of you. Don't neglect to come at once. . . .[19]

(3) Isidora to Sarapias her daughter, many greetings. Before all else I pray for you and your child in the presence of Our Lord Sarapis. You know that I am despondent on account of your brother. I have not received his deposits because I've been sick. They've [fixed] days for receiving them. As to what you said: Send a *chiton* for the little one—if I find a trustworthy person, I'll send it. Or if the gods will, I'll come to join you. Whatever I have, belongs to you and your brother.

I hear you have quarrelled with your husband on account of your father. He hasn't stayed with me because it's winter. Send him to his own place. If I go upcountry, I'll manage him again. I'm waiting for Apollos. Perhaps he'll enlist in the army. [But] whether he enlists or not, I must go upcountry.

Write to me soon about your wellbeing. If you want to write a letter, it's in the house of Serenos, Skambys' brother, that I await his obeisance, on the Bay of Sarapis. Salute the father of the children and the children. Salute Thausarion. Salute your children. Salute Peeous and Pemes. Do not force me to reproach you, Onnophris, for her unpleasantness. Apollos salutes you and your children.[20]

The address of this third letter is "Deliver to Onnophris, priest . . . from Apollos, son of Salibotas". Priests or priestesses of temples or other prominent citizens were used as convenient persons to whom a letter might be addressed. We find a soldier suggesting to his sister at Antinoopolis that he will from then on send his letters to the priestess of the Temple of the Hermonthites "as she is well known". In the above address the priest is presumably better known at Alexandreia than Isidora.[21]

(4) To Stephanos from Hephaistion. On receipt on my son Theon's letter drop everything and come at once to the homestead because of what has happened to me. If you pay no heed, as the gods haven't spared me, so I won't spare the gods. Goodbye.[22]

This is written on the verso of a fragment from a petition, apparently addressed to the strategos and complaining of injury by a brother in connection with a land-division at Kerkethouris. The attitude of open violence against unhelpful gods was definitely

Egyptian. One writer states that he hasn't washed himself or worshipped the gods out of fear of some uncertainty or delay; another that he will refuse the god any devotion unless he can complete his son's education.[23] These people considered the relation between them and a god to be one of exact reciprocity; if the god manifestly failed to play his protective role, the worshipper felt himself free of all obligations.

9

More People on the Nile : Business

ADMINISTRATIVE matters often appear in the papyri; and at
times we see the officials at work and hear about arrangements
being made for them. In the 3rd century: "Diogenes to his
brother Didymas, greeting. I went to Achillas and inquired about
you, and he said: He's at Psobthis. So, knowing your zeal, I
write to you so that you may lend a hand to Apis who is collecting the revenues of Takona, and show him hospitality—so that
on his return he may bear witness of it to me. Goodbye."[1] Later
in the same century an official Gerontas wrote to his "Lord
Brother Ammonianos" about the same village: "Yesterday I came
to Takona and engaged in the induction of the other liturgical
officials so that the tax-collection could proceed. I wonder that
no one has brought me a letter from you, and I am disturbed
because of it, as I don't know how the household is or how affairs
are going with us and in the city. Hasten then to write back to
me on all matters, for you have many persons of the postal service
or of the village who are coming to Takona. As for the tax-
collections, if . . ."[2] (Takona turns up again in 671 A.D. in an
account of expenditure drawn up during the Persian occupation:
"For the price of 50 mirrors bought for the use of the estate bath
at the village of Takona and for 80 more mirrors for the bath in
the village of Ophis, total 130 mirrors, at 3 folleis each . . .")[3]

Business-matters keep cropping up. In 2 B.C. Antas wrote to
Faustos, "Take over from Pothos the total number of reeds and
let me know how many bundles you have received, and put them
in a place safely so that we may take them on the journey up.
Deliver a certain number of them to one of our friends so that a
friend may deliver them safely to me, and if you can . . . give
your attention to it. . . . I bought from [? Pothos] the 1,000

42. Horse in Water

bundles for 15 drachmai. Don't forget. Goodbye." For someone so concerned about safety, his directions are very vague.[4]

In A.D. 38 Ammonios wrote to Aphrodisias, friend and agent, in the Arsinoite nome: "I wrote a letter to Herakleos the herdsman about supplying you with a donkey, and also instructed Ophelion to supply you with another and send me the loaves. You have sent me 3 art. I therefore ask you to do the best you can to send at once the remaining 3 art. and the relish, as I'm on board the boat. As for the pigs' fodder and the rest of the price for the hay, make provision till my arrival. I expect to make up an account with you. I have given you every allowance. Press your wife from me to attend to the pigs, and yourself attend to the calf. Above all, Aphrodisias, send me the loaves and the relish; and if you will, write to me to whom I am to pay a further 20 dr. for hay and fodder. Goodbye."[5]

The reference to the boat suggests that Ammonios moves up and down dealing with his properties. We have three other letters of his to the agent, dated two years later. "I received a letter bidding me send for the loaves on the 5th. I'll then send the donkeys to you without fail on the 8th. Please do your very best to secure me the unguent of lentils. Don't neglect this for fear

we think you've become all at once estranged from us. Salute
Thermion your sister and your children. Goodbye." Next he
wrote in haste, forming bigger letters. "Kindly order the loaves
to be made and the olives to be pickled, and send me word so that
I may send for them. Get the corn in the granary moved because
of the flood, the whole lot of it. Greet Thermion and your
children. 5th year 21 Soter. I've written to you in a hurry."[6]

The fourth letter brings out further the range of his activities,
also his love of relishes. "Diomedes son of Pholos says you've
given him nothing on account of Saras. Please then send me the
child at once and come to Boubastis on the 4th—or on the 20th
by the Egyptian calendar—as I'm grape-pressing there. And buy
me some relishes on the 8th and bring them to Berenikis-of-the-
Shore on the 10th—that is, the 26th. I'm grape-pressing there, so
come. Zenodotos made many charges before Pholos. . . . Please
send me the child by one of the guards. Greet Thermion. Collect
the loan of 40 dr. with the 6 dr. interest, and for the rest anything
that may be owed. 4th year, 28 Drusieus. Bring also 4 art. of
loaves."[7]

Pressure on one hand to get on with the job and excuses on
the other hand for some delay or error: these are the characteristics of such business-letters. In the 2nd century:

Sempronios Clemens to his Most Honoured Apollinarios, greeting.
I got your letters from your father, Julius Sabinus, from whom I
learned that you declare, not that I was unable to attend to your
affairs, but that, as you assert, I was unwilling. And of course on this
point I understood, but all the same I'll set out my justification. The
delay arose in the fact that Valerianus, not of his own wish, but
because our wife contradicted our orders to him, went off straightway
to her.

Since in this situation you enjoined on me with considerable earnest-
ness to write to you, so that thus no further reason for delay should
still remain, I remark that under pressing need I am going up to
Antinoopolis and will write to you from there in reference to this
matter. And if perhaps Fortune allows me to out hither from Antinoopolis, there is no delay. For I'll write to you at once after this distraction,
so that you may not be worried about your affairs. In this way I'll
show you how I'll never again neglect anything.

[2nd hand] I pray you are well together with all your household.[8]

In the same century a man writes from Alexandreia about property-matters and an affair that was probably legal:

N . . . nas to Thaisarion, very many greetings. Before all else I pray for your health and make obeisance for you hourly in the presence of Our Lord Sarapis. I want you to know, sister, that I didn't write a letter to Koprous. I informed her of everything by word of mouth. When she went upriver, the affair had not yet come to a conclusion, but now, I thank Our Lord Sarapis, everything has turned out well. But the [official] communications have not come out. I am expecting them.

Know that our brother Ptolemaios has sold all his property, namely the share that falls to him of the 8 ar. near the village Sebennytos, to Philoxas the cavalry-man; and [his property] in the hamlets Pammebeis, Pemes, Tbounis, Kollauthis, Psens, and Pilipite, and the share which falls to him of a palmgrove in the hamlet of Okes—all this has been sold to Heras, your son.

And now, but for my being in Alexandreia, he would have sold all your property and mine and our mother's. But I thank Ptolemaios, husband of Heuremon's daughter: through him everything was accomplished. He used me like a brother. If Sarapis permits and I receive the communications, I'll come to join you.

I also gave Kopreus all this information by word of mouth, so that she might tell you. If you know that the village-secretary has put me into a liturgy, inform what kind of a liturgy he has put me into. And if anyone has injured you, let me know his name by letter. Give many salutations to my brother Ptolemaios and to Diodora and to Longeionos and to . . . and to Gemella, and many salutations to my mother. [2nd hand] I pray for your health.[9]

In another letter of this century we find the friendly address belied by the bitter tone. "Herakleides to his dearest Hatres, greeting. Without my writing to you, you should have sent me the 20 dr. by Saetas, for you know I paid them here to my partners. But you've waited all this time without paying me. So be sure to give this sum at once to the bearer of this letter and thus save me too from trouble. See then that you don't do otherwise and so force me to come and dispute with you about it. For indeed I found you at Paomis the other day and wanted to welcome you warmly, but you wouldn't stay, oppressed as you were with a bad conscience."[10]

A group of family-letters from the early 2nd century show what seem to be a fairly normal set of preoccupations and movements. Sarapion has at least three sons, Eutychides, Heliodoros, Anoubion. First, however, we find him writing to a sister (or wife) Selene. "Until I hear you're safe as to the affair about which I sailed down, I'll remain, but I hope, if the gods will, to escape yet from the prittleprattle and to return home after the 15th. See that the empty jars are bought and the slaves give attention to the sowing of our private land and the cultivation, and in particular look after the woven stuffs, so that we may not have any cross words. You've shown very little concern for me by thinking I've received the deferment-payment and could meet my expenses out of that. I accordingly borrowed money from friends. For out of the 200 dr. you sent me by Heliodoros, 54 dr. were spent on taxes and the boatfare to and fro. I've sent you my letters by both the slave of Sarapion and the son of the royal-scribe. Goodbye, sister Selene." (The Sarapion in the last sentence is another man with the same name as himself.)[11]

He also writes to his son Eutychides. "It was unnecessary for you to write to me about the wages of the labourers. You are acting for yourself. Ascertain then—it's the safe course—how much Polis pays his labourers and pay yours the same, and let Horion the priest give you the money for the labourers. To-morrow I'll send Achillas to you so that you too may come to Hermopolis. Goodbye."

Eutychides writes to his father: "Before all else I salute you and thank you for telling me of your health. Don't be worried about the young barley. I've sold it. As to your jars, I'm writing to let you know that I'm not forgetting. I have bought for you a 100 sweetsmelling jars. I arranged about the green fodder. . . . When I arrived on the spot, they . . . and with great difficulty I made them set to work at the former rent, as you wrote in your instructions. As for the woven stuffs, several days before you write (?) to me, I'll send them. No news yet about the green fodder. I beg you to write about your health to me. There is no advance in the price of wheat beyond 7 dr. Goodbye and please write to me continually about your safety." To his brother Heliodoros he writes: "The elders made an attack on us and carried their boldness so far as to seize Peteus by night while he was with the cattle in the fields, on the grounds that he was an elder, though he wasn't on the official list nor had he been appointed by the village-scribe. I ask you then to check the other elders (?), to vindicate Peteus, and draw up a petition complaining of Petepsois son of Phatres and Demetrios son of Tekoous as insolent fellows and busybodies. The elders on the official list are Petepsois son of Phatres, Mires son of Mires called Tothes, Mires son of Pasion, Mires son of Petosiris, Demetrios son of Tekoous, Porementhis son of Harmodios." It seems that they were attempting to force him into acting as elder, though it is possible that they were accusing him of having illegally posed as one. Elders had responsibilities in the collection of taxes.

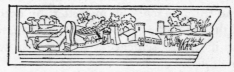

43. Country scene

Eutychides also writes to his brother Anoubion. "Before all else I salute you and Sarapaion and Selene and Eudaimonis. In the next place I beg you not to forget me in my absence, but to look after everything as if it were your own. You will get from Hermophilos 20,000 . . . if it should happen that we do not sail up suddenly. The Master himself wrote on the 3rd warning me to sail up with the folk of Kousia on the 16th or when he chooses. . . . What happened to us in connection with the magistrates you have probably heard or will hear. As to the jars for the festival, see that they are paid . . . the corn to the sons of Pallas [and] Krion. Salute Heliodoros Exakon. Salute Apollonios the cobbler and Ploution. I pray for your health and that of your children."

Some business documents fill out the picture of the family's interests and activities. Kastor son of Panechotes made a proposal to Eutychides for the sublease of 7 ar. in two parcels in the Hermopolite nome for two years. Besides an extra payment in money and corn, the first parcel was to pay 36 art. wheat the first year, 28 art. barley the next, the second parcel 24 art. barley the first, 24 art. wheat the next. Anoubion had a contract with Chairemon in letter-form for the lease of 12⅔ ar. in two parcels near Hermopolis for two years. In the first year the crop was to be hay and arakos, with payment of 250 dr.; in the second year, the crop was to be wheat, with payment of 85½ art. of it. The wheat was to be measured out, half by the measure used in the temple of Athena, half by the measure dochikon. A receipt shows that Anoubion paid a year's rent to Chairemon for land in the Lower Suburb near Magdola Mire. Another receipt shows that he paid a year's rent to Demetria also called Taseus and her son Areios, who acted as her guardian and wrote the document for her as she was illiterate.

An account of receipts and expenditures for Epeiph includes the name Selene. The first 14 lines give receipts, starting with a balance of 183 dr. 3 ob. from the previous month and recording payments made by various persons. The total is 644 dr. 4 ob.: a sum that fails to agree with the figures, which add up to 544 dr. 7 ob. Then comes a list of payments for different purposes, of which the total is given as 465 dr. 5 ob. Here again the arithmetic is hard to reconcile with the figures, though the balance left when expenses are taken from receipts is correctly stated as 178 dr. 6 ob. Then we get a further receipt of 100 dr., the expenditure of which is accounted for. Payments are made to individuals without explanation, but we find also 80 dr. 2 ob. for sheets of papyrus; 20 dr. for cushions; 34 dr. to a tax-collector over some delay with a donkey. 8 dr. to a granary-guard; 8 dr. for a nurse; 100 dr. for travelling expenses, 60 dr. for a ring; small sums for oil, salt, a writing tablet, cheeses, spices, and 20 dr. for a present to a daktylistes, surveyor. Another account, probably by a member of the family, includes a reference to Eudaimonis as well as to a sailor, a *ploion*, and a shepherd.

To the late 2nd century belongs a draft-agreement, which modifies a previous contract by which the writer appointed a representative to collect a debt owed to him in Alexandreia.

Today I appointed you by public deed drawn up through the Record Office here as my representative to collect from Gaius Memmius

Cornutus, also called Polydeukes, who is at Alexandreia, my share of the sums owed by him to my said father's heir, his nephew Herakleides also called Amoitas. But it so happens that I have been paid the debt in full.

I acknowledge that the contract of representation has been made with you for the sole purpose of your issuing a receipt to the officials without receiving anything, and for cancelling the mortgage, because I have, as aforesaid, already received the money as stated in the autograph receipts which I have issued, and I make no claim on any matter whatever.[12]

And here are two letters of the 2nd century (the second perhaps of the early 3rd), which show how complicated the business informations which were exchanged could be. In the first letter we get a glimpse of the Oxyrhynchite pawnbroking trade.

(1) Dionysios to his mother Tetheus, greeting. I've received all the letters about which you write, and as for the wheat that the collectors have demanded from you, it is to be paid, but I had forgotten to make any order for payment. I have however paid in full the naubion [tax mainly for canal-clearing] and the other taxes. Don't be worried at the matter about which I write to Theon not being carried out and at the length of engagement over Pausirion's business to no purpose. . . .

Please receive from Chairemon the bearer of this letter 112 dr. of silver and redeem my clothes, with 8 dr. to meet the interest, and keep 4 dr. for yourself for the festival's expenses. If I had more, I'd have forwarded a further sum. I've borrowed to send even this. So pay him the money and get my clothes back safe, and put them away in a secure place.

Don't worry about us. There's nothing wrong with us and we're on good terms with each other. Theonas salutes you. Salute the boys Apion and his brother Hermatois, Dionytas, those with Nike and the little Thaisous, all those with . . . , Heras and his household, Leontas the proud fellow and his household, those with Taamois, and Thermoutharion. Goodbye. 20 Caesareus.

Send me word about this straightway after the festival: whether you got the money and whether you recovered the clothes. Salute Dionytas and Theon.[13]

(2) Apion to his son Apion and his dearest Horion, many greetings. Before all else I pray for your health and that of your children and wives. All that I wrote in the other letter—so I won't have to repeat it—assume that I wrote also to Horion.

I've sent you by Eutyches of Ision Thryphonis three orders for payment: two for the cultivators of Maximos, the third for Diogenes son of . . . Issue them at once before Phaophi so that they won't be later than the due time. Others were sent to Panechotes the lawyer. Get these from him and pay him 64 dr.

Sell the grass-seed and ask . . . whether he wants the man from Tampitei. Let my revenues paid through the cultivators be put on deposit at the store-house or else kept in safety in the possession of the cultivators. Then, if the gods will, we may, if they're neglected, have no complications with our adversary, or the cultivators must bear the risk.

Don't lease the house of . . . to anyone but a woman who intends living in it. It's [wrong] to expose such a house to youths—so we won't be caused botheration and annoyance.

Tell Zoilos the cultivator from Sento that in accordance with the agreements he must look after the money. Tell the twins also to take care with the small change. And likewise tell Apollonios and Dionysios, if you can send to Paberke in the eastern toparchy to Pausiris the donkey driver, that, as they arranged, they're to pay me the jars of wine and must keep their pledge.

Get from Harthonis the priest the 20 art. of wheat, and from Zoilos the Sento cultivator the 5 art. of wheat he borrowed from me. Look at the strategos' office a letter of the dioiketes written in the month of Thoth about the substitution of other names for mine in drawing lots for the post of collector. Tell Serenos at the camel-shed that he is to take care of the money. Tell Hermias, scribe of the collectors of money-taxes at Ision Panga, to issue an order for the wheat he owes me or for the amount he approves. Let Herakleides son of Heramiskos pay the 6 art. of wheat on deposit. Tell Dionysios son of Epimachos, ex-chief priest, that I petitioned the dioiketes about the revenue so the fine of Sarapion son of Phanias might be reduced.

Salute Statia my daughter and Herakleides and Apion my sons. Salute little Serenos and Kopreus and all our household individually. Amarantos and Smaragdos salute you. I pray for your health.[14]

Apion was certainly a very busy man. Here is a shorter note of the same period. "Valerianos to Sokrates, greeting. You must come down here quickly, for a friend of mine, Auliatos, promised me to settle the affair for you at once, if you come down to beg off from it. Then see to it that you don't delay, in case Iulius sails off suddenly. You will please him also, for he's a stranger. Your daughter salutes you. Goodbye."[15]

L

In the documents forming the archive of Fl. Abinnaios, who commanded a frontier-post on the edge of the Libyan desert, we find a letter from Apollos, who has gone to Alexandreia, acting as Abinnaios' agent. "To my Lord Father Abinnaios, Apollos. Before all else I pray Almighty God that you may receive my letter in good health, with your household. In accordance with your instructions for me to Alexandria and ascertain what the ever-memorable Eisas received from the tenant of your house, I found that he had got in in accordance with your letter 230 myriads, and he has given the tenant notes of hand for them. See then, I have sent you both the note of hand that Eisas gave for the 230 myriads, and the whole account for the house and the loaves. And from the month of Pharmouthi till now, Piste took over your house and the bread. For Eisas resembles country-folk; and he handed it all over to Piste, and—this further matter—Eisas also received from . . . aleios, in accordance with your letter, 50 myriads and 2 keremia of wine. Greetings to you all by name. I pray for your health for a long time."[16]

The phrase "resembles country-folk" is odd; there might be a reference to *stationes agrariae*, sentry-duty on active service, as contrasted with *stationes castrenses*, sentry-duty in camp. The meaning would then be "Eisas is like soldiers on guard". In any event a compliment is intended.[17] The loaves seem certainly to be part of bread-issue made out of the imperial treasury to owners of houses in Alexandreia like the *panis aedium* of Constantinople. We have another note from Apollos: "To my Lord Father Abinnaios, Apollos. Before all else I pray you may receive my letter in good health. Please my Lord Father come here . . . and meet on a happy day together with Constantios your son; and

44. Country scene

meet Adamantios and his wife and his sons and Papos and his wife. I pray for your health for a long time."[18] There is also a letter from Alypios who is at Arsinoe: "To my Lord Father Abinnaios, Alypios. As I couldn't at the moment find a clean sheet of papyrus, I've written on this—the back of a memorandum about estate-business. Please my Lord Father request back from Asklepiades the two solidi of mine that he has on loan, and send them to me to the city. And furnish Zakaon with 2 art. of corn, and when I winnow you will get an equal quantity back from the same Zakaon."[19]

Ptolemaios writes to Heron, his son, a boundary-inspector, in the early 3rd century, "Up to today we didn't find a buyer. I am ceding everything to Didymos on condition I get a third part of the loan and of the rest. Except that I've had a dispute with Ptolemaios, we would have left long ago. He was enraged when he came down, so I am writing to let you know. Salute your children and all your household and Tais and her children. I pray for your good health."[20] Areios in the Arsinoite wrote to an agent on agricultural matters, "You neglected the business of the axles when we were in need of them. All the same, provide the purchase now. As well as the 4 dr., give the 100 . . . I sent you a sack of flax. If you want the shepherd to have 3 fleeces so you may send them, give them to him. Send also more wine to Dionysias, then the price may go towards the digging of the olive-yards, as Dios has gone on a journey to Alexandreia. Goodbye."[21]

Apion in the same century wrote to his son Horion: "I arrived in Alexandreia on the morning of the 29th and I now write to you, my son, to salute you and your sister and daily on your behalf I supplicate the Lord Sarapis. As to the work you're carrying on, I feel no anxiety, knowing that you'll fail nothing that is urgent, especially the irrigation of the farms. We are putting in hand the uncompleted deed. As for our own business, I have done nothing so far . . .".[22]

Now and then traders appear. "Greeting, Ischyrion. Receive through the traders with Herakleon 40 dr., so that you may separate the field-rue by means of the palmtrees, especially the palm of Mikras and the one east of the hut adjoining the courtyard. Try to get a pair of oxen for irrigating the vineyard, or two pairs, as I am coming to you myself on the 13th. So make careful use . . ."[23] Middlemen, *endocheis*, also appear. They received goods from the shipowners, *naukleroi*, and passed them on to the traders, *emporoi* (not retail-salesmen like the *metabolai* of the last letter).

(1) Hermes to his most esteemed Serapiakos, greeting. I stored away the wine of the first vat without separating the fragrant part, of the second I previously found and put aside 30 fragrant jars. The other vats I did not store away, as the middlemen said they would wait till Tybi 5 when the fragrant should be established and accurately known.

Of what was stored I found the first vat 1 drinkable, . . . acid, 1 entirely. . . . Of the second, 5 drinkable, . . . acid. Of the third vat in the . . . orchard likewise 2 drinkable. Of the fourth vat, 1. These I found in receptacles outside part of the . . .

In order then that they may not be lost, tell me if you want them sold. For they can't be carried up without being sold off. I had much argument and complication with the men who took the donkey, as they asked for an earnest. In the end I asked for the mna, as you thought right.

I have sent you 16 cheeses, 4 of which are from the former herdsman. I let him go for this very reason and . . . the animals. Please send some baskets to my house . . . Tybi 1.

Send the leases of the vine-dressers so that they may begin the pruning. [2nd c.][24]

(2) Horion to Serenos greeting. You haven't sent the middlemen as I instructed you. You haven't even written whether they set off, so that I might make preparations. Nor whether Diogas the wool-dealer came, so that we might have his advice. I instructed you to ask about the purchased corn, whether the amount is being completed, and to meet Ptolemaios the sitologos and send his account, getting it from Apollonios and Heras, so that our household may not be troubled. So do this even now, and be at the pains yourself of coming here, so that we may make up the accounts of the rents. If the inspectors came, tell Nikephoros . . . [3rd c.][25]

Wine-dealings are fairly common. Here is a 4th-century fragment with a Christian symbol close to the upper edge:

To my Lord and Beloved Father Phamaeis, Bes the winemerchant, greeting. Before all else I many times greet you and my mother Thermouthis and your household—avert the evil eye—each one by name. You did well to send me . . .[26]

We have encountered various persons with god-names, Isis, Dionysos, Horos, Aphrodite, as well as with names that incorporate a deity's name (Dionysios, Herakleides, Sarapias and so on); it is fitting to strike a winemerchant with the name of the jolly god Bes. Here are two letters concerned with wages and payments:

(1) Aurelios Stephanos to Aurelios Chairemon, his brother, greeting. As I was setting out for Alexandreia, I paid the price of yokes, 60 dr., to the rope-weaver Petobastis in Herakleos' presence, and the price of manure, 40 dr., at Chysis in Kopreus' presence, and the 48 dr. I had with me to Kale for Kopreus. So don't fail to cast the manure on the land. I agreed to pay 100 dr. for 25 art., in Kopreus' presence. So you are to give him the remaining 12 dr.

Don't fail to go there, to help my wife till I return, and for the sake of the irrigation. I found Aithiopas and all goes well with him. Salute all our friends. I pray for your health.[27]

(2) To my Lord Brother Isidoros, Kollouthos, greeting. You aren't acting well in being reluctant to send the wages for threshing through Alobai. And you haven't declared the full amount of barley . . . Be so good as to come surreptitiously with them. The moment is a good one. [2nd hand] I pray for your continued help.

With this last note is the Christian symbol, the chi-rho or labaron which is not found in Egypt before the 4th century.[29]

An odd letter of the 6th or 7th century mentions a travelling moneychanger. Georgios, a landlord's agent, writes to a friend whom he calls Dioiketes: "Immediately and at this very moment let your True Excellency send me here Theodoros the collector, for the noble moneychanger expects him to go down to Alexandreia. But by all means bring him with you and arrive with all speed the day after tomorrow. For I can no longer endure the noble moneychanger, the Lord knows, bothering me. By all means come the day after tomorrow with the said collector."[30]

A puzzling but interesting letter throws light on the commercial activities of Christian groups at the time (264–82 A.D.) when Maximos was bishop of Alexandreia and things were fairly peaceful for the Church. The writer is a business-man who moves between Alexandreia and Rome, and perhaps Arsinoe; he himself is probably an Arsinoite, at the moment in Rome. His relation to the Alexandrian chancery is obscure, but the bishop and his assistants seem to act as depositaries for the sums of money with which X deals. X is of some importance, however, and is able to give orders involving several communities. Group 1 are in the Arsinoite nome: the letter is addressed to them and they are X's main instruments in getting goods turned into money at Alexandreia. Group 2 are at A. . . . and include Nilon or his sister and Father Apollonios (probably a title of respect), who are to get some service from Group 1 at X's request. Group 3 is at Alexandreia and include the bishop, Theonas (his assistant presbyter and later successor), and his lector. Here Primitinos is waiting to get money from Group 1 so that he may sail for Rome; and here too is probably Agathoboulos, whose relations with Group 1 are managed by X, as well as the unnamed man (Y) who is accused of deliberate delays in his own interest. Group 4 are at Rome.[31]

The relation of the groups or communities is unclear. But Group I is apparently to arrange for a shipment of barley to some unspecified person. X complains that Y has delayed (on payment) and forced him into the position of promising to cover the losses of Group I. That Group is asked to buy bread, and with it some service is to be rendered to Nilon and Father Apollonios in Group 2. Some persons (perhaps the two last-mentioned) have written that money be forwarded to Group 1; and this money, X directs, is to be brought to Alexandreia. Group 1 is to buy linen of some sort before bringing the money to Primitinus, as X has agreed. The linen bought in the nome is to be sold in Alexandreia for a certain sum to be handed on to Primitinus or the bishop. Another sum (? for travel expenses) is to be given to Theonas who will hold it for X, who is to settle certain differences between Group 1 and Agathaboulos.

What is important for the light thrown on Christian communities of the later 3rd century is the role of the bishop and two leading members of the Alexandrian hierarchy, who serve as banks or depositaries for Christian business-men. The bishop is to get a fixed sum, which is to be transmitted to Primitinus; another sum is to go to Theonas, who will hold it for X. What is not brought out is whether the bishop and his assistants are themselves financially involved. X is possibly a cleric, for instance a deacon, who is concerned with supplying the material wants of various Christian communities.[32]

The papyrus seems devised so that it could be folded up as a sort of amulet. If the outer margins were turned in over centre (where is a text from *Genesis*) a verse from Hebrews became visible on the top fold. The broken-up text reads:

. . . to send the barley . . . from the same account lest they consider what has been said . . . from supplies sent to him from Alexandreia. With all his excuses, delays and procrastinations I can hardly believe he didn't deliberately plan this. Now if the accruing profit doesn't properly balance the account, I myself guarantee that I'll make up for it.

If you wish, sell some bread . . . to Nilon and Father Apollonios at . . . They have written that the money would be delivered to you at once. Bring this money to Alexandreia, after buying linen there in the Arsinoite nome. For I promised Primitinos that the money will be handed over to him at Alexandria.

. . . from Rome, 8 Pauni.

You did right, Brethren, in buying the linen. Some of you . . . travelling with them to Bishop Maximos and . . . his lector. And when you have sold the linen in the city [Alexandreia], deliver the money to Primitinos or to Bishop Maximos and get a receipt from him.

As for travelling expenses . . . after selling the bread and linen, I beg you to give the money to Theonas, so I may collect it when I come to Alexandria towards my own expenses. Be sure, Brethren, to do this as soon as possible so that Primitinos may not be held up at Alexandria . . . on his way to Rome. . . . And I shall arrange things harmoniously between you and Agathoboulos.

These commercially entangled communities have moved far from apostolic poverty and renunciation of money-making. Not that there had ever been any simple social situation. Hermas had spoken of Christians "confused with business-affairs and wealth."[33] And Alexandreia may well have taken a lead in attempting to reconcile the Christian idea and commercial activities. Here, around 200 A.D. Clement, himself a rich man, gave his sermon on Wealth in which he sought to dissolve the clear injunctions of the Gospels in allegory and moralising. His words show that there was still a strong feeling among large sections of the faithful that it was impossible to be wealthy and to carry on money-making work if one was an honest Christian. He says:

The causes that make salvation more difficult for the rich than for the poor are very complex. Some, hearing the Lord's saying about the camel and the needle's eye, despair of eternal life and give the world its way; they wander further than ever from the path to heaven, without any inquiry as to what rich people the Teacher named, or how the impossible with men becomes possible after all. Others, though they may understand this, neglect the works that lead to salvation, and take no measures to realise their hopes. I speak in each case of the rich who have come to the Saviour's power. With the uninitiated I have no concern.

If then we love truth and love the brotherhood, we shall neither despise nor condemn the rich who have received the call, nor yet come cringing to them for our personal advantage. Our first aim will be to rid them of their despair, and to show them, by a true explanation from the Saviour's words, that they are not wholly precluded from the inheritance of the Kingdom. Secondly, when this baseless fear is removed, we shall further enlighten them as to the way and the deeds and the disposition, by which the Christian hope is to be secured.

45. River scene, with Crocodile

The means of ending the despair of the rich man and the contempt in which he is held by the common Christian is the insistence that the Gospels are not to be taken seriously in their explicit statements. What has scared the rich man off?

Just this, "Sell all that thou hast". And what does that mean. It is not, as some have interpreted the words off-hand, a command to throw away his property and to abandon his possessions. No, he was to banish from his soul his convictions about wealth, the anxiety, the disease of mind, the cares, the thorns of this life, which choke the seed of life eternal.

Thus Clement made the Church at Alexandreia safe for the landlords, traders, bankers, and shipowners, and opened the way for the sort of thing we find in the letter cited above.[34] Not that the objections were easily wiped out. Clement himself in his *Paidagogos* takes the command of Christ in its direct sense.[35] Even when admitting the rich, he insists on the role of the poor as their "bodyguard".[36] He makes incidental criticisms of the traders and their like—the dealer who has two prices. And he denounces the taking of interest from a brother.[37] But generally his influence was to moralise away the precise command. We may compare the effect of the passage from the Gospel, which Clement is at such pains to water down, on another man of Egypt—Antonios, who, hearing it read out in church, was so hard hit that he sold all his property, gave it to the poor, and turned to the hermit-life in which his example had such a powerful effect.

10

More People on the Nile : Law

WITH such a litigious people many journeys up and down the Nile were caused by lawsuits. "I received Thrasyboulos' letter at Kanopos. So I haven't yet obtained the documents, but they are being collated. Apis the advocate hasn't examined the documents yet, but has kept delaying day after day. Since your departure on the 16th Sabeinos has been dealing with the business. I told Philomousos to go to you. Send a decoction of cabbage in the load for Ptollas. Homeros sends his best wishes, and Tahermas and Phileros and his wife. Take care of yourself so you'll stay in good health. Goodbye.—To Thrakidas."[1]

In A.D. 115–6 two brothers Diogenes and Nikanor made an agreement about the journey that Nikanor was to take. They had been carrying on a lawsuit with Menestheus, son of Horos, about the ownership of a slave named Thaisous or Thaesis, whom they claimed to have inherited from their mother. The strategos of the nome heard the case and sent it on to the Prefect. Nikanor agreed to attend the Prefect's court, with full power to act as his brother's representative.[2]

Now, to take a more complicated sort of case that involved movement: we have the final part of a speech in defence of a woman, Hermione, accused of attempted poisoning and fraud over a supposed mortgage.

It was from his own house he came out saying he had been poisoned; when he came out from Hermione's house he told nobody of noticing anything nor did he have the least suspicion, but it was from the house of himself and his son and future heir that he came out with the statement of being poisoned.

He had indeed reasons for administering poison to himself, which many others have had in choosing death rather than life. For he was ruined by creditors and at his wit's end. But if anyone really plotted against him, his son is the most likely culprit.

Why he brought the accusation is now evident. He may indeed have had other troubles during his stewardship, but the case shows that he was jealous of her [probably Dionysia, Hermione's daughter] without her knowledge and called himself her husband. But as she didn't think him worthy of this title, he suffered like a lover and didn't want her to outlive him.

If they assert that the slave Smaragdos has disappeared, being himself accused of having stolen the mortgage—he only declares that a mortgage was made so that it might be stolen: since it is impossible for something to be stolen when it never existed at all or could exist—nor can a mortgage have been drawn up, as the buyer did not know how to write, nor did the present defendant Hermione—nor does a stranger, when another woman is registered as mortgagee, himself issue a deed of mortgage. So from whom could he say that he had received the mortgage? From whatever quarter he got it, it was invalid. And if a slave has run away, that is no argument against his master.

46. Country scene, with Drinking Party

Moreover the division also helps to show that there never was any mortgagee. Persons registered as mortgagees have only their name inserted in deeds and do not claim the property registered in mortgage; but the buyer has clearly claimed the property and enjoyed it ever since she bought it: while he, as he has sold it, has no longer been enjoying it, but has been administering the mother's property as a steward and attacking my clients.

If they state that a joint agreement was made between the daughter and Hermione for 150 jars, to be produced from these vineyards which she [Dionysia] bought, we reply that all this has nothing to do with the plaintiff. If the daughter did come to an agreement with the mother, that provides them with no pretext for calumnies.

The agreement however did not happen at the same period, but nearly a year later, and the provision of 150 jars is not at all a security for 4 talents, since they are the interest on only one talent. Again, if there had been security given to the supposed seller, would the daughter have pledged herself to the State by another deed when she was liable to be deprived of the property whenever he chose?

The facts of the provision are as follows: Hermione had three children, Aphro . . . , Dionysia, . . . Dionysia begged her mother not to leave her with only what had been already used up, but to give her something, since she was dependent on merely a single resource. At that Hermione paid her $1\frac{1}{2}$ talents. But Dionysia did not want her mother in her lifetime to be deprived of that sum, so she paid this provision yearly instead of interest; and the statement of this is contained in the mutual agreement.

Dionysia claimed to have bought a vineyard from the plaintiff's father, while the plaintiff insisted it had only been mortgaged to her, and accused Smaragdos, slave of Dionysia or Hermione, of having made off with the bond of mortgage. The defence replied that the mortgage had never existed and was a mere invention of the accuser. The four talents seem to have been the sum which (according to the plaintiff) had been borrowed by Dionysia from her mother and then advanced to him on the vineyard's security; the 150 jars of wine were then the interest on the money that Dionysia borrowed. The defence replied that the jars were paid to the mother as interest on a talent and a half which she had given her daughter. To strengthen the case against Hermione she was further accused of having tried to poison the plaintiff. The defence replied that the latter was in a desperate state, bankrupt and mad with unrequited love for Dionysia; and stressed the fact that he came reeling out of his own house, not Hermione's, with the cry that he had been poisoned.[3]

The document does not name the accuser, and gives no clue as to the verdict. But luckily another document, dated a year later, seems certainly to fill the picture out. Here Sarapion petitions the epistrategos, enclosing a petition to the Prefect and its answer. Dionysia and Sarapion have disputed the ownership of some land; she said that she bought it from his father, and he said that she held it only on mortgage; he also said that her mother Hermione had tried to poison him. The epistrategos Claudius Quintianus referred the case to the Prefect and ordered the disputants to proceed to Alexandreia. Dionysia went, but not Sarapion. After waiting some time in vain, she petitioned the Prefect Flavius Titianus for permission to return home. He referred her back to the epistrategos, now Julius Varianus. So she restated her case in the document we possess.[4] "Since my opponent even now is absent and the time for sowing is close at hand and the repairing of what the river has swept away requires my presence, I beg you, if you please, to allow me to sail back and have the case decided by you on the spot."

Her petition to the Prefect is worth citing since it puts her case succinctly and amplifies her complaint about a diastrously heavy flood:

. . . Dionysia daughter of Chairemon, her mother being Hermione, inhabitants of Oxyrhynchos. A certain Sarapion, son of Mnesitheus, of the said city, charged my mother Hermione before Claudius Quintianus, late epistrategos of the Heptanomis with poisoning, and at the same time invited a claim to certain property of which he declared himself cheated, but which I Dionysia bought in accordance with official contracts, paying the price for it to his father when alive and to the said father's creditors who held the land on mortgage; and he asserted that it had been registered in security.

The epistrategos referred the matter to your Beneficence and my mother happened to die before the trial. So, as a result of the epistrategos' letter ordering me and Sarapion to sail down to Alexandreia, I presented myself here; but Sarapion paid no attention to the instruction to sail down.

Since then news has reached me while staying here that all my property has been lost through the excessive rise of the Most Holy Nile, buildings, lands, and dykes. I entreat you, my Lord Prefect, in the continued absence of my opponent, to permit me to sail back and obtain justice there—so that I may not in addition to the loss of my property also perish of hunger, and that I may obtain redress.

On the strength of the documents Sarapion seems the guilty person: an impression supported by his prolonged absence from the Prefect's court.

Another papyrus of the first half of the 2nd century brings out the difficulties besetting anyone who lost documents in this society of careful legalities and registrations:

. . . letters of recommendation to the epistrategos, in case he reaches you first. I also instructed the soldier Antoninos, who was in service to the epistrategos Vindex along with me, and who has now sailed up with the epistrategos, to help in the whole thing. All the same I've now sent you a letter to him.

The documents about the slaves I haven't so far found. Actually neither the deed of sale from you to Achilleus nor that from Achilleus to the lady now gone to her rest has been found with me. Achilleus too is absent from home, and I can't make it all out, as I'm not accustomed to throw away any papers at all, let alone important ones. Further, the person who bought the slave from you, a petty pleader at the court of the dikaiodotes, after continually promising to inform us of the sale's date, has let us down.

If you can recall the date and the office through which it was concluded, let me know—and search through your papers to see if the deed of sale to Apollinarion isn't there, and send me word if you know who was the scribe that made out the conveyance from you to Achilleus. It hasn't been found with the scribe Potammon.

To stop anyone molesting you in the meanwhile, I've written to the strategos' secretary, introducing the young Herakleides and explaining the matter, so that he may devise some other means till I send you the documents or come in person. Stick by your letter about Sarapion as a justified action on your part, to those questioning you and to Sarapion himself, appreciating the importance of the matter.

And if you sail down with all good luck, fetch an excellent bed to

47. Two Ibis in marsh

send to Philos for his excellent behaviour towards us, or any other gift you think suitable. I pray for your health, sister. My best wishes to Herakleides and Isis. Ptolemaios sends his too. 28 Mechier.[5]

Complaints about delays, as we have seen, are common in all spheres of action. They abound in the world of the law. "Sabeinos to . . . Narion his mother and to Demetrous, greeting. I want you to know that since the day I sailed down to Alexandreia I have found most of the days free from public business and up till today I have endured intolerable delay in the matter of my suit. It happened that the former archidikastes had departed, and we are awaiting the new man. As soon as he is brought here, with god's help I'll leave without delay. Since the day I came up, I have been with Antonios and everything goes well. Salute Aphrodisia and Thermoutis and Tasoucharion and my friend Ptollas. Antonios salutes you all as well as the children. I pray for your good health.—To Karanis, to the house of Sabeinos the [husband] of Demetrous."[6]

Women had their own problems. "I arrived in the city on the 9th. I ask you, if you can, send me one of your group, as I need him to be my legal representative. A woman isn't permitted to engage in a lawsuit without a legal representative. Know that if you help me the affair will have a successful issue. So that he may come quickly, know then if I suffer injury, you also are going to be hurt, but if we win you will have the profit."[7]

But a man too, through illness or some other disability, might not be able to attend the assizes. The following document was drawn up at Oxyrhynchos in A.D. 135, with blanks left for the name of the representative and the date to be filled in.

Apollonios son of Apollonios son of Diogenes, his mother being Tanechotarion also called Euterpe daughter of Diogenes, of Oxyrhynchos, acknowledges to   of the said city (the contract taking place in the street) since he is unable through sickness to make the voyage to the assize of the nome that he has forthwith appointed   to represent him in the inquiry to be held against him before his Highness the Prefect Petronius Mamertinus or the epistrategos Gellius Bassus or other judges and to carry out everything concerned with the trial; for he gives his consent on these terms. The agreement is valid.[8]

Perhaps Apollonios felt better, or decided to face the accusation, or failed to find anyone ready to represent him.

A letter of the 3rd century brings out further the nuisance caused by failures to attend assizes. "Having ascertained precisely about your safety and what was done regarding you when the Prefect was in the district, Theochrestos informed me of your doings in the Kynopolite nome and that the person you accused didn't turn up—but that he later came forward in this district and said to him that he'd attend on the return journey, and after this neither of you came. . ."9

A husband held up in Alexandreia (late 3rd or early 4th century) tries to explain things to his critical father. "To my Lord Father Origenes, many greetings from Trophimos. Before all else I send many good wishes to you and your wife Kopria and Isidoros and Phoullon and Helene and all our friends individually. You wrote to me in your letter I've got the name God's Gift [Diodoros] because I boast so much. I've sent you money. But I don't boast of what I sent you through Philoxenos. If you've sold the various things I sent you, write to me so I may send you some more. I've been idle here two months or I'd have sent you all some more. The money I collected I'm holding for the trial. For I'm still waiting for the memoranda. You write to me: Petition against Polydeukes. If the memoranda turn up, I'll petition against him and against Sarapadoros. If you feel like it, send me a pout of oil. You wrote to me: You are staying in Alexandreia with your darling. Write and inform me who my darling is. I pray for your health."10

Many officials, minor or important, kept on moving up and down the Nile; but the one regular progress with considerable pomp was that of the Prefect on his tour of inspection. A letter

48. Riverside

dated about A.D. 50 describes such a tour—of the Prefect or the Dioiketes, the chief financial officer. Starting from an unnamed place, presumably Alexandreia, the official went first to Pelousion, then through the nomes along the eastern side of the Delta, the Tanite and Sethroite nomes, Arabia (eastern Egypt), and another nome Auia (called An in hieroglyphics), on to Memphis. After that we went direct to the Thebaid, returned through the Heptanomia, the Arsinoite nome, and other nomes of the Delta missed out on his outward journey, ending in Alexandreia.[11]

There had been itinerant courts under the Ptolemies. They were replaced under the Romans by the assizes held periodically by the Prefect at Pelousion, Alexandreia, and Memphis. The business there dealt with included, besides the trial of lawsuits and the like, a general submission and examination of the reports and accounts of the nome-officials. Much inconvenience was caused by the need of litigants thus to travel to the assizes. Here is a declaration on oath about an appearance in court, dated A.D. 284–6

To Aurelios Philiarchos, strategos of the Oxyrhynchite nome, from Aurelios Zoilas son of Theogenes and Tauris, of the Illustrious and Most Illustrious City of Oxyrhynchos:
I swear to by Fortune [Tyche] of Our Lord Gaius Valerius Diocletianus Caesar Augustus that I will present myself before our Most Eminent Prefect Marcus Aurelius Diogenes when he auspiciously visits this place or the neighbouring nome, and will bring an action in his court against the komarchs from the nome now present . . . on account of the . . . which they wrongly . . .[12]

The papyrus breaks off as it comes to the grounds of the action.

However, things were made easier by the practice of delegating many prefectural powers to local and other officials. Also, as we see from the above letter, the Prefect during his tour was able at times to hold his conventus for Upper and Middle Egypt at various towns along the valley.

Not that litigants were the only persons who had reasons for complaint. Rowers had to be supplied by the localities. A letter of 338 complains of a failure in the duty:

To Flavios Eusebios logistes of the Oxyrhynchite nome from Aurelios

M

Papnouthis son of Paumis . . . of Oxyrhynchos, pilot of a Public Towing Vessel of 700 artabai burden, through me his wife Helene.

It is the custom that a single boatman should be provided from the city to serve on the said state-vessel. I have several times asked Eustochios . . . of the tribe which is at present responsible for this duty to provide a boatman for the current year, who will help in the service of the public corn-supply. But he puts it off day after day, and has not provided a man. For this reason I send this petition, requesting your Grace to send for him and compel him all the same to assign me a boatman.[13]

Here the boat, *ploion polykopon* (many-oared), is being used for state cargo, but other texts suggest that the term also applies to a gala-ship kept at the exclusive service of the Prefect on tour. A special impost was demanded for its upkeep.[14] We meet also in 229 a superintendent of the Prefect's boats, who probably was in charge of boats carrying the imperial post. In our text he is dealing with the alum-monopoly, but this can have been only one of his many duties:

Aurelius Domitius, Superintendent of the Prefect's Boats, etc., to his dear friends the Aurelioi, Sarapion also called Apollonianos, Diogenes son of Sarapion, and Ptolemaios son of Ptolemaios, all three ex-magistrates of the City of Oxyrhynchos, superintendents of the alum-monopoly—greeting.

The six five-day accounts of the alum-monopoly, from 1st to 5th Thoth of the present year, which you have sent, two for the Dioiketes' Department, one for the Roman Archives, one for the Procurator of the Nome, one for his Bureau, one for the Oikonomoi, were received by me on the 20th of the month and forwarded.

I pray for your health, dear friends.[15]

Further, the localities had to provide provisions and other goods for the visit of the Prefect. Apparently an album was prepared in the district where the Prefect stopped, and the list was revised every year:

(A.D. 145-7) From the Secretaries of Hermopolis. Since you ask for the names of those who are to supply and prepare necessities for the Auspicious Visit of the Most Illustrious Prefect Valerius Proclus, we submit the names of those already listed except those exempted by special warrant, and we name substitutes for those drafted into other duties and for those who have died, as follows:

Supplying white bread and vegetables, 4 names from the previous list and 3 others to take the place of 1 dead and 2 on other duties.

Supplying veal, pork, and other commodities, 12 names from the previous list and 7 substitutes provided for 8 others assigned to other public liturgies.

Supplying wine and sour wine, 5 names as previously listed.

Supplying hay, chaff, and barley, 3 names ditto.

Supplying wood, charcoal, torches, and lights, 5 names ditto.

Supplying geese, 2 names ditto.

Supplying oil and lentils, 1 name and 1 substitute.

Supplying fowl and game, 1 name and 1 substitute.

Supplying olives, pickles, cheese, and other goods from the general store, 2 names.

Supplying vegetables and fish, 3 names.

Supplying riding-donkeys and . . . , 2 names.[16]

The amount assigned to each nome was apportioned by assessors to each village. Though the barley dealt with in the following document was for a squadron at Koptos, the procedure in requisitions was the same as in other cases where the Prefect was concerned.

(A.D. 185) To Damarion, strategos of the Hermopolite nome, from Antonius Justinus, duplicarius, dispatched by Valerius Frontinus, Prefect of the Heraclian Squadron stationed at Koptos.

I have had measured to me by the elders of the village of Terton Epa in the Upper Patemite District the proportion imposed upon their village out of the 20,000 art. of barley which his Highness the Prefect Longaeus Rufus commanded to be bought up from the produce of the past 24th year for the requirements of the aforesaid Squadron, of barley, measured by the official standard at the time appointed for measuring, one hundred art., total 100 art. of barley, in accordance with the division made by the assessors of the nome. And I have issued four copies of this receipt.[17]

Visits paid by the strategos of the nome also led to requisitions from individuals to cover his entertainment.

(2nd–3rd century) To Thonis, poulterer. Provide for the visit of the strategos 4 fowls at ten drachmai.[18]

Here, however, the goods seem paid for, as in a receipt of 219, in which a greengrocer of Oxyrhynchos acknowledges that the strategos has paid him through his freedman Theon, "the value of gathered vegetables supplied by me from the month Tybi of the present 2nd year to Pharmouthi inclusive in the said 2nd year at the rate of 8 dr. per month, in all for the period of 4 months thirty-two dr. of silver, total 32 dr., which I have received through the bank of Sosias on the south of the colonnade in the paved avenue."[19] (No doubt, however, officials or great men acted callously, as Polemon in Ptolemaic times, who wrote to the lesonis or chief administrator "of the great god Sebnektynis, greeting. You will do well to provide on my behalf three rooms, with covers and all necessaries, as we are arriving with the whole household. In every way watch out that on our arrival there is not the least negligence. Keep well.")[20]

Various letters mention the Prefect's tour. We have seen how a soldier of the Pselkis garrison was afraid of striking the Prefect's flotilla if he went off downstream. In the 2nd century a writer, addressing his letter "to the house of Pausanias, ex-clerk of the City (of Oxyrhynchos), for Athenarous daughter of Kerdon," said, "Please receive through Kerdon for Dionysios 4 kotylai of unguent, a basket of dessert containing 100 figs, and ½ chous of oil, of which you are to give 4 kot. to the said Dionysios and keep a kot. for yourself. Greet your mother and Matris and her children and all who love you. I am going to Koptos with the Prefect." He does not make clear if he is attached to the Prefect or is somehow going to get a place in his boat.[21]

Later in the same century another writer mentions casually his journey with the Prefect. He does not seem in the retinue; we may assume that in the considerable number of officials and menials accompanying the Prefect, it was possible for odd travellers to find a place on the boats.

Sarapion to his most esteemed Antonios Minor, greeting. As I was sailing down to Alexandreia in haste, I happened to go to the lodging which is in Memphis of the employees of your estate, so that I might write to you from there—and I found no one who was going to you.

When I sailed upriver with the Prefect and fell in with our friend Marcus, I sought to discover if you were there. And since I didn't find you, I made assiduous inquiries after your health, and I went up-country delighted to learn that you were well. I write to you now, then, most esteemed friend, first to salute you and my lord Ammonia-nos and all your kin, and next to ask you all by all means to lend me through Morion's men three fullgrown cows, fine and large of body, as I am about to plough land that has lain fallow. That's why I need them.

So that you may carry this out for me with dispatch, I beg you to let me know their price and I'll send it to you from here. I haven't been able to give the price, since it's uncertain, to Morion's man, who is in a hurry to get away. . . . was bought.

(2nd hand) I pray for your good health, my lord, together with that of my lord Ammonianos and all your kin. Send me the cows by all means, as I have need of them for the farms. And if there is any reason for going to Alexandreia, come to me by all means, for I am now about to go there, with the gods' help.[22]

Again in the late 2nd century or early 3rd a woman wrote two letters together:

Thaisarion to Serenos and . . . her brothers, very many greetings. Before all else I pray for your health and make obeisance on your behalf to Our Lord Sarapis. I want you to know I received from Nilos . . . Yourself then receive from him a bundle of reeds and sandals—4 pairs for Herais, 2 for Serenos, 1 for Ammonios, 1 for . . . and rouge. When out sister . . . send me a letter at once. I salute Ammonios and Sambous. Ptolemaios and Alexandros salute you all.

Thaisarion to Serapous her sister and her brothers, very many greetings. Before all else I pray for your health and make obeisance on your behalf to Our Lord Sarapis. I want you to know that our brother Prolemaios went upcountry in the morning at . . . hour on 9 Epeiph. I used for his dinner whatever you sent me. Please send me the half—2 jars of radish oil—of the same value as that I used. For I have need of them when I give birth, and after all he is your brother as well. Ammonios sailed up with the Prefect as a member of his staff, and wherever he may be he will visit you. If my mother decides to come back with him, let her make herself ready. You have not even thought fit to write me one letter. Send me a jar of salve. . . .[23]

Here the brother is on the staff, but it seems he can add his mother to the passengers on the return journey.

For the 4th century we have an order to an agent; "Give

Gennadios the carpetmaker for the price of a carpet on the occasion of the Duke's visit 2,250,000 denars, equivalent to 1,500 talants. I pray for your health. The 45th, 27th, and 11th years, 8 Tybi." The date refers to three local eras (starting in 307, 325, and 341, and distinct from two other Oxyrhynchite eras dated from 324 and 355, which soon superseded the others). The writer, Athanasios, must have been an official or a magnate; for even with the depreciation of the billon coinage at this time (A.D. 352) the carpet was costly.[24]

11

The Insatiable Sea

WE saw that the Apsu of the Sumerians, the Nun of the Egyptians, the Okeanos of the Greeks, were at root the same cosmic image. In Babylonia the Creation-myth assumed a supreme importance. In the primeval world there was only Apsu, the sweet-water Ocean, and Tiamat the salt-water Ocean; from them the gods were born. The two Oceans are disturbed by the noise of the younger gods, and Apsu plans to kill them. Defeated by Ea, she is enclosed in a sacred chamber, where the young god Marduk is born. Tiamat in time takes up the conflict, together with a horde of monstrous creatures. Marduk finally kills her in single combat, splits her in half—one half becoming the sky, one half the earth. Guards are charged not to let her waters escape.

In Ugaritic myth the highgod El, often called Bull El, lives in his field at the source of the rivers; his son is Baal, fertility-god, the Rider of the Clouds. Baal is at feud with Yam-Nahar, god of seas and rivers. Yam sends messengers to demand the surrender of Baal, and the council of gods agrees. Baal, however, refuses to give in. He attacks Yam and defeats him; but at the insistence of the goddess Ashtoreth (Astarte) he spares him. In Greek myth we noted that Homer and Aischylos preserve the memory of an antagonism of Okeanos and Zeus. Is there anything similar in Egyptian tales?

There is indeed. A tale, written perhaps under Horemheb, on the borders of the 18th and 19th dynasties, tells of a god's battle with the Sea.[1] Unfortunately it is very fragmentary and many details remain obscure. I give here a full version so that the reader may appreciate the ingenuity with which scholars have made sense of it.

his two bulls. I will worship you . . . I will worship the . . . I will

worship the Sky . . . seat . . . the Earth . . . Ptah . . . the Earth. And
the Earth was content. . . . I will discover his . . . Then they bent down
like . . . Then each embraced [his comrade . . .] after seven days. And
the Sky . . . descended on . . . the God of the Sea. And . . . the Earth
brought forth . . . the Four Regions of the [Earth . . .] in his midst
like . . . [his] sovran throne. And he . . . brought him the tribute . . .
before the tribunal. Then Renenutet [Renutet, harvest-goddess] bore . . .
as sovran . . . Sky. See, the tribute is brought to him . . . his . . . or
indeed he will take us as prisoners . . . our own . . . Renenutet [brought
him] his tribute consisting of silver and gold, lapiz-lazuli [and tur-
quoise, filling] the coffers. Then they said to the Ennead: Bring it
about that . . . the tribute of the God of the Sea, so that hearken for us
to all the words [of the Earth?] and we may be protected by his hand.
Is it that he . . .

For they are afraid of [. . . the tribute] of the God of the Sea. Bring it
about . . . the tribute of the God of the Sea . . . bad. And Renenutet takes
a . . . Astarte. Then . . . say . . . birds, hear what I want to say. Do not
do away . . . another. Come, let's go and find Astarte . . . her house,
and cry under [the window of the room where] she sleeps. And say to
her: If you are [awake . . .] if you are plunged in sleep, I will wake you
up . . . the God of the Sea as sovran over the . . . the sky. Come to them
at the [moment . . .]Asiatics. And Astarte . . . the daughter of Ptah. So
. . . of the God of the Sea, the . . . Go yourself with the tribute of the
[God of the sea . . .] Then Astarte wept . . . lord was silent. . . . Lift up
your face and . . . outside. Then [she] bore . . . the . . . sang while
laughing at him. . . . [The God of the Sea] saw Astarte who was seated
on the margin of the Sea. Then he said to her: Whence do you come,
daughter of Ptah, raging and violent goddess? Have you torn the
sandals that are on your feet and have you rent the clothes that were on
you, going and coming as you have done across the sky and the earth?
Then [Astarte] said to him . . . [the gods of] the Ennead. If they give me
you [daughter . . .] them. And what will I then do against them, I?
And Astarte heard what the God of the Sea had said on his side. She
set about going before the gods of the Ennead at the place where they

49. The Seth Animal

were. And the great ones saw her and rose up before her. And the lesser ones saw her and lay down on their bellies. And the throne was given to her and she took her seat. And there was brought to her . . .

Earth . . . the pearls . . . And the pearls . . . the messenger of Ptah went to tell these words to Ptah and to Nut. Then Nut took off the pearls from round her throat, and she put them in the scales . . . Astarte. O my . . . this quarrel with the Ennead. Then he will send and demand the ring of Geb . . . in which is the scales. Then . . . my basket of . . . of the God of the Sea . . . on the gates . . . gates. Went out . . . If they came again . . . and he [will come] to cover the earth and the mountains and . . . to fight with him because . . . he sat down, coldly. He will not come to fight with us. Then Seth sat down . . .[2]

One thing appears at first reading. The main character is the God of the Sea, who is demanding tribute. There seems a general fear of this hostile god. Then, with a close scrutiny, a sketchy outline of the myth appears. Renutet takes tribute to the Sea and also seems to send a messenger (a bird?) to Astarte, who is bidden to go with the tribute. Astarte weeps. The Sea watches her on the shore and asks whence she has come—whether her journeyings have worn out her sandals and clothes. (In Egypt she was considered the daughter of Ptah, a goddess of wrath.[3]) Then we find the Sea addressing Ptah and saying that if the Ennead give him the hand of Astarte, no attacks from him are to be feared. Astarte hears his words, goes to the Ennead, who greet her with respect and grant her a place as a newly-elected member. (Perhaps she acts as an intermediary between the Sea and the other gods.) In the following fragments we seem to find the Sea renewing his demands. Nut, at Ptah's request, tries to pacify him with gifts. But the Sea still rages and threatens a great Flood that will cover earth and mountains. Finally Seth seems sent on to fight with him.

We are reminded of the Babylonian and Ugaritic myth, especially the latter; for the Sea is there a god like Yam, not like Tiamat, and the Ennead's deliberations suggest the Ugaritic council of gods with its waverings. Astarte appears to come from the Land of the Asiatics; and the very fact of this intrusive goddess in an Egyptian tale suggests a borrowing from the Near East.[4] There is further the myth of a seamonster, Hedammu, who ravages the

land with his gluttony, till he is seduced by Ishtar and his depre-
dations are ended: while a Hurrite legend mentions the triumph
of the stormgod over the seagod.[5] In the myth of Illuyanka, the
Hittite dragon, we find a mixture of the themes of dragon fighting a stormgod and of monster lured by a goddess.[6] But we are
forced back to the myth of Yam and Baal for the best parallel.[7]
There is no exact reduplication of details, but the general
similarity is striking.[8]

The Sea in the Egyptian tale is called *Ym*. This new word for
sea appeared about a century before our tale was written. The
earliest known example occurs in the year 47 of Thotmose III
(c. 1450 B.C.); thereafter Ym soon became the usual term for sea
or lake, displacing the classic term meaning the Great Green.[9]
It was clearly brought in by the soldiers of the Asian campaigns,
the seamen and traders, and the hosts of captives. At the same time
new cults were introduced, those of Astarte, Anat, Reshep,
Hurin, Qadesh, Ishtar, and others.[10] From early in the reign of
Amenhotep II (c. 1435) Astarte took her place in the Memphite
area, at Perunefer where Phoenicians frequented the port; and till
a late period her cult flourished at Memphis.[11] Our tale, with its
elevation of Ptah to supreme deity, has certainly had a Memphite
origin.[12] Astarte thrust her way into Egyptian myth. In *The
Contendings of Horos and Seth* she becomes the daughter of Re, the
Heliopolitan god, who there has the supreme position; and Neith
advises Re to give his daughters Anat and Astarte to Seth to
repay him for the loss of the throne of Egypt to Horos.[13] (Though
there is here no link with the Sea-myth, it is of interest to find her
associated with Seth.) We learn also of a myth in which Anat
and Astarte "conceive but do not bring forth".[14] But only in the
Sea-myth does she play an important part; and it seems likely
that this myth was composed when she was still a new-arrival at
Memphis, but had attracted much cult-attention. Her place in
the pantheon was thus explained and justified.[15]

Seth and Astarte appear in association in a text of Ramses II
connected with a foundation on the Syrian road: "His West is
the House of Amun, his South is the House of Seth, Astarte is
found at his rising, Uadjit at his North." On an architrave from
the gate of Sesac we find, "The . . . of Astarte, the Bull of Seth-

Mentu, the son of Mentu active with his arm . . . " The mutilation prevents us from knowing what the king was for the goddess.[16]

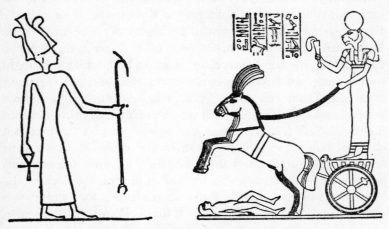

50. Astarte: as war-goddess lion-headed in chariot

Ym had already been personified in *The Tale of Two Brothers*. There Bata warns his wife (created for him by Knuum) not to go out or the sea will carry her off.

She dwelt in the house while he spent the day in hunting desert-game, bringing it back and setting it down before her. And he said to her: "Don't go outside, so that the God of the Sea [Ym] may not carry you off; you would not be able to save yourself from him, for you are only a woman after all. My heart is placed on the top of the umbrella-pine, and if another finds it, I must fight with him." And he revealed to her everything about his heart.

And many days after that Bata went to hunt, as was his daily habit. Then the young woman went out to walk under the umbrella-pine that stood beside the house. And lo, she saw the God of the Sea rolling his waves behind her. She began to run away and went back into the house. But the God of the Sea called to the pine: "Catch her for me." And the pine snatched off a tress of her hair and brought it to Egypt. . . .[17]

Though *The Two Brothers* is composed as a sort of folk tale, it has a clear mythological content not far behind it. Bata is the god Bata; his brother Anup is Anubis; and the episode of the Tress belongs to the myths of Isis—we have seen the divine Tress with its cult at Koptos. Bata, a local god, came late into the pantheon; he was invoked in a poem on the war-chariot of the king and called Lord of Saka (in the Kynopolite nome, Middle Egypt); and he can be shown to be apparently a form of Seth. Here then at last we touch a link of Seth with the Sea-god conflict.[18] In the tale Bata is changed into a bull, which is brought to the king with Anubis on its back, and later treacherously sacrificed. From obscure references in various religious texts we can make out that the bull-transformation was important in his myth. Seth (Bata) changes into a bull; Anubis captures and chastises him, then puts on his back the things he has stolen: hence, we are told, the name of Saka. The same papyrus also mentions that Osiris is set by his son Anubis on the back of the Seth-Bull who is Bata. At Edfu we read, in a long litany, this comment on the name of the Dog Nome, "You are Horos who took up his Father from the funerary hill and set him on the back of the Bull"—there is here a pun on the name Saka, metropolis of the province, and Horos is evidently the Horos-Anubis of the 17th nome. A further reference occurs in a geographical notice where the king brings to Horos of Edfu the territory of the Dog-nome: "for he is he that strikes the bulls, for whom is laid low the bull of sacrifice and enslaved the backbone of Chaï [Seth]". At least we can make out the identification of Seth, Bata, and Bull, in a violent conflict with Horos-Anubis.[19]

More importantly still, in the medical Hearst papyrus, written at the start of the Eighteenth Dynasty, a formula dealing with the "Asiatic Disease" states that "even as Seth has conquered the Sea, so Seth will conquer you, you Asiatic one, so that you will not pervade the limbs of X, the son of Y".[20] Here the Sea is called the Great Green; the name *Ym* is not yet known. For the Egyptians of the time the Mediterranean was the expanse of water joining the Delta and Phoinikia: the Great Sea of Syria.[21] This connection of Sea and Syria helps to suggest the image of Seth repelling the Asiatic Disease as he repelled the Sea. Seth also in early days was described as a Ship that carried Osiris (or Osiris-King) over the Waters of Death.[22] We may further note the way in which myth had become entangled with history. Seth against the Sea was emotionally identified with the Egyptians against the invading Hyksos, who like the Sea in the myth exacted a heavy tribute.[23]

There was a contradiction in the historical application; for the Hyksos had had an important cult of Seth, so that he represented in historical terms the attackers, the engulfing Sea, not the rescuer, the uprising national forces. It seems that it was at this Hyksos-period and its immediate aftermath that Seth became a widely-held emblem of any invading, attacking, and destructive groups. In the period of the Persian invasion, and no doubt in more hidden ways under the Ptolemies and the Romans, Seth stood for foreign oppressors. A few later texts will give us some idea of the fury of hatred that was concentrated thus on Seth:

They chase out the Perverse-of-nature: "We send you in misery back to the land of Asia. Egypt obeys Horos and leaves you wounded. They will repeat the evil that you have committed. They will condemn you to fire."[24]

In such ritual threats nobody would mind the contradiction of both expelling a god and consuming him by fire.

[Thoth speaks:] Remember what you [Re-Harakhti] have ordered when making the law you have set on the conduct of men, on the statute of the gods, and on the king's counsel in his palace, and the charter I have made by order of the Lord Atum, giving Egypt to Horos and the Desert to Seth, when the Lands were shared out between them: to hate violence, love justice, and put the Son on the seat of his Father.

Behold, the wretched Seth has arrived on the highways. He has come to pillage with his hand. He has schemed to carry out rapine by force, as it has been done formerly, destroying cities, ruining their sanctuaries, setting tumult in the temples.

He has committed crime, renewed evil, raised up riots once again. He has cast disaster into Memphis' great sanctuary. He has fomented revolt in Memphis. See too, he has penetrated into Memphis' Sarapieion. He has cast disaster into the temple of Ipet [the hippopotamus-goddess]. He has cut the sacred tree of Saosis down. He has caught the fish that swim in the Great Lake. He has hunted the animals, taken the birds in snares in the temple of he who presides over the Houses [Horos of Chemmis].

He has stridden with long strides into Het-Web [Pure Castle:

where] his voice has sounded beside the Ennead of the gods. He has stirred up war, he has aroused uproar, by the gods of Menesowet. He has begun again to commit a grave offence on the river banks of This. He has cast tumult into Busiris, the town and the nome of Mendes are laid desolate. He has overrun the Castle-of-Spirits at Mendes. He has raised his voice and shouted inside its walls.

51. The god with Ass-ears

He has taken off the sacred tree of Sais of Neith. He has caused havoc in the jewellery of the temple. He has raised up riots in the cemetery and massacre in the town of Kheraha. He has brought in what Atum abominates in the temple of the Ennead of the gods. He has provoked warfare, he has cast tumult into Amun the Great's temple in the nekropolis. He has planned war, he has made conflict rise in the temple of the Spirit of the East [Septu]. He has shown himself at Saft-el-Henneh [Castle of the Jujube-tree], he has traversed the district of Chenen. He has damaged the sacred Jujube-tree whose verdure is the land's prosperity.

He has invaded the sacred Grove of Saosis where stands the acacia in which are Life and Death. He has desired to eat the sacred Cat in the presence of its mother Bastet. See too, he has fed upon mullet in the cities of the Spirit of the East. He has set out in expedition against the Theban nekropolis in the presence of Re who is in Heaven. He has regaled himself on the Ram in the temple of Amun the Great. He has set his hand on the sacred plant in the presence of the Ram of Mendes.

He has made a slaughter of people at Busiris in the presence of Onnophris the Justified [Osiris]. He has fed on the abdu-fish; he has eaten mullet in the Great Hall of Heliopolis. He has suppressed the service, he has stolen the offerings in the palace of the Sole Lord who has no equal. In his palace are heard murmurs against all the gods. Nobody gives them worship at the requisite moment. He has hunted the falcon, he has caught the itenu-fish in the presence of Shu and Tefnut. See too, he has caught the Bull Apis in a lasso in the presence of the Creator of Beings. He has drawn out all the milk of Horos' fostering Cow, he has hunted the sacred cow, the god's Mother. He has suppressed the service of the Lake of temu-trees, he has dried up the Lake of the Sacred Cow.

He has conceived the scheme of setting up as Brigand and wants to impose himself on all by his efforts. Misfortune begins at the place where he is found. It is the reversal of what you [Re] have commanded.[25]

All the allusions cannot be made out; but the compiler is clearly heaping up all the blasphemies he can think of. The national war is translated into a conflict of deities, and the destroyer is not a foreign god but is Seth, the fomentor of dissention and murder inside Egypt. We must remember that the people in general were not admitted to the temples; they merely worshipped the representations on pylons, the sacred animals, and the like. Some sacred sites were specially taboo, for instance the little isle of Bigeh near Philai, where no humans at all were allowed. On its borders no hunting or fishing might go on, and the air must not be disturbed by voice or sound, for fear that Osiris would be woken from his Last Sleep. His temple at Het-Web and the sanctuary at Mendes were similarly guarded; and no doubt there were many more such sites. If foreigners forced their way into sacred spots of this kind, the horror would be great; the frame of things, it would seem, was about to break unless the pollution was wiped out.[26]

The conflict of Seth and Horos went far back and seems connected originally with the warrings and struggles that brought about tribal unity, the unity of the Two lands. It became entangled with the Osirian myth; Seth was made the killer of the saviour-god and Horos his son, who fought Seth and justified his Father. Such an important myth, or series of partly-fused myths, was naturally revalued and given new overtones with each great experience of national disaster and revival.[27] The idea that history re-enacts a primal event—as each important rite, by stabilising the universe afresh, re-enacts the first creation—is clearly brought out by the statement that Ptolemy V despatched the Egyptian rebels at Lykopolis in the Delta with the same ritual as that with which in primeval times in this very place the gods Re and Horos, son of Isis, had put their rebels to death. Perhaps here this interpretation was in part made because of the strongly nationalist aspect of the revolt; it used the traditional Egyptian images against the nationalists. But in any event it shows a typical mode of thought.[28] Since Horos looms so large as the champion against evil monsters, it is worth while glancing in some detail at Seth's solar role, so opposed is it to the later conception of him as the evil one. His place in the solar boat is brought out in the funerary papyri and on the coffins of the great priests and singers of Amun. Thus, in the papyrus of the chantress Her-Uben, the solar boat is drawn by four jackals and four uraeus with hands. A great serpent rears his head up before the boat, but Seth stands in the prow, ready to drive his lance in its jaws. In the middle of the boat is Re-Harmakhis on a throne with falcon-head and solar disk, surrounded by a serpent. Below, in mummified form, are falcon-headed Horos and Ibis-headed Thoth.[29]

Seth has the same role in litanies.[30] In a scene at Medinet-Habu the enemy flee before Ramses III's chariot: scared "as if Seth in his fury laid low the Enemy at the prow of the boat Sektet".[31] Here are some more texts:

Do not go out this day at sunrise. This was the day when one saw Sebek killed by Seth at the prow of the great boat, on this day.

[Hymn to Sungod] The two sons of the Nile have killed for you the serpent Nik. Nubti [Seth] with his shafts.

Rise up, Seth beloved of Re, rise up in your place in the boat of Re, he has received your justified heart. You have laid low [the enemy] of your father Re, each day.

You sail towards your two heavens without enemies, while your burning breath has devoured the serpent Neha-Her. The fish Decher guards the water of your boat, while the fish Abdu has announced to you the serpent Unti. Nubti strikes him with his shafts when he has . . . the heaven and the earth of his storms. His magic is powerful to repel his enemies, his lance is planted in the serpent Ubenro.

Horos at his place as guardian of the helm and Nebed [Seth] transfixing the Enemy.

But at the moment of evening, he [the snake-foe of Re] turned his eye against Re. Then he brought about a halt in the two crews and a great shock in the boat's course. (Then he swallowed up one cubit and three palms of the great water; then Seth launched against him his spear of bronze and made him vomit up all that he had swallowed.)

52. Seth and Horos teaching the Pharaoh (Seth as archer)

Then Seth bent against him. Words that he pronounced like a magic
formula . . .[32]

The bracketed sentence is met only with the New Kingdom.

One magic papyrus says of the monster, "The god of Ombos
[Seth] sharpens his shafts in him, he shakes sky and earth by his
thunder-storms, his magic powers are mighty, conquering his
enemy, his axe cuts up the wide-mouthed dragon." Another:
"Stand up, Seth beloved of Re, stand at your place in the ship of
Re! He has received his heart in justification; you have daily
thrown down [the enemies] of your father Re." A Greek papyrus
addresses Seth as "hillshaker thunderer hurricane-raiser rock-
shaker the destroyer who disturbs the sea itself."[33]

To return now to Seth and the Sea. A medical papyrus of the
19th dynasty (c. 1250 B.C.) has a formula to be recited over the
swallower of a potion. At the end, dealing with the interventions
of Isis and Nephthys, it says: "They are efficaceous for it, as that
which is in the divine Falcon, as when one strikes the bird 'hy, as
when the Sea hears the voice of Seth." Seth is here considered to
have decisive power over the Sea.[34]

The Voice of Seth has power because Seth is a stormgod. He
is Lord of the Storm in the Pyramid Texts.[35] At the end of the

N

Contendings Re says, "Let Seth, son of Nut, be confided to me, so that he may dwell with me and be as my Son; he will thunder in the heavens and one will be afraid of him." In *Unawen*: "See, Amun thunders in the heavens and causes Sutkeh [Seth] to [rave] in his season." Ploutarch makes Typhon [Seth] the cause of thunder and lightning.[36] The Rhind mathematical papyrus states, "Year 11, 1st month of Flood Season, 3rd day, Birth of Seth: the Majesty of this god has given thunder." In coffin texts he is Lord of the Northern Heavens.[37] His beast-sign is used as determinate for words expressing atmospheric disturbances. He has the epithet Great of Roaring.[38] The Pyramid Texts say: "N ascends to heaven. Heaven rejoices for him; the earth quakes for him; the tempest drives for him. He roars like Seth. The guardians of the parts of heaven open the doors of heaven for him. He stands on Shu; he upholds the stars, in the shadow of the walls of god."[39] That is, the deadman go up to heaven as a storm. Seth as the storm-power is thus far earlier than the Sea-myth and owes nothing to an identification with Baal.

Seth's association with the bull probably comes in main part from his role as thundergod. In the Pyramid Texts, Seth is identified with the various sorts of bulls that appear in a sacrificial rite; and another passage says, "He has slain for you like a bull him who slew you."[40] Usually the context is one of storm and violence. "May you let N pass by through the Divided Opening. If you drive N back, he will drive you back. Horos fell because of his eye, Seth suffered because of his testicles."[41] (The Divided Opening has the determinative of a place-name, but it suggests a lightning-split in the heavens.) "N is a heartbeat, son of the heart of Shu, wide-outstretched a blinding light. It is N who is a flame before the wind to the ends of heaven and to the end of the earth, as soon as the arms of the lightning are emptied of N. He travels through Shu and strides through Aker He kisses the red crown, the divinely-created. Those who are in the arbour [? heaven] open for him their arms. N stands in the eastern side of heaven; [where] there is brought to him that which ascends to heaven. N makes a separation of the tempest."[42] Here there is no doubt of the image of heaven-ascent as a lightning-stroke; then N stands in heaven. As a lightning-flash he cleaves the storm-clouds and drives them apart. As the Seth-animal appears as a determinative there is certainly a reference to the conflict of Horos and Seth—the lightning here is the spear of Horos and the storm-roar is the voice of Seth wounded and screaming in pain. (The lightning-weapon must originally have been Seth's; now it is turned against him and he is the sacrificed roaring bull.) The god Aker personifies the two doors of the earth, the east and the west, through which the Sun passes; he was represented as a double sphinx with human heads, as a lion, as two lions seated back to back. In another text the deadman threatens, if refused entry, to smash the heavens in a Sethean fury. "He will let loose a tempest on those who did wrong, and a flood over the Ancients; then will he strike away the arms of Shu under Nut, and N will put his arm on the wall [of Shu] on which you [Seth] lean."[43]

53. Horos spearing the Hippopotamus

Seth, like other gods, could raise or calm storms. In our Sea-myth he presumably fought the Sea as the storm-god or thunder-god and wielded the thunderbolt. A storm in a sea-region could be imagined as a battle of heaven and the waters. Indeed, it could be interpreted as a repetition of the original creation-act. In the Teaching of Merikare (known in three manuscripts of the Eighteenth Dynasty, but going back to an original of the late First Intermediate Period, c. 2070), there is an account of Creation: "He has created for their sake heaven and earth, he has checked the greed of water, he has created air to make their nose live."[44] The word for greed is *snk*, determined by a crocodile; and the passage has therefore been taken to mean that a watermonster or crocodile-of-the-waters was defeated. But no *snk*-monster is known, and the crocodile appears as determinant with other words meaning greed, voracity.[45] In the creation-account the protagonist who tames the Sea is a creator-god, not named but probably the sungod; in the Sea-myth and the medical papyri, he is Seth.[46]

The transfer of roles from one god to another in myths, and the splitting of a single figure, such as the creator-god here, into several figures, is nothing unusual. The core of the Sea-myth is then a creation-story, which has been elaborated and detached, with the addition of further motives. The choice of Seth as the champion of the gods is no doubt determined by his position as thundergod and by his role in the solar boat.[47] There he stands in the prow and tackles the enemy of Re, who seeks to obstruct the course of the sun—the giant serpent, Apepi.[48] This monster is connected with the Sea. He swallows up the water necessary for navigation.[49] In a hymn to Amun, Amun's Eye pierces the snake and makes him give up the swallowed Ocean. Elsewhere we find a tortoise as the beast that threatens to swallow down the Nile-flood.[50]

If we look back at the very fragmentary opening of the Sea-myth, we can see that it seems to have been made up of a creation-story.[51] Both the solar and the Memphite theologies knew the myth of the Insatiable Sea and worked it into their rival doctrines of creation. In all ancient religions, as generally in tribal cosmologies, the sea is the realm of death. Ploutarch tells us:

The Nile flowing from the North and swallowed up in the South by the Sea is said to have his birth in the lefthand region and his death in the right. For this reason the priests abominate the Sea and call salt the Foam of Typhon [Seth], and it is one of their prohibitions: not to put salt on the table. They do not speak to seamen or make use of the sea, and they keep the ox away from the sea; and from this cause mainly they reject fish and write up: Hate fish. At any rate at Sais, in the forecourt of Athena's temple, there was sculptured a child, an old man, then a hawk and next a fish, and at the end, a river-horse, and it

means symbolically: O you that are coming into life and you that are
going out of it. . . . For this reason the old man . . .

By the hawk they mean God, by the fish Hatred, on account of the
sea [as above stated], by the river-horse Impudence, for that beast is
said to have killed his father and raped his mother. And the saying of
the Pythagoreans that the Sea is the Tears of Kronos, seed, may seem to
imply the impurity and unsociable nature of the same element.[52]

A similar attitude appears again in his account:

Egypt was once Sea. Hence many places in the mines and in the
mountains are found to the present day to contain shells; and all
springs and wells, of which there are many, have brackish and bitter
waters, as though being a stale remnant of the former sea which had
collected there. But in time Osiris got the better of Typhon [Seth].
That is, a good season of rains came on the Nile and drove off the
sea, brought the flat ground to light and filled it up with alluvial
deposits. A thing which can call on the testimony of our senses. For
we see even now the River perpetually bringing down fresh mud. . . .[53]

It is a far cry from these Egyptian fantasies to the scientific
universe of Lucretius; yet the concept of the Sea pervading
his poem has many affinities with that which we are tracing. For
him the sea possesses incessant motion and measureless expanse.
The movement of the atoms in the void is like that of the sea;
the universe is a "sea of matter". The troubled human condition
is again a sort of sea, a chaos of passions—anger, love, sheer
uncertainty, tides of war. Atomic compounds are like ships,
intruders on the inexorable sea, beaten and wrecked by violent
waves. The dying universe is running on to the rocks in wreck.
The sea is death, the inescapable law of dissolution. Yet against
the cruel sea stands the earth of Venus, secure and blest with light.
The phrase "into the coasts of light" refers to this endless conflict
of sea and earth, destruction and stability; it expresses the
movement across the bounds between land and water.[54]

We could hardly claim that there is any direct Egyptian
element influencing Lucretius; his ideas here, however, could at
least in part be connected with many aspects of Greek thought.
(Ploutarch cited the Pythagoreans to illustrate Egyptian notions
about the sea.) But no doubt Egypt contributed its quota to the
mass of mythic ideas and images which the Greeks took in and

partly rationalised or made the basis for scientific hypotheses. To bring out the extent to which the imagery of Apsu-Nun-Yam-Okeanos lay deep in ancient religious thinking we may pause to consider how Yahweh of Israel was also a fighter with Ocean and its monster. Here again the conflict is closely linked with creation-myths. In Psalm 89 we read: "Thou dost rule the raging of the sea. . . . Thou didst crush Rahab like a carcass." Yahweh as stormgod tames the sea. "He plants his footsteps in the sea and rides upon the storm." "By his power he stilled the sea."[55] (In Ugaritic texts Asherah walks on the sea and Baal rides in the clouds.)[56] The elemental struggle is transferred to the fight of Yahweh's people against the power of Egypt. Rahab is the monster of chaos, and the "fleeing serpent" whom Yahweh pierces is her dragon-companion Leviathan; she in turn becomes Egypt, the threatening imperial nation, and is used to represent her even when the storm-imagery is dropped. "For Egypt's help is worthless and empty, therefore I have called her Rahab who sits still."[57]

54. Astarte as Sphinx

As Rahab becomes Egypt, her dragon becomes the Egyptian pharaoh. Hophra is "the great dragon that lies in the midst of his streams". He is told that, Leviathan as he is, he will be dragged from his river with a hook and thrown into the wilderness to be devoured by beasts and birds of prey.[58] Isaiah declares: "In that day Yahweh with his hand and great and strong sword will punish Leviathan the fleeing serpent, Leviathan the twisting serpent, and he will slay the dragon that is in the sea."[59] The dragon here seems Egypt, while Leviathan may be Assyria or Babylon. The description of Leviathan exactly follows a Ugaritic text where Mot tells Baal that he'll overcome him. "You smote Lotan the fleeing serpent and destroyed the twisting serpent, the accursed one of seven heads." (We are reminded of the seven-headed dragon of *Revelation*.) The political use of

Rahab-Leviathan in Israel pairs off with the political use of Seth in Egypt.[60]

The deep-rooted notion of Yahweh as conqueror of the waters appears in many other spheres of the Old Testament. The festival of the autumnal equinox seems the setting of Habakkuk's prayer: "Was thy wrath against the rivers, Yahweh? was thy anger against the rivers or thy indignation against the sea? when thou didst ride upon thy horses, upon thy chariot of victory?" "The mountains saw thee and writhed; the raging waters swept on, the deep gave forth its voice, it lifted its hands on high." "Thou didst crush the head of the wicked" and "trample the sea with thy horses, the surging of mighty waters." Psalm 29 ends: "Yahweh sits enthroned over the flood."[61]

In passing we may note a tale of the conflict of Nile and Sea, though it has no link with the tradition we are examining. Seneca tells us that G. Balbillus, Prefect of Egypt under Nero, who wrote a book on the country and his journeys there, declared that during his prefecture there was a regular battle of dolphins from the sea and crocodiles from the river in the Herakleotic Mouth, the largest of the seven main outlets. "The crocodiles were defeated by their pacific foe, whose bites are harmless. The upper part of their body is covered with an impenetrable cuirass, proof against even the fangs of the larger animals, but the lower part is soft and tender. The dolphins plunged under the water, and with the aid of the sharp fins that stand up on their backs, they wounded their adversaries and disembowelled them, moving in the opposite direction. After several crocodiles had been destroyed, the others fled as from a defeat. Nothing is bolder than a crocodile before a fugitive; nothing more timid before a bold attack."[62]

It is of interest to note also a fragment of a tale from the Middle Kingdom about a herdsman who saw a goddess. (A scribe was cleaning a papyrus for reuse and left twenty-five lines from the book's middle.) There are two advents of the goddess, with a lyrical passage, perhaps of alternate songs, coming in between:

Behold, I came down to the pool near this pasturage and I saw there a woman. She was not of the race of mortals. My hair stood on end when I saw her curled wig and the smoothness of her skin. Never will I do what she said. Awe of her is in my body.

I tell you: Go, bulls, let us pass on. Let the cows cross and the goats rest by them near . . . the herdsmen at their rear. Our boat for the bulls and cows has reached its destination, and those of the herdsmen skilled [in magic] recite this waterspell:

My soul is glad, herdsmen, you men! I'll not be driven from the marsh this year of the high Nile which gives commands to the Back of the Earth [the uplands] so well that pool from river we can't tell.

Return to your house. In their place the cattle stay. [O high Nile] come. The fear of you I felt has gone away. The terror you inspired is dead: the wrath of the goddess Usrit, the fear that the Two Lands' Mistress bred.

And when the earth grew bright at early dawn, it was done as he said. The goddess met him as he went to the head of the pool. She came with her clothes stript off and her hair disarrayed. . . .

The fear of the water-spirit seems in some way linked with the fear of the high Nile, which despite its awesome aspect brings benefits. We are reminded of the Homeric *Hymn to Aphrodite* in which herdsman Anchises is afraid that if he mates with the goddess he will lose his manhood. (Succubas of various kinds are widespread; and in Arab incantations we find that if the lovely princess of the Jinns offers marriage to the man who has invoked her, he need not consent; but if he does, he becomes impotent. But here, as in the *Hymn*, the reference is more precise and may be linked with the seduction of Enkidu in *Gilgamesh* as well as Innana's attempt on Gilgamesh himself. Enkidu is sort of satyr, Gilgamesh's nature-self, and has thus some affinity with the Herdsman.)

In the Egyptian tale the goddess is an aspect of water and in some sense of the high Nile; she is thus different from the Astarte whom the Sea demands. But the link of a love-goddess with water in its dangerous aspect is worth noting.

12

Flood and Thunder

THE sea appears as the underworld in the ritual-myth of Adonis. Little gardens were made, particularly by women, in pots, shells, or vases. The seeds of plants or flowers (wheat, barley, fennel, lettuce) which sprouted in a few days, were put in; and the kepoi were probably set on the roofs of houses. The plants dried up and withered as quickly as they had grown. Then the kepoi were thrown into sea or well; and the pots or shells kept as memorials. In late times, no doubt through the influence of the Osirian cult, the rite was seen as one of resurrection; but the meaning of the surrender of the kepoi to the sea seems certainly to be simply that of the going-down of Adonis into death, into the underworld. Theokritos describes the festival at Alexandreia, and though he stresses the yearly return of Adonis (in the sprouting seed) he also shows that the going-down is the return to the world of death:

> In the morning we'll all of us gather with the dew
> and carry him out among waves that break on the beach
> with hair let loose and clothes falling down to our ankles
> and naked breasts, we'll strike up our shrill sweet song.
> You only Adonis, men say, of the demigods
> may visit the earth as well as Acheron River . . .[1]

Cyril of Alexandreia tells us: "While Aphrodite wept Adonis' death, a choir moaned and lamented over her; when she came up from hell and said she had found him she sought, they rejoiced with her and began to dance. This scene has been played up to our own days in the temples of Alexandreia."

The Egyptian legend of the Flood sent to destroy the earth is not like that of Sumeria, Babylonia, Israel, or Greece, with their heroes Zisudra (Atrakhasis in Akkadian), Utnapishtim, Noah, and Deukalion.² Here Re is the highgod. He grows old, his bones turning to silver, his limbs to gold, his hair to lapis lazuli. He hears the evil things that men and women are saying, and bids his retinue, "Cry out and bring me my Eye, and Shu and Tefnut, and Geb and Nut, and the Fathergods and Mothergods who were with me when I was in Nun, together with the god Nun himself. Bring these here secretly to me, so that men and women may not see them and be stricken with fear in the hearts. Come then (Nun) with them to the Great House, and let them declare their counsels. As for me, I will go from Nun into the place where I caused myself to come into being, and let those gods be brought to me there."³

So the gods were brought in and drawn up each side of him. He told them that men were plotting evil against him. Nun advised him to let his Eye go against the plotters. Re replied that they had fled into the mountainous deserts in fear of what they had said. The gods repeated that he should send his Eye out against men, in the form of Hathor. He did so, and Hathor slew men and women in the desert. He then told her that she had accomplished her work, and she declared, "When I gained mastery over men and women, it was very gratifying to my heart". So he said that he would do likewise and make mankind few in number. Thus Sekhmet (here Hathor as the Eye of Re) came into existence. She devoured men as her evening meal, so that she might wade in their blood—beginning from Hensu (Herakleopolis).

Re bade the gods, "Cry out and call to me swift and speedy messengers able to travel as fast as the shadow of the body". Then he told these messengers to go to Abu (Elephantine) and bring him pomegranates. The fruit were mashed in a mortar and mixed with the barley for beer that the women servants had crushed. The mixture was like human blood; and seven thousand pots of this beer were made.

Early in the darkness of the night Re ordered the soporific beer to be poured out over the fields till it was four spans deep. Then at daybreak the goddess set out. She found the flooded fields and her face looked lovely there. She drank and became drunk and forgot all about men and women. Re bade her come in peace and gave her the name of Amit. He said, "At every holy time and festival of the year, vessels of the sleep-inducing beer will be made—as many as there are serving-women". Thus in primeval times was established the custom of brewing this kind of beer for Hathor-festivals, as many pots as there were hand-maidens of Re.[4]

The priest reciting this text must wear new garments and white sandals, must wash in the waters of the Nile-flood, paint a figure of Maat (Truth) on his tongue with green pigment, and purify himself with a ninefold purification lasting three days.

The red waters covering the land seem the Nile-flood. At the end of July the deposits brought down by the Blue Nile give a reddish tinge to the river. The myth explains the miraculous change to blood or beer. According to Alexandros of Miletos, who in the last century B.C. wrote a book about the Jews, the Egyptian priests repeated the magical act at the pharaoh's orders in their efforts to outdo Moses' powers. Moses with his wand had made the Nile copiously overflow.[5] Naturally the Christians, with the miracle of water-into-wine at Cana at the back of their minds, attributed the colour-change of the Nile to Moses. Apollinarius mentions it in one of his psalms, and St Willibrod

55. The Henu Boat of Seker: Deadman kneels before it (BD Ani, ch. lxxiv)

in the 8th century recalls it when he and his companions are
dying of thirst in a desert-place.⁶

In Egypt a letter of bishop Dionysios (A.D. 216) writing of the
ravages of the plague and of the fighting that resulted from the
revolt of the Prefect L. Mucius Aemilianus, "As in the time of
Moses, the waters are changed into blood".⁷ Late in the 4th
century Epiphanios states that on 11 Tybi (6 January) the springs
and streams of water are changed into wine; "many witnesses
affirm that this happens in Egypt".⁸ Actually the reddening
occurred in the summer; but the civil calendar, as fixed under
Augustus, had artificially arrested in January the festival associated
with the colour-change. The Christian tradition later accepted
this date and made it that of the miracle of Cana. "On 6
January, in memory of the miracle performed by Christ, certain
springs and the very river of Nile take the colour of wine or are
changed into wine."⁹

The reddened waters had a special magical quality. In a
recipe for Divine Water we find that strong vinegar was added
to sulphur until "the liquid has the aspect of blood". The running-
red of the Nile must have helped to bring about the myth of
Osiris murdered and dismembered in the river. The yearly
festival of the death, resurrection and triumph of the god at
Abydos took place at the beginning of the 4th month of the
Egyptian year, when the waters were receding and the fields
emerging ready for cultivation: a natural moment for the rite of
rebirth. The Corn-Osiris, represented in ritual as a small clay
figure mixed with seeds that germinated in a few days, was
defined in texts as green, with upstanding penis. Thus the
Jumilhac Papyrus (Ptolemaic or Roman period) shows the penis
vertical, parallel with the shoots of grain.¹⁰ But the idea of his
Nile-murder may well have been stimulated by the red phase,
though we do not find support for this thesis in the texts. Red
rain or water turning red are always ominous in myth and
legend, e.g. the Thames turning blood-red on the eve of
Boudicca's rebellion. Celtic legend provides examples of a hero's
death foretold by red water. Welsh springs have tales of their
water flowing red in connection with the death of hero or saint.
Wells in Cumberland were said to run red on the anniversary of

Charles I's execution. Bloody rain in ancient times, as in the *Iliad*, expressed murder or some disastrous change polluting the elements.[11] It seems unlikely then that the red Nile was not linked with the murdered Osiris, even if the dire moment found no ritual expression. However, we may note that in the later periods the earth is imagined as the god's body and the flood is his sweat, "the fluid that comes out of Osiris"; Ploutarch speaks of the Flowing of Osiris.[12]

If we consider the very many Flood-legends, especially those of the North Americans, we see that they are at root Creation-myths. The universe begins as water; the problem is to explain how solid land appears. Thus the Maidu myth begins:

When this world was filled with water, Earth-Maker floated upon it, kept floating about. Nowhere on the world could he see even a tiny bit of earth. No person of any kind flew about. He went about in this world, the world itself being invisible, transparent like the sky. He was troubled. "I wonder how, I wonder where, I wonder in what place, in what country we shall find a world!" he said.

"You are a very strong man, to be thinking of this world," said Coyote. "I am guessing in what direction the world is, then to that distant land let us float," said Earth-Maker. The two float about seeking the earth and singing songs, "Where O world art thou?" "Where are you, my great mountains, my world mountains?"[13]

They find a drifting birdnest and stretch it out with four ropes, east, west, north, south.

When the floating-in-water episode is detached from the creation-moment, the situation is interpreted as the result of a punishment sent on the world, which brings about a return of the primal ocean over all things; and the quest for the world-mountain involves a rediscovery, not a discovery, of the earth. Egypt did not have a Flood-legend proper, though it had all the material for it; perhaps Plato knew something of this fact when he stated that Egypt was saved from the Flood.[14]

It is interesting to look at the *Timaios* where he tells of the wisdoms brought by Solon from Egypt. An Egyptian priest, discussing the periodic destruction of earth by fire, says that the high-up sites suffer most. "In our case, the Nile, our Saviour in other ways, saves us also at such times by rising high. And when on the other hand the gods purge the earth with a flood of water, all the herdsmen and shepherds who are in the mountains are saved, but those in the cities of your land are swept into the sea by the streams. Yet, in our country, neither then nor at any other times does the water pour down over our fields from above; on the contrary it all tends naturally to well up from below." There is certainly here a genuine Egyptian tradition of the Nile-sources, and possibly a retort by some Egyptian priest to Greeks or Near-Easterners with stories of a world-flood. It would suit Egyptian pride to smile and declare that the unique nature of the Nile saved Egypt from the disadvantages of other lands.

56. Deadman (Ani) spearing the Black Pig: for the pig as responsible for Horos' wound
Derchain, *Sources Orient. V, La Lune*, 1962

Plato's description of Atlantis, with its three concentric rings of sea and two of land, reflects the Egyptian and Sumerian pictures of the original world-mount. Suggestions have been made that his account of Atlantis' destruction was based on a genuine legend with fact behind it: probably the destruction of the city of some 30,000 persons on the island of Thera about 1500 B.C. by a violent eruption which buried it in thirty to fifty feet of volcanic ash. If this surmise is correct, the transformation of Thera into Atlantis with its world-mount and surrounding waters is all the more significant.[15]

There is also a tale given by Ammianus Marcellus about the

Syringes, the underground tombs of the Theban area. "There are also subterranean fissures and winding passages called syringes, which, it is said, those acquainted with the ancient rites, who had foreknowledge of a coming Deluge and feared the memory of the ceremonies might be destroyed, dug in the earth in many places with great labour; and on the walls of these caverns they carved many kinds of birds and beasts and those countless forms of animals which they call hieroglyphic writing." This interpretation had perhaps grown up from some garbled account by guides trying to explain things to Greek and Roman tourists. The idea of the need to eternalise the rituals in words and pictures, and the image of the deadman having to cross a dangerous water on the way to the spiritworld, may have coalesced in this confused rationalisation.[16]

All the ingredients of a legend of Flood-disaster were present in Egypt, we noted. As illustration we might take Utterance 254 of the Pyramid Texts. Here the two opening sections deal with a summons to Re (or Atum) to make place for the dead king and a threat that world-order will be thrown into confusion if they refuse; then comes a prophecy of the disorder after the king's resurrection so that he may journey at ease over the sky.

If you do not make room for N, N will put a curse on his father Geb. The Earth will no more speak, Geb will no more be able to defend himself. N eats for himself, bit by bit, whomever he finds on his way. The *hn.t* pelican announces, the *psd.ti* pelican comes forth, the Great One arises, the [three] Enneads speak: A dam shall dam up the earth, both boundaries-of-the-cultivation shall be united, both riverbanks shall be joined, roads shall be closed against passengers, stairs for those who would ascend shall be destroyed.

The Earth ceases to speak: is dead and cannot produce. The *hn.t* pelican is a goddess; the *psd.ti* is connected with both Ennead and Osiris; as Osiris he comes out of the water, out of the grave. The Enneads then make the prophecy. The whole Nile-system will be disrupted and the high desert-lands will meet, obliterating the cultivated areas. The links with heaven are cut, except for the triumphant deadman who uses his magic knowledge to go as a "tempest of heaven"—also the Bull of heaven. He reaches the spiritworld in a boat and takes there the helm or oar that propels it.

We have here the elements that need only to be extended in narrative to develop an account of disaster and disorder brought down on a guilty world, with the one righteous (or magically secure) man surviving in his ark and regaining a stable universe. The intense way in which ritual-myth is concentrated round the funerary ritual of the king instead of being more communally expanded is the explanation of much in Egypt that differs from other lands.

Indeed, from Chapter CLXXV of the Theban Recension of the *Book of the Dead* it seems that an Osirian legend of the Flood was developed. This chapter is striking in that it contains no spells, prayers, or magical names; it consists of short conversations between the deadman and certain gods, and dialogues between the gods. The copy in the Papyrus of Ani was written at Thebes under the Nineteenth Dynasty. It opens with the cry:

What is it that has happened to those who have become like the Children of Nut? They have fought battles, they have upheld strifes, they have done evil, they have created hostilities, they have made slaughter, they have caused trouble and oppression. Truly in all their doings they made the great become feeble in all our works. O Great Thoth, declare strongly that what Tem [the Setting Sun] has commanded shall be performed. You shall not see iniquity, you shall not be pained, for their years are nothingness and their months are drawing to an end, even while they are working mischief.

I am your writing-palette, Thoth, and I have brought you your ink-jar. I am not one of those who work iniquity in their secret places. Let not evil happen to me.[17]

The text then goes on to lament over the Underworld where the deadman has come. "There is no water or air in it. It is a depthless abyss, dark with the blackest darkness, and a man wanders helplessly in it. There is no joy whatever in it, no rest for the heart, and the pleasures of love cannot be enjoyed there. But let the glory of the Beatified be given to me instead of water and air, and the satisfaction of the pleasures of love instead of cakes and beer." Finally Tem promises him millions of years and Thoth, as the tongue of the Great God, acting for Tem, declares that he is going to make a Flood. "I am going to blot out everything I have made. The Earth shall enter into the watery abyss of Nun by means of a raging Flood and will become even as it was in primeval time. I myself shall remain together with Osiris, but I shall transform myself into a small serpent which cannot be apprehended or seen."

Now the Nile is to rise and cover all Egypt. Nothing will be visible but water. Then Osiris will sail over it in a boat like Re, and will travel to the Island of Fire where Horos is established on his Father's throne.

57. Deadman aids the Ass against the Serpent

There seems a general affinity with the elements discussed in the Pyramid Text; and in the mutilated version of the chapter in Ani's papyrus it seems that the destruction of mankind was in fact decreed by Tem and carried out. But the picture of a disastrous Flood in the Pyramid Text and in the *Book of the Dead* is closely linked with rites of resurrection and salvation; and does not appear to have been detached as a myth standing in its own right like that of Deukalion or Noah. The dominant role of the Nile-water is to save and nourish; the destructive aspects are not forgotten and are conjured up at moments of ritual, but it is heat and drought that stand out as dangerous and liable to crush mankind. The destroying power is supremely lodged in the lion-headed Hathor-Sekhmet. Sekhmet, wife of Ptah at Memphis,

O

was taken to represent the destructive power of the sun. To some extent then the myth of Re and Hathor expresses the way in which the Nile saved the long fertile strip of Egypt from becoming desert like the sun-stricken sands on either side; and Sekhmet has her affinities with Seth, lord of the eastern desert. A stele tells us how Thotmose IV, hunting, was drawn to the region of the Sphinx of Ghizeh and stopped there "when the hour for allowing some respite to his servants had come". The spot was "near the sphinx of Harmakhi near to Sokar of Ghizeh; of Renutet of the town of Djeme of the North; of Mut, Lady of the Door of the North and of the Door of the South; of Sekhmet who presides over the desert".[18]

58. Hathor; Anat

The Sphinx of Ghizeh, sentinel of the border of the western sands, was the Lion that reigns by terror on North and South, and is still called by the Arabs the Father of Fear. There is thus an affinity with Sekhmet, the lioness of carnage, who guards the entry of the eastern desert and spreads her dominion over the Two Egypts. We may further compare Neb-nery, the first guard in the twenty-one gates of the spiritworld to be passed by the deadman before he reaches the Fields of Ialu in Osiris' domain. Unless the deadman knows his name, all the gates of the secret places are barred against him. He generally has a vulture head, though the vulture is normally female. In the funerary papyrus of Nu, Nery however is female: "the lady of terror and destruction; she knows the words that repel the storm and save from perdition those that pass on her road". In the papyrus of Nebseni, Nery is male, lord of the North and South and the Red Earth (the Sethian desert): "the great devourer of millions of years". His habitation "is the Lake of Unt in the Iat. Misfortune to him, who, being impure, wishes to pass. He will fall at once under his knife." Nery is in fact the devourer of all things sacrificed. "He prepares the block of sacrifice and nourishes himself on the entrails of his victims."[19]

An ostrakon from Karnak, engraved with the name of Menphtah, interestingly brings out the ways in which Hathor, normally a figure of love, song, dance, the sistrum, could become ferocious. We find the cryptographic phrase "the lover of Ptah" (Hathor) on the ostrakon. Sehkmet, we noted, was the true consort of Ptah; but Hathor in her own form, or in the form of some goddess (such as Mertseger, Renutet), was often associated with Ptah in the cult of the Theban nekropolis. From the love-songs we see that she played a role like his, as the providence of lovers, and both gained the epithet "comely-faced". They thus were joined in popular devotion, and folktale made them lovers.[20]

Hathor was a very ancient deity—a sky-goddess; a cow-goddess and nurse of Horos; a beneficent mother-figure or lady of the underworld, who received the dead. But as lion-goddess she showed a fierce aspect. A legend told how Re the Sungod lost his Eye (the sun itself).[21] The lost or alienated Eye turned against the god. We have only late versions in which much has become confused; but we can make out certain points. The Eye, identified with Tefnut or Hathor, has left Egypt and gone off to Nubia, where it lives as a wild lioness. The solar potence has become a mere ravaging force. Re sends Shu and Thoth to fetch the Eye back. Wandering through Nubia, they find her at last in the eastern mountain of sunrise, Bwgm, the Place of Finding.[22] She is reluctant to return, but the emissaries persuade her, especially Thoth with a wise speech. She comes home via Philai, Edfu,

Esneh, Dendera. She is appeased at Bigeh before entering Egypt and turns back into a peaceable goddess when she again has contact with Egyptian soil in the region of the Cataract. As Tefnut, she is received with music, dancing, and banquets, and marries Shu. The memory of her return is celebrated thereafter in the towns mentioned.[23] The sacred baboons (who greet the sun each morning) saluted and guided her and in Heliopolis she was reconciled to her father.

The tale was connected with the battle of Re and Eye against evil or rebellious men. The temple of Ombos boasted of being: "The place of Shu at the beginning, to which his father Re came, hiding from those who plotted against him, when the wicked came to seek him. Then Shu made his form (like that) of Horos, the fighter with his spear; he killed them immediately in this district. The sungod's heart was glad over this, over that which his son Shu had done for him."[24] Then came Nuu (?), the one without eyes, to the district "as a lion great of strength to avenge his father Re again".[25] Then again Tefnut with Shu on her return from Bwgm came to the place. (In a fragmentary demotic papyrus the goddess appears as an Aithiopian Cat and Thoth as a Little Dog-ape, and their encounters are the frame for all sorts of amusing and edifying passages. This version seems Hellenistic and was perhaps meant for dramatic recitation; the papyrus is dated 1st or 2nd century A.D.)[26]

59. Hathor-Tefnut as the wild lioness welcomed by Thoth

The ancient background is suggested by a creation-myth known from a copy written in the later 4th century B.C. but which seems to go very much further back.[27] Here the Creator defecates Shu and spits (or pisses) out Tefnut. The next lines are obscure, but for some reason the Eye followed the pair into the abyss of Nun as they separated out. The three gods were thus lost to the Creator. "Shu and Tefnut rejoiced in the abyss where they were. They brought me my eye [following] after them. When I had united my members, I wept over them, and men and women at once came into being from the teardrops which came out of my eyes." Meanwhile, the god has made a second Eye in place of the first, which is enraged on finding this out. The whole myth seems aimed at explaining how the One God breaks up into the universe, emitting Shu and Tefnut as space, air, moisture, and then losing the Sun in this new creation, attempting to replace or balance it with the Moon, weeping over his loss and his regained wholeness, bringing mankind into being, and then producing earth, sky, and the structure of things. The Egyptian feels that it is necessary to explain why the Sun does not stay all the while in the sky, but goes below (as it is interpreted) into the underwaters, and is thus temporarily lost to sky and earth. A primeval estrangement is imagined, with the Moon-Eye created in an effort to find a substitute for the lost Sun-Eye. In the later versions, where the cosmogonic sense has long faded out, the Eye or Sun and the One God or Universe are at odds and this conflict is used to explain and reflect the social and political discords among men. The rebellious Eye finally becomes the instrument of divine vengeance on rebellious men.

Perhaps it is this feeling of something gone wrong, of contradictions and inexplicable discords, that gives Hathor her dual nature, benign and nurturing, savage and destructive. No doubt at the same time all sorts of convergences and fusions of cults help to bring about the complexity in such a figure. And in any event a Mother-goddess can be both preserver and destroyer, giving life and sustenance, and at the same time rending and killing.

The same text as that which tells of the Runaway Eye tells us of Re falling into sickness. Re says, "By my life, my heart has

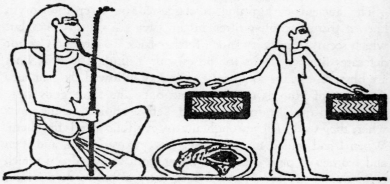

60. Solar Eye in the Waters

become very weary to be with them. I have killed them, but it is a case as though I was not (?) Is the stretching-out of my arm a failure?" (The persons he has killed are his enemies; who they are is not made clear.) The gods in his company bid him not to yield to his weakness and tell him that he was powerful when he so willed, but Re insists, "My limbs are weak for the first time". Nut turns herself into a cow and takes Re on her back. Men see him aloft on the heavenly cow and ask him to return so that they may overthrow the enemies who plotted against him. But Re goes to his palace (? in the west) and darkness comes over the earth.

When the earth became light in the morning, those men came forth with their bows and their [weapons] for shooting the enemies [of the sun]. The Majesty of this God said: Your sins are behind you [forgiven]. The murderers are too remote for their murderous plans. Thus originated the [rite of] murdering. . . . The Majesty of this God said to Nut: "Put me on your back to raise me up."

Re creates the celestial fields with its stars. Nut complains of the weight and Re tells Shu to put himself under her.

We also find an account in which the god is driven from earth by a serpent or by serpents. As usual it is not clear if the separation occurs as part of the creation or after it, and what is the relation of the serpents to the cosmic serpent who daily threatens to swallow the sun; and the whole thing is aimed at producing a strong spell against snake-sting for the man who knows or repeats it. But however we interpret these difficult texts, they certainly seek to explain the separation of the gods from earth, in which men and other creatures or forces rebel and are overwhelmed by some kind of nemesis.[27]

We can now glance back at the prophecy of Neferty which we cited in the first chapter for a picture of the disaster caused by the Nile's failure. The poet is linking natural disorder with political anarchy, and is describing the raids of nomads during the First Intermediate Period. The pallor of the Sun, twice mentioned, is an essential point, and is linked with the statement that "Re will separate himself from men": a situation that creates anxiety in particular for the region of Heliopolis, the centre of the solar religion. The world is reverting to chaos. "What has been made is as if it had never been made", "every good thing has disappeared", and "Re has now to begin again creation". Men have resort to violence and make arrow-heads in metal; the rich are thrown down and the poor are exalted. Periods of drastic social change are seen as a breakdown of cosmic order, a form of world-end, during which the gods retreat farther away from earth and mankind.[28]

Legends of destruction thus tend to gather round the sun-power whether involving Re or his fiercer aspects in Hathor-Sekhmet. Despite all the praises of the Sungod, there is a deep fear of him; and because he debilitates, he is also imagined as

61. Sky-Hathor or Heavenly Cow

himself growing debilitated. Both gods and men at different times plot against him; and the legends hint at successions of supreme power such as those we find in Greek myth. Yet in worship Re remains unchallenged—apart from the strange episode of Amarna and the conflicts of cult-centres which end by fusing him with Amun, and so on. With all the threats of world-end through fire and water, no decisive myth appears to have evolved.

Before we leave this section, we had better glance further at the storm-character of Seth. His power over weather is brought out by Ramses II's *Stele of the Marriage*. This tells of the pharaoh's marriage with the king of Kheta's daughter. First the Kheta (the Hittites) refuse to join other Asian princes in bringing tribute to Ramses, who then goes to war and devastates the rebellious land; Kheta offers yearly to bring tribute, but is always repelled. Then the king of Kheta tries to force a pardon by sending both magnificent presents and his eldest daughter to the pharaoh. Learning of his act, Ramses sends an escort to meet the princess. The time was winter and the weather was bad in Asia. The pharaoh, by the intervention of the god Sutekh (Seth), achieves a miracle and holds back the storms. The mission, accompanied by the escort, arrives in Egypt in the year 34, in the 3rd month of winter, amid great joy. (There is a gap here in the text, but clearly

62. God with ass-ears; Horos and defeated Ass-Seth; Horos victor

the princess pleases the pharaoh and becomes queen of Egypt, ushering in an era of good relations between the two countries.)[29]

The campaign of devastation might be that of the battle of Qadesh in the year 5. But we know there was a treaty in the year 21; so it seems the rebellion was later and the events occurred in the years 21–34. That there are facts behind the tale is confirmed by monuments referring to the queen as "daughter of the king of Kheta"; a stele (Abu Simnel, year 35) alludes to the arrival of the Hittites with their presents and the princess, and insists on the marvellous nature of the alliance.[30] We are also told in another inscription that the king of Kheta wrote to the chief of Qedi to invite him to set out for Egypt to gain the pharaoh's favour, for Sutekh was refusing their offerings and depriving them of necessary rain. "God does not accept the homage of Kheta and Kheta sees no more the water of heaven."[31] On the *Stele of Marriage* the king of Kheta says, "Our country is devastated, our master Sutekh is wroth against us, the sky gives no water in our presence". And here is the full passage about the pharaoh and Sutekh:

His Majesty discussed and deliberated with his heart about the army: "What is their situation, with these folk that I have sent, and who are gone on a mission to Syria, during these days of rain and snow which come in winter?" Then he presented a great offering to his father Sutekh and prayed to him thus: "The sky is on your hands, the earth is under your feet. All that is produced is your will. [Then stop] the rain and the northern wind and the snow, till the wonders come to me which you have despatched." His father Sutekh heard all his prayers. The sky grew calm, summer days arrived . . . his soldiers were all happy, their body expanded, their heart was joyous.[32]

Sutekh was a west-Asian god of unclear origin; he seems, however, to have been the special god of the Hyksos and so in Egypt was fully identified with Seth. His name was even determined by a god with the head of the Seth-animal. In our stele Sutekh-Seth seems merely used as the highgod or baal of West Asia, with special reference to the Hittites.[33]

Seth we then see was well suited for the champion who defended the gods—the order of the universe—against the encroachments and violence of the Sea, the aboriginal chaos threatening to engulf all things. As stormgod he seems to have been early identified with iron; for until the New Kingdom when iron was mined and used industrially, the only known iron was that got from meteorites. Such iron was worked by the predynastic folk, as is shown by some beads with a high nickel content.[34] Meteorites are widely imagined to be thunderbolts and we may take it that the ancient Egyptians had this idea of them—as also of certain fossils and other stones, especially belemnite, which have a shape like that conventionally given to Zeus' thunderbolt. Belemnite is not found in Egypt, but another fossil, lithodomus, of much the same shape, does occur, and there is a big pointed fossil Nerinea Reuieniana, which is common in the rocks at Letopolis. At Akmim the sign ◁ o ▷ was the symbol of the nome and of the god; and Letopolis was the other home of this sign. Both places were thunderbolt-cities.[35]

The Opening of the Mouth of a deadman was an important rite, usually done by the *sm*-priest. The Chief Opener lived at Letopolis and was the highpriest there.[36] In early times the mouth was slit open with a stone knife (copied from the forked flint-knives of predynastic days). The type lasted on, but was in historical times superseded by iron in various forms.[37] Pyramid Texts run:

I open for you your mouth. I open for you your eyes, N. I open for you your mouth with the *nwa*, the *mshtiw*-hook of iron, which opens the mouth of the gods. Horos opens the mouth of this N. [Horos has opened] the mouth of this N. Horos has opened the mouth of this N

63. Solar Eye in the Waters

with that with which he opened the mouth of his father, with that
with which he opened the mouth of Osiris; with the iron that comes
out of Seth, the *mshtiw*-hook of iron that opens the mouth of the gods.[38]

[The Children of Horos] have raised you up, perfect . . . opened your
mouth with their iron fingers.[39]

At the same time the Pyramid Texts see the deadman as himself
becoming iron and set among the stars:

N equips himself with his iron limbs. N voyages over the sky to the
Marsh of Reeds. N makes his abode in the Marsh of Offerings, among
the imperishable stars in the following of Osiris.[40]
The hands of N support Nut, like Shu, even the bones of N which are
iron and his imperishable limbs, for N is a star, the light-scatterer of
the sky.[41]

This last passage is preceded by statements that the deadman has
escaped death even as Seth escaped the day, the halfmonths, the
months, and the year of death "by ploughing the earth".

The *Book of the Dead* (papyrus of Ani) thus describes the
Opening of the Mouth. By this time Seth has become the binder
of the mouth, though it is his iron that still opens it.

The god Ptah shall open the mouth and the god of my town shall un-
fasten the swathings, the swathings which are over my mouth. There-
on shall come Thoth, who is equipped with words of power in great
abundance, and he shall untie the fetters, even the fetters of the god
Seth which are over my mouth. And the god Tem shall cast them
back at those who would fetter me with them, and cast them at him.
Then shall the god Shu open my mouth and make an opening into my
mouth with the same iron implement with which he opened the
mouth of the gods. I am the goddess Sekhmet and I take my seat on the
place by the side of Amt-ur(?) the great wind of heaven. I am the great
star-goddess Saa who dwells among the souls of Anu [Heliopolis].

Later in the mouth-opening the priest used a chisel of iron; and
still in Roman times iron was used.[42] We have several of the
tools.[43] The reason why iron was thought to have a great magical
power for such an operation did not derive merely from its
hardness. Flint for instance was harder. The association with the
sky, stars, storm, lightning and thunder was the key-thing. The
sky-iron was thought to own the blast-power from which it

64. The Sons of Horos

originated. Falling-star, meteor-fall, thunder-blast were all identified. In the early tale *The Shipwrecked Man* we read:

A star happened to fall and those under the place it fell went up in fire. It occurred when I wasn't with them. They burned without my being among them. I [almost] died because of them when I found them in a single heap of corpses.[44]

Thus, the Sioux of North America thought that lightning entered the ground to scatter thunderbolt-stones in all directions —flints which when struck emitted a spark of fire.[45] In Peru, Catequil the thundergod, child of the Heavengod, set free the Indians out of the earth by turning it up with his golden spade: he split the earth and enabled the original men to emerge from the earth-womb. In the thunder-burst he hurled from the sky small round stones which were preserved as fire-fetishes and used as love-charms—to kindle the fires of love.[46] The protective power of iron is seen in the way that it was thought to ward off fairies; in East Prussia, to save a child from being fairy-changed, the people used steel from which lights were struck or anything such as flint from which fire could be educed.[47]

In West and North Africa meteorites were considered to be dropped by God; fresh milk was poured on the place where one was found; and the sword forged from it was held to kill whom-

ever it touched. Hausas who would swear falsely by the Koran
hesitated to do so when they had called on Aradu (Thunder):
they feared to be struck dead in the next storm.

Hence the link of iron with the Children of Horos, who belong
to Letopolis and who are also the four stars of the body of the
Great Bear, which was the standard of the Letopolite nome.[48]
Coffin Texts of the 1st Intermediate period and later texts verify
that the iron was meteoric. From the 1st Intermediate period iron
has a star or another sign as determinate. The star was an integral
element. The other determinate brings out the blast-power of
the iron blocks; for we find it connected with the *mshtiw* of Seth
and with Horos' Enemies, Seth and his followers.[49] It was also
used as the sign on the standard of the Kabasite nome, the 11th of
the Delta, where Seth seems the patron god. It expresses the
stormgod and the iron that comes out of him, the explosive
splitting power of the bolt. A word meaning "break up" at
times takes the place of the nome-capital's sign. In short, iron
with the star and the blast-power sign reveals its meteoric origin,
its supposed nature as a thunderbolt.[50]

The heavenly original was the constellation called by the
Greeks the Great Bear, by the Egyptians the Foreleg of the Bull,
which we later find identified with Seth. (In the temple of Sethos I
it is represented as a complete Bull.) The Egyptians saw the
typical pattern of the Bear at the moment when it rears up on
the east of pole and when it turns upside down above it. Because
iron was thought to come down from above at times of violent
storm-clash, the sky itself was considered iron. The meteors were
apparently fragments chipped from the vault. In Pyramid Texts
the Double Doors of heaven through which the deadman goes
are of iron.[51] He cleaves the iron and wins heaven.[52] The heavens
are seen as hard walls. "When he ascends to heaven, when he
ferries over the vault, for life and joy, also when he traverses the
foaming sea, destroying the walls of Shu. He ascends to
heaven . . ."[53] The heavenly throne of the dead king is iron; and so
is his sceptre.[54] His bones and limbs become iron, as we have
seen. The connection of iron-sky and stars is stressed. "The bones
of N are iron and the limbs of N are like the stars, the imperishable stars."[55] The dead pharaoh descends on "ropes of iron"—a

65. Constellations, showing Thoueris, the Stretched Rope, Horos, Bull, Combats

term that perhaps expresses the flight of shooting stars across the sky. Among the Australian tribesmen, as among many other groups at what I have called the shamanist level, the deadman or the shaman climbs up to the sky on a rope, and a shooting star is said to be the rope thrown away by the spirit which has no more use for it.[56]

The idea of the sky as solid and composed of metal or stone is very widespread at the tribal or shamanist level. It is held by the North American Indians and the South Sea Islanders.[57] The Zulus held the sky to be a rock encircling the earth, with sun, moon and stars inside it, and the folk of heaven outside. *Kalevala* tells how Ilmarinen forged the sky of the finest steel and set the moon and stars in it.[58] The Maoris thought that rain came down through a crack or hole from the reservoir above.[59] Herodotos says that the Greek settlers in Libya came to a place called Apollo's Fountain and the Libyan guides told them, "This is the place for you to settle in, for there is a hole in the sky".[60] Podaleirios asked at Delphoi where to settle. "On receiving an oracle that he should settle in the city where, if the encompassing heavens were to fall, he would suffer no harm, he settled in that part of the Karian Chersonnese which is encircled by mountains all round the horizon."[61] Strabon, citing Ptolemaios son of Lagos, says the Kelts on the Adriatic, who went to Alexander the Great for a treaty, were asked what they most dreaded and replied that it was the falling of the sky.[62] The Germans and others had the same fear of the sky falling.[63] In 179 B.C. in a great storm the Danubian army fled saying that "the sky was falling upon them". An Irish medieval oath ran: "If the sky does not fall with its rain of stars upon the face of the earth when we are camped," and goes on to envisage an earthquake and the sea overwhelming the earth. In the *Arabian Nights* we read, "He cast at me a shooting star of fire . . . and he cried out at me so terrible a cry that meseemed the skies were fallen flat upon me and the mountains trembled at his voice". In Egypt itself we find stated a condition "Nut will fall to the ground", in the early Middle Kingdom, and in the Twentieth Dynasty, Neith threatens, "The heavens will crash to the ground".[64]

Among some Australian tribes to kill the totem-beasts would bring the sky down: for example, in Central Australia, Mangarkun-jerkunja of the Arunta lizard totem was the alcheringa hero who transformed the prehuman shapeless creatures into men, and for anyone there to kill a lizard would have this disatrous effect of shaking the frame of things. The Western Arunta believe that the first couple originated out of two stones thrown out of the sky by a spirit, a great strong old man who lives far away to the north.[65] Creation and taboo mingle in the myth of the Mabuiag people on the Western Islands of Torres Straits. At a camp in Pulu the boys and girls twirled round on the beach with extended arms, though forbidden by their parents; a great stone fell from heaven and crushed everyone on the island save two lovers who fled to Mabuiag; by biting a piece of the *kowai* tree there they stopped the stone and became the primal parents of the island's population.[66] Among the Melanesians, Quat, the ancestor of the people of Alo Sepere, was born of a woman-stone without a father; he fought the ogre Quasavara, whose head knocked against the sky; the ogre fell on his face across the earth and turned to stone.[67] Among the Yoruba of West Africa, Shango the thunder-god, called the Stone-caster, flung down the stone-hatchets which were kept as sacred objects.[68]

We see then that there is nothing unusual about the ideas that the Egyptians held of the sky. What was unusual was the elaboration and precision of their mortuary ritual, which reflected the shamanist journey into sky or underworld.

Seth's *mshtiw*-hook or iron spear was used to repel the evil serpent from the solar boat from the Eighteenth Dynasty on.[69]

(Horos too uses iron weapons against his foes and his mother proposes to use a blade of iron against Seth.[70]) Ploutarch says that the Egyptians called iron the "bone of Typhon [Seth]"; and we saw the Pyramid Texts spoke of the iron coming out of Seth.[71] Kaw was an important site of the Seth cult. A New Kingdom stele is there addressed to Seth. One of the Wah-ka coffins has on it the name of Seth. Wah-ka was governor of the Aphroditopolitan nome, in the eastern part of which, near the village of Antaios, Isis and Horos revenged themselves on Seth.[72] Nephthys was often called Seth's wife, and her husband was worshipped here in Roman times as Antaios.[73] At least as early as the Eighteenth Dynasty Seth was established in the Hypselite nome opposite Kaw a little to the north.[74] At Kaw were found in large quantities huge bones set in heaps, heavy, mineralised, metallic in lustre. They were mostly of hippopotami, one of them a complete skull. They were wrapped in linen, scattered in the tombs, and were evidently sacred.[75] A stele addressed to Seth shows a hippopotamus in a papyrus-swamp.[76] (Ploutarch says the Egyptians depicted Seth as a hippopotamus, and cites a figure at Hermopolis, where he is shown as this beast, "upon which stands a hawk fighting with a serpent; by the hippopotamus signifying Typhon, by the hawk power and virtue, which Typhon frequently gains by force and never ceases to be dis-

66. The Smith of Horos; Horos and the Bull-leg

turbed by his own wickedness and to disturb others. For this reason, when they sacrifice on 7 Tybi, which they call *the Coming of Isis out of Phoinikia*, they stamp on the consecrated cakes the figure of a hippopotamus bound.")[77] So it is clear that the Kaw bones were sacred to Seth and were considered to be iron. They were his iron bones.[78]

These bones were considered iron because they were imagined to have come from the sky, the stars. The stars can be taken as bones in tribal cosmogonies: thus the Arunta and the Loritja in Australia called the blue sky the Flesh, the night-sky with its stars the Bones, and the vault the Stomach of the heavens—with a Back out of sight in the beyond.[79] We must not forget the Egyptian Constellation of the Bull-leg, which represented Seth and his bones of iron. Later Horos was represented attacking it, aided by the hippopotamus-goddess, Ipet. The once-triumphant thunder-god has been displaced by Horos and sinks to the role of the sacrificial bull, whose roars express the defeat of the evil principle.[80]

Before we leave this section, we can glance at the one historical instance of an Egyptian magician who claimed to control the weather. He was Harnuphis, a *magus* attached to the army of Marcus Aurelius. The emperor and his troops in the Danubian campaign of A.D. 174 were surrounded by hordes of Quadi at a spot where they ran out of water. The Quadi, beaten off, retired to the hills, which they fortified; they felt confident that the Romans, unable to retreat or advance, would be broken by the heat and the drought. Then rain fell. While the Romans were busy drinking or giving water to their horses, the Quadi attacked and seemed about to triumph, but at that moment a terrific thunderstorm of hail and lightning struck the Quadi, yet missed the Romans. The Quadi, caught as they were swarming down the slopes, panicked, were driven off, and surrendered. The credit of the storm was given to Harnuphis, who had invoked Hermes Aerios at the crucial moment.[81]

Not that history was unanimous on this point. Capitolinus merely says the prayers of Marcus Aurelius gained water for his soldiers; the column raised by the Senate at Rome gave the

P

praise to Jupiter Pluvius; and Christians sought to take over the miracle by insisting that one of the legions was composed of their brethren, who, with the emperor's consent, offered up prayers and induced the storm, so that thereafter they were called the Thundering Legion.[82] We can discount this last claim since the Legion had long owned its epithet and Marcus Aurelius later treated Christians with severity. Harnuphis was a real character. An inscription has been found at Aquileia on a limestone altar, describing him as a *hierogrammateus*.[83] The altar is dedicated to a *thea epiphanes*, certainly Isis. The phrase suggests a direct manifestation of the goddess, though it doesn't prove that Harnuphis claimed the advent for himself.[84] Hierogrammateis or sacred secretaries were known in Egypt: consulted in divinations, dealing with temple administration and the selection of priestly candidates, the Apis Bull or other holy animals, and acting as custodians of cosmological knowledge and practical lore. We hear of them being consulted in time of plague.[85] An astrological calendar of the late 2nd century declares: "This is a favourable time for chief priests. It produces many sacred scribes of gods and kings, and gives long life to each."[86]

Harnuphis then seems indeed the sort of person to come forward with claims of rain-control or to assert afterwards that he was responsible for the fortunate event. We are told that Marcus Aurelius did consult Chaldeans about the passion that his wife Faustina felt for a gladiator.[87] The Hermes that Harnuphis invoked corresponded to the Egyptian Thoth-Shu—a Graeco-Egyptian fusion of Hellenistic days of Hermes with Shu to

67. The Rain Miracle (aurelian column)

produce an atmospheric god of the elements.[88] Thoth has his water-connections as a moongod. Tradition gave the Nile-flood a lunar date. Aristotle thought the Nile flowed more strongly at the renewal of the moon and its last quarter. Plinius says the Nile started to rise "at the new moon after the summer solstice". And Eumenes made Mercurius (Hermes) the origin of the Nile. An adept of Thoth-Hermes might well consider himself to own power over the sources of water on earth or in the sky.[89]

13

Boats on the Nile

THE Hellenistic and Roman periods saw a great increase in river-traffic and the use of river-systems for carrying goods. There was consequently a considerable development in boats or barges devised for rivers. A large number of the different kinds of boats are illustrated in the mosaic of Althiburos in Africa. Here many names of Celtic and Italian craft are given, but no Egyptian; the catalogue had been made up in Italy from a Hellenistic (not Alexandrian source) by someone who knew Italy and Gaul.[1] We are told that Aurelian increased the number of river-boats on the Nile, no doubt to cope with the grain supplies.[2]

If we look at the names used for Nile-boats we find that *naus* is rare and that the commonest word is *ploion*, of which diminutives also appear. *Ploion* can be used for vesels of sea, river or lake—though when it is used of a sea-ship it almost always refers to the corn-ships going to Byzantium and is late (4th century).[3] We find boats defined as *hellenikon* in the 2nd and 3rd centuries, with some contrast, it seems, between Greek and Egyptian types.[4] A receipt of 286 was made out by "the pilot of an Hellenic Boat belonging to the heirs of Teiron, 350 art. burden":

I have received and embarked on the aforesaid boat in accordance with the instructions of Ulpius Cyrillus the Most Eminent Katholikos, from Aurelios Dementrianos and however he is styled, *dekaprotos* of part of the Middle Toparchy, 75 art. of new pure and sifted barley belonging to the village of Herakleion, which I will transport to the Most Illustrious Alexandreia and deliver to whomsoever I am ordered to deliver it, and I will produce the certificate of the delivery, because I have been paid all the expenses.

This receipt is valid, there being three copies of it, of which I have issued two to you, the strategos, and one to the *dekaprotos*, and in answer to the formal question I have given my assent.[5]

Other words we find are *skaphopakton* (*skaphos* means *hull* and is used for *ship*; *pakton* is a light boat) and *platypegia* (apparently some sort of barges: *platys* means flat broad):[6]

(Transport-account 3rd century) Psobthis in the Lower Toparchy: for the barges of Kronion 299 dr., desert-dues 27 dr., crown-tax 1 tal. 897 dr., desert-dues 672 dr., wages of camel-men 516 dr., desert-dues 21 dr., freightage of barley to Alexandreia 618 dr., desert-dues 52 dr., total 1 tal. 2712 dr.[7]

We also find the *thalamega*, ships with cabins or holds. Thus in accounts of the transport of wheat and beans by water to Memphis of the late 1st or early 2nd century we find two columns, one dealing with a *pakton*, one with a *thalamegon*—the first carrying

68. The Althiburos mosaic

550 art. of wheat, the second 540, so that the difference in burden seems slight. Other items include repairs, examination-dues, charges to a banker, commission, exchange, fees to interpreter and clerks, 14 dr. 4 ob. for a rudder, tips.[8]

We also find a differentiation of boats by epithets ending in -egon to express what they carried: *kopregon*, dungboat; *oinegon*, wineboat; *xylegon*, timber-boat; *lithegon*, stone-carrier; *nekregon*, corpse-boat.[9] There were also boats used in processions, with gods in their cabins; these were borne by pastophoroi.[10] Thus in a tax-receipt (A.D. 196) we read:

"Paul to Apion, nomarch of the Arsinoite nome, through Heron agent, for the *dekanos* of fish-vendors, through Sokemis and the other principals for the 3rd year sixty dr., total 50 dr., for the beer tax individually assessed similarly eighty dr., total 80 dr., for the boats of the image-bearers, similarly one hundred and twenty-four dr., total 124 dr."

Fishing-boats are mentioned several times.

(6th–7th century) Will your True Brotherliness kindly have the damaged fishing-boat you speak of repaired, since, as you say, its rudder is broken and there is need for it to be mended; for I want to send it to Alexandreia. Please send also a messenger to the harbour for this purpose.[11]

(7 c.) . . . so that he may write to the headmen [of . . . to restore] our cattle without a fight, and . . . we may depart and bring the equivalent of the cattle. I exhort you to write to me and I exhort my Lord to write also to the headmen of Inner Laura that they may bring on their part ten other persons and we may depart together and bring the equivalent of the cattle. For thus it seemed good in the sight of my master, their dioiketes, in order that when our master the landlord's agent, who is with you, arrives, they may jointly reconcile us. And behold, he was not . . . until he comes, master. As you wrote to me yesterday about a boat, let him know, master, that there is no boat in our harbour except the fishing-vessels, master.[12]

Two neighbouring villages are in some rather violent dispute.

There were also the boats of the river-guards, who watched the Nile and the canals, seeing to the orderly carrying-on of commercial activity and exchange, and concerned that the dues and taxes should be paid.[13] We have a declaration of A.D. 218–22

made to the strategos by some of the guards of the Hermopolite
nome who swear to watch over the river for a defined period
"on the customary *skaphe*, skiff, together with the soldier dele-
gated to the task".[14] *Kynegides* seem hunting-boats, perhaps of the
kind that Diodoros mentions when telling of hippopotamus-
hunts.[15] "Being both a river and a land animal, it spends the day
in the streams, exercising in the depths, while at night it forages
round the countryside on the grain and hay. If then it was prolific
and reproduced each year, it would wholly destroy the farms of
Egypt. But even it is caught by the united effort of many men,
who strike it with iron spears. Whenever it shows up, they converge their boats upon it, gather around, and wound it repeatedly
with iron barbs (harpoons); then they fasten the end of a rope of
tow to one of the barbs imbedded in the creature, and let it go
till it dies of loss of blood. Its meat is tough and indigestible, and
none of its inward parts edible, neither viscera not intestines."[16]

Texts sometimes speak of the sunboat as rowed. "The gods who
dwell in the Eastern and Western Horizona bear you along, and
those who are in the Sektet Boat [of Evening] row you on." At
the 9th Hour of the nightsun-boat's passage through the Underworld the sailors in the boat ladle up water with their paddles for
the spirits to drink. But we also find the sunboat towed. "The
Southerners, the Northerners, the Westerners, and the Easterners
tow you, adoring you as the primeval one who came into existence by himself." "The spirits of the Westerners drag you on the
road which is in the sacred land." A Pyramid Text which is in
effect a song of triumph in honour of the young ruler of a district,
tells how he returns home from a victorious campaign: the gods
"bowed themselves before N. in homage [saying]: His mother
conducts him, his home-town tows him, *hai*, let go your rope".[17]

Hodega ploia or pilot-boats appear in a charge against an official,
who is said to have requisitioned certain persons to work in one
of them without having a diploma (certificate?). Their job seems
to have been of a hauling or towing kind.[18] Herodotos mentions
towing in the difficult reaches above Elephantine. "Riverboats
have to be hauled along by ropes, one rope on each side, much as
one drags an ox. If the rope parts, the boat is gone in a moment,
carried away by the force of the stream."[19]

Skaphe or skiff is found, once called three-oared.[20] The diminutive is *skaphidion*; we meet one of 60 art. burden, used for carrying a corpse.[21] The characteristic Nile-boat, the *baris*, is thus described by Herodotos:

The Nile boats used for carrying freight are built of acantha wood (the acantha resembles in form the lotus of Kyrene and exudes gum). They cut short planks, about three feet long, from this tree, and the method of construction is to lay them together like bricks and through-fasten them with long spikes set close together, and then, after the hull is done, to lay the deckbeams across on top. The boats have no ribs and are caulked from inside with papyrus. They are given a single steering-oar, which is driven down through the keel; the masts are of acantha wood, the sails of papyrus. These vessels cannot sail upriver without a good leading wind, but have to be towed from the banks. For dropping downstream with the current they are handled as follows: each vessel is equipped with a raft made of tamarisk wood, with a rush-mat fixed on top and a holed stone weighing some four hundredweight; the raft and the stone are made fast to the vessel with ropes, fore and aft respectively, so that the raft is carried rapidly on by the current and pulls the *baris* (as these boats are called) after it, while the stone, dragging along the bottom astern, acts as a check and gives her steerage-way. There are a great many of these vessels on the Nile, some of enormous carrying-capacity.[22]

The *pakton* was lighter and could be taken to pieces, then put together when again required. The term has not been found before the late 1st century A.D., for instance in the transport-account cited above for barges.[23] Again: "The *pakton* is being prepared so that I may transfer the wine of Silenos" (3rd century). A 4th-century list runs: "2 Saite jars, 5 palmwood boards of the *pakton*, 2 couches, a new flagon, a new . . . , a small basket with 2 small knives at the bottom, 1 pot, 1 casket, some small nails of the *pakton*, a kettle-handle."[24] However, a connected form, *paktonitai* occurs in a fragmentary account probably of A.D. 17–18 so the use of the name be much earlier than appears. *Paktonitai* probably means shipwright, *pakton*-maker. In Byzantine times there was a guild of *paktonopoioi*, *pakton*-builders.[25] Among other things, *paktones* were used in the wine-trade.[26] Various adjectives mark out the employment of others; thus we meet a *xylopakton mikron*, a small timber-*pakton*.[27]

Ploion, as we noted, is the common term, often used no doubt in no precise sense. Thus it is used in a letter of the 2nd–3rd century: Severos writes to Euploos asking him to send word if the vintage is done or not, so that the boat may be despatched; if it's done, to come with the news himself and then the boat will be sent off at once.[28]

A *kydaron* seems a small boat which was used to carry State-grain as far as the wharves where the big *ploia* lay. In A.D. 211:

To Sarapion also called Phanias, strategos of the Oxyrhynchite nome. I Tithoes son of Sarapion and Ptolema, of Phakousai, corn-lader of the said Phakousai, swear by the Fortune of Severus and Antoninus the Lords Augusti that I will provide the *ploion kydaron* belonging to me of 150 art. burden for the lading of the government-corn whenever the boats collected in accordance with the order of lading arrive, so as to incur blame in no respect.[29]

Diaremata seem much the same sort of boat, which was needed on the stretch between the Nile and Alexandreia, where the big boats could not enter the canal.[30]

We have already had many glimpses of the things carried in the boats, whether as large cargoes or as incidental conglomerations. We learn much of the uses made of the boats by contracts of transport, sales in the form of long leases, declarations of various kinds.[31] Also of the amounts that the boats could carry.

To Didymos strategos of the Oxyrhynchite nome, from Posidonios also called Triadelphos, master of 8 boats carrying 40,000 art. in the Administration of Neapolis:

I have received and had measured out to me by Dioskoros son of Onnophris and Didymos son of Pausiris, sitologoi of the Psobthis District in the Lower Toparchy, the amount ordered me by you and Horion also called Apion, royal-scribe of the said nome, in accordance with the message of his Excellency the Procurator of Neapolis from the Public Granaries of the said village at the River Tomis of wheat from the produce of the past 19th year of Our Lords the Emperors Antoninus and Geta Pii Augusti, unadulterated with no admixture of earth or barley, untrodden and sifted, including a percentage of $1\frac{1}{2}$ art. ... thousand eight hundred and forty art., total .840 art., by the public

measure . . . and according to the prescribed measurement . . . which I
will carry to Alexandreia and deliver to the officials of the Administration safely, free of all risk and damage by ship. . . .[32]

Neapolis was important for the transhipment of corn from the
Nile to Alexandreia. Other shippers of its Administration had
five boats with a total burden of 23,000 art., and three with a
total burden of 15,000. The pilots of six different river-boats
who in the 3rd century petition the strategos about freightage-
charges declare they have together a cargo of 4,500 art.[33] In the
range of single boats mentioned we find a *skaphion* of 60 art. to
a *kekouros* (a grain-ship) of 10,000.[34] This latter was of Ptolemaic
days. The size also naturally varied. A wood-carrying *skaphe* is
35 yards long and 11 wide. A receipt for payment made by
some *naupegoi*, shipwrights, for the construction of a *ploion
hellenikon* of about 200 art. burden, shows a boat apparently
30 cubits long, 6 wide, and perhaps 3 deep.[35]

We cannot be sure that in each case the declared cargo is the
same as the boat's capacity. Once we find 75 art. in a boat with
the capacity of 350. But no doubt in many cases the wish to
gain as much profit as possible has led to a boat being well
filled up.[36] A letter-writer of the 4th century, saying that he has
chartered a boat, adds, "I pray that a lot of timber can be found
that it can be filled; for it's a big boat."[37]

In some inventories of ships that we possess, again, there is
probably an equivalence of cargo and capacity: for example, a
3rd-century account of timber deals with six boats carrying logs
and boughs (one boat is the *thalamegos* of Silbanos). A list of the
late 4th or early 5th century sets out cornfreights borne by boats

69. Nile as Rivergod (ossuary at Rome)

defined as *ploia* or *losariai*, with names of the owners and the captains.[38]

However, the cargo is undeniable evidence only for a minimal capacity. *Agoge* is the technical term for burden or tonnage; *gomos* for the total effective cargo. *Gomos* indeed is used in the sense of boatload, cartload, load in general.[39] We find "those who had the load" often mentioned in 3rd-century inscriptions with reference to the stone-cutting at Kertassi on the Egyptian–Nubian borders.[40] Also load-presidents and load-priests, who seem members of a cult-association occupied in the transport of stone.[41] *Phortion* is also used for freight.[42] In a set of customs regulations of the 2nd–3rd century, *phortion* appears as a unit of measure in calculating according to weight. Also: "If the tax-farmer desire that the ship should be unloaded [*ekphortizein*], the merchant shall unload the cargo, and if anything be discovered other than what was declared, it shall be liable to confiscation. But if nothing else be discovered, the tax-farmer shall repay to the merchant the cost of unloading."[43] Sometimes the word "full-up" is used— "77 art. which I will carry to Alexandreia and will deliver to the Administration at Neapolis a full [complete] and undamaged cargo."[44]

The cost of carrying goods on land by beasts of burden was much greater than that of carrying them by ship. This point is stressed by a writer asking for the liberation of shipwrights arrested by a police-chief. The men were needed for refitting a ship in grain-transport. There were docking charges, but the rate was not high. Payments seem to be made monthly. In 169 we find 2 dr. 1 ch. paid on three cargoes.[45]

We lack any clear account of the parts and equipment of a boat, or the way the boats were worked and organised. However, much fragmentary information can be gleaned from the various documents. Thus, we have three contracts of *misthoprasia*, sales of boats in the form of a long lease, dated A.D. 212, 291 and 570. The first deals with an Hellenic boat of 400 art. burden, with all appurtenances, which is leased for 60 years; the second, with a timber-carrying *skaphe* for 50 years; the third, with an Hellenic boat for 50 years.[46] The examples cover more than three and a half centuries; and the aim seems to be to hold the nominal ownership while in fact selling the boat. To own a boat gave a man certain privileges. Legislation in favour of shipping that served the Roman corn supply goes back at least to Claudius; and it has been surmised that even under the Ptolemies shipowners had a privileged position.[47] What exactly the privileges were, however, is still unclear; and the fact that one of our sale-leases deals with a timber-ship shows that the desire to be able to figure as a ship-owner was not limited to the corn-trade. Also the lessee might perhaps avoid certain legal disabilities. Thus, if a creditor sought to seize the ship, he might escape sequestration and the resultant tying-up. The document of 212 runs:

Harmirymios also called Melas son of Teras and Senaies of Tentyra the metropolis (acknowledges) to Pbekis son of Pebos son of Pbekis, his mother being Senthotmenis, of Panopolis, that Pbekis has leased to Harmirymios also called Melas by this deed of leasehold sale for a period of 60 years from this present stated day the Greek Boat belonging to him of 400 art. burden more or less—supplied with mats and furnished and decked throughout, with mast, yard, sail, ropes, jars, rings, pulleys, two rudders with handles and brackets, four oars and five punting poles with iron tips, hatches, landing plank, windlass, two iron anchors with iron flukes and one single-armed anchor, one measure, a balance, a Kilikian cloth, a cup-shaped skiff with two oars and provided with the usual fittings and an iron spike, at the rent agreed upon between each other for the 60 years of 1 tal. 2,000 dr. of silver.

Of this sum Pbekis has received on the spot from Harmirymios also called Melas 1 tal. of silver, and the remaining 2,000 dr. of the rent Harmirymios also called Melas will deliver to Pbekis when he visits the Panopolite nome, receiving from him the boat-builder's receipt and other previously acquired securities for the said boat, in order to preserve the rights derived from these Pbekis issuing to the said Harmirymios also called Melas the proper receipt for the said 2,000 drachmai. . . .[48]

Note that the "rent" is paid in a lump sum. The document of 291 begins:

Aurelios Nemesas, of the Lower Division of the Cynopolite nome, resident in the metropolis near the Akantheion, aged about 50, with a scar on the sole of his left foot, acknowledges to the Aurelii Pates and Aniketos sons of Aniketos and Ta . . . , of the Oxyrhynchite nome, that he, the acknowledging party Aurelios Nemesas, has with this agreement sold under lease for 50 years from the present day the *ploion hellenikon* belonging to him of 70 art. burden, with its entire equipment and mast, sail, and yards, decked throughout and . . . , at a rent of 21,000 silver dr. making 3 tal. 3,000 dr., which he has received from hand to hand out of the house. . . .

Both boats are covered with a deck from prow to stern over its whole length.[49] Other boats have a cabin with an awning or protection of reeds.[50] Seams appear to be smeared outside with tar or pitch.[51] Boats like the *hellenikon* and the *skaphidion* seem general transport ships using sails, with a minimum of rowers. The latter were brought in for manoeuvring, not for normal navigation.[52]

Persons seem to have owned bits and pieces of boats. A mast appears in a list of property. A small mast and boat-timbers are among the articles over which an inheritance-claim is waged. And in another such dispute, the half and the quarter of a boat are mentioned.[53] In 378 we meet an order to a wine-dispenser, probably in the service of a private land-owner, to give wine to two sawyers in return for boat-repairs. We also have a contract

70. Fishers and Nilotic Creatures

for boat-building and some fragmentary accounts of ship-building.[54] In 535 a contract was drawn up between Aurelios Menas, shipwright of Oxyrhynchos, and two other Aurelioi, Anoup and Victor, also shipwrights. "Whereas you consented with me for the exercise of shipwright's craft on the boat, the condition being that you should work 45 days for each solidus and 2 art. of loaves and 20 pounds of meat and 6 sextarii of oil and 6 double measures of wine, and that you should be unmolested by the Public Authority in your craft, and after the whole boat has been completed, you should share . . ." The loss of the end of the document makes the point of the agreement impossible to make out; for a contract has already been signed and the present document was to supplement it in some way. Perhaps it was found that some important point had been omitted or that something had gone wrong, necessitating a readjustment. The two men were to receive both wages and maintenance in the form of food (presumably calculated to last out for the 45 days). This combination of money-payment and allowances was fairly common in contracts for service. The guarantee against official interference was likely to have been financial. The tax-quotas of individual workers were levied, not directly by the State, but through the guild. Menas may have contracted to meet the liabilities of his employees; or he may have been promising help or protection in case some question about the right of entry into the guild in question was raised. The document tells us nothing about the boat.[55]

Parasema or ensigns were used on the river-craft. A private boat is mentioned as *asemon*, without a sign. Two boats described as *acharaktoi* were probably without encaustic paintings.[56] The ensigns represented tutelary deities or sacred animals on the bowsprit. We hear of Thalia, Ibis, Isis, Pantomorphos, Tyche.[57] Pantomorphos may be Proteus with his transformations, but is more likely a deity with multiple animal shapes.[58] A return of temple property (for the Oxyrhynchite and Kynopolite nomes, 213–17) mentions "a rudder of Neotera" from Neotera's temple. This is hardly likely to be a rudder carved as the goddess; probably it is the rudder of a ship with Neotera shown as the *parasemon*— perhaps a ship with some sacred purposes; otherwise it is hard to see why it should go into the temple amid statues, lamps, spoons, pens, bracelets, pendants, armlets of gold and silver.[59] An odd epithet of a *ploion* is *agriochenprumnis*, "with a wildgoose as terminal ornament". Here the figure is more in the nature of an ornament.[60]

The liking of the Egyptians for a finely decorated and well-built boat is lyrically brought in the Edfu description of Horos' galley. The chorus cry, "Steady, Horos, do not flee because of those in the water, do not fear those in the stream. Do not hearken when he [Seth] pleads with you." The chorus and onlookers add, "Hold fast, Horos, hold fast!" Then Isis speaks to him: "Take to your war-galley, my son Horos whom I love, the nurse that dandles Horos on the waters, hiding him under her timbers, the deep gloom of pines. There is no fear when backing to moor, for the good rudder turns on its post like Horos on the lap of his mother Isis. The mast stands firmly on the footstep like Horos when he became ruler over this land. That beautiful sail of dazzling brightness is like Nut the Great when she was pregnant with the gods. The two lifts, one is Isis, the other is Nephthys, each of them firmly holding what appertains to them on the yardarms, like brothers of one mother copulating in wedlock. The rowlocks are fixed on the gunwhale like the ornaments of princes. The oars beat on either side of the ship like heralds when they proclaim the prize-fight. The planks adhere closely together and are not parted one from another. The deck is like a writing-board filled with the images of goddesses. The baulks in the hold are like pillars firmly in a temple. The belaying-pins in the bulwarks are like a noble snake whose back is hidden. The scoop of real lapis-lazuli bales out the water like fine unguent, while the *iyh*-weed scurries in front like a great snake into its hole. The hawser is beside the post like a chick beside its mother." The chorus and onlookers shout, "Hold fast, Horos, hold fast!"

The text is also a good example of the poetic quality which pervades Egyptian ritual and the highly dramatic nature that often appears in the treatment. "Let us hasten to the Pool of Horos that we may see the Falcon in his ship." He is setting out to harpoon Seth.

We have a list of tolls or fees that were to be collected on persons or goods moving between Koptos and a port of the Red Sea. The toll may have been exacted in return for convoy service and protection on the desert-roads.[61] Many of the persons dealt with were connected with boats—captain, look-out, guard, sailor, shipwright's assistant; and perhaps we may add the whore. The two items of freight were mast and yardarm. Why only these? we may ask. Did other nautical gear get through free? And where were the items going? One commentator has thought the mast was being carried to the Red Sea for a ship that needed repairs. The Red Sea was treacherous, but would its ports get their supplies of wood from the Nile Valley which was so poor in timber useful for constructions? From early times acacia had been there used, of native wood, for ships; but there had also been a need to import timber from outside.[62] The Ptolemies were keen to control Cypros with its forests and Lebanon with its cedar-woods.[63] The ports of the Red Sea could get strong timber from the east. The Greeks knew of ships built of teak on the Persian Gulf from at least the 4th century B.C.; and in Roman times teak was among the woods exported from India to that Gulf.[64] So the mast reported at Koptos was most likely teak or some such wood coming in, not acacia going out.

A mast could be leased out:

(299 A.D.) Aurelia Sarapammon daughter of . . . os and Tapausiris from the village of Mounchintale in the Lower Toparchy and her nephew Theodoros son of Romaios and . . . kon, both acting through me Pausirios son of Sarapion and Soeris from the same village, to Aurelios Hierakion also called Dionysios son of him likewise named, ex-prytanis, councillor of the Illustrious and Most Illustrious City of Oxyrhynchos, greeting:

We acknowledge receiving from you in full the rent on my ship's mast which you had for the period from 16 Pharmouthi to 15 Pharmouthi of the current year 15, 14, and 7, and getting back from you the mast in sound condition, and we neither make nor will make any claim about anything whatever at all.[65]

The mast had been rented for a year, April to April, with the rent paid a month later, in May.

We have various accounts of timber being carried, without

indication as to its use; for ship-building or other construction jobs. Thus in the 2nd century: Aurelios Perikles to his brother Serenos. "I greet you first of all, my brother, and acknowledge the receipt of all the woodblocks. Send me now two more small camels on the 3rd or 4th of Phamenoth. The boat sails on the 20th. Write to me, brother, if you have need of anything for the places that lie on the Nile, I'll send it to you at once . . . don't delay the boat, but if you don't send the camels, write at once that you're not sending them, so I can let the boat go. I trust that you, your wife and children, and the other members of your household are well."[66]

Boats too were used for carrying bodies to the place of embalming; but they do not seem to have been of any special type. Normally the cargo would be light, though at times there might be a fair number of corpses. An ill-spelt letter of the last century B.C., written on a red potsherd which has the inside blackened with resin, runs:

Pekhytes son of Ammonios to Psenpseeine, greetings: See how you can come down so that you may sail down with me to Koptos, for I've written to Apollonios' people about the bodies from Koptos, so that you may come down with me and we may take away the bodies lying there. There remain twelve lying there. The islanders who came from Syene went off . . . for them, saying: Unless you come down we'll give them to Heron. If you're unwilling to come down yourself, send your brother so that he may come before the bodies [?spoil] so that we may sail down the next day. Goodbye, 4 Epeiph.[67]

The name of the man addressed means: the Son of the Physician.

14

Ferries and Sailors

So far we have not dealt with ferries. In ancient times the owner-ship of a ferry was a mark of independent status. A man remarked with satisfaction on an Edfu stele of the Hyksos period, using conventional phrases, that he had "crossed [the Nile] in his own ferryboat, ploughed with his own cattle, trodden-in [the seed] with his own asses, made a garden of his own trees". In Graeco–Roman times the right to operate ferries was at least at times granted as a concession by the State. In a complaint of about 15 B.C., which incidentally tells us of irrigation works carried out by Augustus in the Delta, we hear of ferry-concessions:

To Herakleides, strategos and overseer of the revenues from Kastor gymnasiarch, citizen of Komas, and from the other katoikoi in the village as well as from the other farmers and from the royal tenants residing in the village:

From Caesar's 16th year, when the State Canal was cut through our village, we of the village, because of this cutting, have a ferry which we use to cross over to carry out our seeding and harvesting. Though the ferryman Patouontes pays the State 300 silver dr. for his concession, Apollos son of . . . tagenes, using [the excuse of examining] the ac-counts, came to the village with a soldier, entered his house, and carried off two new garments that he found there, although Patouontes owed nothing. The latter, oppressed by the tax-collectors, has appealed to us. . .[1]

There are many Ptolemaic references to ferries, including tax-receipts.[2] A receipt of A.D. 150 was issued by two tax-farmers at Oxyrhynchos and certain villages for the year to two men, Achillas and Apeis: 200 dr. "for the revenue of the ferryboats at Pankylis". Later another 100 dr. was paid, making up the full sum due.[3] In the 2nd–3rd century the private account of a land-owner mentions the "allowance for the boat for the return of irrigation-watchmen."[4] A Coptic ostrakon from Medinet Habu runs: "From the time we depart we shall pay jointly for any matter that occurs, and as for any passenger who embarks with us, half his fare is for me and half for you."[5]

Achilleus Tatios, the romancer, gives us a lively picture of brigands in the more swampy parts of the Delta and the ferryboats used there:

There is always plenty of water standing about the haunt of the robbers. When it floods the land, it forms lakes and these stay undiminished when the Nile goes down, full of water and also of the water's mud. The natives can walk or row over them, but only in boats big enough to hold a single passenger. Any sort that is strange to the locality is choked and halted by the mud. The ones in use are small and light, drawing very little water. If there is not water at all, the boatmen pick the craft up and carry it on their backs till they again reach water.

Amidst these lakes lie islands dotted here and there. Some have no houses on them, but are planted with papyrus, and the stems grow so close there is only just space for a man to stand between. Over the head of this thick jungle the leaves of the plant make a thick cover. So robbers can slip in, make their plans, devise ambushes, or lie in lairs, using the papyrus-plants as their fortifications. Others of the islands have cabins on them and with the close huddling of the huts they have the look of a town protected by lagoons.

These are the resort of the buccaneers. One, larger than the others and with more cabins on it, was named, I think, Nikochis. They all gathered there, as it was their strongest fastness, and gained heart from their numbers and from the strength of the position. It was made a peninsula by a narrow causeway, a furlong on length and twelve fathoms broad, on either side of which the lake-waters entirely girdled the town.[6]

That this picture is not a mere fantasy is proved by a papyrus of the last years of Ptolemy Philadelphos and the reign of Euergetes. Here we find piracy on the Nile and a state of extreme insecurity. There is even mutiny in the fleet. The king makes the police responsible in cases where those who shelter deserters or brigands cannot be detected. Various preventive measures were taken:

curfew, no navigation by night, obligation to moor for the night at points designated by the police and there to submit to the surveillance of guards. Sailing after dark could be done only under control, except in cases of bad weather or some urgent service of the king. To defeat corrupt officials, all goods had to be transported on the Nile and boats had to carry *symbola*, documents duly registered to attest the payment of taxes.[7]

The light boats, made from ancient days of papyrus, are mentioned by Lucan in a quick summary of the river-craft of the empire: in Spain, Italy, Britain and Egypt:

> When the Sicoris leaving the plain had banks again
> osiers of hoary willow were stepped and plaited
> into small boats, which, covered with oxskin, rode
> high on the swollen stream, with passengers carried.
> The Venetian skims on the flooded Po; the Briton
> on his broad Ocean; and when Nile covers the land,
> the boats of Memphis are framed of thirsty papyrus.[8]

In another episode of Achilleus Tatios' romance we meet a ferry or hired boat:

We hired an Egyptian boat; for we had just a little money which we happened to have kept in our belts. And we started along the Nile for Alexandreia. We meant to stay awhile and thought it barely possible we might find some of our shipwrecked friends had turned up there. We got as far as a certain town when suddenly we heard a great uproar. "The herdsmen!" cried the sailor and tried to turn the boat round and sail back. But already the place was full, full of terrifying wild men, all tall and dark—not quite black like an Indian, but more like a bastard Aithiopian—with shaven heads, small feet, and gross bodies. All spoke an outlandish jargon.

71. Pygmies in Boats

"We're done for," cried the helmsman and brought the boat to a standstill. The river is very narrow there and four of the robbers boarded the boat, took everything that was in her, and snatched our money from us. Then they tied us up and shut us up in a little hut.[9]

Again, Heliodoros in his romance, describes Meroe:

The people that evening began to cross over the river Astaborras, some by pontoon-bridge, others in ferryboats made of reeds, which were moored in large numbers at many points along the bank to provide direct crossings for people who dwelt at too great a distance from the bridge. These boats move at a high speed owing to their light material and load; for they can carry only a burden of not more than two or three men. They are made of split reeds, each half of a reed forming a skiff (*skaphion*).

A letter of the late 3rd century shows us travellers hiring a ferry: "Saras and Eudaimon to Diogenes the younger, greeting. We have been advised by the most noteworthy Ammonion to send for a ferryboat on account of the road's uncertainty. So we send you this message in order that if they agree to send while you're there, you may obtain what is necessary; and if not, that you may dispatch a report to the strategos and the guardians-of-the-peace. You know what hospitality requires, so get a little . . . from the priests and buy some incense and . . . We hear that you've been two days in Herakleopolis. Don't lose any time in dealing with your charge when you've got what you went for. It's no use if a person turns up too late for something that demanded his presence. Ammonas and Dioskoros the cooks have gone to the Oxyrhynchite Nome on the understanding that they would return at once. As they are delaying and might be needed, please send them off at once."[11]

For regular ferries at crossing-places of any importance the state-monopoly seems continued from Ptolemaic days—though in one case we find a ferry belonging to the community of georgoi of a village. In return for its use they promise to carry out "the summer labours and all other sowing".[12] Tax-receipts mention ferry-guards.[13] Indeed we find guards or watchmen of all sorts in both Ptolemaic and Roman times: field-guards, desert-guards, river-guards, canal-guards, tower-guards, harbour- or

wharf-guards, as well as prison-guards. Thus we hear of harbour-
guards at Kaine or the Grove of Arsinoe.[14] A receipt from a pilot
(2nd–3rd century), issued to the guards of a wharf in that Sacred
Grove and to the sitologoi, acknowledged the lading of 19½ art.
of wheat.[15] In 150, a guard of the desert canal of the Division of
Polemon, aged 55 years, resigned his office to a younger man, of
19 years, on account of business distractions: "on account of
anxieties". There is no reference to salary, nor is any consideration
cited.[16] We know, however, of payment from another papyrus.[17]
In a receipt for various taxes from Soknopaiou Nesos, dated
115–7, the same person for two years pays guard-tax, tax for
guards of the watchtowers, tax for river-guards, poll-tax.[18] About
160 the village-elders of Philadepheia, who were appointed by
the epistrategos on the nomination of the village-secretary, and
who were under the jurisdiction of the strategos) complained:
"Since the arrears of this village are no small sum and since we
have great need of assistance because many officials of the village
do not pay attention to the collection of taxes and especially the
field-guards, we beg that they be investigated by you so that the
exaction of the taxes may proceed with greater care."[19]

Large numbers of Egyptians must have been used to handling
rivercraft large or small. How important water-work was from
the outset is shown by the way in which the nomenclature of
boat crews was early transferred to the companies of workmen
engaged on other jobs, for instance the building of pyramids,
temples, tombs. The workers were divided into three classes: the
main crew named after the king himself; the divisions or watches
of this group, each named after a part of the boat (port, starboard,
bow, stern, and *imy-nfrt*); and a further division into small sub-
gangs with names like pyramid, boat, enduring, north—this latter
at Meydum.[20]

Boat-matters appear in the proverbial sayings. The drunken
man is told, "You are like a broken steering-oar in a ship, obedient
on neither side".[21] The schoolboy is told to be diligent at writing
and not like the unhandy sailor: "He does not keep his eye open
for adverse winds, he does not search the waves. If the outer rope
is let go, the . . . rope hangs about his neck. When he pulls the

rope . . ." Apparently he tangles himself in the ropes and gets them in a mess. In a *Praisegiving to Amun* we read: "I will declare his might to him who fares downstream and to him who fares upstream." An ancient saying runs: "If falsehood walks abroad, it strays; it does not cross over in the ferryboat"—that is, it does not take the direct route. And ferrying comes into the love-songs of the New Kingdom:

> I voyage downstream in the ferryboat,
> my bundle of reeds on my shoulder I bear.
> I'll go to Memphis and there
> to Ptah, Lord of Truth, I'll plead.
> Give me my sister tonight:
> O the stream is wine
>   Ptah is its reeds
> Sekhmet its lotus
>   Earit its bird
> and Nefertem its flower of grace.
> Through her beauty the dawn is bright,
> Memphis a dish of love-apples
> set before the Fair of Face.[22]

Sailors are quick with their fists. Their fights are represented in the decorations of the mastabas of the Old Kingdom. Such conflicts have been read, no doubt incorrectly, into the tale of the competition between Seth and Horos with boats. Apparently there is to be a race with the boats; but the result turns on a sort of pun. The boats are to be stone-boats—an ambiguous term that could mean boats made of stone or boats for carrying stone. Seth's boat of actual stone sinks, while Horos's boat of plaster-covered cedar floats. Then Seth changed into a hippopotamus and tried to make Horos's boat founder; Horos struck at him with his harpoon, but the Ennead said, "Don't strike him." We have here a folk tale in which the winner is a sort of riddle-reader.[23]

A papyrus of 135 B.C. shows us sailors in a brawl: "To Demetrios, one of the diadochoi, hipparch over men, and epistates from Paalas son of Harmais, ship-guard of the barge (thalamegos) of Apollonios, one of the first-friends and strategos and superintendent of revenues. On the (?30th) Phaophi of the 36th year, the said barge being at anchor, certain persons approaching in their own boat came to anchor outside it and broke away some of our gear. When I rebuked them so that they might keep clear, they leaped on board with unseemly shouts and gave me many blows—with the result that in the scrimmage I lost a cloak worth 300 dr. of copper as well as the smashed gear, which was also worth 3,000 dr. of copper. I beg you therefore to give orders..."[24]

Among the sightseers who wrote their names in the Valley of the Kings there was one sailor Psemmonthes, a nauarchos (commander) Ktistes, and a chief-of-rowers Alexandros.[25]

The sort of odd jobs coming the way of a sailor in private employ is brought out by a letter of the late 4th century—dated by the handwriting and the very low value of the *myrias*.

To my Lord and Brother Horion from Hermias. I am surprised if my messenger finds the landlord's boat with you. If however through some carelessness he finds it there, lose not time in sending the sailor to the city at once with the attendant I have sent. See that you don't neglect this.

If the weather is calm and he can't bring the boat back today, let the sailor himself return so as to make a bond—for I'm not a little worried. If you neglect it, our house is likely as a result of the land-lord's absence to be brought to a critical pass through the tiresome Ammonios the speculator and the prefect's assistant.

If you have any silver coins with you or solidi, send them to me quickly; for I owe on account of so many obligations and I'm no longer trusted, unless I behave fairly. Send and tell your people to deliver to me the rest of the wind and $1\frac{1}{2}$ units of the general account. The solidus now stands at 2,020 myriads; it has come down. Don't neglect to send the boat or the sailor today, I pray for your lasting health, Brother.[26]

We see a man caught in the uncontrolled movement of inflation that came over the empire.

Earlier, a letter of A.D. 338 from a pilot dealt with the duty of Oxyrhynchos to provide a sailor for a state-vessel.[27] A fragmentary official letter of the Herakleopolite Nome, A.D. 311–12, addressed to the heads of seven villages, appears to deal with the exemption of a sailor, 26 years old, from service in the state transport-service and with the provision of a substitute. The villages were doubtless jointly responsible for producing the sailor.[28]

Before we go on to look at the corn-ships in more detail, it will help us to get an idea of the restlessly busy life on and round the Nile by looking at some documents of pharaonic days. Then, as in Graeco–Roman days, love-anxieties and boat-troubles were liable to be entangled. In a papyrus of the late Eighteenth or early Nineteenth Dynasty the scribe Meh sends good wishes to the scribe Yeh the younger. "May you do things and may they be successful, and may you get credit for all you have done. Further, give your attention to the officer Merrymose. Now see, I am sending Merrymose to the Mayor to say: Look for those two boats which Pharaoh gave him, and have them looked for everywhere for him. Also give your attention to Merrymose when he is there with you. Don't let him be treated as you treated me when I was here in Memphis, with half the provisions being kept by you for their price in cash. Further, the Chantress of Amun, Nefrese, says: How are you? how I long to see you! my eyes are as big as Memphis because I'm hungry for the sight of you, but here I am praying to Thoth and the gods of Pi-Djehuty: May you be well! may you live! may you get credit for all you have done." Meh adds: "Will you get Merrymose to bring me a roll of papyrus, also pieces of good ink, and don't let bad be brought, and write to me all about your health."[29] We see that the subject-matter of letters going up and down the Nile did not change much over the millennia.

We have part of the logbook of a ship near the end of the Twentieth Dynasty.[30] It opens, "(Year 7, 1st) winter month, day 17, nearly two months of voyage from No", Thebes. Then "departure from the Harbour of Heliopolis" and arrival at "the Harbour of Memphis". A one-day voyage. Day 18: nothing happened. The logbook merely records, "2 months 1 day of voyage from No and [2 days] Harbour of Memphis". This sort of entry goes on for five days. Then Day 23 adds, "Day of the . . . of the Noble Staff of Amun to . . . at eventide". (This Staff was an object invested with the god's divine nature. In another papyrus we read of someone who "went downstream in the Noble Staff": that is, in the boat specially kept for it and given this name for short.[31]

Our boat was not the special one, but it may have been carrying the Staff, as it seems to belong to the highpriest. The event which the logbook mentions might have been a ceremonial visit of the Staff to the Memphian Temple of Ptah; but more likely what is recorded is the arrival of the boat Great Staff at Memphis.)

Day 25: still moored at Memphis. Some 5,000 fish and 200 bundles of *isr*-reeds were received from the boat of the butler. Also: "received: brought by the guard Amenkau: 4 *msh* and 1 *mdkti* of *nhh*-oil, total 5 (vessels), amounting to 262 hin: 55, 55, 61, 41, 54, total 266". The objects are vases. The discrepancy between 262 and 266 was apparently explained in a section of the papyrus that is hard to decipher.

Then comes the "account of trading in . . . Syria". Was there a Syrian merchant in Memphis? *Neheh*-oil was at times a foreign product, possibly from Syria. "Two [read: three] loincloths of Upper Egyptian cloth, each worth 22 *hin*, amounting to 66 *hin*, 31 tunics of coloured cloth, each worth 3 *hin*, amounting to 93 *hin*, 3 loincloths . . . each worth 21 hin, amounting to 63 hin, 6 . . . each worth 20 hin, amounting to 60 hin (*sic*). Total, 282 hin. Received 262, remainder 20." The *neheh*-oil is exchanged for a number of garments—though it is not clear whether it is bought or sold. Probably it is bought. The voyage seems thus at least in part a trading venture. (There is an account of a similar exchange of garments for oil on the verso.) The highpriest barters textile products of Upper Egypt—no doubt the work of the Weavers of Amun—for oil from Syria: oil that would be needed for the temple-lamps.

Day 26: 2 months 10 days out of No, 10 days at Memphis. Day 28: "Departure from the Harbour of Memphis and arrival in the Harbour of the Castle of the House of Osiris. Waiting for the scribe Paraemheb. Day of departure of the Great Ship of the Noble Staff of Amun from Memphis." Day 30: "day of the transport of Mut the Great, Mistress of Asheru"—a festival in which her statue seems to have been taken for a row on the Sacred Lake of Karnak. She was Amun's consort. The boat was still waiting for the lost scribe. We learn that he, with ten others, had been sent on some errand on the 20th day of the 4th month of the Flood, "1 month 11 days ago".

72. River scene

On Day 1 of the 2nd winter month the boat sails again—evidently only a short distance—and arrives at the Harbour of the Flat of the Castle of the House of Osiris, where it stays five days. Day 1: departure of the guard Amenkhau and two others in search of the scribe. But he is still missing on Day 3. Another search-party, of four men and a boat, go out. "Given to them rations for the boat in which they ate, 1 *khar* [? corn]. Given to be issued as rations for the boat in which they are to take to Heliopolis in order to search for him there, 3 khar: total 4 *khar*, and *Khay*, ½ khar; total 4½ *khar*." Then comes a list of five men previously sent on the quest, and a list of men with the scribe. The entries then break off.

On the verso is part of the purser's accounts. "List of the freight which is in the boat of the highpriest of Amun in charge of the scribe of the treasury Hori and the scribe Paraemheb and the guard Amenkhau." The list contains *nhh* oil, wine, *mimi*, *prt-kn*, ropes of *wd*-fibre, and fish. Against them is entered: "fish 5,000: issued 2,000, remainder 3,000". In the next list various articles (oil, papyrus-rolls, etc.) are equated in value with various garments. Again we get the impression that the boat was bartering textiles for other wares. A list headed "Reedwork brought by the sailors of the crew in charge of the scribe Paraemheb" includes *isr*-reeds and ropes, 3 of 1,000 cubits and 27 of 500, all of the *wd*-plant. It seems that the crew were kept busy making cables out of reed they cut.[32]

Another papyrus that apparently belongs to the reign of Ramses II is a somewhat similar logbook, though less systematic. It notes the boat's whereabouts, all the movements, the contributions made by various officials, and the issue of rations to groups dependent on the boat. The boat itself seems sent by the high-priest of Memphis to Per-Ramessu (probably at or near the later Pelousion).[33]

15

The Corn-Ships

THE corn-trade was highly organised already under the Ptolemies. A long memorandum of the late 3rd century B.C. about the management of various departments of the royal revenues declares: "Take care that the corn in the nomes, with the exception of that expended on the spot for seed and that which cannot be transported by water, be brought down. . . . It will thus be easy to load the corn on the first ships presenting themselves; and devote yourself to such business in no cursory manner. . . . Take care also that the prescribed supplies of corn, of which I send you a list, are brought down to Alexandreia punctually, not only correct in amount but also tested and fit for use."[1] And here is a letter authorising the embarkation of the corn levied from certain *kleroi*: "Give orders for the delivery through Killes to Horos, on the state-barge of which the master and pilot is the said Horos, of the corn levied on the holdings of Alexandros and Bromenos and Nikostratos and Pausanias; and let Killes or the shipmaster write you a receipt and seal a sample and bring it to me."[2]

Shipment was carried out by the corn-official, sitologos, and supervised by the antigrapheus (checking or copying clerk) of the royal-scribe, and an assistant from the financial department.[3] A papyrus describes the handing over of the *deigma*, sample, to the guards on board, who would bring with them from Alexandreia, the destination of the cargo, the necessary vouchers from the chief of the harbour-store there.[4] Next came the taking of the royal oath by the skipper, and the exchange of receipt and counter-receipt between him and the officials.[5] The receipt was made out in triplicate (for strategos, oikonomos' assistant, and checking-clerk).[6] We possess material on the transport of grain to the store-house at Syene for the provision of the soldiers there.[7]

The sitologos dispatching the wheat sent off a certificate of shipment, a report countersigned by the royal-scribes' assistant, to the
consignee of the cargo and the sitologos of the store-house at
Syene; also a notification of the shipment to the central sitologos
and banker of the Thebaid. On some occasions the consignee was
represented at the ship's unloading by a sort of harbour-master,
who then reported back to him and at least sometimes to the
central accounting office. In cases of wreck or trans-shipment a
report also went to him so that he might give instructions to the
oikonomos and harbour-master. We have a report that among
ships leaving Letopolis that under command of Totoes with a
cargo of 1,126 art. of wheat (sent from the Tentyrite to Syene)
"has suffered shipwreck under the isle of . . . in the Southern
Toparchy of the Letopolite on this very day".[8]

Under the Romans shipments of the grain exacted as tribute
were made in barges along the canals, then transferred to bigger
boats for the Nile. There is some evidence to show that the cost
of carrying the grain along the canals was borne by owners of
private and katoikic land in the Fayum and also at Hermopolis.[9]
A document of 22 June 163 (A.D.), dealing with some money
transactions between a man, Didymos, and some camel-drivers,
does not mean that he hired or paid them; they were paid by the
government on the completion of work and the presentation of
accounts. Pabous is lending money on the security of wages due,
with payment to be made "at whatever time they receive the
phoreta". We happen to have another document, dated 3 August
163, soon after the job was done and the camel-keepers had been
paid. One of them, Pabous, found it convenient to repay only a
half of the loan and asked to keep the balance for some three
months. So he signed a note at the regular rate of interest for half
the amount of the original loan. (Loans with no interest, not paid
when due, were liable thus to have interest charged on them.)
The cost of porterage at Ptolemais Hormos was met by the state,
which may, however, have recouped itself by an assessment on
the nome.[10] For the cost of shipping the annona or tribute by
Nile-boats we have an account of the 2nd century, dealing with
loads from Oxyrhynchos to Neapolis. It is worth citing in full to
show the varied items:

Account: for the boat of Triadelphos 3,400 art. of wheat at 21 dr. (per 100) 712 dr. To the same 4 dr. per 1,000 12 dr. Carriage of 171 art. of wheat transported . . . the drying-place at 4 dr. per 100, 6 dr.

Price of a jar (wine) sent to the assistants and soldier 8 dr. 1 obol. To the elders of Ophis for the wages of 11 workmen employed in lading, 6 dr. 2 ob. To Aphynchis, granary-guard, as his salary since Tybi 18 dr. more. Total of expenditure, 762 dr. 3 ob., of which a half is (381 dr. 1½ ob.).

For the boat of Horion son of Ammonios 1,500 art. and for the boat of Pausiris son of Apollonios 500 art., total 2,000 art., at 21 dr. (per 100) 420 dr. Payment to Horion pilot the sum given, 8 dr. Price of jar sent to the assistants and the soldier 8 dr. 1 ob. Price of 2 more jars sent to the sailors 16 dr. 2 ob. Price of vegetables to the same, without bread, 4 ob.

To the elders of Ophis for the wages of 7 workmen employed in lading 4 dr. To 1 workman assisting beyond (?) the ½ art. and embarking corn for 3½ days 5 dr. Total of expenditure 466 dr., of which a half is (233 dr.).

Sum of the whole expenditure 1,228 dr. 3 ob., of which a half is 614 dr. 2 ob.

To Dioskoras 3 ob., for which he shall render an account. Price of 2 jars expended upon us alone from Phamenoth 27 to Pharmouthi 15, 16 dr. 2 ob. Expense of . . . together with the price of oil for the same period 8 dr. 4 ob.[11]

The charge is 21 dr. per 100 art., with an extra charge of 4 dr. per 1,000 art. The official who is rendering the account to a superior seems to refer to the group of officials at the river-port as "us alone", who did not drink excessively with two jars for some nineteen days. His arithmetic is not exact; he puts 712 for 714 and 12 for 13½. Horion the pilot is probably different from the Horion with the dispatch-order.[12] Soldiers appear to be normal

73. Discharge of Cargo

on the corn-boats.[13] Half the charge for transport is paid on leaving the dock, the other half no doubt on safe delivery.

The soldier on the corn-boat played an active part in the transactions; for we find him acting as the intermediary in a receipt that concerns the sitologoi of a village and three helmsmen on a cargo-boat—one of them a Jew, "son of Jacob".[14]

Owners of boats had the right to inspect granaries and may have had a limited right to oversee transport from there to the docks, probably to avoid unnecessary demurrage charges. In the 3rd century a centurion writes to the acting-strategos: "As soon as you get my letter, send the heirs of Apollonios, magistrate of the Toparchy of Thmoisaphos, so that there may be no fraud in the lading through any neglect of yours. I have sent for this purpose not only the officer of the guard but also the other councillors (dekaprotoi), so that we may be able to get on with the lading quickly at any point I may require."[15]

To the 2nd–3rd century belongs a letter from a higher to a lesser official. "The bearer of this letter is the captain Panemouos. Please see that his freight is embarked with all despatch and let it consist of what you have in hand, ready-selected for lading. Send up the inspectors yourself to the examination, getting a donkey from the police-chiefs. After this give him your best attention, let him see the granaries, and prepare the overseers and other officials concerned, whose names have been given to you by Harpokraion, so that there may be no delay. My best wishes for your health, dearest friend."[16]

The duty of providing lighters for loading boats seems to grow as a liturgy in the 2nd century, as we see from the letter about a kydaron already cited.[17] The annona was handled by a guild of private drivers, who were required to maintain at least three donkeys owned by the state. Antinoites were left exempt.[18] By the 3rd century the burdens were greater than the benefits.

[A.D. 207] To Subatianus Aquila, Prefect of Egypt, from Totoes, styled as having Senpetsiris as his mother, of the City of Oxyrhynchos. Since your ingrained justice, my Lord Prefect, is extended to all men, I too, who have been wronged, turn to you and beg for redress. The matter is as follows.

I happen to be registered in the metropolis in the Camp Quarter and am always styled by the name above written, in accordance with which I was some time ago designated to the duty of guard, which I blamelessly discharged, and I have as well paid my yearly personal dues, living a quiet cultivator's life. I have been incorrectly designated by Herklammon, the present district-scribe of the first tribe, for the post of Public Donkey-Driver in the said city, a most onerous service, under another name, Sbikis son of Harmiysis and Taseus, and have had booked to me by him property of the value of 1,200 dr. which I do not possess.

Therefore, my Lord, as I have been forced to take up this post of Donkey-Driver although I am wholly without means and am not at all subject to the present district-scribe, our Quarter having presently to serve in accordance with the lot drawn for the districts by his Excellency the epistrategos Geminius Modestus, and have been lawlessly and recklessly designated by Heraklammon, I beseech you, if it seems good to your benign Fortune, to hear me against him, for it appertains to your power to punish unjust and lawless deeds of daring, so that I may gain my rights and be able subsequently in the year that devolves upon me to take up the service with which I may be entrusted.[19]

It seems that the civil service's efficiency has merely slipped up in one instance; but Totoes' indignation and fear transform the act into one of extreme villainy.

Members of guilds seem to get the same rate of pay as private shippers. The officers of the guild of shippers in the Arsinoite nome in 155 acted as sureties for the owner of a private lighter in his carrying out of a state-contract; and there is no sign that the guild had any control over private shipping in the nome.[20] The cargo seems to be 22 logs; the rate from Theadelpheia to Boukolon was 33 dr. $1\frac{3}{4}$ ob. per 100 art. of the lighter's capacity. A total of 266 dr. $1\frac{1}{2}$ ob., with a deduction of $6\frac{1}{2}\%$, possibly a banker's discount for payment in advance. (The same discount is made in a clothing requisition of A.D. 138.)[21] As at this time wheat was selling at 8 dr. per art., the rate of transporting it from Theadelpheia to Boukolon by water seems about 4 art. per 100.

In the Fayum, to provide the necessary transportation, we often find camels and donkeys brought in from other nomes.[22] In general the supervision was under the strategos or the royal scribe, who always issued the orders for payment. In the 3rd century the dekaprotoi at Karanis had general oversight of shipments from the granary to the river.[23] The cost of taking grain from field to granary was met by the owner or tenant of the land.[24] But how the responsibility fell for transport on to the dock is more obscure. In the Fayum owners of private or katoikic land may have had to pay to get their grain to the boats at Ptolemais Hormos, while the state paid for that of tenants of public lands.[25] For the 2nd century in 155 the state paid over 14,000 dr. for camels and donkeys with grain from the Theadelpheia granary to the canal, where the barges took in for Ptolemais Hormos.[26] The payments were made by the state but the farmer had to meet the bill.[27] In the 3rd century private owners had to pay the charges for transport; what the public tenants did we do not know.[28]

Granaries were established at the most convenient sites where the tribute-grain was stored under control of the sitologoi, whose office was a state-liturgy. Perhaps they had some privileges as bankers in compensation; they also stored grain for owners and made payments on order from their deposits. We do not know if they got any commission or could keep any of the fees exacted in the collection. Guards of the threshing-floor also held office as a liturgy.[29]

The sitologoi were in charge of the grain only after it arrived at the granaries. They issued receipts and kept a daily record of what came in.[30] Also they sent in reports at intervals of five, six, or ten days; monthly reports on receipts and shipments; and a summary at year's end. In the 3rd century samples of grain were taken to Alexandreia by a special agent.[31] But the sitologoi were still themselves responsible for the deliveries at Neapolis being up to the sample and in good condition.[32] They also distributed seed and loans on the order of strategos or royal scribe, under whose jurisdiction they were.[33]

The matter of the grain-tribute is naturally one of the best documented; and here we shall keep to a certain amount of illustrative texts, which will fill out the generalisations. A document of A.D. 42, consisting of 22 columns, gives a daily account of the movement of cereals out of a port-of-concentration. Here we find a cargo of 200 art. of lentils for Ptolemais Hormos, with no charge for transport; a cargo of 1,000 art. of lentils of katoikic origin, with again no charge; 216 art. of lentils consigned to the Alexandrian Herakleides, who seems the owner of a big river-boat waiting at Ptolemais Hormos. This time a shipping charge was made: 9 art. of lentils, of which 7½ were put to the account of the sitologos "for water or camel transport", and 1% went to Polemon, owner of a small canal-boat. The state apparently paid, the 7½ art. being perhaps the payment from Pelousion to the port, the rest going to meet the cost for transport on to the Hormos. The next shipment deals with a boat of 900 art.-burden (owned by Herakleides with Secundus, centurion of Legion III, as super-cargo) which was being loaded at the Hormos. On two different days shipments were made from the port in small boats owned by Polemon and Aphrodisias. On 2 Mesore, 783½ art. of lentils were shipped; on 4 Mesore the balance of the cargo, 117½ art., was forwarded by the lighters of the same two men; the freight cost was paid and entered in the total of naula or water-shipments. If we assume that half was paid at Oxyrhynchos, and the rest on delivery, the cost of shipment from the port of concentration to Ptolemais Hormos was 16½ art. per 900.[34]

Thus, in one case, there was no freight-payment; in another the rate seems 1½ art. per 216 art. of "bought lentils"; in a third payment of 8¼ art. was made for the delivery of 900 art., also "bought". The first case shows the katoikoi paying the cost from the place of concentration to the Hormos; in the other two cases the state pays. Comparison with donkey-transport proves that water was much cheaper. The sitologoi mentioned were of Philoteris, Doulos (?), Hiera, Autodike, Theadelpheia, Berenikis, Magais, Polydeukia, Pyrrhia, Dikaiou Nesos, Tristomos, Arsinoe, Pelousion. A pilot is in charge of a cabin-boat called the Ision of Disokouridu.[35]

A document of Philadelpheia, dated around 96, gives us the total of grain-receipts up to 1 Epeiph, then monthly receipts from Epeiph on are summarised.[36] A fragmentary day-book of revenue shows us a register of corn-payments set out according to days and villages.[37]

A customs-house register dated 1 October 104 for the month

Thoth, with five columns. The end suggests that the whole thing was a month's report; if so, only three days are missing (at the start).[38] Three days, the 10th, 12th and 26th of Thoth, are marked as "Hermes"—a term used for days when no work was done or happened to come along. A considerable variety of objects are mentioned. Of food-stuffs: oil (25 entries: 106⅔ met.), black beans (16: 106 art.), green dates (6: 12 art.), vinegar (5: 12 ker.), juicy dates (4: 16 art.), green olives (3: 5 art.), garlic (3: 8 chlibia), arax or wild chickling (2: 10 art.), dried fish (1: 1 chlib.), lentils (1: 4 art.), orobos or bitter vetch (1: 4 art.), barley (1: 1 art.), fine salt (1: 1 art.), wheat (1: 1 art.), vegetable seed (1: 4 art.), white-leaves, probably some kind of fodder (4: 4 onoi). Total duty, 641 dr. 1½ ob.[39]

Animals are a horse, a bull, five donkeys. Other items include iron and katharma (apparently a grade of iron that has not been refined), copper, baskets (or reed, palm leaves and the like), wood fuel, wool-fleeces.

Where the customs house stood is not known. The text does not tell us if the things are being brought in or taken out—except with lentils and wheat, which are imports. Anyway, most of the commodities could have been produced anywhere in Egypt. The lack of reference to boat or river suggests that the place was not on the sea or the Nile; since camels do not appear, there was no link with the Oases, which were too far off for donkeys. If the olive oil was being exported, the location would lie in the Fayum, where Strabon says the only oil-furnishing olives grew; and as there seems a reference to a harbour-master, we may assume the connection with a port on the Nile. Some similarities with other accounts suggest that the destination may have been Memphis and the customs house on the northern border of the Fayum. Much oil, we know from other sources went through Soknopaiou Nesos.[40]

One of the points suggesting Memphis is the examination-fee connected with the wool. Here is a freight-account about 100.

Memphis account, 29th: Account of a wherry (pakton): 550 art. of wheat, 44 dr.; repairs, 6 dr.; tax, 4 dr.; examination-dues, 4 dr.; to the banker, 1 dr.; commission, 5 dr.; exchange, 1 dr.; to an interpreter, 2 dr.; rudder, 14 dr. 4 ob.; a guard from the land and for a boat (kydaron), 4 ob.; to clerks, 4 dr.; to Artemeis, 1 dr.; affidavit, 4 ob.; examination-dues for a libation (tip), 2 dr.—total, 91 dr.[41]

As we noted above, with regard to a document of 155, addressed to some State-bankers, guild-officers might act as sureties for the skipper-owner of a lighter with a government-contract; but beyond that we do not know much of the relations of the guild to its members, the *navicularii Niliaci*. In the Ptolemaic period the naukleros, if prevented by an average from going, say, to the Thebaid for grain, could demand that the strategos of the Arsinoite nome where he landed should authorise him to load the amount of grain which, according to his credentials, he was supposed to load in the Thebaid; but we do not meet this right in the Roman period.[42]

Members of the guild of captains at Alexandreia could arrange with the official administering the annona at Neapolis about the way they divided the nomes among themselves. The naukleroi and the strategos could then fix shipments by agreement; and if cargoes did not arrive promptly at the docks, the naukleroi could create difficulties for the strategos—as we see from the following letter of 118:

Papeiris to the most honoured Apollonios, strategos of Apollono-polite Heptakomia, greetings. I want you to know the procurator assigned me to your nome alone at my own request and with the consent of Bessarion, with my private freighter of 4,000 art. burden.

But after I was assigned, I was detained to officiate as priest for the Pilots' Guild. You will do well, my dearest friend, to co-operate with

74. Cattle Crossing Ford of River

my men, as I cannot be present to pay my respects to your most esteemed self in person, and trust me as one able to render you service. You are not ignorant of my owning other boats with a total capacity of 80,000 art. burden, so that I could sweep your nome clean. Know, sir, that if a man acts as priest of the Pilots' Guild . . .[43]

The sitologoi, as well as receiving what was due to the state, undertook the storage of grain for private individuals; the public granaries thus show a close analogy to the public banks. We have orders addressed to them by a non-official authorising the payment of a quantity of grain to another man; and receipts for such payments.[44] A receipt of 134, issued by the keepers of the public record-office at Oxyrhynchos to the sitologoi of certain districts in the nome, states that they had registered various account-books of the latter.[45] We have also a statement by sitologoi that they had registered their account-books with officials appointed to carry them to Alexandreia.[46]

In 139 the official (probably procurator) in charge at Neapolis reported to the strategos of the Herakleid division of the Arsinoite nome: "With reference to the despatch of the annona from your district under the supervision of Besarion son of Heron, the supercargoes have received the customary release and weighing-toll, with the exception of Satabous, freedman of Sallonios Papeis." It appears that all the cargoes measured up to the sample of wheat sent from the nome except that of Satabous.[47] The forwarding of samples is known in the 3rd century, and was probably in use earlier.

On a roll, dated about 140, which seems to have come from a Fayum record-office, we find six fragmentary charters. In at least two cases the owners were Alexandrians; the commodities transported seem Mendesian olives, trunks of palmtrees, and cereals.

This charter is to be free of all charges save for festivals, angary [impressment], and tips, which shall be discharged by Tryphon [pilot]. The balance of the contract he shall receive on the discharge of the cargo. There shall be no charge for demurrage if he arrives on the day of a festival, but if he is detained more than . . . days, he shall receive . . . dr. per day. Tryphon shall provide a sufficient number of sailors and complete supplies for the boat. He shall anchor at the safest and designated anchorages at the proper hours, and if he does not deliver the cargo, he shall pay the prescribed penalty. He will be ready to sail on 6 of the present Tybi.[48]

The clause requiring safe anchorage is unusual and suggests that piracy or civil unrest was to be feared. (The river-guards had the checking of piracy as a main function.)

Transactions about wheat were often complicated. A document of 149 deals with 8¼ art. bought through the agency of a bank; and as the wheat is stated to be part of grain bought by the government for military and other purposes, the buyer probably held some post connected with grain-buying. The seller's daughter was involved.[49] The orders and notices of transfer which we noted above were negotiable documents if endorsed by the payee with his signature and a further order to pay. Thus we find a transfer-notice of 158–9 endorsed by the payee Sarapaion in favour of Herakleides, who in turn endorsed it in favour of Zoilos. These successive endorsements required no further reference to the office of the sitologoi. The documents circulated freely and thus functioned almost as a paper currency.[50]

The sitologoi of a nome were responsible for a cargo till it was delivered at Neapolis. The grain was generally inspected before shipment, and we find the office of cleaner of the public grain in the Fayum.[51] A report of 188 shows that samples were made:

Antonios Ailianos to the strategos of the Diospolite nome in the Thebaid, greeting. Since the cargo was despatched from the nome under you in charge of . . . ausis son of Sipos and his companions, amounting to 2,000 art. of wheat, appeared at the weighing of the samples to have been adulterated, I ordered that the amount of barley and earth in half an art. of it should be ascertained, and it proved to under measure by 2 % of barley and likewise ½ % of earth.

Accordingly exact at your own risk from the sitologoi who shipped the wheat the difference on the whole amount of the corn, 50¾ art. of wheat, and the extra payments and other expenses, and when you have added this total to the account of the administration, let me know.[52]

The extra three-quarters of an artaba represents the fee of 1½ % exacted in pilots' receipts.

A receipt of 190–1 seems to be from a sitologos, as he undertakes the registration of what are apparently the account-books. "To Neilos stated as the son of Soeris, and to his colleague in the collection of the corn-revenues due at Talao and in the district near Sinary for the produce of the past 30th year, greeting. I have received from you as my salary 400 dr., I being responsible for the registration of the books."[53] A return by sitologoi to a strategos in 194-6 deals with the repayment to the state-granary of a loan made to an ex-official, which he had apparently taken on so as to be able to pay certain dues; perhaps his position as an exegetes had led to his being assessed for an extra-contribution.[54]

Two documents of the late 2nd century give us glimpses of the transport of grain on land. About 180-92 a member of the guild of camel drivers complains from the village of Karanis to the strategos about an officer of the guild who tried to make illegal exactions. Grain from Karanis seems to be delivered at a Nile harbour by camel or donkey.[55]

Antonios came wanting . . . which my wife Aphrodite owns . . . two camels; and when I didn't yield, he inflicted many blows on me. More, while I was away, he exacted from Polydeukes, my wife's son, a minor, 2 dr. on the ground they were paid by all per camel.

And today when I asked him for transportation for . . . at the rate of . . . dr. per art. which he had exacted from all the village, he used the utmost insolence towards me and even threatened me with danger to my life. In fear that he might carry out his threat, I fled to this village of Pharbaitha in this division, and I present this petition asking for it to be filed, so that I may be given a hearing against him and that I may prove on the appointed day . . . hence his theft may be made evident.[56]

Another complaint, this time a donkey-driver, is dated about 197. Here the strategos seems to connive at the breaking of the law that a public donkey-driver carrying grain must maintain at least three beasts.

Aimilios Satornilos to the strategoi of the Seven Nomes and of the Arsinoite except Oasis. Greetings. I observe that the corn-lading is much neglected by you. Each of you commanded by us to have wheat in the storerooms disregards our commands—with no other excuse than that there is a lack of those whose duty it is to transport it.

In my opinion, then, I have often given instructions for them to be brought up to the required number; but you have taken no notice of my instructions. You have made other excuses and co-operated in wrongdoing with the donkey-drivers. You bring the latter up to the required number, but you don't force them to keep the requisite number of 3 asses. Hence it comes about that they are given the regular fee for transport, but the fisc doesn't get adequate service.

To prevent this state of affairs from easily continuing, if there is in the future a number who do not possess the requisite quota, and others who do, I order you to compel each donkey-driver to keep 3 asses, and to brand each donkey. Thus the drivers will be forced to keep 3 donkeys and you can catch the drivers out in their thefts. I bid you farewell.[57]

About this time the position of donkey-driver was clearly becoming burdensome.[58]

16

More on the Corn-Trade

WE now turn to the 3rd century. Many documents belong to the late 2nd or early 3rd, such as this letter from a minor official to a superior with directions for the lading and inspection of wheat.

Paesios to his dearest Archelaos, greeting. This letter's bearer is the captain Oanemouos. Please see that his freight is taken aboard with all despatch, and that it consists as usual of what you have in hand and selected for lading. Send up the inspectors yourself to the examination, getting a donkey from the police-chief. After that, give him your best attention and let him see the granaries and prepare the overseers and other officials concerned, whose names have been given to you by Harpokration, so that there may be no delay. My best wishes for your health, dearest friend.[1]

Difficulties of transport come up in a despairing letter: "They have the excuse. If you are sure you want to transport the corn to Pepsa, write how we are going to transport it. I have today been sitting here three days and Apollinaris has not sent me . . . after I went there. . . ." However, it is not clear whether the annona was in question.[2]

A judicial process of 208 takes us to the village and its granary. The case has come up on 11 April before the Prefect on a tour of inspection following his conventus. The strategos of the nome has been accused by the prytanis (president of the council) of Oxyrhynchos, who appears doubtless as spokesman of both the city and the villages of the nome. The charge is that the strategos is responsible for the late delivery of taxes-in-kind through failing to carry out the customary system of clearing the granaries. The system seems to have been that at floodtime the granaries of villages situated on the Tomis canal (the Bahr Youssef) were first emptied; then a method known as to *kata passalon* was operated— the villages being cleared in order from south to north, and the grain taken to the ports from a given area only after the granaries lying south of it were dealt with. The aim was to stop the grain from accumulating in the north of the nome and bringing about congestion in transport and delays in delivery; no doubt also to share out the burden of transport most easily and efficiently be- tween the Nile-barges and the donkey-teams:

Extract from the minutes of Subatianus Aquila in the Oxyrhynchite Nome. Among other matters: Ailios Ammonios, prytanis, said, "This Canal of ours which lies adjacent to the Inundation has an inflow and over-abundance of water. We ask that at that time vessels should be sent and the canal-villages cleared by means of this canal, and that after that the traditional system according to peg be worked, starting as in the usual practice with the Upper Toparchy, and that each granary be emptied and the grain transported to the normal destination."
    Aquila said, "What is the Peg System?"
    Ammonios replied, "Each area begins from the South."
    Aquila said, "From the Upper Toparchy?"
    Ammonios replied, "Yes. That has always been the usual procedure and has been maintained: namely that there should be no jumping from village to village, but that they should be cleared in keeping with the rise of the water and the villages adjacent to the Tomis Canal be dealt with first."
    Aquila said to Didymos the strategos, "Why wasn't this done?"
    Didymos replied . . .
    And he said to Didymos the strategos, "Where are the present ar- rears, those not yet despatched? In what district?"
    Didymos the strategos said, "In the Lower Toparchy."
    Aquila said to Ammonios, "If you were exposing some misde- meanour, I should have reprimanded him. It is hardly a matter to be questioned that this needs careful attention."[3]

The Prefect both approves the system and exonerates the strategos —though his grounds for this have been lost. The term peg- system is odd. Perhaps the *pessalos* was a measuring stick, and the order in which the granaries were cleared was worked out by the height of the floodwater as shown by the sticks in the various villages: a rational application of the Nilometer-system. The term "jump from village to village" no doubt means: "clear the granaries in a coherent way so that the grain didn't pass to and fro chaotically from village to village". Another Oxyrhynchite document is addressed to a strategos named Didymos: an acknowledgement by a shipper of the receipt of grain for transport to Alexandreia—the corn having been taken aboard from the village Psobithis on the Tomis Canal.[4]

We have a list of officials for the villages Athena and Anoubias in the Arsinoite nome for 209–10; evidently the sites were close together, probably in the south of the Division of Themsites. The list was submitted by a komarch for the current year, presumably to the strategos. A few names have been struck out and another put in by a second hand; in two cases men have been transferred from one category to another. The functionaries listed are village-elders, police chief, guards, inspectors, night-watchmen, policemen, men with the task of promoting peaceful government and safe deliveries to the public granaries, overseers for irrigation, sowing, harvesting and the like.[5] An affadavit of 221 was addressed by a citizen of Alexandreia owning land in an Oxyrhynchite village, Sesphtha, to the strategos of the Hermopolite nome. Though the man thus holds a quite subordinate post he sets his own name before that of the strategos in the superinscription.[6] He goes on:

Whereas I have acted as assistant in the collection of the corn-revenues of the Nome under you to Apollonios your chief officer, I swear by the Fortunes of Our Lords the Emperors that I shall stay with you and not absent myself from Hermopolis till I have fully discharged for you the collection, performing it honestly and in all good faith, otherwise may I be liable to the consequences of the oath. I Aurelios Hierax also called Melas the aforesaid wrote the body of the document with my own hand and swore the oath.[7]

In 236 the captain of a privately-owned ship of 250 art. burden, unmarked, chartered it to a senator of Arsinoe for loading 250 art. of vegetable seed to be carried from the Harbour of the Grove there to the Harbour of Oxyrhynchos for 100 silver dr. free of all charges: 40 dr. down and 60 dr. on delivery, with 2 days for loading and 4 days at Oxyrhynchos; after that, if detained, 16 dr. daily as demurrage.[8] About 250 we find an order sent from the procurator of Neapolis to the strategoi under the epistrategos of the Seven Nomes and the Arsinoite about "the search for the property of captain Hierax, debtor of the administration of the annona". He had defaulted and his property was to be seized. Whether or not the guild was liable for the failure of a member at this period is not known.[9] For 260 we have a letter two komarchs to the strategos of the Kynopolite nome nominating a man "for the conveyance of samples of the wheat belonging to the state which is being conveyed to the Most Illustrious Alexandreia". They present him "as a man of means and suitable, at our own risk"; he is aged 30 and owns property worth 500 drachmai. Prefixed, in a space left blank for the purpose, is a notice from the strategos certifying the publication of the appointment.[10] We here have a definite statement that the samples were taken to Alexandreia in the 3rd century.[11]

On 23 July 264 there was made the acknowledgement of the return of a boat which had been provided under the general orders of the Prefect; it is addressed to an eirenarch (peacekeeper) and undefined official, and shows a new aspect of the eirenarchs' powers. Doubtless their police-work included requisitioning.

To Calpurnios Horion, the most worthy eirenarch, and to Aurelios Achilleus also called Ammonios, the most eminent: Aurelios Herakles son of Theon, mother, Tryphas, from the City of Oxyrhynchos, boatmaker. I acknowledge that I have received from you the boat [*pakton*] with its two willow-wood oars, which I provided for the lading of the State-corn in accordance with the Letters of our most illustrious Prefect Claudius Firmus; and in answer to the question I have made acknowledgement.[12]

We can see from repayment-clauses of loans-in-kind that the harvest was usually threshed and divided by the end of Pauni; large shipment of grain would thus be made in Epeiph. The date here (29 Epeiph) fits into this scheme. We cited above a document in which a man promised to produce his boat when the transports arrived. The date was Mesore, 211. That year, then, the transports had not arrived by the end of Epeiph; the harvest must have been late or the Nile slow to rise.[13]

About 284 there was a sudden convening of the council of Oxyrhynchos by the president to deal with urgent business. Whether the notice was sent round to the councillors or was posted up in some public place, we do not know. The president had an unusually long list of municipal titles.

From Aurelios Eudaimon also called Helladios, formerly eutheniarch, kosmetes, exegetes, hypomnematographos, councillor of the Most Illustrious City of Alexandreia, ex-gymanasiarch, councillor, prytanis in office of the Illustrious and Most Illustrious City of Oxyrhynchos.

The matter of the Transport of Provisions for the Most Noble Soldiers does not allow of even a brief delay. For this reason, and because Letters from his Excellency the Dioiketes Aurelios Proteas, as well as from his Excellency Ammonios, are urging us on this question, and the Boats to receive the Supplies are already at Anchor, it became necessary to call a Special General Meeting of the Council at a suitable place, so that a Discussion may be held on this One subject, and the Obligations performed as soon as possible.

Accordingly, so that everyone, informed of this, may willingly carry out his council-work today, the 15th, the Letters are publicly exhibited. I thought it right that you should know by this Proclamation that I have instructed you, being now in possession of the facts to assemble quickly in view of the Orders (since no other subject remains for the Present Meeting) and vote on the Elections of those who are to serve.[14]

This notice proves, as one would expect, that the president called the meetings. From other papyri of the 3rd–4th century we know that the liturgies to be discussed at the meeting would include the supervision of the transport by water and the care of the provisions as they were brought out of the store-houses and carried to the Nile. The State has already provided the boats, which would take the cargoes probably to Babylon. The meeting was no doubt to be held on the same day; but no exact time or place is stated. We must assume that they were fixed by rule, and that there was a regular Council Hall. The exhortatory tone of the notice suggests, as we have every reason to believe, that the councillors did not enjoy their duties and evaded them where it was safe to do so.

In 284 itself we have a letter from three agents for the delivery of army annona. They had been asked by the strategos, with whom the Prefect and the dioiketes had been in touch, for the receipt of a large quantity of bread delivered to some military and naval detachments. They therefore forwarded the original receipt, with a copy that they asked the strategos to sign. The grain had been delivered in Panopolis "in accordance with the certificates presented by you, to the mobilised soldiers and sailors, 38,496 modii of bread".[15]

A document of 292 takes us back to the threshing-floors:

To Claudios Dioskourides, also called Chaireas, ex-strategos of the Diopolite Nome, strategos of the Oxyrhynchite Nome, from Aurelios Papontos son of Theon and Aurelios Horos son of Archailaos, both Komarchs of the village of Ision Panga for the present 8 (equivalent to 7th) year.

Having been instructed by you to hold secure the crops at the threshing-floors on our lands until the dekaprotoi have received payment in full of the public taxes from each person, we accordingly agree, swearing by the Fortune of Our Lords Diocletian and Maximian Augusti, to be on the watch and to allow no one to touch the produce until each person has paid to the local dekaprotoi the amount due from him—the measurements being made so that no complaint may result. Otherwise may we be liable to the penalties attaching to the Oath.[16]

State-priority had been established in Ptolemaic days; and we find it carried on into the Byzantine epoch, when the landlord here, as in many other matters, took over the powers of the State.[17] An official of the 5th or 6th century writes to a cultivator: "Since the nurse of the Lord Sophronios is owed rent by Psoeios the fugitive who cultivated her land, allow no one to touch what is left at his threshing-floor or the green crops till she has received her rent in full. I have to direct this letter to you, and if I learn that anyone has taken anything of his, I shall demand from you personally all that is owed to her by him."[18]

As an example of an order for payment of annona we may take this document of about 293. Sarapion is an overseer of the military bread supply:

Zoilos to Horion, greeting. Deliver to Sarapion, exegetes and superintendent of bread for the annona, on behalf of the under-cited villages, for the 1st and 2nd assessment: Plelo the remaining 6 art., Psobthis in the Middle Toparchy 18 art., Xenarchou the remaining 15 art., Takolkeilis 18 art., Mastingophorou 10 art.—total 67 art. of wheat by the 10th measure, reckoned to them at the rate of 300 dr.[19]

Wheat is rated, we see, at a considerably lower figure than is to be given soon afterwards in the Edict on Prices.

And here are a few documents of the 3rd century without precise dates. In a papyrus from seven pilots of ships with a total capacity of 4,500 art.—three privately-owned ships are mentioned with figureheads of which only that of Isis is decipherable—"we request that orders be issued for the payment of the obol fee for the shipment of 4,567½ art. of the harvest of the past 1st year which we transported on our river-boats". What this obol-fee was, we do not know, it may have been for pilotage or a freight-charge.[20] An expense-account dealing with a freight of jars of wine runs:

For 400 jars at 4½ ob., 300 dr.; examination-dues, 4 dr.; expense of carriage of wine, 36 dr.; tax, 24 dr.; rudder, 12 dr. 4½ ob.; clerks, 8 dr. —total, 385 dr. 2 ob. Extra payments on this: 30 dr.; exchange, 2 dr. 1 ob.; affidavit 3 ob.—total amount, 418 dr. Timber, 14 dr. 2 ob.; to a beneficarius, 4 dr. — total amount, 436 dr. 2 ob. To a boat 4 ob.; . . . 4 ob; receipt, 1 dr. 1 ob.; to an examiner, 1 dr. 1 ob.; to a soldier on guard, 2 dr. 2 ob.[27]

We have seen the soldier, *stationarius*, in connection with the corn-ships; the *beneficarius* was a soldier seconded for some special duty. Another transport-account, dealing with two villages of the Oxyrhynchite nome:

Psobthis in the Lower Toparchy: for the Barges of Kronion, 299 dr.; desert-dues, 27 dr.; crown-tax, 1 tal. 897 dr.; desert dues, 673 dr.; wages of camel-men, 216 dr.; desert dues, 21 dr.; freightage of barley for Alexandreia, 158 dr.; desert dues, 52 dr.—total, 1 tal. 2,712 dr.[22]

A similar kind of account is made up for Takona.

The problems from the level of the farmer are illustrated by a letter. "To my Lord Zoilos from Dionysios, greeting. The dekaprotos is harassing us a lot about the lading of the corn. So send us Dionysios. He knows the account of the measuring, and we did the lading on the journey up. And now he worries us, and the farmers who have no animals he worries about fodder and about expenses. Send him, for he knows the account, so that he may also get animals. You have written nothing to me about Phoinike. So write, that I may learn the order. Write to me also about the river-workers for the reed-plantations: where we can find them. I pray, lord, for your lasting health."[23]

The dekaprotos worried others; but he himself was often worried about the burden of his office. In 299 a man made an appeal at the Prefect's orders at being appointed as dekaprotos; and then applied to the katholikos.[24] Here one dekaprotos appointed another; and though such nomination of a successor by the outgoing official was unusual, we find it occurring again in 316 when three local collectors of corn-dues give the praepositus of the pagus the names of the men to follow them. One of the three is renominated: Aurelios Herakleios son of Pekoous of the village of Dositheou.[25]

We will not follow the corn-boats into the Byzantine period, when the State both weakens and hardens. But here is an anxious letter from the later 5th century addressed to a cleric, "the most reverend and pious lord Pamouthios. I urge our ever-young Father to send me the boat at once so that I may stow Agathinos' corn aboard, and I'll send a messenger to Sinkepha for the men and camels. Vouchsafe to inquire of the most pious Bishop about the transport-charge for the camels. So don't neglect to attend to this. . . . Many salutations to your Piety my Lord Master."[26]

17

Holy Water

WE may now turn back from the practical aspects to the part played by the Nile in men's thoughts and emotions. Source of life for the Egyptian, the river was also an omnipresent danger. In the ancient text, *The Man who was Tired of Life*, we read:

They who built in granite and constructed halls in goodly pyramids with fine work, when the builders became gods [i.e. died], their [memorial] stelai were destroyed, like the weary ones who died on the riverbank through lack of a survivor, the flood having taken its toll and the sun likewise, to whom talk the fishes of the banks of the water. Listen to me: behold, it is good for men to hear. Follow the happy day and forget care.

A peasant ploughed his plot and loaded his harvest aboard a boat, towing it when the time of festival drew near. He saw the coming of the darkness of the northwind, for he was vigilant in the boat when the sun set. He escaped with his wife and children, but came to grief on a lake infested by night with crocodiles. At last he sat down and broke silence, saying, "I weep not for yonder mother, who has no more going forth from the west for another [term] on earth; I sorrow rather for her children broken in the egg, who have looked in the face of the crocodile god ere they have lived."[1]

He mourns, not for his lost wife who is now at rest in death, but for the children she might have had. The fishes of the bank are those lurking under the bank's shadow where a hastily thrown-in corpse would fall.

Yet the Nile remained the beloved river. "A most beautiful sight it is," says Seneca, "when the Nile overflows across the fields. The plains disappear, the valleys are hidden, only the towns stand out like islands. There is no communication across the face of the earth except by boat; and the less land is visible, the greater joy is felt by the people." It was still what the praises, engraved on the rocks at Gebel Silsileh at Ramses II's command, declared to all men: "the living and beautiful Nile . . . father of all the gods".[2]

We have seen some of the laudatory terms used of the Nile. The waters were often said to be peculiarly sweet and fresh. An

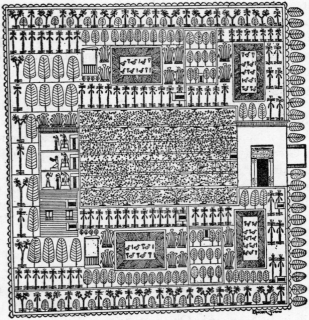

75. House, Garden and Ponds

inscription at Kalachah stated that Nilewater was "sweeter of taste than any other river".[3] Diodoros argued that a proof of the Nile having passed through the tropics was "the excessive sweetness of its waters; for in the river's course through the torrid zone it is tempered by the heat, and that is the reason for it being the sweetest of all rivers, as by the law of nature that which is fiery always sweetens what is wet".[4] Philostratos made his Apollonios declare that he refuses to consider the Egyptians the source of the wisdoms which in his opinion came from the Brahmans of India: to give the Egyptians the credit would be to confer on them a greater boon "than if that were to happen over again which their poets relate, namely if the Nile on reaching its full were found to be with honey blent". (He pays his own tribute to the torrid zone, saying that the Indians "were more subtle in their understanding, since such men as they live in contact with a purer daylight and hold truer notions of nature and the gods: they are near to the latter and live on the edge and borders of that thermal essence which quickens all into life". We see here the same line of reasoning as that which made the Aithiopians a people living close to the gods and owning a fuller revelation of things divine than others in more temperate regions.)[5] Pescennius Niger said to a man who, on the borders of Egypt, wanted wine, "What, you have the Nile, and it's for wine you ask!" Spartianus adds, "The sweetness of this water is such that the valley's inhabitants do not ask for wine." In fact the inhabitants in Greek Egypt did ask for wine; if Egyptians perhaps it was beer they drank.[6]

There was a legend the Nile once tasted of honey for eleven days. And in Latin we find the name Melo for the river—a usage going back to Ennius. Ausonius calls papyrus "Melo's white page".[7]

Athenaios cites authorities for the sweetness and venom of the Nile: "Theophratos says in his treatise *On Waters* that Nilewater is very fecundating and very sweet, and that for this reason it relaxes the stomach of those who drink it with the natron mixed in it. In his treatise *On Plants* he says that there are places where the water is prolific, for instance at Thespiai, but that at Pyrrha it sterilises. Also among fresh waters he says that some are antagonistic to generation of one or more offspring, as that of Pheia or of Pyrrha. A drought once having been produced in the region of the Nile, the water of the stream became poisonous and killed off many Egyptians."[8]

Works were written on the virtues of Nilewater.[9] One author said that the floodwater with its soda salts regulated intestinal functions and menstruation, and helped childbirth.[10] Another said that it aided digestion and nutrition.[11] It was thought to aid human reproduction as well as helping the fertility of animal and plant. Aischylos, who seems to have been much interested in

Egypt, sang the Nile's fecundating powers in a chorus of the *Suppliants*, and in the opening of the *Persians* referred to "mighty Nile's life-engendering coast".[12] Twins were thought to be common in Egypt, even 3, 4, 5, or 7 children at a birth.[13] Goat bitches normally bore two kids; in Egypt they bore five.[14] The land was *polyketes*, rich in monsters; *zoogonos*, generative.[15] And an unknown poet sang:

> Iarbas first arose, the Libyans say,
> out of the desert plains
> which the loins of Zeus had pierced in a gush of sweetness
> and the Nile fattens Egyptian mud to this day,
> bears creatures fleshed with the wet heat,
> and teems with living bodies still.[16]

The floodwater was in fact rich in mineral and vegetable salts, though the ancients seem to have known only the first. They further did not know that by soaking through the soil it lost part of its nutritive value. When the flood was low, a harmful excess of mineral salts could result.[17] Pliny tried to explain the presence of salts (*sal, flos salis, nitrum*), which are usually of sea-origin, by suggesting that here *sal* "is formed by the penetration of the sea itself in the soil enriched as I believe by the Nile".[18]

We meet Nilewater used in magical medicine around 1500 B.C., to cure a man who is sick or who has been burned: especially when the loins or thighs were affected, since from these parts of Osiris' body the Nile flowed. (His efflux seems sweat, blood, semen. "Your flanks are the two vases from which the Nile takes its source" and "the Nile is between my thighs".) In the 2nd and 3rd centuries A.D. when magic was very flourishing, we find recipes like the following: "Go to a place which the Nile has just left open before anyone has walked there or a place washed by the Nile on all sides or which has been flooded by the Nile in some other chance-way."[19]

The Greeks indeed found Nilewater too strong and difficult, even apart from its muddiness during the flood.[20] Filter-vessels, called *stakta* (drops), were used at Alexandreia and doubtless elsewhere. They were "pierced on all sides with holes, close together and very small, through which the troubled water,

oozing out, becomes purer and clearer".[21] In the Delta, at
Athribis, in an area protected as a nekropolis up to the Thirtieth
Dynasty, have been the remains of a Ptolemaic construction in
crude brick, which was repaired under the Romans in the 1st
century A.D. It was linked to an aqueduct and seems certainly to
have been used for filtering on a large scale. Platforms of brick
held and isolated beds of sand, through which the water percola-
ted.[22] Hydraulic systems were also used, as we see at Hermopolis.
There water was filtered through a series of cisterns arranged in
echelon.[23]

Nilewater was exported and drunk abroad. Texts show that the
traffic had begun by Saite times.[24] Dinon in his work on Persia
said the Great King had Nilewater brought and kept in his
reserves as a sign of power. Ptolemy II sent it to his daughter
Berenike who had married Antiochos II of Syria: "The only
river he wanted his daughter to drink."[25] In such cases the water
seems to have been thought to have some magical virtue; and
perhaps the belief in its fertilising potences was what made the
trade profitable. Aristeides of Smyrna in the 2nd century A.D.
declared, "It does not spoil, when kept in Egypt or exported
beyond the frontiers. The Egyptians are the only people we know
who fill jars with water as others do with wine, keep it three, four,
or more years, and draw pride from its age as with wine." The
trade was still going in the 19th century. Gérard de Nerval said
that Nilewater was much favoured at Constantinople; the Sultan
drank no other water; and it was considered to be good for
fecundity. It was expensive and sold in bottles.[26] The water was
also naturally needed at home and abroad for ritual purposes.
Jars made in the form of Sarapis must have been used to hold the
holy water. We meet corporations of water-pourers for
nekropoleis: two women call themselves "of those who pour
libations for Sarapis"; and the ritual-vase for the water developed
a cult of its own.[27] In the late Ptolemaic period, together with
Sarapis, Isis, Anubis, and Harpokrates, there was worshipped at
Delos a god Hydreion, with the epithet *epekoos*, "he who hears
prayers".[28] In the so-called House of Isis at Pompeii a reservoir
seems built for Nilewater. "The water used to sprinkle the
Temple of Isis was supposed to be that of the Nile," said Servius,

the commentator on Virgil; and six hydriai, forwarded to the highpriest N. Popidius Natalis, might have held Nilewater.[29]

We noted earlier how pervasive and all-important was the use of Nilewater in the ritual of Egyptian temples, for aspersions, purifications, libations of all kinds. The holy water was taken at floodtime. The temples had ponds and wells inside their precincts into which Nilewater was brought by a canal or some other such connection. Strabo says that at Abydos was a spring "lying at a great depth, so that one goes down to it by vaulted galleries made of monoliths of remarkable size and workmanship. There is a canal leading to the place from the great river, and near the canal is a grove of Egyptian acantha, sacred to Apollo." As his account comes straight after that of the Seti temple (Memnonion), he was probably referring to the Cenotaph, which we have already considered. In his days the Central Hall would no doubt have already been partly filled with sand, and he may well have mistaken the pitchroof for a vault—recalling the pairs of large blocks roofing the Transversal Room as monoliths, partly under the influence of the Central Hall's roofing stones where daylight did come in through the unfinished structure. The remark about the Canal may be an inference from the rise and fall of the waters at the same time as the Nile. An ostrakon confirms that Abydos was connected with the Nile by a canal which may have come up to the edge of the cultivated area in front of the temple.[30]

In Hathor's temple at Dendera was a "water chamber", and we find chapels such as the Neilaion of Hermopolis, adjacent to the Sarapeion, together with a construction called the *komasterion*.[31] The latter was a covered channel, and despite its name (meeting-place of *komastai*, who in Egypt carried sacred images in procession) it does not seem to have often had a cult-use. Rather it was used by the temple-personnel concerned with the nilometer that was attached to many sanctuaries—though at the flood-festival komastai may have gone down it at the moment of the proclamation that the Nile was rising at the god's order. A papyrus shows that jars of wine were stored there at odd times.[32] The measure, the nilometric cubit, was probably set in a rock-cut cavity near steps that went down to the nilometer or well.[33]

Temple-pools have been excavated at Medamud and Tod. That

at Tod was constructed in sandstone: a rectangle with the longest side parallel to the temple and with steps for the sacred boat on the backs of men to go down to the varying water-level. Both sites had a double pond, and the water came up from a central well. One pond was built inside the other: we may compare the boat-sanctuary in Ptolemaic temples, which is a building inside a building. The upper pond was made to hold the waters of the risen Nile; the lower one to hold the waters at their normal level. There are two sets of stairs. One, of descent, starts at a little distance from one of the angles and follows one of the long inner walls of the upper platform; it comes down to a landing along one of the small sides, at the middle of the wall. The second staircase, for going-up, was set symmetrically on the opposite wall. A platform for processional or other movement ran round the top of the lower pond. The two staircases continue on the pond-axis. From mid-wall they go straight down to the centre of the pond, doubtless right down to base of the central well's construction. A flooring of slabs stepped down to the centre was noted at this level. The depth of the upper pond was 6·65 metres; the orifice of the well was at least 9 metres from the platform above it.

The temple, which was abandoned at the end of the 4th century A.D., seems built in the Roman period. Decorated stones from a

76. The Baboons of Thoth fishing Souls

temple of the New Kingdom were used; they mention Sebek-Re, Gebelein, and Sumnu (on the opposite bank of the Nile, north of Armant). In the 5th century part of the temple was inhabited and part was used as a stone-quarry; the pond-area was filled up and at different times (perhaps 8th century and sometime before the 12th) it housed a press and was used for a tree-plantation.[34]

Such details however give us no notion of the way in which a temple had its charms enhanced by water and greenery. We can get some idea of the aesthetic involved by glancing at Maru-aten at Amarna.[35] Here indeed a special stress was put on beauty; but as in many other aspects of Akhenaten's creed the basis was traditional even if there was a sort of free development on that basis. Was the maru a pleasure-resort or a sanctuary? All maru in texts are connected with solar deities.[36] The earliest example is recorded on a stele of Amenophis III from the temple of Meneptah in West Thebes. "A place of flourishing (or recreation) for my Father Amun at his beautiful festival. I built a great temple in its midst like Re when he rises on the horizon. It is planted with all flowers. How beautiful is Nun in his pool at every season. More is its wine than water, like a full Nile, born of the Lord of Eternity."[37]

Perhaps the main architectural feature was an *ssdt* window where Horos appeared in the shape of the sacred falcon. At Edfu-Behdet the building seems to be near the southeast corner of the main temple, opposite the Mammisi. A falcon was chosen every year from the creatures reared in the precincts and presented to the people by the statue from this Window of Appearances, which was similar to those in the royal palaces of the Eighteenth, Nineteenth and Twentieth Dynasties.[38] At Amarna, however, as the Aten was not anthropomorphic and was represented solely as a sun-disk with rays, no sacred animal would be used. Here gardens were laid out round the sacred buildings of the Maru-Aten, with eight beds on either side of the central pathway to the water-court. "Your rays nourish every garden," cry the solar hymns of the city. "When you rise they live, they grow by you."[39]

The reference to Nun is interesting and shows how the sacred pools were felt to own an Oceanic virtue. Here the Nun-waters must have been in the ponds, the channel running round a kiosk-isle, and the T-tanks in the Maru-Aten. The kiosk, built on an artificial isle, seems to stand for the Aten coming up out of the primeval Nun, the Isle of the Middle. The other such man-made isle which we know, that of the Osireion of Sethos I at Abydos, is also oriented northeast-southwest, and again must symbolise the world-hill rising from the waters. In the suncult of Heliopolis the water for lustrations was brought from a sacred pool in the precincts of the sun-temple; and this pool also was Nun, the waters from which the sun was born.[40] We can understand how a sacred pond like that of Tod, where the water seemed to rise up direct from the underworld, would be indeed Nun for the worshippers.

Further, the longitudinal axis of the large lake is the same as that of a long quay projecting at its west end and that of the front temple at the east end. There seems here a connection with the viewing of the Aten in his daily course: especially at evening when he started on his night-voyage. Does this axis symbolise the Nile? The hymns support the suggestion. During the day "your rays are in the midst of the Great Green Sea"; "the Nile comes forth from the Underworld for Egypt"; and "you make the Nile in the Underworld, you bring it out as you wish to preserve your people alive". Also, Amenophis says, "Nun is beautiful in his pool at every season".[41] An old lustration-formula at Edfu, Philai, Dendera, identified the Nilewater with Nun out of which the sun rose, and spoke of it as "daily giving birth to the King like Re".[42]

There are also eleven tanks interlocking about thirteen square bases. A passageway of painted plaster runs round them, on which appear panels, each with two plants. But at one place, where we expect a tank, the ground is filled in level with the passage-floor. This place is not in the middle of the row, but lies on the main axis of the kiosk, with 4 tanks on the west and 7 on the east. No doubt kiosk and tanks were the sites of the monthly Mswt-'Itn festival; the tank would start the series off in Tybi, then would come the 4 tanks on the west of the main alley, then the 7 on the east.[43] The initial (consecration) feast of the Falcon of Hor-Re was held in Ptolemaic times in his Maru at Edfu on 1 Tybi; and the sun-hymns, after the reference to flowers and gardens, go on: "You make the Seasons in order to create all your work: winter to bring them coolness and heat so that they may taste you."[44] The kiosk and the eleven tanks would then represent the seasonal progress of the Aten, in promoting flowers and plants, as the Zoological Garden in the north of Amarna would bear testimony to another aspect of the god's creative energy.[45]

Where a temple was built back from the river, on the desert cliffs, water was carried by men on their backs. We have the accounts for transporting water for festivals in the Sarapeion at Memphis. The charges rise to 24 dr. per voyage for the months April, May, June. As men drank beer and wine at the festivals, the water must have been for cult-purposes. (Here they may well have been a connection with the sanctuary of Astarte inside the Sarapeion where water would be needed for her spring-festival.)[46] Apart from aspersions, libations, purifications and the like, Nilewater was used in the incubations where a god visited the worshipper during his sleep. At Kanopos, the devotees of Sarapis Hydreios slept round the edge of a pool; and an Aithiopian poet, writing in Greek at Kalabsheh in the far south, tells us that in the course of such an incubation dream, "I seemed to bathe my body in the bed of the stream, pleasantly caressed by the Nile's abounding waters".[47]

The most interesting aspect of the waters is their power of reviving and resurrecting. A Pyramid Text sees the moment of flood as that of resurrection: "The watered fields are satisfied, the canals are inundated for N on this day when his spirit is given to him, when his might is given to him. Raise yourself up, N, take to yourself your water, gather to yourself your bones."[48] Here are two Utterances. Horos makes a libation and offering to the dead king; then comes a libation with *kbhw* water and a fumigation with incense:

This is your cool water, Osiris. This is your cool water, N, which went forth from your son, which went forth from Horos.

I have come, I have brought to you the Eye of Horos, that your heart may be refreshed by it. I have brought it to you. It is under your soles. Take to yourself the efflux (sweat) which goes forth from you. Your heart shall be weary thereby.

To say 4 times when you go forth justified: Libation, 2 pellets of natron.

To say: Osiris N, take to yourself this your libation, which is offered to you by Horos, in your name of He-who-is-come-from-the-Cataract. Take to yourself the efflux which goes forth from you.

Horos has made me assemble for you the gods from every place to which you go. Horos has made me count for you the Children of Horos even to the place where you were drowned.

Osis N, take to yourself your natron, so that you may be divine. Nut has made you to be as a god to your enemy in your name of God. Hr-rnp-wi recognises you, for you are made young in your name of fresh water.[49]

Kbh means to cool or to be cool. The form *kbh.w* is plural to express the drops of which water is composed, but is used as a singular to mean cool-water.[50] *Kbh.wt* personified fresh libation-water, as we saw:

N rows in the *hnbw*-boat where he takes the helm, towards the field of the two lower heavens, to the beginning of this land of the Marsh of Reeds. His arm is taken by Re, his head is raised up by Atum, his forward cable is taken by Isis, his stern cable is seized by Nephthys. Kbh.wt places him at her side. . . .[51]

In this form she is the daughter of Anubis, and she approaches the deadman with her "four *nms.t* jars, with which she refreshes the heart of the Great God [Re] on the day of awakening. She also refreshes the heart of N with them to life, she purifies N, she censes him."[52] Both forms of the name probably refer to the same serpent-goddess, the Cool One. The word *kbh.w* is also a place; it defines heaven as a place. Its mythical origin must have been in the Cool Waters of Elephantine; a cosmic site with its earthly equivalent in the semi-mythical source-hole of Bigeh (finally taken to embrace the whole region of the 1st Cataract). *Kbh.w* is identified with the Nilewaters in which the viscera of Osiris were found and which were supposed to come from the stars of heaven as star-dew or night-dew or the sky-water on which the stars sailed. So *kbh.wt* herself became a star. "The stars follow your beloved *Kbh.wt*."[53] *Kbh.w* is thus simultaneously Nilewater, the birthplace of Re, the whole of heaven or especially the east. Like heaven it has its double doors. It is both the means

77. Deadman (Ani) and Wife standing in water and scooping it up to drink; he holds a
sail (symbolising air or wind), she a fan; two young and one mature palm (ch. lviii)

of transfiguration and of spirit-journeying, and the goal of the
process or journey.[54] *The Book of the Dead* deals with the problem
of facilitating the access of the deadman to the "land of fresh
water".[55] In a tomb of a prince of the Twentieth Dynasty in the
Valley of the Queens we see Nephthys pouring water on the
palms of her hands for the deadman's benefit. As Mistress of the
West, she says, "I give you water of Epet-sut (?), which is the
Great Inundation manifesting itself".[56]

In the *Book of the Dead* (papyrus of Ani) there is a Chapter on
Drinking Water in Khert-Neter, the Otherworld.

The *am khept* priest, Hefer-uben-f, whose word is truth, says: I, even I,
am he who comes forth from the god Geb. The waterflood is given to
him, he has become the master of it in the form of Hapi.

I, the *am khent* Nefer-uben-f, open the Doors of Heaven. Thoth has
opened to me the doors of Qebh [the heavenly waters]. Lo, Hepi, Hep,
the two sons(?) of the Sky, mighty in splendour, grant that I may be
master over the water, even as Seth had dominion over his evil power
(?) on the day of the storming of the Two Lands.

I pass by the Great Ones, arm to shoulder (?), even as they pass that
Great God, the Spirit who is equipped, whose name is unknown. I
have passed by the Aged One [or Great One] of the shoulder (?). I

am Nefer-uben-f, whose word is truth. Osiris has opened to me the Heavenly Water. Thoth-Hapi, the Lord of the Horizon, in his name of Thoth the earth-cleaver, has opened to me the Heavenly Water. I am master of the water, as Set is master of his weapon. I sail over the sky, I am Re, I am Ru. I am Sma. I have eaten the Thigh, I have seized the bone and flesh. I go round about the Lake of Sekhet-Ar. Limitless eternity has been given to me. Lo, I am the heir of eternity, to whom everlastingness has been given.[57]

Here Hapi-Nun has been lifted into the sky, the underworld into the overworld, because of the idea of immortality through ascent to the stars. But the deadman's need of libation and drink-offering, and the identity of the sacred Nilewater with Nun, is stressed all the same. Incidentally, the way in which Seth's power over water is repeated—where we would expect the deadman to be linked with Horos—shows how the association we discussed in the chapter on Seth and the Sea persisted after the myth-connections were forgotten or ignored. In the corresponding chapters in the papyrus of Nu, we read, "Hail, Bull of Amentit!" and "I am the paddle which is equipped, wherewith Re transported the Aged Gods, which raised up the emissions of Osiris from the Lake of blazing fire and he was not burned".[58]

In Lower Nubia it is still the custom to pour periodical libations of water on the graves of relatives. We find women visiting the

78. Meroitic Funeral Stele showing water-offerings

graves every Friday (the Moslem sabbath); a red polished hand-
made bowl at the head of the grave, and a palm-rib, stript of
leaves, stuck at either end with a third rib laid on the grave itself.[59]
The practice is certainly a survival from very ancient Egyptian
times. In the tomb-chapel of Methen, who lived near the end of
the Third Dynasty, is the prayer: "Grace granted by Anubis who
presides in the nekropolis, a Coming-forth to the Voice there by
all his villages on the wag-festival (18th of 1st month) . . . the
1st day of the month, the 1st day of the halfmonth, the 1st day of
every week." (The Egyptian week consisted of ten days, a third of
a month.) An inscription, perhaps of the Sixth Dynasty, runs: "A
Coming-forth of the Voice for him in his tombchapel at the
monthly and halfmonthly festival, on the 1sts of the seasons, the
1sts of the months, the 1sts of the weeks."[60]

The tradition was fully alive in Graeco-Roman times. An
important feature of the Osirian cult at the 1st Cataract was the
libation made by Isis at the burial-place of her husband. On the
1st day of the week she crossed the Nile from Philai to Bigeh and
poured out her drink-offerings in the Holy Place (called the
Abaton by the Greeks), where stood Osiris' tomb overshadowed
by the *iwy*-tree, and a grove with its 365 offering tables. A regular
attribute of Isis as the chief officiant was *kbh.t*, the female liba-
tioner.[61] It was doubtless in the role of wife that she made the
weekly offering. In Greek and demotic we find the prayer that
the dead "may take water on the table of offerings behind Osiris"
—"the fresh water come from Atum".[62] The Greek term is
psychron hydor. The deadman from his tomb asks the passer-by for
"fresh water".[63] The wife of a priest of Ptah complains in the
hieroglyphic inscription of her funerary stele: "The living water
that the earth gives to everyone . . . is now for me only a water
stagnant and dead. . . . Let me be given running water to drink."[64]
A 2nd-century stele cried, "Let Isis shed upon you the holy water
of Osiris".[65] A tomb at Thebes makes the appeal: "Let Osiris
grant you light dust above and cool water to drink."[66]

A Greek of Thebes (?) in Roman times asks his friends and
companions in arms to pour on his tombs some drops of Nilewater.[67] And in a catacomb of Kom el-Chugafah the sarcophagi
were supplied, beside the mummy-heads, with thin metal tubes to

carry water to the deadman's mouth; in a corner of the catacomb there was a cistern to provide the water.[68] In burials of the Ptolemaic epoch which are purely Greek, no such arrangements can be found; the idea and mechanism are Egyptian. Egyptian ideas, mixed with ideas from Syria and Mesopotamia, later combined to produce Christian fears of suffering from thirst in death and hopes of easing it.[69]

Thrice in the calendar at Dendera (10 Thoth, 30 Phaophi, 20 Tybi) the procession of Hathor came from the precinct of the great sanctuary and went to the cemetery, where the Aspersion of the Dead was carried out. In a scene on the terrace of the temple at Philai we see the officiant pour out water on the Osirian mummy. Water-pouring processions shown as lines of Hapis we discussed earlier are common in the temple-representations.[70]

The Isiac reverence for Nilewater inevitably angered the Christians as a parody of their own feeling about baptismal water. Firmicus Maternus told the Egyptians: "In vain you think that this water you venerate can save you. It is another water that makes renewed men be born."[71] On the other hand Greek devotees of the mystery-cults used Nilewater as a symbol of regeneration and immortality, Porphyrios promises those who practise virtue that they will "drink the beautiful waters of an Eternal Nile".[72]

18

The Beautiful Festival of the Valley

GREEKS, moving up the Nile, could see many remarkable religious festivals and rites. First in the Delta, at places like Sais, Mendes, Bouto. If they sailed all the way up to Syene they had the chance of seeing Ptah embark for the temple of Hathor of the Sycamore, Anubis in his procession at Siut, Osiris at Abydos on his way to Nadit or Pagar, and Hathor at Dendera on her way to Edfu. At Thebes they might come upon the squadron of Amon, Mut, Khonsu and others sailing the Nile or the big canals, with Montu arriving at Erment. Horos Behut-t might be sailing from Edfu; and at Syene was Anukit voyaging from the Cataract. Together with the gilded boat of the gods there would be a fleet of lesser vessels carrying priests, troops, devotees.[1]

After the sacred bull Apis has died and received a splendid burial, the priests charged with this duty seek out a young bull with similar body-markings to those of his predecessor. When it is found, the people cease their mourning and the priests who are tending it take the young bull first to Neilopolis. There it is kept 40 days. Then they put it in a state-barge fitted out with a gilded cabin, and lead it as a god to the sanctuary of Hephaistos [Ptah] at Memphis. There, for 40 days, only women may look at it. They stand facing it and pull up their clothes to show their genital parts; but after that they are forever forbidden to come into the presence of this god.[2]

Of the great festivals the one which most strongly brings out the vivifying and regenerative values of Nilewater is the Beautiful Festival of the Valley at Thebes.[3] This celebration seems to have died out in the last Ptolemaic days, but elements of it persisted in the funerary practices. Under the Ptolemies there was a category of priests, *Choachytai*, who seem certainly to be the descendants

T

79. A god carried in his processional boat

of the Servants-of-the-Ka via the Pourers-of-purificatory-water of the Saite and Persian epochs. The Greek word *Choachytes* means pourer of drink-offerings, doing its best to express the act of purification by water which completed the purification by incense-fumigation in the funerary ritual. *Choai* implies libations; but the Egyptian procedure was unlike anything in Greek funerary practice.[4] The Choachytai were then primarily mortuary priests concerned in particular with liquid offerings; but they were also entrepreneurs of funeral processions. Various documents clarify, not without raising difficult points, their status and their relations to the *taricheutes*, who embalmed the mummies. In 270 B.C. the taricheutes Phagonis received from a dead person's father the material needed for the corpse's embalming, and put it in the hands of a choachytes. The terms of the document suggest that the latter had some kind of right-of-control over the articles in question, and that the taricheutes was in some degree subordinate to him.[5] A demotic papyrus contains the fragmentary rules of a priestly corporation, in which the choachytai were interested. The group seems the fraternity of Opet; and the choachytai are described as attached to the Amun of Opet without the usual addition "in the West of Thebes". A rule deals with the case where a choachytes goes to the 35 days of burial-process furnished with stuffs (shrouds and bandages) and a bed; but there the materials may be provided for the mummifying of a group-member by the other members together with the family, and not for a client in the ordinary sense. However, another rule states that the choachytai must not sell the embalming linens of a mummy in its tomb, nor a cover (?) nor a litter. The first two items belong to the contents of the tombs administered by the choachytai; the third item seems to show that they also had at their service the instruments for burials.[6]

A third document suggests that the *nekrotaphoi*, the corporation who stowed the mummies in their tombs, were paid by the choachytai; for they complain at not getting their dues and blame the latter. It is possible then that the bereaved families paid the expenses of a funeral in a lump sum, and that the choachytai then paid out a part of it to the nekrotaphs and perhaps even the embalmers. The Greek term for the last-named means salters, but the demotic term is nobler, calling them readers or lectors.[8] Perhaps they recited certain prayers during their work; Porpyhrios says that they invoked the Sungod after the taking-out of the viscera.[9] A strange inscription on a tomb-wall in Alexandreia has in Greek: "the lector of the monkey"—which reminds us of the "lector of the ape", the embalmer of Thoth's monkeys at Thebes.[10] The embalmers exercised in relation to their clients the role of Anubis beside Osiris; they were impure but respected: "worthy of every honour and consideration," says Diodoros, "associating with the priests and even coming and going in the temples without hindrance, as being undefiled".[11] They had the right personally to reside on the right bank of the river; but they had to carry out their trade on the other bank, in the Memnonia.[12] The choachytai, who seemed to control at least certain aspects of burials, and also were called in demotic Openers of the House (tomb), may also have had the same sort of role in the embalming processes. Ptolemaic tomb-paintings show us a priest reciting prayers during those processes.[13] The choachytai may offer up prayers such as that which Porphyrios attributed to the taricheutai; for by his time the former officiants seem to have disappeared. Under the Ptolemies the choachytai may well have exercised a general control or supervision of all that happened to a dead man after he was handed over for disposal. Certainly it would have simplified matters if the dead man's family had only to deal with a single person, whom they paid for seeing the whole thing through. Often they resided at some distance and sent the mummied body along by water. Further in the weakened condition of Amun's priesthood, suspected of nationalist views, the choachytai seem to have sought ambitiously to extend their controls in the necropolis, which was however under a President who must have had some sort of organisation at his orders.[14]

A lawsuit provides information of the relations between the embalmers and the choachytai.[15] Hermias is the plaintiff, and his lawyer Philokles tries to argue that the two groups were in effect one. He wants to prove that a ruling that governs one of them applies to both, and he declares that the choachytai have deposed corpses (*nekroi*) in Hermias' house. This house stands on the dromos of Hera (Mut) and Demeter (Ipet), for whom corpses are objects of abomination, as also are all persons who deal with them. It seems unlikely that the advocate is wildly exaggerating and calling a fully-mummified body a corpse. So we had best conclude that at least some of the buildings owned by the choachytai were mortuary depots where for a necessarily short time the dead bodies, treated in some provisional way, were kept. (The head seems to have been treated with some resinous layer while the body was left in a natron bath.)[16] The opposing advocate in the lawsuit, Deinon, makes no distinction between corpse and mummy, but argues that the choachytai were not embalmers, whose liturgy was quite distinct. That is, his clients did not disembowel the body, put it in natron, coat it with the final embalming products, and roll it up in shrouds and bandages.[17]

We know of them only in the nekropoleis of Thebes and Memphis. And they seem to die out in the late Ptolemaic era. Thebes suffered badly in the periods of warfare in 88 and 29 B.C.; the burial system could no longer carry on at its previous level. Egyptians on the whole were impoverished, and the specialised groups could not continue to function: paraschistai (corpse-openers, who also disappear) embalmers, nekrotaphs (grave-diggers), and choachytai. Only the corporations of embalmers and diggers carried on; and under the Romans the diggers took over the role of generally conducting the funerary business.[18]

The dead person's urgent need of water is illustrated by the curses inscribed on the statue of Wersu and his wife from Koptos in the Eighteenth Dynasty (probably under Amenhotep II):

The Superintendent of Mountain-Country, Wersu, dead.

Grace given by the King and Osiris Lord of Bousiris, the Great Lord, Lord of Abydos, that he give funerary meals, bread and beer, oxen and fowls, thread and cloth, incense and oil, all good and pure things on which a god lives, and the drinking of water at the swirl of the river, to the Ka of the Superintendent of the Mountain-Country of Gold of Amun, Wersu, dead.

Grace given by the King and Anubis presiding in the Divine Kiosk, that he may grant the receiving of daily food to the *ka* of his wife whom he loves, Sit-Re, dead.

Wersu says: As for any one who violates my corpse in the tomb-pit, who drags my statue from my tomb-chapel, he shall be punished by Re, he shall not receive water at the drink-stand of Osiris, he shall not bequeath his goods to his children, for ever.

He who trespasses on my place, who injures my chapel or drags out my corpse, the Ka of Re shall punish him, he shall not bequeath his goods to his children, his heart shall not have satisfaction in life, he shall not receive water in the tomb-pit, his soul shall be destroyed for ever. The land is wide, it has no limit. Do for yourselves as I have done. A soul is spiritualised [or glorified, benefited] by what has been done for it [or what it has done].

That which is offered on the altar in the house of Min, for the Super-intendent of the Mountain-Lands of Gold, Wersu, dead. That which is offered on the altar of the house of Isis, for the house-mistress, Sit-Re, dead.[19]

We see that the god of the mountains is Amun-Min.[20]

In the papyrus of Nebseni the dead man is pictured standing while a libation of cool water is poured on him and an attendant.[21] The idea is stated in chapter cx of the *Book of the Dead*: when the dead man arrives in Sekhet-Hetep with its intersecting canals: "May I eat there and drink there, may I plough there and reap there, may I fight and copulate there, may my words be mighty

there, may I never serve as a slave there but be ever in authority."
What he was most afraid of was that he might be forced to drink
his own urine and eat his own excrement. A Pyramid Text
declares:

Pure is the tongue which is in his mouth. The abomination of N is
dung; N rejects urine. N loathes this abomination. The abomination
of N, it is dung; he does not eat that abomination, just as at the same
time Seth shrinks from these two companions [Re of the sun, Thoth
of the moon] who voyage over the sky, Re and Thoth, take N with
you so that he may eat what you eat, drink what you drink.[22]

Another text is a spell that describes a lynx defending the dead
man against a snake: "She scratches you [snake] in your eyes so
that you fall in your dung and slidder in your urine. Fall, lie
down, slidder away, so that your mother Nut may see you."
In the papyrus of Nu (early Eighteenth Dynasty) we read:

The things which I abominate I will not eat. What I abominate is
filth, I will not eat of it. . . . Let me not fall down upon it, let it not
light on my body, let it not touch my fingers and my toes. . . . I will
not tread on it with my sandals. O do not send filthy water [urine]
over me.[23]

Mixed with the fears of having to eat and drink impurities was
the fear that living persons would intrude on the tomb to excrete
or urinate there. In the tomb of Ankh Ma Hor we read: "All that
you would be able to undertake against this tomb of mine in the
nekropolis will be equally carried out against your property; for
I am a priestly ritualist, excellent and instructed, for whom no
excellent magical recipe has remained secret. All persons who

80. Sky-boats

have entered into this tomb to satisfy their needs, after having eaten the abomination, which an excellent spirit holds as abominable, without having been purified for me as suits an excellent spirit that does always what pleases his master, I will seize him by the neck like a bird, I will put fear into him so well that the spirits and those of the earth will behold him and tremble. . . ."[24]

In the Theban Recension of the *Book of the Dead*, chapter 51 is on "not eating filth in the Underworld", with a vignette of a man seated before a table of food (Saite Recension); 53 is on not eating filth or drinking polluted water; 55-6 on giving air to the dead, with vignettes of the dead man holding a sail or sails; 56 is on snuffing the air in the earth, with vignette again of a sail; 57-9 are on snuffing the air and mastering the waters of the Underworld, with vignettes of the dead man holding a sail and standing in a running stream, or drinking water in a running stream. Before Osiris the dead man made 38 denials, of which numbers 33-4 were: "I have not stopped water when it should run. I have not made a cutting in a canal of running water." Then in the Negative Confession he made 42 denials, which included: "I have not fouled water."[25]

Documents show that the commonest offerings for the dead were wine, milk, and especially water. For water purified and also appeased the thirst which threatened the dead man with destruction.[24] From the time of the Ptolemies the custom of liquid offerings is proved for the Theban nekropolis. Tombs at El-Assasif had racks with jars on each side of the entry to the grave; the same system was found in the late burials in the tomb of Petosiris. Probably these vessels, together with stoves for incense and sacrifices, were the *epipla*, furniture, which the choachytos Osoroeris in 125 B.C. complained had been stolen from graves left in his charge by contract. He estimated the value at 10 talants of bronze: not a large sum at this time, though such pots were valuable enough to raise the question whether the *tymborychoi*, graverobbers, would not think them worth looting. However the *epipla* may have been articles of funerary furniture such as were still to some extent set beside the mummies. Osoroeris was responsible for the preservation of the objects and had to repay the families concerned.[27]

A short liturgy for one Mutritis shows thatshe received water, wine, and milk when drink-offerings were made to the gods of Djeme: Amon-Re and the great Osirises there. One Dionysios received water on a table of offerings after Osiris-of-the-Lake. Four texts mention the dead receiving drink-offerings; three of them add food—though this may have been due to religious conservatism in the use of phrases.

You receive daily from Khons-Shu in Thebes, offerings and food. You receive cool water, *kbhw*, from Amenophis of Djeme on the first day of every week. (1st c. A.D.)

You ascend on the first day of every week so that your soul may live on the effluxes that issue from Osiris at the hands of Amenophis. (1st c. B.C.)

You eat and drink in the sacred Tei. You receive cool water at the hand of Amenophis on the first day of every week. (1st c. B.C.)

You receive water on the offering tables on the first day of the week when offering is made to Onnophris. (1st c. A.D.)

Water is given by grace of Amenophis who as god of Djeme, Western Thebes, was associated closely with the nekropolis and its inmates. A passage similar to those above is found on a Ptolemaic stele from the island of El-Hesch; and the leading formula of the texts on the Meroitic tables of offerings seems to be concerned with the supply of water. On the monument of a

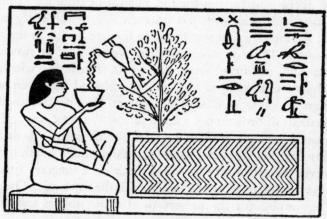

81. Deadman at the Tree and Spring of Life

deified drowned-man of the early Ptolemaic era we read: "You receive water from your Two Sisters at the beginning of [each] week in which there is a *per-kherew* [invocation for funerary offerings] for ever."[29] In a dedication of Euergetes II on the second pylon at Karnak the dead are told not to worry about nourishment since there is a great abundance on the altars of the Theban gods.[30]

It is unlikely that the choachytai and those who took over from them were available every day. The payments for purifications, *agneiai*, suggest that they were not always on the job, at least for this or that dead man. However, one of the three texts mentioned above states that the dead got their solid food daily, their water on the first day of the week. But such treatment was perhaps the prerogative of the dead of rich families, of the important characters whose statue would have been taken into a temple where the highpriest would assure it the share of the offerings which was reserved for it. By Ptolemaic times, whatever had been their previous status, the choachytai served as funerary priests during the Festival of the Valley.[31] Some scholars have seen that rite, the *diabasis* or crossing-over of Amun, as a festival of the dead; others have denied it. But whatever the full meaning of the ceremony, the aspect of the release of the dead, a sort of renewal or pledge of resurrection, seems certainly present; and this aspect it was that concerned the choachytai.[32]

Once a year, perhaps in Pauni, the king or his representative saw to the carrying-out of a panegyris for Amun that included a voyage over the Nile to the west bank, to the region now called the Memnonia which included the various funerary temples and the hills at the rear. The *diabasis* repeated on the Nile the voyage of the celestial ship of Re on the sky-water; and this aspect was no doubt the main point of the ceremony. In texts or scenes the emphasis is on the least detail of the sacred boat's construction, its maintenance and embellishment. The Usirhat was not a mere ferry. The canals often shown in representations of the funerary temples of the Thebes of the West were capable of floating the great boat of Amun to the temple-doors. It would have been easier to take the bari, the small boat-shrine with the god, on the shoulders of porters; there must be a religious reason for the

Usirhat. Amun-Min, in contrast, travels by land, uncovered under his awning; thus he arrives at Luxor or shows himself at Medinet Habu or the Ramesseum. Unlike other gods he has no veils and must be viewed as he goes. But Amun here is a Sungod and the *diabasis* expresses the daily journey over the skies and into the underworld; he goes down into death to be resurrected and to spread his reviving power.[33]

The dead thus cannot but share in the rite and its benefits. The aspersion of their tombs is not at this moment a temporary relief of their thirst; it is a purification and a resurrection, identifying them with the sungod. In the third crypt at Dendera we read:

For Takha, it is the divine nekropolis of Re. And his name belongs to him from the beginnings. The procession of this magnificent god is made to come out so that he may make his voyage in his Beautiful Festival to the Divine Nekropolis of Takha in the new moon of Pachons. Aspersion is poured, vivifying the Aufu, in the presence of this god.[34]

Frescoes in the tomb of Amunmosu show the arrival of the Usirhat from Karnak with the "substance" of Amun-Re. We see it travelling on the great canal that linked the northern region of the Memnonia with the Nile. "This is the Boat of Amun-Re, King of the Gods, who is in his name of Usirhat." To meet him, from the funerary temple, advanced the enthroned statue of Amenophis I. "He comes to see his Father Amun-Re, King of the Gods, in his Beautiful Festival of the Valley."[35] At Gourneh we see what follows. The bari of the god has been taken out of the Usirhat. Those of Mut and Khonsu have also come from their boats. On route, the bari and the sacred image of Queen Ahmes Nofritari have joined the procession. Like the statue of Amenophis, that of Seti I has come out of its temple and gone before the King of Gods. His bari has joined that of the troop of gods. They have all arrived at the Memnoneion, set on the extreme right of the picture. The reigning king Ramses II emerges from the temple to adore Amun-Re. The spirit of dead Seti I, come from his Dwelling of Millions of Years, is there behind Ramses, with a benedictory gesture, asking the great god to accord his graces to the well-beloved son.[36]

To attach a precise meaning to the rite is difficult. Is it like the Night of Soker at Medinet Habu, in which a dead god is about to resurrect? is Amun-Re, imagined as the sun, come to a new life after the yearly death of the actual sun? or is the god merely going through a process of renewal? No doubt the festival had drawn in many elements, just as Amun has drawn in Re the sungod and absorbed him. We cannot go far wrong if we see a strong tinge of resurrection, of rebirth out of water, in which even the humblest of the dead buried in the Valley had some share—though it was the kings and the great men who gained the direct benefit.

In ritual-myth the daily birth of the sungod from the womb of the sky-goddess and his morning wash were inextricably entangled. The king himself underwent lustration before he could officiate in the sun-temple; then, later, in any temple. Since he embodied the sungod, the idea naturally arose that he was reborn through the water. He was not only washed in the House of the Morning, but submitted to an elaborate toilet; he was fumigated with incense, cleansed with natron, anointed, clothed, crowned, given his sceptre, then presented with food. Lustration as both a purifying and a regenerating act was closely connected with the sungod.[37]

82. Horos of the Eastern Desert

There is one more aspect of this Festival at which we may glance. The first book of the *Iliad* tells of Zeus going to the Aithiopians. A scholiast says: "At Diospolis [Thebas] is said to exist a very great temple of Zeus. The Aithiopians come there to take the image of the god at a certain time, with the other deities of the country and in their company they traverse the Libyan region, where they celebrate magnificent festivals for 15 days."[38] It appears to be an effort of Alexandrian scholarship to reconcile the account in Homer with the facts of the Festival; but there may be also a vague memory of the period of Aithiopian domination at Thebes and the role there played by Theban princesses allied to the Aithiopian dynasty in the cult of Amun. The fortnight is a detail added to make the Festival fit in with the *Iliad*, though there could be festivals of this length of time. According to the calendar at Medinet Habu the great rite of Amun at Thebes lasted 23 days.[39]

From Diodoros we learn how the linking of Homer and Thebes had gone further.

As proof of the evidence of Homer in Egypt they bring forward various bits of evidence, and especially the healing drink that brings oblivion of all past evils, which was given to Helen by Telemachos in the home of Menelaos. For it is obvious that the poet had gained precise knowledge of the nepenthic drug which he says Helen brought from Egyptian Thebes, given her by Polydamna the wife of Thon. They allege that even to this day the women of that city use this powerful remedy, and in ancient times, they say, a drug to cure anger and sorrow was discovered exclusively among the women of Diospolis—and Thebes and Diospolis, they add, are the same city.

Again, Aphrodite is called Golden by the natives in accordance with an old tradition, and near the city called Momemphis there is a Plain of Golden Aphrodite. Likewise, the myths related about the mating of Zeus and Hera, and of their journey to Aithiopia, he also got from Egypt. For every year among the Egyptians the shrine of Zeus is carried across the River into Libya and then brought back some days after, as if the god were arriving from Aithiopia. And as for the mating of those deities, in their festal gatherings the priests carry the shrines of both to an elevation that has been strewn with flowers of every kind.[40]

The passage in the *Iliad* he has in mind runs:

> The Son of Kronos clasped his consort in his arms,
> and under them the divine earth sprouted forth
> fresh grass and dewy lotos, crocus, hyacinth . . .

Nonnos has a passage describing the embraces of Zeus and Hera which is an elaboration of this; but he does not link it with Thebes or, indeed, any locality.[41] No one at Thebes ever said that Amun went to Aithiopia, but it is possible that his priests were flattered by the attempt to set the mating of Zeus and Hera there, and gave it some vague approval. With memories of Napata and of Djebel-Barkal where Amun had a great temple, they may have felt that after all Amun-Zeus had his Aithiopian connections and that his journey symbolised an outgoing into all his sanctuaries.

The mating in Homer occurs on Mt. Ida. At Thebes the only place at all corresponding was the burnt rocky walls, the steep cliff, of the Asasif. Here—an unusual thing for Egypt—we see the contours of a true mountain with summit. Perhaps the two shrines of Amun-Zeus and Mut-Hera were taken there. Mut indeed was thought to have come from Nubia or Punt, via the Wadi Hammanat; she was a very old goddess, mentioned on a cylinder inscription of the First Dynasty, and among her titles was Queen of Nubia. She was a world-mother and supposed to own both male and female genitals; and was identified with Hathor. We must note also that from the time of the Priest-Kings (21st dynasty) the king's daughter was consecrated as Wife of the God, while remaining a virgin. The Divine Wife gave the cult an erotic note by playing on her sistrum to the god, sitting on his knee, and putting her arms round his neck. Her court con-sisted of Amun's concubines, also virgins. Earlier in the New Kingdom, we meet Queens who were the Pharoah's wife and the mother of his children, and who were also in purely ritual terms the Wife of the God Amun; but the Divine Wives, in a more definite sense, arrived only with the Libyan, Aithiopian and Saite kingships.[42] They were also called the Hand of God, referring to creation-myths in which a god brought the world into being by masturbation. In the ritual-myth on Setu I's Cenotaph at Abydos we read near the end: "Then his hands became a vagina . . . Atum says: This is what came forth from my lips and what I spat into my hand, which was a vagina. Shu, Tefnut, Ka, Vagina." We may examine this myth a little further, since it helps us to understand Egyptian processes of thought and illuminates the erotic atmosphere of the Amun-cult in the period in question. The Hands-of-God presumably caressed the divine statues.

Neber-Djer, Lord of the Limit or Temu, Sungod of Heliopolis, declared, in a papyrus dated about 311 B.C., "I thrust my penis into my closed hand, I made my seed enter my hand, I poured it into my own mouth. I shat in the form of Shu, I pissed in the form of Tefnut."[44] The inscription of Shabaka states: "Ptah's Company of Gods are before him as Teeth and Lips, being the Seed and the hands of Tem. The Company of the Gods of Tem came into being through his Seed and his Fingers."[45] The theme goes back to the Pyramid Texts. "Atum created by his masturbation in Heliopolis. He put his penis in his fist to excite desire. The twins were born, Shu and Tefnut."[46] We also hear of Re creating the Sudanese by thus sending out his seed. One important effect of these ideas and images—first, the ejaculation into the hand, then the swallowing of the sperm—was a belief that the Word or Logos that afterwards came out of the mouth was the reborn seed, a creative force. This notion was clearly brought out in the text dealing with the relation of Ptah and Tem. "The Company of the Gods are the Teeth and Lips in the Mouth, which assigns names to all things and from which Shu and Tefnut have gone forth. The Company of the Gods create the sight of the eyes, the hearing of the ears, the breathing of the nostrils, and make announcement to the Heart. The Heart is what makes any information come forth and the Tongue is that which repeats what the Heart has thought out. Thus all the gods were created, and Tem and the Company of the Gods, but every Word of the god exists through that which the Heart has thought out and the Tongue commanded." The idea of the Creative Logos has evolved: an evolution that involved the shift from the comprehensive Mother to the self-sufficient (masturbating) Father.[47]

But to return to Amun and his priestesses. It is noteworthy that the ithyphallic Min had now become identified with Amun, and he possessed a strong fertility-aspect and rites that probably

involved mating. The erotic note then which surrounded Amun
in these periods may have helped to bring about the later intrusion
of the Zeus-Hera sacred marriage into accounts of the Festival of
the Valley. It is indeed barely possible that some sort of sacred
marriage, or the suggestion of it, was actually introduced for a
while into the voyage of Amun through the Valley of the West,
of death and of rebirth. Flowers in garlands and bouquets were a
common part of Egyptian ritual in general, and would naturally
attend such a rite. It would be pleasant if we could prove that a
baseless belief in Homer's borrowings from Thebes led in time
to the addition of a touch of Homeric colouring to an Egyptian
ceremony there. God's Wife took part in the Festival. Queen Ese
of the Twentieth Dynasty records: "On his Beautiful [Festival] of
the Valley while one was in the great forecourt of Amun, to
establish the name of the God's Wife, Pure of Hands, of Amun-Re,
King of the Gods, Mistress of the Two Lands, the god's Votaress
Ese. . . .[48]

Indeed we can carry our surmises further. Hathor as Lady of the
Underworld received the dead in the West, just as she daily
welcomed the dying sun in the evening glow. On the left bank
at both Thebes and Memphis she was the guardian of the
Mountain of the Dead. At Thebes we meet also Dehnet-Amentet,
the Peak of the West, who was identified with both Isis and the
serpent-goddess of the nekropolis, Meretseger.[49] Three monuments of the Nineteenth Dynasty interestingly record appeals to
her; they belong to a group set up by lowly draughtsmen, scribes
and attendants of the nekropolis, and express a sense of sin,
regret, and contrite humility which makes them unique in
Egyptian religious history. Nefer'abu calls on Meretseger
"Lady of Heaven, Mistress of the Two Lands, whose good name
is Peak of the West":

> Giving praise to the Peak of the West,
> homage to her Ka.
> I give praise, hear my call.
> I was a just man upon earth.

Dedicated by the Attendant in the Place of Truth, Nefer'abu, justified:

> an ignorant man and foolish
> who knew neither good nor evil,

I did the transgression against the Peak
and she chastised me.
I was in her hand by night as by day.
I sat like a woman in travail on the bearing-stool.
I called on the wind and it did not come to me.
I was tormented by the Peak of the West, the Mighty
   One,
and by every God and every Goddess.
Mark, I will say to great and little
who are among the workmen,
O beware of the Peak.
For there is a Lion within the Peak.
She smites with the smiting of a savage lion.
She pursues him that transgresses against her.
I called on my mistress,
I found that she came to me with sweet airs,
she was merciful to me,
after she had made me behold her hand.
She turned again to me in mercy,
she caused me to forget the sickness that had come
   upon me.
Lo, the Peak of the West is merciful
if one calls on her.
Spoken by Nefer'abu, justified, who says:
Mark, and let every ear hearken,
that lives on the earth:
Beware the Peak of the West.

We do not know what the transgression against the Peak was. It may refer to some specific offence or a general term for what the speaker feels to have been sinfulness or backsliding. The two other addressed to Meretseger are short:

Praised be in peace, Lady of the West, the Mistress who turns herself towards mercy. You cause me to see darkness by day. I will declare your might to all people. Be merciful to me in your mercy.

Great Isis, Mother of a God, Lady of Heaven, Mistress of all the Gods, Lady of children, of many forms.

The great Peak of the West who gives her hand to him she loves, and gives protection to him who sets her in his heart.

The latter stele, of Nektamun, has a representation of the Peak as

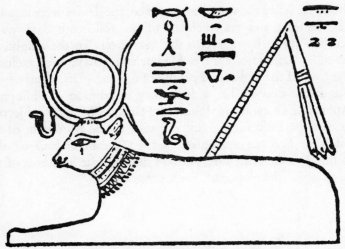

83. Hathor the Heavenly Cow

two slopes of a hill running down from right and left, and enclosing near the top a sort of parallelogram, in which four coiled serpents, forming a cornice, stand out in relief. A goddess with horns and stands on one of the slopes.

Meretseger had a healing cult in which incubation was used; but we do not know how long this lasted. Her worship, however, revived under the Ptolemies, always under the form of a serpent-deity, Agathodaimon. We have a demotic graffito from the Valley of the Queens, dated 122–1 B.C., which holds a proskynema to Agathodaimon; and she figures on the reliefs of Kasr el-Agouz. Her rose-tinted Mountain continued sacred. A graffito calls it the Holy Rock; and another, near the Valley of the Queens, calls it the Holy Place. Even in a Byzantine text we read of the Divine Mountain of the Memnonia; and monks and hermits were attracted, exorcising the ancient daimons.[50]

Meretseger-Isis, as Lady of the West may well have been identified also with Hathor; and Hathor had her sacred marriage with Horos at Edfu. The festival of their union is described on the back of the two pylon towers of the temple. She made her visit to Horos from Dendera; and from the 3rd to the 1st century B.C. the occasion was one of the greatest religious manifestations

U

in the Sa'id. After the sacred fleet arrived, the deities were installed in the temple; and one incident of the following days was a procession made by desert to the nekropolis, to the height. At Thebes, her temple of Deir el-Medineh may have been included in the tour of the *diabasis*. A plaque of opaque glass, clearly from a foundation-deposit, has a dedicatory inscription of Philopator to Aphrodite Ourania (no doubt this Hathor). We may conjecture then that the Edfu hierogamy and visit to the Mountain of the Dead have become attributed to the Theban *diabasis* or that something of the same sort, perhaps through the influence of the Edfu rite, was developed at Thebes.[51]

19

The Blessed Drowned

IN view of the high opinion of Nile-water we are not surprised to find that those drowned in it were considered to be blessed.[1] The usual word for a drowned person in Ptolemaic or Roman texts is *hsy*, which was taken over in Coptic and appears in Greek as *hesies* or *esies*.[2] Derived from the term are many names borne by Greeks, such as Hasies, Hesies, Piesies, Phesies, Thasies, Taphesies.[3] And it appears as qualitative in an Aramean text found in Egypt, probably of the 3rd century B.C.: "Be blessed, Tabah, daughter of Tahapi, perfect in Osiris the god. You have not done aught to men and on earth you have not uttered calumnies against men. You are blessed before Osiris, take water before Osiris. Adore *na Ma'ati* (Isis and Nephthys) and be among the *hacie* . . ." This Tabah may well have been drowned, though we cannot prove it.[4] Many illustrations of the use of *hsy* in magical papyri of the first four centuries A.D. have been found, in connection with apotheosis by drowning.[5] We meet "Osiris the divine drowned", the "blood of the drowned", the use of Hsy as a proper name. Asies, the praised or blessed one, in a euphemism for drowned. The condition of having been drowned is shown by the determinative of water added to the name on mummy-labels. "I am Horos son of Isis who goes on board at Arkhah to put wrappings on the amulets, to put linen on the Drowned one, the Fair Drowned one of the Drowned."[6] Earlier in the Ptolemaic transfers of mummies and funerary services the same word occurs. There are two cases in the mummy lists where a named mummy is accompanied by "his drowned one," *pa-f hsy*. This addition suggests that the nameless drowned person was not a relation but an unknown corpse which had been piously buried by the tomb-owner with a possible eye to aid or praise in the otherworld. The term *pa-hery*, the superior master, is also so often used with *hsy* as to seem a special title of drowned. One expression for drowning is "to do the pleasure, *hst*, of Re".[7] To return to the magical papyri, we read of the burning of the bones of a hesies (? Osiris) who was three days and three nights in the river, and who was carried by a stream to the sea; and are told how to take a cat and make it hesies by plunging its body in water. A spell to induce a trance, *Solomon's Seizure*, has an invocation: "Come to me, you that have become hesies and carried off by the river." In a lovecharm said over the head of a doll the words *isee Iao* may represent *hesies* and *Yahweh*.[8]

84. The Deadman and Herhaf, the god who took him to the Island of Fire where Osiris reigned (BD Ani, Budge, pp. 280, 288, 316, 435, 578, 584, 588)

Obviously the idea that the drowned man had in some special sense become Osiris, drowned by his murderous brother Set, played an important part in the beliefs that grew up round the *hsy*, and in the reverent treatment Herodotos records as being paid to the corpse.[9] The myth of Osiris' drowning existed at the time of the Pyramid Texts. "Horos has counted the gods for you, so that they cannot get away from you from the place where you were drowned. Nephthys has assembled all your limbs for you. . . ."[10] The Texts also speak of Osiris being found by Isis and Nephthys on the bank or shore, and on the bank of Nedyet.[11] Possibly two traditions can be made out: one in which Osiris is tied, smitten, killed, and one in which he is drowned, perhaps accidentally.[12] The drowning tradition appears on the Shabaka Stone of the Thirty-fifth Dynasty: "Osiris was drowned in his waters"; and in the Osirian water-ritual Seth appears carrying Osiris, so that he may have been looked on as having drowned the god.[13] The Shabaka stone may have been a copy of a much earlier document of more perishable material.

According to Diodoros, Horos too was drowned—thrown in the water by the Titans: a Greek way of identifying him with Dionysos Zagreus. Isis, however, used her magic and medicine, and raised him into immortality.[14] We cannot find this story in an Egyptian text, though Spell 113 of the *Book of the Dead* tells how Horos' hands were cut off and cast into the water as the result of his mother's magical curse.[15] And this act of Isis presumably relates to her son's having decapitated her, as we learn elsewhere, when he and Seth were fighting or playing as hippopotami in the river, and she interfered on Seth's behalf. The two gods also appear in the water when they fight in ships; Seth's ship sinks and he turns into a hippopotamus; the gods stop Horos from harpooning him.[16] (We seem in these tales to have reflections of a sacred hippopotamus-hunt in ritual-myth.)

The *Book of Gates* describes the passage of Re's body, Afu-Re, on the night-boat of the sun through twelve serpent-guarded gates. The eighth into which Afu-Re is towed by the usual four gods is in charge of Nun himself. Before them stands the Dweller in Nunu, with bowed shoulders, leant on a staff. In the lake (or series of lakes or lagoons) are four groups of beings (bathers, floaters, swimmers, divers) who are bidden "praise the soul of Re which is in heaven, and his body which is on earth". Afu addresses them and gives breath to their nostrils, telling them all offerings shall be made to their souls which will never die. They shall enjoy peace in their waters; and they shall be fed like Re whose body is on earth and whose soul is in heaven. These seem certainly to be men who have been drowned. (It has been suggested that the priests and theologians did not know how to deal with the drowned—how to arrange for their bodies being rejoined to their souls—and thus handed the matter over to Re in his night-journey.)[17]

In late times Isis was drawn into the system. A drowned woman became an Isis. In 257 B.C. the priests of Aphrodite (Hathor) at Aphroditopolis wrote to Apollonios the dioiketes: "In accordance with what the king has written to you, to give 100 talants of myrrh for the burial of the Hesis, please order this to be carried out. You know the Hesis is not brought up to the nome unless we have in readiness that they need for the burial, because . . . on the day of her death. Know that the Hesis is Isis, and may she give you favour in the eyes of the king."[18]

The Dendur temple was built in honour of two men, the Agathodaimon of the place, Petesi, and the Master, Pa-her, sons of Quwper, who were deified after drowning and worshipped. The temple dates from the time of Augustus. Titles include the Great Praised, the Otherworld One, Praised in the Otherworld, Greatly Praised in the Otherworld. Save in one case, the epithets are preceded by the name Osiris.[19]

In the account of the Fishing of Osiris' Viscera out of the Waters, we find our term *kbhw*. *Kbh.wt*, as the waters of Osiris' death and resurrection, seem to have a ritual location in the embalming chamber conceived as the place of purification.[20] Of the dwarf Djedher we read: "I am the dwarf who danced in the Sarapeion, *Kmt*, in the enclosure of the Place of Purification, *Kbh.wt*, on the day of the Festival of Eternity."[21] On the later sarcophagus of the priest Imhotep: "The doors of heaven are opened for me, the doors of the Land of *Kbh.w* are opened for me." Heaven may refer to the Chapel, and the Land of *Kbh.w* to the area where the embalming chamber stood.[22]

With the ambivalence that often appears in these sacred matters, drowning was also an expression of doom, nemesis, punishment. The wicked are at time drowned in the otherworld.[23] An evil serpent may be drowned as well as burned or pulverised. "Down upon your face Apepi, enemy of Re. Be drowned, be drowned, be vomited upon."[24] On earth too drowning might be a penalty. A Twelfth-Dynasty inscription declares, "There is no tomb for him who rebels against his majesty: his body is thrown into the water."[25] The pharaoh Nebka burned the body of an unfaithful wife and had her ashes thrown into the river. (The adulterous townsman had been held down seven days under water by a crocodile which came to life from a waxen image made by a priest learned in magic.)[26] An inscription of the Twenty-second Dynasty or a little later says, "The doer of evil is thrown into the harbour".[27]

A list has been compiled of persons who seem to have become blessed or deified by drowning. We see that from the Thirtieth Dynasty, under Osirian influence, a drowned person became the Master or Mistress, and the Praised one.

(1) *Nes-min:* on a sarcophagus of the Thirtieth Dynasty, from Koptos. He is called "The Good *Hsy,* Excellent in the Otherworld."[28]

(2) *Tewt-tewa,* also from Koptos, "The Greatly Praised in the Other-world". In the inscription he appeals and the gods reply.

(3) *Di-Webastet:* on an anthropoid limestone sarcophagus from Koptos, early Ptolemaic. The roughly-cut inscription runs:

"Words to be recited for [*lit.* by] the Osiris, the Greatly Praised, Excellent in the Other-world, Di-webastet, Triumphant:

"Your soul enters in at will and you go forth as you wish in the presence of Osiris of Koptos, who is at the head of the House of Gold. Is opened for you Heaven, is opened for you the Earth, is opened for you the Duat, are opened for you the Beautiful Ways in the Other-world. Your soul enters in with Re. You are powerful like the Lord of Eternity. Nepyt, she gives [things pure and] beautiful, and cakes. Hapi, he gives you water. You live, you live, you live. Your soul lives. You receive cool water and incense in the Otherworld, Di-webastet, Triumphant."

Osiris of Koptos at the Head of the House of Gold is mentioned also in (1), showing this House was especially associated with the drowned. Nepyt, grain-goddess, makes various offerings; she and Hapi do not appear in any other of these texts.[29]

(4) *Her-sedjem,* daughter of Ta-(ent)-osiris; a woman of Panopolis in the Ptolemaic period: a spinner, *msn,* of the temple of Thoth-sedjem, "the great god who is in Panopolis". She died in her twenty-seventh year. "You are a *hyst* who passed by the execution-knife without the head being removed." Her mother and her daughter were both still alive.

She is shown standing in adoration before Osiris, Isis, Nephthys, Horos who protects his Father, Anubis, and Min-Re: kneeling before the Ibis of Thoth-sedjem and an altar-stand with lotusbud twined round its support; and seated on a chair before her daughter and an altar-stand on which is a lotus-bud. Standing, she wears a long garment

85. Shades swimming in the deathwaters

with fringed edge, armlets, wristlets, cone and lotus on head, collar. At the extreme top of the stele are the emblem of heaven, winged solar disk with uraei, and two anubis-jackals, each with a collar.

She is the Praised, the Greatly Praised, the Otherworld One.[30]

(5) *Pnephoros*, Graeco-Roman: the Beautiful of Face. Perhaps a deified man, he became identified with the crocodile-god Sebek (Souchos) and was worshipped in the Fayum at Theadelpheia and Karanis. At the first site he was called the Great God, the Crocodile; and at times, Psempnephoros, the Son of Pnephoros. At Euhemeria the god Pnephoros and others were revered. In the southern temple at Karanis he had his cult with Petesouchos, apparently another divinised man linked with the crocodile-god.[31]

The innermost main room or sanctuary there had a big altar on which a mummied crocodile was shown. When not shown, the croco-dile was kept in a deep vaulted niche in the northern wall of the room outside the sanctuary. Opposite the niche and in the southern wall of the same outer room is a smaller vaulted niche—perhaps for a smaller mummied crocodile. Possibly here Pnephoros and his son both had their cults, Pnephoros being the larger crocodile.[32]

Apart from the fact that the crocodile represented Seth tearing Osiris when he tore his victim in the water, it had by its nature a special water-connection. It is often called "he who is in the water". In a vignette of the papyrus of Har-uobn, a young priest-ess, daughter of the highpriest and king Men-hepr-re of the

Twenty-first Dynasty, we see her stretched on the ground in adoration of the crocodile-god opposite her and at the same time drinking water. Three tombs of Deir el-Medineh show three dead persons similarly prostrated, with text ". . . drink water near the tree". There is a tree in the papyrus (perhaps a fruiting sycamore) by the priestess and another by Sebek.

(6) *Her:* on a wallpanel of sandstone from some temple, probably Nubian and of the time of Augustus. He is shown standing, a bearded man in kilt, with a fillet of rosettes on his head (tied in a knot at the back) over a wig, in front of which is the uraeus; a collar is round his neck; and behind him hangs an animal tail. In his right hand he holds the Ankh, the life-sign; and on his left (missing), a formal bouquet and *uas* sceptre. On each leg, attached by two cords, is a greave with lionhead—not necessarily a sign that he is a soldier. His divinisation is stressed by the emblems he holds, and the heaven-sign above him. We read: "Hail, the Osiris, the Praised, the Otherworld One, Praised by Isis, Her, son of Pa-sheri-ment, born of Ta-sherit."[33]

(7) *Anon:* a man on a sandstone stele, probably Nuban. He stands, bearded, in a *shwy* kilt, collar, plain filler over wig with uraeus in front; holds ankh, bouquet and sceptre; and wears armlets and wristlets. He also has lionheaded graves on legs. On top of a lotus-shaped altar are two cakes and libation vase with running water. The stele is in form of a shrine or templedoor on top of which is a winged solar disk, surmounted by a row of uraei wearing disks. Two panels, meant for inscriptions, are not used. Roman period.[34]

(8) *Anon.* This man stands unbearded, in an himation. On his head is a plain double fillet over a wig with uraeus in front. On the wig is a cone with lotus; in the hands are ankh and sceptre. Behind, another lotus-sceptre supports a falcon wearing the crown of Upper and Lower Egypt. In front, an altar-stand with offerings.

(9) *Anon:* on a stele in form of shine or temple-door, on top of which is the winged solar disk with uraei.

The beardless man stands with plain kilt, fillet over wig with uraeus. Right hand (?with ankh) missing. Collar with pectoral below; armlets. Bouquet and sceptre in (missing) left hand. Lotus-shaped altar with offerings: cakes, calf, libation-vase with running water.

(10) *Ta-sherit-(ent)-pi-wer:* on sandstone stele, probably Nubian. She stands in long transparent dress with serrated edges; a plain fillet over a wig with uraeus in front; wears collar, wristlets, armlets; holds ankh, lotus bouquet and another ankh. Altar-stand in front, with two

cakes and libation vase with running water. Her name means the Child of Pi-wer.[35]

(11) *Pa-amen:* on a Nubian stele of sandstone. He wears plain fillet over a blue wig, on top of which is a sort of crown; there seems no uraeus, but there is a false chinbeard held in left hand with a falcon-headed sceptre. The sign of heaven is above. Right hand has an ankh and nearby is a jackal. "Words spoken by the Osiris, the Greatly Praised, the Otherworld one, Pa-amen, Triumphant, son of Pa-her-iw, Triumphant, born of the Lady of the House, Shetet-ti, Triumphant."[36]

(12) *Petesi and Pa-her:* already mentioned for their temple at Dendur in Nubia. The scenes show Augustus making offerings to them. Petesi's consort is shown but is unnamed. The headgear of the trio include solar disks and uraeus. Petesi is coloured blue, Pa-her green (as often Osiris). The consort may be a wife or a goddess linked with Petesi after his death. Inscriptions show him as the local god of Dendur and Pa-her of Qelet (*Klt*).

In the temple they are shown standing or seated, always kilted and holding ankh and sceptre; when standing they have an animal-tail behind. Petesi is beardless, Pa-her has a false chinbeard. The consort stands in long transparent garment with ankh and sceptre, collar, armlets, wristlets. The bouquet which is almost always associated with the drowned appeared often in the temple.

Epithets: The Greatly Praised, the Otherworld One, Praised in the Otherworld, Greatly Praised in the Otherworld, the Agathodaimon of Dendur (Petesi), the Master (Pa-her). Osiris precedes all but the third.[73]

(13) *Antinoos,* the favourite of Hadrian, whose drowning may have been deliberate. There is a story of an oracle predicting a heavy loss to the empire, so Antinoos drowned himself to save Hadrian.[38] The death is said to have occurred on the site where Hadrian founded the city of Antinopolis or Antinoe. He decided to raise his lad to be a "throne-companion of the gods of Egypt". So, in Greek towns he might appear as a comely melancholic youth; in Egypt he was an Egyptian god. The Mausoleum at home, dedicated to him by Hadrian, was Egyptian and bore hieroglyphic inscriptions. He was still revered in the 3rd century as a healer and miracle-worker.[39]

(14) *Isidora,* a girl of the 2nd century, who was drowned and had her tomb at Hermopolis, not far from Antinoe.[40]

(15) *Asklepias,* a small girl who was drowned and had her monument in the Sarapeion at Saqqara. There is no indication, however, of divinity and the main interest lies in the Greek inscription: "Asklepias aged 5 years has departed a *hesies.*"[41]

This list must not be taken as certain in all its items. Some of the persons were without any doubt drowned: for instance, Antinoos and Isidora. And there is a fair probability for all. But we must recognise that the group of the Drowned belong to a wider category of the Blessed and of the *Hryw*. The *Hryw* of which we find a cult at Thebes in the Ptolemaic, may be described as the Saints and Martyrs of Osiris. Petesi and Pa-her included in our list of the Drowned, are martyrs of Osiris, but the second is also a saint, who becomes a local god. The *Hryw* cult seems to have its origin in ancestor-worship but has developed into a cult of the Witnesses to the Osirian faith. Naturally those who die the Osirian death-by-water are in the forefront of the martyrs.[42]

Herodotos says that the same beatitude was attributed to persons eaten by crocodiles (doubtless because they were usually dragged under the water). But in fact we find a considerable dread of crocodiles, though Ailian repeats especially of Omboi: "When their children, as often happens, are carried off by crocodiles, the people are overjoyed and the mothers of the unfortunate victims are gladdened to go about in proud reverence, as having indeed produced food and a meal for a god."[43] His reason seems certainly wrong. It was the divinisation, not the feeding of a god, which begot the joy. However, where the crocodile was worshipped, there may have been a sense of the eaten person having become identified with the god; and Pnephoros with his cult in the Fayum may have been originally a crocodile-victim rather than simply a drowned man. Why one such victim should achieve a cult instead of a mere monument is something to which we have no clue. The same query applies to the two drowned men at Dendur—and to a few other cases where we find men (not drowned) deified for no apparent reason: for instance, two normarchs of the Twelfth Dynasty at Qaw (Antaiopolis).[44]

The belief in immortality or beatitude by drowning spread beyond Egypt. Tertullian knew of the hesies.[45] A rabbinic document of Alexandreia, which cannot be later than the 1st century A.D., the *Apocalypse of Josuah son of Levy*, declares that in the first section of Eden are the Martyrs and in the second the Drowned.[46] We may thus infer that the Egyptian belief had spread by the late Ptolemaic era and infiltrated into the ideas of

Greeks, Romans, Jews: in time it was thus transmitted to the Islamic and Iranian religions.[47]

Not unnaturally it affected the legend of Moses, who was taken up out of the Nile-waters. *Exodus* ii, 10, shows that the writer derived his name from the Hebrew verb meaning to take or draw out.[48] The name was thus interpreted as a participle meaning the Extracted One. The scholars in Alexandreia, however, sought for an explanation in Egyptian, noting that Pharaoh's daughter was Egyptian, not Hebrew. They based their positions on the Greek text, the Septuagint, where the name was transcribed as Moyses. Philon took over their ideas and stated that the princess gave him the appropriate name Moyses, "because she had taken him from the water; for the Egyptians call water *moy*".[49] He thus dealt with only the first half of the name. Josephos completed the interpretation: "Because he had fallen into the River, for Egyptians call water *mo* and those saved from water *hyses*."[50] And he repeated the etymology in *Contra Apion*, where he used *moy* for water and did not cite *hyses*, though he described Moses as "saved from water". (The original manuscript seems to have had *eses*.)[51]

A result of the use of the form *moy* for the Egyptian *mw* (water) was that at times *ses*, not *yses*, was taken as the second half of the name Moses; and this *ses* was interpreted as an Egyptian word for "to be saved" or "to take out". Josephos did not mention—probably did not know—that the water-saved was in fact dead. He may have known, but have preferred to mit this unpleasant aspect; hence his blurring of the etymology in *Cotnra Apion*. Anti-Jewish writers in Alexandreia could hardly have failed to seize on the point. Clement of Alexandreia knew the full bearing of the terms, for he wrote: "Some authors call Moses the person who has died by water." Moses would then become a twice-born person, who died and was reborn.[52]

There can be little doubt that in this devious way the ancient scholars were getting back to the origins of the legend of Moses; for the rejected babe, who crosses water (in boat, chest, and so on) or who is cast into water and drawn up from it, is a very widespread motive attached to culture-heroes. Kyros, founder of the Persian empire, was cast out as a babe and reared by a herdsman or dogbitch; Strabon says his name came from a river. Sargon, the first Mesopotamian empire-builder, was put by his mother in a chest of reeds and thrown into the river; Chingis Khan, who welded tribes into a vast Mongol empire, was locked in a chest and set afloat on the sea. Many more such tales, some purely mythical like that of Perseus or Scyld Scefing of *Beowulf*, others attached to historical personages who led their people through some great crisis or unification, could be cited. There is no doubt that the tale of Moses belongs to this series and that the water-birth is a symbol of death-rebirth drawn from initiation-ritual. It is felt that a person who initiates some momentous change must have undergone this passage through the elements, which is in various degrees conceived as a regeneration or divinisation.[53]

The *hsy* achieves a new birth into the otherworld; the culture-hero achieves a new birth into this world, drawing his strange energies from his immersion in the spiritworld.

86. Isis and Nephthys with the mutilated body of Osiris

It is in the light of the general pattern attached to culture-heroes that we must view the analogies found in the careers of Horos and Moses.[54] There may be some direct Hebrew debts to Egyptian myth, but there is also certainly the fact that the legends of both heroes draw on a universal pattern. Thus, the babe-Horos is threatened by Seth; the babe-Moses by the pharaoh. Horos is hidden in the reeds of the Delta by his mother Isis; Moses is hidden in the reeds of a river (a branch or canal of the Nile) in the Delta by his Levitic mother. Moses comes from the water; Horos (in his late guise as the newborn sun) is fed by humidity.[55] Horos is raised by the local goddess Uadjit while Isis is elsewhere, he grows "strengthened by means of exhalations, clouds and mists"—while Moses is confided by his mother to her daughter.[56] (Anubis too, according to Ploutarch, was exposed by Nephthys his mother from fear of her brother Seth who had copulated with her; he was found and reared by Isis.)[57]

Horos killed his mother in a fit of anger; Moses killed an Egyptian who struck one of his compatriots. Horos retired to the borders of the sea, into the mountains; Moses on leaving the valley of the Nile entered the mountainous region of the Madian. Horos appears in an oasis where Seth joined him; Moses reached an oasis or steppe, where he found himself in the presence of Yahweh. In exile Horos went towards the tree, *shen-i-ucha* (perhaps a thornbush); Moses in exile neared a spiny bush from which came flames. Horos was in charge of the herd of his father's cattle and at one moment he found himself in the isle Hery-ieb; Moses pastured the herd of his wife and came to Mt. Horeb. In the mountains Horos was assailed by Seth, who struck him on the back, snatched out his Eyes and buried them in his rock—or gave them to the Sun as two luminous lotus; Moses hides his face on the mountain from Yahweh, then comes down, his face glowing with light. (Yahweh covers Moses' face with his hand and says, "It shall come to pass, while my glory passes by, that I will put you in a cleft of the rock while I pass by".)[58] The Eyes of Horos were buried in the depths of the mountain of the thundergod; Moses stayed some time in the hollow of Yahweh's mountain, amid fire, smoke and thunderstorms.

This second set of correspondences are by no means exact and are gained by a rather arbitrary selection of details from the highly complicated myth or myths of Horos' Eyes and his conflict with Seth.[59] Seth is indeed a god of thunder and storm; but his confrontations with Horos are not of the same kind as the encounter of Moses with Yahweh. What we have are general themes of danger, withdrawal, ordeal. What is more striking, however, is the episode of hand-contamination which occurs with both Horos and Moses. Horos lies with Seth at his invitation and passes his two hands "between his thighs", making Seth ejaculate his sperm. One of his hands is polluted and is replaced by a healthy one, that Isis brings into being. "She will draw out for him (from his body) another hand of equal value."[60] In a variant both hands are thrown into the water and taken out, apparently in a purified or renewed form, by crocodiles; they are then put back on Horos' body.

In *Exodus*, iv, 6, we read: "And the Lord said furthermore to him: Put now your hand into your bosom. And he put his hand into his bosom; and when he took it out, behold his hand was leprous as snow. And he said: Put your hand into your bosom again. And he put his hand into his bosom again; and plucked it out of his bosom and behold, it was turned again as his other flesh." Yahweh explained that these events symbolise Moses' taking of the water of the river and pouring it upon the dry land. "And the water which you take out of the river shall become blood upon the dry land." (These words remind of the idea that the Nile-water turned blood-red.)[61] Seth, we may note, was connected with both leprosy and snow in Egypt.[62]

Mutilation-motives often go back to initiation-ritual, in which the initiate's body is mutilated in some way or a part (*e.g.* finger or foreskin) cut off. Here both the episodes seem to go back to initiation-rites, though they have been developed in different ways. Moses confronts the Father who gives him the lore of a new life; Horos struggles with the initiation-monster or adversary and gains a new body (expressed by a part of it). Both heroes are injured, polluted, and purified. Horos in the end saves and justifies his Father; Moses gains a new fertility-power over water. They have successfully passed through their ordeals.

The drowned person, we have seen, was thought to have won a state of deification or beatitude. Drowning was thus an extreme and more active form of a passage through which everyone hoped to go in due time in order to move from earth to other-world. Moses' miracle in the parting of the waters may be taken as an episode symbolising a collective movement from one level of life to another: an escape from danger, death, servitude into the freedom of a new situation leading to the Promised Land. We have seen how the Egyptians imagined a complex series of underworld rivers, with the ultimate haven of a blessed land of ease and security. The sky had its river along which the sunboat sailed, the earth had its Nile, the Tuat had its river of death or night. From the Old Kingdom the priests (taking over the shamanist function of guidance through the spiritworld) composed spells, incantations, and prayers for the use of the souls making the journey. The ideas of the geography of the otherworld were codified in works like the *Book of Coming-forth by Day*, the *Book of the Dead*, the *Book of Gates*, the *Hours of the Night* in *Ami Tuat*, and so on. We shall not here follow the complicated voyages of the dead as set out in such compilations which aimed at covering all the possible dangers and obstructions to be met. Instead, we shall take a document which brings out more directly the emotion of the individual faced with the death-passage.

Nehemesrattaui was a woman musician of Amun; and her hopes are recorded on a stele of painted wood of the late period. The statement takes the form of a Decree in which Osiris orders the gods what they are to do as the pharaoh ordered his subjects.

Royal Decree made by his Majesty the King of High and Low Egypt Unnefer [to the] Great Gods in the Domain of the Beyond (to the) Spirits in the Hall of Osiris, [to the] Praised Ones in the Great Hall, [to the] followers extended beside Osiris, the great judge in the Domain of the Beyond, [to the] Gods and Goddesses who dwell in the mound of Djemet, [to the] Silent Souls in the West of Thebes: Divine Decree saying: "O all these Gods of the Beyond together [four times], obey the words of Amun-Re, Lord of the Thrones of the Two Lands, President at Ipet-isout, of Atum Master of the Two Lands and at Heliopolis, of Ptah who is in the South of the Wall, Lord of Ankhtaui, of great Nun, Father of the Gods, saying:

When the Osiris, female musician of Amun-Re, Nehemesrettaui [Rettaui has saved you], daughter of the Divine Father and Seeker of the Udjat Ankhpakhered and born of the lady musician of Amun-Re Isisurt, will enter by you, bring it about that she [has access] to the First Hall of the West. It is the Palace of the Universal Master that you reserve for her, for her who appears in the Nekropolis as Re rising above the Earth. See [that she is accorded] the adoration and [the rite] Sa-ta at her command, and that she is permitted to rise up by bed. Her chapel is pure and she has no fear.

Bring it about that she repulses her enemies, that she imposes herself by the fear she inspires: may she be strong! Raise her above the souls of the gods. Let her have access to the pure sanctuary of Re within which she meets no impurities.

Unite her to life, make her young in age. Let her steps be firm, her force efficacious, let her become a noble among nobles.

Open to her the source of life, ensure that she crosses the water, her throat rising above it. Let her [have access] to the secret sanctuary, seeing that she is surrounded with the influence of him that is in the South of the Wall. Let her [have her place] in the great bed, Isis weeping Nephthys lamenting for her, being protected by the influence of Osiris, Chief of the West, Unnefer. Give her the right to all dignities, since she is under the influence emanating from Re Harakhti with the speckled plumage, coming out of the Horizon. Put her in the presence of Useret, since she is in the protection of Amun-Re, Lord of the Throne of the Two Lands, Presiding over Ipet-isut.

She is this great god whose terror fills the nekropolis. For she has passed the great gates in the Domain of the Beyond where she appears at each instant, the Osiris, female musician of Amun-Re, Nehemesrattaui, born of the Lady Musician of Amun-Re, Isisut.

She is this god, great and noble, for she has reached the Sacred Earth in perfect state. Her heart is just, no fault has been found in it, and the guardians of the balance have absolved her. May her Ba [soul] perch at the place she loves, while her body remains at Thebes.

Words to be said by the Osiris, female musician of Amun-Re, Nehemesrattaui: O constructors attached to the mound of Djemit, silent souls, in the noble tree *nsd*, open for me the gate into Otherworld, the whole of it. Let me be granted to enter your home.

It is reported to the Masters of the Beyond in the Decree that the Lord of the Gods has made, that I am an *imakh* of his town, praised by the god of his town. Look deep inside my body; no fault is to be found there.[63]

She belongs to a sacerdotal family. The upper part of her stele is surmounted by the winged disk; below the dungbeetle Kheper holds in his claws the rising sun, flanked by two uraei (one with the crown of Upper Egypt, one with that of Lower Egypt). On left and right are the jackal companions of the dead on their journey, Anubis and Upuatu (who represent the North and the

x

South); each holds between his front paws the baton *sekhem,* and on his back the whip with multiple lashes.[64] Above each deity, and at each side, the soul-bird Ba worships. In the second register we see the dead woman in an ample white fringed robe; she is sandalled and lifts her left hand in homage. Her right she has given to Anubis who introduces her to Osiris. He holds a document, doubtless the decree.[65] The woman here swims or wades across the death-waters. Normally there was a ferryman. The Pyramid Texts have several references to ferrymen. "Iw, ferryman of the Marsh of Offerings, bring for N this (boat). N goes, N should come, the son of the Morning Boat whom she bore before the Earth, his happy birth, whereby the Two Lands should live, on the right side of Osiris."[66] "Ferryman of heaven in peace, ferryman of Nut in peace, ferryman of the gods in peace, N comes to you, so that you may ferry him over in that ferry in which you ferry the gods over."[67] At least one of the names given to the divine ferryman was Anti.[68]

Diodoros tells him that corpses were ferried across a lake in a baris to a sort of trial of the deadman. The boat was "in the charge of the boatman whom the Egyptians in their tongue call *charon*". (No word at all like charon is known in Egyptian for a boatman.) He again says that the ferryman of the dead is called a *charon*.[69] He wants to prove that the Greeks got their ideas of the death-passage over water from Egypt; and in that point he may have been correct enough. It is significant that Charon does not appear in Homer. Indeed, we have no early reference to him at all, the earliest known being in the epic, *Minyas*.[70] He may have been a figure in popular beliefs which Homer ignored and which came into literature via Orphism.[71] True, the death-ferryman was well known in the Sumerian and Babylonian world. Gilgamesh was ferried across the waters of death by Ur-shanabi, who piloted the ship that survived the Flood. An ancestor of Gilgamesh, Meshkingasher, uses the phrase that "he ascended the mountain and passed through the sea" to express his death and deification. In an incantatory text we hear of a dead man voyaging in a ship under the guidance of the king of Dilmun (Ut-napishtim, the Flood-hero) to the place of death-judgement; the passage is obscure, though the relation to some sort of funerary ritual is clear.[72] But in view of what we have noted about Okeanos and Nun, Charon may have derived at least in part from figures like Anti, mixed no doubt with imagery from the Near East and shamanist concepts from the tribal past of the Greeks themselves.

Perhaps it would not be amiss to end this chapter with a spell of the Roman period, in which we can make out the detritus of many of the religious ideas and images we have discussed. We find purification, Agathodaimon, fire in the lake of heaven with the great god in its midst, Moses on the mountain (with his Burning Bush), a great god on the mountain, liquid turning red:

You go to a dark clean recess with its face open to the south and you purify it with natron-water and you take a new white lamp in which no red earth or gumwater has been put and place a clean wick in it and fill it with true oil after writing this name and these figures on the wick with ink of myrrh beforehand. And you lay it on a new brick brick before you, its underside spread with sand, and you pronounce these spells over the lamp again another seven times. You display frankincense in form of the lamp and you look at the lamp. And you see the god about the lamp and you lie down on a rushmat without speaking to anyone on earth.

Then he answers you by dream. Behold its invocation. Formula: Ho, I am Murai, Muribi, Babel, Baoth, Bamui, the Great Agathodaimon, Murabho, the . . . form of soul that rests above in the heaven of heavens. Tabot, Bouel, Mouihatahi (?), Lahi, Bolboch, I, Aa, Tat, Bouel, Yohel, the first servant of the great god, he who gives light exceedingly, the companion of the flame, he in whose mouth is the fire that is not quenched, the great god who is seated in the fire, he who is in the midst of the fire that is in the lake of heaven, in whose hand is the greatness and the power of god: reveal yourself to me here today in the fashion of your revelation to Moses, which you made on the Mountain, before whom you yourself did create darkness and light—I pray you to reveal yourself to me here tonight and speak with me and give me answer in truth without falsehood. For I will glorify you in Abydos, I will glorify you in heaven before Phre, I will glorify you before the Moon, I will glorify you before him who is on the throne, who is not destroyed, he of the great glory.

Peteri, Pater, Enphe, O god who is above heaven, in whose hand is the beautiful staff, who created deity, deity not having created him. Come down (in) to me into the midst of this flame that is here before you, you of Bouel, and let me see the business that I ask about tonight truly without falsehood. Let it be seen, let it be heard, O great god Sisihoout, otherwise said Armioouth, come in before me and answer me what I shall ask about, truly without falsehood. O great god that is on the mountain of Atuki (of Gabaon), Khabaho, Takrtat, come in to me, let my eyes be opened for any given thing that I shall ask about, truly without falsehood . . . this voice (?) of the Leasphot, Nebhet . . . Lilas.

Seven times: and you lie down without speaking.

By gazing hypnotically at the lamp-flame, the spell-maker is presumably liable to see the godform in the blurring brightness, and also to feel himself to be that godform, surrounded with a shattering lustre. The magical unguent is thus prepared:

The ointment which you put on your eyes when you are about to inquire of the lamp in any lamp-divination. You take some flowers of the Greek Bean. You find them in the place of the garland-seller, otherwise said of the lupin-seller. You take them fresh and put them in a *lok*-vessel of glass and stop its mouth very well for 20 days in a secret place.

After 20 days, if you take it out and open it, you find a pair of testicles in it with a penis. You leave it for 40 days and when you take it out and open it, you find it has become bloody. Then you put it on a glass-thing and put the glass-thing into a pottery-thing in a place hidden at all times.

When you wish to inquire of the lamp with it at any time, if you fill your eyes with this blood aforesaid, and if you go in to pronounce a spell over the lamp you see a figure of a god standing behind(?) the lamp and he speaks with you about the question you want; or you lie down and he comes to you. If he does not come, you rise and pronounce his compulsion. You must lie down on green reeds, being pure from a woman, your head turned to the south and you face to the north, and the face of the lamp likewise turned north.[73]

20

Tourists at Thebes: the Memnonion

EGYPT saw many visitors during the Roman period, some coming out of curiosity and for pleasure, others on administrative work or business matters. The inhabitants of the Nile Valley, also, as we have seen, did much travelling about. Thebes (Luxor today), with its Valley of the Kings and Memnonia, in particular attracted visitors who often left graffiti. On the right bank at Karnak lay the temples of Amun and Mont, with that of Mut to their south; a couple of miles away, close to the river, stood the New-Kingdom temple (now in the midst of Luxor). A traveller described in 1892 the approach:

The great rosy barrier of the Libyan hill, just now apparently right across our path, seemed as the river turned eastward, to come up close and run parallel with us, and the heights of Kurnet-el-Gurnah, broken into terraces of yellow-pink limestone, slopes of grey débris and shining cliffs of sunny whiteness, became a wall upon our right hand. On our left, the Arabian chain of ghostly lilac hue, rose through the haze in peaks that reminded us of the Cumbrian hills, and seemed to lie beyond a heaving desert of utter barrenness, five miles to the eastward.

The banks of the Nile dwindled, and sloped with a gentler slope, and already the husbandmen had utilised the fruitful gift of the gracious river, and the lupin patches and light-green corn and darker clover, had spread a verdurous carpet on either side of the shining water-way. Presently, as we entered up the "straight" that takes the voyager to Thebes, a voice at my side said, "There is Karnak," and, lifted above the palmgroves and acacia trees, dim but forcible, the great square propylon and part of a temple-wall were seen upon the eastern bank. Then, unmistakable among the feathery groves of tall trees, an obelisk was seen.[1]

On the left bank were the great funerary temples, Medinet Habu out to the south, the Ramesseum in the middle, and Deir el-Bahri and el-Qurna more to the north. At the mountain's floor, under the Theban peak, lay the private cemeteries: Deir el-Madina, Qurnet Murai, El-Asasif, Sheikh Abd el-Qurna—with such tombs as those of Menna, Nakht, Ramose, Rekhmere. Finally, in the hollow of the wadies, stretched the Valley of Queens, and yet more west, the Valley of the Kings.

Little is known of the place's origins. Its period of glory began with the Middle Kingdom, from the 2nd millenium B.C., and especially with the revival of the national spirit after the expulsion of the Hyksos invaders. Amun had his centre here, and here kings built their palaces and their homes of eternity. Thebes declined after 664 B.C. and political power shifted to north to the Delta.

How did the area of the nekroplis get the name of the Memnonia? Attempts have been vainly made to find an Egyptian name which was thus Hellenised. Memnon, like the Aithiopians, was known to Homer; and Memnon doubtless played a part in the *Aithiopis* of Arktinos of Miletos, of which we know practically nothing. The *Theogony* presents Memnon as king of Aithiopia; but Mimnermos put that country in the east, and poets and historians installed Memnon in Elam. Sousa became the Town of Memnon. Aischylos put the Aithiopians near the Indians and gave Memnon a woman of Sousa for mother. Diodoros made Memnon the general of Aithiopians and Sousianoi both in the Trojan War. As late as Quintos Smyrnaios Memnon was an Elamite, though others took the easy solution of accepting two Memnons and two Aithiopiai.[2]

The Egyptian terms which have been suggested as underlying Memnonia mean variously Place of the Dead, House of the Dead, Place of the Abysses, the Villages, and Religious Structures (Mennou). Some of these words may have played their part in evolving Memnonia, but we must also allow for the strong wish of Greek scholars to link Homer with Egypt, and in particular with Thebes. The name seems to go back to Kleitarchos in the early 3rd century B.C.; Herodotos knew nothing of it. In the wish for symmetry, the Memnonia of Sousa was described as a palace, and the same term was used for the Egyptian building.

Indeed, we find a graffito scrawled by a Greek at Abydos saying that there he had "come to the Memnoneion" during the Ptolemaic period.[3] Strabon sets the Memnonion at Hawara, in the so-called Labyrinth, the funerary temple of Amenemhet III, but adds that he had seen similar structures at Abydos and Thebes. The term had thus come to mean little more than a fine Eastern palace of an ancient kind.

However, it finally settled on the western part of Thebes. At Karnak and Luxor the great sanctuaries remained active through the Ptolemaic era until curbed by the troubles of the last century B.C. The plural noun Memnonia shows that the whole complex of sacred buildings was covered; but Memnon himself was associated with the colossos of Amenhophis III—perhaps because, as we have noted, there had been considerable links between the Aegean and Egypt in his reign.[4] The finest of the Syringes, No. 9, became Memnonian, because its builder Rameses VI had the same end in his Horos-name as Amenophis; and under the Romans the collective term was applied to all the visited Syringes. The final event fixing Memnon at Thebes and identifying him with Amenophis III was the discovery, in the last century A.D., that the colossos emitted musical sounds at dawn.

Possibly Ptolemaic propaganda had much to do with the linking of Memnon with the great Egyptian funerary temples. Thus

87. The Deadman wanders on the Eastern Mountains

Memnon was removed from Sousa and used as a symbol of the ancient association of Greeks and Egyptians.[5] However, even if this interpretation pleased the Greeks, it had elements which the Egyptians could not but dislike; for the Aithiopian Memnon was killed at Troy by a Greek hero; and in fact the Theban priests refused to allow the colossos to be taken away from Amenophis III.[6] The tale of Memnon thus could not serve to conciliate the two groups, as did the legends of Makedon son of Osiris and Nektanebo father of Alexander the Great.[7]

The fame of the speaking statue does not seem to have spread widely. Ovid, narrating the myth of Memnon, does not mention it; nor does the geographer Mela under Claudius, though he deals with Thebes. We have however the account of the phenomenon by Strabon, who visited Thebes in the years 27–4 B.C. and did not name Memnon. The first writer we know who did is the elder Plinius in his work published in A.D. 78. After that there are many references, in Juvenal, Dion of the Golden Mouth, Tacitus, Loukian and others.[8] Germanicus had visited the site in A.D. 19, but left no inscription. In November 130 came Hadrian and his wife; and later, Septimius Severus. Then falls silence. The last dated inscription is of 5 February 196. Only the rhetoricians, using past material, make references: Philostratos, Himerios. Ammianus Marcellinus, who knew the Syringes, ignores the singing statue.[9]

Here is the account of Strabon:

Now it is only a collection of villages, a part of it being in Arabia, where was the city, and a part on the far side of the river, where was the Memnonion. Here are two colossi, near to one another, each made of a single stone. One is preserved, but the upper parts of the other, from the seat up, fell down when an earthquake occurred, it is said. Once every day a noise, it is believed, like a slight blow, emanates from the part of the latter which remains on the throne and its base. And I too, when I was present at the places with Aelius Gallus and his host of associates, both friends and soldiers, heard the noise at about the first hour (after sunrise). But whether it came from the base or from the colossus, or whether the noise was purposely made by one of the men standing all round and close to the base, I cannot positively assert. On account of the uncertainty of the cause, I am led to believe anything rather than the sound issued from the stones thus fixed. Above the Memnonion, in caves, are tombs of kings, rock-hewn, about forty in number and marvellously constructed: a spectacle worth seeing.

Pausanias tells us:

I am confirmed in my view that the Megarians used to be tributary to the Athenians by the fact that Alcathoos seems to have sent his daughter Periboia with Theseus to Crete in payment of the tribute. On the occasion of his building the wall, the Megarians state, Apollo helped him and placed his lyre on the stone; and if you happen to hit the stone with a pebble it sounds just as a lyre does when struck.

This made me marvel; but the colossus in Egypt made me marvel far more than anything else. In Egyptian Thebes, on crossing the Nile to the so-called Pipes [Syringes], I saw a statue, still seated, which gave out a sound. Most people call it Memnon, who, they say, from Aithiopia overran Egypt as far as Sousa. The Thebans, however, claim that it is a statue, not of Memnon, but of a native named Phamenoph, and I have heard some say that it is Sesostris.

This statue was broken in half by Kambyses; and at the present day, from head to middle, it is thrown down. But the rest is seated, and daily at sunrise it makes a noise, and the sound it is most like is that of harp or lyre when a string has been broken.[10]

The account that Philostratos gives is also worth citing. It gives us, not a personal testimony, but a picture of the sort that had been romantically worked up. It also mentions the fact that Memnon was supposed to be the son of Eos, the Dawn: a mythological detail that did much to make the dawn-music seem right and exciting.

. . . they went on to the sacred enclosure of Memnon, of whom Damis gives the following description. He says that Memnon was the son of the Dawn, and that he did not die at Troy, where indeed he never went, but that he died in Aithiopia after ruling the land for five generations.[11] His countrymen, being the longest-lived of men, still mourn him as a mere youth and deplore his premature death.

The place where his statue is set up resembles, they tell us, an ancient marketplace such as remain in cities that were long ago inhabited, and where we come on broken stumps and fragments of columns, and find traces of walls as well as seats and jambs of doors and images of Hermes, some destroyed by the hand of man, others by that of time.

This statue, says Damis, was turned towards the sunrise and was that of a youth still unbearded. It was made of black stone, with the two feet joined together after the style in which statues were made at the time of Daidalos; and the figure's arms were perpendicular to the seat pressing upon it; for though the figure was still sitting, it was shown in the very act and impulse of rising up. We hear much of the attitude of the statue and of the expression of its eyes and of the way that the lips seemed about to speak; but they say there was no opportunity of admiring these effects till they saw them realised. For when the sun's rays fell on the statue, as happened exactly at dawn, they could not restrain their admiration. The lips spoke at once when the sun's beam touched them, and the eyes seem to stand out and gleam against the light as do those of men who love basking in the sun.

Then they say they understood that the figure was one in the act of rising and making obeisance to the sun in the way men do who worship the powers above, standing erect. They accordingly offer a sacrifice to the Sun of Aithiopia and to Memnon of the Dawn; for this the priests recommended them to do—explaining that the one name was derived from the words meaning "to burn and be warm" (aitho) and other from his mother. And having done so, they set out on camels for the home of the Naked Philosophers.

Nothing is said of the surviving dawn-voice, though it is well attested by the inscriptions. Strabon thought the broken nature of the statue to be due to an earthquake, doubtless thinking of that of 27 B.C., which ravaged the Theban region; but there may already have been a fissure splitting the stone as the result of the fire that devastated the site of the Kom el-Heitan

88. Sun-boat and Two Trees

during one of the sieges of Thebes. The colossos leans over, 2° 40′ out of the horizontal.[12] The noise, which is described as sharp, metallic, twanging, was perhaps the result of the change of temperature at sunrise affecting some part of the broken stonework. A Koptos inscription speaks of the Voice and Trumpet of Memnon's Stone.[13] The sound could happen several times in the same morning, and inscriptions record it as heard from sunrise up to the third hour. Certain slabs of the Edfu temple, in our own days, have been noted to emit under the rays of the rising sun a series of sound sharp as a revolver-shot and fading to a clear vibrant sigh.[14] The cessation of Memnon's voice, it has been suggested, came about through an effort made by Septimius Severus to have the colossus repaired.[15] The emperor may have wanted to increase the lustre of the pagan hero as part of his anti-Christian programme. The Christians on their side took the voice as a work of the Devil. St Jerome insisted that the statue was silenced at the coming of Christ.[16]

Apart from one demotic proskynema, all the writings are in Latin or Greek. They are rather careful inscriptions than graffiti jotted down, and have a far larger proportion of verse-effusions than are to be found on any other site. (Loukian jokingly makes the statue itself utter seven verses—but puts the story in the mouth of a professional liar.)[17] Visitors came mostly in summer, especially between November and March; some had travelled from afar—Side, Sardeis, Caesarea Panias. Of the soldiers, some were stationed at Thebes; one had been domiciled at Korinth, others at Vienna in Gaul. Many tourists came with their families: wives, children, brothers; and some came several times. Some dozen women set their names down. In general the interest seems in the marvellous event, and a sort of hero-cult is established— but not of a serious religious kind.[18] No attempt seems made to use the Voice for oracular purposes, despite the oracular quality attributed to it. Indeed, what is vindicated is Homer and his poems. Hence the way in which on the whole the response is literary. The Roman soldiers may state their visit in dry formal tones, though even they at times yield to a certain cultural excitement. The main visitors are as intent on noting their own reactions as on admiring the statue.

The association of Homer and Thebes went so far that Diodoros assumed he had visited Egypt and had special knowledge of this town, and a character in Heliodoros' romance asserts that he was born in Thebes:

"Let Homer be styled, my friend, a native of this or that country by different people, and let any city claim to be the sage's birthplace, in fact he was our countryman, an Egyptian, and his city was Thebes —with its hundred gates, in his own words. His reputed father was a prophet, but was actually Hermes [Thoth], whose prophet that reputed father was. For when the prophet's wife had the duty of performing some traditional rite and was sleeping in the temple, the god lay with her and begot Homer, who bore a mark attesting this unequal union. From the time of her delivery, one of his thighs [*ho meros*] was overspread with hairs of great length: whence he got his name, as he wandered and chanted his poems among various nations, and especially among the Greeks. He himself does not mention his real name, or even that of his city or race; but those who knew of the hairgrowth affecting his body fabricated his name from it."

"And what was his object, Father, in keeping silent about his native land?"

"Either he was ashamed of being an exile—for he was cast out by his father when about to be selected as one of the young men consecrated to divine service, the bodily blemish making him be considered a bastard—or else he kept silent as a crafty trick for winning favour everywhere by hiding his real city."[19]

The first datable comment is that of Servius . . . Clemens, who in A.D. 20, remarked, "I heard the Voice of Memnon and returned thanks". In 67 three soldiers noted, "we heard Memnon, 11th Year of Nero, 16th of the Kalend of April, at the . . . hour". Then, about 71–2, the Prefect of Egypt heard the Voice at the first hour. On 18 March 72, at the 2nd hour, "I, L. Iunius Calvinus, Commandant of the Mountain of Berenike, heard Memnon, together with my wife". (This officer had control, not only of the Gebel Zabarah, near the town, but of the whole roadway between Koptos and the port on the Red Sea.) Eleven more inscriptions were made before the reign of Hadrian. The persons include a Prefect of the Camp, a centurion who records thirteen dates on which he had heard the Voice (twice on one of the days), a Prefect of Egypt's wife, a cohort's Prefect, another centurion, two Prefects of Egypt. The verses begin. Paion of Side tried a couplet: "Wreckers have damaged your fine frame in vain. For still you speak: myself I heard the strain." And then another: "You speak, Memnon: I was told it long ago. Now on the spot, with my own senses, I know." T. Petronius Secundus, Prefect, in formal Latin tells how he "honoured Memnon with the undercited Greek verses". The verses, however, hardly do him much honour. "Memnon, a part of you here still sits: you spoke, feeling from Leto's Son the burning stroke." Another commandant of Berenike, also officer of a Gaulish squadron, had a try in Latin: "And the sonorous sound of Memnon sighed, which from the lifeless husk he breathless effused, with my own ears I heard and recognised." He was struggling for rhetorical paradoxes which eluded him. Like Paion and others he wanted also to stress the fact of having personally heard the miraculous voice, which by its very nature had a sort of oracular effect without actually saying or prophesying anything.[20]

For Hadrian's reign we have thirty-five inscriptions. Some are brief statements. We meet three Prefects of Egypt (one of whom heard the Voice four times); three strategoi (one with his wife who heard twice); an army officer who was a neokoros of the Great Sarapis and a pensionary at the Mouseion of Alexandrie; a Prefect of a cohort; four centurions; a military tribune; two epistrategoi; two royal scribes (one with wife and two sons) and an assistant; an idiologos and a archidikastes; a Prefect of the Alexandrian fleet.[21]

I, Lucius Funisulanus Charisius, strategos of the Hermonthite-Latopolite Nomes, I heard Memnon twice, before the 1st hour and at the 1st hour, accompanied by my wife Fulvia, 8 Thoth, 7th Year of Hadrian Our Lord. (5 Sept. 122).

Funisulanus Charisius here, strategos of Hermonthis and Latopolis, with his wife Fulvia, has heard you, Memnon, manifestly sound, at the hour when your Mother in tears spreads on your body . . . offering, libation and . . . he himself sang these verses to your glory: As a child I learned how Argo gained a Voice, and for the Oak of Zeus a Voice was found. But you alone I've seen, with my own eyes, cry out and send abroad a strident sound. And he engraved this poem for you . . . after having spoken to you and . . . wholly as a friend.[22]

By night I came for the Voice of divinest Memnon. And, Catulus, Chief of the Thebaid, I heard it.[23]

I, Pardalas of Sardeis, heard you twice. I'll make a record also in my books. Wreckers have damaged your fine frame in vain . . ..[24]

The strategos Celer was here, but not to hear Memnon. He was here in the very midst of the dust of the mounds to consult the oracle and make an act of worship. Memnon understood and uttered no word. But Celer returned to the place where he had been, after an interval of two days. On his arrival he heard the Voice of the God.[25]

> In the Theban plain, along the deep-eddying Nile
> your voice, Memnon, was heard by Gallus who came
> upstream—the sandy Thebaid is his command.
> It rang like the bronze of warriors pierced with blows.
> The son of Peleus conquered the son of the Dawn.
> As at Troy, by Simois' banks, his arms were clanging
> when down he was stricken and stretched in the dust of the land,
> now rings the colossal stone where the Nile-stream flows.[26]
> Ah, what a great wonder I see with my own eyes.
> That must be a god there, a ruler of the skies—
> and he cries aloud and the world is spelled at the cries.
> Such marvels no mere mortal could devise.

—*By Areios, Homeric Poet of the Mouseion, after hearing Memnon.*[27]

But most interesting is the group of inscriptions connected with Hadrian's visit. "Sabina Augusta, wife of the Emperor Caesar Hadrianus, in the course of the first hour, heard Memnon twice. . . ." "I, L. Flavianus Philippus, I heard the divinest Memon, while the emperor Hadrian also heard him, during the second hour, twice." On the first day, Memnon made no sound; next day Sabina went along with the poetess Balbilla and Memnon politely spoke; then Hadrian heard the voice. Balbilla describes the sequence: "On the first day we did not hear Memnon. Yesterday Memnon kept silent to receive the husband, so that beautiful Sabina might return. You are charmed, Memnon, by our Queen's loveable beauty. But at her arrival a divine cry broke out, for fear the King would be angry with you. Too long in your boldness you had held his august true wife. So Memnon, dreading the power of great Hadrian, began suddenly to utter a cry, which she heard with delight."[28] Balbilla was in Sabina's retinue; and she claims in her verses to have as grandfather Balbillus the Wise, who seems to be Tiberius Claudius Balbillus, Prefect of Egypt and astrologer; and to be of royal descent. Her mother, Balbillus' daughter, had married one of the sons of Antiochos IV.[29] Seneca praised highly Balbillus' literary powers, and the granddaughter clearly hoped to follow in his footsteps. She wrote three other poems on Memnon. The cry she described as sharp, "as if something bronze was smitten".[30] And she gave her mythological account:

When in company with the Augusta Sabina I was beside Memnon:

> You, Memnon, son of Dawn and hoary Tithonos,
> seated before the Theban City of Zeus—
> or Armenoth, Egyptian king, for whom
> the learnèd priests their ancient tales unfold—
> receive my greeting. Sing and welcome in turn
> the reverend Wife of Emperor Hadrian.
> Your tongue, your ears were cut by an impious man,
> barbarous Kambyses, who in turn was killed
> by the same sword that struck God Apis down.
> But safely still your statue will laugh at doom,
> now in my songs it's saved, enshrined, fulfilled
> by me whose ancestors were pious-souled . . .[31]

After Hadrian come eleven datable inscriptions: a squadron commander with wife and son; a beneficiarius; a consular legate of a legion; an imperial procurator; a Prefect of Egypt who had come the second time and heard the sound twice.[32] Marius Gemellus, centurion, left three inscriptions in verse, coming with his wife and children, and wishing himself Good Luck. "You've been endowed with speech by the rosy-fingered Dawn. . . ." "Which of the gods has inflicted such an outrage?" and so on. Maximus Statilius, writing in Latin, sought, less boldly than Balbilla, to associate himself with the god.[33] "The poet Maximius Statilius hears harmonious Memnon, and offers his poems: for dear to the gods is the Muse." "The Voice of Memnon strikes my ears as well: let each pronounce the poet Maximus' name."[34] Another assertive poet wrote in Greek:

I am a Sophist.
Memnon knows how to speak like a rhetor, knows how
   to be silent.
For he knows the force of speech and silence, both.
At the sight of the Dawn, his Mother with saffron veil,
he made a sound sweeter than any melodious word.
Falernus, poet and sophist, wrote these verses
worthy of the Muses, worthy of the Graces.[35]

Some forty-five inscriptions cannot be dated.[36] They include the
usual sprinkling of soldiers and officials (epistrategos, arabarch,
archidikast), an athletic victor, some women—Julia Saturnina,
Dionysia—and a man who makes a proskynema for his wife
Apollonarion. Two women poets appear.

Hail, Son of the Dawn, you gave me a favouring word,
Memnon, because of the Muses whose care am I,
I, Damo, lover-of-song, and my lyre to please you
will ever sing, O holy one, your power.[37]

Caecilia Trebulla wrote three sets of verses:

Hearing Memnon's holy voice, I thought of you,
Mother, and prayed that you might hear it too.[38]
Before, we only heard his voice,
but now he greets us as old friends,
Memnon, son of Dawn and Tithonos.
Have speech and sense been given the stone
by Nature who framed the universe?
Kambyses broke me, the stone that you behold,
a statue modelled like an eastern king.
I had a voice to tell my sorrows of old:
Kambyses robbed me of it, and today
I make complaints obscure and flittering,
vestiges of my state long passed away.[39]

On the whole Trebulla is modestly the best of the versifiers on
the colossos. Here are some others:

I, Petronianus, honour you in elegiacs, and make the god a gift of
poetry. My father Aurelius, I'm an Italian born. Then give me, lord,
in return a lengthy life. Many folk come to learn if Memnon keeps

a voice inside the remnant of his body. And he, without his head and torso, sits, speaks and complains to his mother of Kambyses. When fierily the Sun sends out his rays, he announces day to the assembled mortals.[40]

I, Achilleus, after honouring holy Memnon and praying that my brothers may hear his voice, depart, but first I leave an eternal word to the divine Ammonian Son of No—a word solidified in stone.[41]

Achilleus was perhaps identifying Memnon and Amenophis III with his title Divine Son of Amun. "No" is an attempt to transcribe the town's Egyptian name; Diodoros says of Thebes that originally "men named it after Osiris' mother" Nut—and the Greek transcription of her name as *Nau* appears in Naukratis. (Other Greeks, we know, attributed the statue to Ismandes, Amenoth, Phamenophes, Phamenoth.)

He, Son of the Dawn, is not without a head, Memnon, since every day at dawn he gives oracles to men who come to him from all the earth so that . . . some having had the experience . . . others full of wonder, they go back to their homelands.[42]

If it is true that Dawn weeps for her dear son, each time, light-bringing she gives splendour to the rising days, exhaling from the earth a roar worthy of a god, known to the divine Homer who told the tale of Troy: I heard on the spot the voice of Memnon. I Julius, centurion of legion, came here.[43]

Homer was seldom far from the minds of the literary inscribers, who like also, we note, to work out some moralising conclusion. Asklepiodotos, poet and procurator, reverses the idea that the Greek Achilleus was really the victor of the Egyptian Memnon:

Sea-nymph Thetis, yet Memnon lives and loudly lifts his voice when warmed by his Mother's torch, here at the foot of Egypt's Libyan range, cut from well-gated Thebes by the flowing Nile—while your warlike Achilleus has now no word to say on the Plains of Troy or in Thessaly today.[44]

There was not an indefinite space for inscriptions; after Hadrian's reign the legs were mostly covered. Gemellus on 8 May 150 had to use the pedestal for his longest effusion—a lowly position that had been previously scorned. Visitors seem to have dwindled; and inscriptions ended under Septimius Severus.

Y

21

Tourists at Thebes: the Syringes

THE Valley of the Kings was known to the Greeks as the Syringes, the Panpipes. Syrinx, pipe, had a varied number of sub-meanings that ranged from catcall or whistle in the theatre to subterranean passage or mine-gallery. Thus the writer in a book of 1871 described the scene at that time:

As I rode through this city of the dead, visiting the tombs which possessed the greatest interest, I endeavoured as I had done in the Nekropolis of the Pyramids, to recall its pristine state; to see it as it was seen by those who constructed and peopled it. The tombs were then everywhere along the Hager, that is, on the first rise or stage of the desert, above the cultivated land. Here, as generally throughout Egypt, vegetable life, and the soil which supports it, do not extend one inch beyond the heigth of the inundation, which brings the soil as well as the water. The stony desert, and the plant-clothed plain touch with sharp definition, each maintaining its own character to the last, just as land and sea do along the beach. From this line of contact to the precipitous rise of the hills there is a belt of irregular ground. In some places this belt is a rocky level or incline, in others it is broken into rocky valleys, but always above the cultivated plain. The whole of it is thoroughly desert, and all of it ascends towards the contiguous range. It is everywhere limestone, and generally covered with debris from the excavations, and from the hillside . . . .

We have rock-tombs elsewhere; but where, out of Egypt, could we find another such city? It is a city, excavated in the rocky plain, and in the mountain valleys. It consists of thousands of compartments, spacious halls, long galleries, steps ascending and descending, and chambers innumerable. It is more extensive, more costly, more decorated, than many a famous city on which the sun shines.[1]

This landscape of galleried rocks was what the Greeks called the

Syringes. Not long before the above description the death-city had indeed been inhabited. Vivant Denon, in his account of the Napoleonic invasion of Egypt, writes: "Shortly after noon we arrived at a desert, which was the field of the dead: the rock, excavated on its inclined plane, presents three sides of a square, with regular openings, behind which are double and triple galleries, which were used as burying-places. I here entered on horseback, with Desaix, supposing that these gloomy retreats could only be the asylum of peace and silence; but scarcely were we immersed in the obscurity of the galleries, than we were assailed with javelins and stones, by enemies whom we could not distinguish, and this put an end to our observations. We since learnt, that a considerable number of people inhabited these obscure retreats, and that probably, from the savage habits contracted there, they were almost always in rebellion with authority, and had become the terror of their neighbours."[2]

Starting with Thotmes I, the Eighteenth Dynasty created the nekropolis. Under Ramses IX of the Twentieth Dynasty, robbers were arrested for looting the tombs. Under the Priest-Kings about 1000 B.C. the nekropoleis were inspected, and the mutilated and despoiled royal mummies were restored. They were carried about from hiding-place to hiding-place. Some were at last stowed in the rock-tomb of Amenophis II; others were hurriedly put into a big tomb already cut in the foot of the western cliff not far from Deir el-Bahri. The decorated tombs, however, remained. The Greeks recorded their interest in graffiti; Egyptians made their comments in demotic; and later the Romans wrote up their names in Latin and Greek scripts. The Christians carried on in Coptic. Sometimes the writers stripped the stucco or spoiled sections of pictures and hieroglyphs. But mostly they chose a white band on the wall, a corner without hieroglyphs, or the empty field of a painting. Strabon speaks of some 40 tombs being known in his day; now we have explored over 60. But 10 was the number visited in Graeco-Roman days. The graffiti are distributed unequally in them. Syrinx 9, the tomb of Ramses VI (confounded by the Greeks with Amenophis III and Memnon) had some 995 out of a total of a little over 2,100. It was in fact the finest, but two other tombs, 2 and 1, near the entry to the royal nekropolis, had 656 and 132 respectively. In 4 were 58; in 6, 46. Less were in 4 and 6 at the forking of the roads. The visitors seldom went further west, passing the tomb of Setnakt (with one Cypriot graffito) on to that of Seti II (with 59) where the road turned back. No Greek graffiti have been found in the tombs opened in modern times; they were closed or difficult to reach.[3]

Visitors arrived along the detours of the meandering valley; the path to Deir el-Bahri did not exist or was little used. No one came in from the west. The tombs of Ai and Amenophis III, robbed in the Pharaonic era, were now unknown or ignored. The entry of a tomb usually got the most graffiti. Here the visitors paused as they came in out of the sun, or before they left the shade to go out. They chose the well-lighted parts near the door for their names, or moved on a little to the first paintings. They used the inner dimly-lit walls less, but now and then one of them stopped to scratch—on till the final cella. Persons with ink used the lighted areas; the graffiti deeper in were done with a point. The columns of hieroglyphs were mostly passed by; halts were made at the paintings while the guide explained; and then it was the tourist found the time to inscribe his name. In 9 the picture of the scene of metempsychosis before the god-judge of the underworld was especially attractive—because the guide stayed there a longer time or there was some magical value in setting down one's name by such a scene. The scarcity of graffiti in the fine tombs of Seti I and Ramses III suggest that they were at this time obstructed in some way; the halls inside the tomb of Meneptah were filled with alluvial soil carried in by storms in the Ptolemaic era.

The staying-power of the tourists was not indefinite. Not all the tombs were visited, but people went to more than one. Some wrote their names in two, some in three or four. There was no system, however. The commonest way was to write in 2 and in 9. The tourists came in groups or alone. About a hundred graffiti show a party of some sort. We find groups of three to five making a proskynema. Doudas mentioned by Zenon in 6 appears alone in 8; Sanktos mentioned by Sokrates as a companion returns the compliment elsewhere.[4] Palladios, signing Aurialos in 9, appears not far off with other companions. (Aurialos is presumably a mis-spelling of Aurelios.)

Palladios dikologos of Hermopolis saw and admired. Aurialos from Egypt saw and admired. Ak . . . as.

Didymos son of Areios of Panopolis and his brothers and Palladios son of doctor Hermeios (or Hermias) of Panopolis, dikologoi, we admired.[5]

We meet groups from some land or town. A pair of Rhodians, four Kappadokians, or three Romans. Groups drawn together by a common interest or profession, such as the two juriconsults or dikologoi cited above. Demetrios of Hermopolis and Heraios sign around a sphinx; both are scholastikoi and probably together.[6] Family-groups are common. Father and son often appear. Potamon came with his father and made proskynema for all the family, mother, brothers, sisters. "Dionysios son of Dorion, Dorion son of Dionysios" runs a single graffito; "Kollouthes, Petenophis son of Kollouthes." Corinthian Charmes and Aristermis son of Charmes Corinthian sign close together.[7] Sometimes father and son sign far from one another, even in different syringes. Three brothers, sons of Moschion, appear in a single graffito; then a fourth son turns up with the father in another tomb.[8] Perhaps we meet three generations in Klemens son of Serenos, Sarapion son of Klemens, Serenos son of Sarapion.

Often a woman writes down her own name and we do not know if she was with others. We meet Romans, Greeks, Asian Greeks, Egyptians, Christian Copts. Some are in groups: Dionysia and Philinna; Myrto and Helile; Thermoutis, Euphrosyne and Larion; Protarche, Moschiaine, with a suite of five others, Sarapion, Aplonarion, Origenes, Koukoullos, Isidoros. Some are mixed with a male company, perhaps by chance.[9] Some, like the men, merely jot down their names; others say they have come in person, that they have visited and seen the sights, or even that they have looked and cut the name.[10] Others let their name be cut by a companion. "Ianuarius, primipilus, I saw and admired the place with my daughter Ianuarina. Good health to all." This note is in Latin, in red ink.[11] Married men put down their wife's name. "Claudius Bassus, also called Himerios, Most Distinguished

Katholikos of Egypt, Bithynian, I visited with my wife Aste."
Didymos came with his wife, but made proskynema for his
brother.[12] Ptolemaios of Bouseiris came with his wife Kypria and
a son of his own name, and "remembered" Menouthias. But we
cannot tell who was present apart from Agathos in "proskynema
of Agathos and of his mother and of his wife and of his children
and brothers and of Sarapion and Dios and his own".[13]

To penetrate into the dark depths there must have been some
kind of lighting. So we must presuppose that guides and visitors
carried torches. "Dadoukios, scholastikos doctor, I came and
admired, and I have come literally a *Dadouchos* [torch-bearer]."
If this graffito is correctly read, the tourist makes a pun on his
name. Another man calls himself *dadouchos* (priestly torch-bearer)
of the Eleusinian Mysteries, but without any reference to the
tombs.[14]

The earliest inscription is dated 278 B.C., recording the visit of a
Rhodian, Euphranor. But, though Ptolemaic graffiti abound at
Abydos, there seems only one other one in the Syringes.[15]
Touristic interest begins with the Roman conquest, under
Augustus, and carries on to the reign of Marcus Aurelius. Christian
inscriptions, however, show that visitors kept on coming and
writing their names till the 7th century. Some of the people who
wondered at Memnon must have come along to the Syringes as
well, but the only person who certainly visited both sites was
Pardalas of Sardeis. The idiologos T. Statilius Maximus, who
visited Memnon, had his name put down in Syrinx I by someone
who "remembered" him, but there is no proof he was present.
The Prefect C. Vibius Maximus visited Memnon, but the
Maximus who twice appears in the tombs as eparchos is probably
a minor official.[16] Notables did not altogether ignore the site.
We find Prefects of Egypt, governors of the Thebaid, two
strategoi, treasury officials, magistrates, army-officers; but one
gets the impression that the Syringes had a rather plebeian quality.
The great men found more satisfaction in the communion with
Memnon through the dawn-twang and set their name and their
effusion on the colossus. At most they glanced at the tombs and
did not deign to scratch their name there. Certainly many of the
lesser folk had their look also at Memnon. Several scribblers

mention it. The Stones in the following verses are the colossus:

> I came here to Thebes and my eyes on the Stones I cast,
> and on the Pipes where I'm spellbound and aghast,
> Philastrios of Alexandreia, a happy day I've passed.

> Ouranios the Cynic, I've admired their art:
> the Theban Pipes and venerable Memnon.

Iasios of Neocaesarea, I have heard Memnon speak and (seen) the singular virtue of the Syringes, something that leaves us speechless, and I have admired the wisdom of the devisers.

> Herakleios admired all the Syringes, but still
> declares that Memnon's the most divine of them all.[17]

In the gorge that sheltered the Syringes the weather was very hot from March on. Only one person wrote his name in Thoth, the season of the flood, hot and humid. He was Papirius Domitianus, strategos of the near Ombite nome; he had apparently called at Thebes on business and took advantage of the visit to make a gesture of homage in the name of his wife and children. Only two wrote, as far as we know, in Phaophi; they boasted of visiting all the Syringes. Hathyr (October–November) was still warm, but easier. Hadrian was at Karnak on the 24–25th, but did not go to the Valley. In all, of the persons who put down the date, eleven came in the four autumn months, twenty-four in the winter, ten or eleven in the summer.[18]

Many soldiers from the Thebes garrison came, some thirty Alexandrians, proud of their city, six persons from the Delta (Pelousion, Bouseiros, Latopolis, Heliopolis), near two dozen from Middle Egypt, near a dozen from Upper Egypt.[19] From Greece came a dozen Athenians, a Delphian, four Korinthians, an Argive, an Arkadian, three Lakonians, and from the Adriatic side, an Akarnaian, an Aitolian, an Epirote. Also half a dozen Thessalians, a Byzantine, a dozen Thracians, two from the land of Scythia and the Tanasis. Men from the isles of Zakynthos, Taphos, Rhodes, Samos, Lesbos, Crete, Cypros; from Asia Minor—Bithynia, Mysia, Galatia, Pontos, Lycia, Peisidia, Kilikia. Many Syrians and even a sprinkling from Armenia, the Caucasus, Persia, Babylon, or from the West—Cyrene, Sicily, Italy, Spain, Gaul

(Marseilles).[20] As only a small proportion can have written up their names and nationalities, it seems clear that the eastern section of the empire was well represented—though we must remember that it was men who had come a good distance who were more likely to feel the importance of the event and wish to commemorate it.

Among men of the law we find five dikologoi and some sort of assistant as well as several scholastikoi (advocates or legal advisers, but also merely scholars, theoreticians in a general way).

I, the scholastikos Bourichios, thanks to Plato, have visited and admired; I have made proskynema for my lord and brother Saprikios the scholastikos. But it is not for that that Plato has bound me to him.

Bourichios scholastikos of Askalon, I have visited, I have judged myself for not understanding the text [logos]. I do not approve of this irritation of yours, Bourichios.[21]

Bourichios seems a scholar rather than a lawyer. He thanks Plato for inspiring him to make the visit, but seems to state that he is linked with Plato for other and deeper reasons. Then in the second graffito he seems to express regret at the limits of his erudition. If only he could read the hieroglyphs, he would penetrate the secrets of those whom he takes to be Plato's masters. The *scholastikos iatros* we noted above was presumably a professor of medicine. Elpidios of Alexandreia was a *scholastikos heistorikos*, probably a professor of history.[22] However, some of the scholastikoi were certainly men of law, as was Isidoros of Alexandreia, who calls himself a descendant of the judges of his hometown and mentions that he came to Thebes "after having studied at Athens".[23]

Several officials of the treasury and tax-collectors appear.[24] A couplet informs us: "The Katholikos Theodoros brought us to this Wonder. We have beheld a most impressive Wisdom." (*Sophia* means craft-skill and general intelligence as well as wisdom.) "Antonios, son of Theodoros, the most Distinguished Katholikos, Citizen of Heliopolis in Phoinikia, I who have dwelt long in Imperial Rome and looked on the Precious Wonders there, I have also seen those here."[25] (The reading may be Antonios Theodoros; then this pompous fellow is the same as the couplet-composer.) Another man more full of himself than of the scene was Nemesianos: "Fellow-citizen of the Divine Poet Homer, of a Family of Imperial Treasurers and Governors, with other diverse functions, Magister and Katholikos of the Diocese of Egypt, I visited and admired."[26]

The army provides an extremely wide range of ranks, from high-ranking officers to trumpeter, doctor, and legionaries.[27] But their records are plain and matter-of-fact. Several grammarians also note down their names, without inspiration.[28] The same comment applies to the rhetors and sophistai. Doctors are comparatively plentiful, but again they lack eloquence.[29] The commonfolk are almost altogether lacking. We find not a single farmer or farmworker, trader or businessman. There are a few servants and slaves in the wake of their masters. Of the slaves, Ioannes and Kion merely put down their names, Euphrosinos added, "slave of the governor Iulius Cassander, I visited the Syrinx and made the proskynema for my master and my [friends]."[30] There is one artisan, a goldsmith, and perhaps one sailor.[31] There is no sign of the choachytai or other funerary officials.[32]

There are a few persons with priestly functions. One has an odd title: Archpriest of the Thebaid. Another visitor calls himself Servitor (therapon) of All-seeing Hermes, but he seems to have been, not a religious devotee, but a learned exponent of the esoteric doctrine attributed to Thoth-Hermes, who remembers the Homeric phrase "all-seeing Hermes".[33]

There remain the poets and the philosophers. Some persons claimed to be poets, one a woman; and we meet a hymn-writer and a composer or copier of tragedies. Others try to prove their talent by providing verses; seven use hexameters, six write distichs, three prefer iambics. We have already seen some of the efforts. Patrikios of Megara speaks of "the marvellous emotions of his heart". Another declares "at the sight my heart was enchanted and this I wrote. . . ." The sophia, the craft-skill and perhaps also the profound conception, and the vast labour expended, continue to affect the observer.

Tatianos Governor of Upper Egypt visited and admired.

O strange Marvel of the Wise Aigyptians

> that awakens now the greatest Astonishment.
> The world's memory, through all the years to come,
> will admire your words and the labours you have spent.[34]

The *logoi* or words may be the hieroglyphs as explained by a guide, or may be the rules, systems, reasons underlying and giving coherence to the *ponoi*, the labours of excavation and decoration. Some scratchers were capable of only the merest tags:

> I, Kleiboulianos, have seen the great Marvel's spell,
> and admired, who in the land of Delphoi dwell.

> I, Besas, have admired the Syringes, things of wonderment,
> but the sight I have most admired is Memnon's great monument.[35]

More promising poems are fragmentary. Mikkalos the hymn-writer, who considers himself a brave and brilliant horseman, crossed the vast sea and travelled with a cavalry officer, curator turmae; but his sixteen lines are mutilated. And lines that end, "I Demetrios the Cynic have said to you hail," open promisingly with an address to the nymphs of the heights, "Nymphs Orestiades who hold the steeps of the Nile . . ."[36]

One moralist could not resist setting out his favourite maxim: "Marinos has said: Be of good heart, no one is immortal." He leads us into the philosophers, where the Platonists were especially strong. "May Plato be propitious to us, here too!" wrote an enthusiast in red ink. We have already seen the remarks of Bourichios. "You have had the happiness to admire, O wise Plato. If only, philosopher Iulianus, you had seen the sage's itinerary!" Julianus seems to be addressing himself. He says that Plato has been here before him to see and admire, and wishes that he had been able to accompany him.[37] Another inscription runs: "I, Dadouchos of the Most Holy Eleusinian Mysteries, son of Minucianos, Athenian, having visited the Syringes, long after the Divine Plato of Athens, have admired and given thanks to the Gods and to the Most Pious Emperor Constantine, who brought this about for me."[38] From another graffito we can supply the name, Nikagoras, and the date, A.D. 326. In excitement, perhaps, the man has forgotten to add his name. More likely, he has deliberately omitted it, considering the title and the name of his father to be enough. We can make out his genealogy. His father, Minucianos, sophist and author, flourished (according to the Suda) under Gallienus; his grandfather, Nikagoras, was also a sophist. We hear of Longinus inviting this latter to a banquet in honour of Plato; Philostratos calls him the sacred herald of Eleusis. The great-grandfather, the rhetor Mnesaios, addressed a report to the emperor Philip about a mission with which he was charged. Now his descendant has been sent on a mission by Constantine, or, more likely, has been given some privileges for his voyage—the right to use the cursus publicus. The rhetorician Himerios praised the dignity of Nikagoras' speech, and called him his father-in-law.[39]

It seems that the Platonists, in visiting the Syringes, felt that they were following in the master's footsteps and beholding in the underground passages and their pictures the source of his eschatological doctrines. The scene of the Judgment of Souls clearly had a special interest for them. Lysimachos signs on the door frame succinctly: "Platonic philosopher."[40]

At least five Cynics wrote up their names: Ouranios and Demetrios, whose verses we have seen, Diokles (signing four times), Paniskos, and Besa: "Besa the Cynic admired: the day was a bad one . . ."[41] One Aristotelian appears: Serenos *peripatetikos*; and there is a Prefect of a cohort described as *mathematikos*, as well as an astrologer and a *magos*.[42]

Clearly the main motive of the visitors was curiosity and a vague sense of awe. "I have come, I have visited, I have seen, I have admired": that is the formula. Now and then we find someone who seems to have been deeply stirred: to have felt that here was a tremendous work of art and technique, with a strong and profound conception lying behind it. At times this feeling of stupendous achievement makes the visitor feel the presence of something miraculous, something with its own inherent and mysterious quality, its *arete*. A few assume a bored superior tone, like the man who had seen the grandeurs of Imperial Rome. "I, Epiphanios, have visited and admired nothing except the stone." There spoke a determined dissident, or perhaps a Christian. "I, Dioskorammon, have seen this madness, *mania*, and I am astounded."[43] But mostly a confused and routine veneration reigns. There is also an indefinite hope of making the visit somehow a matter of good augury, and the writers use some phrase or other that seeks to divert on to themselves a touch of the great power they feel present in the tombs.[44] (With the Christians this becomes an overt wish for a long life.) Two men boast of their good health; and though the terms suggest the ex-voto thanks for cures found in the great healing centres, the Syringes were certainly never such a place.[45] There is no sign of anything like what went on at Abydos where Bes took over from Osiris and multiplied cures. The great prestige of Memnon, we saw, affected the pilgrims, and the tombs themselves were Memnonian.[46] The most decorated and best kept, that of Ramses VI, was attributed to Memnon, we noted, and was the most visited.

Perhaps it was a sense of inexplicable potences and sanctities that led many visitors to attempt various kinds of anagrams and verbal twists. Berthopgeis seems written for Poregebthis; Paphis ho Psemmagios seems to become Pabhis amtoseimops; Dionysias, onausisid.[47] Jottings of what appear to be meaningless words are perhaps ciphers to which we have no key: *Mtemodo* or *kkpspheooia pskchi*.[48] And we meet twice, in tomb 9, a line that seems best interpreted as the precise Greek equivalent of the modern jeer, "Does your Mother know you're out?"—presumably addressed to Memnon, though it may represent some private joke among a group of tourists.[49]

Finally we may glance at Deir el-Bahri with its sanctuary of healers dominated by Imhotep-Asklepios. Here on the left bank opposite Karnak the hill-range describes a vast amphitheatre which marks the heart of the Theban nekropolis. The funerary temple of Hatshepsut, the Eighteenth-Dynasty Queen, is its noblest monument, magnificently linked with the mountain out of which it is partly carved; and almost all the visitors who cut their names there were certainly in hope of a cure or benefit of some kind from the medical triad now considered to be installed there. A few, however, may have been curious to have a look at the scene and note the *aretai*, the miracles. Thus, the strategos Celer, who made an inscription on Memnon in June 123, had doubtless come for some such purpose. He does not name his nome, but we may assume it was that of Funisulanus and Chairemon, the Hermonthite-Latopolite, at the time including the Memnonia. Funisulanus dates his inscription September 122, so that Celer appears to have been making a tour soon after his appointment. The inscriptions at Deir el-Bahri show him accompanied by his children; we know under Trajan important works of irrigation were probably undertaken on the left bank, and Celer may well have felt that he should make an inspection. Being near Deir el-Bahri, he looked in, perhaps out of curiosity, perhaps because it showed his zeal to note what was happening in a place of popular pilgrimage which might easily become a centre of muttering nationalist discontent. Also, he may have felt the visit would enhance his popularity. As for the Ramesseum and Medinet-Habu, the scarcity of Greek graffiti there shows that these sites also failed to attract the tourists.[50]

22

Perseus-Min

THERE are many more aspects of the Nile that we could explore: aspects of daily life connected with fishing, the papyrus-industry, hunting, work on the embankments, gardens and their pools, and aspects of myth such as the cosmogony of the lotus and the life-death of the Phoenix. But they must be left for treatment elsewhere.[1] To round off this book we shall glance at Perseus, a Greek hero who somehow became lodged at Panopolis on the Nile; for this theme will serve both to fill out further what has been said of the relations of Greece and Egypt, and to provide an appendix to the myth of Seth and the Sea.

Herodotos said that at Chemmis (Panopolis) was "a square of enclosed ground sacred to Perseus the son of Danae. Palmtrees grow round it and there is a stone gateway of great size surmounted by two very large stone figures. Within the enclosure is a shrine containing a statue of Perseus. According to the local legend, Perseus is frequently to be seen in the neighbourhood, and also within the temple. Sometimes a sandal which he has worn, three feet long, is found: a sign, they say, of the approach of a period of great prosperity for all Egypt. In the worship of Perseus, Greek rites are used, athletic contests with all the usual events, and prizes of cattle, cloaks, and skins. When I asked why it was that Perseus revealed himself only to the people of Chemmis and why they alone of the Egyptians held games in his honour, the answer was that Perseus belonged by birth to their city; Danaos and Lynkeus, they said, were Chemmites before they sailed to Greece, and from them they traced Perseus' descent. More, when he came to Egypt from Libya with the Gorgon's head (which is the reason that the Greeks also adduce for his going there), he paid a visit to Chemmis, having previously learned the name of the place from his mother, and there acknowledged all his kinsmen. On his arrival he instructed them to hold games in his honour, and so they did so."[2] He also states that "the Ionians maintain that Egypt proper is limited to the Nile Delta, a stretch of land running along the coast from what is called Perseus' Watchtower to the Pelousian Saltpans", and inland to Kerkasoros. He also describes Xerxes as appealing to the Argives not to fight against him, since they had a common ancestor in Perseus, from whose son Perses the Persians were descended.[3]

Generally we can see some point, even if a stretched one, in the identifications of Greek and Egyptian gods; but this case of Perseus seems to provide no easy analogy in Egyptian cult or myth. Yet Herodotos' account is circumstantial and seems based directly on what he was told or saw at Chemmis (Akhmîn, Panopolis). Indeed one important part of it—that dealing with the games—has complete historical verification. A strip of tanned calfskin from the town reads in large uncials of about A.D. 100: "The Sacred Triumphal Universal Olympic Contest of the Celestial Perseus in the Great Paneias."[4] Papyri further prove the existence of the Games and their attribution to Perseus Ouranios.[5]

89. The earliest known representation of Perseus and Andromeda
(Corinthian amphora)

In Greek myth Perseus has two great deeds: the slaying of Medousa and the rescue of Andromeda from the ketos or sea-monster. The Medousa-episode is clearly much earlier than the other. It alone is known to Homer, Hesiod, Pindar. The Andromeda-tale seems to come in during the 6th century B.C. We can perhaps trace it back to Pherekydes, who seems to have worked in the 5th century; but what his sources were, we do not know. The earlier vases, metopes or reliefs, deal with Medousa; the first known representation of Andromeda and ketos appears on a black-figured amphora; Corinthian, of the second quarter of the 6th century. Perseus is shown nude with a pile of stones at his feet and one in each hand; Andromeda (with her lower part lost) has her hands full of stones, ready to help and supply him. No sword is to be seen. Of the monster, labelled Ketos, we see only the huge head with gaping jaws and stuck-out tongue. Perseus wears shoes with two little curved wings. The story, however, does not yet seem popular. It next turns up on a red-figured hydria, Attic, dated to the third quarter of the 5th century. Aithiopian slaves set up pillars. Andromeda is in Amazonian dress, with long sleeves and tight trousers under a short chiton; she is supported by two slaves, and others bring toilet articles, perfume-jars, mirror, stool, casket, cloak as funereal-bridal gifts. The virgin is the bride of Hades. Her father Kepheus sits sunk in grief; he and his daughter both wear the high cap of oriental royalty. Perseus, still invisible, stands behind him with spears, his hand to his brow in a gesture of compassion.[6]

The difference between the first primitive-looking scene and the polished setting of the second is striking. Now the Andromeda-scenes all show the influence of stage-settings, in particular the plays by Sophokles and Euripides. The heroine is bound in various ways: to pillars or tree-trunks, to an ornate chair (in a late vase). Rocks seem added from the more realistic stage-effects of Euripides. Sophokles' play may be dated perhaps about 442 B.C.; generally it seems that it was about mid-5th century that the theme became widely known. (The one Greek vase-painter with an Egyptian name, Amasis, painted Perseus and Medousa on an Attic jug of the mid-6th century, with no hint of Andromeda.) The original Perseus has all the signs of the culture-hero that we discussed in connection with Moses. He is rejected, thrown into water, is rescued, returns to claim his heritage, is subjected to ordeals, makes the spirit-journey into the otherworld, Okeanos, and comes back with the token of his victory. The Andromeda-episode has every appearance of an accretion, a repetition of the monster-slaying motive in a weakened and romanticised form. What interests us here is the fact that it was set on the Red Sea, in Aithiopia. Can we find any connection between it and the cult of Perseus at Chemmis?[7]

First, what god at Chemmis was Perseus identified with? The great god at Chemmis, as at Koptos, was Min, the fertility-god. Has he any affinities with Perseus? First we may note that the pantheon of the town consists of Min, Aper-iset (Triphis, a goddess of love), Hatendotes, and a deity of the Osirian cycle (Osiris, Isis, Nephthys, Anubis, Ptah-Sokar-Osiris).[8] A stele cites Min, Triphis, Osiris and Isis, with three special deities: a form of Horos, Haroeris, and Kolanthes.[9] A list of local cults on the wall of the sanctuary at Hibis cites for Chemmis: Min, Horos (as above), Osiris, Isis, and an odd monster (bull, crocodile, and some sort of bird) with the name Hor-whose-heart-burns-up.[10] As for an Egyptian basis in the name Perseus, various unconvincing efforts have been made: Per-se as Son of Isis or peh-resou the runner. A happier clue is provided by a scene at Esneh.[11] We see Caracalla pouring two vases out to the two deities of Chemmis, Min and Repyt (Triphis): "Min, Sovereign of the South, Horos the Victorious, Lord of Panopolis, Min-the-Watcher, such is the name he is given."[12] The Watcher or Guard is 'ouerche, and this epithet of the god can be found in a considerable number of names, Orseus, Orses, Ouersenouphis, Barsanouphis. In the marches of Min, the routes of the eastern desert out from Koptos, such names have been found in comparatively large numbers: twenty-one with the divine name -orses: Senorsis (4), Orsenouphis (11), Senorsenouphis (5). So, by the addition of the article to the epithet wrsy, we get P-orses, P-orseus.[13]

Here we find the one plausible link of the name Perseus with an Egyptian god-name. The main objection is that we have no evidence of the epithet being common in Min's cult at Koptos and Panopolis. The name of the latter town shows that the main

Z

90. The Perseus-Andromeda theme after the dramatic representations (amphora, Naples Mus. 3225)

identification of Min was with Pan. However, the large number of personal names compounded of -*orses* suggests that Min the Guard or Watcher had much popularity; and we must note the place-name mentioned by Herodotos in the Delta, Perseus' Watchtower.

We know no tale about Min that at all suggests the rescue of Andromeda from the *Ketos*.

In a late story, taken from the *Aigyptiaka* of Thrasyllos of Mendes, we are told that, "In the course of a civil war the Nile-flood failed and the people suffered from famine; the Pythian [Apollo, perhaps here identified with Re] gave an oracle promising fertility if the king offered his daughter as an expiatory sacrifice to the gods. Crushed by misfortune, the king led Aganippe to the altar. When she was cut into pieces, he, Aigyptos, mad with grief, threw himself into the flood."[14] An Arab writer, Ibn Abd-el-Hakam, who died in A.D. 871, said there was a custom in Egypt of throwing a young girl into the Nile on 12 Pauni (6 June), which the Arabs suppressed.[15] In view of a total silence otherwise about any such custom, we must suppose the whole thing a misunderstood folktale or an exaggeration derived from some rite of taking the statue of a goddess (Isis, Hathor, Neith) to the banks of the river to encourage the rising waters. In a 19th-century account of "cutting the canal" at Cairo we read:

The dam is constructed before, or soon after, the commencement of the Nile's increase. The Kahleeg or Canal, at the distance of about four hundred feet within its entrance, is crossed by an old stone bridge of one arch. About sixty feet in front of this bridge is the dam, which is of earth, very broad at the bottom and diminishing in breadth towards the top, which is flat, and about three yards broad. The top of the dam rises to the height of about twenty-two or twenty-three feet above the level of the Nile when at its lowest; but not so high above the bed of the canal; for this is several feet above the low-water mark of the river, and consequently dry for some months when the river is low. The banks of the canal are a few feet higher than the top of the dam. Nearly the same distance in front of the dam that the latter is distant from the bridge, is raised a round pillar of earth, diminishing towards the top, in the form of a truncated cone, and not quite so high as the dam. This is called the " 'arooseh" (or bride), for a reason which will presently be stated. Upon its flat top, and upon that of the dam, a little maize or millet is generally sown. The 'arooseh is always washing down by the rising tide before the river has attained to its summit, and generally more than a week or fortnight before the dam is cut.[16]

The cone, with its maize-bride, reminds us both of the primeval hill and of the gardens of Adonis; and the custom has a feeling of antiquity. Something like it could beget tales such as those of the virgin thrown to the waters.

We can hardly doubt that such a widely-spread tale-type as that of the girl offered to the waters or the water-monster was present in Egypt. The myth of Seth fighting the exorbitant Sea which demands Astarte is a simple example, still close to ritual bases. From Aithiopia itself in the last century came the legend that Axum was once the seat of a serpent king, who demanded daily a virgin. At last came Saba's turn. She was rescued by a "celestial warrior in earthly form". But the serpent's saliva fell no her foot, causing ulcers and lameness. Acclaimed queen, she crossed the sea to Solomon, who cured her and also got her with child. Her son was Menelek, from whom the kings of Gondar traced their line. In a Nubian tale, the hero saves the king's daughter from a crocodile that stops the river.[17] The relation to water is here of interest; for in a late tale (given by Pausanias of Damascus) Perseus, visiting the Ionians settled near Mt Silpion, encountered a severe storm that caused the river Drakon (Orontes) to overflow and flood the land. He called for prayers, which brought about the fall of a ball of lightning that stopped the storm and checked the river.[18] Strabon sets here the conflict of Typhon and Zeus. Typhon, a *drakon*, fled from the thunderbolts, furrowed the earth, and plunged underground; the Orontes then sprang up from the hole. Egyptian ritual-myth abounds with fights against monster-snakes, who seek to impede the deadman or to swallow up the sun (Seth once swallowed the crescent moon), but strangely we do not find a fight to control the water-sources. The rite of destroying figures of the demon-snake Apepi was carried out in time of storm, heavy rain, or black-red clouds obscuring the sun. When Seth swallowed the moon, Nut speared him and made him vomit it up; but the great spearer of the snake of evil is Horos.[19]

A terra-cotta of a man struggling with a snake has been found near Mopti in the valley of the Niger in the Sudan, with two more similar pieces, rather fragmentary. The man has been crouching down and strives to disengage his right leg and rise up. The date is hard to settle, and we cannot be sure whether a ritual event or some accidental attack by a snake is being represented. The fact of three examples suggests rite or myth.

It is interesting to note in North Africa, at Daura and Songhay, the legend of a young hero killing a water-spirit, Dodo, variously described as a monster, a wildbeast, a snake, a bird. In one version the hero saves a virgin from death and causes the custom of human sacrifice to be abolished. The cult, however, survives in connection with the bori or spirit Sariki Rafi. In the Songhay version the hero is Za; in Daura he is Makass-Sariki (Sariki-killer). The origin of the cult seems to lie in the East Sudan, where a similar sacrifice to a water-spirit is said to have existed. Za, it has been argued, is the same as the Egyptian god Sa, and means also Life and Bull. The Hausa, whose name has been taken to mean People of Sa and whose western advance has been dated around A.D. 1000, may have come from either Meroe or Siwa.[20]

According to Malalas, Andromeda was exposed to Poseidon himself; Nonnos merely says that this god sent the monster. Manilius says that the land was flooded on account of something that angered Neptune, and the oracle ordered the sacrifice of the daughter. Thus in these late accounts we do find a certain link between Andromeda and Aganippe, and the monster appears as a faded form of Yam. Ploutarch mentions that Typhon-Seth, in his plot against Osiris, was helped by a "queen coming from Aithiopia, whom they called Aso". This mysterious figure suggests at least some kind of romance-accretion in the myths of Seth-Horos-Osiris. As a sort of consort of Seth she might be Nephthys or Thoueris. The latter, as a sorceress in a magical papyrus of the 3rd century A.D., is described as Cat (?) of Aithiopia, Lady of the Uraeus, Sekmet Lady of Ast. If Seth were the hero, we might look back to the Ugaritic myths where Anat helps Baal and even takes part in the fighting; she causes Mot's death and later claims victory for herself over Yam, Mot, and Fire. We may recall that on the early vase-representation of Andromeda, she is shown helping Perseus to stone the ketos and is no helpless victim as she later appears.[21]

But we are no nearer to Min, who is in some respects a strange god with his strong fertility-aspects.[22] Only after Amun-Re draws him into Thebes under the Twelfth Dynasty does he quite fit into the interrelated pantheon of great gods. We cannot here examine him in detail, but will select some aspects that may have some bearing on our quest. First there is his link with the Red Sea and the Eastern Desert through Koptos and its roads. At Koptos have been found three very ancient colossi, perhaps the oldest large-scale sculpture of Egypt, which are unlike anything else in the tradition.[23] These standing nude figures were found in the ruins of a temple, and can hardly be other than Min or associates of his. They are ithyphallic (that is, have erect penises), but not in Min's traditional pose in which the right hand is raised with outstretched hand—the royal flail above it. This attitude has not been explained but appears in an engraving on a prehistoric sherd.[24] Here the left hands are in the position of ithyphallic Min, but the right arms hang down against the sides. The clenched hands are broken, but perforations show they held something—a penis made of a separate bit of stone; part of one survives in one statue. One statue has the remains of a beard, not the plaited beard normal for an Egyptian god, thin and tip-curled, but a bigger type.[25] The Koptos head has whiskers but is too battered to show if it had a moustache. Apart from the beard, the head is hairless, with high short skull—again unlike the heads of other Egyptian gods, which wear crowns of emblems. (Ptah and Khonsu have narrow skull caps to which the beard is fixed, or are swathed like mummies.) Altogether the fashion is quite unegyptian, though it is known in Assur and the sole one in Mari.[26] For date, the First Intermediate period has been suggested. We cannot, however, find any Egyptian works with which to relate it, though the stone is limestone from Turah and the statues were consecrated in the Koptos temple. The nearest analogy are the semi-divine attendants of the Mesopotamian fertility-god Abu, or the companions of the Bullman on the cylinder seals.[27] As Min was a Bullman and a fertility-god, the analogy may not be illusive; and Min, as Watcher and Lord of the routes to the Red Sea, may have had some important early links with Mesopotamia.

The statues themselves confirm the connection with the Red Sea at this early date. They wear only a multiple girdle. Along the right sides, below the fists, reliefs are pecked out. The subjects differ to some extent on each figure. The smallest figure has what has been seen as a stag with stick sticking from its mouth; below it are two pteroceras shells. The stag-head seems to stand upright on its mouth as if fastened to the stick; the shells, too, are set upright, with their mouths to the right. The second figure has two incised poles bearing the Min-emblems; below are the two saws of sawfish of the Red Sea, and two indistinct shapes that may be more pteroceras shells. The third figure has two Min-emblems, with an additional pole; below are again the saw of a sawfish and the shells. Above the right shell and under one of the

poles, shortened to fit in, is a bird—perhaps an ostrich. Below
the shells are two more panels. In the upper one is the forefront
of an elephant, his feet resting on hills; and to his right is what
seems the tail and the wing of a bird. Below is the forepart of a
hyena and a bull. These also seem to have their feet on a hill.[28]

91. Min's Primitive Shrine

The Min-emblems prove the link with Min; the other designs
are here alone connected with the god, but they point to a strong
association with the eastern desert and the Red Sea. (There are
no sea-creatures whatever in Egyptian hieroglyphs.) The belt
has no parallel in Egyptian art, but again points to Abu's attendants. The significance of such forms in Mesopotamia seems to be
heroic. They are related to the heroes who fight with beasts and
who are favourites of Early Dynastic and Sargonid seal-cutters;
such heroes are naked, save for multiple belts, and are bearded—
though not hairless.[29] The names of the Bullmen are not known,
but similar beings appear in the texts of Ras Shamra. In the
Hunts of Ba'al we hear of the creation of some demons: "They
have horns like bulls and a tail (?) like the powerful [bulls] with a
face of Ba'al." Called the Devourers, they seem related to the
man-faced Sumero-Accadian bull. Ba'al is perhaps the same as
Hadad, who was assimilated to a bull—though such an assimilation was anciently the prerogative of all the great gods, who thus

expressed their invincible force.[30] Whether the Koptos figures stand for Min or associates of his, the revelation about his cult is the same.

There is further evidence for a mixture of Egyptian and Mesopotamian elements early along the Red Sea. Sumerian ships may easily have gone out of the Persian Gulf along the shore of Hadramaut, through the Straits of Bab el-Mandeb, on to the Red Sea up as far as Sinai. These latter areas may be Magan, "the place to which ships went". A strange knife-handle has been found at Gebel al-Arak, on which a figure with feet ending in snakes looks Babylonish and there is a mingling of pre-dynastic Egyptian motives with a technique that resembles Mesopotamian work of Naram-Sin's period.

Does this rather point to an antiquity of Babylonian art much greater than that of Egypt? For the figure of al-Arak, presumably contemporary with predynastic Egypt, is perhaps that of a Semitic rather than a Sumerian Babylonian. As a god, though somewhat resembling Gilgamesh, he is unknown to Babylonian iconography, and if he is Elamite what is he doing in this galley, unless Elamites navigated the Red Sea in predynastic times? He looks like some god of the desert influenced by Mesopotamian-Elamite ideas brought to the coast (of Magan?) by sea, and represented by a predynastic Egyptian artist.

Min was a Bullman. The emblem in front of his archaic chapel was a pair of bullhorns; he was called the Bull of his Mother and the Strong Bull, and was represented by a white bull at his festival of art in Thebes.[31] Bull-horns still crown his bearded effigy in the shrine of a Roman stele from Koptos. Not that he is the only god with bull-forms in Egypt. Bull-imagery is fairly common in the Pyramid Texts. We meet the Bull of Heaven six times (perhaps some star, also the dead king, and a door-keeper of heaven and of the underworld), Geb as the Bull of Nut, Seth as a Bull (collapsing "because of his [lost] testicles"), the Bulls of Atum (who freshen N "more than the flood which is up to his breast"), the Bull of the Gods (here the Ferryman Looker-behind-him, a strong and faithful servant).[32] The Great Bull is often Re. The dead king is called the Wild Bull or the Great Wild Bull. A Double Bull stands at the double doors of heaven. The Great

Bull is described as the Pillar of the Serpent Nome (the obelisk of Re's city, Heliopolis): a reference to the Pillar of the Two Fighters, Horos and Seth—and the Bull of Heaven is linked with the Column of *kns.t*, a pair of which were at Heliopolis, thought to support the sky.[33] In other texts Osiris is the Bull who impregnates, and the Bull of the Two Sisters (copulating with both Isis and Nephthys). Horos is called the Bull of his Mother.[34]

But though Seth also has a strong Bull-element, Min is supremely the Bull of the Egyptian pantheon. As in the Near East, however, the religious imagery of the Bull goes deep and goes very far back, so that any god may use it for a moment to express a special influx of power. The phrase about Horos cited above appears much more often and more decisively in connection with Min, who is said to impregnate his mother, to be the most virile of the gods, the young bull impregnating his mother, to beget his own father and impregnate his own mother. We do not need to see Horos borrowing here from Min, though in later times he may well have been affected by Min's system of imagery. In a fragment from one of the Ramasseum papyri we find: "Hemen [mated with?] his mother Isis; he got his sister Nephthys with a daughter." Hemen is here equivalent to Horos; the two gods are linked in a Pyramid Text.[35] And so we find Horos as the mater of mother and sister as early as the

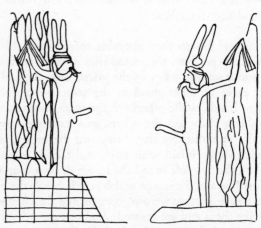

92. Min in his Beauty with his aphrodisiac lettuces

Middle Kingdom. But the bull-nature of Min is essential; with Horos it is peripheral. Bull-power is especially connected with fertilising energies and storm-blast. Min, of all Egyptian gods, brings these two elements together most obviously and richly. It is Seth's position as a storm-god with a thunder-voice that makes also a genuine Bull-god.

As a Bullman related to the Mesopotamian Hero we should expect Min to have myths of struggles with beast-monsters. But this, as already noted, we do not find. However, there seems good reason to find in certain festivals of Min the kind of ritual struggle not uncommon in Egyptian religion. At Bouto, we learn from a stele of the Roman period:

... you who come from the Marsh of God at the time when the plants are verdant to do adoration in the Festival of Horos and bring help to Min when he comes forth to his shrine-throne, pulled by horses, decorated with a red fillet, adorned with a pectoral, when all those who are in front of his shrine-throne tremble, seeing him in danger (?), but he comes forth safe, the disheartened one who is inactive is raised [in mind] when he has seized his lance and attacked his enemies. The people are given over to Him-whose-heart-is-wearied [Osiris].[36]

Though called a Festival of Horos, this is really one of Min. There seems an affinity with the festival at Papremis (probably in the north-western Delta, near the northern Chemmis and Bouto) which Herodotos describes:

In Heliopolis and Bouto they assemble merely to hold festival; but in Papremis they perform the sacred rites as well, as in other places. When the sun is setting, a few of the priests busy themselves with the image, but most of them stand in the temple-entry with wooden spears in their hands, while others offer prayers, more than a thousand men, all holding clubs like the others, and standing crowded against them. On the previous day they bring out the image, which is in a small wooden shrine inlaid with gold, and take it to another sacred building. And the few left round the image draw a four-wheeled cart bearing the shrine and the image which is in it, while the others, standing in the entrance, prevent it from going in, and the votaries, calling on the god, strike them and are resisted. And so a great battle with clubs follows, and they belabour each other's heads. Many, as I believe, die from their wounds, but the Egyptians denied that any one was killed. The natives say that this festival originated as follows:

The Mother of Ares lived in the temple, and Ares, having been reared away from home and having grown to manhood, returned with a desire to mate with his mother. His mother's servants, never having seen him before, did not let him approach, but drove him away. But he brought men from another city, and handling the servants roughly, entered in to his Mother. Thus they say arose the custom of this fight in the festival in honour of Ares.[37]

This ritual combat is often taken as being waged by Seth and Horos; but Herodotos speaks of Ares and Horos he equates with Apollo.[38] He has no certain identification for Ares. One possible equation would be with Montu-Re, the warrior god who steers the sun; the foe would then be the snake-monster Apepi.[39] But a case may be put up for Seth. Herodotos says the hippopotamus was sacred in the nome of Papremis; and Ploutarch says that creature raped its mother. It was sacred to Seth and his consort was Thoueris, the hippopotamus-goddess. But the Mother here seems more likely to be Isis, whom Horos rapes and who at one point favours Seth. The god of the rite shades off into Min, the other mother-mater. At Bouto the fight is to keep Min in the temple; here it is to keep Min or Seth out. (People were killed at Bouto; not so at Papremis, says Herodotos, though he clearly thinks his Egyptian informants may have been covering up darker aspects of the event.)[40]

We cannot then be sure, but we have the feeling that at this late period Horos and Min are closely connected in many ways, and myths of one god are entangled with those of the other. Min certainly had advents or comings-forth as important moments in his cult; and this fact may well underlie Herodotos' remark about the apparitions of Perseus at Koptos, even though he sets them in the neighbourhood as well as in the town. (A fertility-god like Min may have had local advents to help the fertilisation of the fields.) Incidentally, a Pyramid Text links Min and Horos of Bouto. "You command men like Min, who is in his house, and the Horos of Bouto."[41] And we must not forget the Hibis list of deities at Panopolis: Min, Horos, Osiris, Isis, and the trifid monster mingling bull, bird and crocodile.

Not only at Koptos and Apu-Panopolis, Min's two special cities, but also at Memphis (especially under the Old Kingdom), at Abydos (Middle Kingdom) and at Thebes (New Kingdom), we find these advents celebrated. The advent was essentially a processional movement of the god's statue, with stops at certain set places. From the New Kingdom the word "rise" instead of "come out" was used for the event. Min rises like a star. Thus, Nebuaui, a dignitary of the Eighteenth Dynasty, tells us on one of his statues that the king bade him "to go and make Horos Father-Avenger [a name of Min since the Middle Kingdom] rise in the House of Min, Lord of Apu, at all the feasts in Apu". The statue is to participate in the feasts.[42] Min is said to "rise" on the funerary temple of Sethi I at Gurnah; in the calendar of the Esnah temple in the Roman period, under 1 Pachon, we find the "rising of Min at each moon". (In this period Pachon 1 and 15, the day of the new moon and that of the full moon, were dedicated to Min or to his Theban form of Min-Amun; on the 1st, Min was taken to the Birth-House, his face turned in; on the 15th with his face turned out—of the naos?[43]) The Birth of Min is mentioned on the Palermo stone (Thinite Dynasties). This seems the original basis of the Coming-forth.[44] The *Book of the Dead* says, "I am Min at his Coming-forth. I have put two plumes on my head"; and from the New Kingdom commentators felt the need to explain. "What is that? Min is Horos Father-Avenger; his Coming-forth is his Birth."[45] The Coming-forth appears in Middle-Kingdom services for the dead; and formulas begin, such as "contemplate the Beauty [penis] of Min after his Coming-forth, and the identification with the Avenging Horos". The Coming-forth is listed at Medinet Habu under Ramses II among the eight Heavenly Festivals of the month; and at Esnah under the Romans there are three mentions. The first links Min with Renutet, goddess of the harvest. The second deals with 1 Pachon, the festival of the local triad, Khnum, Nebunut, Hika, when Min-Amun was carried in procession with his face "turned in" to the Birth-House, and participated at the side of Hika, together with the Father Khnum, during the festival days. The third deals with 15 Pachon, when Min had his face turned out.[46]

We may add here a few more words on the association of Min

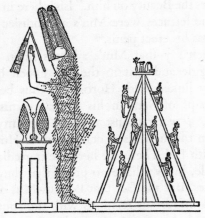

93. Min and his Mast

and Horos. In the great festival of Min, when a sheaf of grain was cut by the king with a sickle, the name in the late periods was not the Coming-forth, but the Festival of Heaven (Dendera) or the Festival of Father-Avenging Horos.[47] During the offering of the sheaf, the hymn cried, "Hail mother-impregnating Min. Secret are your dealings with her in the darkness," and ended, "Min is justified before his foes in heaven (and on earth) by his judges (or in the assembly of judges), the tribunal of each god and each goddess." At Philai we read, "King Min, powerful Horos, accumulating offerings in the Abaton," and on a stele of the Thirteenth Dynasty, in a hymn addressed to Min: "Your heart is united with the king, as the heart of Horos with his mother Isis when he impregnated her and consecrated his heart to her, when his side was close against hers without ceasing." This text is again found at Edfu, and is repeated in one of the two hymns on the pylon of the Ptolemaic temple at Athribis.[48] Ploutarch says the Egyptians have the habit of calling Horos Min.[49] In the Ramasseum we find him connected with the fight against Seth: "The flame goes out towards Seth and his companions," and "Min is triumphant".[50] The epithet Father-Avenging also shows him as Horos fighting with Seth; and in a calendar redacted or written under the Nineteenth Dynasty we read: "Min of Koptos goes this day in procession with the Lettuces [and] with his

Beauty; Isis sees the Beauty on him." Isis is here in a sexual relation to him; for the lettuces were Min's aphrodisiac and the beauty she stared at was his erect penis.[51]

We may then say that Min's advents often had a dramatic aspect of struggle and that in the late epoch he was in some respects closely linked with Horos. He thus becomes a foe of Seth and perhaps of Seth in his animal forms (especially the hippopotamus, a water-monster). His own myth of mother-mating led him through his association with Horos into a love-relationship with Isis. There are here the ingredients of a sort of Andromeda-tale, but we have no proof that they ever coalesced along those lines. But the fact that Perseus-Min of Panopolis and Koptos had his important relations with the routes and ports of the Red Sea, and that the Andromeda-tale was set on the Red Sea, must surely have some significance. But was the original setting of that tale the Red Sea and Aithiopia?

23

Perseus of the Sky

THE original setting of Perseus' exploits was the Oceanic Spirit-world, and we find this tradition continued on vases which use leaping dolphins to mark the location. Later, the usual attempts were made to give a definite geography to myth, and the Gorgon was linked with Libya. The Andromeda-tale was given two settings, one on the Red Sea, one on the Palestinian coast, at Joppa.[1] The earliest reference to Andromeda occurs in Herodotos, who sets her in the Persian area. Perseus, visiting her father Kepheus, got her with child and left his son Perses with her, as Kepheus had no other male heir, and Perses became the ancestor of the Persians. Herodotos also says that Xerxes adduced this genealogy in order to induce the Argives not to fight against him. We may therefore assume it was widely current in the 5th century and earlier. If Xerxes really knew of it, he must have been informed by Greek exiles or friends. Herodotos, however, makes no reference to any rescue of the princess from a monster; and it seems more than likely that he knew of no such story. The first definite location of the rescue that we know occurs in Euripides' *Andromeda* (412 B.C.), and there the setting is Aithiopian. Not for about a century do we meet the Joppa-setting.

However the evidence is extremely confused. Joppa was said to get its name from Aiolos' daughter Ioppe, whom some writers made the wife of Kepheus king of Joppa or Syria. (Andromeda's parents were Kepheus and Kassiopeia.) Mela says there were altars in Joppa inscribed to Kepheus and his brother Phineus; and we hear of a monster's skeleton on show in the city or by the rock where the girl was chained—on the rocks were shown the marks of her chains. Phineus was made an Aithiopian by Ovid; but he and his brother are also called sons of Belos, and it has been

argued that his name is a variant of Phoinix, the ancestor of the
Phoinikians. Euripides himself seems to make Kepheus the son of
Phoinix or of Belos. Hellanikos made Kepheus rule over the
Chaldeans; and if we look back to Hesiod, we find Kassiepeia
bearing Phineus to Phoinix.[2]

The weight of evidence does thus seem to place Andromeda
in the Near East rather than the Red Sea. Perseus was in much
favour as a city-founder; and in the Hellenistic period there was
much mythmaking in order to provide a good hero for a city.
Ake-Ptolemais, a Phoinikian city, shows Perseus with gorgonhead
on one side of a coin-type, his curved sword on the others, in the
3rd century A.D. He was said to be the founder of Tarsos, and
Salamis in Cypros is called by Nonnos the City of Founder
Perseus. Under the Romans Aigeai claimed him as founder. He
appears on coin-types of Tarsos, and other Kilikian cities:
Anemourion, Iotope, Katallia, Koropissos—the Koropissos type
shows Perseus, Andromeda, and dead monster. His cult at Ikonian
goes back at least to the last century B.C. However we sort out
with any precision the dates of Perseus' association with any of
such sites, it is clear that his identification with Ba'als, who had
their monster-slaying myths, was at least as early as later 6th
century B.C., even if it was in the Hellenistic and Roman eras
that the connections proliferated. So the tale of Perseus rescuing
Andromeda was a late variant of the great creation-myth we
discussed earlier. Perseus was the descendant of Seth fighting Yam.
Whether we approach him from the angle of Egypt or the Near
East, this point holds.[3] Far back, beyond all the genealogies and
the associations discussed above, we come to the legends about
Kadmos migrating from Phoinikia and Danaos from Egypt.

One of the picturesque details given in the Joppa-tale does,
however, tell in favour of the Red Sea. Near the shore there was a
spring of reddish water that had got its colour from the monster's
blood. Pausanias says that the hero there washed the blood from
his hands. Philostratos, however, says that the blood pouring
from the monster gave the Red Sea its name: Pontos Erythros
(the name is known to Herodotos for the whole Indian Ocean)—
Mare Rubrum for the Romans.[4] We should expect some such
myth to account for the name, though the comment of Philo-

stratos is no doubt a wild guess. In any event the tale of reddened
waters belongs to the series we discussed above, in which a spring
or stream turns red after some murder, the immersion of a cut-off
head, or the like. It would be interesting if we could link it with
the reddened Nile, but we cannot. Another important item in
this myth and its representations is the sickle-sword or harpe that
Perseus comes to hold. The first vases (starting with a Boiotian
pithos decorated in relief) show him with a straight sword. The
harpe first appears on an Attic black-figured neck-amphora of the
last quarter of the 6th century B.C.; Perseus is shown flying over a
dark mass of mountains with snow on their crests.[5] In literature
Pherekydes, contemporary of Herodotos, describes him as harpe-
wielding. The harpe links him again with both the Near East and
Egypt. It is found in the Ras Shamra texts: used by Anat against
Mot and by Mot against Aleïn. The word here is *hrb* (Hebrew
hereb): not knife or sword but sickle. *Harpe* may be derived from
it, and perhaps the Harpies with their crooked claws came from
the same root. But that root may well have been the Indo-
European *sirpe*, sickle. Samson's ass-jawbone was perhaps a *hrb*;
for no doubt there were bone-sickles, of which only the wood-
mountings have survived.[6] The *hrb*-harpe was a thunder-weapon.
We see it in the hand of a god who also brandishes the axe and
lightning-flashes: in Hittite sculpture near Malatia, dated about
1200 B.C.[7]

In Egypt the name was *hopes*.[8] New Kingdom texts shows a
belief in its inherent virtue. It is the weapon in particular for the
king, replacing the archaic club. "I am valiant as those who own a
hopes", and till the Ptolemaic period it held this special victorious
quality.[9] The Greeks translated the phrase which encloses it as
hoplon niketon, the weapon of victory.[10] In a tale about the taking
of Jaffa by a general of Thotmose III named Djehuti, the royal
club which the king has confided to him is so sacred that for
wanting to see it the prince is destroyed. The Egyptians get the
place by craft and the tale ends, "And it was the strong hopes of
pharaoh—life, health, force—that gained possession of the
town".[11] In the representations that general Horemheb had made
in his tomb at Saqqara (left unfinished when he became pharaoh),
we see him presenting to the king an Asiatic delegation come to

ask for aid against the Khabiri (Hittites): "[Send us] your strong hopes with the order of Amun."[12] A campaign is commanded, and the interpreters tell the delegation, "The Great-of-Courage will send his hopes ahead of him". The victory of Sethi I over the nomads infesting the road to Palestine was attributed wholly to the king's hopes.[13] On the walls of the Karnak temple we read of "the disaster inflicted by the strong hopes of the pharaoh—life, health, force—among the guilty ones of Sos, from the fortress of Tjaru [el-Kantara] to Pekana'an [Gaza]".[14] In representations of the preparations of Meneptah on the eve of the counter-offensive against Libyan invaders, we see Ptah appearing to the anxious king in a dream: "Take then this—giving him the hopes—and you will get rid of the disquiet you feel."[15]

The texts do not explain why the *hopes* has such a great virtue; but in view of the general evidence about the *harpe* we may assume that it represents the might of the thunderbolt. Min's ritual naturally involves a sickle in his harvest-festival; but though we do not find the hopes attributed to him, as a stormgod and bullgod he has a strong character of victorious power, of triumph in war. In the hymn to Min under Ramses III: "I am Min standing upon the mountains, after conquering all lands." In Ptolemaic times we find Min-Slayer-of-his-enemies-Resheph.[16] A hymn of the Nineteenth–Twentieth Dynasty calls Min the Great Bull and speaks of him "opening the rainclouds, the wind on the river".[17] The Bull of the Sky was also identified with the pillar or pole supporting the sky.[18]

As Perseus at Panopolis was always called Ouranios, Heavenly, in connection with his Games, the nature of Min as a sky-bull, a sky-pillar, a storm-power wielding the harpe-hopes of the thunderbolt, we may glance further at his pole, his mast. In the Sixth Dynasty Pepi II devoted a new town to Min's service, and the decree says: "My Majesty has commanded the setting-up of a pole of foreign wood. . . ." Such a dedication to Min involved freedom from the king's jurisdiction.[19] A Saqqara temple represents the setting-up of a Min-pole in this reign; and from the New Kingdom the scene becomes familiar—invariably linked with Min or his counterpart Amun. The title is "the setting-up of the Pole of the Bull (or the Bull of the Pole)."[20] Under the

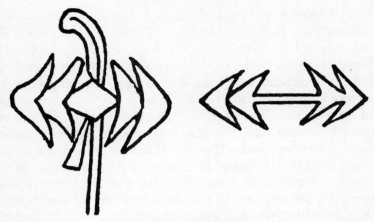

94. Min's (? thunderbolt) sign

Ptolemies we hear of Min "setting up for himself the Shrine of the Bull".[21]

The shrine was composite. A pole was linked by a cord to a small hut behind it. At first the hut stood alone, but by the Twelfth Dynasty the pole was added. Bullhorns were set on the pole: always the crescent-shaped pair represented on bulls. There was also a coil of rope which was itself sacred and which stood alone in the Third Dynasty; in the early Fourth it was coiled into the branches of a stick; then early in the Sixth it was raised on a pole and given a crest. Other sky-gods had poles. Khnum was said in Ptolemaic days to put "Nut under the sky like a great pillar of air".[22] A pole named *wh* was worshipped at Kousai, where Hathor was called by the Greeks Aphrodite Ourania; it was personified by a bull and is at least as old as the Old Kingdom.[23] In Syria we find Aphrodite Ourania as a meteoric goddess, at Aphaka near Byblos; and in Cypros at Salamis Aphrodite had the *harpe*. Her sanctuary there was in use from about the 12th century B.C. and scarabs of Egyptian origin have been found in it, as well as a phallos.[24]

Min as a sky-ascender also appears in the rite of erecting a mast before Amun-Min.[25] We see the construction in two successive scenes on pillars of the chapel of Sesostris I at Karnak. First comes the foundation-rite. A forked pole rests inclined on the fork of a shorter pole: it is the central mast of Min's tent—or at least its lower half. The title runs: "To consecrate (or offer) the red vases and the Amun-goose." This goose is the bird offered in foundation-rites.[26] The second scene deals with the erection or rather the consecration of the erected mast. The king holds his sceptre in his right hand before the mast in the normal gesture of consecration. The title runs: "To erect the mast of the *zhn.t* [tent] for Amun-Re." The mast is set upright and held by two lateral stakes with forks. The head of the mast is forked too. The raised mast is thus forked in a series of representations. In the temple at Luxor under Amenophis III, in the hall of four columns preceding the sanctuary of the sacred boat, on the west wall, in the third reister, we again see the consecration, with the formula that was omitted by Sesotris: "Strike, four times." The king here, like Sesostris, wears the white crown of the south. Min was a god of the south, and perhaps it was as lord of the south that the king carried out his cult. The mast is here made of two poles set end to end; each has a fork and the two forks are interlocked. This is the only example of such a mast.

There are many scenes where only the lower half of the pole has been fixed and this section ends in a fork. The pole thus shown was taken to be the whole tent-pole; but no representation of the tent shows the pole sticking out in a fork. These scenes of the single-forked pole then must deal with the first half of the operations; and the pair of scenes at Karnak explain the method used. The word *zhn.t* seems connected with matting; the tent was plaited with reeds—the sort of portable cover suited for the desert.[27] The image of the *zhn.t* accompanying its name is a thin tall cylinder with no door; but when set up behind the god it is often flanked with a proper Egyptian façade. We thus see the fusion of the desert-watcher with the established god at Koptos and Panopolis. Sky-ascents of one kind or another pervade Egyptian religion; but Min as thunder-god standing on the mountains has his special position as a sky-climber. Mt. Bakhau was thought to support the sky as early as the Middle Kingdom.[28]

Horos is often described as flying in the myths of his battles.

Lifting Heaven. Utterance. Your heaven belongs to you, O Bhdti

[Horos], brightly-coloured one. You fly in it [as the Winged Disk], you alight on the prow of the boat of Re-Harakhti . . . . The King of Upper and Lower Egypt is on his seat, lifting up heaven, supporting the god of Behdet. . . . He is like Shu who lifts up Heaven. (Edfu)

The myth is of the Winged Disk and tells of the conflict of Horos of Behdet and Seth. Near the beginning we are told:

Horos of Behdet flew up into heaven as the Great Winged Disk, and therefore he is called Great God, Lord of Heaven, to this day. When he saw the enemies in heaven, he approached them as the great Winged Disk. He stormed against them before him, and they neither saw with their eyes, nor heard with their ears, as each one slew his fellow in the twinkling of an eye, and not a soul lived.

It is perhaps not irrelevant to note that Perseus, who also flies about in his exploits, has the Cap of Hades, which gives invisibility. The myth—a late one from Edfu—also includes much fighting on water:

Now the foes descended into the water and became crocodiles and hippopotami. And Horos of Behdet in his boat voyaged on the water. Then the crocodiles and hippopotami came and opened their mouths in order to attack the boat of Re-Harakhti. (Horos and his followers bring harpoons and ropes, and smite the foe and bring away 651 of them.) . . .
    Then he saw his enemies, some of them fallen in the Sea and some of them fallen on the Mountains. And Horos of Behdet assumed the form of a manfaced Lion crowned with the triple crown, his arm being like flint, and he hastened after them. . . .
    Then those foes fled before him, their faces being turned to Lower Egypt, from Lahun to the edge of the Sea, for their hearts were faint. . . . And Re said to Horos of Behdet: "Let us sail to the Sea so that we may drive the enemies, whether crocodiles or hippopotami, from Egypt." And Horos of Behdet said: "As you desire, Re, Lord of the Gods." Then he sailed after the remainder of the enemies which was in the Sea. Then Thoth recited the spells for protecting the boat and the boats of the harpooners, to calm the Sea when it was stormy. And Re said to Thoth, "Have we not travelled over all the Sea?" Thoth said: "These waters shall be called Waters of Travel from this day." . . .

Seth appears as a roarer; hence the name of the Place of the

Savage Cries. He turns into a roaring serpent, so that the serpent of a town is called the Roarer. And after the fight in the district of Hebenu the priest is called by a name written down with the figure of a man standing on the back of a Bull and stabbing down with his spear.[30]

We may now pause to glance at Perseus again. From the outset he is a flier, with winged ankles; and this aspect is stressed by Nonnon, who as a native of Panopolis must have known all about the Games there. Perseus appears often in this epic, mainly in connection with his battle against Dionysos—as was natural enough in a work entitled *Dionysiaka.* The struggle between these two figures is less known than Perseus' fight with Medousa and the ketos, but seems to have its link. As a sky-deity he fights the chthonic Dionysos. Deinarchos says that he killed Dionysos and buried him at Delphoi—hence the god's tomb there. A scholiast says that he cast him into the Lake of Lerna, which was perhaps the Hydra's lair. Pausanias and Nonnos set Perseus at Argos, and the story falls more into the usual pattern of the city-authority resisting the invasion of the orgiastic earth-cult. Now Dionysos is the winner. Euphorion says that the god and his wild women defeated Argos in the war against Perseus, and Kephalion that Perseus fled and took refuge in Assyria, where Belimos was king. Pausanias tells us that the women who fought for Dionysos

95. Pompeian painting with Perseus in a Dionysiac dance

against Perseus were the Haliai, the Sea-women. Altogether, the conflict reminds us of Horos of Behdet against Seth—except that in the changed setting Dionysos in the end has to come out as the conqueror.[31]

Nonnos sets Andromeda in the Red Sea. Hera beholds:

> along the Red Sea
> the tangled heap of Andromeda's smasht chains,
> the rock in the sand, the Earthshaker's horrible
> monster,
> Bitterly she averted her eyes not to glimpse by the
> sea
> the bronzeforged harpe of Gorgonkiller Perseus.[32]

Throughout he stresses the sky-nature of Perseus.

> Winged Perseus came to my house the other day . . .
> Nimblekneed Perseus waving his winged foot
> kept his course near the clouds, a wayfarer treading air,
> if truly he flew. But what use if ankle-swinging
> he windswam with that odd oarage of legs
> then crept on tiptoe, keeping a noiseless footfall . . .
> Pereus was ferrying over draughty Libya,
> swimming on wings and circling in the air
> a quickfoot knee . . .
> When may a ground-footfarer catch a winged air-
> voyager? . . .
> He flew into the mellay . . .
> Over Bromios head
> Perseus flew in the air, flapping his light wings.
> But Iobacchos lifted his frame, rose wingless
> high up near the heavens, with larger limbs, above
> Perseus flying, and near the sevenrayed sky
> put out his hand and touched Olympos and crushed
> the clouds; and Perseus quivered in fear, beholding
> the right hand of Dionysos out of his reach
> touching the sun, grabbing hold of the moon.[33]

It must have been because Perseus was so strongly ouranios that his myth managed to monopolise so much of the sky. Not only the hero, but Andromeda, Kassiepeia, Kepheus and the ketos were all raised aloft as constellations—the only example of such a related group among the stars. How, when, and why this happened is extremely obscure. No one has even asked why such a vast importance was given by Greek astronomers to the Andromeda-myth, or how they succeeded in convincing people in general that so many constellations should be allotted to it. We may say as a limit that there was no sign of the group before 575 B.C. Thus it has been argued that probably Plinius was right in attributing the introduction of the Zodiac among the Greeks to Kleostratos. The sky was already divided thus into twelve zones when the Perseus-constellations were worked out, for they had to make room for the Ram and the Fishes. So the date must be before 550, but not much earlier.[34] This reasoning, however, is by no means watertight. There is general agreement that the Zodiac has a Babylonian basis. We have several Babylonian and Assyria lists. That nearest the Greek is not later than the 8th century B.C.; it includes the Bull-of-Heaven, Twins, Crab, Lion, Corn-ear, Scales, Scorpion, Archer, Goatfish, Waterman, Canal, Farm-labourer (our Ram).[35] The Greek Zodiac was perhaps devised in the 4th century, with the constellations much earlier; it was in Hellenistic times that the Egyptian decans were brought into a fixed relation to the Babylonian Zodiac (which is attested in Egypt only in the Ptolemaic period).[36]

As far as the literary and iconographic evidence goes, we should expect the constellations to have been worked out at the earliest in the late 6th century, and to have been established by the mid-5th century. Euripides at least was well aware of their existence; and the growing popularity of the Andromeda-legend about that time supports this dating. We can say at least that the evidence from astronomy does not contradict it. But we still have no clue as to why the Perseus-group about this time invaded so much of the sky.

However radical was the allocation of this group to the constellations, it must have had antecedents. The constellations in question, even if renamed, must have been already to some extent marked out.[37] But it is difficult to draw a precise map of the Babylonian and Egyptian constellations. As far as we can make out, the skymaps in Egyptian tombs and the Babylonian tables

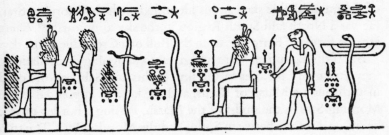

96. Decanal Stars

do not show the same groups divided out in the same way. In pre-Zodiacal days the Egyptians divided the sky into 36 sections, which they called Bakiu and the Greeks Decans; each decan had its god and corresponded to ten days of the wandering year of 360 days.[38] In a sky-map of the Eighteenth Dynasty, in the tomb of Senmut (Hatshepsut's architect):

In the centre of the northern hall appears the bull-headed constellation Meskhetiu—our Great Bear—and the circumpolar star groups. Across the sky the twelve ancient monthly festivals are drawn, each in a circle with its norm of 24 hours, and below, the celestial bodies of the northern sky pass in procession. Opposite, in the southern skies, Orion stubbornly turns his face away from the smiling Sothis, who chases after him beckoning fruitlessly year after year. Above them in turn come the lists of the Dekans with the name of Hatshepsut herself introduced among the heavenly beings.[39]

It is perhaps incorrect to look for any stem of constellations in the most ancient Egyptian sky. The gods became stars, not constellations.[40] Certain stars have strong god-associations and developed myths. We have already glanced at Sothis, the Dog-star. Sah, who has been identified with our Orion as well as the star Canopus, forms a triad with N and Sothis in the Pyramid Texts; he was called "the fleet-footed long-strided god, pre-eminent in the land of the South", and was merged with Horos and Osiris. He was a heavenly ferryman and was depicted as running with his face turned round. Lion-headed Shesmu, who hacked into bits the bodies of the Osirian damned, was set in the 16th decan.[41] Horos is the star that ferries over the sea, the chief of the imperishable stars and is identified with the Morning Star. He has a North and South Region in the sky as on earth.[42] There are also forms of Horos spearing the Bull or a Crocodile in the sky.

But if the Egyptians were not given to designing constellations, they saw many pictures in the sky. Sothis and Sah lead the dead man through a Marsh of Reeds, and the latter is appointed as the Morning Star in the midst of the Marsh. Passing a border-guard, he sits on a throne between Sothis and the Morning Star. The two stars lead him to the Marsh of Offerings north of the Marsh of Reeds; here there is an island with the tree of life, and the stars like swallows fly over. On the Winding Watercourse the face-behind ferryman is united with N and ordered to ferry him over.[43]

In many ways the most important group of stars was what we call, after the Greeks, the Great Bear. We have already considered it in connection with the iron sky, Seth as meteoric iron, the Skybull, the Foreleg of the Bull, and the iron instrument for opening the mouth of the dead man and restoring his life. Here was the home of Seth as Lord of the Northern Sky. (In a tale written in a late Egyptian idiom we hear of Horos as Lord of Lower Egypt, living at Memphis, and Seth as Lord of Upper Egypt, living at Shas-hetep. They fight, Horos as a youth, Seth as red donkey. Horos, winning, cuts off Seth's leg.)[44] Ploutarch calls the Great Bear the soul of Typhon and iron his bone.[45] The Beduin of the Western Desert still use the name of the Leg for it. Opposing the Foreleg or Mshtyw was a constellation called the Uplifter of Wings or Claws. The wing-claws are represented by raised arms, which are the essential feature. The Uplifter seems to have been part of what we now call Cygnus, probably the Greek Ornis. Like the Foreleg, the Uplifter gave its name to one of the instruments used for the mouth-opening rite, but not, it seems, till the New Kingdom. The figure of the Uplifter stretches a cord between his two raised arms.[46] The cord is at times carried straight through to the Foreleg: for instance, in the tomb of Senmut; but in the Ramesseum the figure has dropped one arm and seems to be throwing or thrusting a spear. By the Roman period there is certainly an attacking gesture. Perhaps the change in the Ramesseum was deliberate and myth has been invading these stars and drawing them together.

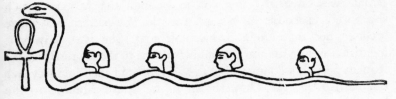

97. The Four Sons of Horos

The conflict of Seth and Horos seems, then, certainly to be invading the area of the Bear and the circumpolar stars. There is Seth lordly in the sky, and every night Horos rises against him.[47]

About 3500 B.C. our polestar set nearly every night and was probably lost in earth-mist, while the Bear was circumpolar throughout the pharaonic period. It therefore served instead of the polestar. Not only was it one of the most impressive constellations; in turning on itself it indicated the pole and was the only constellation of any importance that never set.[48]

We are close to the Perseus-group in Bear and Cygnus. Cassiopeia, like Cygnus, faces the Bear from the other side of the pole, at about the same distance. Together they stand out as a specially brilliant trio. Cassiopeia may well be the man who stretches out his arms in Seti's tomb between the Bull and the Uplifter. At least by the Graeco-Roman period the tales of Horos and Seth in conflict have invaded this area; and the idea of a hero attacking a monster is at work. The originating point of the Perseus-figure, it has been suggested, was the little cluster of stars that came to be taken at the medousa-head he carried in his left hand.[49] At places like Koptos and Panopolis the Horos-figure could easily be identified with Min. Connected with the Foreleg was a Hippopotamus-goddess, who, in this sky-role of hers, was shown with a crocodile on her back. She was Thoueris or Taurt, the Great One, a mother-goddess, who protected both the living and the dead, a heaven-goddess, Eye of Re, and especially a protectress of women in childbirth. In the last-named role she remained very popular in Graeco-Roman times. She was the wife of Seth, Ploutarch says, and she might thus have been the raped mother of the Papremite rite which we discussed.[50] While the male hippopotamus remained a Sethean creature of evil, the female was essentially benevolent—though the way in which she bore a crocodile on her head in the sky-pattern may have inclined her there to a Sethean element. She was, however, identified with Mut and Isis; and if we are to see, in the Graeco-Roman period, a conflict of Seth and Horos in the night-sky, we can perhaps see the Thoueris–Isis figure as contributing to the image of a woman for whom the gods fight. (Magical love-papyri speak of Isis' longing for Horos.)[51]

Here, however, the argument begins to fade out in tenuous conjectures. But there does seem to be some ground for holding that elevation of Perseus Ouranios of Panopolis to the skies in a fixed position owed something to the development of Horos-images of monster-conflict among the circumpolar stars. What remains more difficult to explain is why and how the elevation was carried out, perhaps around 450 B.C. The unity of the conception, involving all the main characters of the Andromeda-story—though two of them, Kepheus and Kassiepeia, were extremely minor ones in the world of myth—suggests strongly a single operation carried out by a single person or by a group with shared ideas. And who in the 5th century had the authority to bring about such a drastic regrouping and renaming of constellations is a question to which there seems no answer.

The Korinthian amphora proves that the legend was known in the later 6th century, but suggests a primitive sort of folktale. The story must have had time to spread and become well known before the fixing of the constellations would be at all likely or possible. We thus come back to the date 450, which preludes the proliferation of the theme in vase-painting and drama. Sophokles and Euripides seem to have done much to popularise the tale, but could not have initiated it. In so far as we can judge, they seem excited by a star-setting which has only recently come up. And if we look at the year 450, we find, oddly, that the Greek world had its eyes turned with much interest on Egypt at that moment. The Athenians had taken advantage of the uprising led by a Libyan chief in the Delta against the Persian lords of Egypt. The generals sailed for the Nile with all their force; after routing a Phoinikian squadron on the Nile, they sailed upriver, joined with the rebels, took Memphis (then the capital), and set siege to its

98. God on Snake

citadel, the White Castle. Part of the fleet raided Phoinikia, the base of the Persian naval power. A squadron of 50 galleys later sailed for the Nile to relieve part of the besieging force; then late in the year, 454, came disaster. The Persians invaded Egypt, relieved the White Castle, blockaded its blockaders on an island in the Delta, diverted the water from the channel in front, and stormed the place. Only a remnant got away across the desert to Kyrene. The relieving fleet was trapped and only a few ships escaped. About the same time a Thessalian expedition failed. In the spring of 450 Kimon tried to retrieve the Egyptian debacle by taking a fleet of 200 ships into the Levant, halting at Cypros and sending 60 ships to help the rebels in Egypt, where a prince was still holding out in the marshes. Kimon beat off a Persian attack, but gained only the respite for a retreat.

Round 450 the thoughts of Greeks, and especially Athenians, were thus turned on Egypt; and Kimon's expedition had plunged into the region, Kilikian and otherwise, where we have also found the trail of Perseus. Perhaps the idea that a Greek hero had once slain a sea-monster in the Egyptian world had a strong appeal at such a moment.[52] The older legend of Herakles slaying Bousiris, the Egyptian king who sacrificed strangers, was an example of Greek propaganda, setting them out as civilisers among barbarians.[53] A short passage surviving from Sophokles' *Andromeda* suggests strongly that the same patriotic moral was there driven home.

> She was slain for the state as a bloody victim;
> for savages have the immemorial custom
> of paying a human sacrifice to Kronos.

He also seems to have shown the rival suitor Phineus as an effeminate oriental, quickly destroyed by Perseus.[54]

This is mere guesswork. All that one can claim for it is that it makes the best possible picture out of the available evidence. Kimon, in 468, had excited great popular interest when he brought back what were believed to be the Bones of Theseus from Skyros—and, straight on his arrival in Athens, played an important part in gaining Sophokles his first victory—one over Aischylos. Perseus was a hero who could be claimed rather by Argos than Athens; but in the 450s Argos had been an Athenian ally and sent a contingent of a thousand men to fight beside the Athenians at the battle near Tanagra. Perseus might then seem a suitable enough hero to represent the superiority of Greeks over Egyptians. We are not sure of the date of Sophokles' play, save that it was well before that of Euripides (412), which displaced it. But the few glimpses of it cited above suggest that it belongs to a period when the Egyptian expedition was still fresh enough in people's minds for its points to get effectively home.

What was happening in 412? Athens was again facing a difficult situation. The Sicilian expedition had ended in disaster; Sparta was hoping to build ships and bring Athens finally down; important islands like Euboia, Chios, Lesbos were threatening revolt; and the Persians, through the satraps on the Asian coast, were offering assistance to Sparta, which was gladly accepted. Thus the old national enemy had once again come into view in connection with an overseas failure, and Perseus might well again come into the mind of Athenians as the hero representing the Greek triumph over barbarians—Perseus against the Persai with whom he was also thought to be linked through Perses—while the Spartans, making a compact with the Persians, would be shown in the role of national traitors.

Such emotions may well have laid behind the revival of the theme, though, from what we know of Euripides' play, the heroic element was at least partly dissolved in romance. If the theme rose to favour as showing the Greek hero putting an end to barbaric human sacrifice and routing the inferior folk, it was as a love-romance that it continued to attract. Loukian tells us how under King Lysimachos, during an epidemic of fever, everyone "went mad with Tragedy, shouting imabics and kicking up a din. They mostly sang as a solo Andromeda's part in Euripides' play, rendering Perseus' speech in song." They went on day after day till held up by a cold spell. The popular actor Archelaos had performed Andromeda for them in the blazing heat, so "most of them took their fever away with them from the theatre; and later, on leaving their beds, they relapsed into Tragedy; the Andromeda kept haunting their memory and his Perseus with Medousa's head still flittered round in everyone's brain". On the Portland Vase, probably made by an immigrant Alexandrian in Italy under Augustus as a wedding-present, the love-romance of Peleus and Thetis is treated, and the heroine is shown fondling the ketos as she greets the young man. Here the sea-serpent has become a mild patron of lovers.[55]

99. Pompeian painting of Perseus and Andromeda: the full romantic setting

A certain verification of our thesis that in the 5th century Perseus as a myth-figure received a second burst of life as the representative of Greek civilisation confronting the "barbarians" of Asia and Africa, is to be found in the part he played in the next century as a model for Alexander the Great. Achilleus and Perseus, together with Herakles, were the heroes to whom Alexander looked as the forerunners or prototypes of his own adventurous aims; and in turn the aura which they lent his deeds helped in bringing about the divinisation of his person. Kallisthenes played his part in this latter development. Alexander was declared to embody Perseus, Herakles, and the Dioscures; and we are told that in Pamphylia the Sea worshipped him. Here, by devious byways, Alexander has become the inheritor of Seth, Baal, and Yahweh. Further, when Alexander made his journey to the Oasis of Siwa with its oracle of Amun, he saw himself as following in the wake of Perseus. Achilleus, who was thought to have faced the Asianic world at Troy, and Perseus, merged with various thundergods and fabricated into the vindicator of Hellenic heroism in the world of Oriental "barbarisms", were the natural guides and models for Alexander in launching his crusade against Egypt and the East.[56]

That Perseus, now seen as an extensive city-founder, maintained his popular position is shown by Loukian's statement that the prophet Alexandros, his contemporary, declared himself to be Perseus reincarnated.[57] In folk-mythology Perseus continued to be a lord of thunder and storm; for we find that right into the medieval period a stone engraved with the sword and gorgonhead was considered to afford protection against storm and thunderbolt.[58]

What then can we say of our discursive examination of Min and Perseus? Nothing conclusive has been proved, but we have learned something of the interconnections of Egyptian and Greek cultures, and have raised several important questions. It seems likely that Min-Horos was identified with Perseus in the early days of Greek penetration, and that folklore about the constellations, born out of broken-down elements of earlier Egyptian astronomy, saw a conflict of Min-Horos and the Sethean monster in the region of the sky where lay the old Bull's Foreleg. Perseus, as the winged adventurer into the dangerous spirit world, easily gathered a story about the rescue of his bride from a monster; and in this story were collected diffused elements of the Yam-battle from both Egypt, Syria, Kilikia. The decisive moment for this story to come up into art and literature was the mid-5th century with the disastrous Egyptian expedition of the Athenian League; and it was probably then that Aithiopia and the Red Sea became the location. The mythical nature of Aithiopia, which we have noted, and the link of Min with the Red Sea, no doubt helped in thus pinning the story down. Sophokles, though not inventing the episode, seems to have given it an importance which it then never lost. The star-links of Horos and Seth provided the impetus for the working-out of the constellations in terms of the contest with the *ketos*; and this new patterning of the sky must surely have been carried out at Athens—though our ignorance of the social organisation of astronomy at the time prevents us from saying how it was done and how the scheme was imposed on the whole Greek world. All we can say is that about the same time as Sophokles' play there was considerable astronomic activity in Athens, where Phaeinos, Euktemon, and Meton were busy observing the heavens and working out systems. Theophrastos says that Phaeinos had some sort of observatory on Mt. Lykabettos, where he noted the solar tropics, and that as a result Meton devised his cycles of nineteen years. Euktemon appears to have especially observed the rising and setting of stars. If we are right in surmising that this group, who would in such a small, close-knit community be in contact with the poets, raised the Perseus–Andromeda story to the skies, we still read in the stars a story which was meant to express the supremacy of Greek culture despite a check to Greek arms. (Meton had a healthy fear of overseas adventures; for we are told that he feigned insanity to escape being sent off in the calamitous Sicilian expedition.)[59]

In our wider quest we have followed the trail of the Nile, considered the ideas that the Egyptians, Greeks, and Romans had of the river, its sources and its virtues, and have looked at the people who in the Roman period sailed up and down, or across, its waters. This has involved us in an examination of the corn-ships and of tourist travellings as exemplified in the Theban area. Continually the search has drawn us into the fundamental questions of Egyptian religion and thought; and we have found continuity between the ancient creation-myths such as that of Seth and Yam, and a late legend such as that of Perseus and Andromeda. In the process we have learned much about the ways of ancient thinking, of the lines on which concepts of the totemic tribe developed into complex and sophisticated world-systems, and have touched on many suggestive points of relationship between Greek and Egyptian modes of thought. The detailed examination made possible both by the wealth of religious texts and of private papyri is something unique in the ancient world, and enables us to see the rich crisscrossing of social and personal aspects in a way that we can mostly only guess at in other areas.

100. Souls of Re and Osiris meeting in Tetu (Busiris): Ani, ch. xvii

"Who is this Divine Soul? It is Osiris. He goes into Tetu and finds there the Soul of Re, the one god embraces the other and two Divine Souls spring into being within the Divine Twin-gods."

Notes

See the Bibliographies of the previous two books for the collections of papyri, etc. Here, at the outset, I should like to pay a special tribute to C. Préaux, for material on the Greeks and Africa; D. Bonneau, for many details about the Nile; Wainwright for the discussion on Min; Rowe, for the list of Blessed Drowned; Merzagora, for material on the Nile-boats.

In the Notes, apart from abbreviations for periodicals, I use the following: B. for Bonneau; LD for Lanzone's *Dizionario*: J.L. for myself; W. for Wilcken and M. for Mitteis; RT for Receuil des Travaux.

1. THE NILE

1. Erman (4) 146 and (5) 193; Maspero (4); B. 406; Moret (6) and (10) ii 13; Pritchard; Bacchi; Roeder (8) 327–39.

2. Posener (4) 1176, 1190–3; Bruyère (1).

3. *Phars.* x 268 ff.; mentions also Aethiopia, Meroe, Philai and *abaton*. "Nature has revealed to no one his hidden source. Men have not been permitted to see the stripling Nile. She has concealed his lairs, for she prefers the nations should marvel than know." States Nile rises at equator near the Seres (Chinese). For Sesostris legend: Diod. i 94, 4; 53 ff.; 73. For the facts: Posener (7) esp. Conclusion. Also Malaise. Orphic *Makrobioi*: J.L. (1) 37.

4. See Moorehead (1), (2) and (3), plus refs.

5. Diod. i 32, 7–11.

6. Branches of Delta: Toussoun.

7. Brooks, *Evolution of Climate* 72 (citing Hume and Craig).

8. G. Murray (3).

9. Butzer (1) and (2); C. Vandersleyen, CE xl 343 f.

10. Butzer (1) 35, also (2) with refs. Name of Lake Moeris: Gardiner, JEA xxix 37; C. F. Nims, JEA xxxiii 92.

11. Griffiths (1) 146–7; Wilson (1) 29; E. Otto (1) 20; Frankfort (2) 50. Nomes: Helck (1) 78. Baumgartel (1) 46 dates district organisations to later phase of Naqada II.

12. Oxy. 1482: SP (Loeb) i 124: God is Zeus.

13. PT 292a–d.

14. Erman (4) 113; Gardiner (21); Posener (7) ch. i. Cf. Pap. Petersburg 1116a, recto: "I captured it like a flood of water" (cf. *Piankhi* 27, 96). "The mudflat (?) is replaced by a flood. There is no river that suffers itself to be

concealed, but it loosens the dam by which it lay hid. [Thus] also the soul comes to the place it knows." As flood recurs and soul returns, God comes back to claim his due(?). JEA i 28, 33 f.

15. Pap. from Kahun, Twelfth Dynasty, Erman (4) 136; Griffith (6) 1 ff.

16. Ramses: *Rec. Trav.* ii 116. Thoth: Pap. Sallier i 8, 2 ff.

17. JEA iii 108.

18. Blackman (6) 289 (Pap. Lansing): some phrases uncertain. In general, Caminos (1); cf. Erman (4) 193 (P. Sallier i 5, 11; Anastasi v 15, 6 ff.), "The worm has taken half the corn, the hippo. has devoured the rest. The mice abound and the locust has come down. The cattle devour and the sparrows steal," etc.

19. BGU 802 i–ii, 13; REg p. 408.

20. Ryl. 243.

21. Lines 120–3; J.L. (2) 115.

22. Petrie ii 13, 19. For Ptol. drainage: SEHRE 281.

23. Tebt. 56; M. *Chr.* 59, 31–3.

24. J.L. (3) 28.

25. Ryl. 80.

26. Oxy. 1834. For Apthous, also 1891, 1959–62, 1994; Eulogios, 1876. Gessias: St. Pal. x 94, 5: prob. not far from Palosis which in 3rd c. was included in toparchy of Thmoisepho (Oxy. 1285).

27. Str. xvii 817.

28. Borchardt, *Abh. Pr. Ak. Wiss.* 1906; GRR i 1290; CIG 4863; REg 1. System seems based on levels not chronology.

29. Str. xvii (788); Plin. v 58: Arist. *or.* xlviii 485 (Dindorf).

30. Vogt (1) cites for years 97–8, 98–9, 101–2, 108–9, 109–10, 132–3, 164–5, 165–6; Poole for 127–8, 128–9. No evidence whether these years good or bad.

31. Oxy. 1211, cf. 519; BGU 362 xv 11 (Arsinoe, Temple of Jup. Cap.); in general, Lumbroso (1) 1–8. Strategos: W. Otto ii 79.

32. Plin. v 58; Oxy. 486 (A.D. 131); Philon in Flacc. 63. An inscription (Preisigke–Spiegelberg 220; W. in *Hermes* 1928 48) of A.D. 18 (?) shows a high Nile; if date is correct, the distribution of grain by Germanicus at Alex. (winter 19) was not through dearth.

33. IGRR i 1110; Dion lxv 9 (A.D. 99); SB 6944 (136); BGU 12 (182); BGU 835 (216); Oslo. ii 27 (244).

34. Str. xvii (788).

35. Mich. 121, 123, 127; *Am. Hist. Rev.* 1935 480. Note lease of land at Ision Panga (after 260) injured by flood and to be given over to grass, Oxy. 1502.

36. Lond. 604. And Lond. 131R and 131V. No definite date for failure in Th. O. 133; Flor. 61 can be any time 48–88.

37. *Paneg.* 31; a gift of wheat to Alex. from Pisidia has no date: OGRR iii 409. And SB 6944; 7468.

38. REg 18–9.

39. Fay 33 (A.D. 163), Euhemeria; Bour. 42 (167), Hiera Nesos, etc. In general, Vandier (3).

40. P. Turin 2131; Revillout *Rev. Eg.* iii 1883, 137. Cf. Kaplony–Heckel no. 14; P. Cair. 30. 713; P. W. Pestman CE xli (82) 317.

41. Kaplony-H., *Tempeleide* 186.

42. War: Giss. bibl. 5; see also BGU 1266; Lewald, *Frankf. Pap.* 14 ff. In general, Berl. *Leihg.* 194. Crop-failure: Mich. iii 182. For *abrochia*, drought: Waszynski, *Bodenpacht* 132 ff. Also Princeton iii 148 (A.D. 172–3); OGI 56. 15; CPH 119 ii 22 (3 c. A.D.); Hib. i 85; BGU 455 (lc. A.D.). Ptol. III remitted some taxes in years of low Nile and famine, OGIS 56 line 18.

More systematic work is needed on the history of Nile-levels. Thus the Meroitic village on the west bank north of Abu Simnel had its earliest houses built on a rather thick stratum of river-mud. It would then appear that not long before the settlement began the Nile had here been flooding; there were no signs of later flood. The problem later seems to have been to keep the sands coming in from the northwest. H. Jacquet-Gordon, CE xli (81) 124. See Trigger further for variations in rainfall and Nile-flood, and sand-pressures in Lower Nubia.

2. THE SOUTHERN BARRIERS

1. Original Nilotic unity: Diod. iii 3–4; Seligman. Neo-Egyptians and Aithiopians: Giuffrida-Ruggeri, *Man* 1916 No. 55.

2. Wainwright (6).

3. Desert route: Strab. 770; H. F. C. Smith. The other great route (that of 40 Days) swerving from Nile went west through oases to Kyrenaica. Rekhmire: Sethe (2) iv 116, 4; de Buck 40. Taharka: Vikentiev (2) 63; Vandier 256. Saite: Petrie (16) ii pl. xlii 15; de Buck no. 24; B. 195 f.

4. In general, H. Junker (4); Emery (2). Kerma: G. Reisner (2); Säve-S. (3). At Sesebi, two lifesize Negro heads: CE 1937, 190–2.

5. Abu Simnel: SB 8544. Expedition: Tod, *Gr. Hist. Ins.* (1946) no. 4; Emery (2) 223; Ditt. *Syll* (3rd ed.) no. 1; Sauneron (5). Karnak: M. Muller (2) i 22 f. (4th Cat.), Préaux (3) 291 (2nd Cat.). Also Hdt. iii 18–25; Legrand iii 23 f.; Hennig (2) iii 201–6; A. Klasens (2) 344 f.; Sauneron (6) 205 f., n. 6; Säve-S. (5). Also MacIver 40. Since the M.K. the fortresses of Semneh and Kumneh at 2nd Cat. protected Egypt from southern attack; there seems no town in this area, but there could be a trade-centre or place of transhipment like Napata or Meroe lower down. For Psammetichos II: BIFAO l 1952 157–207; Wainwright JEA 1952 75–7; Shinnie 32–4 (who calls Pnubs Argo, 37). For inscr. see L. H. Jeffery, *Local Scripts Archaic Gr.* 1961 355.

6. Strab. 822; Dunham (6). For the whole of this section I rely much on Préaux (2). Under Sixth Dyn., Uni, governor of south, organised the digging of 5 canals through the parts of the 1st Cat. most intractible for navigation.

7. Hdt. ii 30; Str. 770.

8. Préaux (3) 292 f.; Hurst 112–17; Wainwright (6). Hdt. ii 19–26 seems not

to know of Aithiopian rain. Greeks in Kambyses' army, Hdt. iii 25; Préaux (3) 302. Also Leclant (1); Wainwright (6) 260, n. 4.

9. Hdt. ii 25; Str. 820.

10. Hdt. ii 29.

11. Hdt. ii 32. Exploration of the south had gone on via Carthage and Kyrene.

12. How–Wells i 177. Via oases south of K., and by a western route, as in Herkhuf's time, one could reach Central Africa without touching Aithiopia: Préaux (3) 295.

13. Sethe (12) and (3) ii 57 ff.; Kees (8); and Griffith (4) 1–4. Egyptian penetration into Lower Nubia, Eleventh Dyn., Emery (2) 139 f.; fortress chain begun by Senusret I, 142–55. Also JEA iii, Clarke, and Gardiner, *ibid*. C. Resiner, *Kush* viii 1960. M.K.: Emery (2) 94, Reisner, *Harvard Afr. St.* v and vi 1923. Hurst 76; Reisner (2) iv–v 538 f. esp. ch. 34. "Land of 12 Ar" (ar = about 7½ miles): under Ptols. the priests of Philai claimed the area had been given to Isis: Bevan 246. A 3rd c. inscr. on isle near Aswan purports to record a gift of the area to Khnum.

14. Préaux (3) 297 f.; Sauneron (6) 176 n. 7 and 187 for Kareima–Meroe. According to observations of Philon, at 16° 25′ (Strab. ii 77). Meroe–Napata: How 174. Dodek: colonised by Greeks under Ptols.: Emery (2) 224. No Roman cities to its south, 235.

15. Sudd: Moorehead (2) 90. *Iliad* iii 37; Strab. xvii 821; i 37, 43; vii 298 f., cf. ii 70; Navarre. Skeletons from Karma indicate an Hamitic population with no perceptible Negroid presence in M.K. (Juncker). Also, Dunham (2) iv 143 f. Much more precise work is required before we dogmatise. Shinnie 155: "Nubia, together with most of the northern Sudan, is today inhabited by a predominantly brown-skinned people of aquiline features having in varying degrees an admixture of Negro, and there is no reason to suppose that the ancient population was very different." For the steady southward movement of Egyptian influences, note linguistic links with ancient Egypt of folk in N. Uganda today (A. Tucker, *Times* 16 Aug. 1967). Breasted, *Anc. Rec.* iii no. 480.

16. Emery (2) 131. Pepi's letter refers to another dwarf, brought from Punt in Fifth Dyn. Yoyotte (3) thinks the expedition was to Dunkul oasis (on the way today from Darfur). For dwarfs in ancient Egypt, Strackmans 622 n. 1.

Thotmose III had canal of Senusret at 1st Cat. cleared and repaired, and ordered Elephantine fishers to dredge it yearly. Egyptians in Nubia and beyond under Amenhotep II: Säve-S. (2).

17. Huy, viceroy of Tutankhamen in Nubia, was invested with seal of office assigning the territory "from Nekhen (El Kab) to Napata": 800 miles along the river: Emery (2) 189; Säve-S. (2) 141–245. Negroes, *ib.* 226–30; Nubians 230–40.

18. Juncker.

19. Préaux (3) 288–90. Evans, *P. of M.* ii 755–7, pl. xii. For relations, Kantor, Vercoutter, Säve-S. 222 n. 1 (against Evans's thesis of direct contacts via Kyrenaika: *P. of M.* ii 756).

Pygmies then as now were hunters of elephants as of marsh birds (*e.g.* cranes): Hurst 112–7, and may have purveyed ivory to Aegean world: Préaux (3) 290 n. 3; P. Demargne; Lorimer, *Homer and Mons.* 95; Dussaud (4) 341 f.; Kantor 85 ff.; Barnett, JHS lxviii 1–25. Aristotle: HA viii 697a4; Strabon denies, i (37, 43); vii (298 f.); xvii (821); cf. ii (700); Navarre. Hekataios (FHG i 10, 266) describes Pygmies disguised and using castanets in fight with cranes. Late example: Philostratos: J.L. (3) 314.

20. Lorimer 94 f. Before the 5th c. B.C. Aithiopia was simply the Hot or Burning Land: Pietschmann.

21. Mallet (1) 10–12 (2) 10–14, 190; Moret (1) 237–73; V. Bérard (1), (2), (3); Gilbert (1).

22. Petrie, *Hist. Eg.* ii 188; C. Smith, CR 1892 vi 464 f.

23 Diod. i 45, 7; Eichstädt rejects.

24. Moret (6) 393.

25. Gilbert 50–7; Mallet (2) 190; Berard (3) 247; Golenicheff, R. T. xxvii 72–112.

26. Maspero (7) 801.

27. *Od.* iv 131; Gilbert 50–2.

28. Gilbert 57–8; Mallet (1) 12; Berard (2) 176 f., etc.

29. Beardsley 9 f. and 76; Préaux (3) 302 f. Conditions in Egypt were bad; a weak Persian domination, anarchy through rebels in the Delta. In general: Diod. i 37, 5; Plin. vi 183; Leider; Rostovtzeff (1) i 381–3 and (2) ii 31 ff. For Cats., Jos. *Bell. Iud.* iv 10, 5.

30. Diod. i 37, 5. Kortenbeutel (1) 17 thinks aim was the mines of Wadi Alaki; Préaux thinks not (3) 263 n. 5.

31. Coin; MacIver 126. Names: SB 302.

32. SB 5111; Sachau no. 47.

33. Emery (2) 225.

34. Plin. vi 18, 3; Budge (13) ii 104–83 (texts). Mines: Diod. iii 12, 4. Fitzler tries unconvincingly to show the mines were of Wadi Alaki.

35. Strab. 786; Wainwright (6) 21.

36. Strab. ii 77; Plin. ii 183 f.; Kortenbeutel 15 f. Garstang found instruments (going back to 2nd c. B.C.) perhaps of observatory: LAAA vii 1914–16 1–24 esp. 4–6, 12: Greek or native?

37. Plin. vi. 183; 48; 180.

38. Griffith (4), *Dakkeh*, nos. 31–2; cf. O. Bodl. inv. 2998, a private letter: "three coming from Meroe". Cf. Roeder (10) 375–8, and ii pl. 23 (attempt to relate to Kandake). Sporadic occupation of Dodek., Roeder (10) i 171; Griffith (4) i 15–32. Lessening Eg. influence in inscrs. of Aithiopian kingdom shown by Meroitic script: Reisner, JEA ix 1923, 69.

39. Strab. xvii 54 (820–1); Plin. vi 181–2; Shinnie 44–8. Queen: (?) Amanishakhete: Shinnie 49. Inscr. at Dakkeh of 13 B.C. by a Meroitic mission; pap. of Milan (*J. R. Hist.* xl 57 ff.) dated 60–94 for fight in desert of Roman ala and Aithiopians. Also, JEA iv 159–73.

40. Stele: LAAA vii 23 ff.; but see Préaux (3) 266 f., esp. n. 4. Head: Shinnie 48, 79; LAAA iv 1911 66 ff.; 1912 74.

41. QN vi 8, 3; also Plin. vi 181, xii 9; Dion K. lxiii 8, 1; Schur 40-5.

42. Pap. Milano 40 (Turner): see n. 39 above; (?) Mich. 203. "Forts" between 4th and 2nd Cats., are square caravan-posts, often with towers, made of drystone; no proof they are Roman.

43. Préaux (3) 268 n. 3; 269 n. 1. Was there Nubian gold in GR Egypt? Strab. 822 cites it. No doubt it was used in exchange for the few GR luxury-objects found in Meroe.

44. Strab. 791.

45. Lefebvre no. 1094 (apostaleis) and 76 (Timotheos Pserkiokometes). The odd inscr. 76 needs more dissection than we can spare it here.

46. Mich. iii 203.

47. Erman (4) 205; Pap. Anast. iv 4, 11 ff. For an arrival at Memphis (2-3 c. A.D.: Oxy 160).

48. Frith 1912 (3rd season); Emery (2) 43. Pselkis was site of the cult of Scorpion-goddess Serquit, who was of Nubian origin: she is in the PTs. The Meroitic king Arqamani left his name at Philai and built at Pselkis, but by the 19th year of Ptol. V, Egyptian rule was re-established over the Dodek., and the only other incursion seems of 23 B.C. Arqamani's chapel is most north of Meroitic mons.; it is part of a temple. Several Ptols. built here, and the forecourt is a Roman addition: Roeder (10). As Ptol. iv also built at Pselkis there seems some sort of co-operation between Meroe and Ptol. Egypt at that time: Shinnie 63. (Bibliog. Meroe: Gadallah, Kush xi 207.)

49. B. 196-8; Préaux (3) 300; Od. iv 477; Il. xvi 174; Strab. xvii 790 (Poseidonios) and i 36—he wants to make Homer the father of geography, as Thoukydides takes him as a great historical source (i 9, 3); cf. Dubois (2) 169-80; Capelle 351. Homer and Egypt: Diod. i 69 and 97; i 12 and 96, 3; i 96, 2; Plout. De Is. 34; Gilbert (1). Zeus and rain: B. 197 n. 6 (who takes the term seriously); Wainwright (7) 13.

50. Diod. i 38, 4 (Agatharkides); Eurip. frag. 228 (Nauck, 2nd ed.), cf. Helen 1-3.

51. Persians: Hdt. vii 69; Trogs., Diod. i 37, 8.

52. Suppls. 559 ff.; cf. Prom. 809 ff. and frag. 300 (Wecklein). Date of Suppls. is uncertain: Oxy. 2256 fr. 3; Merkelbach (1) 101 no. 1075; J.L. (1) 92-5. Snowy top of the Ruwensori: Hurst 208; Préaux (3) 299.

53. Arist. de inund. Nili 194 and 306 n. 2; frag. of Archelaos, etc. See Berger 141-5 for authors and snow-theory; he thinks Anaxag. referred to condensation, but see Capelle 339. But we cannot tell if Anaxag. was building on a mythical or rational basis, or merely recording what had been seen. Préaux (3) 300.

54. De mens. iv 107; B. 201; Strab. xvii 1. 5. Thasian coins in Egypt from 6th c.: Roebuck. From S. Arabia (?) J. Pirenne. M.A. Inscrs. et B.L. xv 1955, 157-76.

55. Anon Flor. 4; Diod. i 39; Rehm 585; Ideler, *Phys. med.* 191; B. 201 f. Hellenistic scholars thought no Greeks went south of 1st Cat. before Ptol. II. See further B. 164–5 (Aristotle), 165–8 (others).

56. Diod. i 39, 7; Préaux (3) 303; B. 199 f.; Mallet (2) 138. Ephoros: B. 165; Arist. of Smyrna, *Disc. Eg.* 70; Seneca, B. 166. Also Nikagoras of Cypros (Aristot. DIN 9) and sc. Ap. Rh. iv 269. Etesian Winds: B. 151–9 from Thales on.

57. Diod. i 40, 1–4; B. 199; Préaux (3) 305.

58. PT 794 ab.; Brugsch (3) 328; Budge (14) 182 f. Also, CT i spell 45, 196c; PT 861b; Sethe AZ lvii 1–50; Brugsch (5) 322.

59. For fuller discussion: B. 2e partie, and Préaux (3).

60. Préaux (3) 306 for Silver Mountain, etc.

61. *Ibid.*, 309–11 for refs. etc.

62. *Ibid.*, 311–12; Strab. xvii 785; Diod. i 37, 9; Nallino, etc.

3. THE SACRED RIVER

1. Heliod. ix 22, 5–6; J.L. (3) 27. For numbers, *Etym. Mag.*, etc.; Neilos: Eustath. ad Dion. *Per.* 222; Abraxas: Barb. Also Campbell.

2. Nonnos xii 23, cf. xxii 276; for Aphrodite, Empedokles frag. 151. Horos: Hdt. ii 144, 2; 156, 5.

3. B. 288 f. Abraxas: PGM viii 51 (Lond. 121); xi 50 (Lond. 124); xiii 647 (Leyd. 395). It is a magical term "in Thoth's language", *kynokephaleite*: PMG *ibid.* 597. See also Budge (21) 179–81.

4. Gardiner (16); B. 219; Mercer (1) 185.

5. De Buck (2).

6. Wängsted 231 (no. 61, 5).

7. Derchain (1) 489; B. 242.

8. Caillaud, *Voyage à Meroe* 1829 ii pl. xvii no. 9.

9. B. 220 f.; Derchain (1) 490; AZ xliv 1907, 114; xlv 1908, 140 f., Erman and Gardiner.

10. Lanzone *Diz.* pl. 198; and Muller (1) 94, fig. 85.

11. Derchain (1) 491.

12. B. 223 f.; bearded Hapi from Tanis, Twenty-first Dyn., B. 226; Maspero, *Guide Mus. Caire* 1915, 152 f.; male and female figures: ASAE liv 1956, 369.

13. Derchain (1) 489; B. 244.

14. Smith, *Eg. Sculpture*, 183 fig. 71; RT 1913, 89 (nos. 43 f., 67 f.); B. 224 (refs.). Note 14 Hapis either side of holy-of-holies in Hathor Temple, Dendera: Mariette (1) 60 and 242.

15. LD iii 175a, 200d, 218d. Neilopolis: Neilos of Hekataios: Steph. Byz., FHG i 277.

16. Lisht: Gautier 36; Griffiths (1) 69. Sia = Intelligence, Griffiths 56. She is in the sun's nightboat, Hu is the steersman: Budge (1) 96. Duality, cf. Griffiths

56 n. 4. Duality as intensification: Breasted (4) 299 n. 2. Hu, also Gardiner, PSBA xxxviii 43, 83.

17. B. 225–6.

18. *Disc. Eg.* 25.

19. Horapollon, *Hier.* i 21, turns to hieroglyphs: the Vases refer to origins from earth, rain, ocean (Nun).

20. B. 226–8. Ramessid impulsion of the cult, 227.

21. Derchain (1) 491.

22. PT 22a; Mercer iv, excursus x.

23. PT, utterance 448 (1048a–1049b).

24. Utt. 303.

25. Utt. 548; Mercer ii 664–6. Adaptation of Utt. 697. Two Enneads, see excursus ii.

26. The *ka* is a complex concept: L. Greven; Faulkner (1). The summary definition here suffices for our purposes.

27. See later on Nun. Niw: Jéquier (4) 60 f.; WB ii 274. If the form be taken as pentilic, line 1346c ends, "the field of the Nunites".

28. She occurs in PT 1180b, 1564a, 2103a, 1285, 1348, 1749, 1995. See Sethe (4) 52. For *hnti : w–s*, see PT 762c, and Juncker (6) vi Bi; (5) 85.

29. Sethe (4) 52.

30. PT 1180c–d; Mercer iv exc. xi. Cf. PT 1140a, 1164b, 1293b, 1365a, etc. Eight are cited, 2012c.

31. PT 138b.

32. PT 1285a–b.

33. PT 765a–b.

34. Utt. 461 (871–4); commanding dead, 318b, 319c; heavenly throne, 1166d. Cf. 2173c, "N is transported over the *hnti*-ocean". Atum's cult was at Heliopolis.

35. Mni. t: 726a, 794c, 872b, 876c, 884b, 1347b, etc.; Muller (1) 148, Smentet.

36. PT 136a and 885; cf. 1446a. As (?) fish: 128a. Warning: cf. CT spell 67, 284 f.

37. PT 468. She greets the dead at a *mshn*-door; *mshn.t* was personification of the brick used by women in childbirth, and so a patroness of birth: PT 1183b. Birthplace of Re, 1180a.

38. PT 255a.

39. Sethe (6) iv 808; Griffiths (1) 73. Sethe says the Cat. of Elephantine, but we may take it to refer to whichever Cat. was being thought of as the source jetting from earth. Further on *kbhw*: Kees (1) 107, 117; Garnot (1) 12 and n. 1; Alliot (2) 80–1 n. 7; Weill (4) 24, notes 2–3; Jéquier (4) 59 f.; Hommel (1) 904 f.; Speelers (1) 166.

40. PT 155b, "an imperishable spirit, like the morning star over the Nile"; 292d, image of destruction by flood of farms; 435a, "a servant, as the Ennead's pelican fell into the Nile, flee, flee!"; see Mercer ii 202, 131. PT 671c, "a holy person who belonged to the Ennead once fell into the Nile", cf. 278b, 226a—

drowning of Osiris; 2047c, "it is Horos who comes forth from the Nile, it is the bull which comes forth from the fortress". Cf. Plout. *de Is*. 38.

41. Blackman PSBA xl 1918, 57–66, 88–91; Jéquier (4); JEA v 117–24, 148–65; Speelers PW iii 37 ff.; Blackman HERE x 477 col. i. PT 1140a–b (cf. 1164b, 1180c, 1293b, 1365a; JEA v 32 pl. v, 19); Mercer PT iv exc. xi for refs. Lake, cf. CT i spell 26, 781. Ntrw: Gauthier, *Dict*. iii 107, cf. PT 544b.

42. Washing: Horos, 1287b, 1980, cf. 1683 ff. Horos and Thoth: 519, 1247. Horos and Seth: 211b, 746b–c. Gods: 921a–c, 1141a–1142b. Bath: 519a–c, cf. 1247a–d, 211c.

43. PT 343a–344b, cf. 937e; exc. xiv, Mercer.

44. Moret (10) ii 5; B. 177, 227; Mercer (1) 185; Budge (1) 235.

45. Utt. 581 (1551–7). *Ssmw* became one of the Decans (16th), cf. 403a, 545b. For later usages, Hoffmann, *Personnamen* 9; see also PT Utt. 334 where the deadman is identified with him; he also appears in the "Cannibal Hymn", see 403a. *Hnti–mnw.t* seems to mean "he who is chief of his department", 285a, 655a, 1549b; but "he who is over his thigh", 1015a, 1719e. The former meaning suits here.

Aker as door: 393, 555, 676, 796, 1014, 1553, 1713, 2202; 1014a as Duat. For Hrti, see 544c and 545b; Hrti and Osiris, 1264c; evil in 350a–b; see also 350, and 445 (ferryman of boat made by Khnum); chief of Letopolis, 1308a.

Isis as falcon: Mariette (1) iv 72; Budge, *Book of Dead*, 151a, 7–8; Budge, *Gods*, ii 205; PT 1140c. For '*Itr.t* palaces (word seems dual), see Mercer iv, exc. 20. Min seems chief of them: 256a, 1998a.

46. Utt. 685. Cataract mountains, Moret in *Bulletin* xxx 734 and n. 16; (6) 8. In general: Kaiser, with exs. of Nun from PT to BD.

47. Brugsch (4) 112.

48. Nagel, BIFAO xxix 86; P. Louvre inv. 3292.

49. Edfu: Chassinat (1) vi 200, 9; B. 229.

50. Boussac, CRAI 1914, 29 and *Rec. Trav*. xxxvii 23 (citing Bissing, etc.).

51. Gardiner, JEA iii 256.

52. Frankfort (1) 45. For serpent protecting sun: Nagel, BIFAO xxix 19–20, etc. (the god in or under it); Budge (1).

53. *Ibid.*, 45–7. As holes for the winds: Mercer (3) 752.

54. B. 229 f.; Derchain (1) 491; Barguet, III, n. 6; Chassinat (1) ii 67, iii 180. Philai: Chassinat (4) 154.

55. Budge (1) 414; P. Leyd. i 350 xix (Hymn Amun); Gardiner (17). The Rocks are also called Veins of the Nile: Sen. QN iva 27; Lucan x 325; Solin. xxxii 10. Krophi and Mophi have been taken as Ker Hapi, cavern of the Nile, and Mou Hapi, water of the Nile: Wainwright JHS 1953, 106; B. 172. Note *scopuli* of Petronius *Sat*. 134.

A few more texts (1) funerary stele 51–48 B.C., dead woman, wife of a priest of Ptah, complains that she lacks "the living waters that the earth gives to whomsoever is on her" (Maspero (7) 113 f.) (2) "the water (is) hidden under the earth" when Nile ebbed (Or. Sib. iv 75; B. 52 n. 1, 111 n. 3) (3) hieroglyphic text as to underground origins of Nile: Stricker 18 f. (4) Duality: "the Nile overflows at his season, supplying with victuals your two sanctuaries, heaven and earth, " JEA iv 127, Saite. (5) Deadman goes up to source, "that the bolts of the door be opened for you—you striding on to the stream at its source, so that you may drink water in front of the *nšmt*-boat in its festival of the region of the *pkr*-tree" *ibid* 124; the spelling for "source" may be a pun-attempt to connect with Elephantine.

56. In making this generalisation about Osiris I do not wish to dogmatise about the full question of his cult's origins. I should like only to say that whatever he was, he was not originally a deified king.

57. Utt. 534, cf. 145–6, 350; Breasted (4) 38. Nedit: PT 1267c; also 721b, 1256b; Sethe (4) 100. Weill argues for a late date: *Bulletin*, xlvi 189–97.

58. Roeder, AZ lxi 61.

4. DOGSTAR, GANYMEDES, PTAH, KHNUM

1. PT 965. Horos as morning star: 805a, 1207a, 1295a, 1871a, 2014a. The deadman sends the Hours on their way: 515a. In general: Parker, par. 157 etc.; Neugebauer (2) ch. iv. Sothis was rep. later as a woman or cow (identified with Hathor) reclining in a ship to express her rule over heavens. When she appears as goddess rather than star, she is rep. as Isis: a woman with star in hand, or standing on dog: esp. associated with Horos who is at times confused with Sopdu the warlike Horos-god, master of Asiatics.

Tablet: Petrie (15) ii pl. v, 1, vi (a) 2; Parker 31 n. 2 and 18.

2. Mercer, exc. vii (Briggs) for refs. Copulation: PT 632, cf. 1636a–b. She is the only sisterwife of N named in the texts. De Buck CT 173e, 48c, 177g; 177i; Derchain (2) 364 f.

3. PT 1437a.

4. Schott (2) 15 (Urk. iv 827); Parker par. 184; CE liii 1952, 364.

5. Mariette i 65b; iii 51, 2; Capart, *Bull. crit. rel. eg.* 1908–9 320; Schott (2) 12–18.

6. Roeder ZAS xlv 22–30 (1908).

7. PT 1116a, cf. 1140a, 1164b, 1180c, 1293b, 1365a. N's mother is Satis, 2209a–b; "N is Satis who has taken possession of both lands", 812a.

8. BD ch. cxxx, 1. Satis had bow and arrows, and wore horns (Sethe, *Urg.* par. 28, thinks of antelope; but she never had a beasthead); Hera to Greeks (Brugsch (8) 299). Mercer (1) 209 says name from root: to sow seed, copulate. She poured Nile waters.

9. Lepsius DK iv 69; iii 171; Roeder *lc*. Also De Buck (1) iv 361 (c. 2000 B.C.).

10. Lepsius DK i 20 (Ptol. II). Also hier. stele, Cairo 22. 180. (Ptol. I); Rochemonteix (2) i 115, 317, 162, 164. Decree of Kanopos: OGI 56, line 36 (Ptol. II).

11. De Is. 38 and 21; B. 264; Porph. De antro 24; also hierog. text, Louvre inv. 2272 (? sailor): Pierret, Rec. insc. inéd. Louvre ii 1878, 84.

12. Oxy. 1380 (2nd c.); Van Groningen (1) on line 144 (composed at Memphis (?)).

13. PGM vii (Lond. i 121); B. 265. "In complete darkness" or "the dark flood" (as fulfilment); teleios used in pap. about the flood refers to completion.

14. Tib. i 7, 21–2; Claudian, etc.; Aratos, *Phain.* 330; Hygin. *Astr.* ii 35; Ps–Eratosth. *Kat.* 33; J. Bayet, *Origines de l'Hercule rom.* 1926, 455. Hymn to Isis on stelai of Kos and Ios: A. Salač, BCH li 3, 378–83. Also Diod. i 27, 4; Plout. *de Is.* 61 (cf. Theon of Alex. *Comm. Ar.* 153) on kyesis as translation of Egyptian word meaning fatness; but Sopet seems to mean sharp, precise (Bonnet, *Real.* iv Sothis 743): reference to precision of advent?

15. Perdrizet TC no. 76 (pl. xvi), cf. pl. xxviii and p. 22.

16. Bonnet *l.c.* 329, fig. 84, and Mus. Berl. inv. 9956.

17. Dattieri 929, 927 (pl. xvii), A.D. 109–10; and 928 (112–13).

18. Neugebauer, Acta orient. xvii 1938, and JNES i 1942; also Parker and H. E. Wenlock, *P. Amer. Phil. Soc.* lxxxiii 1940.

19. Iseum: Moret (1) 165; Dion K. lxxix 10 (early 3rd c.) shows it was still there. Table: E. Scamuzzi, *Mensa Isiaca* (Publ. Torino V) 1939; it may be 2nd c.

20. NA x 45; Hubaux–Leroy 24. Orion assimilated to Horos as to the Nile: St. Pal. xxi par. 154.

21. Diod. i 87, 2–3, cf. Horapollon i 39. For protective dog–god, separate from Anubis, see Theban BD ch. clxxxii; Budge (1) 29.

22. B. 91–3, 269.

23. Met. xi 11. Also Sch. Arat. *Phain.* 33; Horapollon i 3 (cf. Sbordone, *Hierogl.* 7); B. 269; BIFAO ii 1902 33 f.

24. Lefebvre (1) no. viii, with refs. Unhappy end: Maspero and M. J. Honti (*Oriens ant.* 1945) 72. Happy: G. Ebers (1) 99; M. Pieper ZAS lxx 1934, 95–7, also Lefebvre citing G. Huet, *Les contes pop.* 41 for the analogies (leap).

25. Life *Apoll. Tyana* vi 26; perhaps "makes investigation of the stream a plague to the ears; "proportions", symmetria.

26. Sc. Arat. *Phain.* 282; Bowra, *Pind. carm.* 1947 fr 294b (Bergk 282).

27. Daressy (7) 4, no, 8.

28. Bouché–L. (2) 146 n. 3; Roscher vi 975, 4 ff.; 976, 50 ff.; Neugebauer (1) 22 f., 27; Boll (2) 389 takes G. as a borrowing from the Sphaira Barbarika. Codex: Boll (1) *Cod. Vat. Gr.* 1291. In Lond. 130 col. vi, G. is "homonymous with the whole constellation", Neugebauer (1) 22–3. See also Virg. *Georg.* iii, 304; Hygin. *fab.* 224; ps.–Eratosth. *Kat.* 26.

29. PSI 488, 10.

30. Philost. *imag.* i 5; B. 231, 338. Note gem (Overbeck, *Kunstmyth.,* *Poseidon*: Gemmentafel iii 3) where P. bends forwards, with Nymphs. Dwarfs: cf. Louk. *Rhet. praec.* 6; Vatican statue, fig. 1 (Loeb Philostr. *imag.*) where Nile rests on sphinx. For statues of nymphs with varying numbers (2, 3, 7, 9, 16, 17) of children: B. 486. Cf. Sib. Oracle where Nile-waters are *thesphaton,* xiii 44 Note use of epineuein in P. Cairo–Boak, *Sel. Pap. Karanis* iv 20; B. 231 n. 5 —for Nile, "to nod, give sign"; for Nile of which one prepares the coming by getting dykes and canals in good condition.

31. CE 1952, 366. Gebelein: Gardiner (3) ii 18*; Steindorff (3) 19.

32. CT (1st Intermed. Period): de Buck 182c–d.

33. *Ibid.* 182k.

34. Sethe (7) par. 127 f.

35. De Buck 182 n–q.

36. *Ibid.* 183b–j. For Hathor's arrival in Punt, Juncker (9). Ihy: this young god has many functions (esp. at Dendera and other temples of Ptol. and R. periods) to rejoice his divine mother.

37. Osiris and flood in CTs: iii 323f–g and 325f–g; in general B. 243 ff.

38. Ptah: Budge (1) 12–22, 158 f., 259–70 (creator); Mercer (1) 148–51. Ptah at height of popularity, Nineteenth Dyn. For rels with Hephaistos, Ptah–Soker–Osiris represented as bandy-legged dwarf. (Soker was a funerary god.) Texts: Gardiner–Davies, *Anc. Eg. Paintings* ii pl. 70; Frankfort (3) 391, n. 36; Naville (5) pl. 38F.; Holmberg 178 no. 224; P. Berl 3048, pl. 83; Holmberg 118.

39. P. Hood (20–21 Dyn.). Nile as Ptah: ASAE xli 149; Budge (6a) 172; LD i 248;

40. Lepsius (1) vi 118; Budge (1) 259 f., as earthgod: perhaps through association with Osiris got his mummified form as god of dead: Mercer (1) 148 f. for name as Opener. Manetho makes the first king of Egypt Hephaistos; the second, Helios his son (Re). Osiris drowned at Memphis: Budge (1) 267 f. Ptah as creator: Roeder (11) 166–8, 55; Budge (1) ch. x and (15) i 146. Tenen: Roeder (1) 166; Sethe, *Urg.* Always in human form: LD passim; Stolk; Daressy, *Statues.* Apis related to Ptah is late. The Glorious Dd. identified with Ptah by time of Seti I: Holmberg (1) 187. Only thrice in PT, 560, 566, 1482. Semitic relations: Ginsberg, *Orientalia,* ix 1940, 1–2, 39–44.

41. Holmberg 46.

42. Two school MSS of Nineteenth Dyn., Turin Pap. and ostr. Budge (1) 385 and (10); Maspero (4); Erman (4) 146; Bacchi; Pritchard; Roeder (8) 327–39.

43. PT 324a–344b, cf. 352a, 1102b and 1084b (canals).

44. Cicero, *nat. deor.* iii 22; Lucan viii 477. Cicero is saying there are several Vulcans, naming five. Ptah is second; the fourth, "whom the Egyptians think it a crime to name is the Son of Nilus;" the fifth is Thoth (worshipped at Pheneum in Arcadia), said to have fled from Egypt after killing Argus, and "to have given laws and learning to the Egyptians" (Hermes). He also says, iii 21, there is a Sun "whom the Egyptians say was of Heliopolis, sprung from Vulcan the Son of Nilus;" and iii 23, a Dionysus who killed Nysa son of Nilus, and a Minerva worshipped at Sais was sprung from Nilus.

45. Barguet 19 f. n. 6; Chassinat (1) ii 67, iii 180.

46. Hdt. ii 28. Khnum in general: Badawi (3); H. Bonnet (1) 135–40; Frankfort (3) 146; B. 232 n. 6; Budge (1) 173–5, 256; Mercer (1) 151–3. Lord of Cool Water at Elephantine. Nile: see Badawi 19 fig. 9; Capart CE 1939, 102.

47. Rochementeix (2) i 115, cf. i 264; Barguet 28; Sauneron (4) 387.

48. LD pls. 336–7.

49. Budge (11) lx–lxviii and 120–41.

50. Name means Ram. Khnum was deified as early as First Dyn., Petrie (15)

i pl. 23, no. 42; occurs six times in PTs; worshipped at other sites, Esneh, Hypselos, Antinoe, Ombos, Edfu, Thebes, Dendera, Herakleopolis; in Nubia: Philai, Debod, Dendur, Dakke, Kumme.

51. Budge (1) 173. Names 174–5.

52. Pl Sallier ii, verse 3 of hymn; B. 233 n. 11, cf. *Genesis* ii 7. Spontaneous generation from Nile-mud, B. 121 f.

53. Budge (1) 173–5; Mariette (1) iv. 81.

54. B. 233; Maspero (5) 66; Budge (1) 175; Roscher iv. 146.

54. B. 233; Maspero (5) 66; Budge (1) 175; Roscher iv 146. Greeks identified Anukis with Hestia; she wore a feather-crown.

55. Sauneron (4) 366.

56. Leclant (1) 205. Colours: Sethe PW iii 2350; Euseb. *praep. ev.* iii 12, 1; B. 233, 235.

57. Budge (1) 480–6; pharoah of text, Neter–Khet in his 18th year; Barguet.

58. We could go further into the relations of Nile with Re and Thoth, sun and moon; and with Osiris. However the Osirian links keep coming up.

5. CRAFT-GODS AND CREATION

1. Delcourt (1).

2. See Delcourt 43–7, etc. for refs. and further details. Also J.L. (1) sv index for names mentioned.

3. J.L. (1) sv index.

4. Again, esp. 175.

5. *Ibid.* 43–6, 49, 87, 98, 159, 178, 184, 198, 216.

6. *Ibid.* 110 f.

7. *Inid.* 179

8. *Ibid.* 180 f.

9. *Ibid.* 182 f.; Rose, Handbook Gr. Myth. 56, 73.

10. *Prom.* 299–302, Prom. as a governor in Egypt: Diod. i 19, 1.

11. J.L. (1) 195 f.

12. Hermet. xiii 17 (Scott); Budé ed. ii 207; B. 411, 238.

13. G. Thomson, *First Philosophers*, 52 ff. with refs.; *Aeschylus and Athens* 352 f.

14. Alexander 44, 43; *Jesuit Relations*, ed. R. Thwaites 1896–1901. For Moaris: Tyler, *Prim. Cult.* 1873 ii 66. Osiris afloat. Usener 39. Colours: Lethaby 37, 125.

15. See J.L.(i) 245, 267, etc., with refs.—the book passim for relation of the Argo to Okeanos, etc.

16. Frankfort (5) 163, and (1) esp. 20, 28–31. Also de Buck (4) and Hall, JEA x 1924 185 ff.

17. Ani, ch. svii, pl. vii–x; Budge (6a) ii 377.

18. Juncker (3) 41 ff.

19. Blessed; Frankfort (1) 30. Abydos: Kristensen (1) 93 and Naville (2) BD xvii 24; Hdt. ii 124.

20. Budge BD 1899, pl. viii; Frankfort (1) 29; Budge (19) pl. cviii; LD ccxi; Sethe, *Urk.* iv 364.

21. Gunn in Frankfort (1) 80. Note the demons are called Brigands (NK) BIFAO xxix 1929, 62.

22. Wilson in Frankfort (4) esp. 54–6; *Urk.* iv 612, also 183, 843; Lethaby 22–4.

23. PT 1100b–1101d; Budge (1) 7 f., 146–51, 438.

24. John Lyd. *de mens* iv 107 (Roeth 264).

25. Drioton (10) 135–9; for dates of different sections, 157 f.; that used here seems Ptolemaic.

26. Chassinat (1) ii 152; iv 36; vi 33.

27. C. de Buck (4) 46.

28. Gardiner (18) 20 (Leyden hymns).

29. De Buck 46 n. 1; Drioton 139.

30. Drioton 147–51. Kamenphis: Theban form of Min. Nun is used for flood; determinatives of Amun show Nun as his manifestation: Sethe (7) pars. 140 and 22, 200 n.1, 201, 203, 230.

31. BIFAO xxv 11.

32. Leyden hymns vi 10–1, see n. 28 above. Town of Life: Gauthier, *Dict.* i 148. Primeval Thebes: Nonnos xli 270, cf. v 86.

33. Brugsch (3) 222 no. 24.

34. Vandier (4) 83; Drioton 150 f. By Ptol. times Thebes claimed to be sole true burial-place of Osiris, though other towns claimed that bits of O. were buried at them: Drioton 152 f.

35. Budge (1) 438–44; Griffith (5); Roeder (11) 150; Muller (1) 76. Goyon (3); Kees (12) 23. See also here ch. 22 n. 38.

36. Stress is laid on his repairs, and on his lake-building. At Aat-Nebes "gods and goddesses, men, princes and (people) might not enter and look on the Mysteries of the Horizon; this was given (ordained) from the time of Re".

37. Tale tells further of Aart being put in sacred lake and changing into a crocodile, becoming the god Sebek at Aat-Nebes. In battle Geb was aided at this lake, into which he rushed, gaining crocodile-legs(?), hawk-head, and bull-horns.

Griffith (5) pl. xxv and p. 72: "Shu had departed to heaven. There was no exit from the palace for the space of 9 days. Now these days were in violence and tempest; none, whether god or man, could see the face of his fellow."

38. Frankfort (1) 83; the rest is fragmentary. Though castration does not occur here, as with Zeus and Kronos, it is not uncommon in Egyptian myth: Seth by Horos (Griffiths (1) 37–9, 130) – PT 679d: "Horos fell because of his Eye, Seth suffered because of his Testicles." The monster Apepi is castrated at the end of the destructive rite: Budge (1) 516–21. For castration as loss of kingly power: Hittite myth of emasculation of bird skygod Anu by Kumarbi: A. Goetze in Pritchard (1) 120, and O. R. Gurney (*Hittites*, 1952) 190 f. See also PT 1462c (scorn of castrated bull as object of admiration), 660c, 661a (obscure, on castrating knife). For anal second-birth, cf., the Polynesian Maui: J.L.(1) 270.

39. *Ibid.* 73–5 (roof of sarcophagus room).

40. *Ibid.* 76. For Shu lifting Nut: A. Rusch; the pictures of the act were used for magic of resurrection: JEA xii 162 f. Nut and the night-sunboat: A. Piankhoff (5).

41. Bonnet (2) fig. 19; Budge (1) 378—see earlier. Budge (1) 367 for rounded eastern end of Tuat.

42. Mus. Mod. Art, N.Y.; Posener (5) 192.

43. Burrows (1); J.L. (4) "Bronze Age".

44. See above on Cenotaph Seti I.

45. Burrows (1) 46–50 (2) 242–8, 251. Libations to god of underworld through drains or pipes at Ur; Eridu founded on the Apsu, etc. Jerusalem: Burrows (1) 53–7 with temple-rock covering the abyss, the source of the flood.

46. Lethaby, 22; Sethe (11) 3 on P. Harris 44; Griffiths (2); see oversimplified statements in Mercer (2), Wilson (2) 54. Kuentz (1) 147 ff. and fig. 2; Budge (1) 71.

47. Chester Beatty, Pap. 1, Gardiner; Spiegel, 115; Grapow (2) 21 f.—for date, going back to MK. In general, also Griffiths (1); Lefebvre (1) ch. xiv. Our section is 5, 5–8, 5.

48. Spiegel 44. Gold, says the text, is still proscribed in his city, capital of 12th Nome: Sethe, *Urg.* par. 53; see also Gardiner (13) ii 70 on its name, City (or House) of Horos the Golden.

49. P. of Tanis (*Two Papyri, Abydos*, pl. x); and Edfu R i 341; Brugsch (4) 1362, cf. Edfu R i 341. In general, Boylan 154–7.

50. Mariette ii 78a.

51. Edfu R. i 129.

52. Brugsch (3) 760.

53. AZ 1895, 120 ff.; BM 5626. Late: Lefebvre, *Petosiris*, 2e ptie. Text 61, 1, 18 (p. 36), etc.

54. AZ 1884, 38 ff.

55. Mercer PT ii 122.

56. Sethe (7) 84 f.

57. PT 265b and 397a–c; Lacau, *Textes Rel. Rec.* 27 p. 218 (BD 174); Kees (13); Sethe (1) 196, 83d and (8) i 280, 18; 282, 1, 5, 12; lv 1224 f.

58. Budge BD ch. 137a–b.

59. Naville, Aa 71, 16–8; ch. 15B, I (Ba) 13–4. See also: Lacau, *Rec.* xix 27 p. 217.

60. Budge, Ani 435, 280, 288: ch. xxiv.

61. Naville 17, 5–11. Cf. Inscr. at Gt. Oasis, Brugsch 26, 22–3 of Amun; and Mariette, Dend. i 55b.

62. Sethe WB; Sallier iv 8, 3–4; cf. tale of Re coming-forth from Nun. In highplace of *Hmnw*, Re won some victory over rebels: BD, Grapow (1) 1st p., 1915.

Note further PT 1216a–1217b: "N went to the great island in the midst of the Marsh of Offerings, on which the gods cause the swallows to alight. The swallows are the imperishable stars. They give N the Tree of Life on which they

CC

live, so that N may at the same time live on it. (Morning Star) make N to ferry over with you, to this your great field . . .".

63. PT 1188a–f. And 1173a.

64. Te Velde 60–1.

6. OCEANIC NILE

1. Capovilla. Minos and Egypt: Diod. i. 61; Aigyptios on Ithaka, *Od.* ii 15. Note name Ogenos for Okeanos (Pherekydes) may have same root as Sumerian Uginna (circle or totality): A. Rivaud Hist. Phil. i 28. Berger (3) 1–2 connects Okeanos with ai, açanyas "surrounding": the skene of aither. Ogenos: CQ xiii 1963 162.

2. L. Deroy 97–103; Mallet (1) 105; Gilbert; Diod. i 45; A. Gellius xiv 6, 4. For Ketes (Proteus) king of Egypt at time of Trojan War: Diod. i 62; river called after Neileus, i 63, though formerly Aigyptos.

3. Il. xx 13 and xxi 195. Diod. i 12, 5 on Okeane. Okeanos and gods, Il. xiv 302. Jane Harrison *Themis* 456 f. B. 143 and Foucart (2) 88.

4. Theog. 338; Pindar frag. 270, cf. 30 (Shroeder, 1900).

5. Servius ad Georg. iv 363.

6. See J. Ball, 9; Heidel 103, n. 39.

7. Hdt. ii 21 and 23; his denial had little effect. Aristeides of Smyrna speaks of 4 branches: Medit., Caspian, Red Sea, Persian Gulf: Foucart (2) 89.

8. Diod. i 12, 5; 96, 7; i 12, 5; 19, 4. Euseb. *Praep. Ev.* iii 3, 6: "The Egyptians believe that their river Nile is the Ocean from which the race of gods has taken birth."

9. John Lyd. *de mens.* iv 107 (Roeth 264). And Strab. xvii 3, 4; Vitruv. Arch. viii 2, 67; Plin. NH v 9 (10); Solin. xxxii 2–4.

Serv. ad *Aen.* viii 712; Dion K. lxxv 13; Amm. Marc. xxii 15, 13; Paus. i 33, 6; PW iii (2) 2449 and ii (1) 252.

Some thought the river came from west: Peutinger Table, section viii (Egypt) c. A.D. 150, though some aspects (absence of Alexandreia) have suggested a much earlier pre-331 B.C. date: Ball, pl. iv. Persians saw Nile as joining Ocean in direction of Indian Ocean: Aristot. DIN 8. For use of analogies in place of fact (up to John of Damascus ix): Foucart (2) 90.

10. Nonnos xxvi 225 ff. (Indos coming from Aithiopian Mtns.—Eastern Aithiopia as Himalayas or Hindu Kush, cf. Od. i 23. In line 230 he has autogenos. *Ibid.* iii 365. Hymn, verse 5; Barguet 58. See J.L. (3) ch. 20.

11. Mionnet, suppl. ix 93, 1837. Roscher sv Okeanos 817 line 49. Nile in general: Mionnet nos. 384, 333, 323, etc.; Eckhel, *Doctr. num. vet.* I iv 39; Méautis (1).

12. B. 145, 239; Diod. i 37, 7; Hier. i 21; J. Ball 9. Also Diod. i 19 and i 12. Epitaph: Jouguet (3).

13. Timaios, Diogenes of Apollonia, Oinopidos of Chios, Ephoros, etc. B. 176–86 for full refs.; see also Seneca QN iii 26 1; iv(a) 11, 26–7; Proklos, *Comm. Tim.* 22e (Proklos 37a); Diod. i 41, 1–2.

14. B. 172–4. Note Solon on Nile waters out of earth; ps–Arist. on Nile 1; Stoics and Seneca, QN iii 5; 9, 1; 10, 5.

Great Cave: Plato, *Phaid.*; Virg. *Georg.* iv 363; Seneca QN vi, 8, 3 and 5; Lucan x 215, cf. viii 828–9; Statius *Theb.* iv 704; Proklos as above; Prokop. *Letter* 136 (6th c. to a friend of Hermop. Magna).

15. Strab. vi 2, 4; *Tim.* 22d (B. 177–8).

16. *Phaidon* 111–4. Plato: F. M. Cornford (Orphism) CR xvii, 1903, 433–45; J. Dörfler, *Wiener St.* xxxiii 1911 177–212; P. Friedländer, etc. Phere-kydes: Damasc. *de princ.* 124; Porph. *de antr.* 31; Jaeger, *Theol. Early Gr. Phil.* 1967 70.

17. Hymn iv 205–8; cf. sch. Lykophron 576; Roussel (2) 287.

18. NH ii 229. Note observations of Eudoxos of Knidos on wells of Pytho-polis, Bithynia (Antigonos of Karystos, 3 c. B.C.); Ephoros on certain lakes, esp. that of Skythopolis of Palestine swelling at time of Nile-flood: B. 185.

19. Roussel (2) 20, 36, 286; *Rev. Eg.* n.s. i 1919, 83; Hymn iii 171.

20. Paus. ii 5, 3; Sch. Pind. Nem. i 4a.

21. Aristot. DIN 6; Strab. xv i, 25; Arrian *anab.* vi, 1.

22. Paus. i 33, 6.

23. Paus. ii 5, 3–4.

24. Lucan x 247–54; B. 179.

25. Pind. *Nem.* i 1; Strab. vi 2, 4; Soph. fr. 676. Inachos of Argolid and Inachos affluent of Acheloos.

26. Mela i 9, 54; Ball 70; B. 175–6. Note also how Nile gets into the sky. The constellation called by Aratos the Potamos (*Phain.* 590) became in Hygin. *Astr.* ii 32 the Nile or Ocdan; in Latin version by Avienus (4th c. A.D.) Flumen invokes the Po and the Nile: *Phaen.* 796.

27. Laistner 7, 87 f.: *Peri Kenodoxia* 8.

28. CPH 7; Méautis (1) 51: Jouguet (2) 383. (For session at Herakleopolis: *Aeg. Urk. k. Mus. zu Berl.* iii 925; W. *Grund.* 56.) Acclamations: T. Reinach, BCH 1897, 543.

29. Oxy. 41: *Okaanai*. Period of joint rule, prob. Diocletian and Maximian. Katholikos (cf. BGU 21 iii 10) not here finance-officer (as in Eusebios and Julian) but has wider sense, a title of the hegemon. The last-named officials, syndikoi, synegoroi, were prob. on the platform.

30. *Life* v 28.

31. *Life* v 6.

32. Tarn (1) for refs. The event was important even if Tarn overvalues; he has much to say of importance about homonoia in the Hellenistic world.

33. *Corpus Hermet.* iv 3–6; Kahane 13 ff.—117 f. for Hermes.

34. Rites: Festugière (1); Kahane (1) 18 f. Grail: Kahane (2). Macrobius (*Comm. Scip.* i 12, 8, Willis): unembodied souls drink oblivion from the constellation of the Krater and are drawn down to earth. *Pistis:* ch. 147 (Horner and Legge 1924, 198); C. Schmidt and W. Till, *Kopt.-gnost. Schriften* i (3rd ed.) 1959, 252 f.; Kahane (1) 16 for Syriac.

35. P. Lansing: Blackman (6) 297: 15, 9 and 15, 1. He has villeins where I put peasants. Posener (4) ostr.

36. Nile in GR times equated with other rivers and given love-affairs and progeny: Ovid. *amores* iii 6, 39; Apollod. *Bibl.* ii 10; Diod. i 51, 3; Phlegon of Tralles (c. A.D. 125) mirab. xxx–i; ps-Plout. parall. min. 38; Cicero, *nat. deor.*, etc.; B. 325–6.

37. Lond. lit. 239; Christians carry on, St. Pal. xv 250a–b, etc.; B. 410.

38. Oxy. 519.

39. Erman (4) 288–91; Pendlebury, *Tell el-Amarna* 150–5; Davies, *el-Amarna* vi, xxvii; Bille-De Mot, *Age of Akhenaten* 1966, 84 f. Cf. the Nile in Heaven, and "the myriads of Niles pouring forth water daily," N. de G. Davies, Rock paintings, Amarna vi, 30, 29.

40. *Life of Moses* iii 24.

41. *Ibid.* i 36.

42. *Helen* 2; Diehl, *Anth. Lyr.* iii 2, 114 frag. 3; Athen. v 203c; sch. Pind. pyth. iv 56 and iv 99. Tibullus i 7, 25 f.; Lucan viii 445. Cf. Ovid. *art of love* i 645 ff., tale of drought in Egypt; Aristenetos of Byz., FHG iv 320; Prokop. *letter* 136.

43. Lond. lit. 239; Cair. Zen. 383, 13; Tebt. 72 iv 71 and 75, 57–8; B. 317–8, 130 n. 1, 171, 332, 410

44. Oxy. 1830, cf. PSI 488 (3 c. B.C.) where figures of two preceding years are given, sent by pragmateutai; also Tehneh inscr. *Bull. Soc. Arch. Alex.* 1921, 47 ff. Apion: Oxy. xvi p. 7.

7. PEOPLE ON THE NILE

1. Tebt. 750–5. Villages in fourth letter are in Div. of Polemon. Tebt. 755. Epidoros also a sitologos. 756 may be of Adamas: ". . . he cancelled it besides not giving to him, and also has entered him as owing 1½ art. for the 7th year. I simply swear to you by Sobnektynis, whatever he exacts from him he will exact unnaturally; and let Menches know the same thing, from whom the exaction should be made. Goodbye." 757, to Herakleides (? same man as that known to Adamas), who seems a sitologos: "Hermodoros, clerk of the collecting dept., has written to me that the local collectors have despatched to him those of the . . . who are in arrears, wishing to . . . the amounts declared due from them, and that you were not to be found at the granaries but were busy with the lading, and alleging . . ."

2. Oxy. 1153; J.L. (3) 46–7.

3. Oxy. 531. "Happily" is *ep' agathoi*: B. 289 f. tries to relate it, and *syn theoi*, to the Nile. But the terms seem to me to express only the increasing sense of the evil-eye fear leading into Christianity. *Moursinon* (*myrsinon*) may be meant to be *morinon*, "mullberry-coloured", cf. CPR i 27, 8. Oxy. 1759 (2nd c.) is letter to an athlete about things the writer wants brought.

4. Mich. viii 496. For mean son and donkey-fare: J.L. (2) 80 f.

5. Oxy. 929. Ninnaros is steward of Apion, strategos (?).

6. Oxy. 936; many unusual words, *e.g. skorseleina*. Col. ii also has money details. "Mother embraces you."

7. Oxy. 937: *ploion*, not likely a stone engraved with boat-relief.

8. Oxy. 1066. Oxy. 1770, son to mother about arrival and sending of various things; mother is asked to come herself or send Thonios (? another son).

9. Oxy. 1158. Loukios (Lucius) in address.

10. BGU 814, Fayum; REg 306.

11. Oxy. 1775. Seems account of the *entolikon* lost.

12. Oxy. 2156.

13. Oxy. 1862: Rheme sellariotes to Marinos scholastikos, cf. 1863.

14. Oxy. 1562, ends with salutations.

15. Oxy. 1933–4; *ploion*. Askalon: W. *Archiv* v 297 (P. Klein. Form. 1204); Crum–Bell *Wadi Sarga* 20. Spain: Oxy. 1862. Gaza: Steph. Byz. for keramoi called Gazitai: here Gazitia.

16. Barnes, no. 3; no. 4 deals with troubles of women and babies, no. 5 with stiffness and cramp. Charm: Gardiner JEA xxiv 164. Also Budge (16) i 509; Breasted (1) ii 371 ff. Cited: Budge (1) 133 f.; (21) 174 f.: magic P. Harris, BM 1002 42. Theban: xxxi (cf. xlviii), lxxxvii. Ani: cxxxviii (cf. cxxxvii, 44 for fear). cf. Gardiner ZAS xlii 12 ff. (ch. 70); Erman (4) 297: "A water-charm is the name of Amun upon the floor. No crocodile has power when his name is pronounced." Cf. Herdsmen's song at El Bersheh: "You (Oxen) stamp the sand, you tread the fodder, you browse on the herbage, your back, good for your body . . . your haunches, healthy your belly, your calves . . . evil is voyaging, pleasant is your disembarking." *El B.* i 29.

17. Oxy. 525.

18. Oxy. 1291.

19. Oxy. 1292.

20. Oxy. 1769.

21. Oxy. 1773; verso has name as Taurine to mother Amatrion.

22. Tebt. 412. Damas *hyperetes*.

23. Oxy. 2153. *Tekton* and *iokodomos; ploion* and *pakton.*

24. Merton 62. See in general J.L. (2) 149; Highet, *Juvenal* 244 f.

25. Oxy. 746.

26. Mich. 498.

27. Oxy. 1219.

28. Harrop, JEA 1962, 133–40. Cf. PSI iii 208 and ix 1041; Oxy. 1162; Greg. Naz. *epp.* 38, 103, 126, 134, 168, 188–9. *Emphyton* usually means inborn by nature, but can mean implanted. The writer cites Matt. 25, 40. *Kata topon:* nome-subdivision or even a religious community.

29. Athanas. *Ap. c. Ar.* 28, cf. 11 and 46; Brightman JTS i 1899, 109. Two kinds: Origen, *C. Cels.* iii 51; Suicer sv *katecheo;* canon xiv, Conc. Nik. pr.

30. Harrop 136 f.; Guignet 6 f. For possible Pauls, etc., Harrop 137–9.

31. Harrop 139 f.; Dupont 119 ff.; Behm 328–35.

32. Clem. Alex. *Strom.* vii 2, 13; Origen *In Lev. Hom.* vi 6; *Comm. in John* i 16, 93; iii 37, 229; x 43, 306; xiii 10, 58; i 18, 113; 25, 153; and *de Princ.* i 2, 12.

33. Tyler, *Prim. Cult.* ii 71.

34. Oxy. 1159.

35. Oxy. 743, 6 Phaophi, 29th year of Caesar.

36. Oxy. 1155. Prefect C. Vibius Max., cf. Amh. 64; Pastophoroi, lower order of priests, W. Otto i 94–8, ii 152; Tebt. 299, 68n.

37. Oxy. 1768.

38. IGRR i 1098; OGIS 675; REg 2. For the channel, Schiff. Channel Philagrianos (IGRR 1099) cleaned under Domitian.

39. BGU 1680.

40. Oxy. 144 and 151; 1440 gold solidi with 720 solidi in Egyptian coin acc. to Alex. standard, plus 45 to make up deficiency in purity.

8. MORE PEOPLE ON THE NILE

1. Oxy. 1154.

2. Mich. viii, Karanis, 467–81; six in Latin, one fragmentary. The order here is 467 (Latin), 468 (Greek), 474, 477, 478, 479, 480, 481, 497. Thonis is village near Alex., Oxy. 1380.

3. See Taubenschlag (1) 327–9 for refs.; also (3) 110 and 81. For mania, cf. BGU iv 1024 4f, 5c, W. *Archiv* iv 1918, 217. Family as accusers, Oxy. 486 and 472 for son as accuser; Tebt. 333 (M. *Chr.* 115) A.D. 216, daughter; Hamb. 10, 2nd c., prob. daughter; BGU 1061, a foreigner. See also, Lumbroso *Stud. e Doc* i 108 ff.

4. Rations: Oxy. 531 cited above: Lond. ii 190; Plout. *Flam.* 5; SIG 578, 54 (Teos, 2nd c. B.C.); Mich. iii 203; BGU iii 814.

5. See Youtie, *Class W.* xxxvii 1943–4, 8 and 10; Barois (13–5).

6. Cf. Gen. Lat. 1; W. Chr. 369.

7. Mich. 497, builder, *ktistes.* See also Oxy. 935: J.L. (2) 225.

8. Lond. 1920.

9. Mich. 502; brother seems in Karanis (2nd c.).

10. SB i 999, 7; Preisigke WB iii 389; Plout. 10, 14; *Etym. Mag.* 552, 12 sv Koptos; Hopfer i 44; Youtie HTR xxxix 1946, 165–7. Agatharkides, *Mar. Eryth.* 108, reports that coral formations off the Troglodyte coast were called Isidos Trichoma: Plin. xiii 51; Plout. *Face in Moon* 25.

11. BD Anu (Budge) 400 f. "Who are great of wailing, masters of needs, who are over a lock of hair in the land of the West. I enter the earth from which I am gone forth," Frankfort (1) 41. Loukian, *Ignorant Book-coll.* 14. See also Budge, BD (Theban rescension) 342, 413; hair of Nu, 176.

12. Fayum, CE 1937, 97–100; dislike of voyage, cf. BGU 380 and Mich. 1367.

13. Mich. 510. The only Apate we know was on Arabian coast of Red Sea: Plin. vi 32, 155. The pap. found in same house as the Tiberianus archive;

three names shared, but probably not the same. Plague: *St. Pal.* xxii 33, 8 f.; Oxy. 1666 (3rd c.); later. Wilche, *Fest. Hirschfeld* 1903, 128 f.

14. Oxy. 1666: "To the Oxy. nome." Amesysia: J.L. (3) 32, 34, 402.

15. Merton 46: ship, skaris; Gessias, cf. Oxy. 1834. "Deliver to my master the all-virtuous . . . Ioannes, Magister, from Ioannes."

16. See J.L. (2) 44, ch. iv in general; exposure, 21, 43–6, 52, 320 f., 327. Also, Philon, *Special Laws* (Murderers) vi; Ptol. *Tetrabib.* iii 9.

17. Oxy. 1216. Child expected, J.L. (2) 74.

18. Mich. 513.

19. Mich. 516, late 3 c.

20. Mich. 514. Kolpos: seems a geog. ref.; cannot be religious: "In the bosom of Sarapis. For army-recruit and visit to Alex., Oxy. 1666 (3 c.).

21. Meyer Gr. Texte 20, 44–9.

22. Oxy. 1065; W. Chr. 120; J.L. (2) 83. "Drop everything," J.L. (2) 40 and Oxy. 2154.

23. Vitelli, *At. e Roma* vii 124, and Bremen pap.; Oxy. vii p. 220. Doesn't bathe, etc.: J.L. (2) 26 f., Oxy. 528.

9. MORE PEOPLE ON THE NILE: BUSINESS

1. Oxy. 1064. Takona: see above, Oxy. 743: it must be near Probthis; it seems on riverbank. See Oxy. 1830, and 1285: in Lower Toparchy when toparchies existed as admin. divs.

2. Cornell 52.

3. Oxy. 1921, cf. 2040.

4. Oxy. 742.

5. Ryl. 229: *ploion*.

6. Ryl. 230–1.

7. Lond. 893: important for rels. of the two calendars, see Lond. 130, Fay. 139, Hohmann 48 ff. Pholos is prob. G. Julius Pholos epistates phylakiton at this date: Ryl. ii p. 118.

8. Mich. viii 486. Fortune: Tyche.

9. *Ibid.* 492: W. Grund. 122.

10. Oxy. 532.

11. Amh. 131–5, 88 (A.D. 128), 87 (125), 105 (127), 104 (125), 126–7. In 135 festival is Thallos. In 87, Athena temple near Hermo p.: W.O. i p. 774. *Dochikon:* BGU 552, etc. (Hermop. pap.), cf. Oxy. 101, wheat "measured by the bronze-rimmed measure containing 4 choinikes used for payment to the lessor or her agents". In 104, rent is in unspecified produce.

12. Oxy. 509. For appointment of rep., cf. Oxy. 94, 97, 261.

13. Oxy. 530. Pawning: cf. Oxy. 114; J.L. (2) 28 f.

14. Oxy. 533. Lawyer, *nomikos;* cultivator, *georgos.*

15. Mich. 506.

16. Bell (1) no. 22 (Lond. ii 244); *Rev. Phil.* ns. xvi 1942 5–21; SP 9023.

17. See previous note. The verb may also be one that means "allocate", Lond. 1827, 11.

18. Bell (1) no. 23 (Gen. 61).

19. *Ibid.* no. 21 (on back of 41): Gen. 52.

20. Mich. 512.

21. Ryl. 245, to Lucretios.

22. Amh. 136. Horion is gymnasiarch of Oxy.

23. Oxy. 1675. Traders are qualified as *schisthontes:* perhaps *schisthentes*—but sense is obscure.

24. Oxy. 1673. Serapiakos, overseer, *epitropos. Metabolai* (changers) are retail-dealers.

25. Oxy. 1669. Middlemen: OGI 140, 6 (Alex.); San Nicolo i 129. For wine, see for ex. Oxy. 1672, J.L. (2) 82. Traders: Cumont (3) 109 f.; San Nicolo 135; Rostovtzeff SEHRE 607 n. 22, 615 n. 35.

26. Mich. 519.

27. Oxy. 934. Yokes, *zeukteria,* app. in connection with a waterwheel (? yoke of oxen that draw it) in Flor. 16. *En Chysei* (village, Oxy. 899) not likely to mean "in a heap" as if the kopros here consisted of sifted nitrous earth (sebach).

28. Mich. 520. For wine, see for ex. Oxy. 1672, J.L. (2) 82.

29. *Byzantion* ii 1925, 448; Lefebvre, *Rec.* pp. xxxiii–iv. For other symbols, Mich. vi 378.

30. Oxy. 1844; see intro. for the two men. "Expect": meaning would be easier as "await his coming before he himself goes down", but this is hard to get from the text.

31. Amh. 3a; W. Chr. 126; Deismann (1) 192 ff. (2) 172 ff.; Musurillo (whom I follow).

32. Primitinos: Preimeiteinos. See Musurillo for full discussion of bishops, etc.

33. *Mand.* x 1. For influence of rich in Clement's days: Euseb. HE v. 21, cf. Loukian *de morte Per.* 13, 16.

34. *Quis Dives;* Tollington ch. x.

35. *Paid.* 274, 271, 439 f., 574, 877.

36. Clem. *Q.D.* 955, cf. Loukian, *l.c.* 16.

37. Clem. 299 and 473.

10. MORE PEOPLE ON THE NILE: LAW

1. Oxy. 1479, late 1st c. Advocate: *synegoros.*

2. Oxy. 97. Prefect Rutilius Lupus (CIG 4948) in 18–19th year of Trajan; the pap. is joined to another document of 19th year.

3. Oxy. 472: seems tried before an epistrategos.

4. Oxy. 486. Endorsed: "If this is true, petition the strategos, delivering (him a copy of this)." Humbert 109.

5. Giss. bibl. 20. Petty pleader: *rhetoriskos.* Cf. BGU 1676; J.L. (2) 129.

6. Mich. 493, 2nd c.

7. Mich. 507, 2nd–3rd c. Artemis to Sokrates. Address is from Harpakysis, prob. her host in Alex. In general, J.L. (2) 71 f. Request for guardian, Oxy. 720 (A.D. 247), etc.

8. Oxy. 726.

9. Oxy. 1667, Dorion to Apion.

10. Oxy. 1160. See J.L. (2) 39; Oxy. 120. Pot, *koukouma* (*cucuma*); darling, *mychos*.

11. Oxy. 709. Conventus: W. *Archiv.* iv 366 ff.

12. Oxy. 1456. Strategos: Oxy. 1260, 1115. For a recent study of the Prefect's jurisdiction: Humbert. Delegates to his court at Alex., Oxy. 59 (A.D. 292).

13. Oxy. 86. Helene is illiterate.

14. Boat: CPH 119 (3rd c.); Oxy. 86 (W. *Chr.* 46); PSI 298 (4th c.); Grenf. ii 82 (400); *ibid.* 80 (402); *ibid.* 81 (403), also 81a; *St. Pal.* viii 774 (572), also Oxy. 149: Cair.-Masp. 136 (6th c.): cf. Wessely, *Sitz. Wien. Ak.* cxlix 1905 21 (4th c.) and Cair-Masp. 58 (6th c.). Upkeep: last-named pap. for *pakton tou Augoustaliou* of Governor of Thebaid.

15. Oxy. 2116; REg 242. Sarapion may be same as in Oxy. 2137 (land lease); less likely 2135. Roman Archives: adjective dubious. What oikonomoi do here is not clear; under Romans official ones were often connected with imperial *ousiai*, cf. Hamb. 8.

16. Lond. 1159; W. *Chr.* 435; REg 376.

17. Amh. 107, cf. (same year) Ryl. 85 and BGU 807.

18. Oxy. 2139, from Spart(iates), Phamenoth, cf. 2140. and the poulterer, 1568.

19. Oxy. 2138.

20. Van Groningen, *Aeg.* xiii 1933, 21–4. The god had a centre at Tebtynis in district of Polemon.

21. Oxy. 529.

22. Mich. 503. Antonios is former royal-secretary of the Greater Diospolite Nome.

23. Mich. 508. Radish oil: Plin. xix 26, cf. Mich. 481, Fay. 95 (intro.), Ross.-Georg. ii 41, 54, etc.; Baudi, *Aeg.* xvii 1937, 406. Much used as cheap: Athen. ii 57b; Reil 138 n. 2. For pleasure at increase in family: W. *Chr.* 419. Staff and *sysitia*, see p. 136 of the Mich. pap. Members of guilds and birth of child: Boak, TAPA lxviii 1937, 215.

24. Oxy. 1431. Eras: see Oxy. 1632 and Oxy. xii p. 89 f.

11. THE INSATIABLE SEA

1. Birch ZAS ix 119 f. 1871; Newberry, Amh. Pap. 1988 pls. xix–xxi; Spiegelberg PSBA xxiv 41–50; Erman (4) 169–71; Ranke in Gressmann, Altor. Texte zum AT (2nd ed.) 7 f.; Roeder (12) 71–3; Gardiner (12) 76–81 and (19) 74–85; Posener (6); Lefebvre (1) 106–13 and (6); Sayce JEA xix 56, Te Velde 122–3.

2. Following Lefebvre and Gardiner: Wilson ANET 14 and Schott (3) 212–14.

3. Astarte: Wiedemann (1) 433; BIFAO xxv 191; Cook 108; Anat and A. for Seth, Chester B. i 3, 4, and index, Griffiths (1). Later times: Hdt. ii 112: JEA xxxiv 84 (Zenon letter about her priests at Memphis); ex-voto, Aimé-Giron BIFAO xxv 191–211, etc. Also: Leclant, Syria 1967 1-67 with refs.

4. Sayce, l.c.; Albright JPOS xvi 18 n. 6. See also Fontenrose 121–216.

5. Friedrich, Ar. Or. xvii 1, 230–54, and JKF ii 149 f.

6. Goetze ANET 125; Albright l.c. 18; Gaster, Bi. Or. ix 84 f.; Fontenrose 133, 191, 259, 283.

7. Ginsberg ANET 129–31; Gaster, Thespis, 133–61.

8. Albright, l.c.; Lefebvre (6) and (1); Virolleaud, 82–4; Gaster, Bi. Or. ix 82–5; Fontenrose 129 ff.

9. Stele of Gebel Barkal, Reisner ZAS lxix 301; Yeivin JPOS xiv 199 n. 33; Gardiner (13) i 7* and 163*. Möller, ZAS lvi 42, dates the myth to reign of Haremheb, end of 14th c. B.C. See also Ugaritic Texts 137, 133, 68; Goyon (1) 374–7.

10. Mercer Eg. Relig. iii 192–203; Bonnet, (1) 55–7; Glanville ZAS lxvi 108 and lxviii 29–30; Säve-S. (6) 37–9.

11. See n. 3 above; also Mercer l.c., Bonnet, Ranke in Griff. St, 415–17.

12. Pap. Beatty i 3, 4.

13. Ibid. 3, 1–5; Magic Harris pap. 3 (8–9): Lange 29–31.

14. Harris vii, Vs. 1, 5 (Seth mates anally with Anat), Dawson in JEA xxii 1936, 107 (4). Astarte comes with Re to see destroyed foe: Chassinat (1) vi 112, xii pls. cxx-cxxi. Anat (Anta) and Astarte: Montet (2) 160, 169. Also, Te Velde, 28, 30, 113, 130.

15. Posener (6) 468.

16. Pap. Anast. ii 1, 1 (iv, vi, 1–10); Biblioth. Aeg. vii 12. And Kemi v 6; Montet (2) 134, 142.

17. Lefebvre (1) 150 f.; Sethe ZAS xxviii 1891 124; Spiegelberg PSBA xxiv 48.

18. Lefebvre (1) 138; Erman ZAS xviii 94; Gardiner PSBA xxvii 1905, 185; Dawson and Peet JEA xix 167; Yoyotte, R. d'Eg. ix 159–9. As Seth: Vandier (6) 5–9. Initiation-rite: Vikentiev, cited Jesi Aeg. xlii 296.

19. Pap. Jumilhac 3, 18–22; Vandier (6) 6; Edfou viii 7, 3; CT iv 351d–352a and Edfou iv 187, 9–10.

20. Gardiner JEA xix 98. Hearst pap. 12–14: "Who is knowing like Re? Blacken the body with charcoal so as to capture the god on high."

21. Unamun i 8.

22. Griffiths (1) 15, 38; Sethe (1) 100; Rusch ZAS lx 39.

23. Posener (6) 469.

24. Drioton (4) 91 ff. Temple of Osiris at Abydos: Schott (2) 4–59; Pap. Louvre 3129; BM 10252 (copied 361 B.C.). Compiler used several pieces: Gebb as head of divine tribunal; also Re-Harakhti. Drioton (4) 94–6.

25. Drioton (4). Louvre col. C, lines 20 ff.; Schott *Urk.* 16-25. I deal only cursorily with Seth as national foe: see Te Velde 109 ff. etc.

26. Access: Hdt. ii 37. Bigeh: Plout. *de Is.* 20; Diod. i 22; Juncker (2) p. vii. Thoth of the abaton: Boylan 168. Abydos: Strab. xvii 44.

27. Griffiths (1) esp. ch. v.

28. Rosetta decree, demotic version, 15.

29. Nagel, fig. 1.

30. Nagel 33-4; De Morgan *Cat. Mons. et Inscrs. de l'Eg. ant.* i 117, 5; Gauthier, *Livre des Rois* iii 92, 420; P. Leyd. i 346 (Leemans, *Mons. Eg. Mus. Ant. Pays-Bas* ii pl. cxxxix); Chabas 102 ff.; LD pl. ccclxxii, 2 and ccclxxxi.

31. Champollion, *Mons.* pl. ccxx.

32. (1) Chabas 78; P. Sallier iv pl. xvii 3, 4; BM *Select Pap.* pl. clx; Budge (5) 2nd s. pl. civ. (2) Erman ZAS xxxviii 20. (3) Erman ZAS xxxi 121. (4) P. Magic Harris v, 8-10; Budge (5) 1st s. pl. xxiv; Lange (Harris) 40; repeated on Hibeh temple, time of Dareios II, Brugsch (11) pl. xxv, 10 (but Seth has been replaced by Horos). (5) P. Louvre 3292, 10, cf. Naville BD ch. xxxix; *Destruction of Apepi* ix 5. For Nubti: Montet (2) 62, 67.

Nagel (2) 67 f., citing Sethe and MIFAO xxiv 80. Cf. BM pap. 10188 xvi 21-2: "the great Ennead that is in the front of the boat of Re, makes you (Apepi) recoil. The spear of Seth is on your nape". See also small wooden ex-voto, Deir el-Medineh, BIFAO xxviii 1928, 38, and rep. from Med. Habu (Daressy (5) 159 court 30): Nagel (2) 66-8. For accord of Seth and Horos in washing dead king: RT xxxix 70. Seth in solar boat, Te Velde, 20, 99-108; against Apophis, esp. 99-107.

33. Muller (1) 107 f.; Harris (axe may be harpoon); Vatican Mag. Pap.; Erman ZAS xxxi 1893, 121. "The god of Ombos (pierces) the serpent with his shafts" Erman ZAS xxxciii 20. In BD ch. xl the serpent attacks the Ass of Seth: Muller (1) fig. 106. The Greek pap. here cited: Muller 104, no ref. For Eighteenth Dyn. on, confusion of Seth and Apepi, Muller 108 f. In late Nineteenth Dyn. "Nubti strikes his arrows into him (Wnti) after he has . . . heaven and earth with his thunder," Lange (2) 40, who unnecessarily takes shaft as spear, since Seth is patron of arrow-shooting, LD iii pl. xxxvib.

34. Med. pap. of Berlin 21, 2-3; Wreszinski (6) i 103.

35. PT 1261a-b; Griffiths (1) 11.

36. Pap. Beatty i 16, 4; *Unamen* ii 19; *De Is.* 55; Hopfner (1) ii 232 f.

37. Rhind 87, 6-7.

38. CT iii 138b.

39. PT 1149b-1151c.

40. Bull Seth, Griffiths (1) 2, 35; sacrificial bulls PT 1534a, 1550a; bull who slew 1977b; testicles 418a, 679a.

41. Utterance 386, a serpent charm.

42. PT 524-6 (Utt. 261). Bull-roar, Muller (1) 103 f.

43. PT 298-9 (Utt. 255); 298b has Seth-animal as determinative. Much more might be said of Seth as imaging the national foe.

44. Voltan, *Analecta Aeg.* iv; Gardiner *JEA* i 34; Scharff (4) 60; Wilson *ANET* 47 (water-monster). Voltan 76 (krokodil des Wassers).

45. Posener, *Rev. d'Eg.* vii 80 f. *Peasant* B1, 178 f.; stele of Israel, 20; Gardiner *JEA* i 34.

46. Sungod: *JEA* i 34.

47. Nagel (1) and (2); Edgerton-Wilson, *Hist. Rec. Ramses III*, SAOC xii 38; Capart *CE* xli 29–31; Derchain, *Rev. d'Eg.* ix 37; P. Anast. ii 2, 6; Griffiths (1) 12, 21. He joins with Horos to fight snake and defend deadman, PT 678a–c; Schott, *Mythe* 67.

48. Pap. Beatty vii no. 5, 4–5; *Amduat* 7th hour; Vandier *Bibl. d'Et.* IFAO xviii 220–5; and above here, Nagel.

49. BD cviii; Sethe *ZÄS* lix 47* and 85; Thoth's magic against Apepi: Naville (1); Boylan 60 n. 4.

50. P. Boulaq xvii 3, 7 and 4, 1. Wille, *Nouv. Clio* v 182.

51. Gardiner (19) 78.

52. *De Is.* 32.

53. *Ibid.* 40.

54. W. S. Anderson *TAPA* 1960, xci; on light and dark 2–5, sea and land 21 f., matter (Lucret. ii 550) and atomic compounds (ii 552), wreck (ii 1174), coasts (i 22 and ii 224); denial that sea created us (ii 1155).

55. Yahweh defeats Sea: *Job.* 9, 8; 26, 12; 38, 8–11; *Ps.* 77, 19; *Isaiah* 19, 1; *Deut.* 33, 26.

56. Cf. *Ps.* 74, 12–4.

57. F. F. Bruce 53–6. And *Isaiah* 30, 7; *Job*, 26, 12 f. and 9, 13; *Ps.* 89, 8–10.

58. See *Ps.* 87, 4: *Ezek.* 29, 3; *Job* 41, 1, 1–3; *Ps.* 74, 14.

59. *Isaiah* 27, 1; and Ugar. Text 67, 1, 1–13; Bruce 65 n. 18.

60. *Rev.* 12, 3. The rebirth of this sort of imagery in *Rev.* is interesting and important: Bruce 64 f.

61. Cf. *Hub.* 3, 17 f.; *Psalms* 66, 18 and 98; *Is.* 42, 10–3 and 51, 9.

62. QN. iv 2; Plin. xix *init.*; Tac. *Ann.* xii 22. He was prefect A.D. 55. Lefebvre 26; Erman (4) 35; Pieper 14; Vikentiev, *L'énigme d'un pap.* (Berl. 3024) 1940; Roeder (12). For Arabs: Doutté, *Magie et Relig. dans l'Afrique du N.* 93; Moslem jurists discussed if such unions lawful, Robertson Smith 50; see also Tremearne, *Hausa Superstitions and Customs* 155.

12. FLOOD AND THUNDER

1. Lambrechts for refs. He argues that the resurrection is a late idea brought about probably by the influence of Osiris, cf. R. de Vaux, *Rev. Bibl.* 1933, 31–56. Glotz *REG* 1920 and Gow *JHS* 1938 180 and 1940 95 for the Fayum Pap. which Glotz takes to speak of a mystery-drama of Adonis (*deikterion* as its hall), 3rd c. B.C. The man buys a Garland for Adonis, but there is no proof of a dramatic show; or if there was one, what it meant. Cyril, *In Isaiam* xviii 1–2; Glotz 205.

See also Frazer, *Adonis, Attis and Osiris.* Henne, *Aeg.* 1933, 3–4 690 deals with inscr. of Dendera, where the garden seems a large vase with flowers—but it's a matter of the great festivals of Choiak (20th at Bousiris) or Hathyr, if we put the rite in the Roman era. For a possible Garden of O. in Philai district: Gunn (1) 34. In general: W. Atallah, *Adonis* 1966.

2. Comparisons in Hooke (2) 133–5. Noah seems raised to rank of deity and the hero of West-Semitic tale of flood was known in Babylon not only under original name of Nah but also in the Babylonised form of Nehum: Lewy 274.

3. Erman (4) 47–9; Budge (1) 463–7; Muller (1) 73–6; Naville, TS Bull. Arch. iv 1 ff.; Lefebvre, *ibid*. viii 412 ff.; Roeder, Urk. 142 ff. Pomegranates is uncertain; mandrakes and haematite (found at Abu) also proposed. Text goes on with more complaints of Re about pain, weariness, and wish to destroy men. "I shall not recover till another period comes." Nut changes into a cow and takes him: Budge 466. It is said that Re's soul lives in all the land, but Seth's only in the Mtns. of the East.

4. Vandier, *Rel. Eg.*, 38.

5. FHG iii 223 fr. 14, cf. *Exod*. iii 1; *Wisdom* ii 6–8; B. 291. Montet (3) 29–34 tries to set under Marenptah, c. 1225–1215 B.C.

6. *Metaph. Ps.* 104, 29 *Life of W*, ii 341 (Teubner 1883) by Theofridus. Epternacensis. For water-miracle and water-into-wine: C. H. Talbot, *A.-S. Missionaries in Germany* 1954, 13 f. and 15.

7. Euseb. HE vii 21 ff.; Scott, *Hermetica* i 68.

8. *Adv. oct. haer*. i, 51.

9. Gretserus, *Comm. Cod. Europalatas*, cited B. 292 n. 1.

10. P. Leyd. x 12, 7–10. Today the Egyptians at some religious festivals make lentils germinate in damp cotton: Sauneron in Posener (5) 204; Jumilhac, *ibid*. 203. See also B. 248.

11. Both Tacitus and Dion K. refer to the red Thames. Here are a few refs. of red waters from the Celtic area: Cuchulainn: E. Hull, *Cuchullain Saga* 246 f. and *Celtic Rev*. xxi 157, x 277 ff.; Hull, FL *of Brit. Isles* 60: esp. connected with Babd the war-goddess. Wells in Wales: *Chronicon Adae de Usk* (Ed. E. M. Thompson) 218 for Llewelyn ap. Griffith, last Prince of Wales; R. Fenton, *Tour in Wales* (ed. Fisher 1917) for Rhys ap. Pewdwr (beheaded). After battles and murders: F. Jones, *Holy Wells of Wales*, 54. Cumberland: Bulwer, *Dict. of W. Cumb.* 1883, 636; W. T. McIntire, *Cumb. Westmor. Trans.* 1945 xliv. Saints: W. J. Rees, *Lives of Cambro-Brit. Saints*, 7, 293, 126; Gould–Fisher, *Lives of Brit. Sts.* i 321–7, ii 160; F. Jones 40 f.; A. W. Wade-Evans, *Life St David* 12, 91; Morris-Jones and Rhys, *Elucidarium* 1894, 109, etc.

Iliad xi 52; Cook *Zeus* iii, I, 478–81.

12. Water from Osiris: Alliot (1) 14, cf. phrase "sweat that comes out of Hapi", *ibid*. 15; "the Nile that comes from the sweat of your hands", Erman AZ xxxviii 1900, 30. Also AZ l 69 ff.; Yoyotte (5) 101. Plout. says Osiris was called the Ocean, *de Is.* 34 cf. 32; he makes Nile flood, 64; is principle of all humanity 33, 36, cf. BIFAO xxvii 1927, 57 and Moret (11) 733; RT x 1888, 186 and i 197.

13. Dixon: *Maidu Myths*, BAM xvii 1902–7 and *Maidu Texts* 1912.

14. *Timaios* 22; Usener 39.

15. Plato says firstborn of Heaven and Earth are Okeanos and Tethys, and speaks of the Circuits of the Soul bound up with the River of the Body (Stewart, *Myths of Plato*, ed. Levy 1960, 262). Note the Council of Gods called by Zeus at end of Kritias' myth, to deal with the corruption by wealth and power: an account in accordance with both Egyptian and Sumerian creation-myths. In *Tim*. Solon tells of the First Man (Phoroneus) with Niobe, and the Flood. Saviour Nile: Julian *or*. iii 119B.

Thera: G. de Beer, *Listener* 15 Sept. 1966; Petrie JEA 1925, 307; *Times* 20 July 1967; R. Carpenter, *Discontinuity* 1967 ch. 2.

16. Amm. xxii 15, 30; also xvii 7, 11. On Solon and Egypt, xxii 16, 22; and Diod. i 98, 1.

17. Budge (1) 197 f.; Naville BD i (Leyd. pap. of Re) and PSBA Dec. 1904. Pap. of Ani: BM 10470 sheet 29, Budge (20) 311 f.

18. Erman (9) 432; Brugsch AZ xiv 1876, 89; Breasted (1) ii par. 814; Kees AZ lxv 1930, 83 f. Sekhmet had her cult at Rehesu, near Letopolis. We have seen her as the yearly Fever. She also appears as Seth's foe: P. Sallier iv, 2, 3; on night of 25 Thoth: "Sekhmet went to the Eastern Mtns. to strike the companions of Seth." Her rel. to Flood-destruction and the New Year: Muller (1) 76.

19. Bruyère (3) esp. 33–5. Nery: C. Campbell 100; male in 4 tombs of Valley of Queens. Nu, cxlvi, Nebseni, xvii.

20. Drioton (11) no. vii, pp. 384–7. Theban Nekropolis: Bruyère (2) 38 fig. 19, 41 fig. 21, 53 fig. 33, 116 fig. 56. Hathor as Lady of N. Sky; CE liv 1952, 363–4.

21. Juncker (9); Spiegelberg SBAW 1915, 876. Also Budge (11) pp. xxiii–xxxii and 14–41; Juncker (1); Sethe (14). Assimilation with Sekhmet: Kees (9) 142 (PT 262b); CT 172d, Hathor, "my heart is that of a lion", ref. to Eye tales. For Cataract, Juncker (9) 35. Bigeh: CT ii 37b; Juncker (1) 82; Sethe (14) 13. Note a version that gives much importance to tale of Fugitive Eye comes from nekrop. of Aswan. Note her closeness to Horos, also the Eye; both at times said to be from the same region of Nubia (Punt); he is at times her son or husband; as lord of Punt he is a liongod. Mercer (4); Juncker (1) 77 and (9) 15, etc. Juncker (5) tries to show Hathor always the wife of Horos.

22. Birthplace of Sun, and of Osiris: Champollion, *Notices* i 172, etc.

23. Muller (1) 86–8.

24. Juncker (9) 54. P. Sallier iv 24, 2 has "The sun's eye (lit. the Intact One), the Mistress who is in the sky as . . . to seeking (that which?) stood before, which was among the wicked ones, for (?) their . . . in the Delta." Muller (1) 383, 84, 76.

25. Muller (1) 86 and 388 n. 28.

26. Spiegelberg (7): this Leyden pap. has the fable of the Lion and the Mouse.

27. Budge (1) 142 f.; Muller (1) 68–70, 76–9, 88; Budge, *Archaeologia* 11

1890, 393–608 and (5) 14 pl. xii. Rels. to texts on Isis and Horos' scorpion-bite: E. Lefébure AZ xxi 32 (1883).

28. Posener (7) 41–3, 155 f.; date 44; Lefebvre (2) 92; Wilson ANET 444 and (3) 106–8 and 111. Sun's failure to shine, in magic texts: Sauneron BSFE viii 13 f. Cf. Teaching of Marikare, Posener, Bi. Or. viii 169.

29. Kuentz (2) esp. 236–7.

30. Breasted (1) iii pars. 407, 410.

31. Ibid. 425.

32. Presumably there was a temporary lull in midwinter. Abridged version has no ref. to Sutekh or weather: G. Lefebvre (5). The main text opens with invocation of Horos the Falcon, Conqueror of the Ombite (Seth); Horos rampart of flint and Egypt. See also Te Velde, 133; and for Seth as stormgod, 25, 42, 85, 90–1, 102–3, 128, 132.

33. Mercer (1) 55, 223; Budge (15) ii 283. Not many gods identified with Seth; in NK at Avaris Set and Baal both rep. with same cult-animal: Budge (15) ii 283. Under R. III, Montu and Seth identified: Nelson, Med. Habu ii pl. 80. Late in NK, Seth's place taken by Apepi, the great serpent. Efforts have been made to prove Seth of Hyksos not an Egyptian god, linking his name Sutekh with Hittite Soutah (WB iv 345; E.S. Meyer, Hist. de l'Ant. ii 301). For Hyksos: Montet (2) 52 ff.—his human form in the Delta.

34. Wainwright (2) 5.

35. Ibid. 5–6; JEA xvii 194 for Akhmim fossils and sign.

36. Ibid. 6 with refs.

37. Ibid., with details.

38. PT 13b–14a, cf. 1747a and 30b; Sethe on PT 30: pair of blocks of iron.

39. PT 1983a–e, cf. 1330a.

40. PT 749b–e.

41. PT 1454a–1455a and 1453a–1454a. Ani: Budge. ch. xxiii, pl. xv.

42. Wainwright (2) 7 n. 1. Roman times: Schiaparelli i 103.

43. Déveria 349, 351. Tutankhamen's tomb: Lacau pl. xl 207; ILN 7 July 1928 4 ff. Lightning-iron in Ceylon, Prior 35. Iron from stone struck by lightning: S. de Sacy Chrestomathie arabe 1827 iii 440. Girls devoted to lightning-deity on Guinea Coast: G. Zundel, Z. Gesell. Erdkunde xii 1877, 417, wearing a zigzag piece. Blastpower in iron: Wainwright (2) 8, on an Arab story.

44. Lefebvre (1) 37; Erman (4) 32 f.; Golenischeff (5); Maspero (2) 104.

45. Tylor, Prim. Cult. ii 262 f. with refs.

46. Brinton, Myths of New World 153; Herrera, Indias Occidentales, Dec. v 4; Prescott, Peru i 86; Markham, Rites and Laws of Incas 16, 81, etc.

47. E. Lembke, Volksthümliches in Ostpreussen 1884–7, 41. Tremearne, Ban of Bori 218.

48. PT 2078.

49. Wainwright (2) 9 for refs. and examples.

50. Wainwright (2) 9 f.

51. PT 907, cf. 1575 (?).

52. PT 305.

53. PT 1121-2.

54. PT 736, 770, etc., also 1562.

55. PT 2051, cf. 1454, 749, 530. Eisler states that the image of the *mshtyw* comes from the Gilgamesh epic where one of the heroes tears off "the right hand" of the heavenly Bull and throws it before Ishtar, who wails over it. He compares Nut with raised hands before the bulls-leg on the Assiut sarcophagus; and the Paris mag. pap. 1285, 130, 1307. At Gilgamesh's orders the head of the Bull is encased in gold and bluestone, and hung up for the god Lugal-banadda. Hence the head as well as the leg of the Bull in the planisphere of Athens Gundel, *Dekane* pl. 13) and the head to be found on the Senmut tomb, Ramasseum, etc. The Foreleg constellation was familiar to the Hebrews, who may well have got the image from Egypt since no constellation of this name occurs in Babylonian star-lists. JEA xxvii 149 f. I cannot check all this. For Seth and foreleg, Te Velde 86-91.

56. Palmer JAI 1884 292.

57. Schoolcraft, *Indian Tribes* i 269, 311; Smith, *Virginia* in Pinkerton xiii 54; Waitz, iii 223; Squier, *Abor. Mon. of NY* 156; Caitlin, *NA Indians* i 180. South Seas: Mariner, *Tonga Is.* ii 134; Turner, *Polynesia* 103; Taylor, *New Z.* 101, 114, 256.

58. Callaway, *Rel. of Amazulu* 393; Burton, *W. and W. fr. Afr.* 454. Castren, *Finn. Myth.* 295; Kalevala.

59. Tylor PC ii 71.

60. Hdt. iv 158, cf. 185 Atlas as sky-support, 185. See J.L. (1) for Atlas, Aitna, etc.

61. Apollod. *epit.* vi 18; Tzetzes *Lyk.* 1047.

62. Strab. vii 3, 8, cf. Arrian *anab.* i 4 6-8.

63. U. Holmberg (Narva) *Der Baum des Lebens* (Ann. Ac. Sc. Fenn. B. 16, 3 1922-3) 10, 17, 19.

64. Livy xl 58. H. d'A. de Joubainville, *Les. prem. inhabs. de l'Europe* 1894 ii 316 n. 2. Burton, *Thousand Nights and a Night* 1885 vi 100 and Macnaughten, *The Alif Laila* 1839 iii 97. Nut: Lacau in Quibell 32. Gardiner (1) 15, 3.

65. W. Planert, ZE 1907, 566; Strehlow, *A. and L.* i 6 and ii 73. K. Englemann, *Die Eingeborenen der Kol. Süd Aust.* 1908, 184.

66. Haddon, *Camb. Exped.* v 22 (also variants). In Mindanao (Philippines) traditional magic lines ended the petrifaction: Beyer, *J. of Sc.* 1913 viii 97.

67. Codrington, *Melanesians* 1891, 155 f.; sacrifices offered at the stone said to be Quasavara.

68. Brown, *Yoruba Lang.* p. xvi; Burton, *Dahome* ii 142. For iron weapons in cosmic battles: Sanchoniathon on Kronos: Euseb. *Praep. Ev.* i 10, 18 (Teub. i 45) cf. Sadidos killing Kronos, "with his own iron", i x 21 (*sideros* could merely mean sword); Zeus, Roscher, cols. 1426-8; Satan and lightning, *Luke* x 18. Further beliefs among Arabs and in Rajputana: Wainwright (2) 13.

69. Sethe, AZ lix pls. 47*, 48*, pp. 75, 85 f; Budge (5) f. 21

70. Schott vi 45; 44 note e; Budge (5) 13; Schott 59, 2.

71. *De Is.* 62.

72. Wainwright (2) 14; Diod. i 21.

73. Golischeneff (2) pl. iii, v.

74. Moret CRAI 1914, 569.

75. Brunton iii 20; Petrie (4) i, 10 f.

76. Brunton iii pl. xxxii, p. 18.

77. *De Is.* 50. In PT Utt. 324, two female demons in form of hippo. and ass are slain: charm against sickness. Two clubs of Horus are involved in slaying the hippopotamus; there seems a Sethian atmosphere. The speaker is a magician. Mercer ii 249. This is the only ref. to a hippo. in PT.

78. Wainwright argues that iron entered little into industrial life till NK; till then iron little mentioned. Now the term iron-of-heaven comes in: Budge (5) pl. xv; Rougé (1) pl. 226; LD iii pl. 194; Wreszinski (2) no. 88. It thus replaces on several occasions the simple use of "iron" in the old formulas: Wainwright (2) 14.

79. Derived from image of the Sacrifice of the Great Beast, where bits of the Body or Bones constitute the universe. Strehlow, *A. and L.* ii 11. Cf. Dieri cosmic legend explaining the killing of Duturunna: skin of kangaroo pegged over with 6 points of orientation, 4 legs, head and tail. Siebert, *Globus* xcvii 1910, 46.

80. Muller (1) 109 f., 59.

81. Dion K. lxxii 8, 4; Leclant BFLS xxxvii 1959, 306; J. and L. Robert, REG lxii 1949, 159 f.; Kubitschek PhW lv 1935, 792; J. Guey RPh xxii 1948, 16–62; Posener *ibid.*, xxv 1951, 162–8; Momigliano RSI lxvi 1954, 518–20.

82. Capitol. *M. Ant.* xxiv; Xiphilin, Abridge. Dion lxxi 9; Legion XII: had been at siege of Jerusalem A.D. 70: N. de Vergers *Essai sur Marc-Aurèle* 1860, 92 f.

83. Brusin, *Scavi* 166 f.; Pascal, *Cults of Cisalpine Gaul* 47 f.; A. Calderini, *Aquileia Nostra* viii 1937, 67–72.

84. Epithet used of Apis Bull, Hdt. iii 27; of Osiris and civilisers of Egypt, Diod. i 17 2; of healers Asklepios and Hygieia, etc. Two Isiac dedications at divine orders in Cisalpine Gaul: CIL v 10 (Insc. It. x, 1, 601); 484 (x III, 1): Pascal 45.

85. OGI 56, 4 (p. 96); 90, 7 (145); divination, Diod. i 70, 9; Suidas sv; admin. Otto ii 138, 159; i 85–8; lore, *ibid.*, ii 233, i 88.

86. Oxy. 465, 171–4, cf. 103–22: Oxy. iii pp. 136, 126.

87. Spart. *Marc. Aur.* xix.

88. Guey, Posener cited above n. 81; Taautos (Festugière (2) iii p. cxliii). Shu and water: Budge (1) 439 (lake).

89. Aristot. DIN 7 and 12, cf. *Analyt. post.* ii 13, 4; Plin. v 9 (10) cf. xviii 47, 2; Plout. *De Is.* 43; Drioton *Eg. Rel.* i 1933, 46; Eumenes *Paneg. Const.* ix (PL viii 629); Euseb. *Praep. Ev.* iii 12, 1; Lucan x 209 and 214 f.; B. 234–6. Thoth: Boylan 184, 197.

13. BOATS ON THE NILE

1. P. Gauckler, *Mon. Piot.* xii 1905, 113 ff.; Assmann JDAI xxi 1906, 107 ff.; Dessau ILS 9456; Inv. d. mos. no. 576. Prob. from an illustrated catalogue of ships, of which remnants survive in A. Gellius, Nonius, Isidorus of Seville. Rostovtzeff SEHRE 1957, 615 f.

2. SHA Aurelian 47.

3. In this chapter I lean heavily on Merzagora: see her pages 111–5 for terms and refs.

4. Some refs. are BGU 812 (2–3 c.), Lond. iii 1164h (3 c.), Grenf. i 49 (W. *Chr.* 248), Oxy. 1260 and 2136, BGU 1663, Cair.-Goodsp. 14 (4 c.), Mon. 4, 5. v. (6 c.). In BGU 812 (cf. Cair.-Preis. 34—A.D. 315) it is contrasted with *ploiaria skaphoplora*; seems contrast of Greek and Egyptian. See for *skaphopakton*, Oxy. 1554 (251) cf. 1555 and 1553; for *pakton*, Reil 88.

5. Oxy. 1260.

6. See n. 4 above; also Oxy. 1652 (3 c.) and Thead. 59, *platypegia*.

7. Oxy. 1652.

8. Oxy. 1650 col. ii. Prob. for a *naukleros* or a pilot.

9. Merzagora 116–20 for refs. and details. We even find *elaphantegos* in Ptol. times: Rostovtzeff, *Archiv* iv 301; Petr. ii 40; W. *Chr.* 452; Muller GGM i 171 c. 83; Merzagora 119 f.

10. Ryl. 196; Otto i 94 f. *Hiera ploia*: Lond. i 122 (4 c.), Otto i 332 n. 4; Theban times, Revillout, *Mél.* 344; gold boat of Osiris, Hib. 27 (301–240 B.C.); *ploion theou*, Lond. ii 266 (1–2 c.); Wessely *Denk. d.k.Ak.d. Wiss.* 1902 (Karanis u. Sok. Nesos 16).

11. Oxy. 1846. See also *Arch.* ii 447 n. 77 (2 c.); *St. Pal.* xxii 183 (? A.D. 138), BGU 10 (192), *ibid.* 277 (2 c.); Rainer 8 (Wessely *l.c.* 15, 72, 74) 2 c., Tebt. ii 347 (2 c.), BGU 337 (2–3 c.)=W. *Chr.* 92, Oxy. 1846 (5–6 c.), Oxy. 1867 (7 c.).

12. Oxy. 1867.

13. W.O. i p. 282; Meyer O. p. 160; Flor. 91 (2 c.); Oertel 272. But I don't want to go in detail into charges, dues, etc.

14. PSI 734; Merzagora 122.

15. W.O. ii 468, 479, 1408, 1564–5; SB i 2084; Theb. O. 77 f., cf. W.O. ii 1408, SB i 2084. Definite shape of boat. Theb. O. 78 (A.D. 100).

16. Diod. i 35, 10; see W.O. i pp. 228–30; Merzagora 123.

17. Budge (1) 393; Naville BD ii 23; H. M. Stewart 87, 89. PT 303b–d. "The ropes are knotted, the boats of N are tied together," 1376a, cf. 802a, 340d, 1742b.

18. SB 7173 (2 c.); Vitelli, cf. W.O. ii 1153; Oertel 262; Merzagora 124 f.

19. Hdt. ii 29. Ropes: rec. for straw and palm-fibre cords (Byz.): Hermop. pap. 36; rope-weaving technique shown, Theban Tomb 260, JEA iii 125 f.; tow-rope, Oxy. 1834.

For other boats, *kasiotikon, stephanikon, poreion, kerkouroi (kerkouroskaphai), taurokerkouroi*: see Merzagora 126–30. They are mostly Ptolemaic.

20. Three-oared, *triskalmos*: Cair. Masp. 151=SB 6778 (3 c. B.C.)

21. Oxy. 1068 (3 c.), J.L. (2) 232, cf. Lond. v 1714 (A.D. 570), Cair-Masp. 151. *Lembos, keletes, kybaia* or *kerkouros*: also seem Ptol., see Merzagora, 128–30. Diminutive, *kybidion*. Skaphe: M. 126.

22. Hdt. ii 96; Mayser i 36; Assmann, *Hermes* xxxi 1896, 180 ff. criticises Hdt.'s account; Merzagora replies 128. See Hibeh 100 (267 B.C.), barley; W. *Chr.* 11 (123 B.C.), armed men on Nile from Hermonthis to Crocodilopolis.

23. Oxy. 1650.

24. Oxy. 1220; J.L. (2) 290. See Oxy. 2153 cited above, pakton with frightened young girl. List: Oxy. 1658.

25. Oxy. 814; and Cair.-Masp. 20 (6 c.), 143, 147, and Hamb. 56 v. (6–7 c.).

26. PSI 948 (A.D. 345), see Oxy. 1650 above, cf. 1651 (3 c.).

27. BGU 812 (2–3 c.), cf. SB 4323, *paktomarion*. *Arsenikos*: does it mean for men (though actually here used for goods—cf. Oxy. 741)? or merely "strong"? Note *arsenikoi kalamoi*, St. Pal. xx 940 (7 c.), BGU 837. Strab. xvii 50 stresses weak structure.

28. Oxy. 1585.

29. Oxy. 1197; Oertel 130. Oxy. ix 219 for dermatites.

30. Prokop. de aedif. vi, 1; Merzagora 133—also for *libyrnoi* or *libernoi*, *lousoriai* (Oxy. 1048, 4 5 c.), *karis* and *haliadion* (both late): M. 133 f.

31. Merzagora 135 for lists of contracts, misthoprasiai, apographai, other declarations; P. Kunkel 1–3 (*Archiv* viii 187–90) 1 c. B.C., etc.

32. Oxy. 1259 (3 copies: 2 to strat., 1 to sit.). Administration: *cheirismos*. Master: *naukleros*. Cf. Oxy. 708 for Neapolis; W. *Chr.* 508–9; BGU 8 ii 29–30.

33. St. Pal. xx 32 (A.D. 231), Oxy. 2125 (220–1) to sitologos of Sko district. Also PSI 1048, *potamia ploia*.

34. Oxy. 1068; Cronert, *Racc. Lumb.* 524. And Magd. 11 (3 c. B.C.); W. *Chr.* 442. Cargo not less than 500 art. in *ploion skaphoploron* (315) C. Preis. 34; 700 in a *ploion polykopon* (338) Oxy. 86. *Prosagogis* with 2500, Lille 21 (221 B.C.); *lembos*, 300, Petrie ii 20 (252 B.C.); *kydaron*, 150, Oxy. 1197 (A.D. 211).

35. BGU 1157 (1 c. B.C.) and 1663 (A.D. 3 c.); Lond. v 1718 (6 c.)—(?) meteorological table.

36. Oxy. 1260 (A.D. 216) and Oxy 1650 (1–2 c.).

37. Flor. 305.

38. Oxy. 1738; other boats belong to Romanos the sailor, Horion the sailor, Pasion, Zoeilos the sailor. List: Oxy. 1048, freight here app. connected with embole. Lusoriae: *Cod. Theod.* vii 17 (Danubian); *Theod. Nov.* 23. See also SB 5953.

39. Oxy, 2017 (5 c.) for logos agoges "of ship of Nonna from Kerkepha in the harbour of Thmoianmounis". *Gomos*: Giss. 54 (4–5 c.), Flor. 305 (4 c.), St. Pal. viii 1094 (6 c.); and PSI 429 (3 c. B.C.). More A.D. refs., PSI 792, Lond. ii 301 (M. *Chr.* 340), Grenf. ii 46a (W. *Chr.* 431), Mey. 14, Oxy. 708 (W. *Chr.* 432), Oxy. 63 and 2135, Lond. v 1759. Also W.O. i pp. 745 f.; Merzagora 138 n. 5; Amh. 138 (M. *Chr.* 342) on two *gomoi* of charcoal on *ploion tamiakon*

of 200 art.; Meyer, *Gr. Texte* 90 n. 3, notes that this excludes sense of cartload and allows only sense of boatload; *ibid.* 21. Volume: W.O. i 1754 f.

40. Fitzler 101 f., 145 ff.; San Nicolo 122 ff.; Otto i 128 ff., 251 ff.; Zucker; Oertel 128 ff.

41. Zucker sees a local designation; Oertel denies; Fitzler thinks it can signify, rarely, the priesthood.

42. Merzagora 139 f. Oxy. 1153 (1 c.), Lond. iii 948 (236), Bad. 85a (2 c.); W.O. i p. 398 (gate of Leuke Kome).

43. Oxy. 36. Merchant, *emporos*; taxfarmer, *telones*. Regulations end: "and they shall receive from those who farm the taxes a written declaration so that they may not be later liable to false accusations". Seems to mean the *telonai*, when not examining the cargo, were to use the written statement by the *emporoi*. See also W.O. i pp. 273 ff., *agogion*.

44. Oxy. 2125 (A.D. 220–1), cf. 1259–60: dealing with embole, Sko District, harbour of Satyros. Thead. 47 (4 c.); odd phrase, isos pleres: W. *Archiv.* iii 116 on Goodsp. 28: 2 c.).

45. Petrie ii 20, i, ii; W. *Chr.* 166 Cost of shipping rarely shown. Shipment of veg. seeds from Arsinoe to Oxy. (115 km. upstream) cost 40 dr. per 100 art.; demurrage charges, 16 dr. a day (prob. giving the earning capacity of craft of 250 art. burden): Lond. 948; REg 271 (A.D. 236). Calculation of freight rates: Robbins and Mich. 4966. For lumber canal from Theadelpheia (?) in Div. of Polemon to Boukolon, barge of 800 art. burden was chartered at a rate of $33\frac{1}{2}$ dr. per 100 art.: P. Col. 1R 4X, REg 260 (155). Lumber from Kelopatris at rate of $4\frac{1}{2}$ dr. per cubit: SPP xx 68, frag. i V 9 Charges in Ross. G. ii 18 are fragmentary. Oxy. 180 (3 c.): order to banker to pay sailor as naulon on 600 art. corn, 40 dr. (20 already paid).

Docking charges: Zeretelli O. 28; O. Strassb. 274. Payment: W.O. 262.

46. Lond. 1164h; BGU 1157; Oxy. 2136. Sale: Mon. 4, 5V (A.D. 581). Equipment, *skene*—Ptol. Zen. 31 (SB 6712), PSI 437—ploia are *akataskeua*, C. Zen 53 (SB 6714). For *katarphia*: Merzagora 143.

47. Ruggiero (1); Pigeonneau 225, 235

48. Lond. 1164b; REg 269. Payment "through the executing bank of Anoubion son of Ammonios, of the Matidian Tribe and the Kalliteknian Deme, in Antinoopolis". Anchors: Merzagora 143.

49. Decked: *sesanidomenon*, cf. Flor. 69 (3 c.).

50. Lond. 1714, ploion *skaphidion*; C. Zen. 13 (259 B.C.) has a skin-cover Contract Mon. 4, *askenon*. Cabin: Merzagora 146.

51. Ruggiero 53.

52. Terms of parts or equipment: Merzagora 142; inventory, SB 1 (3 c.), Reil 123 f., Merzagora 146 f. Late term is *phikopedalon*: (?) ship with *pedalion* steering-oar, rudder) in form of fish called *phykos*: Mon. 4, 5 v. *Katotion*: lifeboat: Lond. iii 1164h (3 c.). With two oars, all necessary equipment, and a hook of iron for catching on to another boat (*obeliskos*), Ruggiero 55. I omit Ptol pleasure-craft, etc. Monastery-boat, Lond. ii 248, etc.

53. Cornell 33 (3 c.) Lond. v 1728 (584–5), Mon. 7 (583).

54. Oxy. 1752, BGU 1663, Flor. 69.

55. Oxy. 1893. For combination in pay: SB 4490, Strassb. 40; only in kind, SB 4503. Taxes: Reil 191 f.; guilds, San Nicolo 24–6.

56. *Parasema*: PSI 1048 (3 c.). Tebt. 486 (3 c., grain-cargo), Grenf. i 49 (W. *Chr.* 248, A.D. 220–1), SB 423 (3 c.). Lond. ii 256a (W. *Chr.* 443. A.D. 15), *skaphe demosia. Asemon*: Lond. iii 948 (236), M. *Chr.* 341 and Meyer JP 43. *Acharaktoi*: Lille 22–3 (Ptol.)

57. Tebt. 486 (2–3 c.), Lond. 256 (1 c. B.C.), PSI 1048 (3 c.), Grenf. i 49: this last is a registration by a man of a boat belonging to his son, a minor, at Antinoe: *hellenikon* of 250 art. Father is the pilot.

58. Crönert, St. Pal. iv 84; Bell (2) 88.

59. Oxy. 1449, 14: *pedalion tes Neot* (*eras*).

60. Mon. 4; *premnes* in pap. Edfu text: Blackman (14). I omit one obscure comparison.

61. N. Lewis (1); OGIS 674, IGRR i 1183. Dittenberger thought the mast going to Red Sea. Red Sea: SEHRE 388.

62. Acacia: Lucas AEM (1932) 385; Hdt. ii 96.

63. SEHRE 381, 385, 1168–70. Ryl. 592.

64. Theophrastos HP v 4, 7; Plin. xvi 80, 221. Romans: *Periplus* 36; War-mington (1) 214.

65. N. Lewis (1); Cornell inv. i 81 (Cornell 45). Both are illiterate. For Aur. Hierakion; Oxy. 1104.

66. Hamb. 54. See *Class. Philol.* xxiv 1929, 42–7. Serenos is here dekadarches, cf. Hamb. 40—though Meyer on Hamb. 54 thinks it an error.

67. JEA iii 197; J.L. (2) 230–2. See also Hamb. 74 (A.D. 173–4); contract PSI 967 (1–2 c.), Oxy. 1068. Corpse-boats appear in payment of *naula*, to which the accompanying letters allude: Par. 18 *bis* (2–3 c.), W. *Chr.* 409; mummy-tickets, Crönert, *Racc. Lumb.* 521–5.

14. FERRIES AND SAILORS

1. Stele: JEA iii 100. Concession: BGU 1188; REg 229. Note also import-ance of the death-ferryman in myth, and the central nature of the image of the god in his boat—an example at random: "Khepri who resides in his boat" (sun-god), P. Beatty 1, 4, 10.

2. Edfu Ostr.: Meyer O. pp. 127–30; BGU vi pp. 122–31 (2 c.). In some cases, *naulon tou oinou*. See also Petr. iii 37; Par. 67; O. Cair. 9761 (Krokodilo-polis of the Pathyrite); Préaux CE lv 1953, 112–4: Sipemous pays bank of K. for ferries of the Path. 4,000 dr. for the year. He may be taxfarmer or ferry-concessionaire. At Edfu some payments are made by intermediary of the farmer, others by those liable to the contributions: BGU 1380–1413 (E. Kühn). We cannot define the tax precisely from the receipts: Heichelheim (2) 189 (3) 347–9. See further discussion, Préaux.

Tax on ferries attested for Fayum too: refs. in Préaux. Also Wallace 189, 434.

Bodl. O. 54–6, 10 (sailors of guard-ship). For such sailors: O. Wilb. 20; Tebt. 802.

3. Oxy. 732.

4. Ryl. 225.

5. Stephanski 82.

6. Ach. Tat. iv 12, 4–8.

7. Hibeh ii 189; officials, C. Zen. 59060.

8. iv 130–6. See Plin. xiii 11.

9. Ach. Tat. iii 9. Note the Hyksos were the Shepherds: Jos. *C. Ap.* 85 f.

10. *Aithiop.* x 4, 6. He mentions 3 rivers there meeting: Nile, Astoborras, Asasobas. The account of Meroe in general accords with Diod. i 33; Str. xvii (821–2), xvi (771) four rivers, (786) three. Cf. Plin. vi 185.

11. Oxy. 118.

12. BGU 1188 (15–14 B.C.), *georgoi*. Also BGU 1208 (27–6 B.C.), Oxy. 732 (A.D. 150), Lips 32 (250): M *Chr.* 93, Oxy. 118 (3 c.), PSI 1082 (?4 c.). Perhaps similar are the boats of Petr. 201 (W. *Chr.* 166), Lille 21, Petr. iii 107a (also Ptol.).

13. Ryl. 185 (2 c.), 193. Riverguards W.O. i 282 f.

14. Frisk 1; Hamb. 17; REg. p. 409. Office of harbour-guard held at Syene by Antonios Malachaios, but after A.D. 145 office leased to contractors: REg p. 493.

15. Tebt. 370, cf. BGU 81. In general, Lond. 256a: *Archiv.* i 145; Oxy. 276; Amh. 138; Lond. 301 and *Arch.* iii 221.

River-guards: see nn. 2 and 13 above, also Flor. 91 (2 c.) ; Meyer O. p. 160 (1–2 c.); Oertel 272. Tower-guards, salary, Frisk.

16. Canal-guards, Tebt. 393.

17. BGU 621.

18. Ryl. 191; also *syntaximon* (laographia), cf. 190 (A.D. 83–4.).

19. Hamb. 35.

20. Rowe (2). cf. *Museum J.* (Philadelphia) xxii pl. vi; and Rowe in ASE xxxviii 391 f.; C. Boreau *Rec. Champollion* 1922, 43 ff.; Montet (4) 395 f.; E. Lefébure, *Sphinx* ix 18 f.

21. Erman (4) 190 and (6), P. Anast. iv 11, 8 ff. and v; P. Sallier i 9, 9 ff.

22. P. Koller 2, 3 ff.; P. Anast. iv 2, 4 ff. and v; Gardiner, Hierat. Texts 38. Amun: Gunn (1) 83 (Nineteenth Dyn.). Proverb; Erman (4) 130, Complaints of Peasant, 4 MSS of MK; Gardiner JEA ix 5 ff. Poem: Erman (4) 245; P. Harris 500 R; Muller (3); Maspero (6) 236–8, etc. Note Nonnos ii 669–71, proverbial saying: life as ferry.

23. Lefebvre (1) 198; H. Goedicke, JEA 1961, 154 against magical interpretation, but wrongly; the basis is a shamanist riddle-contest. Spiegel (1) 53 links with sailors fighting.

24. Tebt. 802. Shipguard: see Eustath. *Od.* 1562, 3b.

25. Baillet 1573 (nautis not sure), 1069, 20.

26. Oxy. 1223. Landlord, georgos, Eparchos, coupled with speculator, is more likely to be in service of a military prefect than an official of the aparchia.

See Antinoop. ii 94 (6 c.): Writer seems overseer or steward (to a landed proprietor or secular dignitary, who lives in Alex.). "With regard to Theon the assistant I found that he was absent and have not conversed with him so far. But I had a talk with Iosephis the assistant of Psobthis and . . . a letter . . . a certain sailor who is getting 6 solidi near you; the same man says . . . that in a letter of yours you told him to compose this letter."

27. Oxy. 86.

28. Michael. 28. Villages seem in 12th pagus, which may have been at least partly same as Koite topos: Boak, Mél. Maspero.

29. Barnes (2).

30. Peet (2): P. Turin pls. lxviii, lxix.

31. BM 10052, 7. See above for rope-weaving, ch. 13. n, 19.

32. "Contribution of the Steward of the Temple of Amun, Ramessesnakt" includes wine, mimi, sti; of Royal Butler, oil, reeds, cable, fish, salt, mimi, etc. Pt. 3: list of "Garnets still remaining, not in the ship" 20. Issues for the boat begin: "Given for seed by the hand of the scribe Petersnamun 30 khar of mimi." "Given in the presence of the Highpriest as sustenance for the workmen in his charge" (incl. 1,000 fish); issue of something connected with "the Highpriest's nets"; seems a plant,(?) wd.

33. P. Leyd. i 350; RT xvii 143 ff., Spiegelberg; Gardiner JEA v 182.

15. THE CORN-SHIPS

1. Tebt. 703, lines 80–7: diagramma stating quantity of corn to be sent by each nome to Alex. In general: Bouché-L. H. des Lag. iv 64; W. Grund. Schubart, Einf. 431; W. Kunkel, Archiv. viii 183. Also Tebt. 704, 750, 753, 825; Lille 53; Strassb. 93–5; Hamb. 17 intro., etc.

2. Hibeh 39 (265–4 B.C.); 42, 98, 117—corn to go to agents of sitologos, receipt of captain for 4,800 art. barley for Alex., return of corn-revenue.

3. Reekmans (1).

4. SB 8754.

5. Pilot's oath: Tebt. 810, 134 B. Symbola of naukleros: Hibeh 98, 156; Lille i 21–4; Petrie ii 48 (iii 116); Tebt. 823–5; Strass. 113.

6. Tebt. iii 825c b and a.

7. See Reekmans further.

8. Reekmans, no. 110.

9. Flor. 387 iii.

10. BGU 607 (A.D. 163); JEA xv 160–3, C. W. Keyes. Phoretron: M. Chr. 142: BGU 69 soldier to pay "as soon as he next gets pay". In gen. Frisk 12ff.; Westermann-Keyes 98 ff.; Ziebarth PW xx 1, 533. Pabous: CPR 16. Loans with no interest: Ryl. ii 176, Oxy. 269. Porterage: Frisk 1 xxii.

11. Oxy. 523. One or other of the charges may be obelismos paid to shipowners or captains on authority of strategos.

12. Taking apostolon to have this meaning, cf. Tebt. 486 (2–3c).

13. Cf. Oxy. 276, 9 for soldier as *epiploos.* Oxy. 1749 (4 c): account for transporting epibatai from near Alex. to Nikiou, Herakleopolis, and Kynopolis. *Epibatai* are perhaps equivalent of earlier *epiplooi*, soldiers or other guards: W. Grund 379. cf. Oxy. 1380.

14. Oxy. 276 (A.D. 77), cf. Lond. 266 R. He is of 2nd Legion; no such legion known in Egypt before Traiana Fortis, not yet created. At this time: 3rd and 22nd. Text may be error for 22nd; otherwise a detachment from one of the two 2nd Legions must have while transferred to Egypt. See for soldier aboard, Oxy. 1651 cited ch. 16.

15. Oxy. 62: *Embole*, yearly contribution of corn, first to Rome, then to Byz. Dekaprotoi of a toparchia: BGU 579; in 3rd c., Oertel sv.

16. Oxy. 63; see also Hamb. 17; Keyes, JEA xv 160. Pilots' receipts have extra $1\frac{1}{2}\%$ added to shipment, Why? It may be the amount of weighing-toll at Neapolis: Grenf. ii 45a.

17. Oxy. 1197; also Grenf. i 49.

18. BGU 1022, with some privileges we do not know.

19. Oxy. 2131; J.L. (2) 289, c.f BGU 970 and 525.

20. Frisk 1; Col. i R4; REg 261.

21. BGU 1564, Philadelpheia: deduction is made on 28 dr. advanced on one account only.

22. W.O. 1091–1125; O. Bruss. 814; REg 261, 266. Under Romans the transportation of grain a liturgy; so strategos yearly on recommendation of village-officials appointed a certain number for *onelasia trionia* (Liturgy of 3 donkeys at village-disposal). Such donkeys were *demosioi* during service and had to bemarked: Ath. 41 (1c.) and *ibid.* p. 271; Oxy. 2182; PSI 1229; Rend. Harris 93; prob. Aberdeen 20. Donkeys did most carrying on land; a load was $3\frac{1}{2}$ art. lentils or beans. When these came from public tenants, a deduction was made: $\frac{1}{2}$ art. per load for supplies coming from Theadelpheia. From Autodike, $13\frac{1}{2}$ art. were deducted from $213\frac{1}{2}$ (61 loads). These sums seem to go to the drivers' guild. (Autodike was nearer the point of concentration, hence difference). But see Kalen, Upps. 49. No deduction when cereals came from katoikoi or private land-owners (assuming latter were marked by having their names put after that of the sitologos). Land-owners may have paid in kind or money for all we know, cf. BGU 242, Flor. 387 iii.

23. O. Mich. 64 ff.; 329 ff.

24. REg ch. iv, 3: sv. *phoretron.*

25. REg 256. Grain from N. Fayum seems to overland to Kerke on Nile: *Aeg.* 1933, 241; W. O. 1091–1125.

26. Frisk 1; Col. 1 R4; no record of amount or load-price. But Reg. 261, cost of 5,627 art. seems 559 art.: $\frac{1}{8}$ art. for load of $3\frac{1}{2}$.

27. Upps. 5 (A.D. 158–9). See also REg 263.

28. Oslo 17 ff. List of Hire of camels, donkeys, wagons, REg pp 405–7; costs of water-transport 407 f. Also Robbins, *Isis*, xxii 1934, 95 ff.

29. I do not want to go at length into the role of the sitologoi. See Calderini; REg 490 f. and ch. iv, 3. In first 3 centuries no proof that tribute was exacted

before the peasants were let take the grain from the threshing-floor. Payment was often made after threshing and peasants often in arrears: SB 5320. A fellow-citizen had liturgy of ensuring delivery of clean grain, honestly sifted; another app. had to guard storerooms and work with sitologoi in sealing them: Ryl. 90. Standard government measures: REg pp. 466–8 and 563.

30. Upps. 3, 4 v.

31. Oxy. 1254; Strassb. 31.

32. Oxy, 708; 1447.

33. REg ch. iii, 9. *Praktor sitikon*: Oxy. 1196; Flor. 358; Amh. 69.

34. A few exs.: Oxy. 813, request for barley cargo, 287, payment of corn by collector for a village to sitologoi of a Division, 383 and 385, corn receipts, 1447, receipt to a woman for corn-dues: all A.D. 1 c. Ryl. 200, sit. receipts (Hermop. nome) with arrears covering 26 years; cf. 201.

35. BGU 802 i–ii, 13; REg 256. See it for many more details.

36. Lond. 900; REg 309.

37. Ryl. 199.

38. Clauson, with refs., etc., cf. Lond. 929 and 1169. On days labelled Hermes, Clauson 273–6; J. L. (3) 30 f. I have no space to go at length into customs matters, so use this register as a typical document. For customs at Hermopolis and Harbour of Memphis: Wallace 258; local customs 268; desert-guards 272–4, 151 f., 155, 268, 462 f., 467 f.; sv index phylakia, etc.; for Ptol. gene-matophyl. 369 n. 21.

39. Clauson for details. *Phylla leuke* may be white clover or some kind of lotus, 269; baskets 268, 276; tarichos 278; *katharma*, SB 4481 (5 c.), 5640 (Lond. 1408) and Lond. 1369 (both 8 c.). Rates of duty, Clauson 256 f.; wool, 263–8; oil 269–73.

40. Clauson 257 f., 267, 262. Wages of 2 Arabian Archers, 16 dr. each.

41. Oxy. 1650; same pap. has similar account for a boat with hold (minus tip and guards); cf. 1650a, much the same but "to a soldier 4 dr.; receipt 2 ob." Cf. also 1651, 2 (3 c.); Corn. 3, 5 (250 B.C.). Searchers, Fay. 104 (3 c.) mentioning Nikopolis; Tebt. 5, regulations for search (goods on Alex. wharf); W. *Chr.* 30 (c. 200 B.C.).

42. P. Col. 1R 4X, REg 260. J.J.P. i 53; *Klio* xxvi 239.

43. Giss. 11; W. *Chr.* 444; REg 257. Lond. 295 (A.D. 118), rec. of camel-driver to sitologoi for hire of camels carrying grain to wharves.

44. Receipts: Oxy. 517, 518, 613, 614–6, 501, 533 (2 c.). Orders: Oxy. 516, 619–32, 163–4, 161, 146, 148, 137, 166–7, 159–60, 158–9, 88 etc.

45. Oxy. 515.

46. Amh. 69.

47. Grenf. ii 45a; W. *Chr.* 431; REg 258: money provided for Libation of Memphis; T.'s ship is 6,000 art. burden. Samples, Oertel 261—see also W. *Chr.* 508–9; Giss 15; Lond. 256 R(a) 17; Hibeh 39 and 98 for sealed samples (3 c. B.C.). Also next ch. here. Oxy. 522 for corn-transport account (2 c.), payments for carrying wheat, winejar for assistants and soldier, to elders of Ophis for wages

of 11 workers employed in lading, to granary-guard, to pilot, for vegetables for workers, etc.

48. Ross-G. ii 18.

49. Tebt. 394, cf. 369.

50. Oxy. 2591. More orders to pay, Oxy. 2588–90 (2 c.); 1539 (2 certificates by asst. of sitologoi crediting payments one private person's account to another, A.D. 179–80, cf. 1540, A.D. 187–8. Grain-receipts: Lond. 315, W, *Chr.* 357, Bacchias District, cf. Lond. 314; B.G.U 1636; Lond. 900–all 3 c.

Upps. 291 (Theadelpheia) A.D. 157–8, acc. of transportation for grain being moved in pursuance of commission issued by strategos, prob. after notif. from procurator in charge of Neapolis that shipping would be available.

Upps. 1, i–iv, SB 7193, REg 315 (1 head. A.D. 164–5), poor harvest: recs. classified under dept. of the administration (dioiketes) and of the imperial account (usiac). Ryl. 202a (Thead. 108) receipt Oxy. 1541 (192) receipt by sit. to 2 persons (one a R. cit.) for payments amounting to 125 art. corn bought for military and perhaps other reasons, cf. Tebt. 369. Oxy. 1842 (307), a counter-receipt for payments of corn to sitologoi of Seryphis.

51. Fay. 23a (2 c.).

52. Oxy. 708, cf. 1447 (44) where payer is woman, not a tax-collector as seems in 287; the dues were prob. not rent of State-lands but land-taxes on other kinds of lands, cf. Fay. 81; Ryl. 202a. Fee: note Oxy 2125 (A.D. 221).

53. Oxy. 514.

54. Tebt. 337. For State-loans to individuals, Tebt. 111, 353, 365, 387. Customs-recs. in and out of Fayum, Lond. 1265–6.

55. Warren 5; *Aeg.* 1933, 241; O. Mich. 329 ff.

56. BGU 242, M. *Chr.* 116, REg 263: to strat. of Herakleides Div., Arsinoite nome: complainant is registered in the metropolis but resides in the village.

57. BGU 15 ii, REg 264.

58. BGU 1566; Oxy. 2131; J.L. (2) 289.

16. MORE ON THE CORN-TRADE

1. Oxy. 63. See PSI 1053 of Oxy., an order for procurator of Neapolis to transport grain from certain granaries to the harbour for carriage to Alex.; "measure is the public $\frac{1}{2}$ art. measure, as ordered, and the additional 1% and $\frac{1}{2}$% to be added. Tebt. 486: corn-lading. Ryl. 209 (early 3 c.): list of corn-dues. The State often made the village-community cultivate domain-land in area of neighbouring villages: BGU 84; Rostovtzeff, *Rom. Kol.* 166 ff., and de Zulueta, *de patroc. vicorum* 71

2. Michaelides 17

3. Oxy, 2341. We do not know what means of transport the peg system was. The canal is Bahr Youssef on W. banks of which Oxy. stood: Pearl (2). It can be identified with Tomis of Lond. 131.

4. Oxy. 1259. For strategos see BGU 1091 and Oxy. 1560.

5. Oxy, 2121. Property-qualification for elders, 800 dr. (cf. Lond. 199, ii

p. 158, with however 600 dr. for chief and policeman; and BGU 6, 400 or 500 dr. for elder); overseers, 100 dr.; persons appointed to keep peace and see deliveries safe, 600 dr. In general, intro. Giss. 58, W. Grund. 342. *Poros* is property, not income. Lists: cf. Ryl. 90 (Kynop. and Lysimachis), Lond. 1220 (Sok. Nesos and Neilopolis), Oxy 2122, Ryl. 89, Fay. 304, Lond. 199, BGU 6, SB 4636.

6. Hamb. 17; REg 266. More docs. for years 211–2, 214, 216, 219: Oxy. 1197, 1259, 1553, 1525, 2119: declarations and reports. The last mentions a monthly report; Flor. 317 has been taken to mean they went daily; Giss. 3 shows in fact the reports covered 5 days.

7. Oxy. 2120, cf. 81, 1196. Also Oxy. 2125 (A.D. 221), pilot's rec. (REg 270), cf. *Gr. Texte* 14; Warren 5 (*Aeg.* 1933, 241); Bad. 79 and 85; Lond. 256R ii and 301; Tebt. 486; SPP xx 32; Oxy. 1259. Report from Psobthis A.D. 222–3, Oxy. 1526. See storage-charges: Oxy. 1443–4, 1526 (all 3 c.).

8. Lond. 948; REg 271. For sponde, a keranion of wine at Oxy. I include this though not corn.

9. BGU 8, W. *Chr.* 170, REg 272, Fayum. Oxy. 1554 (251) declaration on oath for surety of boat-owner, cf. 1555 (260–1).

10. Oxy. 1254. Notice: Flor. 2, W. *Archiv* iii 530

11. Strassb. 31 (prob. 3 c.).

12. Oxy. 2568; he is illiterate. Cf. Oxy. 1197 (given above) Mesore 211. For willow: Merton i 19. Nome-comarchs not attested before the 4th c., see Oxy. xxxi p. 114. Nome: Oxy. 2107, 2343, 80, 118, 1662, 2333; village, 1505–6, also Amh. 146, PSI 47, Iand. 25.

13. In general, Börner 30 ff.

14. Oxy. 1412; titles, Oxy. xii pp. 28–30. See Jouguet, *Vie M.* 379 and 374. Babylon, cf. Oxy. 1261. For liturgies: Lond. 948; Flor. 75, W. *Chr.* 434; *St. Pal.* i 34: all acknowledgments by kybernetai to councillors as to rec. of corn for river despatch. Naukleria: Rostowjew, *Archiv* iii 223 (Giss. 11), W. *Gr.* 379 and Oxy. 1261, 1259, 1260; C. Preis. 34.

15. Oxy. 1115. For modii read loaves (?); chorosai, mobilised?

16. Oxy. 1255.

17. Ptol., Tebt. 27; Roman, Rostowjew, *l.c.* 213 f.; W. Gr. 215 f.

18. Oxy. 1107: "Deliver to Ioannes, assistant, from Eudaimon."

19. Oxy. 2142, cf. 1115. Lond. 1260: contract of conveyance of freight.

20. PSI 1048 (Oxy.), REg 273. Oxy. 522 has an unspecified charge (4 dr. for 1,000 art.); and for obol exacted by sitologoi in payments of grain, see REg ch. iv 3 on prosmetroumena.

21. Oxy. 1651, cf. 1650 and 62. Stationarii (incl. centurions, decuriones, beneficiarii) used for police-purposes: W. Gr. 413 f.

22. Oxy. 1652. Crowntax, *stephanotika*, is obscure. If a variant of *stephanika*, the addition of a percent. for desert-guarding is odd; but it may be taken as an epithet of (*ploia*). Platypegia=barges, cf. Thead. 59, BGU 781. Camel-drivers: Lond. 295 (A.D. 118).

23. Oxy. 1671.

24. Oxy. 1204, J.L. (2) 302 f.

25. Oxy. 2124: "Well-to-do and suitable for the service."

26. Oxy. 1871. Sitologoi, 2–3 c.: Lond. 217, 346, 351, 290, 315, 471, 439, 180. Distrib. of seedcorn: 256 (A.D. 11–5). 4 c.: Aur. Isid. Arch. nos. 50 f., 11, 45–7, Oxy. 2113–4, 2124, etc.

Oxy. 2347 (362), skipper guarantee. Skipper declaration, Oxy. 87 (342). For 6 c.: Oxy. 133, 127. Throughout here, examples are illustrative, not exhaustive, as this is a very large field.

17. HOLY WATER

1. Faulkner (2) lines 60–80: refers to onset of N. wind with rain and cloud. Towed: literally "dragged a voyaging".

2. QN iv 2, "the sole hope of Egypt." Inscr.: Wiedemann (4) 146 f.

3. REG 1884, 286–90.

4. Diod. i 40, 4; against, ibid. 7. Cooked: Orib. Coll. Med. 22, 5 (purified). Aristotle in Strab. xv i, 22; fresh from distance, Lucan x 219 ff., etc.

5. Philostratos, Life Apol. vi 11.

6. HA xi 7, cf. Heliodoros iv 18, 3; Pescennius died A.D. 195. See also, Plout Q. Conv. viii 5, 13; Heliod. ii 28, 5; Hermet. xiii 17; Anth. Gr. ix 386, 4; Lond. Lit. 239, 29; Seneca QN iv(a) 2, 30.

7. Manethon (Loeb) 36, 38; John of Antioch, Hist. vel Arch. 385, 20; also George Synkellos; Chronog. 552, 1, 102. Melo: Servius ad. Georg. iv 291; Festus 124; Auson. epig. iv 75; Symm. i letter 14. Eupotos: Aisch. Prom. 812. Potimon hydor: Euseb. praep. ev. iii 11, 48. Flowering: Bacchylides, Lyra Gr. iii p. 114. Cf. Pindar frag. 198 on the Tilphousa; Athen. ii 15 (41 c.) says it killed Teiresias.

8. Athen. ii 15 (41e–f); goes on to say thunderbolts cause saline nature of the Karian river with sanct. of Zeus Poseidon by it. Theoph. frag. 159 Wimmer; plants, ix 18, 10.

9. Onesikritos, c. 330–327 B.C.; Aristotle; Theophrastos; Rufus, doctor 1–2 c. A.D.

10. Orib. i 5, 3, 15; Theoph. fr. 159.

11. Syntagma, ed. Sethe 109; Dion. Orb. Desc. 221; Eust. Comm. Dion. Per. 226; Aen. ix 31; GGm ii 216.

12. Suppl. 855; Pers. 33; also Sen. QN iii 25, 11; Plin. vii 3; Orib. 22, 5 (8 children at a birth).

13. Strab. xv 1, 22; Plin. vii 3; Aristot. HA vii 5, de anim. gen. iv 4; A. Gell. x 2; Solin. i 51 (Trog. Pomp.).

14. Ailian NA iii 33.

15. Theok. xvii 98; Hippolytos, Ref. omn. haer. v 7, 5.

16. Edmonds Lyr. Gr. iii fr. 131, 21. Cf. also Pomp. Mela i 52; Heliod. ix 22, 5; Strab. xv 1, 22; GGm ii 216; Dion. Orb. desc. 227; AP i 100. Bull Apis: Plout. 10, 5; Ail. NA ci 10.

17. Theophr. fr. 159: iodes, harsh.

18. Plin. xxxi 39, 6, cf. 42, 1 *flos salis*, which has a bad smell, is found in Egypt and seems brought by Nile.

19. B. 285. Berl. hierat. 3027 xi 14 (c. 1450 B.C.). Texts: Lexa ii 32 and P. Ebers 69, cf. use of Nile "hymn", Préaux, CE xx 1933, 364 f. Pap.: Eitrem, *Pap. Mag. Gr. de Paris* i 29 (1923): *kataklysmos*.

20. Orib. v 5, 1. The Greeks found harmful microflore and microfaune in it.

21. Rufin. HE xi 26, cf. Heliod. ii 23, 1 and iii 11, 3.

22. Michalowski (1). At first used rainwater at Naukratis, then at Alex.; also canal water drawn-off through decanting pools.

23. Badawy (4), cf. Suppl. ASAE 1949, 41. In gen., Cagnat, *Man. d'arch. rom.* i 88–90; Vitruv. viii 6, 15. Cinders used: Plout. *plac. philos.* iii 16.

24. Hdt. iii 6.

25. Athen. ii 67a, 74b; Plout. *Vit. Alex.* 36d. Ptol. II: Polyb. fr. 154 Hultsch; Jouguet, *Hist. Nat. Eg.* 54. To prevent poison? to help pregnancy?

26. *Disc. Eg.* 116. And Nerval, *Voyage en orient* 1869 ii 207. B. 104–9.

27. Perdrizet TC 76; Roussel (2) 286. See further B. 282. Women: P. Louvre 22 (*Sorapei*).

28. Roussel no. 152; Perdrizet (2), 49; Weber *Terrakotten* 24. Epekoos, cf. Obsequens (Nilus): Plin. *Paneg.* 31, 6. For vase in cult and reps., B. 282–4; also coins. Osiris: *Sethianische Fluchtafeln*, ed. Wunsch 86; *St. Pal.* xxi par. 455 (Hopfner). Aspersion: Servius ad. *aen.* iv 512; ii 116; Juv. vii 527. Libations: Apul. *Met.* xi 20; Porphyr. *de abst.* iv 8 (to flute music); G. Lafaye 96; Cumont (1) 437; Heliod. ii 23, 1. Often in pharaonic times the ankh is near the rep. of water; the undulous design (water flowing from vase) can be replaced by succession of ankhs and the vase itself be an ankh: Donadoni (1).

29. B. 281. Nilewater in houses: Verhoogen CE ix 1934, 39–41. Temple. V. Tran Tam Tinh, *Culte d'Isis à P.* 1964, 34. Serv. *Aen.* ii 116. *Hydriai:* CIL iv 2660. "I offer you the Flood in a jar of gold," Eighteenth Dyn., Brugsch WB 989.

30. Frankfort (1) 32; Strab. xvii (813); Petrie (17) 2. As the brickvault had collapsed for the most part, there would have been a lack of light.

31. CPH 117 Verso ii 9–12; B. 380.

32. B. 380. Komasterion as meeting-place, SB 5051 (Taposiris), used metaphorically of heavens as place of procession: P. Mag. Paris i 1608; P. Mag. Leyd. W. 17, 27, etc. Procession: Oxy. 519 (2 A.D.), cf. 1265 (4 A.D.). Jars stored: Mich. 123 recto Ia 19; C4; d.

33. A. Rowe (3) 492.

34. De la Roque (4); *Médamud* 1929 pl. ii and p. 63. Heights of flood 1 c.: Dykmans (1) ii 1936, 29. Chinese ceramics in Theban tombs seem of 12th–15th c.

35. Badawy (2).

36. Gunn, City of Akhenaten i 156–9. Chabas defines as place of temple where the divine statues were set when oblations made to them: *Etudes sur l'ant. hist.* 1873 417 f.; place of viewing the solar gods, Gunn *l.c.*; Fairman in Pendlebury *City of A.* iii 208.

37. Badawy (2).

38. Alliot 584, 603, 569 ff. See J.L. (3) ch. 17.

39. Breasted (4) ii 81 f.; iii 44–8, 77 f.

40. Blackman (5) and PSBA xl 88.

41. Badawy 61 f.; Breasted 325–7.

42. Juncker (10) 67.

43. Badawy's convincing interpretation.

44. Edfu: Alliot 592, 607. Hymn: Breasted (4) 327.

45. Semitic origin of Maru Aten suggested: Badawy 63, who also compares the Festival House of the Mesopotamian Gods on a riverbank and its role in New Year Procession, 64.

46. Calderini (1) 159–8 B.C. Astartideion connected with the katoichoi: her cult, Louk. de dea syria 48 f., festival would be in Pachon: Calderini 685 f.

47. Kanopos: Von Bissing BSAA xiv 1929, 49. Poet: A. H. Sayce (1), etc.

48. PT 857a–858a.

49. Utterances 32–3, cf. Utt. 423, an expansion; and PT 1180a–d where Re is awakened. Libation water is a substitute for the lustral washing of the dead body. Utt. 34–6 deal with natron and purification. For washing of dead: Blackman (14): "You go on your way to cleanse yourself in the Excellent Pool", etc.

50. Mercer PT iv, exc. x; Kees (1) 107, 117; Jéquier (4) 59 f.; Speelers (3); Hommel 904 f.; Garnot (1) 12 and n. 1; Alliot (2); Weill (4) 24 and nn. 2, 3.

51. PT 1346a–1348a. Cited also p. 44; see also 48.

52. PT 1180b–1181b. Her name is written with determinative of 10th nome of Upper Egypt (4 jugs) and she was equated with the uraeus-serpent goddess Wad.t, though she originally rep. the serpent of the abaton. Cf. PT 1176–82, 1138, 1141.

53. PT. 1285a.

54. PT 525 ff. A god to king: "I bless you so that you may be able . . . to revive like the Nile flood," De Buck (3), Frankfort (3) 107. "Drink water at the wish of the heart" LD 799; "enjoy water" (Cairo 20469) signifies the dead has found life in the beyond.

55. Budge (3) vi, chs. lx, lviii.

56. Tomb 53: a fairly common Ramessid motive. Yoyotte JEA xliv 1958, 27. Times: ASAE 1952, 197, BIFAO 1949, 184, Capart (3); Parrot 102; Hassan ASAE 1928, 4 f.

57. Budge Ani, ch. lxi, pl. xv, pp. 442–4. For am-khent priest in opening of mouth, Budge (21) 192 ff.

58. Nu chs. lxiiia–b, ibid 445 f.

59. Weigall (2) pl. iv 2, 3; Gunn (1) 31. Palm-ribs, Lane, Mod. Egs. 1895, 486. Moslem visits to dead: Galal, Rev. Et. Islam. 1937, 136.

60. LD ii pl. 5; de Rougé (1) pl. xxxviii; Mariette, Mastabas, 433, cf. perhaps PT 1067c.

61. Juncker (3) 18, 51. Offering: 9 ff., 16, 55–7 (milk). Kbh.t: 13, 55–6.

62. I. Levy J. As. 1927, 288; B. 279 n. 2. Atum: A. B. Kamal (1) 63 no. 22069.

63. CIG 6717; Levy 299 with exs. Egypt and Italy. Dolger 170 n. 78.

64. Maspero (7) 113 f.

65. Sarapias, stele of Mex: Neroutsos (2).

66. SB 5718 (combining Gr. and Eg. formulas), also SB 335, 5037.

67. Jouguet (3).

68. Schreiber BSSA xv 1914, 12; at Ras Shamra installations to take water to dead go back to period of Eg. alliance (1440–1360 B.C.): Schaeffer, Ugaritica 1939, 30. In parts of Nubia, still pots of water set near tombs: Blackman, JEA iii 1916, 31 ff.

69. Parrot (1–3). See J.L. (3) 58, but repeated here.

70. Foucart (1) 31–5.

71. *Prof. Rel.* ii 5.

72. See Euseb. *praep. ev.* xix 10, 2–3.

18. THE BEAUTIFUL FESTIVAL OF THE VALLEY

1. Foucart (1).

2. Diod. i 85, cf. Strab. xvii 16. The Bull Apis, Hap, was worshipped at Memphis as incarnation of Osiris and the second life of Ptah. Boubastis: Hdt. ii 59.

3. J.L. (3) 60 f.

4. Bataille (1) 246 f.; Foucart 29; Gauthier BIFAO xiii; Griffith, P. dem. Ryl. iv p. 16; v p. 17; W. UPZ i 38; Spiegelberg P. dem. Berl. p. 9.

5. Spiegelberg (6); Reich; Bataille 247.

6. P. dem. Berl. 3115; Bataille 247 f.; Otto i 100 n. 4; W. UPZ ii 37 n. 7 and 38 n. 10.

7. UPZ 185; Bataille 248 f. and 238; No value in UPZ i 102, 7–8.

8. P. de, Berl. 3116/2/23; UPZ 180a/3/9; and P. dem. Ryl. xi p. 123; xiv p. 128 and 122 n. 1.

9. Porph. de abst. iv 10; Otto i 107.

10. SB 2009; and P. dem. Ryl. xi p. 122.

11. Diod. i 91, 5; UPZ i p. 48; Cumont (3) 139. A royal *prostagma* protected them: Batialle 219.

12. UPZ 162/8/9 and p. 72 and 84. UPZ 162/2/25, p. 76, cf. 162/4/28; Otto ii 290 n. 3.

13. Paintings: Dawson JEA xiii 1927, 46. Demotic: Spiegelberg, P. dem, Berl. p. 9 n. 2. *Haidios oikos.*

14. Bataille 273.

15. UPZ 172/2/19; Peyron, *Pap. Gr. R. Taur. Mus. Eg.* 40–2; G. Maspero; Bouché-L. (1) iii 159 and iv 218 ff.; Bataille 249–52.

16. Dawson 43.

17. But see P. dem. Louvre 2409 (Memphis) year 21 Philopator, where one of contracting persons appears as both taricheutes and choachytes. Revillout, *Rev. ég.* i 129 n. 2; AZ xviii 1880 115 f. For clients of choach., Bataille 252–4; their revenues, etc., 254–7; social rank, 257–61; admin. of nekropolis 271.

18. Bataille 261–4. Nekrotaphs may always have been entrepreneurs in Ptol. times at lesser sites.

19. Griffith (9). The Egyptian idea was that the man not the soul was agent of his deeds, good or evil, on earth.

20. Other curses: Sottas. Few from the NK and none so detailed as ours here, save that of Seti I at Redesia: Sottas 128.

21. Budge (1) 347.

22. PT 127b–129a, cf. 718a–c. And 440d–441b.

23. Budge (1) 337.

24. Capart CE 1939, 103 f.; Blackman (13) esp. 58 f.; Garnot (5) till end of OK. Cf. CE 1939, 38, tomb of Nekhebu (OK architect).

25. Budge (1) 298–300. First declaration ends with "I have washed" 4 times.

26. Thirst: Deonna (2). Purifying: as such it appears in rites of opening of mouth, burning incense, and natron, in tomb of Petosiris (Lefebvre 132). General carrying-on from Pharaonic times of funerary customs: W. Schubart, *Einführ.* 470; J. Ste-Fare-Garnot, *Religion Eg. ant., bull. analyt.* 1939–43 (1952) chs. x–xi, 188–229.

27. Bataille 266; Foucart (1) 22 f. Dawson, *Aeg.* ix 108, sees in purchases of kythrai confirmation of his ideas on the great jar in which corpse was bathed in natron: JEA xiii 43. These kythrai cost 2 obols in Wessely's text, and 1 dr. in P. Amh. Pottery had a low price (REg p. 471), so Dawson may be right: Bataille 215 n. 1. Solid food in repast of dead: Bataille 267; animal sac. 267; burial rites 267 f.

28. See J.L. (3) 57, repeated here: P. dem. Cairo 31170; 31172; JEA iii 1916, 33, cf. P. dem. Cair. 31171, 31175, 31176; Spiegelberg AZ liv 1918 86–92. See also Totenpap. Berl. 3162 (*Buch. v.d. Verwandlungen*) 3, 3–5; Möller (1) I 6, 11, and p. 85; Mariette (4) I ii, pl. ix; Leyd. pap. T 32, 7, 8; El-Hesch, Juncker (3) 57. Meroitic: Griffith (8) 42–6 and 83; Shinnie 113, 146.

29. Rowe (1) 292. Text has Two Brothers; seems an error.

30. Drioton ASAE xliv 1944, 149 f.

31. Bataille 269; Vandier (1) 117. Feast of dead; birthday celebrations at tombs; *agapai* and *episemoi hemerai:* J.L. (3) 56 f.

32. Peyron (P. Turin p. 85); Brugsch (10) 44, yes; Steindorff, UPZ ii 86, no. Funerary cult celebrated in nekropolis: Bataille 270.

33. Foucart, *passim*, esp. 108–15 for texts; *diabasis*, 45 ff.

34. Foucart 113 f.

35. Tomb 19 wall C; Foucart 207 f. Boat: CE liii 1952, 45.

36. Foucart 207–9. Soker, an old god of dead, with cult at many sites, Memphis with Ptah, Abydos with Osiris; in Ptol. times a mere shadow of Osiris. He appears 18 times in PT.

37. Blackman (6) 206 f., also (7–11) for lustrations and purifications. Baptism of king: Gardiner (21).

38. Sch. *Il.* i 43 (Dindorf 54): *xoanon.*

39. Foucart 9–11. Ethiopians were remembered; the Demotic Chronicle

(Spiegelberg 1914), a medley of prophecies, records the hope of hero to come out of Aithiopia and deliver the Egyptians from the Ptolemies.

40. *Nepenthes pharmakon, Od.* iv 220 f.; Diod. i 97, 7–9. *Synousia* of Zeus and Hera.

41. *Il.* ii 346 ff.; J.L. (3) 321 f.

42. Nubia: Juncker (1) 68 f. Petrie, *Anc. Eg.* iii 1917. Cylinder: Petrie *Anc. Eg.* ii 79 no. 85. Titles: Budge (15) ii 30. Genitals: Mercer (1) 209. She was also worshipped at Napata (for dominance of Theban NK religion there, with Amun at head: Shinnie 141). Mut = vulture in predynastic Egypt: Brugsch (7) i Bl. 39. There may be influences of Near East and Babylonia in Divine Wives of Amun, though the link with Min may have helped.

43. De Buck in Frankfort (1) 86.

44. Budge (1) 142: Pap. BM 10188.

45. Budge (1) 15.

46. PT 1248a–d, cf. 1818a. See Mercer PT ii 412 on 814a: deified Vulva as his Hand.

47. Budge (1) 15. Griffiths JEA xliv 1958, 124.

48. Czerny JEA xliv 1958, 32.

49. Gunn (1) 86–8; Erman (7) and (8) 78 ff.; Breasted (4) 349 ff.; Maspero (9). Second text is also of Nektamun, not necessarily the same man. For possible afflictions of blindness, Gunn 89. Erman describes the scene as a gorge. Place of Truth may be part of Theban nekropolis, not the whole as Brugsch and others have thought: Gunn 84 n. 3, see also Clère. In general: Bruyère (2) and (4).

50. Bruyère (2) 220, 276; Ptol. stelai, 276–9; *prosk.*, Spiegelberg, *Demotica* ii 26; D. Maller, *Le K. el-Ag.* 73. Later graffiti: *Mél. Glotz* ii 497; BIFAO 1939, 131—and BIFAO 1939, 145. Byz.: Lond. i 77, 27 (p. 231) cf. Deissmann, *Licht.* 189; BIFAO xxxviii 136, 146–7; Bataille (2) nos. 89 and 172. Conditions at times of first Christian communities: J. Doreste, *J. Asiat.* 1948, 257 ff.

A serpent covered Meretseger's head, as reminder of the punishment of those who offended her; snakes swarmed on her hill-flanks. She was involved against snake-bites: cf. Moses in *Numbers* xxi 7–9.

51. Alliot (1) esp. 517 (procession); height, 511; de Wit (4). In general, JEA xxxv 98–112, xxxvi 63–71, Blackman and Fairman. Also Fairman, *Bull. J. Ryl. Lib.* xxxvii (1 Sept. 1954); Drioton (12). Alliot is against the dramatic interpretation; sees a religious service, not a festival. But even so there could be a dramatic element, which could have effects outside the sanctuary proper. Note Hathor was in the temple at Deir el-Medineh, where the Ptols. were *synnaoi*: this may have been a point of stop in the later itinerary of the Festival: Bataille 90. The Festival was still active in 117 B.C.: UPZ 162/3/1–3. There were two sanctuaries of Hathor in the nekropolis in the pharaonic period; also in Ptol. period (one an important structure built by three of the kings): Bataille 94–7. Plaque: Hayes JEA xxxiv 114–15.

19. THE BLESSED DROWNED

1. Brief treatment in J.L. (3) 216–23. I here draw on the list of Rowe (4).
2. Griffith (7).
3. Griffith (7) 132; Preis., *Namenbuch.*
4. Levy 288; CIS no. 141 (incorrectly taken as a request for O.'s fresh water). Leibovitch (1) 302. Obscure here.
5. Griffith (10) 38.
6. *Ibid.* 53, 38 f. (Spiegelberg, *Eigennamen* 7*, on Berlin pap. 3116), 73; 52 on *hsy* and Osiris; 37 "If you wish to bring in a drowned man, you put a sea-karab-stone (?) on the brazier." Moret RT xvii 92 f.: *hsy* as the Great Submerged and the Greatly Praised. For *hsy* before name of a god, as singer: "The revered, the singer of Sarapis, Hep-men . . .", Spiegelberg *Demot. Denkmäler* i 1904, 12 pl. 1, no. 31086. Variants: E. Chassinat, RT xxii 11, xxi 61, 65; Rowe 11. *Hsy* as beatified, not merely drowned: Leibovitch (1) 301.
7. Griffith (10). 132 ff.; Rowe 6. And Griffith (10). 133.
8. Preisendanz PGM I v 270–3, and iii 1. Also I iv 875.
9. Griffith ZAS xlvi 134; Erman (5) 423; Von Bissing RT xxxiv 37; M. A. Murray ZAS li 135; Spiegelberg ZAS liii 124 f.; Kees (10); Wiedemann, *Anthropos* xxi 1926, 9 and n. 9; Hopfner (2) i par. 789, ii pp. 65 f., par. 130; index p. 168 sv. *Ertrinken, der Ertrunkene (Esies)*=Osiris, *Ertrunkener.* Also Budge (18) i l ff.; Elliot Smith and Dawson, *Eg. Mummies* 1924, 132.
10. PT 615c–616a, cf. 24d. Griffiths (1) 6, adds 766d: see 7 nn. 1 and 4 for problems of translation. PT 620b, Horus appears "in his name of *Hnw-boat*".
11. PT 2144a–b, 1008c, cf. 1500a.
12. Farmer (1) 205.
13. Shabaka: 8; 19 ff.; 62 ff. Also RT xiv 1892, 14 and Sethe (1) 38. Breasted ZAS xxxix 44, 50, pl. i, ii, 19, cf. 62.
14. Diod. i 25, 6; Griffiths (1) 101.
15. De Buck CT ii spell 158; Sethe (13) vi; Griffiths (1) 48.
16. Sallier iv 2, 6; Chester B. i 8, 9; CT ii 37b–c, cf. ii 38g; ii 414. Griffiths (1) 46 f; *Contendings* 13, 2–11.
17. Budge (1) 373, (6a) i 157, also (2).
18. PSI iv 328; Loeb SP ii 411, taken to refer to sacred cow worshipped as incarnation of Hathor.
19. Rowe 7 f.
20. Moret (7) 37–41, 49 n. 2.
21. Maspero (8) 7; Rowe 16.
22. ASAE xxxviii 190 n. 1. MK version, de Buck CT i 75. More refs. in Leibovitch (1) 30 f. The Gates of the Land of Kbhw open to the dead: Maspero (8) ii 7 and Rowe 10.
23. Erman–Grapow WB ii 122, sv. *mhw*; Rowe (1) 182, text iii, refs n. 4; Budge (17) text vol. 139; Budge (5) i 102, 105, 224–9. Drowning of evil serpent: Budge (17) 105; *mhr*, drowned (16) 317 f.
24. Budge (1) 520, (17) 105, (16) 317 f. In general Kees (10).

25. Moret, *Rec. Champ.* 1922, 336; Kamal ASAE xxxix; Lange (1) ii 149 line 19.

26. Erman (4) 38; Lefebvre (1) 76 f.: Pap. Westcar.

27. Budge, *Rec. Champ*, 436. Sacrifice: Rowe (4) 295. At Asyut, a saying: "He who dies drowned dies a martyr," Rowe 296.

28. List from Rowe (4), see him for refs.: List A, plus pp. 291–303.

29. Nepar, male counterpart of Neper: Gardiner (1) no. 1 1931, 25 n. 1.

30. Name: Ranke 250 no. 19. Temple, Rowe (4) 28. Mother and daughter: Drioton, *Ann. Inst. Philol.* iii 1935, 139.

31. See more details, Rowe 293.

32. Niches: Boak, *Karanis 1924–31* (1933) 52 pl. x B (1–2); Grenfell–Hunt, *Fayum Towns* 22, 30 ff.; Boak 19; Breccia, BSAA xvi 1918, 20 102; Lefébure ASAE x 162; xix 39 CRAI 1908 772. Papyrus: Kuentz (4), Bruyère (15) nos. 3, 218, 290.

33. For analogies, Rowe 17 f. Note rose-coloured lotuses as crown of Antinoos. Greaves with lionheads: Roman relief of Antaois (sic.) and consort (Edgar (6) no. 27572); Maspero (*Guide Mus. Caire* 1915 254 no. 1200) thinks them Sarapis and Isis: from Luxor; G. Daressy i 178, ii pl. xxxvii no. 38696: Amun-Re (Pantheus). Rowe suggests the two lionheads are a play-writing of *phty*, the Strong One (? epithet of drowned). Budge (1) 132 (Leyden), the all-god of the magician with lion-headed knees.

34. Altar lotus-shaped with two buds springing from it, cf. Lepsius v pl. xxv.

35. Name: Ranke 386 no. 16; equated with Senpoeris.

36. Rowe 21 f., also for another late stele.

37. Blackman (12); Sethe HERE vi 1913, 651. Bouquets: Blackman pls. xx, xxxiv, lvii, lix, lxvi, lxxxvii. Green: *ibid.* 82 n. 2. See also Weigall (2) 82 f. El-Amir calls Klt Kurtah.

38. See J.L. (3) 215–8. Substitute sacrifice, Wainwright (7) 74, 4 f., 29, 51, 57 f., 89. See Calendar of cult-offering, 2–3 c., Oxy. 2553: birthday.

39. Lucas and Rowe, ASAE xxxviii 144 n. 5; Erman (3) 241 f. and (1) 423; Gayet, *Mus. Guimet, Bibl. de vulg.* xxx 53 ff.; Jouguet *Ann. Inst. Philol.* 1935, 232; Sethe HERE vi 1913, 651 f., etc.

40. J.L. (3) 219 ff. Also Graindor BIFAO xxxii 97 ff.; SB 740–1; Eitrem *Symb. Osl.* xviii 127 f. and *A. f. Religionwiss.* xxxiv 313–22; Jouguet, *Mél. Capart* 1935, 231 ff.

41. E. Egger (1); W. (3). List of epithets, Rowe (1) 8 f. Osiris generally stands before the Drowning Title, at times after it. Note Isis' title the Excellent One. Maspero (8) ii 1939, 91. For drowned and Theban choach., Bataille 30; under Osirian influence the drowned, *hypobrichios*, becomes the Master (Phri) or *hsi*.

42. M. el-Amir.

43. HA x 21; Plin. on the Tentyrites also, viii 93.

44. Wainwright JEA xxiv 144.

45. Levy REG 1923, p. lviii (*De Bapt.* v); REG 1922, pp. lii–liv.

46. Levy, JA ccxi 310.

47. Leibovitch (1) 303; Levy; El-Bokhari, *Trads. islam*, titre lvi, ch. 30.

48. Czerny (1), also Gardiner (14).

49. *Life Moses* i 17 (Cohn).

50. *Ant. Jud.* ii 228 (Naber); perhaps he wrote moy.

51. C. Ap. i 286 (T. Reinach). Under *moy*, the Eg. term for water was also introduced into the lexikons: Suidas, Hesych. Eses: Nestle, *Z. f. alttest. Wiss.* xxvii 1907, 112.

52. Czerny 352 f. for details and refs.

53. J.L. (4) 194–6.

54. Vikentiev, drawing on Exodus and P. Chester Beatty i, also Plout. *De Iside*. See him for refs. Though he gives some wider analogies, he has no idea of the worldwide pattern.

55. Plout. *de Is.* 11.

56. *Ibid.* 38 and 40; Ex. ii 3 f.

57. *De Is.* 14.

58. Vikentiev for refs. Eyes: Chester B. x 3; *de Is.* 55 (swallows and gives Eyes to sun). But the problem of the Eyes is highly complex, e.g. Griffith (1) 28 ff. *Shipwrecked Sailor* 60 f. for covering face at advent of serpent of fire. Lotus-eyes: CB x 4 f.

59. Vikentiev tries weakly to find an analogy of Anti losing toes and Moses bidden to take off his sandals.

60. CB xi 7. In general, Griffith 48; Spell 113 from BD (two hands).

61. Hebrew word for breast can mean garment-fold or part of body, inner or outer: Vik. 26 n. 3. Cf. Greek *kolpos*. For leprosy: R. Bennett, *Disease of Bible* 29 f.

62. Kuentz (3) 215, 232–4. Burning Bush later seen as Mary: Chitty 169. Mention of Re in Exodus?: Gunn in *Eg. Relig.* i 33 f.

63. Zayed. The father has a priestly title of late epoch: WB iii 471, 11. Two other stele with same text; five known in all. To Usirur and Hariesis, Paiuher (Amun priest) and a woman. Usirur (mother, also a Lady Musician of Amun) is first prophet of Amun-Re (he also appears in large libation-vase, Louvre, with prayer to Nut). We see in text a transfer of royal power to individuals, cf. Sacred Tree of Heliopolis, once royal, now found in individual tombs: Sethe, *Urk.* 1906, 276, 11; J. Lieblein, *Livre Eg.* 1895, pl. xlvii 13.

64. Zayed sees only Upuata, but the pair are more likely U. and Anubis: Budge (1) 214. Zayed also calls them dogs.

65. Also Isis, Nephthys, Horos, Hathor, Upuatu.

66. PT 1 93–1194b; Erman (4) 8; Sethe ZAS liv 2. Cf. 1183a, "O Nwrw, ferryman of the March of Pa't".

67. PT 383–384b. Also 445a, 597b, 599a, 946b, 118b, 1193a, 1441a, 1737a, 1757.

68. Ferryman: ASAE xli 1942, 343 f., Anti: confusion with Antywy in 10th nome (of the Serpent); Budge (1) 24, 108.

69. Diod. i 92, 2 and 8.

70. Paus. x 28, 2. *Charon* sv. Roscher; Lawson *Gr. FL* 114; N. P. Politis, *Meletai* 1904, i 612; F. de Ruyt, *Charun* 1934 (Etruscan).

71. Note Hercules fighting Charon to carry him over Styx: Virg. *Aen.* vi 39; Servius, *ad loc*; and Norden.

72. Hooke (1) 47 f. Ebeling (1) 14. Ritual goes back at least to mid-2nd millennium B.C. For an example of initiation as a passage through water, A. C. Hollis *The Nandi* 1909, 56.

73. Griffith (10) v 45 f. Godnames invoked are written twice. In margin: "Behold the spells you write on the wick Bakhukhsikhukh, with figures." Greek *Kyamoi*: Diosk. ii 105, abominated by Pythagoreans, Aristoph. *Frogs* 195, etc. Plant: Theophr. CP iv 14, 2. For Moses further in magic, Budge (21) 176.

20. TOURISTS AT THEBES: THE MEMNONION

1. H. D. Rawnsley, *Notes from the Nile* 162 f.

2. Bataille (1) 1–21, for refs.; Goosens; Gilbert (2); Pley; Hüsing.

3. Gr. Abydos no. 563.

4. Gilbert (2) 48; also Bataille 18–20.

5. C. Robert, *Gr. Heldensage* iii 1185; Pley PW xxix ter, 647; Bataille 21.

6. CIG 4727, 4731.

7. Letronne (3) 82; Bouché-L. iii 23 f. Memnonia (for W. Thebes) is not used by Diod, or sch. Homer A425 (Dind. 54), or Anton. Itin.: Garofolo 7 f.

8. Ovid. Met. xiii 576 ff.; Strab. xvii 46; Tac. *Ann.* ii 61; Plin. xxxvi 58; Juv. xv 5; Loukian *Tox.* 33, *philops.* 3 and 33; Ptol. iv 5; Dion. Per. v 252, etc.

9. Bataille 155 f. refs. Philostr. *Life Ap.* vi 4 (based on Damis); Hdt. iii 4 (Memphis!); Himer. *ecl.* 20, 3, orat. xvi 1. A late trad. (sch. Juv. xv 5; Tzet. *chil.* vi 64) said Kambyses broke the statue to find secret of the voice.

10. Paus. i 42, 3. Str. C 816. Musical stone: cf. Ovid, *met.* viii, 14, AP, Planudean App. 279.

11. An Egyptian retort to the Homeric version?

12. Bataille 157 f.

13. Letronne 156. *Echos*: Louk. *Philops.* 33, cf. CIG 4721, 4723, 4725; Letronne 102–4, etc. Against Letronne: Steindorff, Baedeker's *Egypt* 1929, 346. Nature of the stone: lower part, a quartz conglomerate from Gebel el-Ahmar or Silsileh, with structure tending to separate out in places when even slight rise in temperature begets a dilation; with resulting sounds of break: Bataille 160.

14. Maspero ASAE x 1910, 14–16.

15. Letronne 38 f.; Maspero (7) ii 311 f.; Milne (1) 61.

16. Letronne (3) 50.

17. Philops. 33; Letronne 30. Demotic: Bernand (2) no. 108; Bataille 161; Steindorff 346.

18. Bataille 164–8 for refs.

19. Diod. i 97, 7; Heliod. iii 14; Louk. *True Hist.* ii 20 jestingly makes him a Babylonian, Tigranes, sent as hostage among the Greeks. Note the god-mating in this tale.

20. Bernand (2) for inscrs. and full analysis; nos. 1–15 before Hadrian. No record here of Germanicus' visit: Plin. viii 46.

The prefect of 15 heard the voice twice on the same day (16 Feb. 104) $2\frac{1}{2}$ hr. and 3 hr.

21. Bernand (2) nos. 16–50.

22. Nos. 18 f.

23. No. 21, possibly epistrategos.

24. No. 22.

25. No. 23: voice, *echos*.

26. No. 36, epistrategos. Deep-eddying, the Skamandros, *Il.* xx 73, xxi 5: applies well to Nile, esp. in flood. M.'s death was not in Homer (*Od.* iv 188, xi 532) but in Cyclic Poets. Roscher, sv Memnon 2653.

27. No. 37. No. 42 also verse, cf. 41.

28. Nos. 28–33.

29. Bernand 91 f.; her brother was C. Julius Antiochus Epiphanes Philopappus, consul 109; Seneca QN iv 2, 13, praises Balbillus' literary powers.

30. She calls Memnon Egyptian.

31. No. 29.

32. Nos. 51–61.

33. Nos. 51–3.

34. Nos. 54–5.

35. No. 61.

36. Nos. 62–108.

37. No. 83.

38. No. 92.

39. Nos. 91–3.

40. No. 72.

41. No. 99. Diod. i 15, 1; Schäfer ZAS xli 1904, 140 f.; Bernand (2) 198 for more refs. Strab. xvii 813: Imandes, Ismandes; Paus. i 42, 3; Kaibel. *Ep. Gr. ex lap. coll.* 988, 992; Euseb. (*Chron.* 68, Koerst) says Amenophis, perhaps following Manethon despite mention of Biblical characters. Note Amenhotep I had in NK an oracle with workers of the nekropolis for clients; his cult was still alive under the Ptols. (Czerny, BIFAO xxvii 1927, 159 n. 2), but no sign of the oracle still functioning or related in any way to the Memnonian voice. No: Gauthier (4) iii 75; Gardine, (13) ii 24; Griffith, *Dem. Ryl.* iii 83, 228, 423.

42. No. 100.

43. No. 101; no. 104: "Afflicted Dawn pours out a scream (*iygeo*) when Memnon floods the air (with his song)".

44. No. 62. Dion Chrys. seems to include colossus among statues lacking inscriptions. He was in Egypt A.D. 69.

21. TOURISTS AT THEBES: THE SYRINGES

1. B. Zincke, *Egypt of the Pharaohs and of the Khedive* 1871, 139–41.

2. V. Denon, *Travels in Upper and Lower Egypt* (transl. F. Blagdon 1802) i 316.

3. Baillet (2): the basis of the account here and for numbers of graffiti. Writers: Strab. xvii 816; Diod. i 46 ff.; Letronne *Rec.* ii 257–9; Paus. i 42, 3; Ail. HA vi 43; Heliod. ii 27; Amm. Marc. xxii 15, 30.

4. 887 and 914; 590 and 233. The names, like many others, recur but we cannot tell if they are of the same persons.

5. 1814 and 1822; dates at times help to relate.

6. 1810 and 1813.

7. 71; 72; 705 and 711, cf. 411–12; 677, 684, 770, 776; 1969, 1975; 2075, 2102.

8. 64; 241—see 226, 1887.

9. 1670, 1614, 1513. Children are mentioned but often we cannot tell if they were present.

10. 828; 634; 194; 1645 (Aplonarios?). Cucullus–Koukkoume appears in Fayum, BGU 255.

11. Antipatra 171; Ianuarius 468.

12. 1247 and 995.

13. 1545 and 1704, cf. 778, Pasios of Pontos "with his household"; 1591, 1535, 1669, etc.

14. 1402 and 1265. Dadouchos also Eleusinian priest: CIG 185. For possible guides: 76, 745, 285.

15. 30 and 66.

16. Last dated graffito that of Count Orion, A.D. c. 537: no. 788. Baillet puts up as strong a case as possible for 901, 1356, 76, 1535, etc. See p. xxii, also xxxiii–xxxix. Pardalas 1745. *Notarius et tribunus voluptatium* (sic.) 769 (p. 618); director of mines 745, etc.

17. 245; 562; 777; 1732. Cf. 1277.

18. Baillet pp. xiv–xxvii.

19. Six from Herakleopolis, dozen Hermop., eight Panopolis, etc.

20. Baillet, pp. xxviii–xxxii for details.

21. 1279 and 1405; 1402 medicus; other scholastikoi, 1861, 1402 (cf. 233, 280–1, 1058, 1242), 1266, 1277, 1810, 1242, 1274, 1279, 1243, 1058, 1516, 1110, 1858, 1360, 1406.

22. 1861.

23. 1836 cf. 1271.

24. Baillet pp. xlii–iv.

25. 1285, 1249, cf. Oxy. 67 for name. See also 1247 Bassus Himerius kath. of Egypt, of Bithyna, cf. rhetor Himerios of Prousa; Baillet CRAI 1922 282–95.

26. 1293, his suite 1295, 1840, 1848. Magistros: of horse BGU 405; 456; of soldiers—in Egypt preceding the dux militum.

27. Pp. xliv–xlvii.

28. Pp. li–liii.

29. Pp. liv–v.

30. 505, 764b, 1929. Servants 1254, 1295; *despotes* 2080, 1840, 1848; *kyrios* 1279; valet 288; freedman 665.

31. 1076, Chrysochous; 1573 sailor?

32. Bataille 174.

33. Bernand p. xl. Baillet 1284; Astakios 1743; *Il.* xv 214.

34. 993, 859, 990 (c. 174), 171, cf. AP xi 201. Hymnologos: 904; trago-diographos 1547; 119 is obscure.

35. Pp. xlviii–li with lists. Patrikios, 1087, pale ink, cf. 1660; Tatianos 1380, black ink.

36. 1427 and 1277, cf. 1403, "I Besas saw and admired the great marvel of the Syringes": scholastikos. Mikkalos 901; Nymphs 319, 3 c. in red ink.

37. 1818, Marinos. Platonists 1263 and 1255; Eudemon (Eudaimon) may be a name, but the translation given makes the best sense. Cf. 1900 and 902.

38. 1265 and 1889. For cult of Plato, Letronne 279–82, and the dadouchos 279–82; Ditt. *Hermes* xx 10 ff.; Foucart, *Les mystères d'El.* ch. vii; Magnien *Les Myst. d'El.* 1950, 158 f. Genealogy: Letronne 173–9, 278–83; Porph. in Euseb. *praep. ev.* x 3, 1 (Henichen 64); Philostr. *Vit. soph.* ii 27 and 33. Letronne imagines a great-great-grandfather: Minucianus I: Fabricius, *Biblioth.* vi 107 f. For M. medicus, cited by Galen: *ibid.* xiii 339. (For Plato deified as Dionysos, a seal "Dionysoplaton": JEA 1948 88.)

39. *Orat.* xxiii and *ecl.* vii 4; he opened a school in Alex. in 369, a prudent but settled foe of Christianity. For Him, and Egypt: Magnien 159. Here Himerios 1247. In Nik.'s graff. *dia Platonos* could mean after Plato or by his favour, cf. 1263. The emperor gave him a viaticum, no doubt certain subsidies —not likely a mission connected with the suppression of the temples as has been suggested (the Council of Nikaia occurring shortly before). See further Baillet, pp. lviii–lix: mostly wild guesses.

40. 1281. Johnson JEA i 181 (SB 6012) on the Mouseion pensionary, also bouletes of Antinoopolis, *platonikos philosophos.*

41. 562, 319; 1542, 1611, 1721, 1735 (Pisides); 172; 1381—difficult passage on Besarion follows, something about averting an impurity: katharma eu . . .

42. 158, 1628; math. 1806, cf. 559; Isidoros astrologos 1172; magos Amsouphis, son of Athas, cert. an Egyptian, 14, 320, 1509.

43. 1613; 1550.

44. Pp. lxxi–ii.

45. 360 and 655, cf. 2107. I do not deal with the Christian graffiti.

46. 604 bis, 999.

47. 311, 477, 1386; see 246d, word-play also on Colossos, Bataille 175.

48. 1062, 1102, 1140, cf. 1987, 1102; BIFAO xxxviii 150.

49. 1922 and 1986.

50. Bataille (1) 177 f. and (2) 124, cf. 123; Nikasios (2) no. 18, and Bernand no. 57. Trajan: Bataille (1) 74.

22. PERSEUS-MIN

1. A certain amount about Gardens is set out in J.L. (3). but there is yet more to be said.

2. Hdt. ii 91. No sign he thought of Min as Pan; for him Pan is Mendes: Sourdille 169. Min–Perseus: Wiedemann 368 f.; Sourdille 55 n. 3, 207–9,

211–13; Drexler; Maspero (3). Gauthier thinks no rel. of Perseus and Min. Kallimachos, *Aitia* (Loeb, fr. 655, p. 277) gives an odd detail of folklore " . . . and a third called after Perseus, of which he planted a cutting in Egypt": a tree called Mimusops, which P. was said to plant in Memphis. That Min was later taken as Pan is brought out by the name Panopolis.

3. Hdt. ii 15, 1; vii 150 (Xerxes) cf. Apollod. ii 2, 4. In vi 54 Hdt. says the Persians claim Perses.

4. Iconomopoulos; JEA xxi 157.

5. J.L. (3) 81, 244, 350 with refs.

6. Woodward no. 9, also 29. Amasis, no. 13.

7. Red Sea and Aithiopia: primarily the plays. Many late refs., Ps-Eratosth. *Kat.* 15 ff., Apollod. ii 4, 3 (? Pherekydes), Louk. *Dial. Seagods* xiv, Philostr. *imag.* i 29; Claudian *Against Ruf.* i 280–4; Ovid. *Met* v, etc. For a lengthy discussion Fontenrose, ch. xi; I keep to what seems most relevant to our quest.

8. Kamal, stele from nekropolis.

9. Scharff (2).

10. Hibis: *Metrop. Mus.* iii pl. 4, v. Esna: Brugsch (3) 756. Triphis (anciently Sprit) is known only from mons. of Saite and GR period.

11. Wiedemann; Montet (1) ii 81; Sourdille (1) 211–13. Per-se: Brugsch in Wiedemann (1) 368 f.; Sauneron (3).

12. Gauthier (8); Juncker (1) 88; Kees (9) 11; de Wit (1) 366. In Twelfth Dyn. Min is the god "standing upon the Mountains", and MK, "he who is upon the Cliffs of the Eastern Desert" Gauthier (1) 190 and (5).

13. Erichsen, *Demot. Glossar* 95; Crum, *Coptic Dict.* 491; Collart (3); Sauneron (7); Goyon (2). Orses Kephalonos Chalkeus at Wadi Hammamat, from small temple in N. wall of Wadi: JEA 1958, 109 f.

14. Ps-Plout. *de fluv.*, *Nilus* xvi (Teubner, *Moralia* vii 308); FHG iii 502. This Aigyptos seems Ramses II: Wainwright (7) 74. Thrasyllus died 36 B.C.

15. Hartland iii for the worldwide taletype; also sv. Roscher, PW, LM, Krappe, etc.

16. 500; see 501 f. on the boat for the festival, with trad. it used to carry the virgin to be thrown in. Cf. Casting on of the Book, Wainwright (7) 75, in inscription at Silsileh (Ramses II and III, and Merenptah). In general Brides of the Sea, Frazer, *Magic Art* ii 150 ff.; Loeb Apollod. i 207 f.

17. Saba: T. C. Plowden, *Travels in Abyssinia* 1868, 84. Hartland iii 25; this tale is Bear's-Son type (pit-episode, etc. omitted), the hero marks heroine with blood of crocodile: the form taken in this tale of the proof or token used against the imposters. Cf. Greek tale of virgin thrown to sea: Athen. xi 15. Tales of crocodile and girl are common in Africa, *e.g.* Zulus, Callaway, *Tales* 56, 58, 349; Senegal, Bérenger-Férand, *Superstitions* ii 19; Bechuana, if watersnake killed, waters go dry: Calloway 290.

18. Paus. Dam. iii 4, 467 f. Silpion: PW 3a 124, close to Mt. Kasios, a home of the gods (worldpillar) with offerings to Zeus Keraunios, Storm–Baal; Fontenrose 75, 133, 143, 277 f., also 73, 130, 173, 212, 214, etc. Note the Mt. Kasios also on borders of Palestine and Egypt, where Typhon's body lay under

the waters, says Hdt. In Ach. Tat.'s romance we hear of a painting of Euanthes seen at Pelousion in Egypt in the shrine of Zeus Kasios: it showed both Prometheus and Andromeda in chains, and A. was in a hollow of the rock, the ketos approaches, Perseus swoops from the air with his sickle-sword. The ketos is like a monster-crocodile: iii 7. Unfortunately we do not know the date of Euanthes.

19. Fontenrose 277 f., cf. Malalas 8 (Dind. 197); Orontes was once called Drakon, Typhon, Ophites: see further J.L. (1) 42–5, etc. Egypt: Budge (1) 517 f.; (10) 1910 i; *Archaeologia* lii. Moon: Budge (1) 522, (6a) 345, and his *Book of Gates* 241, 268.

20. RA 1961, 1, 203–9; no jewels or clothes: is the man a captive? The incision round ankles seems rep. fetters, not ornament. TC originally painted brown: it can hardly be the Laokoon motive. A. J. N. Tremearne *The Ban of the Bori* 1914 411–18; also his *Niger and West Sudan*. The bori mount the dancers in the rites and possess them.

21. Malalas ii 36 f. (Dind.); Nonnos xxxl 10; Manil. v. 540 ff.; Goold 14 f. Plout. *de Is.* 13 (spell), Griffith (10) xii 22. Anat: Fontenrose 136. For Kassiepeia and her quarrel with Nereids, see refs, *ibid.* 295; here again we get the fight with the Sea, but the form is essentially Greek: *phthonos* and *hybris*, cf. various myths of similar conflict with Hera, Aphrodite, Muses, Apollo, etc. Note Nereids with the *Ketos*: amphora, Naples Mus. 3225.

22. Eight appearances in PT and these not very important: 256a; 424b thunderbolt; 953c "love N like Min"; 1712b (with Horus-Ha, a god of the West); 1928c; 1948a "raise himself up like Min"; 1993c, link with Horos of Bouto; 1998a, double palace (cf. 256a).

23. Baumgartel (2); found by Petrie 1893–4, see his account; Capart (2) 216–20.

24. Scharff (5).

25. Perhaps like that of King Djoser on statue for serdab of the Step Pyramid, but face is shaven (beard seems artificial) there; at Koptos the head is whiskered.

26. Tell el-Hari: Frankfort, More Statues from the Diyala Region pl. 12, 120; (6) 29.

27. Following Baumgartel; he suggests intrusions at this Period, *e.g.* Bes, and growth of Osiris' popularity; he takes O. as of Asian origin, which I think dubious.

28. Prob. shells (now lost) on second figure.

29. Frankfort (6) 11 f. Note Bullman from Umma (*ibid.* 115) naked but for multiple belt, bearded: type appearing with human-bodied heroes in beastcombats on seals. Head here has hole for horns to be fitted; legs lost below knees, may have been taurine as thighs have dowel holes for lower legs. Rivet near end spine for tail? Statue ithyphallic like Bullman of seals. Head too damaged to tell if hairless.

30. Dussaud (3). Hadad, *ibid.* 19. Koptos was a possible line of invasion from Near East via Red Sea: see discussion, R. Englebach ASAE xlii 193–221, though he inclines to the Delta. He does not mention the Min statues. Also Petrie,

History 1924 3; *Making of Egypt* 77. JEA 1963 23. Al-Arak: *Fdt. Piot, Mém.* 1916, Bénédite; M. R. Hall, JEA viii 252.

31. Gauthier (1) 176 ff. *Koptos* pl. 22a.

32. PT: heaven 332a–b, 397a, 803a, 1432b, 2059b, 2080c; Gebb 316a; Seth 418a; Atum 701a; Ferryman 925a.

33. Mercer PT iv exc. xix. Bull of Light is stargod, and king as *shd*-star of gold is one of his adornments, 889d. In Sumerian myth the Bull of Heaven was a foe, killed by Gilgamesh and Enkidu. Re and king are both called Bull of Ennead; Re is also Great Wild Bull and Bull of Splendour.

34. Griffiths (1) 2,133, 46, 49, 91 f. See 91 for refs. as to Osiris, Horos, Min, and possible rel. to Bata tale. *Edfou* i 404, 8 has Min as "Bull of his Mother, who is over his staircase . . ." For steps connected with Min-Amun (as with Osiris) in temple of Mut at Karnak, etc., Gauthier (1) 28 f. Hymn, Twenty-second Dyn., to Min shows at Karnak a monthly rite, on 10th day celebrating him as Min-Amun (Bull) impregnating his Mother: P. Berl. 3055; Gauthier 11.

35. Jacobsohn (1) and (2) 3 f.; PT 1013d; Barnes (1) pl. 18 and p. 27; Vandier (7) 8–10. Jacobsohn thinks Horos and Min were early linked in mystery of Bull of His Mother and both got the mother-mating from the kingship (PT 388, mating with Nekhbet or Hathor, Jacobsohn (1) 21): this is most unlikely and shows the widespread wrong-headed effort to exalt the rituals of kingship instead of seeing in them a particular concentration and usurpation of initiation-rituals, creation-rituals, etc.

36. Drioton (13) 3 fig. 1; Cair. 85932, 5–9; Drioton (14) 10 f.

37. Hdt. ii 62–3: he may be softening the original statement of incest: Stein, see Powell sv; Griffiths (1) 86. A. W. Lawrence 178 sees here a fight of Seth and Horos, citing stele of Ikhernofret, cf. Groningen (2) iii 142; Hornblower *Man* 1937 174, who cites the fight at the raising of the djed-pillar (shown in NK Theban tomb): Brugsch (3) v 1190; A. Fakhry ASAE xlii 1943 pl. 39; further Griffiths (1) 86 ff., including site of Papremis. Note Hdt. iv 190a on fight near Lake Tritonis, described as Eg. in origin; cf. Plato *Tim.* 24B. But the rite seems indigenous, the goddess "Athene" like Neith: Bates, *Eastern Libyans* 205 ff.

38. Hdt. ii 156, cf. rape of Tefnut by Geb, cited earlier: here the conflict is with followers of Apepi and Re. No identification: Linforth 6. Links of cults of Montu, Amun, Min: JEA 1965 135.

39. Sayce, *Anc. Empires* 160. Shu as claimant: Lawrence 179; Wiedemann 264 (Gr. pap. Leyden), Ares as Onuris (cf. Sourdille 187 n. 1 and Kees (12) 23) who could be identified with Shu: Juncker (1) 169; Griffiths JEA lxxv 23.

40. Sourdille 188 f.; Griffiths (1) 89. But Thoueris was beneficent; no tale of Seth raping her.

41. PT 1993c; associated with form of Horos, 1712b.

42. Gauthier 16 n. 2.

43. *Ibid.* 16 and 9–11. He sees no lunar or astronomic rel. as do Brugsch and Kees (AZ lvii 1922 131 n. 5); says they misread date at Med. Habu. He

thinks the two processions are really festivals of local god Khnum and triad: with Min as the son Hika.

44. G. thinks the Bull of Min (Palermo stone, Thinite Dyn.) is prototype of Coming-forth.

45. BD ch. xvii; Grapow 18–21; Hassan 141. Earliest Comings-forth see end Third or early Fourth Dyn. In festivals, Memphite nekropolis, it is generally 7th after the rite of flame (or lamps), though the order is not strict; it can come after the setting-up of altars with fire, the great festival, or after Sed. Not in PT.

46. Gauthier 23–5. From NK, stelai and tombs in general cease to list various festivals in which the alimentary service of the dead, but there are a few exceptions. Calendar Med. Habu, Ramses II: among festivals lists 8 generally called the Heavenly Feasts of the Month, with details of offerings (48 feasts a year); the second is Min's Coming-forth, between feast of 29th lunar day and that of New Moon. Medical P. London xvi 40: festival of Min as occasion of joy for children: seems the Coming-forth (Wreszinski (4) 164, 213). List at Thebes, Amun, seems to have Coming-forth in Pakhons: Rougé (2); Gauthier (1) 25–8.

47. G. 30–3. Min at Sais, important since it became the capital: RT xvi 48; Speelers. Rec. Insc. Eg. Mus. R. Brux. 88 no. 334. Birth-house: ? Mammisi.

48. G. 70. Hymn: 230–41. Philai: Brugsch (3) 756; hymn, Lange (4). Edfu: Dumichen (7) i pl. xxxvii; Piehl, pl. xlvii, o; Chassinat ii 390 f. Athribis: Petrie (10) 21 pl. xxxi g.

49. *De Is.* 56. Plout. has a Greek (not Egyptian) play on words: *Horos* and *horomenon*, what-is-seen: Parthey (1) 101; G. 33 f.

50. G. 223.

51. Verso, P. Sallier iv: BM 10184 Budge (2) pl. clxi 3 f.; Chabas 80; Budge (5) ii pl. cv 3 f. From Twelfth Dyn. the combined expression: "see the beauty of Re-Min" RT ix 32 f.; under Eighteenth, Min of Apu often called Min-Re (ED iii 29d, ii 164b and 166; Kees RT xxxvi 53, at Apu-Aknmim; Mariette (3) i 39a, ii 20c at Abydos). In GR times, many places: Dakkeh: Roeder (4) 78; Edfu: Chassinat iii 275, 278; Athribis: Petrie (10) pl. xvii and xviiia; Budge, Cat. passim; Kamal, stelai from Chemmis; Brugsch (8) 36. But Min-Re not met at Koptos. Solar link makes Min from Eighteenth Dyn. Master of the Heaven, Great God Master of the Sky: LD iii 29d. This is a different relation than Min as stormgod.

23. PERSEUS OF THE SKY

1. Fontenrose 275 ff. gives a convenient set of refs., but goes too far in trying to fit all the monster-combats into a general pattern of the Near-East Dragon-Fight. He therefore makes as little as possible of the Red-Sea connections. Sayce (2); Hartland, etc.

2. Fontenrose 277 n. 1, 276 n. 2 for various refs. and further relationships of the sort here mentioned. Earliest known source that set A. at Joppa is ps-Skylax GGM 79.

3. Fontenrose, 278–80, refs. Efforts to reconcile the opposing statements: Plin. vi 29, 182, says Syria was part of Kepheus' Aethiopian kingdom; Strab. i 2, 35 (42 f.) says some locate the Aithiopia in Phoinikia; Tac. *Hist.* v 2 says a band of Aethiopians fled from the tyranny of Kepheus and founded Jerusalem, becoming the Hebrew nation. Other writers saw Aithiope as a cognate of Iope: EM 473, Steph. Byz. 220 (Holst), LM ii 294; Tümpel, *J. Class. Phil. Suppl.* xvi 1888 127–220 (who gives the Perseus myth a Rhodian basis). Note how name Kassiepeia has by-forms Kassiope and Kassiopeia.

Note the Hellenistic cult of city-founders, *neoi ktistai*, linked with Tyche: *Mél. Syriennes* (Dussaud 1939) 287 f.

4. Springs of blood: Paus. iv 35, 9; Philostr. *imag.* 1 29, 2.

5. Woodward no. 14; also 19, 28, 30–2. Pherekydes: *Zeus* ii 71. Harpe used in cosmic struggles by Zeus; by Herakles against monsters. *Sirpe*: H. Levy, 177 ff.; Hesiod, *Works* 571.

6. *Syria* xii 205, 219.

7. Wainwright (1) 152, 157. Marduk's harpe: Hopkins 348.

8. Michailidis (1) 60–5.

9. *Urk.* iv 974 f.

10. WB iii 270, 5; Ptol IV's trilingual decree line 34.

11. Wiedemann (3), cf. Spiegelberg RT xxv 184–90; P. Harris 500H; Gardiner (12) 82–5; Peet JEA xi 225.

12. H. Schäfer: *Ber. Preuss. Kunstsamml. J.* xlix 1928 Heft 2 34–40.

13. Michailidis 63.

14. Wreszinski (5) ii pl. 34.

15. Muller (2) i pl. 17/32. Proper names compounding *hopes*: Mich. 65. Aphrodite and *harpe* in Cypros: RA 1959 (1) 97 f. Kronos in magic: S. Eitrem, *Mél. Bidez* 551–60. Sickle naturally used in Min's harvest rite.

16. Gauthier (1) 190; LD iv pl. 11a; JEA xx 152 f. In general, Wainwright (1) for more on bull, mountain, thunder; rel. to Horos 162.

17. Wainwright (1) 161; JEA xvii 185–95, xx 150. Not from association with Min; it is much earlier.

18. Wainwright (1) 163 ff., esp. 168; cf. PT 280, 283, 792. Min-pillar as personal name: Murray, index vi col. c; Ranke, *Personnamen* 17. Wainwright (7) for *wh*: 10, 17 n. 1, 23; bull 23 n. 4, 107, pillars 106 f.

19. Sethe Urk. i 292; Moret CRAI 1916 326, 328 ff.

20. ASAE xxvii 56 f.; Wainwright (1) 64 n. 2; Ptol., LD iv pl. xlii, b; Mariette (1) i pl. xxiii; Rochemonteix (2) i pl. xxvi, b and ii pl. xl, b. Cf. Asherah-pole of Palestine; Attis-pole etc.: Irminsul with bull and pole. Variations, Wainwright 165.

21. Petrie (10) pl. xviii.

22. Petrie (11) pl. ix 2, x 3; Wainwright (1) 165 n. 7; Juncker *Giza* i 151 no. 17, fig. 23b and pp. 150 f. no. 22. More details and relations to Wadjet, Wainwright 166 f.; cord as magically uniting, etc.

23. Khnum: JEA xx 142, 146, 148 f. Nut: Daressy RT xxvii 87, 192, cf.

Mariette (1) iv pl. 23b. Wh: Blackman, *Meir* i 2 (Sethe *Urg.* 16 sees it as not of sky); bull OLZ 1932 cols. 521 ff.

24. Aphaka: Sozomen EH ii, 5 (Migne lxvii 948); Wainwright ZAS lxxi 43. Feathers: Blackman *Meir* i 3, ii pl. xviii 2. Feathers as Air: JEA xvii 194 f. Aphrodite: n. 15 above, also Schäfer CRAI 17 Oct. 1958, Picard 31 oct.: graved seals, *favissa*, mysteries said to founded by Kinyras, highpriest hereditary; a mystes gave money for sacred lore, got a phallos and some salt. Wainwright 167 for more on meteorites and pillars. In general *Zeus*, J.L. (1), etc.

25. Lacau (4).

26. Kuentz: *Archives Mus. Hist. Nat. Lyon*, xiv 1926.

27. Lacau; PT 130a and 2100, "Horos has woven (or plaited) his tent over your head". Lacau for cord and cone of basketwork.

28. Sethe ZAS lix pl 44* and p. 74; JEA xviii 165.

29. Fairman (1) 22–8: much aetiology in this myth as may be seen from the citation. Waters of Seeking 33; Lake of Combat 32; Seth as hippo. of red jasper 33; elsewhere he is the red hippo. See n. 44 below.

30. *Ibid.* 30 f. Astarte 29, "And His Majesty went. A. being with him."

31. Fontenrose 388 n. 31; 399 nn. 32–3.

32. Dionys. xxxi 8–12; *drepane*, 20. Cf. frag. Sophokles' Andromeda "on steeds or wherries are you voyaging?"—he seems to come floating over sea.

33. *Dionys.* xxviii 291; xxv 31–5; xxxi 9–11; xlvii 566 and 655–663, cf. xlv 235, xlii 205 ff. Andromeda, Kassiepeia, Kepheus appear mainly in rel. to constellations. Perseus and Tarsos: xviii 291, cf. xiii 461. For Perseus and Dionysos, refs. in Guthrie, *Greeks and their Gods*, 170–1.

34. Goold. Kleostratos: Fotheringham (1).

35. Fotheringham (1) 78; Weidner 39 f., 122.

36. Neugebauer (2) 82, 102, 140, 170, 188; he thinks, against van der Waerden (*Af. Orientforch.* xvi 1953 22), that Signs were not yet introduced by 419 B.C.; Dicks (1) 26 f. The exact division (12 sections of 30) was certainly worked out in Babylonia, some time after 450 B.C., perhaps not till 4th c.

37. Webb (2) 58–63 says they were formerly called King, Seated Lady, Fettered Lady, Bearer of the Demon's Head, but gives no refs.

38. List of Decans: Budge (15) ii; (1) 245 f.; also Slolely and Neugebauer (3).

39. Winlock, cited Budge (1) 246.

40. Briggs.

41. Budge (1) 241–3.

42. Briggs 45 f.

43. Briggs 47.

44. Naville (1) xxiv; Chassinat vi 219–23, xiv, clxxxii–iv; Brugsch (3) 609 f. For Mshtiw in PT, Briggs 47 f. Fairman (1) also Seth as red hippo. pursued by Horos. Horos says to Osiris, "I have torn out his leg. The leg of Seth. The four-threaded web." *Ramasseum Dram. Pap.* 108 cf. 126. Seth is several times dismembered in PT, being slain as a bull: 1007a, 1543a, 1976a, 418a; Griffiths (1) 34 f., 2 n. 6, 33. In the end his pieces were said to be distri-

▪ted throughout Egypt, following pattern of Osiris: Fairman (1). For head
▪d leg of Bull: Wolters, Eph. arch. 1892 221.

45. *De Is.* 62. More on Mouth-opening, Wainwright (8). Biot, *J. des
▪vants* 1855 465 f.; Brugsch (5) 343.

46. Anker or Onuris also stretches a cord but lifts one arm: Daressy (1)
▪025, 38028, 38023–4. Why is the cord stretched? to fetter as we see the forces
▪f Apepi fettered (Budge (1) fig. on p. 377) or to direct a magical force (*ibid.*
▪g. on p. 374, spell-weaving with nets or cords)?

47. Senmut: Wainwright fig. 3; Ramesseum, fig. 6; fig. 4, Seti's tomb, has
▪xtended cord; Ptol. rep. at Philai omits cord, LD iv pl. xxxv, b. Senmut's is
▪arliest rep.; but the Uplifter was recognised and named long before Nineteenth
▪yn. More reps.: Twentieth Dyn.: Brugsch (5) 125 figs. AB, 126 no. 4. Ptol.:
▪D iv pl. 35b. Roman: Brugsch (5) 7; Wainwright 357 n. 9 on Petrie (10)
▪l. xxxvii. Theban rep. of cord as spear: Lockyer 151, *ibid.* 147–9 for Thigh
▪nd Seth.

48. Lauer 182 further. Early link of stars (esp. circumpolar) and Underworld: Kees (1) 91 ff., 131. Letopolis and Great Bear: Wainwright (3) and (7)
▪0, 22 f., 76.

49. Buttmann cited Webb (2).

50. Thoueris and childbirth: J.L. (3) 205 f. Plout. *de Is.* 371c, 50; 358c, 19.
Papremis: Griffiths (1) 89; she turns from Seth to Horos, 103, 105. Budge (1)
243 takes the thing on which her foreleg rests to be the Great Mooring Post,
PT 794c; but Mercer takes that to be Isis, the Great Stake. The object is a magical
knot connected with her powers to bind and unbind. Only one ref. to hippo.
in PT (Utt. 324) deals with two female demons (?diseases) in form of hippo.
and ass, who are slain. (It opens with greeting to doorkeeper of Horos at
arrival of N, who is to hail Horos, or H. and Osiris.)

51. Roeder LM v 878–82, 888–903; Griffith (10) xii 22.

52. Sophokles had a connection with Kimon, it seems from the tale that in
468 the casting-vote of K. and his colleagues (returning from Skyros with bones
of Theseus) gave him victory over Aischylos: Plout. Kim. 8; *Marm. Par.* 57.

53. Griffiths (3).

54. Phineus: Ovid *Met.* v 19 ff.; Hyg. 64; Malalas; Kedren. i 23B; John.
Ant. vi 18, 4, 544 f.

55. Louk. How to write hist. 1. Haynes (P. Vase). See Ashmole, JHS 1967
1–17 for a fuller interpretation; he suggests the ketos may be part of Thetis,
representing her metamorphoses. In any event the ketos is unmenacing.

56. Arrian. *anab.* i 12, 1–2; ii 3, 2. Ps-Plout. fort. Alex. ii 12. Kallisthenes:
Curt. viii 5, 8; Plout. *Alex.* 33; Polyb. xii 23, 4. Sea; Kall. *script. rer. Alex.*
(Didot) fr. 25 p. 19; Plout. *Alex.* 17; Arr. i 26, 2; Wilcken *Alex.* 102; Tarn
Alex. 374, 357—cf. Xen. *anab*, i 4, 17 on Euphrates recognising Kyros. Carfaux
and Tondriau, *Culte des Souverains* 1956 127, 131, 135; Str. C 814.

57. Louk. *Alex.* 11 and 58.

58. Wright, *Archaeologia* xxx 450 no. 20; Paus. Dam. iii 4, 468M; De
Sculpturis Lapidum (13 c.) i 20.

59. Ailian VH xiii 12. Theophrastos (Loeb ii 393) tells us: "Good astronom
have been found in some parts: for instance, Matriketas at Methymna observ
the solstices from Mt Lepetymnos, Kleostratos in Tenedos from Mt I
Phaeinos at Athens from Mt Lykabettos, Meton, who made the calendar cy
of 19 years, was the pupil of the last named. Phaeinos was a resident alien
Athens. Other examples of local astronomers could be given." Euripides, wi
his obvious interest in all the branches of thought and research in his perio
may well have known Phaeinos, Meton, Euktemon.

That Sophokles dealt with the constellations is proved by Eratosthene
Katast. 16, cf. *Aratea* of Germanicus Caesar: Ellis, *J.P.* iv 267, Maas, *Commen
in Arat.* 215, 257, and Hygin. *poet. astron.* ii lo. See also attempt to reconstruc
the play: Kuhnert, Roscher, iii 1994 and Petersen, JHS xxiv 104 (from BN
hydria E 169). The fragment *sareton* suggests the garb of the Persian King, bu
the word might be used merely to suggest oriental majesty.

Bibliography

Ahmed Bey Kamal see Kamal. Alexander, H. B. N., *American Myth.* 1916. Alliot, N. (1) *Le Culte d'Horos à Edfou au temps de Ptol.* 1954 (2) *Rev. Eg.* v 80. Amir, M. el-, JEA xxxvi 81–5. Andrae, W., *Die Fest. im Nahen Osten.* Avennes, P. d', *Hist. de l'art eg.*

Bacchi, *L'inno al Nilo* 1950. Badawy, A. (1) *Hist. of Eg. Archit.* 1966 (2) JEA 1956 58–64 (3) *Der Gott Chnum* 1937 (4) RA xlviii 1956 140 ff. Baikie, J., HERE ix 1917 220. Bailey, K. C., *The Elder Pliny's Chapters on Chemical Subjects* 1932. Baillet, J. (1) *La régime pharaonique* 1913 (2) *Incsrs. gr. et lat. des tombeaux des rois ou syringes* 1926 (3) CRAI 1922 282–95. Ball, J., *Eg. in class. Geographers* 1942. Barb. (Abraxas) *Homm. Deonna.* Barguet, *Stèle de la famine à Séhel.* Barns, J. W. B. (1) *Five Ramasseum Pap.* 1956 (2) JEA xxxiv 1948 35–9. Barois, *Irrigation in Eg.* (House Dept. Misc. Docs ix 1888–9 no. 134). Barucq, A., ASAE xlix 183–202. Bataille, A. (1) *Les Memnonia* 1952 (2) *Inscrs. gr. du temple de Hatshepsout à D. el-B.* 1951. Beardsley, G. H., *The Negro in Gr. & R. Civilisation* 1929. Behm, J., *Das Bildwort vom Spiegel, I Kor. xiii 12.* Bell, H. I. (1) *Abinnaeus Archives* 1962 (2) JEA xxxiv 1948 82–97. Bérard, V. (1) *Les Phéniciens et l'Od.* 1927 (2) *La Résurrection d'Homère* 1930 (3) *L'Od. d'Homère* 1931. Berger, H. (1) *Gesch. d. wiss. Erkunde d. Gr.* 1903 (2) *Die Geog. Frag. d. Erathosthenes* 1880 (3) *Myth. Kosmogeographie d. Gr.* 1904. Bernhard, M. L., RA 1956 (1) 129–56. Bernand, A. (1) with O. Masson, REG lxxx 1–46 (2) with E. Bernand, *Inscrs. de Colosse de Memnon* 1960. Besnier, DS sv *navicularii.* Bevan, E., *Hist. of Eg. under Ptols.* 1927. Bilabel, *Die gr.-aeg. Feste.* Bingen, J., CE xxx 1955 no. 59 130–3. Birch, S. (1) ZAS iv 1866 89, on to viii 1870 73 (2) *Select Pap. in Hieratic* (BM). Bissing, von (1) *Das Re-Heiligtum d. K. Ne-Woser-Re (Rathures) III: Die grosse Festsarstellung* 1928 (2) AZ xli 87 ff., (3) with Muschler, *Die Mastaba des Gem-ni-Kai* 1904–5. Blache, V. de la (1) CRAI 1896 456–83 (2) *ibid.* 1897 520–7. Blackdon-Fraser, *Hieratic Graff. from . . . Hatnub.* Blackeney, E. H., *The Eg. of Hdt.* 1924. Blackman, W. S. (1) *Meir* (2) JEA iv 1917 (3) *Man* xxv 65–7 (4) *The Temple of Derr* (5) RT xxxix 45 (6) with Peet, JEA 1925 Oct. 284–98 (7) JEA xi 201–9 (8) JEA v 117 ff. 148 ff. (9) PSABA xl 57, 85 (10) RT xxxix 44 (11) HERE x 476 (12) ZAS xlvii (13) *Temple of Dendur* 1911 (14) ZAS xlix 1911 54 (15) JEA v 117 (16) with Fairman, JEA xxx 5–22. Blinkenberg, *Thunderweapon in Religion and Fl.* Blümner, *Technologie.* Boak, with Petersen, *Sokonpaiou Nesos.* Boeser, with Holwerden, *Beschreibung d. aeg. Samml. d. N.R. Leiden: Stelen.* Boll, F. (1) *Beitrage z. Ueberlieferungsgech. d. gr. Astrologie u. Astron.* 1899 (Ak. Wiss. Münch. 1 77–140) (2) *Sphaera* 1903.

FF

Bonneau, D., *La Crue du Nil* 1964. Bonnet, H. (1) *Reallex d. aeg. Religionsgesch* 1952 (2) *Bilder-atlas: Aeg. Relig.* Bono, F. de, ASAE 1951 li 59–91. Borchardt (1) *Grabdenkmal d. k. Sahure* (2) ditto *Ne-user-re* (3) AZ xlii 82 (4) *Statuen u. Statuetten, Cat. Gen.* Bouché-Leclercq, A. (1) *Hist. des Lagides* (2) *L'Astrol. gr.* 1889. Bourdon, C. L., *Mém. Soc. roy. Géog. d'Eg.* vii 65–72. Boussec, H., RT xxxiii 1911 61–3. Brandon, S. G. F., *The Saviour God* 1963. Breasted (1) *Anc. Records* (2) *Hist. of Eg.* (3) *Dawn of Conscience* 1933 (4) *Development of Religion and Thought in Anc. Eg.* 1912 (5) BIFAO xxx (Mél. Loret) 709–24. Breccia, E. *Mons. de l'Eg.* GR. Briggs, R. E., in Mercer PT iv 38–49. Bromehead, C. E. N., *Procs. Geolog. Assn.* lvi 2 1945 85–134. Bruce, F. F., in Brandon. Brugsch, H. (1) *Matériaux . . . du Calendrier* (2) *Drei Fest-Kalendar* (3) *Thesaurus* (4) *Dict. géog.* (5) *Aegyptologie* (6) *Geog. d. alt. Aeg.* 1857 (7) with Dümichen, *Rec. mons. eg.* (8) *Religion u. Myth.* (9) *Abh. Göttingen* xiv 1868–9 177 (10) *Lettre à de Rougé* (11) *Reise nach der grossen Osae El Khargal.* Brunton, *Qau and Badari.* Bruyère, B. (1) *Docs. de fouilles* xviii 1952 (2) *Mert Seger à Deir el Médineh* (3) CE liii 1952 31–42 (4) *Fouilles IFAO* ii 2, 12 (5) MIFAO liv, with Kuentz. Buck, A. de (1) *Coffin Texts* (2) *Orient. N.* 1948 1–22 (3) *De Godseienstige Beteekenis van de Slaap* (4) *De Eg. voorstellingen betreffende den Oerheuvel.* Budge, E. A. W. (1) *From Fetish to God* 9134 (2) *Eg. Heaven and Hell* 1925 (3) *Book of Dead* 1910 (4) *Mummy,* 2nd ed. (5) *Facsimiles of Eg. Hieratic Pap.* 1910 (6) *P. of Ani* 1894 (6a) ibid. 1913 (7) *Nu* (8) as (1) (9) *Book of Dead, Hunefer, Anhai,* etc. 1899 (10) *Hieratic Pap.* BM 1924 2nd ed. (11) *Legends of the Gods* 1912 (12) *On the Hieratic P. of Nesi-Amasu* 1891 (13) *Eg. Sudan* 1907 (14) *Guide Eg. Coll.* BM 1909 (15) *Gods of the Egs.* 1904 (16) *Eg. Hierogl. Dict.* 1920 (17) *Chapters of Coming Forth by Day,* Text 1898 (18) *O. and Eg. Resurrection* (19) *Greenfield Pap.* (20) as (6a) (21) *Eg. Magic.* Burdeau, J., etc., *Aspects of l'emp. rom.* 1964. Burrows, E. (1) in Hooke, *Labyrinth* 1935 (2) *Orientalia* i 1932. Burton, R. F., *The Thousand Nights and a Night* 1885.

Cagnat, *Inscr. gr. ad res rom. pert.* Calderini, A. W., *Aeg.* xiii 1932 674–89. Caminos, R. A., *Lit. Frags. in the Hieratic Script* 1956. Campbell, B., JEA xvi 1930 6–9. Capart (1) *Thèbes* 1925 (2) *Les débuts de l'art en Eg.* (3) *Bull. Crit. Relig. Eg.* 1906–7 236. Capelle, W., *Die Nilschwelle,* N. J. Kl. Alt, xxxiii 1914 317–61. Capovilla, G. (1) *Aeg.* 1959 290 (2) xl 1960 1. Carter, H., *Tomb of Tut Ankh Amen.* Caulfeild, *The Temple of the Kings at Abydos.* Chabas, *Le Calendrier des jours fastes et néfastes* 1870. Champollion, *Grammaire ég.* Chassinat (1) *Temple d'Edfou* (2) with Palanque, *Assiout* (3) *Mammisi d'Edfou* (4) BIFAO iii 1903 154. Chenet, G., *Mél. Syriennes* 1939 i 49–54. Chitty, D. J., *The Desert a City* 1966. Christophe, L. A., *Temple d'Amon à Karnak* 1955. Clauson, N. Y., CE ix 3–4 240. Clédat, J. (1) BIFAO xvi 201 (2) xvii 103. Clère, J. J., BIFAO xxxviii 173–201. Clermont-Ganneau, *Rec. d'Arch. orient.* v 300. Collart, P. (1) BCH liii 76 (2) with Jouguet, *Petites recherches sur l'écon politique des Lag.* 1925 (3) BIFAO xxxi 102–4. Cook, S. A., *Religion of Anc. Palestine in Light of Arch.* Couyat (1) CRAI 1910 525–42 (2) with Montet, *Inscrs. du Ouadi*

Hammamat MIFAO xxxiv (3) BIFAO vii 1910 15-39. Czerny (Černy), J. (1) ASAE xli 1942 349-52 (2) *Anc. Eg. Relig.* 1957.

Daressy (1) *Statues de Divinités: Cat. Gén.* (2) *Textes et dessins magiques* 3) *Notice du temple de Louxor* (4) ASAE ix 1908 (5) *Notice explic. des ruines de Méd. Habou* 1897 (6) ASAE xiii 1913 109-114 (7) BIFAO xii 1916. Dattari, *Nummi Alexandrini Augg.* Davies (1) *Mastaba of Ptahhetep and Akhethetep* (2) *Tomb of Amenemhet* (with Gardiner) 1915. Deismann (1) *Light from Anc. East* (tr. Strachan) 1909, 2nd ed. 1910 (2) *Licht von Osten* 4th ed. 1923. Delcourt, M., *Hephaistos.* Demargne, P., *Ann. Ec. HE de Gand* ii 1938 51-2. Demel, H., *Mitt. Anthrop. Gesell.*, Wien lx 1930. Deonna, W. (1) *Artibus Asiae* xiii 3-4 1949 347-74 (2) RHR cxix 53-81. Derchain, P. (1) CE xl 487-94 (2) CE liv 358-68. Deroy, L., *Mél. I. Levy* 1955 87-121. Devéria, *Le fer et l'amant* (Maspero, *Biblioth. ég.* v). Dicks, D. R. (1) JHS 1966 26-40 (2) CQ ix 306. Dietrichson, L., *Antinoos.* Dolger, F. J., *Antike u. Christentum* v. Donadini, S., *Ann. Scuol. Norm. Pisa.* II vi 1937 1-11, 166-8. Drexler (1) Roscher II 2 Abh sv *Min* 2980-2 (2) Suppl. ASAE cahier 11, Edfu (3) *Bull. Inst. Eg.* xxv 1943 (4) *Les Fêtes Eg.* 1944. Drioton, E. (1) *Médamoud, les inscrs.* 1926 (2) with Vandier, *L'Egypte* (3) REgA ii 172-99 and l 133-7 (4) *Le Théâtre Eg.* 1942 (5) *L'Amant de l'Art* xxviii 200 (6) *Rev. des Confer. fr. en Orient* xiii 459 (7) *Arts asiat.* i 96 (8) *Rev. Hist. du Théâtre* vi 7 (9) *Rapp. fouilles Médamoud* 1924-5 (10) ASAE xlv 111-62 (11) ASAE xl 305-427. Dubois, C. (1) *Rev. de Philol.* xlix 1925 60-83 (2) *Géog. de Strabon.* Dümichen (1) *Der Grâbpalast des Patuamenap* (2) *Geog. Inschr.* (3) *Hist. Inschr.* (4) *Baugesch. d. Denderatempels* (5) *Altaeg. Kalenderinschr.* 1886 (6) *Kalend- opferfest-Listen, Med. Habu* 1881 (7) *Altaeg. Tempelinschr.* Dunham, D. (1) *Sudan Notes and Rec.* 1947 (2) *Royal Cemeteries of Kush* i 1950, ii 1955, iii 1952, iv 1957, v 1963. Dupont, J., *Gnosis* 1949. Durbach, *Choix des inscrs. de Délos.* Dussaud, R. (1) RHR c 86 (2) *Les Religions des Hittites etc.* (3) RHR cxiii 1936 5 (4) *Mél. Glotz* i. Dykmans, G., *Hist. écon et soc. de l'Anc. Eg.* .

Ebeling, *Tod und Leben.* Ebers, G., *Das alte aeg. Mârchen.* Edgar, C. C., *Zenon Pap: Cat. Gén.* Edsman, C. M., *Ignis Divinus* 1952. Egger, E., RA ns xiii 103. Eichholz, D. E., *Loeb Pliny NH* x. Emery, W. B. (1) *Archaic Eg.* (2) *Eg. in Nubia* 1965. Erichsen, W. (1) *Acta Orient.* vi 1928 270-8 (2) *Demot. Orakelfragen* 1942. Erman (1) *Aeg. u. aeg. Leben* (Ranke) (2) with Grapow, WB (3) *Mârchen d. Pap. Westcar* (4) *Eg. Lit.* (Blackman) 1927 (5) *Die Relig. d. Aeg* 1934 (6) *Die aeg. Schulerhandsschriften* 1925 (7) *Sitz. preuss. Ak. Wiss.* 1911 xlix 1086-1110 (8) *Handbook of Eg. Religion* (9) *Sphinkstele, Sitz. Berl.* 1904.

Fakhry, A. (1) ASAE xxxix 709-23 (2) *Inscrs. of Amethyst Quarries at Wadi el Hudi* 1952. Fairman, H. W., JEA xxi 1935 26-36. Faivre, J., *Canope, Ménothis, Aboukir* 1917. Farina, G., *Bilychnis* xx 1923. Faulkner, R. O., JEA xli 1955 141-2. Festugière (1) HTR xxxi 1938 1-12 (2) *Hermès Trismegiste.* Feuardent, *Numismatique: Eg. Anc.* Firth, C. M., *Arch. Survey of Nubia* 1912, 1915, 1927. Fitzler, *Steinbrüche u. Bergwerke im ptol. u rom. Aeg.* 1901. Fontenrose, J.,

FF*

Python 1959. Fotheringham, J. K. (1) JHS 1925 xlv 78–83 (2) xxxix 1919 164–84. Foucart, G. (1) BIFAO xxiv 1924 (2) BIE xxv 1943. Fränkel, H., GGA cxcii 198. Frankfort, H. (1) *Cenotaph of Seti I at Abydos* (2) *Birth of Civilisation in the Near East* 1951 (3) *Kingship and the Gods* 1948 (4) *Before Philosophy* (1949 Pelican) (5) JEA xii 157–62. Friedlander, P., JdAI xxix 1914 98. Frisk, *Bankakten*.

Gaillard, with Daressy, *La fauné momifiée: Cat. Gén.* Gardiner, A. H. (1) *Chester Beatty Pap.* (2) *Tomb of Amenemhetep* (3) *Eg. Grammar* (4) with Peet and Černy, *Inscrs. of Sinai* (5) as (1) (6) *Hieratic Pap.* BM 3rd s. (7) *Cairo Sc. J.*, Fév. 1914 41–6 (8) JEA ii 125 (9) PSBA xxxiv 1912 257–65 (10) *Notes on the Story of Sinuhe* 1916 (11) JEA iii 99 and v 127, 242, x 94, xix 122 (12) *Late-Eg. Stories* 1932 (13) *Anc. Eg. Onomastica* (14) *Eg. Miscellanies* (15) in *Legacy of Egypt* (Writing and Lit.) (16) AZ xlv 1908–9 140 f. (17) AZ xli 1905 2, 12–42 (18) AG xlii (19) *Griffith Studies* 1932 74–85 (20) JEA i 100 (21) JEA xxxv 3–12. Garnot, J. S. F. (1) RHR 1941 5–26 (2) *J. de psych. norm. et path.* 1948 463–72 (3) *La Vie relig. dans l'Anc. Eg.* 1948 (5) *L'Imakh et les Imakhous* 1943 (5) *L'Appel aux Vivants* 1938. Garofolo, RT xxiv. Gauckler, P., *Mon. Piot* xii 1905 113. Gauthier, H. (1) *Les Fêtes du Dieu Min* 1931 (2–3) *Le Personnel du dieu Min* 1931 (4) *Dict. des noms géog. contenu dans les textes hierogl.* (5) *Kemi* ii 41–82 (6) *Mél. V. Loret* (BIFAO xxx) (7) *Temple d'Amada* (8) BIFAO iii 179. Gautier, J. F. (with Jequier), *Fouilles de Licht* (MIFAO vi) 1902. Gayet, *Temple de Louxor*. Gesenius-Buhl, *Hebraisches HandWB*. Gilbert, P. CE xxvii 1937 47–61. Gisinger, F. (1) PW 1937 sv *Oikoumene* (2) ibid. *Periokoi* 883–7 (3) ibid. 1957 *Nachträge* 1285–6 (4) ibid. Suppl. Bd iv 1924 604–12. Golénischeff (1) *Die Metternichstele* (2) AZ xx 1882 135 (3) *Hammamat* (4) RT xiii 1890 75–96 (5) ibid. xxviii 80. Goodspeed, *Pap. from Karanis*. Goodwin, *Frag. of GR work upon Magic*. Goold, *Procs. African Class. Assn.* ii 1956 10–5. Goosens, G., CE 1939 336–9. Gordon, P., *L'Image du Monde dans l'Antiquité* 1949. Goyon (1) ASAE xlix 337–92 (2) *Nouv. Inscr. rupestres du W. Hammamat* 157 (3) *Kemi* vi 1936 1–42. Grace, V., AJA i 1946. Graindor, M. P., BIFAO xxxi 1931 1–29. Grapow, H. (1) *Relig. Urkunden* 1915 (2) *Sprach. u. Schrift. Formung aeg. Texte*. Greene, J. B., *Fouilles . . . à Thèbes*. Greipl, N., *Philol.* lxxxv 159. Greven, L., *Der Ka in Theologie u. Königskult* 1952. Griffith, F. L. (1) *Hieroglyphs* (2) with Petrie, *Two Hierogl. Pap. from Tanis* 1889 (3) *Stories of the High Priests of Memphis* (4) *Cat. Demotic Graff. of Dodecaschoenus* i 1937 (Les Temples immergés de la Nubie) (5) *Antiq. of Tell el-Yahudiyeh* (6) *Hieratic Pap. from Kahun and Gurob* 1898 (7) ZAS xlvi 132 (8) *Karanog* (9) JEA ii 5–7 (10) with Thompson, *Demotic Mag. Pap. of London and Leyden* 1904. Griffiths, J. G. (1) *Conflict of Horus and Seth* 1960 (2) JEA xlvi 1960 122–3 (3) ASAE xlviii 1948 409–23. Groag, *Vierteljahrschrift f. Socie. u. Wirtsch.* ii 1904 481–510. Groningen, van (1) P. Oxy 1380 (thesis 1921) (2) *Herodotus Historien*. Gueraud, O., BIFAO xli 1942 141–96. Guignet, *Les procédés epist. de S. Greg. de Naz. comp. à ceux de ses contemp.* 1911. Gunn, B., JEA iii 81–94.

Hall, *Cat. of EG. Scarabs* BM. Hartland, E. S., *Legend of Perseus* 1894.

Hassan, S. (1) *Hymnes relig. du ME* (2) *Sphinx* (3) *Excavations at Giza* vi pt i 1946. Haynes, D. E. L., *The Portland Vase* 1964. Heichleheim, F. (1) *Aeg.* xiii 1933 187–92 (2) PW 1933 sv *Monopole* (3) *L'écon. roy. des Lagides*. Heidel, W. A. (1) *Hecataeus and the Eg. Priests in Hdt Bk II*, Mem. Amer. Ac. Arts Sc. xviii 1935 (2) *The Heroic Age of Science* 1933. Helck, W. *Untersuch. zu d. Beamtentiteln* 1954. Hennig, R. (1) *Klio* xxiii 1929 256–76 (2) *Kulturgesch. St. z. Herodot*, RhM 1934. Hermann, A., *J. f. Ant. u. Chr.* ii 1954 44–6. Hess, J. J., *Der demot. Roman v. Setne-Ha-Mus* 1888. Hill, G. F., *Cat. Gr. Coins: Lycia, Pamph., Pisidia*. Hogarth, D. G., *Authority and Archaeology*. Hohmann, *Zur Chronologie d. Pap*. Holmberg, MS., *The God Ptah* 1946. Hommel, F., *Ethnol. u. Geog. d. A.O.*, 1904, 1926. Honigmann (1) PW 1936 555–66 (2) *ibid.* 1926 149–202. Hooke, S. H. (1) *The Siege Perilous* 1956 (2) *Middle E. Myth*. Hopfner, T. (1) *Plut. über Isis u. Os.* 1940–1 (2) *Gr.-Aeg. Offenbarungzauber*. Hopkins, C., AJA xxxviii 341–58. How, W. W. (with J. Wells), *A Commentary on Hdt.* i 1928. Humbert, M., in Burdeaux. Hurst, H. E., *Le Nil* (transl. Guieu) 1954. Hüsing, G., MVAG xxi 35–68.

Iconomopoulos, REG ii 1889 164–8.

Jacobsohn (1) *Die dogmat. Stellung d. Königs in d. Theologie d. alt. Aeg.* 1938 (2) *Die Bewusstswerdung des Menschen in d. aeg. Relig.* 1951. Jahn, K., PW suppl. vii A2 1948 sv *Trogodutai*. Jéquier (1) BIFAO vi 1908 35–8 (2) *La frise d'objets des sarccoph. du ME* 1921 (3) *Mél. V. Loret* BIFAO xxx (4) *Considérations sur les Religions eg.* 1946. Jouguet, P. (1) *L'Imperialisme macéd. et l'Hellénisation de l'Orient* (2) *Vie Municipale* (3) REG ix 1896 433–6 (4) *Mél. Glotz* ii 493–500. Juncker, H. (1) *Die Onurislegende* 1917 (2) MdDAI ix 1952 89 (3) *Das Götterdekret über das Abaton* 1913 (4) JEA vii 1921 121–132 (5) *Der Sehende u. blinde Gott* 1942 (6) *Bericht . . . Grabungen auf d. Friedhof d.A.R.* i–viii (7–8) omitted (9) *Auszug d. Hathor-Tefnut aus Nubien* 1911 ABAW (10) *Die Stunden-wachen in den Osirismysterien*.

Kadish, G. E., JEA lii 23–33. Kahane, H. and R. (1) *The Krater and the Grail* 1965 (2) ZfD Alt. lxxxix 1954 192–4. Kahrstedt, U. (1) *Uber Gesandtschaften aus fremden Ländern*. Kaiser, O., *Die myth. Bedeutung der Meeres in Aeg., Ugarit, u. Israel* 1959. Kamal, A. bey, *Stèles ptol. et rom., Cairo*. Kantor, H., AJA lvi 1–103. Kaplony-Heckel, U., *Demot., Gelelen-Urk. d. Heidelberg Pap-Samml.* 1964. Kaufmann, C. M., *Aeg. Terrakotten*. Klasens, A. (1) *A magical statue base in M. of A. Leiden* 1952 (2) *Jaarbericht Ex Or. Lux* x 1945–8. Kornemann, PW iv 381–480, sv *Collegium*. Kortenbeutel, H., *Der aeg. Süd.-u. Osthandel* 1931. Kraeling, E. G., *Brooklyn Mus. Aramaic Pap*. Kristensen, W. B., *Het Leven uit de Dood*. Krüger, O., *Ptol. u. frühröm. Texte* 1929. Kuentz, C. (1) BIFAO xvii 121–9 (2) ASAE xxv 181–238 (3) RT xxv (4) ASAE xxviii 103–72. Kunkel, W. AfP viii 185.

Labib, P. C., *Die Herrschaft d. Hyksos in Aeg. u. ihr Sturz*. Lacau, P. (1) *Sarc.*

antér. au NE (2) ASAE i 1950 221 (3) ASAE lii 1952 185 (4) CE lv 1953 13–22. Lafaye, G., *Hist. culte div. Alex.* Laistner, M. L., *Christianity and Pagan Cultures* 1951. Lambrechts, P., *Mél. I Levy* 1955 207–40. Lane, E. W. *Manners and Customs Mod. Egs.* (1st. ed. 1836; 5th 1860), Everyman ed. Lange (1) with Schäfer, *Grab.-u. Denksteine d. mittl. Reich* (2) *Der mag. Pap. Harris* (3) *Das Weisheitsbuch des Amenemope* (4) SPAW 1927, 2, 231–8. Langlois, *Numismatique des nomes d'Eg.* Lanzone, R. V. (1) *Diz. di Mitologia:* LD (2) *Les Pap. do Lac Moeris* 1896. Lasseur, D. le, *Les déesses armées dans l'ant. class. gr. et leurs origines asiat.* Lauer, J. P., BIFAO lx 1960 171–83. Lawrence, A. W., *The Hist of Hdt. of Halicarnassus* 1935. Leclant (1) BIFAO xlix 1950 193–253 (2) *Bull. Soc. fr. d'Egyptol.* xxi June 1956 29–39. Lefébure, E. (1) PSBA viii 200 (2) *Sphinx* viii 10 f. (3) Bull. hist. et philol. 1905 (4) *Sphinx* xi 1908 1–25. Lefebvre, G. (1) *Romans et Contes eg. de l'époque pharaon.* 1949 (2) *Hist. des grands prêtres d' Amon à Karnak* (3) ASAE x 1910 Crocodilopolis (4) *ibid.* 152 (5) ASAE xxv 34–45 (6) CRAI 1946 496. Legrain, *Temples de Karnak* (ed. Capart) 1930. Legrand, P., *Hérodote.* Leibovitch, ASAE xl 1940 301–3. Leider, E., *Der Handel von Alex.* 1934. Lenormant, *Lettres assyriologiques.* Lepsius, *Denkmäler.* Lesquier, J., *L'armée rom. d'Eg.* 1918. Lethaby, W. R., *Architecture, Nature and Magic* 1956. Letronne (1) *Rec. des Inscrs. Gr et Lat. d'Eg.* (2) *Recherches geog. et crit. sur le livre de mensurae orbis terrae* (3) *La Statue Vocale de Memnon* 1833. Levy, H., *Die Semit. Fremdwörter im Gr.* 1895. Lewis, N., TAPA 1960 xci 137–41. Lewy, J., *Mél. Syr.* 1939 i. Lexa, *La magie dans l'Eg. ant.* 1925. Lieblein, *Dict. des noms hierolg.* (2) *Dict. noms propres.* Lindsay, J. (1) *Clashing Rocks* 1965 (2) *Daily Life in Roman Eg.* (3) *Leisure and Pleasure RE* (4) *Short History of Culture* 1962. Lockyer J. N., *The Dawn of Astronomy* 1894. Loew, J., *Die Flora der Iuden.* Loret, V. (1) RT xii 109–111 (2) *La Flora pharaon.* 2nd ed. 1892. Lucas, A. *Anc. Eg. Materials and Industries* 1948. Lumbroso, G., *L'Eg. des Gr. e dei Romani.*

MacCulloch, J. A., HERE vi 1913 42. Mace, with Winlock, *Tomb of Senebtisi.* MacIver, D. R,, with Woolley, *Buhen* 1911. Mahler, AZ xlviii 89. Malaise, M., CE xli (82) 244–72. Mallet, D. (1) *Les premiers étab. des Gr. en Eg.* 1893 (2) *Les Rapp. des Gr. anc. avec l'Eg.* 1922. Margoliouth, JRAsiatS 1890 677–731. Mariette (1) *Dendérah* 1870 (2) *Mons. divers* (3) *Abydos* (4) *Pap. ég. du Mus. de Boulaq.* Maspero, G. (1) *Contes pop. de l'Eg. anc* 1905 (2) transl. Johns. (3) *Philol.* i 179 (4) *Hymne au Nil* 1912 (5) *La myth. ég.* 1889. (6) *Etudes ég.* i 3, 1883 (7) *Hist. anc. des peuples or.* 1921 (8) with Gauthier, *Sarcoph. des époques persane et ptol., Cat. Gén.* ii 1939 (9) *Et. de Myth. et d'Arch.* ii 402. Maspero, J., with G. Wiet, *Matériaux pour servir à la geog. de l'Eg.* Mayser, *Grammatik d. gr. Pap. aus d.Ptolemäerzeit.* Meautis, G., *Rev. de Philol* xl 1916 51–4. Meister, K. *Eranos* xlvi 94–122. Mercer, S. A. B. (1) *Relig. of Anc. Eg* 1949 (2) *Earliest Intellectual Man's Idea of the Cosmos* 1957 (3) *Pyramid Texts* 4 vols (4) *Horos, Royal God* (5) *Etudes.* Meredith, D. (1) CE xxviii 126 (2) xxix 103 (3) xxx 127 (4) JEA xxxix 99 (5) JEA xliii 56–70. Merkelbach, R. 1, AfP xvi 1956. Merzagora, M., *Aeg.* x 2–4 1929 106–48. Meulenaire, H. de, *Bibl. or.* xvi 1956 106. Meyer, E., *Gesch. Alt.* 3rd ed. Michailidis, G., ASAE xlviii 1947 47–75. Michalowski,

JJP xi–xii 1957–8 185–9. Mionnet, *Descr. des médailles ant.* Moldehnke, C. (1) *Etudes arch . . . à Leemans* 1885 (2) *Uber die in altaeg. Texten erwähuten Baume u.d. Verwerthung* 1886. Möller, *Die bieden Totenpap. Rhind.* Montet, P. (1) *Géog. de l'Eg. anc.* (2) *Le Drame d'Avaris* 1941 (3) *La Bible et l'Eg.* (4) *Les scènes de la vie privée* 1925. Moorehead, A. (1) *The Blue Nile* 1962 (2) *The White Nile* 1960 (3) *No Room in the Ark* 1959. Moret, A. (1) *Rois et dieux d'Eg.* 1925 (2) *Du caractère relig. de la royauté pharaon.* 1902 (3) *Mystères ég.* 1913 (4) *Du sacrifice en Eg.* (5) *La mise à mort du dieu en Eg.* 1927 (6) *Le Nil et la Civil. ég.* 1926 (7) *Le Rituel du culte divine journalier en Eg.* (8) *RHR* 1908, l, 86–7 (9) *J. Asiat.* 1912 xx 73–113: 1916 vii 271; 1917 x 359 (10) *Hist. Nat. ég* 1932 (11) *La légende d'Osiris.* Müller, W, *AfP* xvi 1956 190–213. Muller, W. M. (1) *Eg. Myth.* (2) *Eg. Researches* (3) *Liebespoesie.* Murray, G. W. (1) *JEA* xi 138 (2) *BIE* xxiv 81–6 (3) *Man* xxiii Sept. 1923. Murray, M. (1) *Saqqara Mast.* (2) *ZAS* li 1914 127. Musurillo, H., *CE* xxxi Jan. 1956 124–34.

Nagel, M. G. (1) *BIFAO* xxviii 33–9 (2) xxix 65–8. Nallino, C. A., *BIFAO* xxx 465–75. Navarre, O., *DS* sv *Pygmaei.* Naville (1) *Textes rel. au mythe d'Horus rec. dans le Temple d'Edfou* 1870 (2) *Das aeg. Totenbuch* (3) *Details relevés dans les ruines de quelques temples ég.* 1930 (4) *Deir el Bahari, the Temple* (5) *Bubastis* (6) *ZAS* xl 66–75 (7) *Goshen and the Shrine of Saft el-Hanneh.* Neroutsos Bey (1) *Etudes sur l'anc. Alex.* (2) *RA* 3rd s. ix 1887 199. Neugebauer, O. (1) with van Hoesen, *Gr. Horoscopes* 1959 (2) *The Exact Sciences in Ant.* 1957 (3) with Lange, *Pap. Carslburg no. 1,* 1940.

Olssen, B., *Pap. briefe.* Örtel, *Die Liturgie.* Otto, E., *Aegypten: Der Weg d. Pharaon* 1953. Otto, W., *Priester u. Tempel.*

Paradisi, U., *Aeg.* xliii 1963 269–77. Parker, *The Calendar of Anc. Eg.* Parrot (1) *Le Refrigerium dans l'au-delà, Bull. Mus. de Fr.* 1936 131. (2) *RHR* cxiv 69–92, 158–96 (3) cxv 53–89. Parthey, G., *Plut. über Isis u. Os.* (ed. 1850). Partsch, J., *Abh. Sachs, Ges. PH Kl.* xxvii 16 1909 553–600. Pearl, O. M. (1) *Aeg.* xxxi 229 (2) *CW* xxxvii 1943–4 10. Peak, W., *Der Isishymnus v. Andros* 1930. Peet, T. E. (1) with Loat, *Cemeteries of Abydos* (2) *BIFAO* 1930 481–90. Perdrizet, P. (1) *TCs Fouquet Coll.* (2) *Bronzes gr. ditto* (3) with G. Lefebvre, *Graffites.* Petrie, F. (1) *Objects of Daily Use* (2) with others, *The Labyrinth,* etc. (3) *Abydos* (4) *Antaeopolis* (5) *Facsimiles of Pap. of Ani* (6) *Six Temples at Thebes* (7) *Amulets* (8) *Nagada and Ballas* (9) *Hawara* (10) *Athribis* (11) *Koptos* (12) *Researches in Sinai* (13) *Memphis* (14) *Tools and Weapons* (15) *Royal Tombs of 1st Dyn.* (16) *Tanis* (17) *Osireion at Abydos.* Piankhoff, A. (1) *Le Coeur dans les textes ég.* (2) *ASAE* xlix 51–5 (3) *ibid.* 129–44 (4) *La Création du disque solaire* (5) *JEA* xx 57–61. Piehl, *Inscr. hierogl.,* 2nd s. Pieper, M., *Das aeg. Märchen.* Pierret, *Inscr. ég., Mus. Louvre.* Pietschmann, *PW* i 1095–1102. Pigeonneau, *L'Annone Romaine.* Picard, C., *Les statues ptol. du Sarap. de Memphis* 1955. Pleijte, W. (1) *Actes VI Congr. Int. Orient.,* Leyden, 4th part, 1885 (2) with Rossi, *Pap. de Turin* 1869–76. Pley, *PW* sv *Memnon,* xv

645–8. Poole, *Cat. BM Coins.* Poland, F., *Gesch. d. gr. Vereinwesen* 1909. Popper, *The Cairo Nilometer.* Porter, with Moss, *Topog. Bibl.* Posener, G. (1) *Princes et pays d'Asie et de Nubie* 1940 (2) *La première dom. perse en Eg.* 1936 (3) CE xiii 1938 259–73 (4) *Cat. ostraka hiérat. litt. de Deir el Médineh* ii f.2 1952 (5) *Dict. of Eg. Civil.* 1962 (6) *Mél I. Levy* 461–78 *Litt. et Politique dans l'Eg. de la XIIe Dyn.* 1956. Powell, *Lex. to Hdt.* 1938. Préaux, C. (1) CE xxvi 1951 354 ff. (2) liii 1952 257–81 (3) lxiv 1957 284–312 (4) *Mél. G. Smets* 1952. Preisendanz, *Pap. Gr. Magicae.* Preisigke, F. (1) *Eigennamen* (2) *Berichtigungsliste* (3) *Gr. Urkunden d. aeg. Mus. zu Kairo.* Prior, G. T. *Cat. of Meteorites* 1923. Pritchard, ANET 372 (2nd ed. 1955). Puchstein, *Epigr. gr. in Aeg. reperta.*

Quibell, *Excavs. at Saqqara* 1906–7.

Raimondi, J., MSRGE iii 1928. Ranke, H., *Die aeg. Personnamen* 1935. Reckmans, T., with van'T Dack, CE 1952 149–95. Rehm, A., PW 1936 571–89. Reich, P. *Jur. Inh.* 10077a–b, pp. 38–42. Reil, *Beitr. z. Kenntnis d. Gewerbe im hellen. Aeg.* Reinach, A. J. (1) DSAA xiii 111–44 (2) *Rapp. sur les fouilles de Koptos* (3) ASAE xi 193 (4) *Cat. Ant. Eg . . . de Koptos, Mus. Guimet de Lyon* 1913. Reinach, T., *Un Code fiscal de l'Eg. rom.* Reisner, G. (1) JEA vl 45 (2) *Kerma, Harvard Afr. St.* vi 1923. Robbins, *Isis* xxii 95. Robert, L. (1) HRH xcviii 56 (2) *Et. epigr. et Philol.* 1938. Rochemonteix (1) *Temple d'Apet* (2) *Temple d'Edfou,* with Chassinat. Roebush, C., *Class. Philol.* xlv 236k47. Roeder, G. (1) Roscher sv *Set* (2) *Debod bis Bab Kalabscha* (3) *Naos: Cat. Gén.* (4) *Dakke* (5) *Aeg. Inschr. Berlin* (6) *Die aeg. Religion in Texten u. Bildern,* 4 vols. (7) *Hermopolis* 1959 (8) *Kulte, Orakel,* etc. 1960 (9) AZ xlv 22–30 (10) as (4) (11) *Urkunden* 1915 (12) *Altaeg. Erzahlungen u. Märchen.* Rogers, R. W. *Hist of Anc. Persia.* Rostovtzeff (1) SEHHW 1941 (2) *Gesellschaft u. Wirt. d. röm. Kaiserzeit* (3) SEHRE. Rougé, de (1) *Inscr. hiér.* (2) *Mél. d'archéol.* i (3) *Rituel funéraire.* Roque, B. de la (1) *Abou Roasch* 1922–3 (2) *Médamoud* 1926 (3) BSRGE xi 1922 113–40 (4) CE 1937 157–62. Rousell, P. (1) REG xlii 137 (2) *Les Cultes ég. à Delos* 1937. Rowe, A. (1) ASAE xxxviii 127 (2) xli 339–41 (3) *Bull. Ryl. Lib.* xxxix 1957 (4) ASAE xl 1940 1–50, 291–303. Ruggiero, R. de, *Bull. d. Ist. d.* DR xx 1908 48. Rusch, *Die Entwicklung der Himmelgöttin Nut* 1922.

Sachau, *Aramäische Pap. u. Ostr.* 1911 San Nicolo. *Vereinwesen.* Sauneron, S. (1) *Les prêtres de l'anc. Eg.* 1957 (2) BIFAO li 1952 41–8 (3) BIFAO lx 1960 11–7 (4) *Les Fêtes d'Esna* 1962 (5) *Rituel de l'embaument* (6) with Yoyotte, BIFAO l 1952 157–207.Säve-Sönderbergh (1) *On Eg. Reps. of Hippo.-hunting as a Religious Motive* 1953 (2) *Aeg. u. Nubien* 1941 (3) *Kush* iv 54–61 (4) JEA xxxvii 53–71 (5) *Eranos* xliv 68–80 (6) *Navy of 18th Dyn.* 1946. Sayce, A. H. (1) REG vii 1894 290 (2) JHS xlv 161–3. Schäfer (1) *Urk. d. aeg. Alt.* (2) AZ xli. Scharff (1) *Das vorgesch. Gräberfeld v. Abusir el-Meleq* (2) AZ lxii 86–107 (3) *Aeg. Sonnenlieder* (4) *Die hist. Abschnitt, Sitz. Münch.* viii 1936 (5) *Die Alt. Frühzeit.* Schiaparelli, *Il Libro dei Funerali.* Schiff, *Festsch. Hirschfeld* 377. Schubart, *En J. an Nil* 1923. Schur, W., *Die Orientpolitik d. K. Nero* 1923. Schwartz, W. J.

class. Philol. cliii 1896 156. Seckel-Schubart, *Der Gnomon* Seligman, *Griff. St.* 1932 457–61. Sethe (1) *Dramat. Texte* (2) *Urkunden d. aeg. Alt.* (3) *Untersuchungen* (4) *Urgeschichte* 1930 (5) *Die Zeitrechnung d. alt. Aeg.* 1919 (6) *Urk. d. gr.-röm. Zeit* (7) *Amun u. d. Urgötter* 1929 (8) *Urk. d. 18 Dyn.* (9) *Gött. Gelhrte Anz.* 1912 705–26. (10) *Pyr. Komm.* (11) *Altaeg. Vorstellungen* 1928 (12) *PW* 1903 256–7 (13) *Sprache f. d. Kennen* (14) *Sonnenauge.* Sharpe, *Eg. Insc.* Shinnie, P. L., *Meroe* 1967. Sijpensteijn, P. J. (1) *Aeg.* xliii 1963 70–83 (2) *Pap. Lugd. Bat.* xiv 1964. Slolely, R. W., JEA xxxiii 102 f. Smith, Elliot, with Dawson, *Eg. Mummies.* Smith, G. F. H., *Gemstones* (1958 E. C. Phillips). Smith, H. F. C. with A. Adam, *Sudan Notes & R.* xxxi 303–6. Smith, W. Robertson, *Religion of Semites* 1894. Sottas, H. *La préservation de la propriété fun. dans l'anc. Eg.* Sourdille, *Hédodote et la religion ég.* Speelers, L. (1) *Les Textes des Pyramides Eg.* (2) *Comment faut-il lire les Textes des Pyr. Eg.?* (3) *Textes des Cerceuils* 1946. Spiegel, *Die Erzählung vom Streite d. H. and Seth.* Spiegelberg, W. (1) *Ein Erbstreit aus d. Ptol. Aeg.* (2) *Die Lesung* in RT xxvi 1904 (3) SBAW, 1926 2 Abh. (4) *Credibility of Hdt.'s Account of Eg.* (4) *Kopt. HandWB* (6) AZ liv 111–4 (7) *Sitz. Berl. Akad.* 1915 876. Stein, A., *Die röm Ritterstand.* Steindorff, G. (1) *The Relig. of Anc. Egyptians* 1005 (2) AZ liii 59 (3) *Gräbfunde d. Mitt. Reichs* ii. Stephanski, E. *Coptic Ostr. from Med. Habu* 1952. Stewart, H. M., JEA xlvi 1960 88. Stolk, *Ptah* 1911. Strackmans, M., *Mél. Smets* 621–31. Stricker, B. H., *De overstroming van de Nijl* 1956.

Tait, *Ostr. from Bodl. Mus.* Tarn. W. W., *Alex. Gt. and Unity of Mankind* 1933. Taubenschlag (1) *Law of GR Eg. in Light of Pap.* 1944 i (2) ii (3) *Strafrecht.* Te Velde, H., *Set God of Confusion* 1967. Therikower, V., *Die hellenist. Städtgründ.* Thomson, J. O., *Hist. of Anc. Geog.* 1948. Tollinton, R. B., *Clement of Alex.* 1914. Toussoun, O., *Mém. sur les anc. branches du Nil* 1922. Trigger, B. G., *Hist. and Settlement in Lower Nubia* 1965.

Usener, H., *Die Sintflutsagen* 1899.

Vandier, J. (1) *La Relig. Eg.* 1949 (2) *Manuel d'Arch. Eg.* i 1952 (3) *La famine dans l'Eg. anc.* 1936 (4) CRAI 1945 214–8 (5) *Actes 21st Congr. Int. Orient.* 1948–9 54 f. (6) RHR cxxxvi 8 f. (7) *Mo'alla* 1950. Vercouter, J., *Essais sur la rel. entre Eg. et Préhellènes* 1954. Vikentieff, Vl. (1) ASAE liv 179 (2) *La haute crue du Nil et l'averse de l'an 6 du roi Taharqa* 1930 (3) ASAE xlviii 21–41. Villard, M. de, *La scultura ad Ahnas* 1923. Virolleaud, *Légendes de Babylone et de Canaan.* Visser, *Götter u. Kulte.* Vitelli, *Racc. Lumbroso* 23–8. Vogt, *Die alex.*

Wainwright, G. A. (1) JEA xxi 152–70 (2) JEA xviii 3–15 (3) *ibid.* 159–72 (4) JEA xvi 35–8 (5) ASAE xxviii 175–89 (6) *Sudan N. & R.* 1947 11–24 (7) *Sky-religion in Eg.* 1938 (8) *Griff. St.* 373–83. Waltzing, J. P., *Etude hist. sur les corp. prof. chez les Romains* 1895–6. Wängsted, *Ostr. dem.* Ward, *Seal Cylinders of W. Asia.* Warmington, *Commerce between RE and India.* Webb, E. J. (1) JHS xli 70–85 (2) *The Names of the Stars* 1952. Wehrli, F., *Die Schule d. Aristot.*,

Heft 1, *Dikaiarchos* 1944. Weidner, *Handbuch d. Bab. Astron.* 1915. Weigall (1) *Travels in Upper Eg. Deserts.* (2) *Antiq. of Lower Nubia.* Weill, R. (1) *Recherches sur la prem. dyn. et les temps préphar.* 1961 (2) *Les décrets roy. de Coptos* 1912 (3) ASAE xi 97–141 (4) *Le Champ des Roseaux* 1936. Wellersly, K., RM xcviii 135–50. Wellmann, *Quellen u Stud. zur Gesch. d. Naturwiss.* iv 4 1935 86. Wessely, BIFAO xxx 1930. Westermann, W. L. (1) with Kraemer, *Gr. pap. in Lib. Cornell* 1926 (2) with Keyes, *Tax Lists and Transport. Rec. Theadelphia* 1932. Wiedesmann, (1) *Herodots zweites Buch* 1800 (2) *Das Alte Aeg.* 1920 (3) *AfRelig.* xix (Waffenkult). Wilcken, U. (1) *Alex. d. Groose u. d. hellenist Wirtschaft* 1921 (2) ZAS lx 86–102 (3) JDAI xxxii 201. Wilkinson, (1) *Manners and Customs of Anc. Eg.* (2) *Modern Eg. and Thebes.* Wilson, J. A. (1) *The Culture of Anc. Eg.* 1951 (2) in Frankfort (4) (3) *The Burden of Egypt.* Winlock, H. E., MK in Thebes. Wit, C. de, (1) *La Role et le Sens du Lion* 1951 (2) *Les Inscr. du temple d'Opet* (Bibb. weg. xi) (3) CE xxxii 1957 25–39 (4) CE July 1956 279–82. Witkowski, *Ep. priv. gr.* Woodward, J. M., *Perseus* 1937. Woolley, C. L., with MacIver, *Karanog, The Rom.-Nub. Cemetery* 1910. Wreszinski (1) *Pap. Ebers* (2) *Der grosse medizin, Pap. 2 Berlin* (3) *Die Hohenprieste des Amon* 1904 (4) *Der Lond. med. Pap.* (5) *Atlas* (6) *Die Medizin d. alt. Aeg.* Wroth, *Cat. Gr. Coins, Troas,* etc.

Yeivin (1) *Inscr. Ugarit de Palest. Qedem* ii (2) *J. Palest. Or. Soc.* 1934 iii Yoyotte, J. (1) *R. d'Eg.* ix 125 (2) BSFE 1950 no. 3 17–22 (3) BIFAO lii 173–8 (4) as (1) 157–9 (5) *Rev. d'Eg.* xiii 1961.

Zandee, *Hymn aan Amon van P. Leiden* i 350. Zayed, A. El-H., ASAE lvi 87–104. Ziebarth, E. (1) *Aus der ant. Schule* (2) *Beitr.* (Hamb., Abh. Gebiet). Auslandskunde xxx, Reihe A (Rechts. u. Staats. ii 1929). Zucker, ASAE 1912.

Indexes

Authors Cited in Text

Gods

Rulers

Officials

Archidikastes, Judicial Official, connected with Records Office, 135, 165, 323, 326. Assessors, 105.

Boundary-inspectors, 153.

Daktylistes, surveyor, 149. Dekaprotos, councillor elected to supervise collection of corn-dues, etc., 218, 248, 261, 263. Dikologos, jurisconsult, 331. Dioiketes, financial administrator under prefect (but also minor officer), 135, 151, 155, 167 f., 260, 300.

Eirenarch, police magistrate, 259. Engineer, 13. Epistrategos, governor of large district, 163–5, 247. Exegetes, civic magistrate (concerned with citizen's status, etc.), 260. Eutheniarch, concerned with food-supply, 260.

Frumentarius (army-commissariat officer), 130.

Gymnasiarch, in charge of gymnasion, 123, 260.

Hypomnematographos ("memorandum-writer", mostly an Alexandrian magistrate aiding prefect in judicial matters), 266.

Idiologos, high financial official, 323, 332.

Katholikos, high financial official in Byzantine Egypt (also lesser officials), 216, 263, 332, 334, 335. Kosmetes, civic official (esp. concerned with ephebate), 260.

Logistes, financial commissioner (by 4th century with administrative powers), 167.

Nomarchs, 29, 305. Notary, 14.

Officials, magistrate's assistant, minor official, 14. Oikonomos, "steward," 168, 242.

Police, 235, 256, 258. Praepositus pagi, administrator of a pagus, 263. Priest, 141, 147, 151, 195, 335. Prefect, 14, 104, 127, 139, 165 f., 171, 189, 194, 246, 256 f., 259, 322 f., 325 (Petronius, 15, 29 f.; Cornelius Gallus, 28); his tour, 166–70; of cohort, 337. Procurator, 168, 223, 252, 327; of squadron, 169. Prytanis (president of town council), 105, 256 f., 260.

Ripuarius, police official (Byz.); name suggests river-bank connection, 14. Royal clerk or scribe (Basilikogrammateus), 123, 147, 223.

Secretary of Town, 168; of village, 236. Scholastikoi, 154, 223, 249, 254. Sitologoi (corn-officials), 154, 223, 249, 254. Strategos, civic governor of nome, etc., 15, 123, 135, 167, 169, 223, 242, 246, 257–9, 261, 323 f., 332, 338. Syndikos, 105.

People in or of Egypt

Abaskantos, 113. Abinnaios, Fl., 152 f. Abraham, 123. Achillas, 143, 147. Achilleus, 163 (Aur.), 259, 324. Adamantios, 153. Adamas, 111 f. Aemilius, 135. Agatheneros, 114. Agathinos, 115, 263. Agathos, 127, 332. Agathoboulos, 156. Agathos, 127, 332. Agathos Daimon, 32. Ahmose, 53. Aimilios Satornilos, 254. Aithiopas, 155. Alis, 14. Alexandros, 114, 136, 171, 238. Alypios, 153. Amarantos, 151. Amasis, 20. Amenkan, 241. Amoitas, 150. Ammonas, 115, 235. Ammonion, 235. Ammonios, 115, 118, 144 f., 171, 231, 245, 277–9. Amyntas, 117. Aniketos, 111. Ankh ma Hor,

Lagos, 122. Larion, 331. Leon, 118. Leontas, 150. Longeinos, 146. Longinus Priscus, 129. Loukios (Lucius), 115.

Makarios, 128. Marcus, 170. Matar, 71–5. Matris, 170. Maximus, 151, 155. Megale, 117. Meh, 239. Melas, 136, 226, 258. Memmius Cornutus, G., 149 f. Menas, 130–2 (Aur.), 228. Menephtah, 201. Menestheus, 160. Merrymose, 239. Metellus, 130. Methen, 277. Mires, 148. Morion, 171. Moros, 9. Moschiaine ,331. Moschion, 331. Mutritis, 286. Myron, 113. Myrto, 331.

Nefer 'abu, 293 f. Nefrese, 239. Nehemesrattaui, 310 f. Neilos, 254. Nemesas (Aur.), 226. Nemesianos, 115, 135. Nikanor, 112–14, 160. Nike, 150. Nikephoros, 154. Nikestratos, 243. Nikias, 123. Nikolaos, 124. Nilon, 156. Nilos, 171. Ninnaros 12, 114.

Oanemouos, 256. Origas, 112. Origines, 166, 331. Onnophris, 113, 141, 223. Osoroeris, 285. Ouranios, 333.

Pa-amen, 304. Pabous, 244. Paesios, 256. Pa-her, 304 f. Paion, 323. Palladios, 330 f. Pallas, 148. Pamates, 140. Pamouthios, 263. Panares, 9. Panechotes, 148, 151. Panemouos, 246. Paniskos, 337. Panisneus, 138. Paomis, 146. Papeiris, 251. Papirius Apollinarius, 133. Papirius Domitianus, 333. Papontas (Aur.), 261. Papnouthis (Aur.), 168. Paraemheb, 241. Pardalas, 324. Pasion, 148. Pasoxis (?) 140. Pates (Aur.), 227. Paulos, 124. Pausanias, 112, 114, 138 f., 170, 243. Pausirion, 150. Pbekis, 226. Pebos, 226. Pedamun, 84. Peeous, 141. Pekhytes, 231. Pekoous, 262. Pemes, 141. Perikles, Aur., 231. Persion, 138. Pertaios, 27. Pesiur, 53. Petepsois, 148. Petesi, 304. Peteus, 148. Petobastis, 155. Petosiris, 111, 148. Petronianus, 326. Petronius Secundus, T., 323. Phameis, 154. Phanias, 223. Phatres, 148. Philargyrios, 127. Philastrios, 333. Phileros, 160. Philiarchos, Aur., 167. Philinna, 331. Philokles, 282. Philomousos, 160. Philos, 165. Philoxas, 146. Philoxenos, 115, 139. Phoibammon, 14. Phoinike, 263. Pholos, 145. Phoullon, 166. Phronimos, 113. Piste, 113. Ploutarchos, 117. Ploution, 148. Polemon, 170. Polis, 147. Polydeukes, 116, 254. Porementhis, 148. Posidonios, 223. Potasimto, 20. Pothos, 143. Primitinos, 156. Protarche, 331. Proximos, 14. Psemmonthes, 238. Psenemmous, 111. Psenpseeine, 231. Psoeios, 261. Ptolema, 223. Ptolemaios, 111, 116, 119, 135, 146, 153 f., 165, 168, 171. Ptollas, 160, 165.

Rekhmire, 17 f., 316. Rheme, 118. Romaios, 230.

Sabeinos, 32, 165. Sabinus, Julius, 145. Saetas, 146. Salibotas, 141. Sallonios Papeis, 252. Sambous, 32, 171. Sampadoros, 166. Sanpat, 128. Sarapaion, 148, 253. Sarapammon, 115, 138 (Aur.), 230. Sarapasto, 140. Sarapias, 117, 140 f. Sarapion, 115, 119, 123 f., 140, 147, 151, 162–4, 168, 170, 223, 230, 261, 331 f. Sarapous, 129. Saras, 145, 235. Serapiakos, 154. Seras, 117. Satabous, 252. Satornilos, 32 f., 130–2. Sbikis, 247. Secundus, 249. Segathis, 132 f. Sekoundos, 113. Selene, 147–9. Sempetsiris, 246. Sempronius Claudius, 130, 134. Sempronius Clemens, 145. Senaies, 226. Senthotmenis, 226. Serenos, 141, 151, 154, 171, 231, 331. Seuthes, 105. Severos, 223. Skambas, 141. Silbanos, 224. Sipos, 253. Sit-Re, 283. Smaragdos, 151, 161. Soeris, 230, 254. Sokmenios, 32. Sokmenis, 220. Sokrates, 151. Sopatros, 121. Sophronios, 261. Sotas, 122. Soueris, 32. Statia, 151. Statilius Maximus, T., 325, 332 (? same men). Stephanos, 141 (Aur.), 155. Subutianus Aquila, 257. Symeonios, 128. Syros, 12, 114.

Taamois, 150. Tabenka, 32. Tabitheus, 130–2, 135. Taeis, 138. Tahermas, 60. Tais, 153. Tamalis, 128. Tanechotarion, 165. Tapausiris, 230. Tarem, 138. Taseus, 138, 149, 247. Ta-sherit(ent) pi-war, 303. Tasoitas, 115. Tasokmenis, 32. Tasoucharion, 135, 165. Tat, 107. Tauris, 167. Techosis, 116. Tekoous, 148. Teras, 226. Terentianus, Cl., 129–36. Tetheus, 150. Thaisarion, 146, 171. Thaisas, 32. Thaisous, 150, 160. Thausarion, 141. Theochrestos, 166. Theodoros, 13, 128, 155, 334. Theogenes, 167. Theokles, 20. Theon, 123, 127, 129, 136, 150, 170, 259, 261. Theonas, 126, 150, 156. Theoninos, 117. Thermion, 145. Thermoutharion, 150. Thermouthion, 128. Thermouthis, 154. Thermoutis, 165, 331. Thmoisaphos, 246.

Places in Egypt

General

ERRATA

Read (figures give page and line): 14.3, Aphthous; 17.15 and 316.6, Rekhmire; 24.2, 29.1, 269.8, Strabon; 15.26, Krokodilopolis; 38.1, Red Sea; 70.20, 333.26, 339.2, Letopolis; 115.12, Philokyros; 115.31, Loukios; 123.4, Hermophilos; 134.20, Neapolis; 146.22, Koprous; 171.2, Ptolemais; 194.3, writes; 246.25, Harpokration; 247.5, Heraklammon; 258.11, Themistes; 265.6, 273.20, Kalabscha; 279.9, Behdet; 290.3, Thebes; 291.36, Seti; 303.18, Nubian; 305.16, Ombos; 317.13, Amenophis; 253.34, Maximus; 341.15, Akhmim; 364.8, Nonnos; 42.4, Behdet; 305.31, Nomarchs.